The Central Asian Civilization
That Bridged the East and the West for
Over Two Millennia

THE TURKS

Volume 1
"Until the 10th Century"

EROL I. YORULMAZOGLU

Copyright © 2021 Erol I. Yorulmazoglu
All rights reserved.

Cover Design: İlknur Muştu - www.ilknurmustu.com
Page Layout: Cansu Poroy - cnspry@gmail.com
Cover picture: Tonyuquq Orkhon Turkish inscriptions from the 8th century

ISBN: 978-1-7366954-0-1
Library of Congress Control Number: 2016921605
Kindle Direct Publishing

To the noble Turkish nation...

CONTENTS

Preface 15
Acknowledgments.. 17
Introduction... 19

Chapter 1 Language and Culture.. 31
    1.1. The Turkish Language 31
        The Historical Evolution of the Language........................ 34
        The Turkish Writing System 36
    1.2. An Enriched Culture 38
        The Use of Silk 39
        Turkish Hot Drinks: Tea and Coffee............................. 40
        The Epic Stories of the Turks 42
        Shadow Theater 43
        Music from Asia 44
        Military Music 45
        Turkish Cuisine... 48
        The Stirrup 54
        Equestrian Arts... 55
        Falconry 57
        Sports 58

        The Turkish Calendar 64
        The Tulip... 66
        Colors.. 67
        Literature 68
        Ceramics and Pottery 70
        Painting.. 71
        Kilims and Carpets.. 72
    1.3. From Tents to Fixed Dwellings 76
        The Evolution of Turkish Architecture............................ 81
        The Seljuk Prototype for Success..................................... 84
        The Ghaznavid and the Delhi Sultanate 86
        The Mamluk Revival of Egypt 87
        The Timurid Renaissance... 88
        The Magic of the Mughals.. 89
        The Iranian Splendor 90
        The Ottoman Magnificence 90
    1.4. The Influence of Religion 92
        Religion and the Military Culture 98
        Turkish Mythology... 102
        Ancient Beliefs and Rituals 111
        Animal Symbolism.. 114
        Number Symbolism 119
        Ancient Funerals 119
        Eastern Influence: Buddhism.. 122
        Transition to the Semitic Religions................................ 124
        Islam.. 127
        The Acquisition of Arab Names 131

Chapter 2   Overview of the Past of the Turks.. 133
    2.1. An Introduction to World History 133
        Earliest Human Settlements.. 134

      Steppe Origins of the War Chariots 136
      Old Civilizations 138
  2.2. Tracing Back the Turkish Past 141
      About the Proto-Turks 144
      Turkish Race 150
      Controversial History 153
  2.3. The Age of the Nomads 156
      The Pre-Islamic Asian Nomads 159
      About the Scythians 161
      Turk versus Mongol on the Steppes 165
      A Note on Native American Origins 166
  2.4. Life in the Eurasian Steppes 167
      The Geographic Locations of the Turks in History 168
      The Turks as Demography Changers 172
      Historic Turkish Titles and Government 176
      State Symbolisms: Flag, Tugh, and Drums 181
      The Pastoralist Nomadic Warriors 183
      Political Establishment of the Turkish Steppe Empires 191
      Heterogeneity of the Steppe Empires 195
      The Silk Road 197
      Women in Old Turkish Society 202
      Major Turning Points 204

Chapter 3 The Rise of the Mounted Archers 207
  3.1. Ancient China and the Nomads 207
      Turkish Tribes during the Hunnish Epoch 210
      Getting to Know Ancient China 214
      The Rise of Imperial China and the Hu 216
      The Great Wall 219
      Han China and the Barbarians 220

The Western World from the Third BCE to the
Fifth Century CE 222
3.2. The Xiong-nu 224
    Who Were the Xiong-nu? 226
    The Tribal Economy 229
    Xiong-nu Society 231
    Xiong-nu Hordes 233
    Xiong-nu Culture 234
3.3. The First Nomadic Empire 235
    The Story of Mo-tun (Mete), the Founder 236
    The Yueh-chih Nomads 240
    The Role of Chinese Women in Peace
    Treaties with the Huns 244
    The Rise of Hun Power 246
3.4. The Split and the Fall of the Empire 253
    The Civil War and the First Split 254
    The Second and Final Split of the Empire 256
    The Fall of the Southern Huns 261
3.5. The Outcome of the Huns 263
    The Survival of the Southern Huns 264
    The Fate of the Northern Huns 265
    Further Split of the Northern Huns 267
    The European Huns versus the Asian Huns (Xiong-nu) .. 269
    The Eastern Steppes after the Huns 271
    The Westward Migration of the Turks 272
3.6. The White Huns 274
    The Origin of the White Huns 274
    The Kidarite Dynasty 276
    The Fall of the Kidarites 277
    The Rise of the Ephtalite Dynasty 278

  Relations with Persia and India 281
  The Fall of the Ephtalite White Huns 283
  Political Aftermath After the White Huns 284
  The Legacy of the Huns in Asia 286

Chapter 4 The Great Turkish Migrations 291
  4.1. The Tribal Movements 291
  4.2. The Black Huns 296
   The Roman Empire before the Huns............................. 298
   The Movements of the Germanic Tribes 299
   The Hun Invasion 300
   The Huns in Western and Central Europe 303
   The Hunnish Civil War and its Outcome 306
   The First "Barbarian" King of Italy................................ 308
   About the Huns and Attila and the Huns..................... 312
   The Legacy of the Huns in Europe 314
   The Aftermath of the Huns in Europe 319
  4.3. The Bulgars 321
   The Splitting of the Bulgar Union.................................. 323
   The Loss of Ethnic Identity... 325
   The Bulgar Legacy in the Volga 327
  4.4. The Avars... 329
   The Makers of Central European Demography............. 331
   The Strength of the Mounted Archers 333
   The End and the Legacy of the Avars............................. 334
  4.5. The On-Oghur Legacy 336
  4.6. The Non-Hebrew Jews.. 339
   Khazaria as an International Power 340
   The Sole Non-Hebrew Judaic State................................ 342
   The Turkish Jewry.. 343

        The Khazar Economy 344
        The Decline 345
        The Rise of the Rus' 347
    4.7. The Wild Warriors 350
    4.8. The Polovtsy 355
        The Kimek Turks of Siberia 355
        The Rulers of the Pontic Steppe 357
        The Qïpčak Mercenaries 358
        Cumania in the Balkans 359
        The Fall of Desht-i Qïpčak 362

Chapter 5   The Masters of the Eurasian Steppes 365
    5.1. Turkish Mongolia and China 365
        The Xianbei 367
        The Political Climate in Northern China after the Han ... 369
        The Juan-juan as the New Nomadic Power 375
        The Relations Between the Nomads and China 378
        Demographic Changes in Mongolia 379
        The Sixth and Seventh Centuries 380
    5.2. The Chinese Turks 381
        The Steppes in the Fourth Century 383
        The Rise of Turkish Power in China 384
        The Turkish Rule of China 386
        The Establishment of Buddhism in China 389
        The Culture of Forced Suicide 391
        The Ensuing Events and the Fall 392
        The Legacies of the T'o-pa Turks 394
    5.3. The Celestial Turks 398
        Connection to the Huns 399
        The Color Blue and Its Significance 401

The Rise and the Division of the State 404
Relations with Rome 405
Relations with China 408
The End of the First Period 411
The Gök-Türk Interregnum 412
The Second Rise of the State.. 415
The Fall and Betrayal.. 417
The Afghani Gök-Türks 418
After the Gök-Türks 419
5.4. The Power Brokers of China.. 420
The Role of Religion 422
The Relations with China 423
The An Lushan Rebellion 424
Post-Rebellion Sino-Turkish Relations............................... 426
The Change in Dynasty and Decline................................... 428
The City Builders of Central Asia.. 429
The Uighur Tragedy.. 430
The Revival of the Uighurs 431
The Tutors of the Mongols... 433
The Conversion to Islam.. 434
5.5. The Desert People 435
Moving to China 435
The Guards of the T'ang... 436
The Fall of the T'ang 437
The Khitan Influence on China 438
The Rise and Fall of the Sha-t'o 439

Chapter 6   Tribal Entities Until the Eighth Century........................ 443
Ancient Turkish Tribes 444
After the Break-up of the First Union 446

The Former Great States 448
The Second and Final Union of Turks 449
The Lost Ancient Tribes 451
Contributions of the Early Nomads
to Settled Civilizations 452

Selected Book Recommendations 455
Selected Journal-Article Recommendations 459
About the Author 461
Appendices 463
Notes 467
Index 533

MAP LIST

1. Scythians and their migration patterns 161
2. The Eurasian steppes 168
3. Important geographic locations across the Eurasian steppes 172
4. Major trade cities and towns along the historic Silk Road 199
5. The Great Hun state in Asia 227
6. The Huns and the Great Turkish Migrations 268
7. European Huns and White Huns by the middle of the fifth century 286
8. Bulgars and their migrations 324
9. Khazar and Uighur Qaghanates by early ninth century 342
10. Turkish dynasties within China 372
11. GökTürk Qaghanate by the end of the sixth century 403
12. Ancient Turkish tribes contributing to Chinese history 446

PREFACE

History is a compilation of humanity's past experiences. To learn from prior successes and failures, all we have to do is look to the past. Many nations first spread across the globe and then evolved over the ages into their current states by interacting with other nations. History tells us about the cultural and political evolutions that our ancestors went through. It is by understanding history that we learn how we reached the current state of affairs in our contemporary world.

In two volumes of this work, *The Turks*, I present the experiences of the Turkish nation mostly based on the references provided by non-Turkish scholars. It is the history of an Asian people—a history that spans more than two millennia, stretching over a large geographic area from the Pacific Ocean in the east to the Atlantic Ocean in the west, from the shores of Siberia in the north to the Indian Ocean in the south. The second edition includes the often-forgotten Turkish mythology as well as Turkish history from the point of view of past Turkish tribal movements or actions Nevertheless, it is a fact that Turks were the superpower of the world not long ago, and it is a fact that they had an impact on the development of prominent civilizations in China, India, Persia, Russia, Europe and the Middle East.

Volume I takes us back to more than two thousand years ago. On the basis of the recorded history as known from the Chinese archives, the ancient Turks were originally from southern Siberia and Mongolia, where they were known to live as pastoralist nomads. They were excellent horsemen, well before the Mongols of Genghis Khan. Upon the unprovoked attack by the Chinese monarch who unified China to initiate the Imperial Period of China, Turks united for the first time under the banner of the Huns, known to the Chinese as the Xiong-nu. This was the official event that marked the entry of Turks into the world history. For centuries, until the application of gunpowder in the military arena, their cavalry remained superb and effective with their unsurpassed mounted archers.

When the Huns were politically divided into two separate states, one came under the influence of the Chinese, while the other remained independent. When the latter group decided to move away from the traditional homeland of Turks, they also triggered the beginning of the great Turkish migrations that lasted nearly a millennium, with Turks moving westward to western Central Asia and then to Europe.

Those who remained behind were still able to make their presence felt in China until the tenth century. Following in the footsteps of the former Huns, first the Gök-Türks and then the Uighurs were able to disturb the Chinese with their military might. The former established the last true union of the Turkish tribal federations, stretching from the Korean Peninsula in the east to the outskirts of Central Europe; its disintegration led to the formation of multiple new Turkish states from Asia to Europe along the vast territories of the Eurasian steppes.

As we will see later in this book, the westward movements of these Central Asian warriors eventually caused the Hungarians to settle in their present-day homeland, and in addition, they led to the evolution of the modern-day demographics of the Germanic as well as Slavic peoples of Europe. In addition, Turks contributed to the early development of the Russian state.

Meanwhile, the fall of the Gök-Türks in the first half of the eighth century weakened Turks in western Central Asia. This condition eventually led to the spread of Islam in their territories. With their conversion to Islam, the future of Turks changed forever.

Dr. Erol Yorulmazoglu
Naperville, Illinois

ACKNOWLEDGMENTS

I would like to extend my appreciation to my friends — including Ms Derya Yelkenci — who have been supportive of my efforts to complete this book, which required nearly four years of research. I am grateful to my wife, Zeynep, for standing behind my work. I am indebted to Dr. Peter B. Golden, professor emeritus of history and Turkish and Middle Eastern studies at Rutgers University, for his invaluable encouragement to publish this book.

INTRODUCTION

Who are the Turks? When Turks are mentioned, most people think about the people from Anatolia, but the Turks are not confined to Asia Minor; they are found across a large geographic area stretching from the Far East deep into Europe in the west. Then who are the Turks? Does the name Turk identify a specific group of people (such as a specific ethnic group), or does it have a unifying meaning for a number of peoples (people with similar backgrounds but separate languages)? In other words, does the name Turk have a similar connotation to the name Latino, which may imply a group of people with different languages (French, Italian, Spanish, and Portuguese) but similar origins? When looking into the long, complex history of the Turks, one can see that the name Turk actually applies to a specific group of people from Asia, but in a manner of speaking, one can also argue that it applies to peoples with similar backgrounds but using different dialects of the same language.

When this ethnonym is mentioned today, one generally understands a Turk to be a citizen of, or a descendant from, the Republic of Turkey. However, as already stated, Turks are not restricted to the geographic area of Turkey. Indeed, Turks are currently found across a large area. In this context, Turks can be from Azerbaijan, Kyrgyzstan, Kazakhstan, Turkmenistan, or Uzbekistan; or from Chuvashia, Gagauz, Tatarstan, Tuva, or Xinjiang; or from Afghanistan, Bosnia, Bulgaria, Greece, Iran, Macedonia, Mongolia, or Russia. In fact, more than half of all people who speak a Turkish (commonly referred to as Turkic) language live outside of Turkey. How is it possible that the Turks live not only in Turkey but also outside of Turkey over such a large geographic area? The answer to this question can be found only in the annals of the long history of the Turks.

The origin of the word Turk is not known. This ethnonym appeared in the earliest Turkish inscriptions, known as the Orkhon inscriptions, from the eighth century, located in the territories of modern-day Mongolia. The word was spelled Türük but was adopted as Türk by the Turks in the medieval period and in the modern age. The Turks of the past were known not by their ethnic identity but rather by their political names, which were borrowed either from the names of their leaders (e.g., Osmanlï—or Ottoman), their tribes (e.g., Uygur—or Uighur), or their totems (e.g., Aq-Qoyunlu—or White Sheep). But the ethnic identity of the Turks survived because they never forgot who they were. In the era when the Turks were establishing states under various names without reference to their ethnicity, Mahmud al-Kâshgharî, a Turkish scholar and lexicographer of the Turkish language from the eleventh century, wrote his famous *Divan-ï Lügat-ï Türk* (*Grand Dictionary of the Turkish Language*), stressing the importance of Turkish identity. Not only were the Gök-Türks the first-known Turkish polity to establish a state under their ethnonym, in the sixth century, but the message they left in the Orkhon inscriptions in the eighth century also carried a Turkish nationalist flavor. The Eastern Romans referred to their land in Central Asia as Turchia, the Greek word for Turkey or "land of the Turk." When the Seljuk Turks in the eleventh century invaded Anatolia under the Great Seljuk Empire, the Greeks eventually came to refer to Asia Minor as Turchia as well. Meanwhile, by the tenth century, Central Asia had acquired a Turkish character. Hence, nearly all Central Asia became known as Turkestan, a Persian word meaning "land of the Turk."

The homeland of the Turks is traditionally known to be Central Asia, which is a vast land stretching from the Caspian Sea in the west to the eastern borders of the Mongolian steppes in the east. Central Asia is an ancient land, in essence a true cradle of civilization. It has been influenced by major civilizations, such as Greek, Persian, Chinese, Turkish, Arab, and even Mongolian. It is known as a crossroads for the transfer of technology. For example, paper-making technology and the knowledge of gunpowder were transmitted from China to the Western world through Central Asia. The land has also been a conduit for the transmission of ideas and faith. Christianity and Islam both reached the outskirts of the Far East through Central Asia. Manichaeism and Buddhism are other faiths that were carried into China by Central Asian nomads.

We should keep in mind that Turkish history began in Central Asia, more specifically Mongolia and southern Siberia, more than two millennia ago and later involved the three continents of Asia, Europe, and Africa. Before we plunge into a long historical journey, we need to clarify the terms Turk, Turkish, and Turkic.

Modern Western scholars have divided Turkish identity into two groups: Turkish (Turk) and Turkic. Within this artificial division, the former group characterizes a person from the Republic of Turkey, whereas the latter signifies any person from another Turkish-speaking people outside of Turkey (such as in Azerbaijan or Uzbekistan). But this division is based primarily on dialect differences. Even though the proper Turkish language itself does not support this division, many Turkish scholars, under the influence of modern Western scholarly works, adopted the word Türki to denote the English word Turkic, which was created in the second half of the nineteenth century. But as we see from the eleventh-century work *Divan-ï Lügat-ï Türk*, by a Qarluq Turk, the word Turk was used to describe all living Turks from any tribal background. Therefore, for Mahmud al-Kâshgharî of the eleventh century, whether a Turk was from an Oghuz tribe or a Qarluq tribe or a Kyrgyz tribe, there was no difference; in other words, they were all Turks. For him it did not matter whether they used different dialects of Turkish; they were still Turks. Therefore, for historical reasons and to explain the past of the Turks in a unified and proper manner, neither Turkic nor Türki will be formally used in this book.

Turkish history started with the successive formation of nomadic empires across the Eurasian steppes. Among the well-recognized early empires were polities known by their Chinese names, such as the Xiong-nu and the T'u-Chüeh (also written as Tu-kiu).[1] The Great Wall of China, which was originally established against these mounted archers (see chapter 3), failed to prevent the military incursions of these Central Asian warriors into China. In Europe, while the classical era (or antiquity) ended with the demise of the Western

Roman Empire, the period of the Middle Ages (or the medieval period) was defined by the Eastern Roman Empire. The Turks played a key role in the fall of each of these empires, and consequently, they made a significant impact on the history of Europe. In fact, as will be explained later, the Huns and the Avars contributed to the development and evolution of modern-day European demographics. Starting in the eleventh century, the Seljuks helped shape the history of the Middle East as they took on the role of the defenders of Islam against the crusaders coming from Europe. Turkish control of the Middle East, which lasted nearly one millennium, also influenced the evolution of the modern-day demographics of the Near East.

Despite Turkish nationalist sentiment making its first recorded historical appearance in the eighth century with the Orkhon inscriptions and later in the eleventh century with the dictionary of Kâshgharî, for the most part, the Turks did not clearly exhibit nationalist goals in their conquests. Perhaps this was the reason that after the fall of the Gök-Türks, they were never again united under one banner. Indeed, ethnic nationalism was not the reality of the past; instead, it is a reality of the modern era. Nevertheless, it is clear that the Turks of the past—even though they may not have used their ethnic name for their states—were still quite aware of their Turkishness. They referred to themselves by their tribal names, but they were also quite aware of their ethnic identity. This is evident in the fact that Babur, the Timurid prince who established the Mughal dynasty in India in the sixteenth century, called himself a Turk in his own autobiography, today exhibited in the British Museum. Even others were well aware of the ethnic identity of the warriors coming from Asia. For example, the Greeks properly referred to the Khazars of eastern Europe and the Seljuks of Anatolia and Iran as Turks.

Early on in their history, European tribal entities did not use their ethnonyms either. For example, when Attila the Hun contributed to the fall of the Western Roman Empire in the fifth century, the Germans were not unified under a single ethnic identity but were rather divided into tribes, such as the Goths, Franks, Burgundians, Lombards, Saxons, and Vandals. Most of them finally came under the control of the Franks, with the influence of Christianity being the unifying force. Indeed, in the Middle Ages, generally speaking, religious faith became the unifying force for most of the tribal peoples.

Just like the early Germans, the ancient Turks were divided into tribal confederations. The nomadic Turks were loyal first to their chieftain and then to the khan (king) of the tribal confederation. In the early eleventh century, for example, the major Turkish tribal confederations were the Oghuz, Kimek, Pečeneg, and Qarluq-Yaghma. Many of these tribes succeeded in forming polities but were united under the name of Islam rather than by an ethnonym. But as mentioned above, the Turks were always aware of their ethnic identity. This is also evident from the eleventh-century (and the first-known) Turkish dictionary, *Divan-i Lügat-i Türk*, which proved the nomads' awareness of their Turkishness. The author of this dictionary demonstrated that even though these tribal entities once had borders with influential cultural centers like that of China and Persia, these tribal people were still able to maintain their mother tongue and their cherished traditions, to which they were strongly attached.

The growth and expansion of Islam in the seventh and eighth centuries did not automatically trigger a Christian response from Europe. But the military successes of the Turks, new converts to Islam, allowed Muslims of different ethnicities to unite under the banner of these Asiatic nomads, who possessed Islamic power for nearly a millennium. Toward the end of the eleventh century, the territorial expansion of the Muslim Seljuk (Oghuz) Turks into Anatolia, a key territory of the Eastern Roman Empire (also referred to as the Byzantine Empire starting in the seventeenth century) at the doorstep of Europe, forced the Europeans to launch the Crusades, which also inadvertently precipitated the endless "Christian versus Islam" rivalry. This interreligious strife, which started in the second half of the Middle Ages, is still very much alive in our time. But interfaith rivalries were seen not only between these two major Semitic religions but also within them. The pages of history show conflicts between Catholics and Protestants in Christianity as well as between Sunnis and Shi'ites in Islam. The Thirty Years' War (1618–48), one of the longest continuous wars in modern history, was fought between Catholics and Protestants within the Holy Roman Empire. During the modern age, wars between Sunni Ottomans and Shi'ite Safavids were carried out mostly to establish political rather than religious superiority over each other. These were battles in which Turks (of Turkey) fought Turks (of Iran). Nevertheless, in each of these instances, ethnic identities were never as important as religious differences as excuses for war.

By the end of the eighteenth century, the indifference toward ethnic identity ended with the French Revolution. This event brought forward the concept of nationalism, which began to spread first across Europe, later, in the nineteenth century, into the Ottoman Balkan Peninsula, and then, in the early twentieth century, into the Ottoman Middle East.

Starting in the first millennium and during most of the second millennium CE, the Turks formed multiple states, controlling large territories across eastern Europe, Africa, and most of Asia, including the Middle East and the Indian subcontinent. In Africa, for example, the Ottoman Turks extended their territories and their sphere of influence from the borders of Morocco to Egypt and then down to Sudan and Ethiopia. Subsequently, by establishing ports along the Indian Ocean's coastline in Somalia and Yemen, they were also able to turn the Red Sea into a "Turkish lake," as they did with the Black Sea in the north. But the nineteenth century witnessed the loss of power of the once-mighty Turkish rulers from Asia. There are no records showing the Turks exhibiting nationalism during the zenith of their power, except perhaps to some extent in the eighth century for cultural self-preservation against China. However, in the late nineteenth and early twentieth centuries, Turkish nationalism came into existence as a survival mechanism when Western (Ottoman) Turks and Eastern (Turkestan) Turks came under attack by Europeans. Though the Turks had been present in the Balkans for more than half a millennium, they were forced to retreat to Anatolia, which they had inherited from their Seljuk ancestors in the eleventh century.

The sixteenth century was an important turning point in the history of the world. Until then the mounted archers of Central Asia were militarily superior to the armies of sedentary peoples. But the emergence of gunpowder as a military tool ended the agelong supremacy of the nomadic warriors forever. During the long period from the sixteenth to the nineteenth century, a vast geographic area from the borders of Morocco in the west to the borders of China in the east was ruled by the three Turkish gunpowder empires of the Ottomans, the Safavids, and the Mughals. In the western part of this Turkish hegemony, the intercontinental Turkish empire of the Ottomans spanned African, European, and Asian territories, whereas Iran was ruled by various Turkmen dynasties, including the Safavids. And finally, the modern-day territories of India, Pakistan, Bangladesh, and parts of Afghanistan were under the control of the Mughals.

Despite this advantage of having strong influence over these large areas, pan-Turkism did not appear to be a political issue in the history of the Turks. The only exception might have been during the reign of the Gök-Türks, as noted in the text of the eighth-century Orkhon inscriptions and in the late nineteenth-century and early twentieth-century publications and declarations of the nationalists of the Ottoman Empire. In either of these time periods Turkish nationalism came into existence only as a need of resistance to the growing threats against the Turkish entities.

In India the Mughal (Timurid) hegemony ended in the nineteenth century. By the nineteenth century, Siberia—the ancient vast territories of the Turkish mounted archers—was completely lost to the imperial armies of the Russian czar. In Central Asia, the ancient homeland of the Turks, the Eastern Turks (Turkmens, Kazakhs, Kyrgyz, and Uzbeks) had to rise against Soviet Russian oppression in the early twentieth century. In Iran more than seven hundred years of Turkish rule ended in the early twentieth century as well.

As this book will illustrate, the Turks once had control over large territories spanning Asia, Africa, and Europe. Their presence in Central Asia since the classical era and their expansion in the medieval period showed their ability to build durable powerful empires and lasting civilizations with amalgamations of multiple cultures.

Tracing the Turks' past into antiquity, before they accepted Islam as their religion, is difficult, because pre-Islamic Turks did not leave much of a recorded history. For the most part, their past can be found in the writings left behind by the Chinese, Romans, and Greeks. The first-known self-recorded historical information from the pre-Islamic era comes from the Gök-Türks, whose eighth-century stone inscriptions are found in modern-day Mongolia. But with the help of historians with expertise in Turkish history, one realizes that Turkish history indeed goes far back into antiquity before Christ.

For one reason or another, many historical sources and historians have made the mistake of attributing Turkish history in specific periods to the

Persians, Mongols, and so on. For example, it is common to see the European Huns of Attila being mistakenly called Mongols, or the Safavids being erroneously referred to as Persians. Such historical mistakes arise from the complexity of Turkish history, which comes primarily from the Turks' usage of nonethnic names for their former polities and from the wide geographical spread of these political entities.

Because of the simultaneous Turkish presence in multiple areas of three continents, Turkish today is spoken across a wide geographic area from China in the Far East to Bosnia in the west, from the vast lands of Siberia in the north to the mountainous lands of Afghanistan in the south.

In the pre-Islamic era, the Turks established large tribal confederations, which were formed by the gathering of small tribes. The individual tribal members were loyal first to their own tribes. In the hierarchy, the *qaghan* (emperor) or khan (king) was above all tribal leaders, and therefore, he was the head of the social structure. Since it was believed that the monarch was appointed by God, he was also sacred to the extent that his blood could not be spilled. But the qaghan could be punished and executed in the event he committed a gross offense requiring the death penalty; for this he was strangled on the basis of knowledge of close-combat technique of war, a practice that was also seen in the Ottoman Empire. Up until the eighth century, the Turkish tribes for the most part remained united under powerful qaghans. But after the fall of the Gök-Türks, the Turks were never united again.

For centuries Turks have been unjustly facing cultural prejudice from Westerners. Always claiming that the start of human civilization has emerged from themselves, Westerners did not only view Central Asians as mere goat herders but also they belittled Asians as a whole. However, while France, Spain, Portugal as well as all present-day Slavic nations were non existent before the ninth century CE, Turks had already left behind multiple stone inscriptions, clearly indicating a sign of civilization.

If we put the Scythians aside, in the West the Turks appeared in Europe initially as the Huns and more recently as the Ottomans. They faced negative bias among Europeans for centuries. Even in the Near East, the Turks were misjudged, owing to political reasons and misinformation. William Ewart Gladstone, British prime minister, was one of the most ardent Turcophobes of nineteenth-century European politicians; his statements clearly portray the anti-Turk sentiments in Europe during the nineteenth century and later: "They [Turks] were, upon the whole, from the black day they first entered Europe, the one great antihuman specimen of humanity. Wherever they went, a broad line of blood marked the track behind them; and as far as their dominion reached, civilization disappeared from view."[2]

But scholars with prudence could put away their biases and acknowledge the Turks' accomplishments. Ernest Jackh, a political scientist from the World War I era, claimed that the negative image of the Turk was a result of European religious bias: "A Christian historian of the eighteenth century wrote: 'European Christians should be ashamed of reaching into the gutter and fishing out those outdated stories of superstitious Oriental Christians.' It is from such sources that common prejudices and misjudgments about 'the Turk' have originated."[3] Giovanni Curatola, a professor of Islamic archaeology and art history at the University of Udine in Italy, has said, "For Westerners, the Turks come from the East. It is unlikely that anyone would question this assumption, and yet the notion is irredeemably tarnished by Westerners' prejudices, our supposed centrality and alleged cultural superiority. This is a major obstacle in understanding complex cultural phenomena. Thus, let's think ourselves as Westerners, and of the Turks as coming from another 'center of the world' or cradle of civilization, a Central Asian one, and as being witness and heirs to those vast lands in all their variety."[4]

The Turks were once known to be a nomadic people, but as they established great empires in the past, their contributions to the arts and architecture eventually earned them many places in the UNESCO World Heritage List, which are provided in volume 2 of this book.

The Turks were the first superpower of the world, at the beginning of the modern age. Today, they are represented by six independent states in the Near East and Asia. One of them, the Republic of Turkey, is a member of the G20, and its economy has been growing at a fast pace. In fact, Turkey has consistently been among the fastest-growing countries in recent years. It is the sixteenth-largest economy in the world and is projected to be among the top ten economies in about a decade or so.

Today, Turkish-speaking peoples are spread across a large geographic area. Officially Turkey and Turkmenistan are the only two modern-day countries that carry the name Turk, but other contemporary countries have Turkish-speaking peoples as well. Among these are Azerbaijan, Kazakhstan, Kyrgyzstan, and Uzbekistan. In addition, there are autonomous republics or territories within China and the Russian Federation that are of Turkish origin. Among these is the Xinjiang Uighur Autonomous Region of China, where the Uighur Turks live. Others are Tatarstan (Tatar Turks) and the Sakha Republic (Yakut Turks) in contemporary Russia. There are also others, as listed in this book. Even though the Turkish Republic of Northern Cyprus carries the Turkish identity in its name, for political reasons it is not officially recognized by the United Nations.

Most nations on earth experienced their histories in fixed territories. Only a few nations traveled across the globe and formed lasting imprints on the places they journeyed to. The British stretched their reach via the high seas, whereas the Turks spread from Asia into Europe and North Africa on land. However, the Mongols were also known to have formed a formidable land-based empire. Unlike the Turks whose presence was felt across the civilized world for more than millennia, the Mongol influence evaporated quickly even though they once formed the largest empire ever. One reason for this is the fact that, in the distant territories they controlled, they did not have the support of the local people, who were from different ethnic backgrounds. Hence, after the death of Genghis Khan, the Mongols quickly faded from eastern Europe and the Middle East and even from China. The Turks, on the other hand, often moved into conquered territories not only with their soldiers but also with their people. But in these conquered territories, they were at times exposed to the influx of other ethnic groups, and thus, many of them were assimilated by the newcomers to their territories or by the more numerous native peoples.

This book is an attempt to present not only some information about the language and the culture of the Turks but also a synopsis of their history, more than two millennia long, over the vast territories of three continents. As this book will show, Turkish history made an impact on the evolution of many other nations' histories as well.

In this book the designations BCE ("before the Common Era") and CE ("of the Common Era") will be used instead of BC ("before Christ") and AD (*anno Domini*). BCE describes events that took place before year zero, and CE events taking place after year zero. The reader should know that this book provides only a glimpse into the complex history of the Turks.

The principal framework of the Turkish world in our modern times has been formed by the historic Oghuz-Qïpčak-Qarluq Turks. However, they themselves owed the foundation of the evolution of the Turkish world to the ancient Oghur Turkish speaking nomads who are represented today by the Chuvash Turks.

Today's Turks are the sons and the daughters of the great conquerors of the past. After leaving their original homeland, modern-day Mongolia, the Turks were dispersed over a period of two millennia across a large territory encompassing nearly the entire Asian continent in addition to northern Africa and eastern Europe. Over time they succeeded in forming multiple kingdoms and empires of various sizes. While some of them did not have a significant historical impact, others had a significant influence on the evolution of modern-day demographics and cultures in the areas where they existed.

Chapter 1:

LANGUAGE AND CULTURE

1.1. THE TURKISH LANGUAGE

Today Turkish is spoken over a large geographic area stretching from southeastern Europe in the west to Siberia and western China in the east. It is considered part of the Altaic language family originating in Central Asia. Characteristics of Turkish include agglutination and lack of grammatical gender. Proper Turkish is also characterized by vowel harmony. Typically all the vowels in any given word must belong to the same vowel group. The vowels are classified as hard (*a, ı [i], o, u*) or soft (*e, i, ö, ü*). For example, in the Turkish word *denizler* (seas), the vowels all belong to the soft-vowel group. In Indo-European and Semitic languages, inflection is expressed by changing the stem of a word, whereas in Turkish the stem remains unchanged, and instead suffixes are added to the word to express grammatical changes. For example, *dagh* (mountain) becomes *daghlar* (mountains); *gelmek* (to come) becomes *geliyorum* (I come) and *geldim* (I came). In the present day, Turkish is spoken as a native language in Azerbaijan, Kazakhstan, Kyrgyzstan, Turkey, Turkmenistan, Uzbekistan, and many locations in the Balkans, Cyprus, the Middle East, parts of Siberia, Afghanistan, and western China.

Although generally considered part of the Altaic family of languages, some scholars believe that Turkish is rather an independent language. Within the currently accepted classification of the Altaic family, the Turkish language is grouped with the Mongolian and Tungus languages. According to some experts, Japanese and Korean are distant relatives as well.[5] In fact, the Altaic hypothesis suggests that Turkish and Mongolian were derived from a common language root known as Proto-Altaic, which branched to yield the modern-day Korean, Japanese, and Tungus languages.[6] Turkish, Mongolian, Tungus, and Korean, having Altaic linguistic affinities, might have lived together or in close proximity of one another in the early ages of history. For this reason, it has also been suggested that Turkish and Korean have closer common linguistic elements than any other Altaic languages.[7] There is an abundance of literature as to whether Japanese is related to Korean as well as to the Altaic languages. Comparative linguistic studies between Proto-Altaic (including Old Turkish/Mongolian) and Old Korean/Japanese have shown a relationship between these languages.[8] It has been suggested that the roots of Japanese can be found in the Altaic family of languages.[9]

The Turks and the Mongols had quite a long relationship in the steppes of Eurasia as nomads before the modern age. These two nations have many common words. However, significant cross borrowings did not occur until the thirteenth century. By the time Genghis Khan brought most of the Turks under his rule in the thirteenth century, the Mongols were far more uncultured than the Turks; therefore, it was likely that they borrowed more words from the Turks than the Turks did from them.[10] For example, words such as *yurt* (nomad's tent, country) and *tengri* (God) are Turkish loanwords in Mongolian; the terms *elči* (ambassador) and *ulus* (country, nation) are also Turkish words adopted by the Mongols.[11] In other words, the ancient historical, political, cultural, and demographic situations favored the Mongolian language borrowing from the Turkish language. An Altaic expert has suggested that nearly 25 percent of Mongolian vocabulary is of Turkish origin.[12] While the first borrowing by the Mongols may have occurred from the Xiong-nu (also known as Hsiung-nu), or the Asian Huns (Turks), subsequent borrowing must have occurred from the Tabgač (Turks) by the Khitans (Turco-Mongols) in the fifth and sixth centuries.[13] The adoption of Turkish loanwords in Mongolian continued during the hegemony of the Gök-Türks and the Uighurs in the eastern Eurasian steppes. Even during the rise of the Khitans in the twelfth century, Uighur Turkish had a significant influence on Mongolian.[14] Indeed, it appears that much of the shared vocabulary between the Mongols and the Turks in the thirteenth and fourteenth centuries actually comprised loanwords borrowed from Turkish.¹⁵ Borrowings continued in subsequent centuries as well. Following the fall of the Mongol Empire in the fourteenth century, Čaghatai Turkish emerged in western Turkestan while receiving some influence from the Mongolian language. This particular Turkish dialect evolved from the language of the Qarluq Turks, who had been in this geographic area for a long time. By contrast, the Mongolian linguistic influence was the greatest among the Siberian Turks of Tuva, Khakassia, as well as among the Turks from the Altai Mountain region since they remained under Mongol rule the longest; however, the Tuva still use some of the oldest existing Turkish words, dating back to the eighth and ninth centuries.¹⁶

Linguists have demonstrated that Proto-Turkic was spoken as early as 3000–500 BCE.¹⁷ Nevertheless, the first-known written record of Turkish is the eighth-century Orkhon inscriptions left by the Gök-Türks in the Orkhon valley in modern-day Mongolia. It provides an example of Old Turkish, also known as the Old Turkic language. Formally we have no records of Turkish predating the eighth century. But linguists have worked to reconstruct the language on the basis of Turkish names and words recorded by non-Turkish-speaking peoples, such as the Chinese and the Greek-speaking Eastern Romans.¹⁸

The earliest example of Turkish actually goes back to the period of the Xiong-nu, or the Asian Huns. According to Chinese documents, the Xiong-nu imperial ruler used the title of *shan-yu*. In the Chinese inscriptions, the full title was noted as *ch'eng-li ku-t'u shan-yu*. This statement has now been reconstructed as *tengri kut'lu shan-yu*, which is translated from Old Turkish as "heavenly blessed shan-yu" or "majesty son of heaven" or "great son of heaven."¹⁹ Linguists have suggested that the word *tengri* (God, heaven), as well as words for animals and plants of the steppes, was later borrowed by the Mongols from Xiong-nu Turkish.²⁰ There is no doubt that the Xiong-nu (Asian Huns) spoke the Turkish (Turkic) language.²¹ According to linguistic evaluations, the European Huns, as the descendants of the Xiong-nu of Asia and the immediate subsequent Turkish-speaking tribes in the Pontic Steppe (modern-day Ukraine), used the Oghur dialect of Turkish.²² Today, Oghur Turkish survives only in modern Chuvash, spoken in the Russian Federation.

In the eleventh century, Mahmud al-Kâshgharî, a scholar from the Qarluq Turks, wrote the *Grand Dictionary of the Turkish Language* (*Divan-i Lügat-i*

Türk), in which he stressed the unity of Turkish dialects and the Turkish world. It not only included extensive work on the Turkish language but also incorporated the first-known map of Turkish-speaking peoples. Even though modern Western scholars have divided the Turkish language and its speakers into two groups—Turkish (Western Turkish) and Turkic (Eastern Turkish)— Mahmud al-Kâshgharî used the word Türk indiscriminately to encompass all speakers of all dialects of Turkish. Indeed, there was never such Turkish/ Turkic differentiation in the history of the Turks. Hence, as stated earlier, to stay loyal to historical evolution, the word Turkic will not be used in this book. Within the context of historical distribution of Turkish tribes, scholars have divided the Turkish language into six major branches, on the basis of its dialects. These are listed as follows:

- Southwestern (Oghuz) branch: Azerbaijan, Gagauz, Turkey, Turkmenistan
- Northwestern (Qïpčak) branch: Balkar, Baškïr, Kazakh, Kyrgyz, Noghay, Qarachay, Qaraqalpaq, Tatar
- Northeastern (Siberian) branch: Altai, Khakas, Shor, Tofa, Tuvan, Yakut
- Southeastern (Qarluq/Čaghatai) branch: Uighur, Uzbek
- Oghur branch: Volga Bulgar, Chuvash (near extinction, owing to Russian influence)
- Arghu branch: Khalaj (now extinct)

THE HISTORICAL EVOLUTION OF THE LANGUAGE

On the basis of the input of linguists and research on historical Turkish states, the following correlations with these branches of the Turkish language can be made:

- Southwestern (Oghuz) branch: Ottoman Empire, Safavids, Seljuks, Aq-Qoyunlu, Qara-Qoyunlu, Golconda Sultanate
- Northwestern (Qïpčak) branch: Golden Horde, Kazakh, Tatar

- Northeastern (Siberian) branch: Yakut
- Southeastern (Qarluq) branch: Uighurs, Qara-Khanids, Uzbeks, Timurids, Mughals
- Oghur branch: Avars, Bulgars, Huns, Khazars, Gök-Türks (?)
- Arghu branch: Khalaj (Delhi Sultanate)

The Huns did not leave any written records behind. What we know about them is their Turkish names and titles as recorded by the Chinese, Romans, and Greeks. The first-known full written text is from the Gök-Türks, written in what is known as Orkhon Turkish. Western linguists are not ready to place Orkhon Turkish, the language spoken by the Gök-Türks of the eighth century, into any specific category. It is also referred to as Old Turkic. In fact, the period between the fall of the Gök-Türks in the eighth century and the rise of the Mongols in the thirteenth century is considered the period of Old Turkish.[23] In this period there are three potential sections. The first consists of East Old Turkic, which includes the language of the Eastern Gök-Türk Qaghanate and resembles Oghuz Turkish; it is believed that at this stage, the language did not show definite dialect breaks. The second is Old Uighur, on the basis of written manuscripts from the ninth century and later appearing to be similar to East Old Turkic, mentioned above. Finally, the third is spoken Qara-Khanid (Qarluq), which was the first Islamic Turkish literary language, written in the Arabic script. The accounts of a Ghaznavid poet contain the first mention of the division of Turkish dialects into Qarluq-Uighur grouping and Oghuz-Qïpčak grouping on the basis of geographic locations of these tribes.[24]

The period of Middle Turkish began in the thirteenth century and continued to roughly the end of the fifteenth century. It is represented by Common Turkish (Oghuz, Qïpčak, and Uighur) and Oghur Turkish (Volga Bulgar).[25] Historically, this period included Khwarezmian Turkish, which later evolved into Čaghatai Turkish, spoken by the Timurids and later the Mughals. The origin of the Čaghatai dialect was the Turkish spoken by the Qara-Khanid Qarluqs. During this period, Qïpčak Turkish (documented in the Codex Cumanicus by missionaries) was present in Mamluk Egypt and in the Golden Horde Khanate.

In the period of Premodern Turkish, beginning in the sixteenth century, Khalaj (Arghu-branch Turkish) completely disappeared. During this time the Čaghatai dialect evolved into the Turkish spoken in modern-day eastern Turkestan and Turkmenistan regions. However, the arrival of Uzbeks speaking Qïpčak-dialect Turkish into western Turkestan created the modern-day Uzbek language with the mixture of the preexisting Čaghatai Turkish dialect in this area. The Kazakh language arose from the Qïpčak dialect of the former Golden Horde Khanate. Meanwhile, in the west, the Oghuz dialect gave birth to Ottoman Turkish and Azerbaijani, which also evolved into rich and distinguished dialects. The modern-day Tatar and Baškïr languages are closely related to the Qïpčak branch of Turkish, whereas Chuvash is the surviving descendant of the former Volga Bulgar (Oghur), which is a distinct dialect of Turkish.[26]

Meanwhile, the Turks who spoke the Siberian branch of Turkish came under significant influence of the Mongolian language since they remained under Mongol rule for a long period, from the thirteenth century until the eighteenth century, when their lands were taken by the imperial Russians. These Turks include the Altai, Khakassia, Tuva, and Yakutia (Sakha). This branch of Turkish dialect still includes ancient Turkish words. Of all the Turkish dialects, probably that of the Yakuts' remains most similar to ancient Turkish, since until the nineteenth century, when they came under Russian influence, the Yakut Turks were practically immune to outside influences as they survived in northern and northeastern Siberia through the ages. Moreover, the names Kyrgyz and Yakut remain the oldest tribal Turkish names surviving into the modern era since ancient times.

THE TURKISH WRITING SYSTEM

The Chinese writing system is based on hieroglyphic characters, but the first Turkish system, as we are aware today, appears to be a runic form that dates back to the eighth century and likely even before. This writing system is alphabetic. It was deciphered by Vilhelm Thomsen in 1893 upon his discovery of stone inscriptions in the Orkhon valley, in modern-day Mongolia. The Orkhon alphabetic signs were called *tamgha* by the ancient Turks; this is an ancient Turkish word used for signs as a form of communication and for tribal marks (for branding livestock, tents, and banners).[27] Although some scholars believe that this alphabet, consisting of ancient Turkish tamgha signs, was a Turkish invention, others believe that it was developed from a Semitic-origin alphabet.[28] However, according to other scholars, the ancient Turkish tamghas of the sixth century, ancient Glagolitic characters of the eighth century, Sarmatian marks of the first century, and zodiac signs all seem to have derived from a common source; these signs are thought to have a magical value strangely related to one another.[29] Similar ancient runic signs have been found on the coins of the Sassanians (third to seventh century), White Huns (fifth to seventh century), and Seljuks (eleventh to twelfth century).[30] The runiform writing system, also referred to as the Orkhon script, was known to a variety of Turkish peoples of the Eurasian Steppe, including the Bulgars, Khazars, Kimeks, Pečenegs, Gök-Türks, and Uighurs.[31]

Before the introduction of Islam into the Turkish world in the eighth century, the Turks used many different lesser-known scripts as well; these included the Hebrew, Manichaean, Brahmi, Tibetan, Nestorian (Christian), and Armenian scripts.[32] In the fourteenth century, there was contact between the Crimean Armenian diaspora and the Qïpčak Turks, among whom some accepted Christianity and used the Armenian script for their writings. It appears that some groups of Qïpčak Turks in the twelfth century chose the Judaic faith and used the Hebrew script, as the Khazar Turks did before them in this region.

Starting in the eighth century, the Arabic script began to establish itself as the new alphabet of the Turks who accepted Islam as their faith. The first examples of Turkish literary works written in Arabic letters are from the Qara-Khanid Khanate of the Turks. These are Yusuf of Balasagun's *Qut-adgu Bilig* (*Wisdom That Brings Good Fortune*) and Mahmud of Kashgar's *Diwan Lugat-i Turk* (*Compendium of the Turkic Dialects*).[33] Beginning in 1927 the Turkish states of western Turkestan began to use the Latin alphabet. On November 3, 1928, the Republic of Turkey abandoned Arabic script for a modified Latin script. However, by the 1930s, all the Turkish peoples of the Soviet Union were forced to use the Cyrillic alphabet. Later, after the fall of the Soviet Union, in the 1990s, the former Turkish Soviet republics of Azerbaijan, Kazakhstan, Kyrgyzstan, Turkmenistan, and Uzbekistan went back to using Latin scripts, while Cyrillic remained an accepted form.

1.2. AN ENRICHED CULTURE

The Turkish culture is a rich basket of traditions that evolved over more than two millennia over a large territory stretching from China in the Far East to Morocco in the west, from the Russian plains in the north to the Arabian Peninsula and the Indian subcontinent in the south. The Turks, even though they were conquerors, did not impose their own customs upon the people they conquered. Instead, they borrowed from the customs of the conquered people to synthesize new forms of their traditions. Consequently, the original nomadic traditions of the Asian steppes became quite complex over the centuries. During this long period, Turkish customs incorporated elements from Arab, Chinese, Greek, Indian, Persian, and European cultures.

The ancient Turks were heavily influenced by their faith of Tengriism, a form of monotheism, which not only affected these nomads in hunting and war but also influenced its followers in the creation of art, known as the "art of the steppes."[34] The Turks initially were exposed to the rich Chinese culture for more than a millennium. The Xiong-nu (Asian Huns) are known to have been the earliest intermediaries of cultural exchange between China and the West.[35] In other words, they facilitated the start of exchanging merchandise between the Far East and the West through the Silk Road. This role was later assumed by the Gök-Türks, who traded between China, the Eastern Roman Empire, and Sassanid Persia. More than a millennium before the British began to purchase silk and tea from China, the Turks were trading their horses for silk and tea.

Until the Turks arrived in the Middle East, the Persian traditions there faced extinction when the Abbasid Arabs pursued a policy of suppressing

Persian elements in the Islamic territories. In fact, the rich Persian culture was in danger of being replaced by Arab culture in its homeland, Iran. But the situation changed in the eleventh century, when the Turks took complete control of Iran and the Middle East, which lasted just short of a millennium. Because of their patronage, the Turks played a crucial role in saving Persian culture from being suppressed by Arab influence. From the end of the tenth century, with the establishment of the powerful Turkish rule of the Ghaznavids across Iran, modern-day Afghanistan, and northern India, the Turkish rulers became great patrons of Persian culture. Subsequent rule by the Seljuks, the Timurids, and later the Safavids took Persian cultural development to new heights. Modern-day Persians owe the Turks, for Turkish support allowed Iranian culture to survive forever.[36]

This section gives a brief overview of Turkish cultural experiences from the past.

THE USE OF SILK

In the classical era and the medieval period, silk was a luxurious commodity used for trade. In fact, silk was the most important lucrative item sought from China across the Eurasian continent. As a result, the trading route between China and the West eventually came to be known as the Silk Road. Even though China tried to keep the art of sericulture a secret to keep its monopoly on the silk trade, silk farming eventually reached Korea, India, and Sassanid Persia. Nevertheless, China remained a major silk producer, unsurpassed in its quality. The spindle wheel was likely invented in conjunction with silk technology linked to silk production during the Chou (Zhou) dynasty (1046–256 BCE) in China, but it was not until the second half of the first millennium CE, it is believed, that the silk spindle wheel and silk technology were introduced in Europe.[37]

Among the Turks, silk was used in textiles, particularly for the clothing of nobles. This was apparent in the famous Turkish caftans, which were similar to the *changshan* of the Chinese in the Qing dynasty. The Russians borrowed the word *caftan* from the Turks, and it became a Turkish loanword in English.[38] Bursa, after becoming the capital of the Ottoman Empire in 1335, eventually became its most important center of raw-silk production and silk-textile making. Then the Ottomans did not have to rely so much on Chinese silk, and silk importation declined over time when Bursa peaked in silk production in the nineteenth century.

TURKISH HOT DRINKS: TEA AND COFFEE

One of the most cherished Turkish pastimes is drinking hot tea. The tea itself is called *chai* (*çay*) in Turkish. This is an ancient word borrowed from the (Mandarin) Chinese. Many European and Near Eastern nations formerly under the Turkish sphere of influence borrowed the word *chai* from the Turks; among these are the Albanians, Arabs, Bulgarians, Croatians, Greeks, Persians (Iranians), Romanians, Russians, and Serbians. The Turks have been drinking tea since the beginning of the Common Era. Today, Turkey is self-sufficient in tea production.

The Turks primarily were responsible for introducing coffee to the world as a delightful and addictive beverage that many of us enjoy today, sipping it from our cups and mugs. By the late sixteenth and early seventeenth centuries, Westerners had become acquainted with the famous Turkish coffee, which was cultivated as a favorite pastime during the Ottoman Empire after the Turks conquered Mamluk Egypt. The English word *coffee* originated from the Turkish word *kahve*, which itself was derived from the Arabic word *qahwah*, meaning an "alcoholic drink or a fragrance,"[39] since the drink provided its consumer a stimulant effect as well as an aroma. The Turkish *kahve* eventually became a loanword in European languages late in the sixteenth century.[40] Coffee was originally discovered in Ethiopia, but in the late fourteenth or early fifteenth century, it was introduced to Yemen.[41] This southern Arabian Peninsula territory, the source of Turkish coffee, was added to the Ottoman Empire in 1538 with the efforts of Admiral Hadïm Süleyman Paša, who was a well-known commander of the Ottoman fleet in the Indian Ocean, thus facing Admiral Afonso de Albuquerque of Portugal a number of times in this arena.[42]

Coffee was consumed in Mamluk Egypt by the early sixteenth century. But the Arabs initially consumed coffee by ingesting crushed coffee beans for the stimulant effect to stay awake longer during religious rites. When the

Ottoman Turks conquered Egypt in 1517, Muslim merchants brought coffee to Istanbul, the capital of the Ottoman Empire. The Turks, however, used coffee only as a beverage.

Hence, the Turks became acquainted with coffee for the first time in the first quarter of the sixteenth century, and by the middle of the same century, coffee had become an integral part of Turkish life and culture. But Westerners were unaware of it. Venetian ambassador Gianfrancesco Morosini in a report in 1585 described his amazement at the Ottoman Turks' favorite pastime: "The favorite entertainment of all Turks—from the important men right down to the lowest of them—is to congregate in shops or on the streets and drink a black liquid called kahve (coffee) as boiling hot as they can stand it."[43] The first Turkish coffeehouses were established in the Ottoman capital Constantinople in the year 1550, and by the end of the sixteenth century, while Venetian merchants were importing coffee into Europe,[44] the consumption of coffee was common across the Ottoman Empire and later virtually the entire Islamic world. Finally, by the seventeenth century, both coffee as a beverage and Turkish coffeehouses had gained social, political, economic, and religious significance.[45] The Turkish style of coffee preparation and use were so unique that when the beverage itself were adopted by Western (European) culture, it was called *Turkish coffee*.[46]

The first Turkish coffeehouse is believed to have opened in the Tahtakale quarter of Istanbul. Nearly a century later, in 1669, Müteferrika Süleyman Agha, the Ottoman ambassador to France, popularized coffee with his guests from Parisian society while hosting them in his opulent mansion.[47] Coffee entered the London market in the mid-seventeenth century;[48] by the late seventeenth century, Turkish coffeehouses were also spread out in the Egyptian countryside;[49] and finally, by the eighteenth century, coffee was everywhere.[50]

Coffee as a beverage today occupies such an important place in Turkish lives that breakfast itself is called *kahvaltı*, which translates as "before coffee." A cup of coffee is consumed for pleasure after a hearty breakfast. The Ottomans successfully introduced Turkish coffee into the daily lives of Western societies. Today's Western coffeehouses, such as Starbucks and others, are the modern versions of the former famous Turkish coffeehouses. Traditional Turkish coffee is served with Turkish delight on the side.

THE EPIC STORIES OF THE TURKS

Although the early Turks did not leave written records until the eighth century, their stories lived on through oral traditions. Starting in the nineteenth century, the oral stories and poetry of Central Asia became of interest to Western scholars.[51] It is now claimed that there is evidence for Altaic influence in Greek mythology and Romance art.[52] The old Turkish epic stories were known as *dastan* (Persian for "tale" or "story"), often written in a mixture of verse and prose, presented by a singer, or *dastanjï*.

There are significant similarities between the stories of the Anglo-Saxon *Beowulf* and the Kyrgyz epic *Er Töshtük*. Even though the peoples who kept these oral traditions were from different racial groups, there was a time when the early Germanic and Turkish nomads were acquainted with each other. As early as the third and fourth centuries, the Huns were in contact with Germanic tribes. The similarities in the motifs and patterns of these epic stories are likely a product of the narrative carried into Europe by the migrations of Central Asian tribes.[53]

The story of Manas, a Kyrgyz epic, is another ancient oral tradition that has survived to our times. It is a powerful and highly developed oral epic poem thought by Homeric scholars to be comparable to the ancient Greek epic the *Odyssey*.[54] Indeed, the Turkish oral epics of Inner Eurasia are so rich that these Asian folktales have been thought to be the sources for Homer's epic.[55] Manas is considered to be a monumental artistic production that draws on the spiritual life and the traditional ways of the Kyrgyz in addition to memorial feasts, bridal events, military campaigns, and so on.

The legend of Ergenekon is an epic story of the genesis of the Gök-Türks. It tells how the tragic experiences of a probable Hunnish royal family brought them from near extinction to becoming a major power (more in chapter 5.3). The story of Alpamïsh is an Uzbek dastan that apparently has parallels with the *Odyssey*.[56] By completing heroic tasks, Alpamïsh wins the heart of his bride, Barčïn. Later Alpamïsh finds himself imprisoned in foreign lands, but he is finally freed through the help of his horse. He returns just in time to stop the marriage of his bride to someone else and proves his identity by wielding his forefather's mighty bow. Finally, the two lovers of the story are able to consummate their marriage. A variety of versions today vary from sixteen hundred verse lines to fourteen thousand verse lines.

The legend of Oghuz Qaghan is another story, about the birth of a tribal group of Turks. It is a form of heroic epic with prose and verse. In this story Oghuz Qaghan becomes the qaghan (emperor) of the entire Turkish world. He starts giving a name to every non–Oghuz Turkish tribal confederation one by one on the basis of merit. Finally, the story ends with his sons becoming the heirs of the Oghuz tribes, which spread across the world.

The oral epic tales of Dede Korkut are a compilation of multiple stories. They present the moral values, social lifestyle, and heroic stories of the Oghuz Turks. Like other Turkish epic stories, these are presented in both prose and verse. They are believed to have originated in the thirteenth or fourteenth century. The tales of Köroğlu are adventure-romance epic stories that seem to have originated in the sixteenth century. Köroğlu is the son of a man who was unjustly blinded (the name Köroğlu means "son of a blind man"). He goes on a quest for justice as a warrior and a minstrel. The stories are about a hero who struggles for the sake of those who suffer under unjust tyrannical rulers. His actions in these tales resemble the chivalry of Robin Hood. Many of these tales live on in the folk songs of Turkey.

SHADOW THEATER

Shadow theater is an ancient form of entertainment that is widely prevalent across a large geographic area from China to India and from Turkey to Egypt and Europe. Although China has a very sophisticated shadow-theater culture and many scholars believe that this art form started in China, evidence to the contrary suggests that the origin of this form of theater is either Central Asia or India.[57] In fact, leather-based shadow-play figures have been found in nomadic graves from the first millennium BCE around the Altai Mountains; hence, it has been suggested that the technique of the shadow theater originated among the nomadic tribes of the Central Asian steppes, and as a result, they were likely the first performers.[58] The flat figures made of leather, felt, paper, cloth, or bark by Central Asian Turkish nomads are thought to have been related to their Tengriist religious beliefs. In fact, a Song dynasty source quoting a T'ang-period observation states that these figures likely represented the gods of the Gök-Türks.[59]

The Turkish *karagöz* shadow play is popular not only in Turkey but also across the former territories of the Ottoman Empire. On the basis of available records, the well-known karagöz shadow theater of Turkey did not appear until the sixteenth century, when the Ottoman Turks conquered Egypt, but this type of entertainment was already in use among the Mamluk Turks of Egypt in the thirteenth century. While tracing back the history of this form of entertainment, the shadow theater does not appear in China until about the tenth century.[60] Although shadow theater was likely used among the (western) Turks at least since the twelfth century, the Mongols in the thirteenth century are believed to have spread this form of entertainment from China to Iran, Egypt, Turkey, and North Africa.[61]

MUSIC FROM ASIA

With such a long history and exposure to many cultures over two millennia, Turkish music evolved into many forms. Turkish folk music (*Türk halk müziği*) is the most traditional and possibly the least influenced form of music in Turkey. The tunes definitely carry an Asian flavor. The most common musical instrument for this form of music is *saz*, which is a string instrument derived from the ancient Turkish *kopuz* of Central Asia. This instrument has become popular across the land that the Turks conquered. Consequently, other ethnic groups borrowed the saz as their traditional musical instrument. For example, the *bozuk* of the Turks came to be known to the Greeks as the *bouzouki*.

Turkish string instruments show great variety, with the two-string *meydan sazï*, three-string *çura*, six-string *bağlama*, eight-string *bozuk*, and nine-string *aşïk sazï*. In the Black Sea region, the most popular string instrument is the *kemençe*, and in the Aegean region, the *kabak* is one of the most commonly played instruments. Turkish string instruments have been played throughout Asia. In fact, the ancestral Turkish steppe instrument *kopuz* became a popular string instrument in Mongol courts both in the east and in the west.[62]

Turkish classical music (*Türk sanat müziği*) is a form that was developed at the Ottoman palace and in major Ottoman cities across the Turkish empire. The tunes for this type of music are a mixture of Asian and Middle Eastern style and thus with Arab and Persian influences as well. Long before the development of European orchestras, Turkish classical music was played by multiple musical instruments, and therefore, it required an instrumental ensemble, at times with a single singer. One of its instruments, the *qanun* (or *kanun* in Turkish and Arabic), is claimed to be a descendant of the ancient Egyptian harp. Although there have been many claims as to the origins of the Turkish *qanun*, it is plausible to think that since the Turks came from Asia, it may have originated in the ancient Chinese instrument known as the *guzheng*.

Turkish wind instruments also show a great variety, including *zurna* (always played with *davul* [drum]), *kaval* (flute), *ney* (ancient mystical flute), and *tulum* (bagpipe). The drum, the traditional instrument of the shaman and a symbol of the cosmos, was the musical instrument of war for the Xiong-nu (Huns) and most recently for the Ottoman Turks.[63] With his Tengriist faith, the nomadic warrior believed the drum and his sword each had a magical soul, making him invincible on the battlefield with a magical power.[64] The Pečenegs' preferred musical instruments were pipes and cymbals.[65] The drum also signified independence. In fact, the depiction of drums on the reverse side of the Osmaniyah Order of the Ottoman Empire was a sign of independence of the empire.

MILITARY MUSIC

Military bands are an ancient Turkish tradition. Even the eighth-century Orkhon inscriptions of the Gök-Türks describe the military band. The Sha-t'o Turks of the tenth century, while reigning in northern China, had a group of musicians reminiscent of the Ottoman *mehter* band, as well as dancers, when going to war, and according to Chinese records, the musical instruments included the "three-stringed Hunnish fiddle" and the Ch'iang (Tibetan) flute.[66] During the period of the Seljuk Turks and the early Ottomans, musicians playing drums and *zurna* in front of the monarch formed the military band, known as *askeri mızıka* or *nevbethane* (nevbet house). In the old Turkish tradition, *nevbet vurmak* meant "to play military music in front of the monarch," who would stand and listen until the end. The group was also known as the *nevbet-i sultani*. The early Ottoman monarchs continued the tradition of listening to *nevbet* while standing until Sultan Mehmet II, the conqueror of Constantinople, changed this tradition. Consequently, the sultans no longer needed to stand to listen to nevbet. The name *mehter*, derived from the Persian word *mihter* (greater), appeared for the first time in the Ottoman court in the sixteenth century, and it replaced *nevbet* permanently. Previously known by its older name, *nevbet-i sultani*, the Ottoman mehter military band became the world's oldest known military band.

The mehter group played with multiple instruments together in an ensemble. There were different types of percussion, wind pipes, cymbals, and bells. Percussion instruments included *kös* (bass drum made with leather stretched over a very large copper bowl), *nakkare* (kettledrum made with leather stretched over two small hand-carried copper bowls), and *davul* (made with leather stretched over both sides of wooden drum hoop). The wind pipes included *boru* (initially made out of bark but later out of copper or brass) and *zurna* (wooden pipe played with straw reed). The other instruments were *zil* (Turkish cymbals made out of copper-tin alloy) and *çevgen* (small bells attached to a brass crescent).

Both the initial battle cry and the thunderous, constant beating of the battle drums of the military band helped the sultan's troops focus on the battle and demoralized the enemy. For the old Turks, the large percussion instruments signified independence and power. It has been noted that when Sultan Selim went into battle in Čaldïran against Safavid shah Ismail, the Ottomans had five hundred *kös* in the mehter. The music of the Turkish military band was played during the siege of Constantinople in 1453, and a European eyewitness of the events reported, "With the sound of drums and other musical instruments they made even the sea emit sounds. Trumpets, however, were seldom used because they did not have many of them."[67]

The *zurna* became a permanent instrument of the mehter, starting in the early sixteenth century. The nevbethane of the Mongol Ilkhanids included *boru* and drums, but that of the Turkish Artuklu Beyliği (emirate) used *boru*, kettledrums, cymbals, and bass drums.[68] Miniatures of the Mongol Ilkhanids and the Turkish Timurids from the fourteenth and fifteenth centuries do not show *zurna*, whereas their Ottoman counterparts from the sixteenth century and afterward do. The use of military bands, particularly employing the use of battle drums, to engage troops was already quite developed in pre-Ottoman Turkish armies.[69] The Ottomans simply elevated this ancient inherited tradition to higher levels of perfection.

It is a well-known fact that the music of the mehter had a deep influence on famous European musicians. By the sixteenth century, Europeans had started to form their own military bands, taking the Turkish example. The use of Turkish drums, cymbals, and triangles in particular were adopted into the Western opera starting in the seventeenth century, with reference to the Turkish context. Christoph Willibald Ritter von Gluck (1714–87), from Vienna, Austria, was one of the first Western composers who made use of the Turkish bass drums and cymbals, especially in passages that he designated as Turkish or in the Turkish style (*alla turca*), where cymbals and drums provided a march feel, with almost every beat emphasized. Franz Joseph Haydn (1732–1809), also a great composer from Austria, is considered the father of symphony. He was a teacher of Beethoven and a friend of Mozart. His second Turkish opera, known as *L'Incontro improvviso* (1775), using the bass drums and cymbals, had a specific rhythmic motive in its Turkish-music passages. But among Western composers, Wolfgang Amadeus Mozart (1756–91), another musician from Austria, is the best-known Turkish-style (alla turca) composer. There are wonderful examples of alla turca in his Violin Concerto no. 5 in A (1775) and his Piano Sonata no. 11 in A Major (1781–83). In the latter, its last movement, known as the Turkish Rondo (also referred to as the Alla Turca), is one of Mozart's best-known piano pieces, imitating the sound of the mehter (the Turkish janissary band). Ludwig Van Beethoven (1770–1827), a German composer studying under Haydn, also used alla turca sections in works such as *Die Ruinen von Athen* (1811), *Wellingtons Sieg* (1816), and the Ninth Symphony (1824). Another composer who used alla turca sections was Italian Gioacchino Antonio Rossini (1792–1868), whose great examples include his famous "Turkish operas," such as *L'italiana in Algeri* (1813). German composer Jakob Ludwig Felix Mendelssohn Bartholdy (1809–47), also known as Felix Mendelssohn, used a specific alla turca rhythmic motive in his world-famous "Wedding March," which is the intermezzo between acts IV and V of his *A Midsummer Night's Dream*, composed for William Shakespeare's play of the same name.⁷⁰ Over time "Wedding March" became popular across the globe, and it has been used in many wedding events. Other examples of the mehter's influence on Western composers include "The Capture of Kars" by Modest Mussorgsky (1839–81), from his *Solemn March*, and the Quartet for Chorus and Piano by Johannes Brahms (1833–97), from his op. 64, from the "Fragen" movement.

TURKISH CUISINE

It requires three important factors to evolve an existing world cuisine into a great one: possession of wealth, acquisition of sophistication, and lively interest in taste. The centuries of Turkish history are proof that the Turks have all three elements necessary to have developed a cuisine worthy of global recognition. The Ottoman Empire, by conquering vast territories across Europe, Asia, and Africa, not only became one of the richest monarchies of the world during its zenith but also acquired culinary sophistication by being exposed to multiple cultures of the world. As for the taste for food, it has always been clear that eating is one of the favorite pastimes and customs of the Turks.

According to early Chinese and European records based on the observations of the chroniclers when the Huns were on their military expeditions, ancient Turks consumed meat on skewers (shish kebab) and yogurt.⁷¹ But the mainstay diet for the nomads was dairy products, since consuming them did not reduce the size of their flocks.⁷² These products included milk (*süt*), cream (*kaymak*), butter (*yağ*), cheese (*peynir*), koumiss (*kïmïz*, from mare's milk), and yogurt (*yoğurt*). The last was also consumed as a cheese-like solid food prepared by straining (*süzme*).

While the Turks borrowed from other cultures to synthesize their modern-day complex culinary art, the nations that they conquered were strongly influenced by their cuisine and dietary habits as well. For example, Turkish dairy products, which are known as staples of the Turkish kitchen, have become part of the cuisines of the nations that they ruled. Greek yogurt is well known in the Western world, owing to marketing, but *süzme yoğurt* (strained yogurt) is actually an ancient Turkish tradition. Yogurt has multiple uses in the Turkish kitchen; it can be consumed plain, with meat, with soup, or as a diluted salted drink known as *ayran*, or it can be used as the sauce for a main dish. It can also be served as a cold side dish with cucumbers and olive oil with garlic; this is known as *jajïk*, or the Greek borrowing *tzatziki*. Yogurt, introduced into the Western culinary tradition with its original Turkish name, is one of the contributions of the Turks to the world diet. In some parts of the Turkish world today, yogurt is also called *katïk*.

Koumiss (*kïmïz*) is a traditional Central Asian nomadic alcoholic drink made by fermenting mare's milk; kefir is produced by fermenting cow's milk. The latter has long been a traditional drink among the mountaineers of Caucasus and was introduced to the Western world in the late nineteenth century.[73] In the production of both, fermentation is catalyzed by yeast and bacteria.[74] Kefir and koumiss, like yogurt products, are a good source of probiotics, which are live microorganisms; they are believed to provide therapeutic and preventative health benefits when ingested. According to clinical studies and case reports, probiotics are useful for medical conditions such as diarrheal disorders (viral, antibiotic induced, *C. difficile* colitis, and traveler's type), irritable bowel syndrome, immunologic/inflammatory disorders (atopic dermatitis, rheumatoid arthritis, Crohn's disease, ulcerative colitis, and prevention of asthma), small bowel bacterial overgrowth, dental caries, lactose intolerance, and high cholesterol, and they reduce the risk of colon cancer.[75] In Europe, yogurt-based drinks with probiotic sources constitute the fastest-growing product category among consumers.[76]

When it was necessary to cull the animals, the nomads would either roast them on a spit or boil them in a large pot called *kazan*. In the winter, since their animals were leaner, giving less milk, they relied more on hunting. Fishing and gathering wild plants on the steppes provided additional sources of nourishment. But overall, animal products, such as meat and dairy products, were the principal sources of the ancient nomadic Turkish diet.[77]

Chopping meat was an ancient Turkish practice used by many different Turkish groups and represented by the same common word, *kïyma*.[78] Uncooked *kïyma* was used to make sausages. Before becoming Muslims, the Turks also made blood (*kan*) sausages (Islam prohibits consumption of blood). Drying meat into jerky (*kak*) was also used as a way of storing excess meat for later use. Small pieces of meat were called *tikkü* or *tikke*, good for stew.

Another Turkish dried-meat item is *pastïrma*, also known as *bastïrma*, which comes from an ancient nomadic Central Asian tradition. It is seasoned and air-dried cured beef. Its name is derived from the Turkish term for "pressed" meat. Under the Ottoman Turks, *bastïrma* gained popularity among non-Turks, and as a result, *bastïrma* is known by the Albanians (*pasterma*), Arabs (*basterma*), Armenians (*basturma*), Greeks (*pastourmás*), Romanians (*pastramă*), and so on with similar words. Although the Western word *pastrami* is said to derive from the Yiddish word *pastrómeh*, this word also originated from the Turkish word *bastïrma*. A typical Turkish breakfast and appetizers (*meze*) for *rakï* (Turkish national alcoholic beverage) may include *bastïrma*.

Turkish breakfast may also be served with *sucuk* (pronounced "sujuk"), a spicy dried sausage and another popular meat item in former Ottoman territories with names derived from the original Turkish; hence, it is known to the Arabs (*sujuq*), Armenians (*suǰux*), Greeks (*soutzouki*), and Romanians (*sugiuc*). *Sucuk* is also known to the Kazakhs as *šujïq* and to the Kyrgyz as *čukčuk*. The Russians refer to it as *sudzhuk*. Often *sucuk* is a product of beef, but it can be made from horsemeat in Central Asia. Among western Turkestan and Volga-area Turks, there is a special type of *sucuk* made with horsemeat known as *kazï*. There are also sausage-shaped confections in Turkey still called *sucuk*.

Owing to their pastoralist lifestyle, the Turks also consumed offal, or organ meats, and other varieties of meats from their animals. Offal is known as *sakatat* by the Turks. It was normal to find the heart, kidneys, liver, testicles, and feet of an animal prepared for consumption. For example, soup made from lamb or sheep feet is known as *pača* soup; when the head of the animal is added, it is known as *kelle pača*. Delicacies can be made from brain and tripe as well. *Kokoreč*, also known as *kokoretsi* by the Greeks, is a specialty made from roasting intestines, preferably from suckling lambs, on a horizontal skewer over a charcoal fire.

Despite having a pastoralist nomadic lifestyle, the ancient Turks did not consume solely meat and dairy products. According to Chinese records, the Xiong-nu (Asian Huns) knew about agriculture. Grain and dried fruit, either cultivated or acquired by tribute or plunder, were consumed by the ancient

Turks. It is noted that the Chinese slaves of the Xiong-nu may have done the farming for them. The Kyrgyz and the Uighurs were also among the ancient Turks who had agriculture in their societies. The words for wheat (*buğday*) and barley (*arpa*) appear to be old within Turkish vocabulary. It is also known from ancient Uighur texts that these Turks had knowledge of making flour and noodles. *Divan-i Lügat-i Türk*, a Turkish dictionary written by Mahmud of Kashgar in the eleventh century, gives more information about the Turkish knowledge of agricultural terms. How long the Turks were aware of this type of lexicon remains unknown. On the basis of anthropological research on the graves of the Asian Huns, it seems the knowledge on agriculture may have been present among the Turks since before the Common Era. By the time mass conversion from nomadic lifestyle to a sedentary one began in the eleventh and twelfth centuries, they already had sophisticated knowledge on agriculture. The discussion of agriculture among nomadic and seminomadic Turks will be presented later in this book.

On cold wintry days, Turks have popular historical drinks that can spice up the taste buds of their consumers. *Boza* is a cold, nutritious, rich, filling drink, whereas *salep* is a hot, milky, relaxing beverage. Both can be consumed with a cinnamon topping. *Boza* is an ancient drink with a low alcohol content (usually around 1 percent) made from fermented grains. Typically it has a thick consistency with a sour taste. It is a common drink not only in Turkey but also in Kazakhstan, Kyrgyzstan, and the former Ottoman Balkan nations. The earliest recorded consumption of *boza* is noted from the tenth century. *Salep* is a popular drink made from the flour of wild orchids indigenous to Turkey. It is nonalcoholic. The Turks discovered this beverage by first grinding flour from the tubers of these wild orchids. It is believed that the drink made from these enchanted flowers demonstrates its healing power in a variety of ailments, including respiratory problems (bronchitis and cough) and gastroenteritis (diarrhea).

There are also cool, fruity nonalcoholic Turkish drinks known as *šerbet*. The word is a derivative from the Arabic root word *sharba*, which also can be found in the names of other drinks known to the Turks, such as *šarap* (wine) and *šurup* (syrup). *Šerbet* comes in a variety of flavors, including honey, fruits, rose petals, and spices. The beverage was very popular in the Ottoman

Empire, and eventually it reached Western civilizations in Europe. Early in the seventeenth century, the Turkish word *šerbet* entered the English dictionary as *sherbet*. Later the French word *sorbet* described a frozen dessert derived from the flavored sherbet. Turkish *šira* is a cool, sweet nonalcoholic drink made from slightly fermented grape juice. It is traditionally served with kebab or grilled meats. Another traditional drink is *šalgam*, which is a fermented but nonalcoholic beverage made from turnips. It can be consumed spicy or nonspicy along with kebabs or with the traditional alcoholic beverage *rakï*.

Mahmud's eleventh-century dictionary also provides information on Turkish cooking utensils such as the *sač* (domed iron griddle) and the *šiš* (skewer). The word *kazan*, which describes a useful utensil for the Turkish nomads, has been known as a large cauldron utlized to produce mass production of food for large groups of people. Mahmud's list of food items made of grain included *ekmek* (flatbread), *kavurmač* (toasted grain), *kavut* (grain fried in butter), *kömeč* (pancake baked in ashes), and *yuvka* (thin flatbread). *Tutmač* was a well-known noodle dish; It apparently had an important place in ancient Turkish banquets. *Mantï* is an ancient dumpling-type Turkish dish that is present from China to Anatolia. In eastern territories it is steamed, and each piece contains meat, whereas in the western Turkish realm, it is boiled in meat broth and served with garlic-yogurt sauce. The Koreans have a similar dish called *mandu*. The later-appearing similar dish in the West is known as ravioli.

Rice was also a popular dish among the Turks of the past. As they moved away from the Chinese sphere of influence to the Middle East, they came into contact with the Persian culture. Once they learned the Persian pilaf method of soaking and steaming rice, they forgot the ancient Turkish word for rice (*tuturkan*) and instead began to use the Persian version, *pirinč*.[79]

Once the Turks entered the Middle East, their cuisine became influenced by their Persian counterparts. *Yakhni* (meat stewed with vegetables) is an example of the Persian cooking appearing in Turkish kitchens. Arab *halwa* (sweet pastry) became popular as well. Even though shish kebab is an ancient way of cooking meat for the nomads on the road, the Arabic word *kabob* replaced its forgotten Turkish counterpart. However, the Turkish word *šiš* entered the English dictionary as *shish* for "skewer." Furthermore, both

Iranians and Arabs borrowed many Turkish dishes into their respective cuisines as well.[80] The Turkish *kavurma*, a dish of fried meat, was adopted into Arab cuisine as *qawurma*. As they ruled over the Arabs and the Persians for nearly a millennium, the Turks continued to develop new dishes that their neighbors continued to borrow from them.

Most dough-related cooking of the Turks was influenced by Far Eastern traditions, particularly from China. One of these examples is *börek*, an ancient Turkish dish made out of dough filled with meat or sweetened nuts and fried on a flat sheet of iron or baked in an oven. Turks also developed the Near Eastern style of baking sheets of filled pastries. Today, *baklava* is a well-known dessert that has been present from the Balkans and the Middle East to Central Asia since the time of the Seljuks. It is believed the word itself is derived from a Turco-Mongol common root.[81]

Ottoman cooking transformed the old eight-layered baklava into fifty- to one-hundred-layered *baklava* by inventing the paper-thin *yufka*, known as strudel or *filo* dough.[82] Pastries led to the development of multiple kinds of *börek* (such as *su böreği* and *Tatar böreği*) and dough-based desserts (*kadayif* and different kinds of baklava). In the fifteenth century, *hošaf*, a compote of dried fruit mixed in cooled fruit juices, was invented. The Persian *yakhni* that the Seljuks fell in love with was taken to new heights by the Ottoman Turks as they developed well-known dishes such as *musakka*, *silkme*, and *imam bayïldï*, in addition to *güveč*. Most of these dishes used eggplant. But the Ottomans went further in developing different uses of vegetables by stuffing them. Apparently the Arabs stuffed eggplants with meat, and the ancient Greeks used fig leaves to wrap around cheese. The Ottomans created a variety of *dolma* (hollowed vegetables filled with a variety of fillings) and *sarma* (stuffing material wrapped with either grape or cabbage leaves) dishes. Virtually any vegetable could be used as *dolma*. The popular Greek dish *dolmades* is a borrowing from the Turkish dish *yaprak dolmasï*, also known as *yaprak sarmasï*, for its grape-leaf wrapping with filling.

The extravagance of the Ottoman palace kitchens was well known. At the time of the conquest of Constantinople in the fifteenth century, Sultan Mehmet II had 40 master cooks in his kitchens. During the rule of Mehmet IV in the seventeenth century, the number of cooks swelled to 370, with an additional 150 bakers. In the nineteenth century, there were more than 400 confectioners. A detailed description of the rich offerings of Ottoman cuisine is outside the scope of this book.

The sophistication and richness of Ottoman Turkish cuisine heavily influenced the cuisine of Turkey's neighbors.[83] While many Turkish dishes were added to different national kitchens in Asia, Ottoman cuisine became part of many Balkan, Mediterranean, Iranian, and Central Asian cuisines.[84] Today, thanks to Ottoman contributions, Turkish cuisine is one of the top four cuisines of the world, together with Chinese, French, and Italian.

THE STIRRUP

The stirrup did not appear to be used during the epoch of the Asian Huns (Xiong-nu) or later, during the period of the European Huns. Hence, both in Asia and in Europe, it seems to have emerged after the Huns ceased to exist as a political entity. But even before then, Turkish mounted archers were masterful horseback riders able to use their weapons while at full gallop. The Huns attacking Roman Europe were described as being glued to their horses, and they were viewed as centaurs. Later, the introduction of the stirrup as a military tool allowed others to develop effective cavalry units as well. It appears that the stirrup was introduced in China during the period of the nomadic empire of the Juan-juan (Asian Avars) between the fourth and sixth centuries, and in Europe it began to be used in the Frankish armies in the seventh century.[85] In fact, the stirrup was introduced in Europe by the European Avars (chapter 4.4).[86]

According to a study of the etymology and usage of the term, the stirrup most likely was used for the first time between the fourth and sixth centuries CE.[87] It was the Turks who first used this crucial medieval warfare piece. For the Turks from the Eurasian steppes (Oghuz and Qïpčak), the stirrup was *üzengü*, while for the Turks of the Siberian steppes (Khakas, Tuva, and Yakut), it was *izenge*. There are ample data to show that the first use of metal stirrups on both sides of a horse by the Turks essentially revolutionized the art of warfare.[88] As a result, the nomadic Turks made a significant contribution to medieval European military history. With the use of this equipment after the eighth century, European monarchs provided land in return for the pledges of armored knights on horseback in times of need for the state.[89] Hence, with the introduction of stirrup and consequently the emergence of the cavalry force in Europe, a new feudal class was born.

EQUESTRIAN ARTS

According to the Chinese, the life of the Turks depended on their horses.[90] The Oghuz hero and his horse were bonded with such strong ties that the two were an inseparable pair. In an Oghuz epic story, when a hero witnesses his horse coming to his rescue, he says, "I do not call thee horse but brother, O truer than my brother."[91] When a hero died, his horse was either burned with him or buried with him, and the horse's tail was placed on a pole (*tuğ*). If a hero's fate was unknown, he was assumed dead, and consequently, his horse was sacrificed and its tail placed on a pole. This practice was present among the Turks at least since the period of the Gök-Türks if not before. Since the Tengriist Turks believed in the hereafter, they also believed that the sacrifice of the dead warrior's horse would allow him to have his beloved animal with him in the next life. Hence, the purpose of this practice was to honor the dead and provide him with a horse in his afterlife. But the practice continued into modern times as well. There are examples of the early Ottomans being buried with their horses. For example, the horse of Sultan Osman II (1618–22), Sesli Kir, was buried in the monarch's mausoleum at Üsküdar Palace.[92]

The Turks were known to take care of their own horses. They were their own saddlers and veterinarians, and this was true for their monarchs as well. In one story, the Uighur qaghan (emperor) was repairing his saddle when the caliph's ambassador was brought in, and Orhan Khan (1324–59) of the Ottomans was known to take care of the shoeing and other services of his own horse.[93]

Throughout history, including in modern times, Turks of various tribes and clans all have been known to be experts in horse breeding throughout Inner Asia. The Kyrgyz were known to have bred large horses, whereas the Bulak raised small horses. The Northern Alayondlu, Alakčin Tatar, Oğuz, Basmïl, and Tukshi bred dappled (*alaca*) horses. Historically, the Gök-Türks raised their hunter horses in the northern plains and the southern desert. The Čiğil bred theirs in Sogdiana. According to Kâshgharî, the Uighur qaghan's horses were found on the Issyk Kül plateau. The Khalaj or the Qarluq raised their horses in the mountains of Tokharistan, while the Čağdal did the same at Fergana, once called the gate of Turkestan.[94]

The horse was a symbol of power for the Turk. The Ottoman Empire reached its zenith with the help of the horse. The Oghuz epics proclaimed that the warrior on foot has no hope, and the cavalry remained the centerpiece of the former Turkish empire's armed forces until the emergence of the gunpowder era in the sixteenth century. Hence, the horse was revered as the defender of the nation and received an equal share of credit with its mounted warrior.[95] In antiquity and the medieval period of Turkish history, the horse was a symbol of royal power. *Alaca* (dappled) horses were frequently used by Turkish royals of ancient times; Central Asian Turkish petroglyphs illustrate such horses. These animals were also considered to have celestial importance.[96]

Among the ancient nomadic Turks, the horse was also considered a symbol of time. The horse was a vehicle showing the passage of time, and this vehicle was mastered by the monarch, who showed his mastery in royal ceremonial ridings. Among the ancient Turks, the god of time was known as Öd or Ödlek. In the old Uighur book *Irk Bitig*, the god of roads (Yol Tengri), the rider of a black-and-white dappled horse, seems to be associated with Ödlek, who is also mentioned in the eleventh-century book *Kutadgu Bilig*. Because the *alaca* (dappled) equine coat color was associated with time, the owner of the dappled horse, the monarch, was also considered the master of time.[97]

The speed of the horse was associated with time as well as with flying. The ancient Turks believed that a warrior could fly on horseback similar to the Greek mythological creature Pegasus. Kâshgharî in the eleventh century mentioned Turkish warriors wearing bird wings on their heads, illustrating this ancient belief.[98] Perhaps this is the reason the tradition of wearing feathers on Turkish hats as a sign of nobility was carried into recent Ottoman times.

Myths of flying horses were common in eastern Turkestan, where bird-shaped saddles were common.[99] Gök-Türk Altaic petroglyphs demonstrate the unique form and shape of Turkish saddles, which seem to have been preserved from Pazïrïk saddlery up until recently, including the Ottoman saddle (*Osmanlï eğeri*).¹⁰⁰ Ancient Turkish horses carried tribal marks, known as *tamgha*; these marks were either illustrative texts or pictograms.¹⁰¹

FALCONRY

It is suggested that falconry originated in Central Asia around 2000 BCE and later spread from there to the East and West.¹⁰² Falconry, also known as hawking, is an ancient art of taming hawks, most likely starting in the Eastern Eurasian Steppe and spreading eastward into China, southward into India, and westward into the Mediterranean world and Europe.¹⁰³ It has been suggested that, on the basis of some Egyptian hieroglyphs, falcons are thought to have initially been used in the hunting activities of the Egyptians as early as 1580–1350 BCE, the period of the Eighteenth Dynasty. But hawks, a symbol of divinity, were not likely part of falconry among the early Egyptians. In other words, there is no proof that the early Egyptians practiced falconry.

One of the earliest records of this ancient sport appears to be a bas-relief from the period of the Assyrian king Sargon II (722–705 BCE).¹⁰⁴ This time period roughly corresponded to the time when Scythians appeared with their Central Asian traditions in the Middle East. There is further evidence that the sport was likely present in Persia around 480–550 CE.¹⁰⁵ But this time corresponded to the appearance of White Huns on the footsteps of Persia. Other early evidence for falconry comes from the Far East. There are definite Chinese records detailing the use of hawks in the hunting activities of Wen Wang of the Ch'u Kingdom (689–677 BCE).¹⁰⁶ In reality all these three time periods appeared to be associated with the rise of the proto-Turks in these respective territories.

In the Far East, falconry was established during the Han dynasty in the first or second century CE, but there is also a mention of this practice in Ch'in (Qin) China in the late third century BCE.¹⁰⁷ The timing of these Chinese records correspond to the appearance of the Huns to the north of China. While it is clear that the Romans did not practice falconry, there are claims that the sport was transmitted to them from the Germans. But it appears that around the year 200 CE and afterward, when the Ostrogoths settled north of the Black Sea, they may have learned this practice from their conquerors coming from the East, the Huns.¹⁰⁸

Falconry as a sport did not achieve popularity as a hunting activity in the West at least until the twelfth and thirteenth centuries.[109] There is evidence that the Sha-t'o Turks, the conquerors of northern China in the early tenth century, used falcons when hunting, and the use of birds while hunting was practiced by the Chinese as well.[110] Birds of prey were also used in the royal hunting activities of the Ottoman Turks. It is said that in the fifteenth century, Sultan Murat II had about one thousand hounds and more than two hundred hunting birds of prey.[111] Under the reign of Sultan Ahmet I, there were 30 falconers (*doğanci*) in Enderun (the Inner Court), whereas in Birun (the Outer Court of Topkapï Palace), there were 271 goshawk keepers (*čakïrjï*), 276 peregrine falconers (*šahinji*), and 45 hawk keepers (*atmajaji*).[112] Today the use of the gyrfalcon by the Kyrgyz and the golden eagle by the Kazakhs as their national symbols comes from the ancient Central Asian tradition of horse-riding falconry.

SPORTS

In the present day, it is difficult to ascertain what sportive activities the ancient Turks may have been involved with, but what is accepted is that archery and wrestling, in addition to equestrian arts, used to be among the most popular traditional sports of these nomadic peoples. Although the Europeans might have first observed horseback riding by the Scythians, the arrival of the European Huns, with their excellence in using the bow while riding their horses, likely permanently introduced both equestrianism and archery into the European arena. Neither the Greeks of the classical period nor the Romans were known to be archers; in fact, whenever the bow appeared in Greece or Rome, it was considered an alien introduction, particularly from the East.[113] However, the Turkish Central Asian warriors of the past were known for their mastery of archery on horseback. The ancient Turks in Europe, such as the Huns, Avars, and Bulgars, gained great successes with their highly mobile mounted archers. The Eastern Roman chroniclers described the Huns appearing to be "glued to their horses," and a similar description was given for the later-appearing Avars in Europe.[114] Roman historian Jordanes wrote that the Huns were excellent horsemen skilled in the use of bow and arrow.[115] Seljuk mounted archers later won great respect from the crusaders.[116]

An archer had a composite bow, his arrows, a *siper*, and a thumb ring. The Turkish composite bow was made of wood, horn, and sinew. Historically, the Turkish bow was the most successfully developed of the composite bows of the Orient.[117] Its skeleton was wood to which strips of horn were glued to its compression site. On its back several layers of sinew fibers were glued. The bow maker produced his glue from the end pieces of tendons being cooked slowly over several days. For the sinew backing, the Achilles tendons of cows were used for flight bows, and steer tendons were used for war bows.[118] The bowstring was made of multiple silk threads with added loops of catgut. However, the early Turkish bowstring was likely made of horse hair.[119] Later, unslung silk was also used. The Turkish archer also used a *siper*, or an arrow guide, which was secured to the bow hand. Its proper use increased the accuracy of the shooter and the power of the draw. The thumb ring was another important accessory; it helped distribute the pressure of the string over the inner area of the end of the thumb and protect the thumb against injury at the loose.[120] Finally, the Central Asian reflex bow, also known as the composite bow, gave its users an advantage over their enemies for its greater maneuverability, wider range, and more piercing power.[121]

Just as the Xiong-nu (Asian Huns) under Mo-tun, the founder of their empire, used "whistling arrows," the Sha-t'o Turks (chapter 5.5) more than a millennium later had similar arrows with "musical sounds" that were produced from holes in the arrowhead.[122] These ancient weapons were also called singing arrows. The arrow in old Turkish culture was a symbol of power, as it was for the Seljuk and Ottoman Turks more recently. Just as modern-day ambassadors present their credentials, Turkish ambassadors or messengers of the past carried an arrow as a sign of authority. A similar custom was also prevalent among the Sha-t'o Turks of the tenth century, and a contemporary Chinese historian stated that this was a foreign custom.[123] Indeed, this was an ancient Turkish tradition.

Turkish archers were known for their ability to shoot over great distances. The advantage of the Central Asian composite bow showed in the traveling distance and the piercing power of the arrow. According to a record, in the art of shooting with the composite bow, Sultan Murat IV (1623–40) was the best of his time but not as good as the famous champion Toz-Koparan

(Dust-Raiser), who lived during the reign of Sultan Bayezït II (1481–1512).[124] In the old days, arrow-shooting competitions were common. For example, Yisüngkä, a nephew of Genghis Khan, was the Mongol champion, shooting at a distance between five and six hundred meters, whereas in the Ottoman Empire, the recorded champions were Iskender Toz-Koparan, with 1,281.5 *gez* (797 meters), and Sultan Selim III, with 1,400 pikes (889 meters).[125]

The Arrow Esplanade, known as Ok Meydanï, in Istanbul was a large field during the Ottoman Empire where Turkish archers showed their skill in shooting arrows over great distances. The great achievers were commemorated with carved marble pillars indicating their names and the distances they shot. At one time the park was full of these pillars. One of the remaining pillars indicates "fifteen hundred cubits" for Sultan Murat IV; another is marked "seventeen hundred cubits" for Toz-Koparan.

In 1794 Turkish ambassador Mahmut Efendi amazed British spectators in London when he shot a short arrow on horseback over a distance of 415 yards against the wind with his short Turkish composite bow, and subsequently he shot 482 yards; none of the British toxophilites could bend his bow as the Turk could.[126] The ambassador's bow today is kept at the Hall of the Royal Toxophilite Society in London. In 1798 Sultan Selim III, with his great strength and skill in archery, was recorded to have shot an arrow in the presence of British ambassador Sir Robert Ainslie to a distance of 1,400 pikes (Turkish measure), or 972 yards and 2¾ inches (English measure). According to another British record by Lord Bacon, a Turkish arrow was "known to pierce a steel target or a piece of brass two inches thick."[127] The success of the Turkish archers of the past was the result of the light, short arrow and a very powerful bow, in addition to great strength and skill.[128] In the present day, however, with technologically advanced modern bows, an archer can shoot longer distances with less strength than was needed to use the old Turkish composite bow.

The origins of the game of polo are not known. But it is considered to have been a sport of ancient cavalry units. In the annals of history, the first cavalry warriors came from the Scythians and the Huns. The earliest known recordings of polo come from Persia in the sixth century, but there are also such recordings from the period of T'ang China (618–907). Although the game of polo is not played in modern-day Turkey, it is known that the old Turks had an interest in this sport. It is a fact that the appearance of polo both in Iran and China corresponds to the rise of Turks in the sphere of influence of these countries.

Today we know that at least the Seljuk and Safavid monarchs engaged in the game of polo. Zahir al-Din Nishapuri, a Persian elite of the palace of the Seljuk Turks, observed Sultan Malik-Shah (1072–92) playing polo.[129] Sultan Ay-Beg, the founder of the Turkish dynasty of the Delhi Sultanate in northern India (volume 2, chapter 1.4), was noted to have died from an accident during a polo game in 1210. In fact, the game of polo was brought to India by the Turkish Central Asian conquerors of the subcontinent. As a result, the northern state of Rajasthan became the center of polo in India. In the present day, the cities of Jaipur and Jodhpur are well known for their skillful polo players. Meanwhile, the famous Meidan-i Shah (Royal Square) in Isfahan, Iran, offered a sandy esplanade for the Safavid monarchs to enjoy polo games with their Turkmen officers. According to Kâshgharî in the eleventh century, *čögen* (persianized form is *čevgen*) was a ball game played on horseback with a mallet-shaped root from a tree called the *bandal*. The details of this game as played during the Qara-Khanid period are unknown. It may have been similar to the modern polo game.

Equestrian sports remain an important part of the traditional cultural life of Central Asians, for whom a horse is a prized possession and horsemanship a much-prized skill. Long-distance horse racing up to one hundred kilometers, known as *baiga*, is practiced by many Central Asian Turks, including the Altai, Bashkirs, Kazakhs, Kyrgyz, Tatars, and Uzbeks. Often the riders are chosen from young male teenagers, sometimes riding without a saddle. The Kyrgyz refer to these races as *at čabysh*. In the highlands Kyrgyz females learn horseback riding starting in their childhood. They have their own races, known as *kyz dzharysh*. In addition, *audaryspak* is traditional Kazakh horseback wrestling, in which the winner has to pull his opponent to the ground while remaining on horseback. This game is known to the Kyrgyz as *oodarysh*.

The old Central Asian folk game known as *kyz kuumai* (chasing the bride) is a race between the groom and the bride, who is given a head start. They race in their traditional wedding outfits, and if the groom is able to catch up to her, he gets to kiss her, but if the bride wins, she has the right to beat him with her *kamči* (whip).

Central Asian Turks, including the Kazakhs, Kyrgyz, and Uzbeks, are known to play a popular ancient equestrian sport called goat grabbing. Among the Kazakhs it is referred to as *kokpar*, derived from the ancient Turkish word *kök-börü* (gray wolf). For the Uzbeks it is *küpkari*, and for the Kyrgyz *ulak-tartysh*. This very popular masculine sport, thought to be related to polo, is played between two teams of skilled horse riders who struggle over a decapitated goat, which the holder tries to place in the opponent's goal. The sport requires not only skill in horseback riding but also strength to carry the carcass, wrestle opponents, and reach the goal. It is played during celebrations of holidays and weddings, as well as at the start of spring (Nowruz) and in autumn after the harvesting is completed.

Another skillful equestrian sport is the Kyrgyz *jumby atmai*, which involves shooting at a target while galloping. The target is often attached to a thread hanging from an inclined pole, and the contestant is expected to break the thread using a bow and arrow. The sport of Kazakh *kumis alu* and the Kyrgyz *tyin enmei* involve picking up as many coins as possible from the ground while riding at a gallop. Central Asian horsemen also enjoy falconry on horseback using falcons or eagles to hunt for foxes and pheasants.

Another historic game is *jirid* (Turkish *cirid*), involving throwing javelins on horseback, and it is still played in Turkey's Erzurum. This game was known to have been played by some of the former Ottoman sultans.[130] It has been suggested that the game of polo is related to the ancient Turkish game of *jirid*.[131] Hunting was also a royal sport for the Ottomans, where the sultans rode their horses with hounds and hawks, an ancient Central Asian tradition (horseback falconry). The ancient Turks were likely interested in other sports, but the scarce records do not provide enough information about them. Chinese records indicate that the Xiong-nu (Asian Huns) were fierce warriors, but they also had diversions such as horse jumping and camel races.[132]

Although wrestling has been and is a common sport for many peoples, such as the ancient Greeks and the Japanese, the sport is also a national pastime for the Turks. It was always part of life for the former Central Asian warriors training in close combat. There are similarities between the traditional Mongolian wrestling *bökh* and the *kïrkpïnar* oil wrestling of Turkey. Both styles of wrestling take place in an open grass field. The annual Turkish *kïrkpïnar* wrestling competition is one of the oldest traditional sporting events, dating back to 1357, during the Ottoman Empire. Unlike the Mongolian version of open-field wrestling, in the Turkish style, the competitors cover themselves with oil from head to toe before beginning their matches, hence adding to the difficulty of the match, which has no time limit. The Tuvan Turkish (from Russian Siberia) wrestling style of *khüreš* (possibly derived from Old Turkish *keriš*, modern-day *güreš*) is similar to Turkey's outdoor oil wrestling, *yağlï-güreš*, without the use of body oil. The *khüreš* is also a traditional sport for modern-day Turks of Turkestan, including the Kazakhs and Uzbeks.

Soccer, known mostly as football outside the United States, is one of the most popular sports around the world. A popular belief is that modern-day football originated in England. In the West, the ancient Greeks dating back to around the fourth century BCE had records of a game where a ball was passed between players mostly by hand. Since the Romans tried to adopt the Greek culture into theirs, this game likely became part of Roman culture as well. By the fifth century CE, the Roman game was known as *harpastum*, but it seems it initially became more popular in Gaul.[133] It is believed that during the Roman occupation of the British Islands, the native Celts also learned about this game. *Harpastum* was apparently played on a rectangular field with two teams, where the objective was to get the ball from one side of the field to the opposite end. The athlete either kicked the ball or passed it by hand. The ball carrier was always at risk of injury since protection of the players was not one of the goals of the game. It appears that the ball game did not survive in the other Roman territories, but when the Romans left the British islands, the Celts continued to play this game in the ensuing centuries. But according to the descriptions, the game was not football (or soccer) as we know it; rather it appeared to resemble modern-day rugby. Interestingly, when the British arrived in the Americas for colonization, they found that the American Indians had their own traditional "football" game.[134] Were the British conquerors of the Americas influenced by what they saw? It is possible. Eventually we see the evolution of rugby being played with both hands and feet in Great Britain and in the American colonies. However, early in the second half of the nineteenth century, the Celtic or British football split into rugby and football. Did this split come as a result of the evolution of the British "football" on the basis of the observations of the British in their colonies? Ultimately, the British Football Association was formed in 1863, and the British Rugby (Football) Association in 1871. In essence the question is whether football (soccer) truly originated in Britain or whether the British learned about it during their presence in the colonial territories?

A form of kickball existed in Asia as well. Indeed, the Chinese Han dynasty in the second century BCE had some sort of kickball known as *tsu chu*, which used to be played during imperial birthday ceremonies. The Japanese also had a ball game called *kemari* by the sixth century CE. These facts demonstrate that kickball or football in one form or another was being played in different parts of Asia.

However, according to Chinese records, kickball was of non-Chinese origin but was apparently played among the Central Asian peoples. These archives indicate that the Sha-t'o Turks in China, including their highest officials, played this sport.[135] They also mention that the ceremony of the ascension of the first Sha-t'o emperor to the throne in 923 CE occurred on the "football" field. Even in the eleventh century, we find in the Turkish dictionary of Mahmud of Kashgar that the Turkish tribal youth played with a round ball in a game known as *tepük*; however, the rules of this game remain a mystery. One fact is certain: football (soccer) today is the most popular sport across the globe.

THE TURKISH CALENDAR

In the ancient pre-Islamic Turkish calendar, as in the traditional Chinese calendar, the years were named after animals, with similar animals as zodiac signs. Whether the Turks borrowed the ancient calendar from the Chinese or the Chinese borrowed it from the Central Asians is not clear. However, it would have made sense for Central Asian nomads such as the Turks to use animal names in their calendar since they used to follow a Tengriist faith, which was based heavily on the power of nature and animals. In the early years of their conversion to Islam, the Turks were still influenced by their pre-Islamic faith. The portal of the Gök-Medrese in Sivas, Turkey, reveals zodiac reliefs of twelve animals (akin to the Chinese calendar), which illustrate the ongoing shamanist Asian influence despite the fact that the building was built in 1271–72, during the period of the Seljuks of Rum, to provide Islamic education. Indeed, owing to their liberal spiritual background, the Anatolian Seljuks created unique sacred art in their buildings with the inclusion of figural representations that are unique and unparalleled in Islamic world history.[136] The stone-carved reliefs of Gök-Medrese were once part of the ancient Turkish calendar from the Tengriist period of Turkish history, particularly from before the Common Era. They include twelve animals, essentially identical to the traditional Chinese zodiac signs; these are the rat (*sičan*), ox (*öküz*), leopard (*pars*), hare (*tavšan*), dragon (*lov*), serpent (*yilan*), horse (*younda* or *at*), sheep (*koyun*), monkey (*maymun*), chicken (*tavuk*), dog (*it*), and pig (*domuz*). The Turkish zodiac was used for the twelve months of the calendar and for the twelve-year cycle, like the Chinese zodiac.[137] The calendar was based on a lunisolar system, with twelve solar months of twenty-nine to thirty days, periodically requiring an adjustment with the addition of a lunar month to keep the calendar's phases with the solar timing. The Uighur Turks were known to have used the twelve-animal calendar at least since the eighth century CE. When the Uighurs began to play an important role in the Mongol Empire's administration and cultural development, they also introduced to the Mongols the use of the Turkish calendar.[138] It appears that the most significant legacy of the Mongol invasion of Iran in the thirteenth century was the introduction of the Turkish twelve-animal calendar, which lasted until 1925, when the last Turkish Qajar dynasty was replaced with the Persian Pahlavi dynasty.[139]

The new year according to the old calendar was marked by Nowruz, meaning "new day" in Persian, which would have been *yeni gün* in proper Turkish. It is no secret that when the Turks were exposed to Persian culture in western Turkestan during their westward migration from the Far East, they became influenced by the ancient traditions of the Iranian world. Nowruz was one of the words the Turks borrowed from the Persian vocabulary. Today Nowruz is celebrated as the new year in Iran and in most of the Turkish world. While Nowruz indicated the equinox and the first day of the old Persian calendar, in the ancient Turkish pastoralist culture, it also signified the beginning of spring, and with it the beginning of a new year as well.

THE TULIP

The tulip today is associated with the Netherlands. But it is known that the first historical sighting of tulips by Europeans was in the Ottoman Empire. The Western word *tulip* was derived from the Turkish *turban*, which itself was a distorted derivative of the Persian word *dülbend*. The word *tulip* came from *turban* because the flower was likened to the large Turkish hat.[140] There is also suggestion that the tulip might have been derived from the Turkish *tülbend*, a cloth that was likely used to wrap around the tulip bulbs for their preservation during the winter months. The tulip was a prominent flower for the Ottoman Turks and was depicted in many Ottoman art forms. But it seems that prior to its use by the Turks, nothing was known about this flower in the Western Hemisphere. Neither ancient Greek nor Roman records mention the tulip. It is known that the tulip is indigenous to Asia, more specifically to the Eurasian steppes. Hence, it is clear that upon the arrival of the Turks to Anatolia in the eleventh century, they brought tulip bulbs along with them.

Busbecq, the ambassador of the Holy Roman emperor, was the first European who used the term *Tulipa gesneriana*, in 1554, and tulips were first mentioned in England in 1578.[141] After the tulip became popular in Europe, Constantinople became an export center for the gardens of western Europe.[142] It was said that Turkish tulips turned English gardens into Turkish seraglios.[143] The tulip entered the European market from Turkey in the late sixteenth century, and consequently, this exotic flower became a commodity among other non-European goods, such as tea, coffee, cocaine, potatoes, and tobacco.[144] But over time, the tulip, which had a significant impact on European consumers, was also changed by the Europeans into what it is today.[145] Ultimately, the Dutch successfully cultivated the flower to its present-day beauty.

COLORS

The ancient Turks of Central Asia used colors to define cardinal directions; these included blue, red, white, and black.¹⁴⁶ Within this old nomadic tradition, *gök* (blue) indicated east, *kïzïl* (red) south, *aq* (white) west, and *qara* (black) north. For this reason, the Mediterranean Sea might have earned its name of Akdeniz (White Sea) for the Turks since it was to the west when they arrived in the Middle East from Central Asia. In an attempt to organize his mounted archers in squadrons according to the directions that they needed to face, the Xiong-nu monarch Mo-tun placed bay or roan horses to the east, reddish horses to the south, white horses to the west, and black horses to the north.¹⁴⁷

Among Central Asians the colors had other meanings as well. Blue was sacred to the Turks as it represented heaven, the celestial world. Hence, the word *gök*, meaning "sky" or "heavenly" as well as "blue," was used for the great god of the Turks, known as Gök-Tengri. At the same time since blue for ancient Turks was considered to be the color of God it also signified infinity as well as sublimity.¹⁴⁸ Turquoise, also known as *Turkish blue*, has historically been a favorite color all across Central Asia, not just for its beauty but also for its talismanic virtue.¹⁴⁹ In the meantime, while blue was used to indicate holiness gray or gray-blue was used for ordinary animals. As it is well known, gray wolf has been considered to be a holy animal for ancient Turks yet they labeled this animal as blue-wolf or "gök-börü" whereas today many Turks refer to this mythical animal erroneously as gray wolf.¹⁵⁰

Red had been accepted as the color of love and happiness. For this reason the bridal kaftans and kadftans of maturity as mentioned by Dede Korkut were in red color, and therefore, the weddings used to be represented by this color as well.¹⁵¹ Yet, the Turks of Turkey have abandoned their traditional red bridal costumes in place of Western white bridal gowns. On the other hand, many brides still celebrate the traditional henna night (*kïna gecesi*) with red costumes or outfits together with female family members from both sides the day before the wedding.

Since the color red represented the blood, it was at times used synonymously with blood. However, red may have represented evil as well. For this reason, evil spirit 'Albastï' was associated with this color, and in addition, the old 'red tongue' term was used to signify villainous language. In old Turkish the word 'al' either signified orange color or very dark red, in which case it used to be accepted at the color of kingship.[152] Among the ancient Turks 'al' was also used for color of banner, nevertheless, due to historical facts this word did not necessarily indicate red color.[153]

Among the ancient Turks the white color represented wisdom and experience. It also signified purity and chastity. In mythological sense this color also meant goodness while black was representative of adversity, ill omen, and evil. Since the word black indicated northerly direction, the Black Sea may have acquired its name for being to the north of the Turks or because it was north was the source of the cold 'black wind' (karayel). If winter was very called, it was also referred to as 'black winter' (kara-kiš). In addition, black for Ottoman Turks was a sign of royalty. For this reason the members of their dynasty applied black feathers to their large turban hats as they also used black fur covers over their shoulders early on in their history.

For ancient Turks the yellow color was not a well-accepted color since it used to be the color of Chinese emperor and Chinese dragon. Yellow also represented evil and chaos. It was also used to label some maladies.[154] For this reason, this color was not commonly used by the ancient Central Asian Turks. Yet, in the thirteenth century affected by Chinese culture the Mongols used this color for the name of Golden Horde Khanate.

"White-red-blue" were the colors of the three banners or 'tuğ' used during ceremonies of shamans, and therefore, they were also among the favorite colors of ancient Turks.[155] As mentioned above, together with black these three colors were used to label major directions. However, the colors black (indicating north) and blue (indicating east) signified 'greatness' and supremacy' among the steppe nomads of Inner Asia, carrying more weight than the colors white (west) and red (south).[156]

LITERATURE

Ancient Turkish literature is based on oral traditions; examples of epic stories were given earlier in this chapter. It is conceivable that the Turks had written works since they were known to use a runic script, but because Turkish history was fluid, with population movements and frequent polity changes, hardly any record of the ancient Turks survived into the modern era. In addition, early Turkish polities were mostly nomadic, and consequently, there were no enduring fixed structures to store their written records. Hence, most of the early information about them has been obtained from the records of sedentary civilizations, such as the Chinese, Romans, and Greeks. The Orkhon inscriptions written in a runic script on stone pillars by the Gök-Türks in the early eighth century remain one of the earliest examples of written Turkish texts. The *Irk Bitig* (*Book of Omens*) is the only known book with the Old Turkish (Old Turkic) text written in the ancient runic script; it was discovered among the manuscripts found in the Hall of a Thousand Buddhas near Tunhuang (also known as Dunhuang), a city in the Gansu province of modern-day western China.[157] This Old Uighur textbook was likely written in the ninth century. Today it is preserved in the British Library in London.

Although the pre-Islamic Turks were generally known to be nomadic or seminomadic people, as will be discussed later, there are records indicating that their steppe empires communicated in writing with China and the Eastern Roman Empire. The Khazar Turks were also another group of sophisticated seminomadic people who used the runic script that the Gök-Türks used. Isaac Ben Abraham Akrish, a Jewish scholar from the sixteenth century, found tenth-century correspondence between (Turkish) Khazar monarch Joseph and Hasdai Ibn Shaprut, an Andalusian Jew and vizier of the court of the caliph of Cordova. Akrish published this material in 1577. In his letter Joseph explained the origin of the Khazars, their geographical location, their disputes with their neighbors, and the story of the conversion of the Khazars to the creed of Judaism.[158]

After the Turks converted to Islam, the first-known Turkish literary works written in the Arabic script came from the Turkish state of the Qara-Khanid Khanate. These were Yusuf of Balasagun's *Qut-adgu Bilig* (*Wisdom That Brings Good Fortune*) and Mahmud of Kashgar's *Diwan Lugat-i Turk* (*Compendium of the Turkic Dialects*) from the late eleventh century. From that point until the early twentieth century, Turkish literary works were written with the Arabic script. We see that many literary works were affected by the cultures and traditions of the local peoples whom the Turks had conquered. For example, the literature of the Ghaznavids of Afghanistan and India became heavily influenced by Persian literature. The same was true for the Mughals of India and the Seljuks and Safavids of Iran. The Ottoman Turks were influenced not only by Persian literature but also by Arabic culture and language. This subject matter will not be elaborated any further, since the scope of Turkish literature, with its wide geographic distribution and historical evolution, has a long discussion material of its own and it is not part of this book. The purpose here was to provide the reader an idea that the early nomadic Turks were able to read and write in a world when the literacy rate was low even in civilized areas.

CERAMICS AND POTTERY

The emergence of the art of ceramics corresponds to the use of pottery, which was already in use by the end of the first millennium BCE, particularly in Iran.[159] But with the help of the Silk Road, we see the use of ceramics from the Roman Empire in the west to China in the east. Particularly in China, the art of pottery reached its peak during the T'ang (618-907) and Song (960-1279) dynasties. During the Abbasid Arab dynasty, Arab and Persian crafters took the art of pottery to new heights. Their works often rivaled the exquisite Chinese ceramics.[160]

In the fourteenth century, the Ottoman ceramics industry was established in Iznik (Nicaea) by Sultan Murat I (1359-89), and Iznik ceramics and pottery thrived during a short period between the late fifteenth century and the end of the sixteenth century under the patronage of the Ottoman court.[161] Under the rule of Suleiman the Magnificent (1520-66), Iznik became the ceramics center of the Ottoman Empire.[162] During the zenith of the empire, from the fifteenth century to the end of the seventeenth century, the empire attracted artisans from all corners of the empire and from Asia, Europe, and Africa. Consequently, a rich Ottoman artistic style was developed, and the works that were produced amazed following generations.[163]

From the fifteenth to the eighteenth century, glazed tile was the primary decorative tool used in Ottoman architecture.[164] Ottoman pottery in the fifteenth and sixteenth centuries had the finest samples that the Muslim world produced.[165] Iznik pottery in particular, with its unique brilliance of glaze and color, reached a new height. Iznik porcelain initially reflected the blue-and-white influence of the Chinese Ming dynasty (1368–1644), but eventually Ottoman artists began to interpret Far Eastern motifs in their own creative ways.[166] Iznik ceramics and pottery later adapted to polychromic character. In the sixteenth century, Ottoman ceramics witnessed the use of turquoise blue.[167] While the use of emerald green and violet was common, in the same century, the use of the characteristic red pigment became popular as well. Concurrently, the application of floral motifs of tulips, hyacinths, carnations, and roses emerged as a new decorative style.[168] The Süleymaniye Mosque, completed in 1557, was the first building where Iznik glazed tiles with red pigments were used.[169] Beginning in the seventeenth century, particularly after the great fire of 1606, the Iznik ceramics industry experienced a progressive decline. But for half a millennium, Ottoman Turkish carpets, textiles, and ceramics were part of European material culture. Furthermore, complex and powerful Ottoman Turkish art left an impact on the artistic expression of Europe for centuries to come.[170]

PAINTING

Miniature painting is popularly believed to be a Persian cultural element even though it is not. Miniature painting, in fact, is an old tradition, and early examples can be found in China. Naturally, Turks migrating from the Far East to the Middle East brought this tradition to their new home in the Levant. The custom of drawing human subjects with slanted eyes continued in both Turkey and Iran. Hence, the human figures in these paintings appeared more Asian than Middle Eastern owing to the tradition brought into this land by the Turks, who primarily provided patronage for this art form in a land where human figures were forbidden by the Arab caliphate in early Islam.

Besides miniature painting, the Turks brought another cultural element to the Middle East. European travelers to Turkey and Iran in the middle of the sixteenth century described their observations of marbled paper, which was later introduced into Europe about the year 1600. For about two and a half centuries after that, this type of decorated paper was used in bookbinding and wallpaper as well as for other decorative work.[171] The source of the marbled paper again appears to be the Far East. The earliest known color-dyed paper was silk paper from China, first described in the third century CE, but the use of marbled paper was noted at least in the early tenth century on the basis of sources from the T'ang dynasty. In Japan the technique, known as *suminagashi*, seems to have appeared in the late Heian period (794–1185) and was likely influenced by Chinese culture.[172] It has also been suggested that this art was already present in Bukhara in Central Asia in the fifteenth century from the Timurid period.[173] But there is evidence that the marbling of paper was practiced in Turkestan in the thirteenth century, well before the appearance of the Timurids; hence, the technique was likely used during the earlier Seljuk period and subsequently in the Ottoman Empire. The marbling of paper, known in Turkish as *ebru*, was common across the Near East as early as the fifteenth century. The name *ebru* likely came from the Persian words *ab* (water) and *ru* (surface), even though the art itself is not Persian. This Turkish tradition was also found in the sixteenth century in the Turkish sultanates in Malwa and Deccan, in south-central India, but according to some scholars, the technique was transferred there from Iran.[174] This would not be surprising, since Persia came under Turkish rule beginning in the eleventh century (volume 2, chapter 2.5).

KILIMS AND CARPETS

Among the hand-knotted carpets in the world, the best known are Persian and Turkish carpets. Carpet weaving is an integral part of the cultures of both Iran and Turkey. While a Persian carpet uses a single-looping knot technique known as the Persian or the Senneh knot, the traditional Anatolian (Turkish) carpet is made with a double-looping knot referred to as the Turkish knot. It has been said that the art of making hand-knotted carpets is a "gift of the Turks to the world civilization."[175] In other words, Turks were likely the inventors of the knotted pile carpet.[176]

The oldest known hand-knotted rug is the Pazïrïk carpet from the fifth century BCE, found during excavations of a kurgan at the Pazïrïk burial site in the Altai Mountains near the intersection of the Altai Republic (Russia), Kazakhstan, China, and Mongolia. This historic carpet piece was discovered during the Pazïrïk excavations between 1948 and 1949 by Russian archaeologist

Rudenko, who believed that the finds belonged to the Scythians. Some Western scholars believe that this was the work of an ancient Indo-European culture. Some believe that the Pazïrïk carpet is a Scythian artifact, but others claim it is more likely to be of Hunnish origin.[177] It has been suggested that this carpet piece likely originated between 300 BCE and the year of Christ's birth. However, taking into consideration the demographic makeup of the Altai area and other characteristic findings from these excavations, it has been suggested that the Pazïrïk carpet was produced by the Xiong-nu (Asian Huns).[178] Hence, it is thought that knotted-carpet weaving originated with Central Asian nomads instead of sedentary civilizations and that this carpet originated in Central Asia rather than Persia.[179]

The women of Turkish tribes before the third century CE were known to knot and weave carpets for their tents.[180] In the fifth century, Priscus, a delegate from the embassy of the Eastern Roman Empire, while giving a description of Attila's tent, mentioned a carpet being in front of the Hun emperor's seat.[181] Even today many Near Eastern nomadic tribes produce hand-knotted carpets, which are part of their heritage.

One of the main motifs of the Pazïrïk carpet was also found in a Seljuk work of art.[182] Indeed, certain motifs of the ancient Pazïrïk carpet were also found centuries later on Seljuk bowls.[183] Furthermore, this historic carpet was not produced with the Persian-knot technique; rather, it was made with the Turkish knot, which apparently has not changed over the ages.[184] This is despite the fact that the Persian knot was already known at the time of Pazïrïk burials, on the basis of a Bashadar saddlecloth made with the Persian knot.[185] The Pazïrïk carpet today is exhibited at the Hermitage Museum in Saint Petersburg, Russia. More recent samples of nomadic knotted-carpet fragments found at Lou-Lan and Lop-nor in eastern Turkestan are from the third to the sixth century CE; these specimens today are at the British Museum in London, and other pieces are at the Museum of New Delhi, India.

Kâshgharî pointed out that the Turks had a habit of tying their horses' tails before engaging in battle. This was also observed in the well-known Battle of Manzikert of the Seljuk Turks in 1071. Late Han Chinese art demonstrates that Xiong-nu horses had either cut or knotted tails, which was a common practice among medieval Central Asian Turks. Interestingly, this detail is also illustrated on the Pazïrïk carpet.[186] Horses with three-dented manes are illustrated in the Pazïrïk motifs, and a similar presentation of horses was common in Altaic, Siberian, and eastern Turkestan cultures. These horses were pictured in northern Turkish petroglyphs, particularly in Sulek and in the Altai regions. In addition, horses with tufted manes were seen among the Anatolian and the Altai Turks.[187]

It is clear that the carpet is an invention of Central Asian nomads. For them the carpet covered the floor of their living area within the yurt (tent) and insulated them from the bare ground.[188] The primary reason the single-knot weaving system did not become popular among the nomads is that carpets woven with this technique were not durable, and the nomads could not afford to constantly look for raw materials to replace their carpets. Instead, they created the double-knot system, which allowed them to produce more reliable and durable carpets.[189] The nomads found their colors from nature; trees, flowers, a variety of plants, and even certain types of soil provided them with an incredible kaleidoscope of color sources. With the introduction of chemically produced aniline dyes from Europe in the late nineteenth century, the production of natural root dyes in Turkey began to decline, but the ancient tradition has been kept alive by nomadic Turkmen communities.[190]

The Turks brought their carpets and their traditions with them while settling in the ninth century in Samarra, Iraq, the capital (838–83) of the Abbasid Caliphate, where they held military power as the caliph's personal mamluk troops (volume 2, chapter 1.2). It has been said that the Turks introduced the legendary flying carpet of the epic story *One Thousand and One Nights* into the Arab world.[191] The Turks are known to have brought the knotted carpet to Egypt as mamluk soldiers, and examples of these items were found at Fostat, an ancient site near Cairo.[192] Some of these carpet fragments can be seen at a variety of prominent museums, including the Metropolitan Museum of Art in New York, the Röhss Museum in Gothenburg, the Arabic Museum in Cairo, the National Museum in Berlin, and the Textile Museum in Washington, DC.

When the Seljuks and later the Ottoman Turks arrived at the Anatolian plateau, they brought a rich variety of Central Asian designs to this new land. Although there do not appear to be any carpet samples from the Great

Seljuk Turks, who ruled their empire from Iran, a few fragments survived from the period of the Seljuks of Rum. Over time, Anatolia has become one of the most important carpet-producing locations in the world.[193] Other places of significant carpet production include Iran, Turkmenistan, Uzbekistan, Afghan Turkestan, Caucasus, India, and China. Ottoman rugs, based on age-old Turkish traditions, incorporated ideas from the refined Seljukid and Timurid cultures and from Safavid Persia to earn recognition as one of the most fascinating art forms of the Islamic world.[194] When the Ottomans conquered Tabriz, the capital of Safavid Iran and one of the most important centers of carpet weaving, they learned about Iranian Turkmen tapestry as well.

The influence of Seljuk-style Turkish carpets in European artworks became apparent when animal-figured carpets became fashionable in the paintings and frescoes of European painters during the fourteenth and fifteenth centuries.[195] Among these examples are Filippo Memmi's *Mary and Infant Jesus*, Ambrogio Lorenzetti's *Madonna and Child Enthroned with Saints*, Giovanni di Paolo's *The Pope Enthroned Attended by Saint Catherine of Siena*, and Bartolomeo's *Scenes from the Legend of Saint Vincent Ferrer*. European artists continued to be influenced by the evolution of Turkish carpets. Starting in the fifteenth century, the geometric designs and, later in the century, floral motifs of Ottoman Anatolian carpets began to show up in Western paintings and frescoes.[196] Examples include Pierro della Francesca's fresco in the Church of San Francesco, Mantegna's *Mother and Child*, and Luca Longhi's *Virgin Mary and Child*. Admiration for Ottoman Turkish rugs became evident in Italy, the center of the Western Renaissance, as many Italian noblemen ordered carpets for palaces and churches.[197] Many of Europe's nobles treasured their Anatolian carpets, and they sought to show off their wealth by having them painted into their portraits.[198]

The Turkmen carpets of Anatolia still carry rich Ottoman traditions. While Turkmen carpets from Central Asia have features characteristic of the nomadic past, carpets from Iran and Turkey reflect multiple levels of sophistication on the basis of their decorations and motifs as well as colors, representing nomadic, village, city, and court experiences.[199]

1.3. FROM TENTS TO FIXED DWELLINGS

Prior to the second millennium CE, the Turks were known as a nomadic people. These pastoralist Central Asian nomads lived in felt tents known as yurt (*otağ*). But archaeological discoveries suggest that the former Turkish empires of the Xiong-nu, Gök-Türks, and Uighurs had urban life as well. The Chinese records support these findings. Indeed, written records and discoveries from excavations illustrate that even though the Central Asians of the past were known mostly as nomads, they also built permanent settlements in Inner Asia.[200] Furthermore, there is a suggestion that the first Turkish urbanization may have started during the Zhou dynasty of China (also known as the Chou dynasty, preceded only by the Chinese Shang dynasty); although this claim is controversial, the ruling class of this dynasty may have been of Xiong-nu (Asian Hun) origin.[201] It is a fact that China's longest-lasting dynasty (1050–256 BCE) was formed by the union of non-Chinese Ji and Jiang clans.[202] The likelihood of the dynasty's Central Asian roots may have facilitated the exchange of information and technology between the settled world of China and the nomads to the north.

Archaeological excavations at an Inner Mongolia site unearthed a Xiong-nu graveyard from the late Spring and Autumn period (770–480 BCE) and possibly the early Warring States period (480–222 BCE) of China. The discoveries were typical Xiong-nu arrowheads, horse fittings, and other metal items, including farming tools. These findings also showed that the Xiong-nu were not purely a pastoralist nomadic people; they pursued agricultural activities, and at least some of them had a sedentary lifestyle.[203] The discoveries of fixed settlements (dating from the third to the first century BCE) south of Ulan Ude, a city in the Republic of Buryatia, a Siberian republic of the Russian Federation, are further proof that the Xiong-nu were not entirely nomadic. Archaeological discoveries in the Abaqan, Orkhon, and Selenga valleys show Xiong-nu kiosk-style dwellings of noblemen with the Chinese technique of brickwork and a heating system made with pipes circulating hot air. It appears that the Gök-Türks and the Uighurs used this architectural technology as well.[204] Many of these structures also have tiles branded with Turkish tamghas. Chinese records claim that the Xiong-nu had fixed dwelling sites, owing to strong Chinese influence. Even though this is possible, the hypothesis completely disregards the fact that even nomads could have had permanent buildings at times owing to their cultural background. The discovery of large Xiong-nu cemeteries indicates that the Xiong-nu culture included fixed dwellings, and many of them did not exhibit Chinese influence at all.[205] Nevertheless, one cannot deny the fact that the Chinese culture ultimately had significant impression upon the nomadic peoples of the north.

There is information about the Di (or Ji) and Jung (or Jiang) tribes, known as the progenitors of the Xiong-nu, living in tents and fixed structures in cities near Chinese feudal city-states in the Zhou (Chou) period (1045–265 BCE). It appears that they had their own city-states, known as the non-Zhou states.[206] Furthermore, the Hien-yün (also a Di group of people), who have been viewed by modern-day scholars as the ancestors of the Asian Huns (Xiong-nu), had their own city-state, Chung-shan, which was eventually conquered by the neighboring state of Chao of the Zhou Chinese.[207] Hence, it is clear that the Xiong-nu, in addition to living in well-known Central Asian dome-shaped felt tents (yurt), constructed fixed dwellings as well. But the majority of the tribal people still lived in their domed felt tents.

When the Xiong-nu polity ceased to exist in the early third century CE, their knowledge of constructing buildings did not disappear. There is historical evidence of trading cities built by the Gök-Türks along the Silk Road in western Turkestan.[208] We also know that the Uighur Turks, as successors of the Gök-Türks, built cities with fixed dwellings;[209] Ordu-Balïq (City of the Army or Imperial City) and Beš-Balïq (City of Five) were among their well-known cities. Although some Turkish dialects use the word *kišla(q)* for "village" (actually this means "winter quarters"), the proper Old Turkish word for a town is *balïq*.[210] Old Turkish had two separate words, *ordu* and *balïq*, associated with settlement places. From Kâshgharî, the author of the first Turkish dictionary of the eleventh century, we learn that the word *ordu* was originally used to describe "a fortified castle and a city from where the monarch ruled." In a manner of speaking, an ordu was a royal city protected by the army. The word *balïq* was similarly used to mean "a fortified city" and was associated with the Turkish word *balčïq* (clay). *Balïq* has been equated with the Mongol word *balgasun* (for Balasagun), in fact also a Turkish loanword in Mongolian.[211]

An ordu in effect was a city modeled on a fenced nomadic encampment. An example of this was seen in the Zhou dynasty. With its non-Chinese origin, the organizational setup of the royal Zhou (Chou) dynasty city was thought to be of Inner Asian origin.[212] In fact, the Zhou royal city was formed by two concentric circumvallations; the inner one had "the throne of the world's monarch," while the outer section had four turrets, representing the four corners of the world. During the Xiong-nu period, fortifications and cities with rectangular circumvallations of earthen walls over wooden posts were built with Chinese techniques. Thus, the concept of the ordu (central imperial city) started among the Xiong-nu.[213]

When Genghis Khan's step-grandson Batu Khan established the Khanate of Altïn Ordu (Golden Horde) in modern-day Russia in 1236, he used the Turkish concept of the "royal city" but incorporated the Chinese tradition of using the color gold (or yellow) for the imperial family. A typical ancient Turkish city was also known as a *balïq*. The capital city of these Central Asians came to be known as an *ordu*, an ancient term dating back to the times of the Xiong-nu with the meaning of "camp of the ruler," but over time, since the Turkish monarch was dependent on his army, the word *ordu* eventually became associated with the army as well.[214] The English word *horde* was derived from *ordu*.

The Ephtalites (White Huns) and later the Turks of western Turkestan and the Khazar Turks continued the Xiong-nu concept of ordu, which was the residence of their monarchs. Within this concept, rather than using felt tents, the Khazar qaghans (emperors) resided in brick buildings.[215] The

Gök-Türks, influenced by the heavy presence of Buddhism, incorporated elements of sedentary forms of worship places into their Tengriist traditions. Such holy places were built on the ordu concept. The Turkish temple for worshipping was called a *tengrilik*, and an *ev-barq* referred to a temple with effigies of dead Gök-Türk noblemen.[216] After becoming Muslims, the Turks applied this concept in building mausoleums, a practice not known by Muslim Arabs, who used to bury their dead in unmarked graves. During the Gök-Türk period, the ordu concept was also used for protection of sacred cities, dedicated at times to a deity and at other times to a royal personality. The central structure was the old Central Asian Turkish temple, which had a cylindrical altar (*yağïslïq*) and resembled a domed tent, with its entrance located between two towers facing the east. However, the towers could have been in the corners of or near the main structure. Within this old architectural concept, in the old temple, construction rooms were later added to the central temple structure, extending the functionality of the building, resembling the future madrassas (Islamic schools). When the Turks converted to Islam, one can hypothesize, they brought their pre-Islamic domed-temple structure to the construction of mosques and madrassas. Clearly, in this evolving Central Asian temple structure, the towers of the ordu turned into minarets.[217] This description of the old Turkish ordu is somewhat reminiscent of the early Seljuk architecture of mosques, where double towers served as minarets on each side of the entrance. Excellent Seljuk examples are today visible in Anatolia. The thirteenth-century Seljuk architectural marvel Gök-Medrese in Sivas, Turkey, which was an Islamic institution, was built on the basis of this pre-Islamic style, with two towers (serving as minarets) on each side of its entrance.

The first mosque and subsequent mosques in the days of Prophet Muhammad did not have minarets; the idea of the minaret may have come from the bell towers of Christian churches during the Umayyad dynasty.[218] In the late ninth century, the architectural design of one of the earliest Islamic buildings of Egypt, the Ibn Tulun Mosque with its minaret, built by Ahmad Ibn Tulun, Turkish governor of Egypt, may have been based on the ancient Turkish ordu concept. However, it has also been suggested that the minaret model was copied from the minaret of the Great Mosque of Samarra, built in the early ninth century.[219] But the influence of the Turkish ordu concept in building the mosque in Samarra could have also come from the powerful Turkish mamluk warriors of the caliph. Using Uighur architecture of temples with slender cylindrical towers, the Qara-Khanid Turks built the first examples of monumental minarets in Turkestan.[220]

In the Uighur Empire, the first city was Ordu-Balïq in the Orkhon valley. Interesting observations from Tamim Bin Bahr al-Muttawi'i, a Muslim Arab traveler, probably in the year 821 CE, provide more information about Ordu-Balïq, where the Uighur qaghan lived. He noted that this thickly crowded city, with twelve large iron gates, was rich in agriculture and busy markets.[221] The traveler also described four large and four smaller towns nearby. He described all the Turks as *zïndïq* (Arabic for "infidel"). The Uighur qaghan's palaces included luxuriously built kiosks in the T'ang Chinese style.[222] The traditional domed cylindrical tents were still important, especially among western Turks, who were away from Chinese influence. The dome was revered among the Turks of the past. Even when they converted to sedentary fixed dwellings, they still used domed structures, whether in woodwork or in masonry, since the dome represented heaven.[223]

Among the other old cities built by Turkish monarchs were Bukhara, rebuilt in the sixth century by Yang Soukh Tigin of the Gök-Türks; Yangï-kent, built in the same century by Oghuz Yabghu; and an unknown island city on Tere-köl Lake, presumably constructed in the eighth century by Uighur qaghan Bayan Čor.[224]

Over time, influenced from their ordu concept, the establishment of geometrically designed palaces and gardens became a trait of Central Asian nomads.[225] The Timurids and later their descendants, the Mughals, also had geometrically designed gardens. In the eleventh century, the first ordu established by the Seljuks at Merv was based on a square design, but influenced by the designs of western Turkestan, the Great Seljuks at Rey built octagonal ordu, and in Konya they had hexagonal ordu. Sultan Mehmet II built his palace (Topkapï Palace) in Constantinople in a quadrangular format, keeping alive the Central Asian ordu tradition.[226]

After the Mongols of Genghis Khan destroyed the ancient city of Ji, his grandson Qubilai Khan in 1267 ordered the construction of a new city in its place, known as Ta-tu (Great Capital).²²⁷ The declaration of Ta-tu as the new imperial city of Qubilai Khan ended Mongolia's role as the center of historic nomadic empires. The city, which was known by its Turkish name Khan-Balïq (King's City) among the Mongols and the Turks, eventually came to be known as Beijing (earlier name Beiping, recently known in the West as Peking).²²⁸ As will be discussed later, the Mongols got their state-building knowledge from the Turks (volume 2, chapter 3.3). One historical fact is that the Mongols are culturally indebted to the Uighur Turks.²²⁹

There is also evidence that the Khazar Turks north of the Caspian Sea had fixed residential buildings and cities.²³⁰ The only remaining city today from the Khazars can be said to be Kiev, the capital of modern-day Ukraine. Kiev was originally named by its founders, the Khazars, as Sambat, a compound word from Turkish *sam* (high) and *bat* (power). In this context the Khazar word *sambat* meant "high fortress." The Eastern Romans added the Greek suffix *as* to make the word Sambatas.²³¹ Interestingly, after the Mongols destroyed the city of Kiev in the thirteenth century, it was rebuilt, and the Tatars called it Menkermen, again created from two words: *men* (high) and *kermen* (fortress).²³² The Oghuz Yabghu lived in a city known as Yangï-kent (under Sogdian influence in western Turkestan, the word *kent* was used instead of Turkish *balïq*).²³³ The Seljuks from the Oghuz Turks, who previously lived among the Khazars, brought their knowledge of ordu-style architecture to the Near East,²³⁴ later contributing to the emergence of Seljuk-style architecture in the Middle East.

THE EVOLUTION OF TURKISH ARCHITECTURE

Beginning in the eleventh century, but particularly in the twelfth century, we begin to see Turkish architectural pieces starting to blossom in Central Asia, Iran, the Middle East, Afghanistan, and eventually northern India. When the Turks came to the Near East, where they encountered the Islamic faith, they also met with the rich ancient Persian culture. Yet from the introduction of Islam in Iran by the Arabs, in the seventh century, until the late tenth century, there is no clear record of Persian culture and architecture in the

Persian-speaking world.[235] Persian culture was indeed suppressed by the Arabs, but it gained liberation with the arrival of the Central Asian Turks as the new leaders of the entire region for nearly a millennium. As the Turks began to establish new dynasties across a large geographic area from Anatolia to Khorasan, they used Persian inspiration mixed with their own Asian elements to create a new form of architecture. The Turks learned to use baked brick from the Persians. Hence, many large buildings were made out of baked bricks rather than stone blocks, as bricks could withstand the earthquakes that the region was prone to.

With the arrival of the Turks into the Islamic Middle East, a new style of wood carving with sloping surfaces appeared as Islamic art with a Central Asian character. At the various courts of the Seljuk family across the entire Middle East, including Asia Minor, Mesopotamia, and Persia, arts and crafts with Central Asian influence flourished as never before. In addition, the arabesque style, known as the supreme achievement of Islamic ornamental design, had its most magnificent development under Seljuk patronage. Architectural works became more monumental and were designed with new ornamental forms as well. The Seljuks also introduced Central Asian-style round and polygonal tomb towers or mausoleums made of brick where tombs were decorated with geometric designs. While Islamic art under the Arabs did not include shapes and forms of living beings, the Seljuk Turks, still carrying their traditional Tengriist and shamanic culture of Central Asia, used the figures of subjects and animals in their architectural decorations. Even mosques illustrated these unexpected representations of animals on their facades. Besides architectural development, many other art forms also excelled under Seljuk patronage; these included calligraphy, painting, metalwork, ceramics, wood carving, and carpet weaving.[236]

When the Turks began to transition to a sedentary lifestyle under the influence of Islamization, they tried to base their fixed dwellings on their agelong cherished traditional nomadic tents. In the old tent-life principle, each tent housed a single family. When the child of the house became older and married, he or she moved to a private tent. This principle was later applied to permanent buildings. Turkish house design was based on the Turkish nomadic tent, known as the *otağ* or *yurt*. However, early houses were built with multiple rooms, each having its own outside entrance; in other words, the rooms functioned like independent tents. Turkish houses with multiple rooms evolved into two-story buildings. The *sofa* was the centerpiece of the house, where the family would get together, like the center area of a tent. This area was the common living area, similar to the living room of a Western home. This was also where Turkish hospitality was shown to a guest. With the growing influence of Islam, the architectural layout evolved to protect women's privacy. Consequently, the first floor, or the ground floor, included a living room for men, known as the *selamlık*. This was where men from outside the family were hosted. The second floor had a living room for the women known as the *haremlik*. The garden of the house was enclosed in a courtyard with high walls to ensure privacy for the women. Today, Safranbolu houses are significant examples of old Turkish houses from the eighteenth and nineteenth centuries, and they have been entered into the UNESCO World Heritage List.

Turkish architecture, which evolved in the past millennium, took two somewhat divergent pathways after the Turks spread over a large geographic area with the help of their military skills. Those who moved westward encountered the Middle East and Europe, whereas those who moved south met with the cultural elements of the Indian subcontinent. When the Turks began to convert to Islam more than a millennium ago, they had their own Central Asian nomadic traits and Chinese influences. With the introduction to Islam, they became acquainted with Arab and Persian influences. The amalgamation of these cultural inspirations led the Turks of Central Asia to create their own unique architectural legacy, which became common across a large geographic area occupied today by the modern-day states of Kazakhstan, Uzbekistan, Turkmenistan, and Iran. As the Turks expanded their control in the Near East, they left more architectural imprints across modern-day Afghanistan, Azerbaijan, Bosnia, Bulgaria, Croatia, Egypt, Greece, Hungary, Iraq, Israel, India, Jordan, Pakistan, Romania, Saudi Arabia, Serbia, Syria, Tunisia, and Turkey. Historically, the Seljuks, then the Khwarezm-shahs and later the Timurids, expanded on the architectural developments over the vast central Eurasian steppes. But Seljuk architecture was the base of what was to come.

In the western Turkish world, the architecture incorporated Central Asian Turkish, Islamic, Persian, and Eastern Roman elements. The first examples of this group found in Anatolia came from the architecture of the Seljuks of Rum, which evolved from the synthesis of Central Asian and Persian influences like its earlier Great Seljuk counterpart. This was followed by Ottoman architecture, which incorporated Eastern Roman inspirations. Meanwhile, eastern Turkish architecture took off with the matured Timurid Central Asian culture, which came from the traditions of the Seljuk and Khwarezm-shah Turks. This unique group later evolved down two paths, Safavid (also known as Persian) and Mughal (also known as Indian) architectures. While the former perfected the Seljuk and Timurid architectures into a unique Iranian style, the latter formed a masterful fusion of Central Asian traditions of structural techniques and decorative designs with those of Persian and Hindu origin.[237] Indeed, the unique masterpieces of Mughal architecture are the ultimate result of the hybridization of Islamic, Persian, Hindu, and Turkish Timurid traditions.

THE SELJUK PROTOTYPE FOR SUCCESS

The Seljuk Turks had conquered Iran and the rest of the Middle East by the middle of the eleventh century, and they quickly adapted to their environment (volume 2, chapter 2.5). Their incredible military successes, including against the Eastern Roman Empire, precipitated the age of the Crusades. The Seljuks became staunch defenders of Islam. Consequently, the resistance the crusaders found in the Seljuks led to the creation of anti-Turkish biased message from their Western contemporaries that lived on until the present day. Consequently, the Turk came to be known in the West as a primitive tribesman, a barbarian, or simply "the unspeakable Turk." If the Turks had willed, they could have forced their Christian subjects to convert to Islam, but they did not. An objective review of history shows that the Seljuks had the rare quality of mercy that only a few nations have.[238] Adding to their Central Asian traditions, these Turks acquired cultural elements from the Arabs, Armenians, and Iranians. They subsequently welded them into a unique new entity, which became known as the Islamic Seljuk culture, from which Seljuk architecture was born.

Turkish architectural development thus officially begins with the Seljuk Turks. During the reign of the Seljuks over Iran, Khorasan, and much of the Middle East from the eleventh to the twelfth century, and in Anatolia from the eleventh to the early fourteenth century, Seljuk architecture essentially became the foundation of Turkish architecture. Under the Seljuks, architecture incorporated more and more intricate geometrical designs, including the technique of squinty, which was brought to new heights.[239] The Friday Mosque of Isfahan is a good example of such influence of Seljuk architecture by the end of the eleventh century. Relief brickwork was also a characteristic of Seljuk work, as was the monochrome system of decoration.[240] However, over time multicolored glazed bricks were introduced. The use of multicolors in Turkish architecture was more and more apparent under the Timurids. Ottoman architecture, by contrast, preserved the monochromic elegance of the exterior for the most part while using lavish multicolored interior decorations. This became one of the distinctive characteristics between western and eastern Turkish architecture. The introduction of colors was followed by the increased use of floral motifs. The use of glazed tiles for architectural decoration in Islamic structures began to appear by the end of the thirteenth century, and the metallic cladding of *mihrab* was in demand by the end of the Seljuk period and during the period of the Khwarezm-shahs.[241]

Seljuk buildings characteristically exhibited simple interiors but opulent portals. The decorative motifs and carvings on stones were lavishly displayed on the entrances of Seljuk constructions. Seljuk mausoleums (known as *türbe*) were built as circular or multifaceted towers with conical roofs. It has been suggested that the shape of the structure resembles the traditional yurt. These stone representation of yurts often exhibited decorative motifs with animal characters from the old traditions of the shamanist past of these Turks. Stone mausoleums were characteristic of the Seljuk architectural landscape.

Despite being Muslims, the Seljuks did not abandon their shamanist character immediately. Even though Arabs outlawed pictures and animal characterizations, Seljuk coins portrayed animal figures. The Gök-Medrese from the late thirteenth century (Islamic school in Sivas, Turkey) exhibits a sculpture of the tree of life at its entrance along with a relief of animal heads representing the Turkish-Chinese astrological calendar, a clear Central Asian trait.

The *caravanserai* was a public building used commercially but also for other community activities. The word derived from *caravan* (trade protector) and *serai* (palace). The Turks also called it *han* (from an Old Turkish word for "house"). These buildings had religious significance as well. Travelers were often given free hospitality, owing to the Turkish tradition. They were constructed by local governors and maintained by a legal endowment known as *waqf*. Caravanserais were built around a central arcaded courtyard, influenced by the layout of nomadic camps.[242] These structures were common along the trade routes.

Wooden mosques from the Seljuk period also provide a very important legacy from medieval Turkish history. The Ešrefoğlu Süleyman Bey Mosque, built in the late thirteenth century, is an outstanding example. The Eskišehir-Sivrihisar Mosque is another good example from this period. The Mosque of Mahmut Bey in Kasabaköy of Kastamonu, built in 1366, is considered the most beautiful example of wooden mosques in Turkey. The Masjid-i Juma (Friday Mosque), or the Congregational Mosque of Khiva, is a large, one-storied mosque with a tall brick minaret (originally built in the tenth century but renovated through the eighteenth century) left behind by the Seljuks.

In short, Seljuk Turkish architecture used the concept of open-space courtyards freely in caravanserais, mosques, palaces, *medrese*s (madrassas or schools), and even houses. Despite the fact that the Seljuks built many urban architectural structures such as these in addition to mausoleums, hospitals, and bridges, they probably preferred to live primarily in their yurts up until the thirteenth century.[243]

THE GHAZNAVID AND THE DELHI SULTANATE

The Ghaznavid architecture that found its way into northern India was based on the traditions developed in Iran by the contemporary Seljuk Turks in the eleventh century.[244] The Ghaznavids added the Turkish-Persian style of construction by incorporating local elements from modern-day Afghanistan and India. Later, the successors of the Ghaznavids in India, the Turkish monarchs of the Delhi Sultanate, continued the tradition. Seljuk Central Asian edifices with four-centered arches and domes soon became standard across the Turkish-ruled Islamic territories. The grandiose Quwwat al-Islam Mosque (Might of Islam Mosque) was built by Sultan Ay-Beg, the first Turkish monarch of the Delhi Sultanate (volume 2, chapter 1.4), to make a statement in India.[245] The Tughlug dynasty (1320–1412) of the Delhi Sultanate developed a new style with geometric designs and strong sloping walls made with red sandstone up to midheight and white marble above. This unique combination of materials and colors was to become a strong influence and basis for future Mughal architecture.[246]

In the fifteenth century, Turkish warrior-saint Ulugh Khan Jahan marked the initial period of Muslim architectural development in Bengal by building a city. The ancient city, known as Khalifatabad, is located today in the suburbs of Bagerhat. An examination of the city's infrastructure illustrates the masterful technical skill in building roads, bridges, and water cisterns. In addition, superbly built mosques, mausoleums, and public buildings decorate the ancient city.

Gol Gumbad (Gül Kümbet), completed in 1656, is an extraordinary Islamic structure with a large-domed square building with towers in its four corners. It is the mausoleum of Muhammad Adil Shah, the Turkish sultan of Bijapur. It was an architectural work created on the basis of twelfth-century Seljuk architectural knowledge, particularly with the use of intersecting arches.[247] The structure resembles the Great Seljuk sultan Sanjar's mausoleum, now located in Merv, Turkmenistan. It appears to be reminiscent of the ancient, or pre-Islamic, ordu concept mentioned earlier.

THE MAMLUK REVIVAL OF EGYPT

Starting in the ninth century, Turkish warriors began to enter the Muslim Arab armies of the Abbasid Caliphate as slave soldiers known as *mamluks*. One of these officers was Ahmad Ibn Tulun, who rose through the ranks to become the governor of Egypt, and subsequently he established the very first Turkish Muslim dynasty, known as the Tulunid dynasty of Egypt, in the second half of the ninth century. The earliest surviving architectural example from this period is the Ibn Tulun Mosque, which appears to be constructed on the basis of the pre-Islamic ordu concept of Central Asia. Later, after the fall of the

Ayyubid dynasty in Egypt, the Turkish Qïpčak Mamluks formed their own Mamluk dynasty of Egypt, threatening the Crusader States of Palestine. Under this dynasty, Turkish (Qïpčak) Egyptian Mamluk architecture evolved in the thirteenth and fourteenth centuries. The successful development of Mamluk architecture owes primarily to the influx of builders and artisans from the Middle Eastern territories that were devastated by the Mongol invasion.

THE TIMURID RENAISSANCE

Starting in 1379, Timur (volume 2, chapter 4.4) began to gather architects and artisans from the lands he had invaded, including Khwarezm, Tabriz, Shiraz, and later India and Syria.[248] The Timurid Renaissance (1405–1506) helped to revive the arts and culture in western Central Asia, particularly in Transoxus (also known as Transoxiana). During this time, architectural development evolved further from the standard Seljuk architecture. The traditional Central Asian architectural traditions continued to change further, establishing the foundation for later Mughal architecture. Timurid architecture was rich in polychromic ceramic decorations. Timurid Samarkand, the capital of the empire, had low mud-brick buildings, each with a courtyard where shade trees grew. There are some 250 surviving buildings from this period of Central Asian history. Timurid public buildings were known for their colossal size in addition to the quality and richness of their decorations, covering facades, and arcaded courtyards, as well as tall minarets and domes.[249] Timurid architecture employed the increased use of color with intricate ground plans and complex vaulting systems.[250] Eventually the architecture that evolved under the patronage of the Timurid rulers came to be known as the imperial Timurid style of architecture, characterized by the unifying force of the geometric action of design, structure, ornament, and space.[251] The Bibi Khanïm Mosque in Samarkand, the Goharshad Mosque in Khorasan, and the Ahmed Yasawi Mausoleum in Kazakhstan are among the many surviving Timurid architectural pieces in Turkestan. By adding to the well-established Seljuk-style buildings, fourteenth- and fifteenth-century Timurid architecture became a key new prototype in the development of Central Asian Islamic architecture, and therefore, it served as a foundation for the subsequent evolution of the artistic achievements of the later Turkish empires of the Safavids of Iran (volume 2, chapter 5.5), the Mughals of India (volume 2, chapter 5.3), and the Ottomans of Turkey (volume 2, chapters 5.2, 5.4, 5.6).

THE MAGIC OF THE MUGHALS

With the establishment of the Mughal dynasty (1526–1858) in India by Babur, the Timurid prince and the last true heir to the Central Asian empire, India witnessed a revival of extraordinary arts and architecture. During the reign of the Mughals on the subcontinent, Islamic art reached new heights. The architecture under this dynasty was the result of the masterful fusion of Turkish Central Asian, Persian, and Hindu inspiration. The use of red sandstone and white marble by the former Turkish Tughluq dynasty became characteristic of Mughal architecture, which dominated the Indian subcontinent for several centuries, strongly influencing subsequent developments in India as well. In the seventeenth century, during the reign of Shah Jahan, Mughal architecture reached its climax. However, the British came up with a fictitious story that Mughal emperor Shah Jahan imported architects and craftsmen from across Asia—including a certain architect, Ustad Isa, from the Ottoman Empire—to build the Taj Mahal. Furthermore, Spanish Augustinian friar Sebastian Manrique, observing the construction of this magnificent edifice in 1640–41, claimed that an Italian goldsmith named Geronimo Veroneo designed it, because only Europeans were capable of building such a magnificent building. But the Taj Mahal was built by Mughal architects Ustad Ahmad Lahauri (from Lahore) and Mir Abd-ul Karim (a favorite architect of Jahangir) under the direct supervision their patron, Shah Jahan.[252] Ultimately, the buildings that Shah Jahan built, including the masterpiece Taj Mahal, were a result of the splendid refinement of an amalgamation of traditions of Islamic, Persian, Timurid (Turkish), and Hindu origin. The Mughal architectural style was later borrowed by the Hindu maharajas, who built their palaces owing to this influence. One other contribution that the Mughals made was the masterful use of white marble, particularly beginning in the seventeenth century. The Taj Mahal, built from unique nonporous Indian white marble, also witnessed the emergence of the art of marble inlaid with precious and semiprecious stones. Today, this art is kept alive by artisans in the Agra area, where the Taj Mahal and other well-known Mughal architectural marvels are located.

THE IRANIAN SPLENDOR

When the Turks rose to power in Iran and the Middle East in the tenth century, Persian culture was suppressed by Muslim Arabs. The arrival of the Turks from Central Asia facilitated the revival of the rich Persian arts and architecture with the mixture the new conquerors brought from the depths of Asia. As stated earlier, the Seljuk Turks were the first to synthesize what was to become the new Turco-Persian architectural style. This became the basis for the future Ottoman and Timurid artistic evolutions. Continued Turkish rule in Iran took the Timurid designs to new heights under the Turkish-speaking Safavid dynasty. Safavid architecture in Iran, particularly from the sixteenth to the nineteenth century, included influences from ancient Persian, Turkish Central Asian, and Arab cultures. The Safavids were affected particularly by Seljuk and Timurid architecture. Eventually, Turkish Safavid architecture was accepted as the standard Persian architecture. After the fall of the Safavid dynasty in Iran, Western architectural influences began to enter Iran. In the nineteenth century, the Golestan Palace became a masterpiece of the Turkmen Qajar dynasty, joining the influences of traditional Safavid architecture with those of Western construction. The Turkish rule of Iran from the eleventh century until the early twentieth century left its mark in Persia with its characteristic unique Turco-Persian-style artworks, which are admired by art lovers around the world.

THE OTTOMAN MAGNIFICENCE

The strong Seljuk influence among the Ottoman Turks lasted well into the fifteenth century. The Yeşil Türbe (Green Mausoleum) of Sultan Mehmet I, built in 1421, still had an apparent Seljuk character. But by this time, the transition to the Ottoman style had begun. Eastern Roman inspirations found their place in the soul of the evolving Ottoman architectural landscape. Even though the Ottoman Turks carried forward the traditions of the Persian, Seljuk, and Eastern Roman arts, they eventually created their own style.[253] Topkapï Palace, the royal seat of the Ottoman Empire for nearly four centuries, was built presumably owing to a nomadic spirit, owing to the vast greenery surrounding the much smaller built-up areas of the palace.[254] The Çinili Köşk (China Kiosk), a civic building from 1473, more resembles a Central Asian structure, like a Timurid edifice. The Ottomans were known for building *külliye*, a complex that often incorporated a mosque, a *medrese* (school), and a mausoleum.

Ottoman architecture reached its climax in the sixteenth century. During this period, Koca Mimar Sinan (1491–1588) emerged as the great master of architects. In fact, he is considered one of the greatest in the history of architecture.[255] Among his known works are the Haseki Hürrem Sultan Bath Complex, the Şehzade Mosque Complex (Prince's Mosque Complex for Suleiman's son Mehmet), the Mihrimah Complex, the Süleymaniye Mosque Complex, the Kïlïch Ali Paša Mosque Complex, and the Sokollu Mehmet Paša Mosque. All are in Istanbul, but his masterpiece Selimiye Camii (Selim II Mosque) is in Edirne. His buildings exemplify the magnificence of the Ottoman grandeur in the sixteenth century. It has been said that he produced 318 buildings, among which the most well known are the mosques of Suleiman in Istanbul and Selim II in Edirne.[256] The Ottomans built on traditional Seljuk architecture by incorporating elements from the Eastern Roman tradition, as well as from the Persian and Islamic (Qïpčak) Egyptian Mamluk traditions. During the nineteenth-century reforms under Western influence, Western architectural influence also became apparent in the newly constructed Ottoman buildings. Hence, many of the newly built Ottoman palaces, kiosks, and mosques began to exhibit the baroque style of the West. Examples are the magnificent Dolmabahče Palace, Beylerbeyi Palace, and the Ortaköy Mosque.

1.4. THE INFLUENCE OF RELIGION

The Central Asian Turks of antiquity and the medieval period worshipped Gök-Tengri (Sky God), who was eternal and could not be represented in any form. Hence, they actually followed a form of monotheism. They also believed in the evil force of the underground god Erlik. They believed in the Tengriism influenced by the forces of Mother Nature, which were ultimately earthly manifestations of Gök-Tengri. Their respect for nature fit well with their nomadic lifestyle. The early Turks also believed in the hereafter. In pursuing military successes, they wanted to impress their ancestors. The Turks buried their dead in graves called *kurgan*, which often included the dead person's horse and personal belongings since they believed in resurrection into the afterlife. The kurgans of the Huns often included mummified bodies, whereas the Gök-Türks and the Oghuz Turks burned their dead along with their belongings before burying them. However, the Turks did not remain Tengriist for long after they began to spread across the vast steppes of Eurasia and came under the influences coming through the many routes of the Silk Road. As the Turks encountered different ethnic groups with different creeds, they began to convert to different religious faiths. Some examples are as follows:

- Gök-Tengriism: the ancient Turks—for example, the Huns (chapter 3) and the Gök-Türks (chapter 5.3)—were among the followers of this Tengriist faith.
- Buddhism: the Tabgač Turks (chapter 5.2) solidified the establishment of Buddhism in China in the fourth and fifth centuries; later, the

Idiqut Uighurs also followed the Buddhist faith, and they facilitated the conversion of Genghis Khan's Mongols to Buddhism.

- Manichaeism: the Uighur Turks' (chapter 5.4) conversion in the eighth century allowed the survival of the majority of the written records of this agnostic religion into our modern times.
- Judaism: The Khazar Turks (chapter 4.6) had the only formal non-Hebrew Judaic state in history.
- Christianity: the Danubian Bulgars (chapter 4.3) were the second group of Turks after the European Avars to adopt this religion in the ninth century, during the period of the First Bulgarian Kingdom in the Balkans.
- Islam: the Oghuz (Turkmen) Turks spearheaded the leadership of this Semitic religion in the Near East for over a millennium, with mass conversions beginning in the tenth century; today, the overwhelming majority of the Turkish world follows this faith.

Starting with the Xiong-nu (Asian Huns), the earliest known religion of the Turks is the Tengriist faith, which, as a Central Asian creed, was common to the later Mongols as well. In fact, this faith was common to the European Huns of Attila and other Turkish tribes arriving in Europe (e.g., Avars, Bulgars, Sabirs, and Khazars), as well as to the Gök-Türks, Uighurs, Kyrgyz, Oghuz, and so on. But in the ninth century, first the Avars and later the Bulgar Turks accepted Christianity over their traditional Central Asian faith. In the Tengriist faith, the ancient Turks believed in Sky God, or Gök-Tengri, who represented good, whereas Erlik, the underground god, promoted evil. God manifested his will through the forces of the nature. The shaman, acting as a medium and a spiritual leader, performed rituals to communicate with the spirits. Similar faiths existed among the American Indians, whose ancestors came from Asia through the Bering Strait at least twelve thousand years ago.[257] During the Ice Age period, the sea level at this strait was much lower, if not below the land. There was no contact between the Old World and these people until the Vikings came about 1000 CE. However, since the ancestry of the American Indians was from Central Asia, it was natural for shamanism to exist among the tribesmen of Americas.

After the Common Era (CE) began, the Sogdians, an Iranian people dealing with trade along the Silk Road, carried Buddhism, as well as Christianity, in its Nestorian form and its gnostic Manichaeist offshoot, to the Far East.[258] The last two forms of faith were considered heresy by Christians at large. Particularly Manichaeism, a gnostic faith, was considered a threat to the religions of Christianity, Zoroastrianism, and Islam; by the sixth century, it was eradicated from the Middle East. This gnostic faith originated in Iran. The Uighur Turks, abandoning their ancestral religion, converted to this Iranian religion in 762, and traditional shamans were also proscribed by the qaghan himself. This religion previously never found acceptance in any land, including Persia, where it originated, but it became the state religion of the Uighur Turks. After the Uighur Empire was destroyed by the Tengriist Kyrgyz Turks in the ninth century, a small group of Uighurs moved to modern-day Xinjiang, where they eventually accepted Buddhism. In the late fourth century, the Tabgač Turks, who formed the Northern Wei dynasty of China, also chose Buddhism over their ancestral Tengriist religion of the steppes. By taking over the northern half of China, they became instrumental in establishing Buddhism in China.[259]

Interestingly, it appears that most of the time when the Turks converted from their ancestral Tengriist faith to another creed, they seemed to lose their ethnic identity. For example, in the case of the European Avars and the Danubian Bulgars, their conversion to Christianity facilitated the disappearance of their Turkish identity within Europe. This process was also catalyzed, in the case of the Avars, by forced conversion by Charlemagne and, in the case of the Bulgars, by their absorption into the overwhelming influx of the Slav population.

Nevertheless, the attachment of the nomadic Turks of the past to Tengriism was part of their cultural identity during ancient and medieval times. Tengriism used to be the common faith of the old Central Asian pastoralist nomads of the Eurasian steppes. The religion did not have an organized religious establishment, nor did it have written guidelines. Its rites were carried out by the rulers but also by individual shamans. It was the dominant religion of the nomads as it was for the Xiong-nu (Huns), Gök-Türks, Avars, and so on. However, there were Turkish tribal unions that followed other religious faiths besides Tengriism.

There are instances where the faith of the entire tribal nation was possibly changed owing to a personal decision of the monarch. For example, in 762, when the Uighur Turks were surrounded by those who followed Tengriism or Buddhism, Uighur Bögü Qaghan declared Manichaeism the official religion of the state. Similarly, in the early eighth century, when the Tengriist Khazar Turks were facing the powerful Christian Eastern Roman Empire in the west and the Muslim Arab Umayyads in the south, their monarch adopted Judaism as the official faith of the land.[260] In both of these instances, both the Uighurs and the Khazars were militarily at their strongest; hence, these faiths could not have been forced upon them.

In the case of the Uighurs, there was no political or military concern from China, since the Uighurs' military might supported the T'ang dynasty, but there was constant exposure to the Sogdian merchants who brought merchandise back and forth between the West and the East.[261] These merchants probably brought Manichaeism with them and convinced the Uighur monarch to make the change. In the case of the Khazars, however, the choice might have been a political one, perhaps to stave off social and religious pressures from neighboring Christian and Muslim powers by choosing another Semitic faith over the others.

There were also tribal federations without a cohesive faith. The Kimek Qaghanate of the tenth century in the Kazakh Steppe, for example, does not appear to have had a unified religious faith; this little-known Turkish polity appears to have had fire worshippers and Buddhists but mostly Tengriists. According to the Eastern Roman chronicler Psellus from the eleventh century, the Pečeneg Turks in the Western Eurasian Steppe were atheists, believing that all events happened by chance and death was the end of everything. But a contradictory Muslim report suggests that while the Pečenegs were mostly fire worshippers, a single tribe converted to Islam through the efforts of a Muslim scholar captive among them. There are reports from Christian missionaries as well. In 1008 Bruno of Querfurt converted only thirty Pečenegs to Catholicism. He also described them as "the most stubborn and cruel of all the pagans."[262] Again according to the records, some of the Pečeneg chieftains entered the service of their adversary Volodomir I, the Rus' prince, in the late tenth century. There are also records suggesting that the Pečenegs were referred to as the Ishmaelites, perhaps a reference to their being associated with Islam.[263]

Regardless of the individual Turkish groups' sporadic conversions, between the eighth and tenth centuries, Turkish tribal confederations of Asia began mass conversions in faith, gravitating toward the Muslim creed. The Qara-Khanids became the first to adopt Islam as their religion circa 900. In Europe, in the ninth century, the Danubian Bulgars became Christians, while their kinsmen the Khazars decided to accept Judaism as their official religion.

Judaism is the oldest Semitic religion, but historically it was followed exclusively by the Hebrews until the ninth century, when the Khazar Turks in the Pontic Steppe, north of the Black Sea and the Caspian Sea, converted to Judaism and became the only non-Hebrew nation accepting Judaism as a national religion. The Krïmchaks were another unique Jewish group, emerging in the sixteenth century in Crimea with their rabbinic Judaic faith. It has been suggested that they descended from the remnants of the Jewish Khazars, but this has not been proven. Whatever their origins, they spoke a dialect close to Tatar Turkish, and culturally they had similarities to Crimean Tatars. Nearly six centuries after the fall of the Khazars, they would not have been expected to speak Khazar Turkish. In World War II, nearly 70 percent of them were massacred by the Nazi Germans.[264]

Christianity seems to have found more acceptance among many Turkish tribes, particularly before the emergence of the Mongols in the thirteenth century. The Bulgar Turks, who were in the Balkans, willingly converted to Orthodox Christianity in the ninth century. In present-day Mongolia, the Karait and Naiman Turks of the early thirteenth century were Nestorian Christians. The populations of the Qïpčak and Cuman Turks before the arrival of the Mongols were split into Christians (those in the west, bordering the Polish and the Russians) and Muslims (their eastern majority). Once the Tatars lost power in the land of the former Golden Horde Khanate, starting in the sixteenth century, they came under pressure of the Russians, and eventually many of them were forced to convert to Orthodox Christianity.

Islam began its penetration into western Central Asia after the Arabs defeated the armies of T'ang China in 751. The fall of the Gök-Türks in the eighth century, the weakening of the Uighurs in the ninth century, and finally the forced departure of the Kyrgyz from modern-day Mongolia in the tenth century kept pushing Turkish tribes westward toward Persian-dominated Muslim areas in Transoxiana and Khorasan in stages. Contrary to popular belief among modern-day Turks, the religion of Islam was not embraced by their ancestors quickly; rather, the process of conversion took at least two centuries. In fact, initially the Turks resisted conversion to Islam, but in the late tenth century, mass conversions began. In the Pontic Steppe, Islam made its way into eastern Europe with the help of Muslim traders. In this area the Volga Bulgars became Muslims in the tenth century. Hence, eventually Islam became the universal religion for the majority of the Turkish world, particularly in the eleventh and twelfth centuries. Also by this time period, almost the entire western Turkestan region became Turkish, nearly completely replacing the Persian elements except for the culture. As a result, the Turkish demographics facilitated for Islam to take deeper roots in Asia.

Today, Turks predominantly follow the Sunni sect of Islam. The Sunni Sufis of the Turkish Yesevi (Yasawi) order were instrumental in spreading Islam in Turkestan. But in the sixteenth century, after Iran came under the rule of the Turkmen Safavids, who established the Shi'ite faith, Iran served as a barrier between the Sunni Ottoman Turks in the west and the Sunni Uzbek Turks in Central Asia. Subsequently, the militant-appearing Naqshbandi order concentrated their efforts to spread their message deep into Eastern Asia. The Naqshbandi movement eventually made its way into Inner Mongolia to spread Islam. In China, Muslims of Chinese ethnicity came to be known as Hui in Chinese.

The effects of shamanism persist in modern times in the vast territories of Siberia. Even though the Yakut Turks who live on the far frontier of distant northeastern Siberia have become Christians under Russian pressure, some of them still practice the ancient Tengriist religion. During the Soviet era (1917–90), shamanism/Tengriism in Siberia were outlawed, but with the fall of the Russian communist regime, these old traditions began to resurface as a basis of ethnic identity, and ample documentation on this faith appeared, particularly among the Yakut Turks.[265]

RELIGION AND THE MILITARY CULTURE

From the early years of Turkish history, the religious beliefs of the Turks had a profound effect on their martial lifestyle. For them, dying on the battlefield was synonymous with honor, and this was part of their religious beliefs as well. From antiquity into the medieval period, most Turks followed a monotheist faith known as Tengriism, which fit their warlike spirit since it rewarded its followers for the number of enemies they killed in battle.[266] It has been suggested that the Tengriist beliefs of the nomadic Huns gave them a form of common magic-religious thought that provided an immense traditional value in keeping them together as one unit.[267] The shaman, believed to be a communicator between heaven and earth, often encouraged the steppe monarchs and their warriors in their quests for military successes. The fighters were indoctrinated in the belief that their bows, arrows, and swords were divinely powered for their victories. Consequently, they thought they could defeat any army in their pursuit of world domination.

Throughout the Middle Ages, Oghuz Qaghan, an epic hero of the legend of Oghuz Qaghan, became a symbol of the Turkish ideal of world domination. The Orkhon inscriptions from the early eighth century show that similar sentiments for the pursuit of global conquest existed among the Gök-Türks. In addition, in these inscriptions, the Turkish ruler claimed that the Turkish state could be brought down not by non-Turks but only by unruly Turks. This actually happened when the Uighurs rebelled against their masters, the Gök-Türks, with the help of the Basmïl and Qarluq Turks. Mahmud al-Kâshgharî from the Qara-Khanid territory in the eleventh century wrote that the Turks were "the selected warriors of God to serve the Almighty," and the Turks of the past generally believed that they were a people chosen by God to lead the world.[268] Ammianus Marcellinus, a contemporary of the (European) Huns, described them as "the most terrible of all warriors." Theodoros Synkellus characterized the philosophy of the Avars as "Life is war." On the opposite end of the Eurasian steppes, Ssu-ma Ch'ien of China said about the Xiong-nu, the ancestors of the European Huns, that warfare was "their natural disposition." The Arab chronicler al-Jahiz in the ninth century wrote that the Turks occupied "in war the position of Greeks in science and the Chinese in art."[269]

The Tengriist Turks believed their ruler was a heavenly appointed monarch supported by Gök-Tengri (Sky God), who was the most high for the Turkish nomads. *Gök* meant "high or heavenly" as well as "blue" (for the sky).[270] Therefore, for the Gök-Türks, blue in all its different tones was the most venerated color. The word *tengri* was used to refer to God, but it was also used as an adjective to mean "divine." For this reason, the Turkish rulers of the early nomads were considered divine or celestial, just as the Chinese emperors were. According to Chinese records, the Gök-Türk monarch, the qaghan, was heavenly appointed and therefore was given the title of "heaven created." Motun, the founder of the Xiong-nu Empire, or the (Asian) Hun Empire, had the title of *ch'eng-li ku-t'u shan-yu* in Pinyin Chinese, which, when transliterated into Old Turkish, took the form of *tengri qutlu shan-yu*, meaning "majesty son of heaven" or "heavenly blessed shan-yu."[271] The Turkish ruler also carried the title *tengri qaghan*, believing that he was invincible as long as the sun continued to shine. The empire was given to the Turks by heaven, or *tengri*. While the Romans referred to Attila the Hun as the "scourge of God," the Hun leader declared he was the heavenly appointed ruler of the world. In written communications between the Gök-Türk qaghans and Chinese emperors, they started by referring to each other with the divine origin of their authority; terms like *son of heaven* and *son of god* were not uncommon.[272] As noted in Greek writings, the title of "God-appointed khan" of the Danubian Bulgar Turks was similar to what has been noted on the Orkhon inscriptions. A similar view of divinely appointed monarchy was seen even after the Turks accepted Islam. The monarchs of the Ottoman Turks considered themselves "the shadow of God on earth." The Mongols, including Genghis Khan, used similar Turkish monarchy titles.[273]

In the Kül Tigin inscription (from Orkhon inscriptions found in Mongolia) from the eighth century, we see that the Gök-Türk monarch Bilge Qaghan stated that his leadership was accepted by Gök-Tengri, and consequently he possessed *qut* (divine power or blessed power). The good force (qut) of Sky God (Gök-Tengri) came upon the earth from heaven to the Turkish monarch, legitimizing his sovereignty. As we learn from the Orkhon inscriptions, the tengri qaghan, having divine power (qut), could transform his warriors into wolves against the enemy, who were sheep. Consequently, we also see the mythological importance of the wolf in ancient Turkish life.

During a Gök-Türk coronation, the nobles would strangle the new monarch a little bit and ask him about the duration of his reign.[274] If, however, a monarch was to be executed for one reason or another, his royal blood could not be shed, since he was heavenly appointed. Consequently, he needed to be strangled.[275] Even in their Islamic faith, when someone of royal blood from the Seljuks or the Ottomans was to be executed, the ancient Central Asian tradition of strangling was followed.

For the ancient Turkish khans, the material world was divided into two sections, the *el* (or *il*) and the *yagï* (or *yaghï*). The former referred to communities living under the rule of the tengri qaghan, whereas the latter described communities showing no allegiance to the khan and living in the lands yet to be conquered by him.[276]

The most important weapon of the steppe nomads was the reflex or composite bow, which was thought to be a Scythian invention.[277] The bow and the arrow were long-distance weapons, whereas the sword and the lance were close-range combat arms. The Avar Turks introduced the scimitar and the spur to Europe.[278] Throughout the early part of their history, Turks took pride in their excellent horsemanship and their ability to shoot arrows with deadly accuracy while galloping at full speed. Chinese military chariots were no match for the superb mounted archers of the Xiong-nu (Asian Huns). These Huns introduced the concept of cavalry to China.[279] According to Chinese sources, for a Turkish warrior, dying on the battlefield was an honorable death, whereas dying from an illness was shameful.[280] These early Turks also despised living into old age; dying from old age was not considered an honorable death. Dying while fighting brought honor not only in this life but also after death, along with a higher status with their ancestors.

The concept of the hereafter was known to the ancient Turks. The martial lifestyle of the Eurasian nomads was strongly influenced by this religious belief. The mounted warriors believed that the enemies they killed would be their slaves in the hereafter. Furthermore, when they died, their tribe either buried or burned their horses with their deceased owners, as they thought that they would need their horses after their resurrection in the land of the dead.[281] The slain enemy, who was to serve the Turkish warrior in the hereafter, was turned into a stone monument known as a *balbal*. The early Turks believed that after the death of the noble warrior, when they placed his dead body in his tomb, arranged like a home, together with his *balbal*s, he would live on for eternity, served by the souls of his slain enemies. More on this will be presented later in the discussion of the funeral practices of the ancient Turks.

The concept of dying for a religious cause particularly to achieve a higher status in the hereafter is also present in Islam, and this is known as martyrdom. The chance for achieving martyrdom in the name of God and receiving rewards in the hereafter fits the aspirations of the Turkish warriors, facilitating their conversion to Islam. Hence, even after becoming Muslims, the Turks continued to believe that they were chosen by God to lead. Meanwhile, the Muslim elite, seeing that the Turks were capable of defending Islam, were quick to accept the Turkish concept of world domination.[282] The poet Gazzi (1049–1130) described the Turks as demons during war and angels at times of peace. Chivalry was an important part of the lives of these warriors. On the battlefield, the Turks and the Franks admired each other; a chronicler of the First Crusade wrote, "The Turks are a heroic people."[283] Hence, after the Turks converted to Islam, dying on the battlefield was considered as honorable as it was for their Tengriist ancestors. Seljuk and early Ottoman warriors particularly, while engaged in a battle, raced with each other, so to speak, to die while fighting to achieve an honorable martyrdom.

In an attempt to reach honorable death on a battlefield as a Tengriist faithful or to reach martyrdom as a Muslim, the Central Asian warriors achieved extraordinary military successes, which led them to believe that they could achieve world domination. In 1071 the victory of Seljuk sultan Alp Arslan over the Eastern Roman emperor Diogenes against all odds gave him the confidence that he could conquer the world, but he was assassinated. Sultan Muhammad of the Khwarezm-shah Turks, after conquering Iran, Khorasan, and Transoxiana, wanted to take the civilized world for himself, but he was not able to take China when he found out that this had already been accomplished by Genghis Khan of the Mongols, who went on to conquer most of the civilized world in the thirteenth century. Tamerlane of Samarkand in the fourteenth century wanted to become a world conqueror, but after he attacked Iran, Anatolia, eastern Europe, and India, he died before his planned march to China. However, Sultan Mehmet II of the Ottoman Turks, by taking

Constantinople in 1453, not only ended Roman history but also turned his empire into a world empire and ended the Middle Ages. The Ottomans, in essence, reached the ultimate ancestral goal of world domination by turning the Ottoman Empire into a superpower, particularly between the fifteenth and seventeenth centuries.

TURKISH MYTHOLOGY

The term mythology is derived from two Greek words, 'mythos' and 'logos.' While the later describes knowledge, the former is about extraordinary tales that may have had significant influence on a society, and within these stories typically supernatural characters have been the principal characters. These legendary tales, not based on facts, often constituted part of the ancient history of a society thus providing an account of the origin of the people in a legendary manner. Thus, mythical stories also carried religious sense in many ways. While the West has been heavily influenced by the ancient Greek mythology and the Far East has been known to have its own mythological past, but in the West, there has not been detailed literature in regards to ancient Central Asian Turks' mythology.

We learn how proto-Turks viewed the universe that we live in from ancient Chinese chronicles. In China of the past sky was thought to be a domed structure while the earth was a rather flat surface with multi-corners swimming in the waters of the oceans. Among the GökTürks and Uighurs domed sky was thought to be a cylindrical structure resembling domed tent of their monarchs. In one of the old Uighur chronicles it was said that the universe was like a tent in which a majestic octagone-shaped tree trunk gave a support to the tent while pointing to four cardinal directions and four intercardinal directions; this view in fact has a direct connection to ancient tree cult within the Turkish mythology. For ancient Chinese and proto-Turks the north star was thought to be the highest point in the sky, and according to old beliefs of the steppes, the palace of Tengri (God) used be there; the stars in the constellation of Ursa Major (Big Dipper) were known to proto-Turks as 'Seven Hans' and the movement of these stars were used by them to determined time.[284]

Proto-Turks also believed that the domed sky was revolving around a golden pile while the sky wheel itself carrying the stars also was turning as a result of which the night's darkness was chasing the daylight. They believed that this wheel that was situated just below the domed sky was forced to turn by the sky-dragon (ancient Turkish: *kök-luu*). Hence, domed sky, sky wheel, and sky-dragon were all symbols of the heaven as well as those of the time. For this reason, since (Sky) God was also known as Öd Tengri (Time God) it was believed that the Creator was also in charge of the time.[285]

In ancient Turkish cultural traits, we find that the word God had been at times synonymous with Tengri, Ülgen, and Kayra Han. However, this did not suggest that ancient Turks were once polytheists. On the contrary, ancient Turks believed only in one single deity known to them as *Tengri*, or God. In the Orkhon inscriptions, God is described as God of the Turks. While Tengri has been the protector of the Turkish nation, the ruling qaghan as God's representative on earth with the attribution of a giver was able to issue punishment and forgiveness.[286] Qaghan was only able to get his throne with the approval by God and thus becoming a liaison between the Creator and the people.[287]

Ancient Turks used the term *Gök Tengri* or simply *Tengri* for 'God.' In the meantime, the word Tengri was also used to indicate the sky where the Heaven was located. Hence, in this context Gök Tengri depending on its utilization could have also meant heaven, also known as *učmağ*.[288] Thus, the color 'gök' in a manner of speaking used to be a holy color for the steppe Turks of the past.

As we understand from the Orkhon Inscriptions Umay was a being receiving 'kut' (power, fortune) to protect the children of the nation as an angel but not as god.[289] The term "öd Tengri," which translates as god of time, has been misunderstood and in fact, it has been taken out of context in these inscriptions. Indeed, taken in its entirety the ancient text refers to the fact that God decides on the time and thus making the human a mortal. In essence there was no such thing as Turkish Pantheon of gods as there was in the West; in fact, the ancient Turks only believed in one God.[290] According to Abbasid ambassador ibn Fadlan's testimony an Oghuz Turk was swearing by 'one God' just as ancient Huns (Xiong-nu) were taking their oaths for their Gök Tengri (Sky-God).[291]

Shamanism is sometimes viewed by the Westerners as an ancient religion that has been prevalent throughout the vast central and eastern steppes of Eurasia as well as southern Siberian territories. The word shamanism is derived from the 'shaman', the person who actually led the practice shamanism among the nomads of the past. Even though it can be said that shamanism had been an inseparable part of the lives of the ancient nomadic Turks, neither the word shamanism nor shaman are Turkish words in origin. It appears that it was the Western anthropologists who coined the term shamanism.

In reality, shamanism was not a religion but rather a practice of communication with the world of spirits and channeling their energies into this material world. Hence, shamans were not men or women of religion but rather communicators with spirits. In fact, with the support of spirits shamans were not only able to improve daily lives of their people but also, they had the ability to heal maladies.[292] On the other hand, the true ancient religion for the Turks in essence was 'Gök-Tengriism' since the ancient nomadic Turks worshipped Gök-Tengri or simply Tengri, who was the only god to whom they sacrificed their animals. In other words, Gök-Tengriism, in a manner of speaking, could have been considered among the first monotheist religions of the world.

While many of the ancient civilizations had deities representing the good they also had deities representing the evil. For example, ancient Persian deity Hürmüz was god of good whereas Ehrimen was the evil god, and neither had power over the other one. On the other hand, Tengri was the one and only god of the steppe Turks of the past whereas Erlik was the devil. Tengri was all powerful and the Creator while Erlik had no power over Tengri because he was created. In fact, ancient Turks practiced a monotheist religion.[293] For the ancient Turks, the ruler of the underworld was Erlik, known as the devil (or Satan) by Christians and Shaytan by Muslims. But the Qïpčaks called the devil Yek, possibly borrowed from the Indian Yakkha through Sogdian merchants or the Chinese.[294]

Ancient Turks had totemism but this practice did not include a deity since Tengri was always the only god. Totems were often chosen from among sacred animals, and thus, a totem could have suggested hereditary relationship with the people and the animal chosen as the totem. A village also likely used its totem as its name, and a totemic animal could not be consumed. Often those who carried the same totem could only marry with another group of people with a different totem. It was also believed that a totem provided protection from outside dangers.[295]

The word *shaman* was applied to the practitioners of shamanism both among the Tungusic peoples in Eastern Siberia and among the Turks and Mongols in the Eurasian steppes during prehistoric and medieval times. A shaman could have been a man or a woman. The Turks used the term *qam* for a shaman, whereas the Mongols used the word *bö*, which was derived from the Turkish word *bögü*, "sage, wizard."[296] The earliest recording of the Turkish word *qam* is found in T'ang Chinese archives mentioning the Kyrgyz Turks calling their shaman *qam*. Among the Muslim Mamluk-Qïpčaks, *qam* was used to mean "doctor" instead of the Arabic term, *tabib*.[297]

In shamanism Central Asian and Siberian Turks used to believe that all live and still objects in the nature had souls of their own, and therefore, these people believed that every object had to be represented as a matter and a soul or a spirit. In addition, for Altay Turks spirits were separated into everlasting spirits known as "tös" and those which were created known as "neme". Then these were then further divided into good (arï) and bad (qara) souls or spirits.[298] Those spirits that had the power to protect or to own the interests of the people were known as "iye". These powerful spirits were also divided into "ak iyeler" for a good spirits and "qara iyeler" for bad spirits.[299] For example, Altay Turks believed that mountains, earth, water and ice had good spirits protecting the health and happiness of the people. Especially good spirits associated with sky as well as earth and water were able to bring bounty, peace, enlightenment.

As opposed to good spirits, bad spirits were able to use their given power to inflict death and destruction and thus spread sadness across the land. Mighty bad spirits (*qara iyeler*) were led by *Erlik* and his subordinates including *Albastï* (*Alkarïsï*) and *Karabasan*. After converting to Islam Central Asian Turks accepted these bad spirits as jinn.[300]

Ancient Turks used to have nature-based 'cults' but unlike Westerners who used cults in their religious practices Central Asians did not worship any being in the nature. In other words, objects such as mountains, trees, water, earth were not considered as gods but they were revered as sacred.[301]

Since water symbolized life for ancient Turks, the water cult used to have an important place in their lives. For this reason, creeks, rivers, as well as lakes were considered to be among living creatures. Those who failed in their duties and rebels were punished by holy soil and water.[302] For these Turks majestic mountains and their flowing waters were considered as residing place for good spirits who offered protection to the people. Central Asians then used to worship at these high-altitude locations and made sacrifices. Hence, these places used to be considered holy to them.

Siberian and Central Asian Turks of the past used to have tree cult and one of the principal examples of this cult was a tree known as the 'tree of life.' However, ancient Turks used to call this tree "Temir-terek" – meaning iron pillar – for supporting the sky.[303] Being unique this special tree used to be considered as one of the central pieces of the Turkish mythology. As long as this tree remained green, it was believed that the earth would also continue its existence. Together with its roots, trunk and branches it used to represent the three layers of the earth and it also facilitated connections between the natural events across the universe. The tree of life was believed to be majestically tall enough to reach God and it was thought to have nine main branches, each symbolizing one of the nine layers of the Heaven. The tree was also a conduit for the spirits in the sky and the underground to reach the surface of the earth. Thus, it served as a communication tool for shamans of the past to contact these spirits. As much as the tree of life was useful to shamans it was also important for Turkish rulers of the past since God given power and good fortune was transmitted to them through this tree. As much as it was a symbol of life, this tree also designated one's pedigree and it also functioned as the symbol of death. According to ancient Turks, even though death ended the existence of the body, its spirit or soul was immortal. Ultimately, this soul was only able to find its path to God (Heaven) or to Erlik (Hell) through this tree.[304] Besides the tree of life Turks also used to believe there were trees that did not only protect families but also there were trees that provided children and protected them through their good spirits. For these reasons, it is clear that ancient Turks used to be a society showing great respect to the tree.[305]

In order to protect themselves from evils and diseases as well as to make special requests Inner Asians used to make 'bloodless' sacrifices to Tengri

(God), and therefore, they used to tie pieces of cloth to the branches of sacred trees to make sure their 'bloodless' sacrifices would reach God. In other words, while the tied cloth pieces themselves were 'bloodless' sacrifices, these trees served as a means of communication with God. Hence, such trees were known as 'wish trees'.[306] These trees also were utilized to make requests by lovers to reach their loved ones.[307]

Turks who lived north of Altai Mountain Range in vast Siberia were not known to have formed states or complex civilizations as their pastoralist kinsmen in the steppes did. Since these Turks resided in heavily wooded territories, they also had a forest cult.[308] While for pastoralist Central Asian Turks forests possessed evil spirits, for those who lived by wooded areas forests had good spirits. Hence, when they went into forests for hunting they used to clean themselves and showed their reverence to the trees.

Based on their mountain cult ancient Turks believed that they received their strength from the mountains, which were considered as precious as their country. Hence, they also believed that these mountains were protected with permission by God by holy spirits. Furthermore, since the peaks of the mountains were closest points to the sky these Turks also believed that Tengri resided in these locations. For this reason, these places were considered holy places.[309] Hence, mountains used to be among religious ceremonial places. In the past one of the best-known holy mountains was the Gök-Türks' mythological Ötüken. There were also others, such as Kut-tag of Uighurs, Altai of Altai Turks, Tien Shan (Tengri tag) of the Huns.[310] In a manner of speaking because of their high altitudes these mountains were viewed as a pillar for the sky and means to reach God in a fastest way.[311]

As part of the mountain cult it could be said that ancient Turks also used to have a cave cult. One of examples was seen among ancient Tabgač Turks, known to Chinese as the T'o-pa. When they used to live by Lake Baikal around the year 260 C.E., the Tabgač were seen to worship in a cave.[312] Perhaps for this reason of having a cave cult, the famous Buddhist caves of Yün-kang in Shanxi and Lung-men were built in Honan during their rule of northern China under their Northern Wei dynasty. Cave cult has also been thought to be part of the stone cult.[313] Based on Chinese archives Asian Huns used to have cave cult as well, and they were known to practice major religious ceremonies led by the Turkish emperor in 'ancestral cave'.[314] Nevertheless, cave cult was also common among Far Easterners and Buddhists.

Cults perhaps arose from the belief that four important elements played significant role in the creation of earth and life. These were fire, air, water, and earth. In a manner of speaking air cult had to do with Tengri residing in the sky. In essence God's residence heaven was located here. Meanwhile, cults of water and earth, as discussed above, were about the ancient yer-sub (earth-water) cult of Turks, which used to be part of ancient Turkish culture. In fact, yer-sub for pastoralist Turks was an important concept defining their understanding and belief of their homeland. Fire on the other hand had a cult of its own.

Fire did not represent goodness or evil alone, and in fact, there was a belief that it may have possessed both characteristics in itself. Turks used to burn large fire during their state ceremonies with the understanding such fire would transmit news or information to Tengri in the sky.[315] Unlike other religions such as Zoroastrianism which accept fire as a holy power from a deity, in Turkish Tengriism ancient Turks merely viewed the fire as a holy means of communication with their Creator. In fact, during state ceremonies in ancient times the "Great Fire" (Ulu-Od) was used as a means of transportation of a sacrifice to Heaven as well as transmission of important news such as the crowning of a ruler to God.[316] Ancient Turks also believed in fire's purifying and healing powers. By jumping over fire they used to think that they would be cleansed from the evil spirits. Furthermore, shamans used fire to heal certain maladies.[317]

Since stone is a solid hard object it used to represent power. For example, the Migration Epic of Uighur Turks has shown that when Uygur emperor gave up the sacred rock of the nation to the Chinese, his people were forced to leave their lands as a result of loss of their strength. Stone was also thought to have special powers in the nature. With the use of dried grass and by hitting two stones together, one could generate fire. Furthermore, a special stone known as *"yada"* stone was used to generate rain when needed. On the other hand, another specific stone known as *"balbal"* was used at the burial place of the Turkish hero to represent every enemy he killed in his lifetime.[318]

Besides the lifeless objects of the nature, the living beings also had a significant place in the Turkish mythology. Particularly animals living in the wild nature such as wolves, eagles, and snakes were especially important. However, it should be noted even though they may have been looked upon as totems, none of these animals had deity characters. Since wolf has already been discussed later in this chapter, we will touch upon the snake and the eagle. The horse as another important animal in the lives of Inner Asian Turks was already discussed in chapter 1.2.

Being able to renew itself by changing its skin the snake at times possessed good and at times evil characteristics in addition to carrying healing as well as deadly powers embedded in its poison. In other words, carrying opposite characters a snake could have possessed a protector spirit while on the other hand having a wicked and deceitful nature as well.[319]

Birds have a special place in the Turkish mythology as well. While the underground world of Erlik was represented by ungodly monsters, birds represented the earth and the sky. In essence birds resided on the trunk (earth) and branches (sky) of the tree of life being in the center of the world and representing the three layers of the universe.[320] Birds did not only serve as a harbinger of the coming of Spring, in other words the new year, but also, they were the sentinels of the Heaven.[321]

The eagle is known as the lord of all the birds and for this reason it was accepted as God's messenger and representative on earth. According Central Asian and Siberian beliefs eagles were known as shamans' mothers or fathers.[322] There were those who also believed that a two-headed eagle (a symbol used by Seljuk Turks) used to lead birds of prey.

According to Chinese records during China's Five Dynasties (907–60) and Ten Kingdoms (902–79) period, Li K'o-yung, the legendary leader of the Sha-t'o Turks (chapter 5.5) was born in an eagle's nest.[323] Unfortunately, we do not have detailed information regarding the eagle legend of the Sha-t'o. But these Turks continued to survive even after their three dynasties in China ceased to exist. In fact, their later practice of Christian Nestorian faith helped them to preserve their cultural identity even though they were under the heavy influence of strong Chinese culture. Finally, in the thirteenth century Sha-t'o Turks reappeared in the historical arena as Önggüt Turks and Aq-Tatars.[324]

In this section we tried to provide only an introduction to a very complex subject of Turkish mythology. However, in order to understand Turkish history and cultural past, it is equally important to have a good knowledge about this subject matter. Having a rich pantheon of good and evil spirits, shamans became useful for Siberian and Central Asian steppe Turks in order to communicate with these spirits on their behalf. In essence, through communications with God and/or spirits ultimate goal was to bring peace, serenity, happiness and good health to the people. Essentially shamans were not in charge in leading religious events.

On the contrary religious ceremonies were led by Turkish monarch. While Turkish qaghan was not only ruler of the material world he was also viewed as a representative of God on earth. On the other hand one of the duties of a shaman was to act in favor of the state by getting help from the world of spirits. However, Eastern Roman sources described shamans erroneously as priests. Based on these records when an Eastern Roman envoy was about to be presented to GökTürk qaghan, a priest (a shaman) first intervened by asking the ambassador to pass in between two fires for purification purposes and to go around the fire to drive away any misfortunes that he might have been carrying.[325]

A shaman was thought to have a special gift for communicating with spirits, helping him or her learn the future, manipulate the weather, and inflict or cure disease. Hence, Turkish shamans were fortune-tellers as well as healers of maladies.[326] In essence, different peoples viewed the shaman differently as a medicine man, sorcerer, or magician. Shamans were called upon only on special occasions and not for everyday practices of religious rites. They were also soothsayers. This was pointed in the Codex Cumanicus, compiled in the fourteenth century, providing information about the Cuman or Qïpčak Turks of eastern Europe.

According to Muslim observers from the tenth century, a *qam*, in addition to functioning as a physician, performed a special process known as *yada*, which gave the performer the power to change the weather with the use of a rainstone.[327] It has been said that when Great Mongol khan Tolui, the youngest son of Genghis Khan, and his troops were encircled by the Jürchen army, he benefited from *yada* to change the weather in his favor with the help of a Turk from the Qanglï tribe.[328] According to an Arab traveler who visited the Uighur Empire in the early ninth century, the Turkish qaghan possessed pebbles with which he could bring down rain, snow, cold, and so on.³²⁹ The Turks, particularly the Kimek, were known to have special pebbles (*yada-taši*), which gave their possessor the power of bringing down rain or snow or to modify the weather, like bringing the cold and so on.³³⁰

For the ancient Turks, the universe was made of *üč kat* (three layers). The underworld or hell was known as *tumaq* or *ič yer* (inner world), whereas heaven was referred to as *učmaq*.³³¹ *Yer* was the material earth in which we live. The holy places in shamanism were found in nature; holy mountains, forests, and rivers were essential components of this old Central Asian religion. For the ancient Turks, the most important mountains included the Altai Mountains and the Tien Shan (Celestial Mountains in Chinese), also known as the Tengri Tagh (God Mountain) to the Turks. The Gök-Türk monarchy lived along the sacred Orkhon River in modern-day Mongolia near the magical Ötüken Mountain, from which the celestial power of qut was transferred to the Turkish monarch for him to be able to rule over the Turkish nation. The name Ötüken, used by the Gök-Türks to define the center of their empire, where their qaghan lived, was also used to define Mother Earth.³³²

ANCIENT BELIEFS AND RITUALS

Information on the religion of the ancient Turks is found in the records of the Chinese and the Eastern Roman Empire. Furthermore, the Turkish oral epics from Asia collected in the nineteenth and twentieth centuries constitute "the world's richest and most instructive treasury of materials" on the shamans and ancient religious beliefs of the Turks.³³³ The Orkhon inscriptions mention Umay (placenta), who was likely an idol protecting unborn souls and young children. According to Mahmud al-Kâshgharî, a Muslim Turk from the eleventh century who wrote the first Turkish dictionary (*Divan-i Lügat-i Türk*), one who believed in Umay would also get a child. But it was Sky God (Gök-Tengri) who gave qut (good fortune or heavenly blessing); for a nomad this meant an abundance of livestock.

According to Eastern Roman Empire sources, the Gök-Türks had a holy mountain (Ötüken, near Orkhon valley) belonging to the qaghan. Though the Turks showed special respect to fire, air, water, and earth, they attributed the word *tengri* only to the creator of heaven and earth, calling him Gök-Tengri.[334] The sacrificial places were often found on the mountains; for this reason for the ancient Turks and Mongols, the mountains were sacred.[335] The Orkhon inscriptions and Chinese records indicate that the Gök-Türks had holy rivers, where they would make sacrifices to Gök-Tengri. Ötüken was known as the sacred mountain, but probably it was not a single mountain but rather a mountain range.

During the rituals it is believed that the shamans, with the help of their drums, would go into a trance; then they would also be able to tell the future and heal the sick by means of a supernatural journey where they would retrieve the sick person's soul from the evil spirits. In the sixth century, an Eastern Roman envoy to the Gök-Türks observed that, during a funeral ceremony, mourners lacerated their faces and sacrificed horses and servants.[336] Among the Xiong-nu, special sacrifices were made during the first, fifth, and ninth months of the Chinese calendar year. The fifth and the sixth days of the month appear to have been holy days for sacrifice for the Huns.

The ancient Turks believed in the presence of a spirit known as *tin* in Old Turkish. It was used for the soul of the living creatures. Since tin was the real person of the dead body, it often received respect from the living tribesmen. The Central Asians also showed respect to the sun and to the moon, such as the ancient referral to moon as *Ay-Dede*, "grandfather moon." The Qïpčak-Cumans had a similar "father moon" concept.[337]

The ancient Turks seemed to consider volcanic lakes on top of mountains as holy. The sacrificial offering of paper horses, paper camels, and other paper animals at a volcanic lake in northern Shanxi was an old Turkish custom, but the symbolic use of paper was a Chinese influence. Although the Sha-t'o Turks of the tenth century were strongly influenced by Chinese culture, they still had a Central Asian character with the preservation of their Turkish customs. For example, in 942, upon the death of the Sha-t'o emperor, a horse sacrifice was made on the Western Mountain (Hsi-shan), very typical of old Turkish religious customs.[338]

Protecting the family as a unit of the tribe was important for the survival of the tribe in general. The social values and order within the tribal system were therefore very important. Murder was punishable with the death penalty. We learn from the Oghuz Turks (Turkmens) that, for the sake of preserving the tribe's survival, even before their conversion to Islam, homosexuality was considered a great sin.[339]

The blood oath was an ancient Central Asian Steppe tradition that was part of the Turkish (*qan qarïndashï*) and Mongolian (*anda*) customs (known as blood brotherhood). In the old tradition, one would use a sharp object to inflict a small cut to either the hand or the finger to cause bleeding; the prospective blood brother would then swallow the blood from the wound, by which act the two people would symbolically become the same blood and flesh. Within this context, taking an oath or swearing an oath in Turkish is *ant ičmek*, "drinking an oath."[340] Possibly the Old Turkish word *ant* or *and* came from the same Altaic word root that gave rise to the Mongolian word *anda*. For the steppe peoples, the preservation of an oath was important. Mahmud of Kashgar from the eleventh century stated that breaking an oath was punishable by death by iron, symbolized by the sword; the stipulation of oath breaking was described in the statement "If I break the oath, may this sword enter blue and come out red." The use of iron was symbolic, giving respect to this metal signifying strength. Furthermore, for the steppe people, iron and the blacksmith possessed great magical power.[341]

Tying ribbons or prayer flags or rags particularly to a tree to obtain blessings or good fortune (qut) is an ancient shamanic tradition that still exists across Muslim and non-Muslim Turkish Asia as well as in modern-day Turkey, where the tree is often referred to as a *dilek ağacï* (wishing tree). This is analogous to wishing wells or pools in Western culture.

The ancient records indicate that the horse was a daily companion of the Turkish *tigin* (prince) or *alp* (warrior), and horse-riding events in funerals and ancestral worship ceremonies—for example, among the Gök-Türks—were also observed. The horse would become a royal vehicle after the king was raised and carried on a felt carpet by four princes (*tigin*) around the tent, and then the monarch would complete the royal riding ceremonial.[342]

ANIMAL SYMBOLISM

The ancient Turks used animals in their symbolism. The wolf was a sign of strength and leadership. The bird was an omen of good fortune for the Xiongnu, whereas the howling of a dog was a presage of a whole year of prosperity for the Bulgar Turks.[343] Just as the wolf and woodpecker had important mythical roles in the birth of Roman civilization, the wolf and crow had similar significance in ancient Turkish popular traditions. In the relationships between lifesaving animals and needy human being, the mythical animals were described as supernatural divine beings. In the Tengriist faith, these animals were likely viewed as envoys of Gök-Tengri, or Sky God, to the material world.

For the Wu-sun and other ancient Turkish tribes, and later for the Mongols, the wolf and the crow, thought to be their ancestors, were venerated animals. The word *böri*, an ancient Turkish word for "wolf," was at times used as a name or a title to show respect for the divine animal. The crow was an object of religious significance among the Wu-sun as well as the Karait Turks, who are thought to have been the descendants of the Wu-sun living in modern-day Mongolia from the eleventh to the thirteenth century.[344]

According to Sima Qian, a Chinese chronicler from the Han period, Kun-mo was the mythical leader of the Wu-sun tribal union. When the shan-yu (emperor) of the Asian Huns killed his father, he left the child in the desert to meet his death. But a crow flew in to bring Kun-mo pieces of meat, and a wolf came in to give him her milk. The shan-yu was impressed, thinking that the child might be a god. He took in the child as his own to raise him as a warrior. When Kun-mo succeeded in becoming a mighty fighter, the shan-yu bestowed upon him the control of his late father's people. Kun-mo organized them into a warrior nation. When the shan-yu died, Kun-mo moved his people away, making them independent and thereby ending the payment of homage to the Huns.[345]

In another version of the same story, again noted in Chinese chronicles, Kun-mo's father was killed by an outsider at the time of his birth. The child was taken away to safety by a tribesman. After putting the child on the grass to look for food, he came back to observe that a crow was feeding the child meat, while a wolf was giving the child her milk. Impressed by what he saw, the tribesman immediately took Kun-mo to the Huns. The child grew up as a warrior commander under the protection of the shan-yu, who later gave Kun-mo a chance to avenge his father. After succeeding in his mission, Kun-mo turned the Wu-sun country into a powerful force under the Huns. Upon the death of the shan-yu, he made his people independent.[346]

Some scholars have postulated that since the Roman wolf story of Romulus and Remus was recorded earlier than the story of the Wu-sun, the legend traveled from the Roman world to Central Asia via the Silk Road, which was not only a conduit of trade between the East and the West but also a route for cultural exchange between the two worlds. Nevertheless, for the ancient Turks living within nature as nomads, even before the Wu-sun were known, the wolf might have been an important folkloric and religious character. While the wolf did not appear to be as important a socioreligious element for the Romans after the foundation of Rome in 753 BCE, the wolf was nearly always a significant mythical animal among the Turks, including the Ting-ling and the T'u-Chüeh. The lack of an older record of the Wu-sun version of the mythical story does not mean that the Roman legend was older, as the story could just as easily have migrated from the East to the West. In a similar fashion one can also debate the origin of the mythical dragon, as it is a folkloric element in China as well as in Europe; more than likely, the dragon was a mythical creature of the Far East rather than one of the West.

Among the T'u-Chüeh (Gök-Türks), the legendary genesis story known as the myth of Ergenekon (chapter 5.3) suggests that the Turks came from an abandoned Hunnish boy who was initially raised by a she-wolf, with whom the young man later consummated his marriage to raise his nation, known as the Gök-Türks. One of the wolf's newborns became the ruler of the Gök-Türks and placed a wolf's head on his flag.[347] Besides the Gök-Türks, many other Turkish tribes revered the lupine figure quite prominently. While the Gök-Türks came from a she-wolf and a Xiong-nu (Hun) boy, the Töles tribe was formed from the relationship of a male wolf with a Xiong-nu princess.[348] Similarly, on the basis of Chinese archives, the Xiong-nu believed that their nation came into existence as the result of the union of a Xiong-nu princess and a male wolf.[349] According to an Iranian historian, the Turks got their bad temper because they were given wolf's milk during childhood illness.[350]

The wolf, one of the most venerated animals in the steppes, was the totem of various Turkish tribes. Siberian wolf figures were used as tamghas by the proto-Turkish Chou people in the first millennium BCE (1050–249 BCE).[351] Owing to the important stature of this animal in Turkish culture, the wolf head (*böri*) was also the earliest known flagpole finial of the Turks.[352] The use of the wolf symbol among the proto-Turks was confirmed by the discovery of wooden wolf-head effigies at Pazïrïk (about the fourth century BCE) and at Noin-Ula (about the second to first century BCE); these pieces were thought to have been used as flagpole finials.[353] The Töles had a wolf-headed deity in their pantheon. The qaghan of the Uighurs, thought to be a tribe of the Töles, also had a wolf pennon to which respect was shown. Despite the fact that the Uighurs abandoned their ancestral Tengriist faith in 762, they still paid homage to the wolf figure on the lupine flagpole finial during their dynasty on the banks of the Orkhon (744–840) as Manichaeists and during their dynasty in Turfan (850–1250) as Buddhists. In fact, the use of the Turkish lupine flagpole finial remained a privilege of the Turkish monarchs from the sixth century to the thirteenth century over a very large territory from the Gulf of Chihli (former name of Bohai, the innermost gulf of the Yellow Sea) in the east to the Volga River in the west, from Gansu (Kansu) to the borders of Persia, including Afghanistan and parts of Pakistan.[354]

According to Chinese records, the Turkish qaghans (emperors) after the sixth century claimed that their dynasties were descendants of the totemic wolf ancestors, and the royal guard officers were called *böri* (wolf).[355] In essence these special warriors were viewed as personified form of wolves; similar lupine symbols were used in subsequent Turkish polities. The werewolf concept was present among the ancient Turks even after they abandoned their traditional Tengriist faith; after all many believed that they were descendants of the wolves. There is a tale in which Bayan, son of Bulgar czar Symeon, could change himself into a wolf at will; this idea persisted even after the Bulgar Turks converted to Christianity. The Russians described the Qïpčaks as having the custom of howling like a wolf before and after a battle.[356] Although the origin of the Chinese name Xiong-nu for the Asian Huns has been explained in different ways, one translation of the term is "howling slaves."[357]

The Turkish use of the wolf symbol on flags was well known in the pre-Islamic era. In addition to their *batrak* (modern word is *bayrak* [flag]), which was a wolf pennon on a lance, the Gök-Türks used a totemic insignia known as the *tös*, which was used by other Turkish tribes of Inner Asia as well. The *tös*, attached to a lance, was formed by a totemic wolf head connected either to the animal's hide and tail or to a bag of textiles resembling the body of the animal.[358] This lupine icon probably took its name from the Old Turkish word *tös*, indicating the anatomical connection between the head and the neck. The Turks also had the *kök-luu*, the celestial dragon, which was a hybrid lupine-draconic monster with a wolf's head attached to a serpentine tail found at a Hunnish burial site at the Noin-Ula kurgans, by the Selenga River in northern Mongolia.[359] Most of the finds from these kurgans are now exhibited at the Hermitage Museum in Saint Petersburg, Russia. The Gök-Türk dragon masks carried pearls (known as *moncuk* in Old Turkish) in their mouths; these were not styled after the contemporary Chinese T'ang dynasty fashion but rather resembled those used by the prior Turkish Chinese dynasties of the Tabgač (Northern Wei) and Hunnish Tsü-k'ü (Northern Liang).[360]

The ancient Turks used animal names in their titles, likely because of the strong influence of their shamanist totemism; examples included *böri qaghan* (emperor of wolves), *boqa qaghan* (emperor of bulls), and *sonkor tigin* (prince of hawks). Among the Yakut Turks of northeastern Siberia, each tribe had an animal totem, which was sacred; hence, the animal chosen as the totem of a tribe could not be eaten, but the totem of another tribe could. Each tribe was named after its totem, and the people adopted that animal's name as their family names as well.[361] The *koč* (ram) was an animal totem representing wisdom and experience; it was used either as a title or to signify a prince.[362] Hence, in reference to old Turkish shamanist practice, the word *kočum* (my ram) in Anatolian Turkish is often used by parents to their sons to mean "my prince." Today the term is also used in Turkey as slang between friends.

Turkish motifs also appeared in Muslim territories beginning in the ninth century, when the Turks were soldiers in Islamic armies. One of these is the depiction of a fight between a man and a bull. In one of the Dede Korkut epic stories of the thirteenth century, Boğaç was a hero who earned his name from his extraordinary strength, with which he could kill a bull with his fist.

A Muslim historian described a Turkish general's indispensable qualities on the basis of the characteristics of a variety of animals: "the heart of a lion, the chastity of a hen, the craftiness of a fox, and so on."[363] Despite conversions into the monotheistic religion of Islam, the Turkish nomads did not readily give up their Tengriist past. Each clan had an animal *ongon* (Old Turkish word for "totem"). For example, even though the tribal entities of the Turkmen Aq-Qoyunlu and Qara-Qoyunlu of the fourteenth century were Muslims, they still had their ancient tribal *ongon* of white sheep and black sheep respectively. In the Muslim Qara-Khanid Khanate, in the year 1068, Yusuf of Balasagun, the author of *Kutadgu Bilig* (*Wisdom of Royal Glory*), hailed the Turkish monarch with the title of Kök Böri (celestial wolf).[364] Timur (also known as Tamerlane in the West), the defender of Islam in Central Asia, remained loyal to his people's Tengriist past by using ancient totemic signs—for example, the draconic insignia of Timur's flagpole and *tuğ* (horsetail standard), possibly derived from the Uighur *kök-luu*, as well as the Ilkhanid draconic arch.[365]

One other important point is that, among the large group of Oghuz Turks, the word *kurt* (worm) in Oghuz Turkish possibly replaced the ancient proper word *böri* in the eleventh century because the Oghuz believed that the wolf was born from the totemic *tös* represented by the wolf head attached to the wormlike body of the dragon, hence the Anatolian Turkish word *kurt* instead of *böri* for "wolf."[366]

While for many other Turkish tribal entities, the dog might have been a lower-importance creature, in Qïpčak religious beliefs, the dog (in Old Turkish, *it* and *köpek*) had a significant place; there were many personal names associated with the dog. Examples include It-Oba (as a clan name) and Qutuz (Qïpčak Mamluk sultan of Egypt). At the time of the Mongol invasion, the Cuman Turks made an agreement with Istvan, coruler with his father, King Bela IV (1235–70), to defend Hungary against the invaders; to seal their promise, they swore over a dog that was cut in half with a sword. This was an ancient practice known not just to the Cumans but also to the Bulgars, as well as the pre-Christian Hungarians.[367]

Ultimately, the horse was probably the most important animal in the lives of the nomadic Turks. The Turkish Muslim polities of the Khwarezm-shahs and the Mamluks of Egypt used an equestrian effigy on their coins despite the fact that Muslim Arabs shied away from using any picture objects.[368] More on the importance of the horse in early Turkish life was discussed within the subject of equestrianism in chapter 1.2.

While discussing animal symbolism among the ancient Turks, one other important matter that will be brought up here is the fact that in ancient Turkish, many animal names had the suffix *lan*: *arslan* (lion), *baqlan* (an unknown animal), *burslan* (probably a leopard), *qaplan* (tiger), *qulan* (wild ass), and *yïlan* (snake).[369] It is still not clear how these animal names were generated using the suffix *lan*.

NUMBER SYMBOLISM

The number seven (*yedi*) was holy to the ancient Turks. A new monarch was presented to Gök-Tengri on a carpet held by seven warriors. For the Gök-Türks, the numbers seven and nine (*toquz*) had symbolic importance as well. These Turks would go around the *yurt* (felt tent) of a deceased person seven times. A newly appointed ruler would be spun round on a felt blanket nine times.[370] In shamanist cosmology, the number three (*üč*) represented three realms: heaven, earth, and the underground. However, later the number nine was added to describe the number of levels that exist between heaven and the underworld. Sky God (Gök-Tengri) resided at the highest level, the ninth level. Nine was also considered a number of luck.[371] After the Turks converted to Islam, the number five (*beš*) became important, representing the five key rites of Islam. Furthermore, the number seven (*yedi*) earned a different significance, indicating the seven layers of heaven in Qur'anic teaching.

ANCIENT FUNERALS

According to Chinese records, a large number of slaves, concubines, and war prisoners were killed as sacrifices during a Xiong-nu nobleman's funeral. The Huns and other Turkish tribal customs allowed horse racing during funerals. The Huns also arranged wrestling matches and galloped their horses during these events. Apparently, playing drums was part of these funeral ceremonies. When Attila died, in his funeral ceremonies, the Huns cut their faces and part of their hair; apparently this was an ancient custom of the Turks.[372] In another old Turkish custom, after a royal man was buried in an unmarked grave, those who buried him were also killed to keep the burial site a secret. When a Khazar monarch died, he was buried near a river, which was afterward diverted to flow over his mausoleum; then his gravediggers were killed following the completion of their duties.[373]

The Chinese reported that, in the sixth century, the Gök-Türks had a tradition of burning their dead together with the deceased's horse, clothes, and personal belongings. But in the seventh century, this tradition was abandoned. Gold and silver items were left in the tomb, and numerous *balbals* in the form of hewn stones were placed around the tomb in a standing position. Today archaeologists have noted that the tombs of Gök-Türk rulers have not been well preserved, but tens of thousands of *balbals* have been found.[374] The stone statues found near Cuman burial sites apparently had a different significance than the *balbals* of the Gök-Türks. These statues, referred to by the Cumans as *sïn*, had bowls, likely for the water of life. According to ancient Central Asian Tengriist belief, this mystical water, nourishing the heroes, originated at the base of the World Mountain of the World Tree, joining the three realms of heaven, earth, and the underworld. These statues have been found on Qïpčak-Cuman kurgans facing the east.[375]

The early Turks cremated the bodies of their dead after covering the faces with a kind of potter's clay. As the body burned, the clay would bake, turning into what was known as a death mask.[376] Excavations of kurgans across southern Siberia have revealed multiple examples of these masks. During a battle, Uighur warriors were also known to wear death masks.[377] This may have indicated that the warriors were ready to fight to the death. Perhaps this is reminiscent of Muslim Turkish fighters wearing an inner shroud (*kefen*), ready to die in battle with the intent to achieve an honorable death.

The burial of a Gök-Türk nobleman was accomplished several months after his death; if he died in spring or summer, he would be buried in autumn, whereas if he died in autumn or winter, the burial would be arranged in the spring.[378] A similar custom existed in other Turkish tribal entities as well.

Chinese records show that Uighur warriors were buried standing up, fully armed, and similarly, the Oghuz placed their dead in a sitting position in a large tomb, wearing their caftans and belts and holding their bows.[379] Just like the Gök-Türks and the Xiong-nu, the Oghuz and the Cuman Turks used *balbals* around their tombs so that the slain enemies' spirits would serve the deceased in the hereafter. The Cumans also buried their dead in a sitting position along with their horses, still alive. According to the chroniclers, during the burial of a Qïpčak nobleman, the deceased was seated in his tomb with his belongings along with his best horse and his best sergeant, both buried alive, bearing a letter to the first of their kings.[380] Similarly, when a Cuman knight died, a large grave site was opened, where the knight was seated in a chair. Then his best horse and his best sergeant were placed in it alive. Before the sergeant went in, he took leave first from his khan and then from the other knights. The khan gave him a letter to be given to the first of their previous khans; the letter would carry much praise for the sergeant. Subsequently, the sergeant would willingly enter the grave, which then would be closed forever.[381] This is an example of human sacrifice and the description of a ceremony for a kurgan burial. But this also shows that the ancient Turks, even before encountering the Abrahamic religions, believed in resurrection and the hereafter. The practice of burial with human sacrifices was also followed by other Turkish groups: Xiong-nu, Gök-Türks, Khazars, Pečenegs, Danubian Bulgars, Yenisei Kyrgyz, Altai Turks, Yakuts, and even early Ottoman Turks. Usually, those who participated in the royal burial party were killed to preserve the secrecy of the grave site. In this ceremony, symbolic communication with an ancestor spirit was considered a religious ritual.[382] Interestingly, the description of a letter in these ceremonies suggests at least some literacy among the Cumans and the Qïpčaks.

The building of mausoleums was not part of Islamic and Hindu religious traditions, but Central Asian Turks such as the Timurids and the Mughals built large mausoleums.[383] However, in the Mughal Empire, Emperor Aurangzeb (1658–1707), son of Shah Jahan, changed the Central Asian tradition by forbidding the construction of roofs on buildings containing tombs. The Muslim Oghuz, such as the Seljuks and the Ottomans, also built notable mausoleums.

EASTERN INFLUENCE: BUDDHISM

Buddhism was born in India in the sixth century BCE. When the teachings of Buddha (563–483 BCE) began to spread, they first reached the oasis kingdoms of Central Asia, particularly in the modern-day Xinjiang Province of China, in the first and second centuries CE, but it was not until the tenth century that China became a largely Buddhist empire.[384] The faith was brought to China by Central Asian nomads. At the end of the fourth century, Chü-shih, a non-Chinese nomadic people, converted to Buddhism in Turfan.[385] The Chü-ch'ü ruling family of the Northern Liang, a Xiong-nu (Hun) dynasty in China, patronized Buddhism in the fifth century.[386] They were defeated by the Northern Wei of the Tabgač Turks in 439 and moved to Kao-ch'ang, where they cultivated the rulers of the Sui and T'ang dynasties until the year 640.[387] These Turks ultimately paved a way for Buddhism to become the major religion in China (chapter 5.2).

The ancient Turks of Central Asia followed largely the faith of Gök-Tengriism. The T'o-pa (Tabgač) Turks, as the nomad conquerors of China, quickly realized that their faith could not be preserved in their new lands. Besides, the Chinese elite viewed shamanism as superstitions identical to those of the ordinary Chinese. The nomads also saw that if they were to accept Confucianism, they would be accepting cultural assimilation. Consequently, these foreign rulers of China brought in another religion to strengthen their position as new emperors. The introduction of Buddhism in this respect was the perfect solution for these monarchs as they portrayed their enthronement as the "coming of Buddha."[388] The Turks of Central Asia accepting Buddhism equated the Tengriist deity Gök-Tengri to the heavenly king (*t'ien wang*) of Buddhism.

The concept of the Four Heavenly Kings of Buddhism as guardians of the four corners of the world was brought to Central Asia before the Common Era by the traveling monks across the steppes. One of these deities, known as the P'i-sha-men (Vaiśramana), the king of the north, was embraced by most Turks, probably because this was a kind of warrior-god, a deity most easily acceptable to the warlike Turks of the Central Asian steppes.[389] Turkish Buddhism is believed to have evolved from the faith originating in Khotan, an oasis town in the Tarim basin in the modern-day Xinjiang Province of China.[390] In the tenth century, the Sha-t'o Turks, like most other Central Asian nomads, followed the faiths of both Gök-Tengriism and Buddhism, but after conquering northern China, they also acquired the religious traditions of the Chinese.[391]

Since Yüwen-t'ai, former commander in chief of the Western Wei (Tabgač) and the founder of the Northern Zhou (Chou) dynasty (557–581) of the Xiong-nu, built a Buddhist temple for the Turks in the name of the great Turkish qaghan Mu-han (553–572), it appears there were some followers of Buddhism among the Eastern Gök-Türks. Ming-ti (556–60), the successor to Yüwen-t'ai, added this inscription to the temple: "The Turk, the great I-ni Wen Mu-Han, in summer, turned to the complete foundation of Buddhism. That was wholly the work of Heaven."[392] Ming-ti went on to praise the Turks' military virtues to show his appreciation for the assistance of Mu-han in the establishment of the Zhou. There is no documented evidence that these Turks had accepted Buddhism as their religion by this time. Nevertheless, there is a suggestion that Taspar Qaghan (572–80) declared Buddhism to be the official state religion of the Gök-Türks.[393] During his visits to Gandhara in 759 and 764, the Chinese Buddhist monk Wu-k'ung noted the presence of Buddhist temples, which were established by Turkish monarchs. But when Hsüan-tsang passed through Central Asia in 629, he noticed the absence of Buddhism among the western Turks.[394] This observation indicates that in the early seventh century, the Western Gök-Türks may not have been following the Buddhist faith, yet a century later, this creed seems to have made inroads among the Central Asian nomads. By contrast, the Eastern Gök-Türks of the first empire period had already been exposed to Chinese Buddhism late in the sixth century through the Northern Zhou (Chou) dynasty (557–81).[395]

T'ang Chinese control of Central Asia, which lasted approximately for fifty years (630–82), ended when Il-teriš (also known as Qutlugh) Qaghan (682–91) reestablished the sovereignty of the Gök-Türks by starting the second period of the Turkish empire. Until the Gök-Türk Empire ceased to exist in 744, the state policy, as can be noted from the Orkhon inscriptions, appeared to be an anti-Chinese one. In their messages on the stone inscriptions, Minister Tonyuquq and Kül Tigin warned the Turkish people against the pacifying influences of the Chinese as a threat to their existence, implying their desire for the Turks to avoid Chinese Buddhism and return to the ancestral faith of Gök-Tengriism.[396] Even though the Gök-Türk inscriptions between 692 and 735 do not mention Buddhism, it is known that these Turks had been exposed to this faith for several decades.

An abundance of Turkish Buddhist literature originated not only from the Kansu corridor, where the Yellow Turks were present, but also from Tun-huang and from the Turfan oasis, one of the main centers of Turkish Buddhism; this faith was likely present in this area at least since the fourth or fifth century.[397] Meanwhile, after the Uighur Empire (744–840) took the lead from the Gök-Türks in the Eastern Eurasian Steppe, in the year 762 Bögü Qaghan abandoned the traditional Tengriist faith and adopted Manichaeism as the official state religion of the Uighurs. Then, after the Tengriist Kyrgyz crushed the Manichaeist empire in 840, the Uighurs fled southward in two directions: one group arrived in the Kansu province of China, and the other settled in the contemporary Xinjiang area, where they formed the Uighur Qočo Kingdom and eventually adopted Buddhism as their official religion.[398] During this time these Turks left abundant Buddhist literature written in the Uighur script. Even after the fall of this kingdom due to the brief Mongol invasion of the thirteenth century, Turkish Buddhism continued to flourish during the thirteenth and fourteenth centuries, particularly in the same area.[399] It should also be noted that the Uighurs spread Buddhism among the Mongols when they also took administrative positions within the Mongol Empire.[400]

While the Uighurs accepted Buddhism in eastern Turkestan, many of the Turks in western Turkestan also converted to Buddhism from their ancestral Tengriist faith. In particular, a significant portion of the Turks of the Yabghus of Tokharistan and the Türgeš Qaghanate (volume 2, chapter 2.2) were already Buddhists when Muslim Arabs tried to penetrate into their territories in the seventh and eighth centuries.

TRANSITION TO THE SEMITIC RELIGIONS

The presence of the Turkish tribes in Europe beginning as early as the third century exposed them to Christianity. But the Huns were not known to adopt this Semitic religion. The European Avars, however, even though they resisted the pressures of conversion, were forced to accept Catholicism by Charlemagne.[401] Hence, they were the first group of Turks changing from their traditional Tengriist faith to the Christian faith. The next group of Turks who felt the pressure to convert to Christianity was the Danubian Bulgar Turks in the ninth century[402] at a time when their Tengriist kinsmen in western Turkestan were being pulled into Muslim Arab armies as slave soldiers. These Bulgars came down to settle in the Balkans in the seventh century when their cousins split and moved into the Volga region in modern-day Russia; these were known as the Volga Bulgar Turks, who abandoned their Tengriist faith in the tenth century in favor of Islam.[403] The modern-day Chuvash Turks, who live in the Chuvash Republic within the Russian Federation, are believed to be the remnants of the European Huns and Volga Bulgars, and they follow the Russian Orthodox Christian faith. The Gagauz Turks are Christianized remnants of the Seljuk Turks living today in Gagauzia in Moldova in the Balkans.

The Turkish tribes became acquainted with Christianity in Asia as well. Central Asian Turks were initially exposed to Christianity through the teachings of Persian Nestorian priests around the year 550, and this was followed by two major conversion events among the Turks; the first took place in 644 with the help of Elias the Metropolitan of Merv, and the later event occurred in 781–82.[404] A third mass conversion to Christianity occurring around 1007 involved nearly two hundred thousand Turks and Mongols, and the Karait tribe is thought to have been among these new converts.[405] This Turkish tribe later emerged as a prominent tribe in Mongolia in the early thirteenth century (volume 2, chapter 3.1).

The conversion process among the Eurasian nomads followed a hierarchical order, starting from the top, since the elite of the tribes, as policy makers, were often more exposed to foreign influences. From a sociology standpoint, the conversion process would have followed one of the three patterns: conversion by voluntary will, conversion due to political, social, or economic pressures, or conversion by assimilation. From the viewpoint of sedentary civilizations, conversion would have offered a valuable tactical advantage—that is, achievement of security by means of controlling the nomadic raiders. Since sedentary armies could not stop incursions by the mounted archers, bringing them to the same faith as the sedentary societies would have perhaps halted these otherwise-unstoppable attacks. Hence, to achieve these goals, missionaries of the sedentary peoples worked hard among these pagan invaders.

There are reports that as early as the fourth century, there were Armenian efforts to convert the Huns to Christianity in Caucasus. In the sixth century, Armenian missionaries led by Bishop Kardost produced a Bible in Hunnish (Turkish). In the seventh century, Syriac chronicles show a group of Turks, possibly Ephtalites (White Huns), converted to Nestorian Christianity. But there are examples of many failures as well. In 528, when a Hunnish chief was convinced to convert to Christianity, he subsequently found death through the rebellion of his heathen people led by his brother. In 619, when Qubrat, the great Bulgar khan, converted to Christianity, it allowed the Eastern Roman emperor Heraclius to weaken Avar domination in the Balkans by forcing the Bulgars to break away from their kinsmen, the Avar overlords.[406] However, subsequent Turkish Bulgar monarchs did not follow Christianity until the ninth century.

The Cuman Turks' occasional conversions to Orthodox Christianity are documented in Rus' chronicles. But conversions by the tribal chiefs were noted particularly in the face of the Mongol invasion of the thirteenth century, as they were likely to set up alliances with the Rus' and other Christians against the Mongols. Following the disaster of the Battle of Kalka River against the Mongols, the Cumans who took refuge among the Russians became Christians and settled among their Slavic neighbors. However, there are also records showing that Catholic missionaries, particularly the Franciscans, were active in converting the Cumans to Catholicism with some success. A Cuman episcopate was established circa 1217–18.[407]

The first decline of the Gök-Türks in the early seventh century eventually exposed the Khazar Turks in eastern Europe to Semitic religions. Even though the Khazars became acquainted with Christianity, they initially preferred to remain in the Tengriist faith. However, when they gave sanctuary to Jews persecuted under the Eastern Roman Greeks and the Sassanian Persians, they became influenced by Judaism, which they later accepted as their state religion (chapter 4.6). The Khazar Turks consequently became the first and the only non-Hebrew people (Gentile) to have the Judaic faith as a state religion, in the ninth century.[408]

Now returning from Europe to the Turkish homeland in Central Asia, we see Islam entering western Turkestan in the second half of the eighth century. But the oasis towns along the historic Silk Road connecting China with Central Asia, India, Persia, and the Near East were critical in transmitting not only merchandise but also knowledge of science and faith, and before the advance of Islam into Central Asia, the land had been exposed to the Christian faith. In fact, Christianity in its Nestorian form passed beyond Persia into Central Asia in the third and fourth centuries, and by the eighth century, it was recognized by people along the Syr Darya.[409] The well-known Central Asian Turkish tribes that accepted Christianity were the Öngüts and the Karaits.[410] The latter group played a critical role in the rise of Genghis Khan and his Mongols as a power in Mongolia in the late twelfth century. There is also evidence that Christianity, particularly its Nestorian form, found acceptance among the Čiğil, a subconfederation of the Qarluq tribal union.[411] In the meantime, while the Uighurs converted from Manichaeism to Buddhism in eastern Turkestan, the Turks in western Turkestan were exposed to Islam when the Muslim Arab armies of the Umayyads came to the outskirts of Central Asia at the end of the seventh century.

ISLAM

At this point it is important to touch upon Islam's rapid seventh-century expansion from the Arabian Peninsula to the Near East and into Asia, where mostly shamanist and Buddhist Turkish tribes were scattered. How did the majority of these Turkish tribes embrace Islam? Did they convert to this faith quickly? What were the factors that made Islam acceptable to the Turks? But first we will elaborate on the political evolution of Islam in the Near East.

When Prophet Muhammad died in Medina in 632, the Arab Muslim community came under the rule of the caliphs of al-Rashidun (632–61). During this period, the leaders were chosen successively from the four companions of the Prophet. The first of these was Abu Bakr (632–34), who was one of the Prophet's most trusted supporters and the father of the Prophet's wife A'isha. Upon becoming the first caliph, Abu Bakr transformed

Medina into the capital of the Arabian Peninsula. He was succeeded by Omar (634–44), who was the father of the Prophet's wife Hafsa. Omar managed to turn the strength of the desert Arabs against the Eastern Romans in Syria and Palestine and the Persian Sassanids in Iraq and Persia. After his assassination, Othman, the Prophet's son-in-law, became the third caliph (644–56), until he was murdered. Ali, the cousin of the Prophet, became the final caliph of the al-Rashidun period. He was also the son-in-law of the Prophet through his marriage to Fatima, the daughter of Muhammad. However, Ali soon found opposition to his rule of the Islamic lands when he realized that Muawiya, the powerful governor of the territories of Syria and Egypt, had his own designs for the state.

Muawiya was a kinsman of previously assassinated Caliph Othman, as both were from the Umayya clan of Mecca. As a result, he was not keen to follow Ali's political leadership. Aware of Muawiya's desires, Ali moved to Iraq to prepare for a confrontation. His army consisted of poorly trained Bedouins against his opponent's disciplined and experienced military force. The first battle in 657 was not decisive, but Ali was murdered in 661. After this assassination, Muawiya established the Umayyad Caliphate (661–750), with the capital in Damascus. But the murder of Ali alienated his loyal followers; they viewed Ali, who was directly related to the Prophet, as the rightful heir to the position of caliph. Consequently, this event marked the initial formal split of Islam into the Sunni and Shi'ite sects. For the faithful of the latter sect, Ali was considered the first imam (religious leader).

Less than two decades after the death of his father, Ali's son Hussein attempted to take over the Umayyad dynasty, but his failure led to his demise, with the public mutilation of his body in Karbala, in modern-day Iraq. This event marked the firm establishment of Shi'ism as a rival Islamic dogma to its Sunni Orthodox counterpart, and Karbala became a holy city for the Shi'ites. Hasan and Hussein, Ali's sons from the Prophet's daughter Fatima, were also viewed as martyrs and were considered the next two imams of the Shi'ite faith. Subsequent imams were all descendants of slain Hussein. While Shi'ism evolved as a more liberal view of Islam, Sunni'ism remained a more rigid orthodox sect. With the exception of the short-lived Shi'ite domination of the Middle East in the tenth and early eleventh centuries, before the arrival of the Turks, Sunni leadership controlled this region for the most part. The Umayyad dynasty, however, in the year 750 relinquished its position to the Abbasid dynasty, which descended from Prophet Muhammad's youngest uncle, Abbas Ibn Abd-al-Muttalib. Shortly after taking control of the Islamic world, the Abbasids moved into western Turkestan, where they met mostly Tengriist Central Asian nomadic people.

The Turks were always known as a martial people. As stated earlier, Tengriist Turkish warriors believed that they would be provided rewards for heroism and chivalry. Their military prowess was their honor. They also believed that, by dying on the battlefield, they would be in a respected place with their forefathers. Although Islam presented the option of martyrdom by dying for God and thereby obtaining a higher status in the hereafter in the service of the creator, the choice to convert from Tengriism to Islam still took over three centuries among the Turkish mounted archers.

However, the conversion to Islam was not always peaceful. Even though Muslim Arab armies entered Central Asia early in the eighth century, it took more than two centuries for the Turks to convert to the Muslim faith. Among the reasons for this delay was the fact that the Turkish territories already had a variety of Semitic (Judaism) and Semitic-derived (Nestorian Christianity and Manichaeism) religions. Furthermore, the Türgiš state of the Turks in western Turkestan resisted the Arab activities in the area. Hence, it was not an easy task for the Arabs to force the Turks to accept the Muslim faith by the sword. But over time Muslim merchants had success in carrying the words and the message of the Qur'an to these Central Asian Turks.

Islam was brought to the Turks by Muslim merchants, and by Muslim mystics known as Sufis.[412] Persian-speaking merchants brought Islam to the Turks for the first time. This Semitic religion emerging from the desert of Arabia eventually had a more profound influence on the Turks than did Buddhism and Manichaeism. As stated earlier, before the advent of Islam in Central Asia, the Turks were exposed to multiple religions in addition to their ancestral Tengriist faith, including Buddhism, Christianity, Judaism, Mazdaism, and Manichaeism. Rather than the orthodox Sunni version of Islam, it was the mystic Sufism version that attracted the Turks to Islam, since they saw similarities between mystic Islam and the mysticism of their Tengriism.[413]

Islam began to make inroads among the Turkish tribal entities between the ninth and eleventh centuries, particularly during the Persian Samanid rule of Khorasan and Khwarezm. Mass conversions began in the latter part of the tenth century.[414] Ultimately, the Sufis were responsible for effectively spreading the word of Islam among the Central Asian nomads.[415] One of the most important Sufi brotherhoods was the Naqshbandiyya, founded in the fourteenth century by Khwâja Bahâ ad-Din Naqshband, a Tajik (Persian) from Bukhara. But the early spread of Islam among the Turks was particularly influenced by the works of Turkish Sufi and poet Khoja Ahmad Yesevi (Yasawi), whose mausoleum today is in Kazakhstan.

Yesevi was a Turkish poet and a Sufi leader previously trained under another Turkish spiritual leader, Arslan Baba, in the early twelfth century. It was Yesevi's popular mysticism that catalyzed the rapid spread of Islam among the Turkish tribes across Central Asia. Because of his efforts, the popular Sufi Yesevi order was established. It has been said that the Sufi who helped to convert Özbek Khan of the Golden Horde into the Muslim faith in 1320 was from the Sufi Yesevi order.

Another famous thirteenth-century Central Asian Sufi was Jalal ad-Din Muhammad Rumi, also known as Mevlana, who spent his life in Konya (Iconium), the capital of the Seljuk Sultanate of Rum in Anatolia. His spiritual legacy has survived into modern times. The Mevlevi Sufi order that was established after his death in Konya is well known today because of its whirling dervishes.

While the Arab views of orthodox Sunni Islam forbid the use of pictures and figures of humans and animals to prevent idol worship, many of the early Turkish converts did not follow these strict rules. Even after they converted to Islam, Sunni Seljuks continued to exhibit the influences of their pre-Islamic ancestral Tengriist religion in their artwork. Under the patronage of the Muslim Turkish dynasties, starting with the Seljuks, miniature painting gained popularity. Often these art pieces included animal and human figures. Because of their liberal spiritual Islamic interpretation, the Seljuks of Rum produced unique artwork in their sacred buildings, including figural representations on the portals.[416] These buildings included mosques, religious schools (*medrese*), and mausoleums (*türbe*). Most of these stone reliefs included animal motifs, but a few included human figures. For example, the hospital of the Ulugh Jami at Divriği and the Alaeddin Mosque at Niğde in Turkey both have human head figures on their portals. The Kaykavus Hospital in Sivas exhibits sun and moon motifs, and the Čifte Medrese of Kayseri illustrates a lion figure. Seljuk tombs also have figures of realistic or surreal creatures. It is suggested that the unique Seljuk mausoleums (*türbe*) have characteristics of Central Asian shamanist rituals with their tent-and-earth-burial theme.[417]

The Orkhon inscriptions from the eighth century tell us that giving to the needy was an important social duty and tradition. The Gök-Türks monarchs are described in these writings to feed the needy and to clothe the naked to make the Turkish people happy and powerful. The obligatory giving to charity in Islam is another aspect of the religion that attracted the Turks to this Semitic religion. As Muslim chroniclers wrote, wealthy Turks were known to give to charity and to social and religious institutions. For the Turkish people and their rulers, the public good and solidarity were more important than any material gain, but ultimately this attitude benefited the public in general, giving rise to their political power.[418]

THE ACQUISITION OF ARAB NAMES

Throughout history, people who have converted from one faith to another have tended to change their names to feel more accepted in their new faiths. Hence, if someone converted to Christianity, the new convert acquired a biblical name. Similarly, new converts to Islam were expected to acquire Arabic names, since Islam arose in Arabia.

From the time Islam arrived in Central Asia in the mid-eighth century until the Turkish people adopted the Islamic faith in large numbers in the tenth century, the Turks mostly continued to use their traditional names, which often had shamanic significance. For example, though Qara-Khanid founder Satuq Bughra Khan in the tenth century acquired the Muslim (Arab) name Abd al-Karim, and Seljuk sultan Tuğrul Bey in the eleventh century took the Islamic (Arab) name of Muhammad,[419] these prominent leaders were still popularly known by their given Turkish names.

When the Seljuks invaded the Middle East, many of their commanders, though they were Muslims, had only loose ties with Islam.[420] In fact, they still carried the influence of shamanism of Central Asia. For example, while Muslim Arabs shied away from using figures of living beings in their art, the Seljuks not only promoted miniature paintings of human beings and animals but also used animals on their coins. While many Muslim commanders changed their names to Arabic or Persian ones, Artuq Bey and his dynasty were among those who continued to use Turkish names.[421] Late in the thirteenth century, Osman Bey, the founder of the Ottoman principality (*beylik*), named all his sons with Turkish appellations—including his successor, Orhan—with the exception of Süleyman. Furthermore, many supporters of Osman Bey, including Qonur Alp, Aqcha Khodja, and Samsa Čavuš, used Turkish names rather than Muslim Arab names.[422]

With the emergence of the Turkish military within the Islamic world starting in the eleventh century, Turkish remained as a language of war, whereas Arabic was the language of religion. At various times in the Islamic world, despite the fact that the Turks established monarchies across a large geography from Algiers to Bengal and from Yemen to Siberia, many local administrators were either Arabic or Persian speakers recording in their mother tongues.[423] In the fifteenth century, Turkish recordings emerged as a result of the regional dominance of the Ottoman Oghuz and Čaghatai Turkish dialects, and the latter became the primary language used by the Timurid and Mughal courts.

Chapter 2:

OVERVIEW OF THE PAST OF THE TURKS

2.1. AN INTRODUCTION TO WORLD HISTORY

Ancient world history is described in different stages of human development, characterized as ages. Each age, however, occurred at different times in different geographic locations, depending on the developmental stage of the native peoples there. The Stone Age, which might have lasted nearly three million years, witnessed the use of stones for tools and weapons. It ended with the discovery of metalworking about 5000 BCE. The Neolithic Age was the last stage of the Stone Age before the discovery of metal use. During this time the beginnings of agriculture and the domestication of the animals were observed. The Copper Age, also known as the Chalcolithic Age, is considered a transitional period between the Neolithic and the Bronze Ages. Copper making dates back nearly to 5000 BCE. The Bronze Age probably ended in the Near East in about the eleventh century BCE, much earlier than in Europe, where it likely ended in about the seventh century BCE.

The Bronze Age was characterized by the use of copper and bronze along with initial examples of writing. Initial examples of advanced urban civilization can also be found within this period. It is suggested that agriculture, with its earliest harvest products of wheat and barley, made its first appearance in Central Asia about 6000 BCE, but the building of irrigation canals, thus allowing more reliable agricultural activities and population growth, occurred three millennia later.[424] Also in this age, pastoralist nomadism began between

4000 and 3000 BCE. Horseback riding may not have started until at least 1000–600 BCE. In the subsequent Iron Age, which began about 1200 BCE, the prevalent use of iron over bronze stands out as a characteristic of this period. During this time metal objects were used as cutting tools and weapons. The manuscript tradition also began to evolve in this period. Alphabets, literature, and the recording of history began in this age. The end of the Iron Age in about the fifth century BCE also marked the end of prehistory.

Prehistory was essentially dominated by the development of human tools and agriculture. Horseback riding also began during this period. The period of ancient history, however, began with the discovery of writing and record keeping. Therefore, there was some overlap with the period of prehistory. Ancient history also began with the development of human civilizations. Mesopotamia and Anatolia are known as the cradles of civilization. This ancient geographic territory, also known as the Near East, has been a witness to great civilizations that helped shape the contemporary world. Chinese culture is nearly as old as that of the Near East, but its earliest developments are not as well known, because there was not meaningful interaction between the Chinese and the West until much later in history. Only a few civilizations made an impact on ancient world history. The Sumerians, the Egyptians, and the Hittites, who were in the Near East, are among the best-known great early civilizations of the world.

EARLIEST HUMAN SETTLEMENTS

The discovery of 'Göbekli Tepe' archeological site nearly fifteen kilometers from Urfa, an ancient city in southeastern Turkey, revealed the presence of massive carved stones about 11,000 years old. The German archeologist who has discovered the site has determined Göbekli Tepe to be the world's oldest temple. This remarkable site is located at the northern age of the Fertile Crescent. It has been determined that these massive stones were crafted by prehistoric people who were likely hunter-gatherers. At the time when this site was originally built, there was no discovery of metal tools yet nor was there pottery either. Instead, the stonecutters at that time used stone tools.

Although there has been no scientific clue for the meaning of carved pictures and symbols, the stones illustrated bas-reliefs of wild animals including boars and lions thus gives the sense that this temple was presumably used for shaman-like rituals. There is no data to indicate who these people were and where they came from.

Excavations at Göbekli Tepe and its vicinity have determined that people in this area began animal husbandry with cattle, sheep, and pigs within 1,000 years of this temple's construction. On the other hand, the discovery of world's oldest domesticated strains of wheat suggested that agriculture began nearly 500 years after Göbekli Tepe was constructed. Based on carbon-dating Göbekli Tepe was built around 9000 B.C.E., and therefore, the age of this site makes it about 6,000 years older than well-known Stonehenge located in Britain. Just to give more perspective, the oldest Egyptian pyramid was built during the third dynasty (2690 B.C.E. to 2610 B.C.E.).

Nevalı Çori (8500 B.C.E.) known as an early Neolithic period settlement near Urfa in southeastern Turkey has the world's oldest known buildings and it is also known for its oldest domesticated Einkorn wheat. Tell Sabi Abyad (7500 B.C.E.) in the Balikh River valley in northern Syria and Jarmo (7100 B.C.E.) in modern Iraq on the foothills of the Zagros Mountains are among the oldest known settlements on earth. Again, these are within the Fertile Crescent territory. Two other Neolithic settlements both in Turkey, Çatalhöyük (7500 B.C.E.) in Konya province and Çayönü Tepesi (7200 B.C.E.) about forty kilometers northwest of Diyarbakır at the foot of the Taurus mountains are among the oldest human settlements as well. In the meantime, the oldest prehistoric Neolithic Egyptian societies are from about 3600 B.C.E. along the Nile River; it was only shortly after 3600 B.C.E. that the Egyptians began to evolve into more advanced civilization leading into dynastic society.

While pottery began in the Fertile Crescent with the start of Pottery Neolithic Period around 6900-6400 B.C.E. thus succeeding the Pre-Pottery Neolithic Period, in China an early form of pottery was discovered from nearly 20,000 years ago, thus making it the world's earliest pottery yet discovered.

Meanwhile, the discovery of Göbekli Tepe also brought a new theory in regards to the evolution of civilization. Until recently most scholars believed that humans first learned farming and then lived in settled communities before building worship places and complex social structures. However, Klaus Schmidt, the German archaeologist who discovered Göbekli Tepe, suggested that it was the construction effort with megaliths that actually paved way to the evolution of complex societies.

In essence this discovery showed that the humans at this point demonstrated transition of their sociocultural life from being simple hunter-gatherers to the beginnings of settled organized lifestyle. This change was then followed by the development of agriculture. As a result, these developments led to the formation of a complex Neolithic society. With the domestication of plants and animals transition to sedentary lifestyle most likely began to occur as a result of economic necessity in addition to coping with climate changes as well as for security reasons.[425] Only about 6000 years later after Göbekli Tepe's construction that writing was discovered in this region as well. Göbekli Tepe was incorporated into UNESCO World Heritage List in 2018.

STEPPE ORIGINS OF THE WAR CHARIOTS

As stated earlier mankind's Agricultural Revolution began with the Neolithic Age about 12,000 years ago. This was the last stage of the Stone Age before the discovery of metal use. It was during this period of time when animals were domesticated. It was also the domestication of horses about 5,500 years ago that may have given an impetus to the rise of pastoralist nomadism in the Eurasian steppes.

It was natural that nomads utilized vehicles with wheels to carry their goods. Indeed, the invention of the wheel was so significant in mankind's history that it facilitated the transport of heavy materials across distances. Hence, this invention was also crucial in providing rise to the evolution of commerce for early human civilizations. It has been thought that the earliest utilization of solid wooden wheel occurred in the Middle East, particularly in Mesopotamia, yet it has also been suggested that carts with wheels may have originated from the Eurasian steppes.[426] In fact, the earliest depiction of a vehicle with two axles and four wheels was found on a pot dating back to circa 3500 BCE, found in Poland, at the outskirts of western Eurasian steppes.[427]

While the vehicles with wheels were initially used at times of peace, it was not until the Bronze Age or about 2600 BCE when battlewagons pulled by wild asses were used by Sumerians in their military campaigns. But their heavy weight and slow movement did not make them practical war machines. On the other hand, the domestication of the horse at about 3500 BCE did not only revolutionize transportation but also communications as well as warfare.[428] It is now an accepted fact that the horse was domesticated by steppe people of the Botai Culture (3700 BCE to 3100 BCE) in the plains of northern present-day Kazakhstan. These ancient Asiatic hunter-gatherers were also consuming mare's milk just as Central Asian Turks and Mongols have been doing for thousands of years. Ultimately, the utilization of horses in place of much slower wild asses for pulling carts led to the subsequent invention of chariots as more efficient war machines.

Based on archeological findings and carbon-dating technology it is clear that the first use horse-powered chariots was seen on the steppes of Kazahkstan. Indeed, the agricultural civilizations began to utilize this technology much later. While the Eurasian steppes were using horse-powered vehicles as war machines earlier than 2000 BCE, the Middle Eastern civilizations did not start using them until 1800 BCE.[429] Hittites provided the oldest written record, known as the Anitta text describing the utilization of chariots at the siege of Salatiwara in Anatolia around the seventeenth century BCE. While the chariots became widely used in Anatolia and the Middle East, the knowledge of this war technology also passed on to ancient Egypt by the fifteenth century BCE. Ultimately, the Battle of Qadesh was the first known recorded battle between the ancient Egyptians and the Hittites in 1274 BCE; the battle became known for its large scale chariot usage. On the other hand, Romans did not use chariots for war but rather for prestigious racing purposes.

On the eastern spectrum of the ancient civilized world China appeared to have adopted the utilization of chariots from the steppe peoples as well. This transfer of technology was not limited to steppe war chariots but also to high-end application of metallurgy from the steppe culture. Indeed, it has been suggested that the application of copper-bronze as well as iron technology entered into China through Kansu corridor from eastern Turkistan.[430] But it was during the period of 1180-1150 BCE that the powerful steppe people Kuei-fang successfully pushed against the expansion efforts of Shang dynasty of China by using war chariots. Hence, with such exposure it appeared that Shang China began to utilize horse-powered war chariots by the thirteenth and twelfth centuries BCE.[431]

Although horseback riding may have perhaps started within the Botai Culture of Kazakhstan, many academicians had believed that this was not started until at least 1000–600 BCE. Yet, the dominant use of horse early on has been seen with the pulling of chariots or other vehicles with wheels. But clearly the true art of horseback riding rose from the steppes of eastern Eurasian steppes. Furthermore, beginning with the early Iron Age (circa 900-600 BCE) the petroglyphs of southern Siberia and northwestern Mongolia illustrate that previously predominant war chariot designs left their place for those of mounted warriors.[432] The fate of these steppe fighters will be discussed later in the third chapter.

OLD CIVILIZATIONS

The Sumerian Empire existed during the Chalcolithic Age, also known as the Copper Age, between the fifth and fourth millennia BCE. The Sumerians are best known for the invention of writing; they were the first people to leave behind written records, with a cuneiform alphabet. The other earliest recordings are from Egypt, about fifty-five centuries ago, and China, about thirty-two centuries ago.

During the Bronze Age, roughly between the fourth and first millennia BCE, the Egyptians and the Hittites had the most powerful and civilized empires in the world. Subsequently, during the Iron Age, ancient Greek civilization flourished as city-states, particularly thriving between the fifth and fourth centuries BCE. During the same period, the Etruscans, situated in modern-day Tuscany of Italy, formed an advanced civilization, which formed the basis for the Roman Empire later. At the end of the height of Greek civilization, Alexander the Great from the Macedonian ethnic group formed perhaps the first far-reaching empire in world history as he stretched his power and Hellenic culture from his homeland across the Middle East to the northern borders of the Indian subcontinent. The Roman Empire followed the fall of the Macedonian Empire.

In the East, Chinese recorded history began with the Shang dynasty as early as the eighteenth century BCE. It is well known that China is home to one of the very old cultures of the world. The short-lived Qin dynasty (221–206 BCE) is considered the first imperial dynasty of China that united the land. In the second century CE, during the subsequent Han dynasty (206 BCE–220 CE), the Chinese discovered paper for writing.

Persians are another ancient people, of Indo-European stock. They first appear in the Assyrian scriptures in the ninth century BCE. The Achaemenid Empire, which existed between the sixth and fourth centuries BCE, is the first-known Persian empire. In fact, the Persians founded the first monarchy in world history.[433] This once-mighty empire was brought down by Alexander the Great.

Above are examples of early sedentary civilizations, which likely resulted from the transformation of nomadic civilizations into sedentary ones. The emergence of nation-states occurred much later. Among the most prominent tribal nations were the Turks, the Germans, and the later-appearing Mongols. In history, only a few empires have existed long enough to have a significant influence on the modern world. The following is a short list of the most influential and longest-lasting empires/states that shaped the development of the world:

- The (Western) Roman Empire (27 BCE–476 CE): 503 years
- The Eastern Roman Empire (395–1453): 1,058 years
- The Republic of Venice (697–1797): 1,100 years
- The Holy Roman Empire (962–1806): 844 years
- The (Turkish) Ottoman Empire (1299–1922): 623 years

In contrast, among the nomadic tribes that carried the tradition of statehood the longest surviving one was that of the Huns. Starting in the third century B.C.E. they continued their existence nearly into the second half of the sixth century C.E. (chapters 3 and 4.2). If we consider that the founders of GökTürk dynasty were in effect from the Huns, then we could stretch Hun political existence well inot the middle of the eighth century (chapter 5.3).

The Roman legacy was the longest-lasting and the most influential one, forming the basis of Western civilization. The Romans were influenced by the Etruscan and ancient Greek civilizations. When mighty Rome was weakened, it split into two separate empires in 395. The demise of the Western Roman Empire in 476 was catalyzed by the attacks of the Turkish European Huns of Attila. The legacy of Rome ended when the Ottoman Turks ended the Eastern Roman Empire (also known as the Byzantine Empire) in 1453.

Although it is common to use the name Byzantine Empire, the official name of the Eastern Roman Empire was Imperium Romanum, Latin for Roman Empire. After all, it was the continuation of the former Roman Empire in late antiquity and the medieval period. But its population comprised predominantly Greek speakers. The Eastern Roman Empire, during its existence, was never called the Byzantine Empire. In fact, the term Byzantine, which comes from Byzantium, the name of the city before it became Emperor Constantine's new capital, was first used by German historian Hieronymus Wolf in his work *Corpus Historiæ Byzantinæ*, published in 1557, more than a century after the empire was conquered by the Ottoman Turks. The people of the Eastern Roman Empire referred to their capital Constantinople as Rome or as New Rome and called themselves Romaioi and their empire Romania.[434] For this reason, the Ottomans referred to Thrace as Rumeli, Turkish for "land of the Romans," and to the Greek inhabitants of the conquered empire as Rumlar, meaning Romans. The term Hellas, by contrast, referred to the ancient pagan Greek tradition and was used as a derogatory term up until the twelfth century.[435] To stay true to history, the Eastern Roman Empire will not be referred to as the Byzantine Empire in this book.

2.2. TRACING BACK THE TURKISH PAST

Turkish history dates back to antiquity, on the basis of ancient Chinese recordings. Since the Turks were largely a pastoralist nomadic people until the twelfth century, they did not leave much recorded history. The first recorded information left by them dates back to the eighth century. Most information about their ancient history comes from the archives of other people who encountered them.

Linguistically, it is believed that Proto-Turkish was spoken as early as 3000–500 BCE.[436] Hence, Turkish is considered one of the oldest languages of the world. In fact, it was spoken long before many modern European languages came into existence. When the eighth-century Gök-Türk inscriptions were written, French was not in existence yet. There is no surviving Russian literary work from the eleventh century, when Mahmud of Kashgar wrote the first Turkish dictionary.

It is not known how different language families evolved separately from one another. Despite the fact that many societies developed independently from each other, the majority of humans share a common hunter-gatherer past. It was only about ten thousand years ago, when the Ice Age ended, that two new lifestyles began to emerge: agriculturalism and pastoral nomadism. The grassland of the Eurasian Steppe, more than six thousand kilometers long from Manchuria in the east to Hungary in the west, became the world of pastoralist nomads. The great nomadic empire of the Xiong-nu in 209 BCE was the first of its kind (chapter 3.2), and these pastoralist nomad warriors along the northern border of Han China marked a new page in history.[437]

According to the Chinese, these ancient Turks were known as the Xiong-nu (or Hsiung-nu in Wade-Giles Chinese), also referred to as the Asian Huns.[438] Until they formed their first empire in the third century BCE on the northern border of China, they appeared to be dispersed as pastoralist nomads across the steppes of modern-day Mongolia, a vast territory also known as the Eastern Eurasian Steppe.

The original homeland of the Turks is thought to be the steppes of contemporary Mongolia, including the territories of the Altai Mountains, a mountain range where modern-day Kazakhstan, Mongolia, Russia, and the Chinese province of Uighur Xinjiang come together. However, it has also been suggested that the Turkish homeland stretched over a much larger area, including parts of the vast lands of Siberia. It should be noted that the word Mongolia in modern times is used as a geographic descriptor and for the land of the Mongols. But modern-day Mongolia was not the Mongols' homeland until after the first millennium CE. They previously lived in the forests of Manchuria. Mongolia, or more properly Outer Mongolia, was the homeland for many ancient Turkish tribes and their tribal confederations.[439] Over time the Turks spread out from the Mongolian steppes to western Asia and to the taiga forests of Siberia to reach the Arctic and Pacific coasts.[440]

Scholars in linguistics have generally accepted that the Turkish language originated in the Altai Mountain region. For this reason it is thought to be a member of the Altaic group of languages. This mountain range is important in Turkish mythology. In Chinese texts, this mountain range is known as the Golden Mountains, but in Turkish, the word *altai* literally meant "red horse" (*al tay*). Just a bit farther west are the Tien Shan, shared by modern-day Kazakhstan, Kyrgyzstan, and China and known to be important to the ancient Turkish world. In Chinese, Tien Shan means Celestial Mountains. The ancient Turks referred to this mountain range as Tengri Tagh, meaning God Mountain.

The earliest known recorded history suggests that in ancient times, most of northern Asia (Siberia) came under the loose control of the Hunnic Turks. When the Turkish tribes began to spread west and northwest from their homeland, they also forced out the Persian tribes residing in the western portion of Central Asia. Over time, as we will see later, all Central Asia stretching from the eastern shores of the Caspian Sea to the territories of the western provinces of modern-day China came under the influence of the Turks. In the Middle Ages, this large territory was named Turkestan—a Persian word that signifies "land of the Turks"; in Old Turkic the term would have been Türk-ili. Currently this territory includes the Turkish states of Kazakhstan, Kyrgyzstan, Turkmenistan, and Uzbekistan, in addition to the (Turkish) Uighur autonomous province of Xinjiang of China.

Responsible for the fall of the Western and Eastern Roman Empires and for establishing historically significant five dynasties in China over 950 years, the Altaic peoples had a significant impact on sedentary civilizations from the Far East to Europe.[441] Over a period of nearly a millennium, the Eastern Roman Empire faced multiple Turkish-origin Altaic peoples, including the Huns, Avars, Bulgars, Khazars, Pečenegs, Cumans, Qïpčaks, Seljuks, and Ottomans. The Mongols also had a brief but significant experience in the West as Altaic conquerors.

Turkish domination over northern and western Siberia lasted nearly until the eighteenth century. Even today fragments of Turkish groups remain scattered across the Siberian territories of the Russian Federation as either autonomous republics or ethnic territories. Interestingly, we find that Siberia might have been named after an ancient Turkish group of people, the Sibir Turks of the fourth and fifth centuries.[442] Eastern Roman Empire records indicate that the ethnic Sabirs (also known as Sibirs) spoke a similar language to that of the Pečeneg Turks, who appeared in historical records much later. The Sibir Turks resided in the western portion of Siberia, just north of the Caspian Sea.

According to another theory regarding the name of Siberia, it originated from an ancient pastoralist Turkish description combining the Old Turkish words *su* (water) and *berr* (unpopulated wilderness); hence, the composite word meant "wilderness with plenty of water."[443] Similarly, the name of Siberian Lake Baikal was derived from *bey* (big) and *kül* (lake), and the name of the Yenisei River originated from the words *yeni* (clear or new) and *sei* (water, from *su*).[444]

ABOUT THE PROTO-TURKS

Rock carvings known as petroglyphs provide information on cultural life in early human history. Central Asia has an extensive amount of these stone recordings. Similar carvings are also found in the farthest point of eastern Europe. Despite the fact that the Huns are considered the earliest part of Turkish history since they formed a state (chapter 3), scholars have traced the earliest findings of Turkish history in rock carvings and seals (*tamgha* in Old Turkish) left by the proto-Turks in a large geographic area encompassing most of central and eastern Eurasia.[445] Early Turkish tribes were spread out throughout this vast geographic area. For this reason, many scholars believe that the Turkish homeland was not restricted to the Mongolian steppelands but rather stretched over two-thirds of the vast Eurasian steppes. While the earliest mention of Turkish tribes can be found in ancient Chinese annals dating back to 2250 BCE, according to the research of sociologist S. Somuncuoglu, the Lena petroglyphs in Siberia dating to 14,000–12,000 BCE are the earliest evidence of a Turkish presence. According to Dmitriy Vasilyev, vice president of the Orientalists' Society at the Russian Academy of Sciences, the Central Asian petroglyphs describe the ancient culture, migration stories, and psychology of ancient Turkish tribes.[446] Tireless expeditions in the harsh geography of Saimaluu-Tash in modern-day Kyrgyzstan have revealed ancient rock carvings associated with the ancient runic Turkish alphabet, therefore suggesting that these thousands-of-years-old carvings and seals are among the earliest remnants of Turkish cultural history. Some of these are claimed to have been created as early as 5000–10,000 BCE or even older, after the end of the Ice Age.[447] The stone carvings and figures that have been discovered across the vast Asian steppes have been attributed to the earliest tribes of the Turks.[448]

Who were the proto-Turks? While some historians consider the Xiong-nu (chapter 3) to be the proto-Turks, others believe them to be even older than these northern tribal people. Indeed, Chinese archives also mention regarding *Jung*, *Ti*, and *Hien-yün* tribes (chapter 3.1), which were all much older than the Xiong-nu. Another question that should be posed is that because of what is clearly missing in ancient records is the physical description of the proto-Turks; how did they look? According to some of these records some Turkish tribes had europoid or Caucasian characteristics but there are records describing other Turkish tribal people having mongoloid appearance as well. Even though French anthropologist Valois (1967) suggested that the Turk was europoid race's easternmost representative, others such as Baker (19740 and Thoma (1975) believed that the Turk was a racially mixed person between europoid and mongoloid races.[449]

Today, the earliest historically known Turks are the Xiong-nu, or the Asian Huns. Chinese archives describe the Huns as having, for the most part, Europoid (or Caucasian) features instead of Mongoloid morphology, and this characterization is supported by archaeological finds in burial sites in Mongolia.[450] But occasionally Mongoloid-appearing features were also found, indicating intermarriages between the Caucasian Turks and other Asian races, such as the Chinese and the Mongols. By the time the majority of the Turks had left modern-day Mongolia, in the tenth century, they were still mostly Caucasian in appearance.[451] The Kyrgyz were an ancient Turkish tribal entity present since the times of the Xiong-nu (Asian Huns). In Chinese sources, their tall warriors are described as being blond and blue eyed.[452] Today, the Kyrgyz, still keeping their ancient tribal name alive, reside in Kyrgyzstan in Central Asia, and they have primarily Mongoloid elements, indicating significant blending of Asian races in their makeup.

Many Western and some Eastern scholars believe that the human remnants with europoid characteristics discovered from excavations in eastern Turkistan as well as Central Asia in addition to southern Siberia were Indo-European origin. The controversy surrounding many of these remnants belonged to tribal nomadic peoples of Scythians (chapter 2.3) and Yueh-chih (chapter 3.3.).

Scythians were once known as warlike mounted archers striking fear into the hearts of great civilizations of antiquity in Near East. Historically, since they spread out across a very large geography, it is plausible to split them into Siberian, Indo-European, and Pontus geographic divisions. Around the seventh and fifth centuries B.C.E. Scythians around Aral Sea had Andronovo Culture, and they clearly had mongoloid elements in their physical appearances. Similar findings were also found from Scythians who once resided in the region of Altai and Tien-shan mountains as well as from those who lived by Pamir Mountains, however, it also became apparent that by the fourth and second centuries B.C.E. they began to lose their mongoloid features.[453]

According to ancient Chinese archives the physical appearance of the Yueh-chih who lived in eastern Turkistan was described to be consistent with europoid look. The same records mentioned that these tribal people, who later formed the Kushan Empire, had fair skin, and they were extremely talented to shoot arrows while on horseback.[454] Mostly based on their physical (Caucasian) appearances both Scythians and Yueh-chih have been thought to speak an Indo-European tongue. Yet, this view came into existence despite the fact we do not have any clear linguistic data available from these ancient nomadic peoples. On the other hand, these scholars seem to share the opinion that these nomads used to belong to an eastern Persian group of people.

Nevertheless, it should be noted that there were among the Turkish tribal peoples from Inner Asia – such as those of the Xiong-nu, Ting-ling, Yenisei Kyrgyz, and even from more recent centuries those of the Kïpčak – nomads who used to have fair skin, blond/red hair and green/blue eyes. In other words, many of these nomads used to have the appearance of Indo-European peoples however they used to speak Turkish belonging to Altai group of languages, which also included Mongolian, Tungus, as well as Korean and Japanese. Hence, it is not possible to classify these obscure nomadic people into a specific racial group only based on their physical characteristics.

Is it possible that nomadic people located in a large geographic area may not have mixed during their migrations with local peoples from other racial stocks? Of course, the logical answer to this question would be a negative one. At this point it is plausible to say that by traveling long distances away from their original habitat ancient nomadic peoples likely came into contact with different races, and as a result, they developed genetically, culturally, and linguistically mixed newer characteristics. Even though these facts are anthropologically very well known, scholars insisted in classifying extracted human remnants from excavations into a specific language group only based on their physical appearances.

Yet, it is quite clear that human artifacts discovered throughout southern Siberian and eastern Eurasian steppes cannot be attached to a specific race and to a specific language group of people only based on the determined physical anthropologic evidence. In identifying the ethnic origins of these nomadic peoples for whom we have no linguistic data, information regarding their social lifestyle and religious practices would also carry significant importance besides the evidence regarding their physical characteristics. Quite interestingly it is a fact that both social lifestyles and cultural elements of Scythians as well as Yueh-chih were very similar to those of ancient nomadic Turks.[455]

In Central Asia while Western and Eastern origin peoples living together began to mix by the seventh century B.C.E. and afterwards,[456] similar cohesive existence and racial mixing in southern Siberia started around the Bronze Age and in the vicinity of Baikal Lake even much earlier than this period of time.[457] In view of these facts it is not sufficient to consider only physical appearance of human remnants from southern Siberia and Eurasian steppes for classifying them with one specific race. On the contrary, in order to determine the ethnic origins of nomadic peoples from the ancient times, history should benefit from experienced researchers of archeologists, anthropologists, and geneticists.

Another important question is that when and how Indo-European peoples have penetrated deep into Asia. The probable entry points of these europoid peoples into the Asian steppes included from north into southern Siberia and modern-day Kazakhstan (Andronovo Culture), from northeast into Altai territory (Afanasyevo Culture), and from west through Bactria and Transoxus into Tarim Basin.[458] Thus, the entry of Caucasian race into Central Asia could be traced back to the Bronze Age and even to earlier times.

The skulls discovered at the excavations at Tarim Basin in early twentieth century appeared to be dating back to first century B.C.E. and up to third century A.D.. The physical anthropological studies demonstrated that these skulls did not only include mongoloid and Indian characteristics but also surprisingly they illustrated Scandinavian features. Later, excavations in the Xiaohe region of western China revealed mummified human remnants that were not mongoloid, and in addition, embroidery artifacts similar to those of Bronze Age Denmark were discovered; carbon dating (C14) of the finds from Xiaohe showed that these were older than 3,800 years.[459] At first scholars believed that these finds were from Celtic-Scandinavian origin people. Assuming these discoveries belonged to a European race, where were the Asians in this part of the continent by this time? While explaining the penetration of an Asiatic race into this territory American Sinologist V. H. Mair claimed that starting with the appearance of Turkish nomadic tribes as early as the third century B.C.E. mongoloid race began to establish itself in this region.[460] Even though Mair and scholars who shared his views believed that the Xiaohe discoveries did not include an Asian presence, genetic studies and especially haplogroup (ancestor determinant) evaluations from these unearthed ancient human remnants illustrated different facts for everyone to see.

The examinations with Y-chromosome (father determinant) on the Xiaohe finds showed that these human remains were matching with those of Uighur and Kazakh Turks (western Eurasian genetic pool) but another interesting discovery included that the studies with mtDNA (motherhood determinant) exhibited the results were showing matches with samples obtained from Turks from Altai, Tuva, and Yakut (Saka) regions in addition to non-Turkish Tungus.[461] As a result of these scientific discoveries, Mair was compelled to revise his prior views by stating that in order to determine the ethnic origins of the societies from Tarim Basin region it would be necessary to conduct detailed physical anthropologic as well as genetic studies.[462]

The haplogroups from the genetic studies performed from the human remains discovered from the excavations at Scythian cemeteries at ancient Pazïrïk region illustrated matches with present-day Altai Turks.[463] Despite these scientific findings many scholars continued to believe that Scythians were likely from Indo-European origin. Nevertheless, genetic evaluations on Scythian remains in Altai region demonstrated matches with present-day Uighur and Kazakh Turks in addition to Samoyed groups from Uralic peoples.[464]

Despite the fact that cultural characteristics of ancient Scythians and Yueh-chih were very similar with those of ancient Inner Asian Turks and despite the fact genetic studies on the human remains from these ancient tribal peoples showed remarkable matches with those of Inner Asian Turks many scholars today still insist on their claim that ancient Scythian and Yueh-chih nomads were Iranian origin peoples. Furthermore, even though these scientists suggest that these ancient tribal peoples spoke an Iranian dialect, to this date there has been no meaningful discovery regarding their spoken language. However, it should be kept in mind that the only clue that makes these scholars stick to their claim is that they still rely on physical anthropological characteristics of excavated human remains.

However, the history of the proto-Turks start even before the first appearance of the Scythians. According to ancient Chinese records Turkish history may have started nearly at the same time when ancient Chinese history began. It is a fact that Shang dynasty (1600-1045 B.C.E.) may have faced an ancient powerful tribal people known as the *Kuei-fang*. These records suggest that the Kuei-fang formed military superiority over the Shang society due to its use of war chariots that the Chinese did not have.[465] However, in the first half of the twelfth century B.C.E. with the adaptation of war chariots into their military the Shang became successful over the Kuei-fang. Later, the Zhou dynasty that replaced the Shang was known for its heavy reliance on these chariots. However, it is also known that the Zhou that conquered China was in fact a warlike foreign tribal entity.[466] During the Western Zhou (1045-770 B.C.E.) period the name of the Kuei-fang was no longer spoken but instead *Hien-yün* (or *Hün-yu*) tribes were in prominence. Yet, it is believed that Kuei-fang and Hien-yün are from the same racial group of people.[467] In addition, during the Western Zhou period of China another tribal group known as the *Jung* (also referred to as Rung) emerged as well. While Western Zhou dynasty was establishing its hegemony over China, it also needed to fight against the powerful nomadic tribes of Jung and Hien-yün, who were the ancestors of the Xiong-nu (Asian Huns).[468] It has been also suggested that the Xiong-nu were actually a branch of the greater tribal federation of the Jung.[469] Ultimately, Jung succeeded in crushing the Western Zhou dynasty by 770 B.C.E., thus leading to the formation of the Eastern Zhou dynasty.[470] Traditionally, the Eastern Zhou period is divided into Spring and Autumn period (770-476 B.C.E.) and Warring States period (480-221 B.C.E.).

With the end of Western Zhou dynasty, the name of the Hien-yün also disappeared from the political arena. While Eastern Zhou dynasty was making efforts to establish its rule over China, a new group of tribal people known as the Ti appeared on the northern frontier. In the meantime, the Jung continued to reside to the west of China. It has been said that warlike Ti and Jung tribal federations were considered to be among the proto-Turks.[471]

Based on Chinese archives Chinese historian Taishan made an interesting claim. In the second half of the seventh century B.C.E. when the western branch of the Jung federation felt security threat from the Ch'in state of China they began to migrate westward. Those who remained behind came to be known as the Yueh-chih (chapter 3.3) but those who migrated away to settle by Ili-Chu basin came to be known as Saka by the Persians and Scythians (chapter 2.3) by the Westerners.[472]

TURKISH RACE

While discussing about the proto-Turks above, we have mentioned that among the ancient Turks there were both mongoloid as well as europoid featured peoples. Based on ancient Chinese records we know that among the proto-Turks there were blond, green eyed and fair skinned people as well. Among these there were tribes like Ting-ling carrying these characteristics. Even more recently from the eleventh century we know that Russian description of *'polovtsy'* (blond heads) was attributed to the Kïpčak Turks who were known to be blond and blue eyed. By looking at this information one can simply think that ancient Turks were europoid race.

However, spoken language Turkish is an Altaic language, which includes Mongolian, Tungus, Korean, and Japanese. If we put Turkish aside, the speakers of the Altaic languages are mongoloid featured people. In this case it would make sense if the Turks were from a mongoloid race as well.

Yet, by looking at Turkish language's origins and by learning about physical characteristics of ancient Turks from Chinese archives there seems to be a duality question as to whether the Turk is from a mongoloid or a europoid race. On the other hand, if the Turks originally were a mongoloid race how come some of them were blond and green eyed?

In the ancient times if we postulate that Turks initially were a mongoloid race, but in order to explain europoid features of some of their tribes, we would also need to postulate that these were likely mixed with europoid tribes at some point time in history. If this truly happened then with which people did they mix? Were these from Persian, German, Slavic peoples of the Indo-Europeans or from the Uralic peoples mixing with these Turks?

These questions can only be answered by conducting detailed, objective archeological, physical anthropological, and genetic research. Since it has been determined that physical anthropological evaluation on archeological finds are not sufficient, genetic cross-examinations in future archeologic studies would certainly make important contributions to understand the origins of the Eurasian steppe and southern Siberian societies.

Because of the fact that some of the Turkish tribes carried the characteristics of Caucasian race another hypothesis would be whether the Turks were not from an Altaic group people but rather from an Indo-European race, and as a result, they eventually became influenced by Altaic speakers as their language turned into Turkish. However, this would not be plausible hypothesis since Turkish language has a solid foundation, and therefore, it cannot be a newly evolved language. In other words, Turks cannot be an Indo-European group of people who later entered into the Altaic family.

Ultimately, we may bluntly conclude that Turks who speak an Altaic language are originally from mongoloid race just like their Altaic speaking cousins are. On the other hand, in order to understand the reasons why some of their tribes carry europoid features it would be necessary to analyze historical data more in depth.

Since they migrated to faraway lands throughout history, Turks must have mixed with other races where they settled. If we trace back to ancient times, among the europoid races who may have given their features to proto-Turks were most likely the Scandinavians. As already discussed above during the excavations of pre-Bronze Age cemeteries at Xiaohe the discovery of human remains with Nordic (Scandinavian) characteristics would backup this suggestion. By using physical anthropological and genetic data Turkish historian Mızrak is supporting this hypothesis.[473]

Most likely in ancient times Indo-European tribal peoples used to live in Asia but with the expansion of mongoloid race they were forced to migrate westward into European continent over time. However, while they lived in Asia, it is possible that some them were mixed with mongoloid races. Indeed, archeological discoveries in Siberia and Turkistan to this date have been supportive of this claim.

In his work *Getica* Roman historian Jordanes described Goths leaving their motherland the Scandza Island to go to the Scythian land known as Oium but at the same time he wrote about his astonishment why his colleague Josephus claimed that Goths were from the same origins as the Scythians were.[474] Since he would not accept Scythians being related to the Goth, Jordanes wrongfully tried to point out that these Germans were related to the Getae people. In a similar manner Roman senator Cassiodorus suggested that Goths were related to Getae as well as Scythians.

In fact, Getae, who first appeared in the sixth century B.C.E., were Thracian origin people who lived by the meadows around the lower Danube basin. These people by being influenced by Scythians they eventually developed their own mounted archers. However, later when the Romans conquered these territories Getae essentially disappeared after the first century B.C.E.. Yet, it has also been suggested that Getae initially originated from Scythians.[475] If this is true, since mounted archery has been a native cultural element from Central Asia, it would not be unusual for Getae people to be related to Scythians who migrated from Asia.

Well before they faced the Huns in the year 375 A.D., Goths had left southern modern-day Sweden territories to take over the steppes in modern-day Hungary and northern Black Sea after the second century A.D.. In the meantime, in order to insult the Huns Jordanes claimed that they originated from the mixture of short human-like creatures and wicked witches chased away by the Goth king.[476] Nevertheless, there have been claims that Goths had some cultural similarities with the Huns. Being apart from other Germanic tribes the ability of the Goths to train horses similar to Central Asians, in addition, the utilization of Orkhun (runic) alphabet by ancient Scandinavians just as ancient Turks did, and finally, their use of mythological symbols such as wolf and crow may all suggest that these two large group of peoples at some point in time in history may have had cultural exchanges.[477] Moreover, by using genetic data from human remains from excavations Mızrak pointed out that the data from Scandinavian territories were matching with those of ancestors of Central Asians from Altai, and he especially stated that the discovery of U2e haplogroups from excavations at Iron Age Hun cemeteries from Mongolia suggested in ancient times ancestors of Turks and Scandinavians must have had genetic mixing.[478]

With this information it is possible to explain why some Turks acquired blond hair and colored eyes making them characteristically apart from the rest of their Altaic cousins. Otherwise, being from motherland of northern Altai and southern Siberia, proto-Turks were known to have a different mongoloid appearance known as *"Turanî"* type setting them apart from the rest of their Altaic cousins.[479] This may have been the result of mixing of mongoloid race with that of Nordic people. This physical appearance as discovered in cemeteries of the nomads has been shown to be present among the peoples of Scythians, Yueh-chih, Tokharians, and Kidarite/Ephtalite (White Huns) traveling from Central Asia to western Turkistan and northern India.[480]

CONTROVERSIAL HISTORY

The Etruscans and the Sumerians are two ancient civilizations that have left deep imprints on humanity's history. While the former established the origins of Western civilization in the making of the Roman Empire, the latter left its mark with the development of writing and the first establishment of the rule of law. Who were these Etruscans and Sumerians?

In Western history, the Roman Empire is the foundation of the Western world. It is apparent that from the time of its establishment, the earlier Etruscan civilization on the northern Italian Peninsula was the primary source of knowledge for the formation of Roman civilization. Recent investigations into the origin of Etruscan civilization (in the Tuscany region of modern-day Italy) claim that the Etruscans originated not from the Italian Peninsula but rather from the East. It has been suggested that the Etruscans migrated to northern modern-day Italy from Anatolia (modern-day Turkey). They perhaps emigrated from Lydia, an ancient civilization in Anatolia. But there are also scholars who claim that the Etruscans may have had proto-Turkish origins.

The advanced Etruscan civilization, which reached its zenith from 800 BCE to about 500 BCE, is considered the foundation of the culture of the

Roman Empire. It has been demonstrated that the Etruscan culture heavily influenced the development of Roman art, architecture, and religion. Etruscan technological knowledge turned the Roman Empire into the most advanced civilization of its time. Etruscan power and civilization flourished in the modern-day Italian province of Tuscany. The Romans called them Tusci, hence the name Tuscany for the land where the Etruscans lived. But anthropological and archaeological studies have revealed that the Etruscans were not native to modern-day Italy. Recent findings suggest that Etruscan origins can be traced to the Near East or to western Asia. DNA findings are supportive of these claims.[481] Even more interesting findings come from genetic comparative studies on men from Tuscany and men from Turkey; the results are astonishing, as they suggest that the Etruscans were genetically linked to Turkey, or to the Turks of Anatolia.[482] During a symposium on the Etruscans conducted in Bodrum, Turkey, during June 2–4, 2007, on the basis of the results of the completed genetic studies, the president of the Turkish Historical Society, Dr. Yusuf Halacoglu, claimed that there is a 97 percent probability the Etruscans are of Turkish ancestry.[483] Furthermore, it has been recently proposed that the Etruscan language is not a member of the Indo-European language family; the Turkish language is not an Indo-European language either. Strangely, it has been suggested that the oldest known Turkish runic alphabet has similar characters to the Etruscan alphabet.[484]

The Etruscans used to cremate their dead, as did the Gök-Türks and the Oghuz Turks. The Etruscan people apparently believed in the afterlife, just as the ancient Turks did. In Turkish mythology, the wolf has a special place as the savior and protector of the nation. In Etruscan mythology, the wolf has a similar place. Indeed, in Roman mythology, an Etruscan wolf saves the twin brothers Romulus and Romus and provides for them. After Romulus prevails over his brother for power, he establishes the first Roman city. Before it became an empire, the Roman Republic was established around 500 BCE.

In the first century BCE, the Etruscans were completely overrun and assimilated by the Romans, who benefited from Etruscan civilization and culture and claimed them as their own to develop the well-known Roman civilization.

The civilization of the Sumerians is much older than that of the Etruscans. The Sumerians thrived between roughly 4500 and 3500 BCE, and their civilization is considered the beginning of history for humanity, even before the emergence of ancient Egypt. They flourished in Mesopotamia, in the area of modern-day Iraq. The Sumerians invented writing with cuneiform characters on mud tablets. They also established the first form of law. Just as the Romans learned from the non-Italian Etruscan civilization, the Semitic Assyro-Babylonians developed their legacy from the non-Semitic, non-Indo-European culture of the Sumerians.

Sumerian is one of the oldest languages in the world. Even though it previously survived in the ancient Near East, the language was not Semitic in origin. In fact, Sumerian, which has no relationship with Indo-European or Semitic languages, has been thought to have affinities with Ural-Altaic languages.[485] Although it has been claimed that Uralic languages or Hungarian may be related to the now-extinct Sumerian language, it has also been suggested that Sumerian words in Hungarian may actually be borrowings from other languages, such as Caucasian or Turkish.[486] According to a proposal, a group of Turks left their homeland in Central Asia to establish themselves in Mesopotamia and formed the Sumerian civilization.[487] On the basis of other points of view, Sumerian may be related to both Uralic and Altaic languages. Experts in linguistics believe that there may be a relationship between the now-extinct Sumerian and Hungarian (Uralic group) and Turkish (Altaic group) languages.

Were the Etruscans and the Sumerians from among the proto-Turks? The early Turks, or proto-Turks, were otherwise known to be nomads. Could they have formed such advanced sedentary civilizations in the early stages of history? Every nation went through a nomadic or tribal past before establishing a sedentary civilization. For archaeologists and anthropologists, the jury is still out on the matter of the origins of the Etruscans and the Sumerians. More evidence is needed on the origins of these great civilizations.

2.3. THE AGE OF THE NOMADS

The Eurasian Steppe has had a significant and lasting impact on human history for more than two millennia. This vast territory stretches from the Arctic Ocean in the north to the Himalayas in the south, from the river valleys of China in the east to the Carpathian Mountains in the west. This large geographic area was once home to warlike pastoralist nomads who contributed to the rise and the fall of many empires. Indeed, the migration of nomadic tribes along the Eurasian Steppe corridor is a fascinating subject for historians and anthropologists at large.

To explain population movements in the Eurasian territories, history has been artificially divided into two different periods of migrations: the first period is between 800 BCE and 1500 CE, defined as the nomadic age, and the second period is between 1492 and 1992, known as European expansion and implosion.[488]

The earliest population movements have been attributed to the westward expansion or movements of the Saka tribes, also known as the Scythians. These migrations included the Tokharians from modern-day Xinjiang. The well-known migratory movements of the Turks did not begin until the Great Hun Empire of Asia (Xiong-nu) began to lose power during the first century CE. Particularly after the second century CE, Turkish tribes began to show up at the doorstep of eastern Europe. The (European) Huns, (European) Avars, Bulgars, Khazars, Pečenegs, and Qïpčaks appeared successively. We know that the presence of the Turkish tribes in eastern Europe followed the fall of Hun power in Asia and the rise of the Avars (Juan-juan) of Asia. The tribal leaders who made the decision to migrate likely considered the following factors: they did not agree with the contemporary leadership in the Asian steppes, they had lost politically to the new rulers of the steppes, or both. Some experts have also cited drastic climate changes that may have made the steppes unbearable for the pastoralist nomads. However, there are no documented climate changes that could have prompted the westward movement of Turkish tribes starting in the first century CE.

Interestingly, the first Turkish comers to Europe were from the Oghur Turkish-speaking group of Turks, again coinciding with the fall of Hun power in Asia. It is known that the Huns of Attila were related to the Utrighur Turks, speaking the Oghur dialect.[489] The On-Oghur Turkish tribes arrived in Europe in the same period as the above tribal groups did. As we will see later in the book, it is now known that the On-Oghurs lent their name to the name of Hungary (chapter 4.5).

The pastoralist Turks proved to be effective warriors in both Asia and Europe. In fact, history has shown that these nomadic people were dynamic conquerors with unchallengeable military superiority over sedentary peoples.[490] Their successes came from their undeniable strength, their use of bows and arrows with unequalled reputation, and their ability to shoot arrows on horseback at full speed with deadly accuracy.[491]

Throughout history the nomads typically followed the steppe corridor to migrate. This corridor, at least for the Turks, began in the northern territories of China, in modern-day Mongolia, then moving westward into modern-day Turkestan and northwest to the Pontic Steppe in the Black Sea area. The Europeans felt the impact of these migrations the most since the corridor for the most part was only one way for the Turks; the exceptions were the Oghuz Turks of the tenth and eleventh centuries (volume 2, chapter 2.5) and the Tatars of the sixteenth century (volume 2, chapter 4.5), returning to Turkestan.. Hence, when the Turkish tribes began their movement, they first populated the Transoxus area (territories of modern-day Uzbekistan, Kyrgyzstan, and Tajikistan), replacing the Persian-speaking peoples there. As a result, this area became turkized, starting with the arrival of the White Huns, known as the Ephtalites (chapter 3.6). Over the following centuries, Turkish tribes began to move in this area wave after wave, solidifying the Turkish character of this territory. Consequently, as mentioned earlier, the geographic area from the eastern shores of the Caspian Sea deep into the western provinces of modern-day China over time became known as Turkestan. However, those tribes looking for other pastures in the steppes kept moving toward Europe. From at least the fourth century, with the arrival of the Huns, there was a Turkish presence in the Pontic Steppe of eastern Europe, and it lasted well into the eighteenth century, when Russian imperialist expansion was at full speed.

With the arrival of Islam in Turkestan in the eighth century, the Turkish nomads came under the influence of this Semitic religion. In about two centuries, they turned into the defenders of Islam against the crusaders from Europe. Islamization also changed the way of life for many Turks as they became sedentary. Consequently, the direction of migration for Muslim Turks shifted from eastern Europe toward the Middle East. Previously, moving to the Middle East via Iran was not convenient for the pre-Islamic nomads, because Iran has a fairly mountainous terrain lacking the pastures that the nomads needed. Therefore, the previous westward movements preferred going north of the Caspian Sea into the Pontic Steppe. During the reign of the Ottoman Empire, also known as the Turkish Empire in European history, the influx of Turkish nomads into Europe continued through Anatolia and Thrace until about the seventeenth century. These nomads were known as *akïnjïlar* (raiders).

At the end of the fifteenth century, the period of European expansion and implosion began. In this new period, the technological superiority of the West over the nomads of the steppes became apparent. Imperial Russia in particular benefited from technologically superior armies as the czar moved into the fertile Siberian territories. By the early twentieth century, the Russian conquest of most of the Asian steppes was complete. However, in 1917 imperial Russia collapsed after the Russian Revolution, also known as the February Revolution of 1917. Then, with the following October Revolution of 1917, also known as the Bolshevik Revolution, the control of Russia was in the hands of the revolutionaries. By 1922 the communist Soviet Union was formed. Subsequently, the Soviet Russians faced fierce resistance from Central Asian Turkish states, which were eventually taken into the Soviet Empire. The Russians continued to migrate into Central Asian territories as they did during the period of imperial Russia. However, with the fall of the Soviet Empire (the last colonialist) in 1992, the implosion period began, and the Russians began to gradually move back to (European) Russia.

THE PRE-ISLAMIC ASIAN NOMADS

Prior to the beginning of the Islamization of the Turkish world in the eighth century, the Turks followed a Tengriist faith while living a nomadic lifestyle in the steppes of Asia. Their faith was Tengriism, a well-known religious faith of the Central Asian tribes of the Turks and the Mongols. The power of the religion came from the universe that the tribesmen lived in. God was known as Tengri and lived in the sky (*gök*). Hence, God at times was also referred to as Gök-Tengri. Shamans were the religious representatives of Gök-Tengri, working as healers but also as mediators between the spiritual world and the earthly creatures. The ancient Turks and the Mongols believed in a Tengriist faith very similar to that of the American Indians, who are believed to have come from Asia over ten thousand years ago. Because of their origin in Asia, there are cultural and religious practice similarities between the American Indians and the ancient Turks and the Mongols, and consequently, there have been claims that there may be ethnic connections between these races.

There is no doubt that the ancient Turks were shamanists, as the American Indians were. Just as the Native Americans did, the ancient Turks wore feathers to symbolize nobility and earned bravery as well as social status. This was also visible in Ottoman aristocracy. The old *sorguč* was a feather-based ornament placed in the turbans of Ottoman noblemen. The number of black feathers indicated the degree of nobility and the awards earned before the advent of the medals in the nineteenth century. Further similarities between the Native Americans and the early Turks can be seen in Native American tapestries, which are nearly identical to Turkish kilims. But these and many other cultural similarities are only similarities, not absolute proof that the Native Americans are related to the Turco-Mongols.

As stated earlier, the history of the ancient Turks is not very well known, since the Turks themselves did not leave written records. We can learn much about them from the archives of ancient China, since the Turks of antiquity were in contact with the Chinese. But it is difficult to identify proper Turkish or Mongol names in Chinese annals, since Chinese recorders modified their original names into Chinese versions. For example, the Huns were known as the Xiong-nu in Chinese, and the Gök-Türks were referred to as T'ü-chüeh. Even if the prehistoric nomadic Turks possessed written records, since they did not have a fixed place to store their archives, like the sedentary Chinese or Egyptians, these records cannot be recovered now. The earliest written information that we have today is from stone-carved monuments from the Gök-Türks. Their alphabet ceased to exist shortly after they fell from power, and the Turks switched to the Arabic script after they adopted Islam. The Uighur Turks, however, used a different script, known as the Old Uighur alphabet, which was later adopted by the Mongols in the thirteenth century with the help of a Uighur adviser of Genghis Khan.[492] This new Mongolian alphabet came to be known as Uighurjin script named after the Uighur Turks.

We know that the early Turks and the Mongols had much in common and their lifestyles, cultures, and religious faiths were similar. As they both had a nomadic lifestyle often living side by side early on, linguistic similarities can be found in Turkish and Mongolian. For example, "horse" is called *at* in Turkish and *aduu* in Mongolian. The nomadic tent is called *yurt* in both languages. For both the Turk and the Mongol, the horse was the most cherished and valued animal. Both peoples made a national alcoholic beverage from the fermentation of mare's milk—this was *kımız* (koumiss) for the Turks and *airag* for the Mongols.

Both the ancient Turks and the Mongols were excellent mounted archers; they could shoot on horseback with their powerful composite bows, an ability that gave them an excellent tactical advantage against their enemies. Their unmatched military skills allowed them to gain military success against their sedentary neighbors. When they were beaten, it was often because they were victims of political trickery. Indeed, the Chinese created divisions within the ruling Turkish class and the Mongolians to weaken their grip on power. Another major reason for the loss of strength was the irresistible power of assimilation. In conquered territories where the overwhelming majority of people were non-Turkish or non-Mongolian, the Turkish or Mongolian conquerors could not hold on to their ethnic identities for long. This was true, for example, both for the Northern Wei dynasty (formed by the Tabgač Turks, a.k.a. the T'o-pa) and the Yuan dynasty (formed by the Mongols of Qubilai Khan) in China, as the ruling class eventually adopted the Chinese way of life.

ABOUT THE SCYTHIANS

The name Scythian was known to the ancient Greeks as *'Skytahi'*, to the Persians and Indians as *'Saka'*, and to the Chinese as *'Sai'*. In the Assyrian records from the seventh century B.C.E., Scythian was known as *'Ashguzai'*. Herodotus, a well-known Greek historian from the fifth century B.C.E., referred to Scythians as *Massagetae*. Scythians on the other hand were known as steppe nomadic people originating from southern Siberia and Altai region of Central Asia.[493]

It has been said that the Scythian history began with the emergence of warlike Jung (Rong) nomadic tribes, which have been considered to be among the proto-Turks.[494] However, as stated earlier Chinese historian Taishan claimed that as a result of the pressure exerted by the Ch'in state the western branch of Jung tribes began to migrate westward during the second half of the seventh century B.C.E. and finally when they reached Ili-Chu basin they were known to the Persians as Saka people and to the Greeks and Romans as Scythians.[495] Those who did not migrate came to be known as the Yueh-chih people (chapter 3.3).

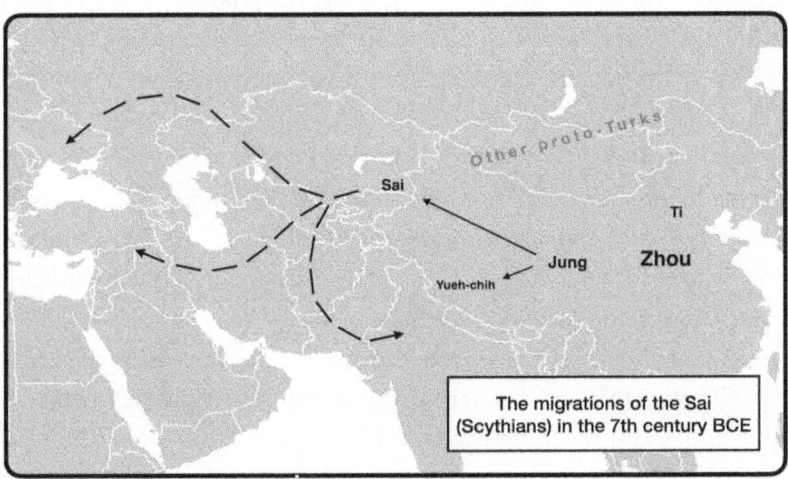

Map 1. Migration patterns of Scythians who left their pastures in the Far East after they separated from the warlike tribes of the Jung people. After they reached southeastern region of modern-day Kazakhstan, they split in three ways, each finally reaching northern India, the Middle East, and the Northern Black Sea (Pontus) Steppes in modern-day Ukraine.

According to the Assyrian records from the seventh century B.C.E. Scythians by this time reached the Middle East. After they attacked their allies the Assyrians and defeated the Medes people of Iranian origin, in the third quarter of the seventh century B.C.E. Scythians occupied the Medes Empire. Subsequently, by entering Anatolia they catalyzed the fall of the Urartu Kingdom. However, by the year 624 B.C.E. Median king Cyxares was able to break the hegemony of the Scythian mounted archers. Yet, one of the legendary successes of these Central Asian warriors was the fact that they were able to stop the Achaemenid invasion of Great Darius into the Scythian territories around 514/512 B.C.E.. Archaeological studies demonstrate that these warlike nomads had military activities around seventh and sixth centuries B.C.E. in Mesopotamia, Syria, Anatolia, Caucasia, and Egypt.[496]

Avesta, the holy book of Zoroastrianism, mentioned that the enemy of the Aryan race were the Tur people who lived along the shores of northern Caspian Sea and in the Kama River basin. The Tur were also mentioned in the eleventh century by Persian poet Firdausi's work Shah-nameh where he referred to them as ancient enemies of Iran. Furthermore, Firdausi coined the land of the Tur as Turan. According to the Assyrian records from 641/640 B.C.E. the Tur people were considered to be the same as the Saka (Scythian) people.[497] For this reason, the 'Turan' term has been associated with the land of the Turks.

In the fifth century B.C.E. Greek historian Herodotus mentioned about the *Massagetae* living as warlike nomads to the east of Araxes River (a tributary of Amu Darya) and considered to be the Scythians.[498] At the same time, he described about a fifth century B.C.E. struggle between Achaemenid emperor Cyrus and Tomris the queen of the Massagetae.

After a while, the Scythians were spread out across a very large geographic territory. Their northern branch covered southern Siberia, Altai region, Kazakh steppes and reaching the Ural Mountains in the west. The southern branch of the Scythians reached from the Pamir Mountains into the middle of the Indian subcontinent, including present-day Afghanistan, Pakistan, and eastern Iran territories. Finally, the western branch of these nomads covered a large area from the Pontus steppes north of the Black Sea to the Danube River basin. Scythian steppe nomads, as mentioned above, most likely originated from Central Asia, and over time, since they spread out across an extraordinarily large geographic area, rather than being from a single racial group they were more likely to have absorbed different racial groups into their nomadic federation.[499] Besides, by the second century B.C.E. their mongoloid physical features were fading away, and this fact alone suggests that during long journeys they must have mixed with peoples from different racial backgrounds.[500]

Earlier in this book (chapter 2.2) the genetic connections between Scythians and modern-day Siberian Turks as well as Uighur and Kazakh Turks were mentioned. Furthermore, the lifestyle, the sociocultural elements and even the burial traditions of Scythians as well those of ancient Turks were very much alike.[501] (In addition to these facts, the famous Pazïrïk rug was found to be woven with well-known double-knot Turkish technique whereas traditional Iranian carpets have always been woven with single-knot technique (chapter 1.2).

Even though their genetic findings as well as their sociocultural elements showed connections with those of ancient Turks, the ancient peoples of the steppes have been often considered to be among the proto-Iranian peoples by some scholars while they are also viewed as proto-Turks by others.[502] Yet, as mentioned earlier, their lifestyle was very much similar to that of the proto-Turks. Nevertheless, it is also a fact that the nomads were very much influenced by the Sogdian Persian culture. On the other hand, their cultural artifacts, other discoveries in cemeteries as well as present day scientific findings all indicate that these people were not likely to be part of proto-Iranian population; more on this subject matter was discussed in chapter 2.2. The Scythians were truly a nomadic people covering a large territory across Asia and eastern Europe. Today, some scholars actually consider the Scythians of the period between the seventh and the fourth centuries B.C.E. to be part of the early Turkish history.[503] Z. V. Togan, a well-known Turkologist, believed that modern-day Yakut Turks living in the Autonomous Saka (Yakutistan) Republic of Russian Federation are descendants of one of the branches of the former Scythians.[504] The Yakuts in our present-day are also known as Saha (Saka) Turks.

During the seventh century B.C.E. Scythians began to exert their influence by advancing into modern-day southern European Russia and Ukraine territories. Cimmerians used to live in these steppes before the arrival of the Scythians. After the third century B.C.E. Scythian existence in western Central Asia began to fade away with the rise of the powerful Hun empire in the east.

In the meantime, Scythians were settling in the Pontus steppes known as Scythia to the historians of the Eastern Roman Empire. Some scholars also believe that present-day Ossetians in Caucasus are descendants of Scythians who were once fierce warriors feared by the Western world. Even though many Western historians believe that Scythian language was Iranian origin, these nomadic people based on their religious traditions were closer to ancient Turks and Mongols.[505] Moreover, even today there is no surviving linguistic data from the Scythians. In order to understand their ethnic and sociocultural origins there is need objective studies not only based on physical anthropologic evaluations but also based on detailed archeological and genetic evaluations.

In 1453 when the Ottoman Turks conquered the last bastion of the once legendary Eastern Roman Empire's legacy, Europeans came to the belief that the Turks were indestructible. For this reason, Bishop Siena and his contemporaries believed that Turks were a nation descended from the Scythians. This conclusion was based on documented observations of the similarities in their customs, clothing, and equestrian lifestyles, including the use of the reflex bow and their related languages.[506]

Today, the history of the Scythians, Cimmerians, and Sarmatians is a subject of controversy among Turkish and Western historians. Despite the genetic discoveries speak otherwise many Western scholars feverishly claim that these ancient tribal peoples were Indo-European origin whereas their Turkish counterparts insist that they were actually from Turkish-Altaic racial group of people. While Turkish historians base their claim on the fact that the cultural background of these ancient tribal peoples was very similar to that of the Asian Huns, Westerners defend their position by pointing to very few ancient Persian words and physical anthropologic findings. It should be clear that nomadic tribes whenever they migrated they were more than likely to be influenced by the culture of the local peoples with whom they met. In other words, if Mahmoud of Ghazna acquired an Arabic name, if Anatolian Seljuk sultan Keykubat took a Persian name, and in the ninth century if Bulgar khan Boris used a Slavic name, none of these facts would suggest that they were not Turks since we know well that they were from Turkish stock of people.

It is an established fact that when the Scythians, Cimmerians and Sarmatians migrated to the west, they used to have very similar traditions to those of ancient Turks of the steppes like the Huns. Yet, it is known that over time these nomads upon settling down eventually were assimilated by the local people. Similar examples are abundant in the Turkish history. Mughals who descended from Tamerlane becoming Indianized starting in the eighteenth century and Danube Bulgars from Oghur Turks becoming Slavicized beginning in the ninth century are among these examples. For this reason, when studying history, it is important to examine the facts with an open mind and in scientific manner.

TURK VERSUS MONGOL ON THE STEPPES

From prehistoric times until the medieval period in this large Asian territory, the Turkish and the Mongol tribes lived as nomads. Throughout history the Turks have far outnumbered the Mongols in terms of total population. In 2018, the Mongol population in Mongolia was just above three million, whereas the Turkish-speaking population approached 200 million. In the early history of Asia, despite the fact that Turks were always an overwhelming majority on the steppes, a powerful khan, whether a Mongol or a Turk, would have been able to gather both Turkish and Mongol tribes under his banner, as Mongol Genghis Khan did in the thirteenth century. In the ancient nomadic traditions of the Asian steppes, a powerful khan, regardless of his ethnicity, would have earned the respect of the tribesmen across Central Asia. After all, shared glory was more important than anything else. Thus, strong khans or qaghans were often able to gather Turkish and Mongolian tribes under one banner in the form of nomadic confederations, such as those of the Huns, the Juan-juan, the Xianbei, and so on. It should be noted that most pre-eighth-century Turkish history is obtained from Chinese, Roman, and Greek archives with the (often-biased) view of the non-Turkish recorders.

A NOTE ON NATIVE AMERICAN ORIGINS

As stated earlier, data show that Native Americans have ethnic connections to the peoples of the Eastern Eurasian Steppe and the Far East. There are cultural similarities between Asiatic peoples and the Native Americans, and linguistic similarities, due to either a common parent language or direct contact while they lived together or both, are also found.[507] There has also been occasional scientific research trying to link the origin of the Native Americans to Asian tribes. What is known is that Native Americans are descendants of the Eskimos and the Asiatic populations who crossed the Bering Strait, which was once a land bridge connecting Asia to North America.[508] These unidirectional migrations occurred on multiple occasions. It is believed that the first wave of migrations took place more than fifteen thousand years ago, the second wave occurred ten to fifteen thousand years ago, and the third wave happened about ten thousand years ago.[509] There are in fact some claims for genetic relationships between these people of the Americas and the people of Asia. Genetic studies have also shown that there is a relationship between Chinese and Native American genetic stock.[510] Furthermore, the discovery of identical molecular findings between polymorphic albumin variants Naskapi (found among the Naskapi Indians of Quebec, Canada) and Mersin (found among the Eti Turks of southeastern Turkey) has led to the conclusion that there is a genetic relationship between these Turks and the Native Americans.[511]

2.4. LIFE IN THE EURASIAN STEPPES

The Eurasian steppes include vast lands from the Siberian forests in the north to the mountains and deserts in the south, and from the Hungarian Plain in the west to Manchuria in the east. It is divided into three areas: the Western Eurasian Steppe (the Hungarian Plain and the Pontic Steppe in eastern Europe), the Central Eurasian Steppe (Turkestan), and the Eastern Eurasian Steppe (present-day Mongolian steppes). Over this large territory, the Turks were known in history as great conquerors. Their power over time extended outside the steppe territories as well. Turkish history has witnessed the formation of a few dozen states. Many of them are not worth mentioning, because they had short life-spans. But the multiplicity of the Turkish states indicates the military character that the Turks once exhibited in world politics. Some of the most significant short-lived states will also be presented later.

Officially the Turks first appear in history under the name of the Xiong-nu (according to Chinese archives), or the Asian Huns.[512] After Hun power eroded in Asia, the clear migration of Turkish tribes toward central Eurasia began. Again in Chinese records, there is mention of the Ting-ling and T'ieh-le tribes associated with the Turks moving westward.[513] Perhaps some of these included the Oghur Turkish tribes, which successively gave rise to the European Huns, Avars, Bulgars, and Khazars. Having formed multiple states over a period of more than two millennia across the three continents of Asia, Europe, and Africa, the Turks certainly had a significant influence on world history. The historical Turkish impact on world politics and cultural developments can be seen in the evolution of global civilization.

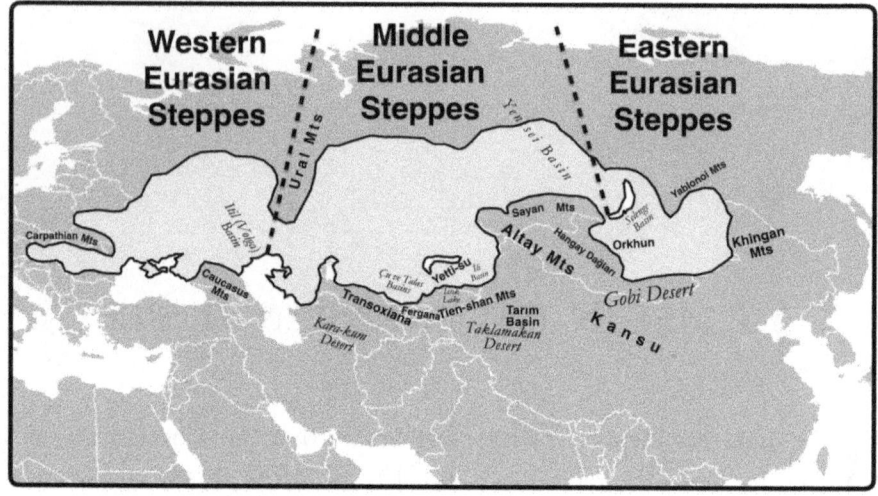

Map 2. The map illustrates large geographic corridor that the Eurasian steppes cover across much of the Asian continent and deep into central Europe.

THE GEOGRAPHIC LOCATIONS OF THE TURKS IN HISTORY

To learn about Turkish history, it is important to understand the geographic areas that are involved in the past of the Turks. Since the Turks speak a language originating in the Altaic family of languages, their origins are believed to be in the Altai Mountain area. These majestic mountains are located where Kazakhstan, Mongolia, and China come together. For the ancient Turkish steppe empires (Xiong-nu, Gök-Türks, and Uighurs)—which were among the first recognized Turkish states in the history—their seat of power was in the territories of modern-day Mongolia. Although this area is referred to as Mongolia, even when describing ancient historical events, the Mongols did not begin moving into this land permanently until the second half of the tenth century, after the Kyrgyz Turks left these steppes (volume 2, chapter 3.1).

In Turkish history, the term Turkestan is often used. As stated earlier, it is a Persian word that means "land of the Turks." The Persians, particularly the ancient Persian-speaking trader people of the Sogdians, used the term initially to characterize the large Asian territory, especially when it was under the rule of the Gök-Türk Qaghanate, also known by historians as the Türk Empire. The territory covers the lands of present-day Turkmenistan, Kazakhstan, Kyrgyzstan, Uzbekistan, and the Xinjiang Uighur Autonomous Region of China. In modern times, the last has been recognized as Chinese Turkestan, and the area of the former countries is collectively referred to as Russian Turkestan. Sometimes these divisions are referred to as eastern and western Turkestan respectively.

Central Asia is another geographic term that is common in Turkish history. It is a large territory in the center part of the Asian continent that includes Turkestan and Persian-speaking Tajikistan. However, the UNESCO definition of this geographic term also includes southern Siberia, Mongolia, western China, and Afghanistan. Western Central Asia, also known as western Turkestan, is overwhelmingly Muslim with its Turkish-speaking states of Turkmenistan, Kazakhstan, Kyrgyzstan, and Uzbekistan; Tajikistan is the only non-Turkish-speaking state. Eastern Turkestan of Central Asia includes Xinjiang Province of China, where the Uighur Turks reside. Eastern Central Asia includes not only eastern Turkestan, with Xinjiang, but also the Republic of Mongolia and the Chinese territories of Inner Mongolia and Manchuria.[514]

Eurasia, a common geographic term in the history of the Turks, essentially means the combined continental landmass of Europe and Asia. The ancient Turkish tribes, starting with the Xiong-nu, moved westward from modern-day Mongolia toward Europe, crossing over the Eurasian Steppe, which stretches from Manchuria in northeastern China to Hungary in eastern Europe, with a northern boundary marked by the taiga forests in Siberia and a southern border defined by the desert belt, which includes the Gobi, Taklamakan, and Qara-Qum. This area witnessed the formation of the largest land empires in the world's history, established by the Turks, the Mongols, and the Russians.[515]

The Silk Road, which was the major communication route between China and the West traversing the Eurasian steppes, served as a trade and cultural exchange link between the major cultural centers of the premodern world. The ancient Turkish tribes used the Silk Road for trading purposes.[516] Western Turkestan, which remains at the center of the Silk Road, was historically divided into smaller geographic areas known as Transoxiana (or Transoxus), Khwarezm, and Khorasan. Respectively, these smaller geographic areas were in the northeastern, northwestern, and southern territories of western Turkestan. Transoxiana, also referred to as Transoxus, is an ancient Greek term meaning "land beyond the Oxus River." It refers to an area between the Amu Darya and Syr Darya rivers that included most of modern-day Uzbekistan, Tajikistan, a portion of southern Kyrgyzstan, and southwestern Kazakhstan. The Arabs called this area Mawarannahr, while the Iranians called the region Turan.

Semirechye, as known to modern-day Russians, was previously known to the Turks as Yeti-Su or Yettisu, meaning "seven rivers." The region took its historic name from the seven rivers flowing from the southeast into Lake Balkhash. It is situated in present-day southeastern Kazakhstan, but the historic area also includes in the south Issyk Kül (Issïk Kül), world's second-largest mountain lake, situated in modern-day eastern Kyrgyzstan. For the nomadic Turks of the past, it was an important territory.

Syr Darya is one of the well-known rivers of Central Asia. It was also referred to as Jaxartes by the ancient Greeks and as Sayhun by the old nomadic Turks. It arises in the Tien Shan, and passing through the Fergana Valley, it empties into the Aral Sea. Amu Darya, also known by its ancient Greek name of Oxus, is another major river of Central Asia; its source is in the Pamir Mountains in Tajikistan. It flows through Turkmenistan and Uzbekistan before ending in the Aral Sea. It was also known as Jayhun by the Turks and Muslims of the past.

Khwarezm is a geographic term that has been attributed to the large oasis on the delta of the Amu Darya. The Aral Sea is on its northern border. Today, the area is shared by modern-day Kazakhstan, Turkmenistan, and Uzbekistan. Khorasan (also known as Khurasan) covered a large territory that includes eastern Iran, southern Turkmenistan, and Afghanistan. These areas in ancient times were part of the empires of Alexander the Great and the Persians.

The Tarim basin is a large area in northwestern China located in present-day Xinjiang. The Taklamakan Desert occupies much of the territory. This territory was occupied or influenced by the Asian Huns until the Han Chinese wrested this land for China in the first century CE. However, at later times the Turks reoccupied this territory, and today it serves as the land of the Uighur Turks.

The Fergana Valley is a historic location along the Silk Road that is situated today between Uzbekistan, Kyrgyzstan, and Tajikistan. Before the valley became part of Turkestan, it was heavily populated by Persian-speaking people. The Achaemenid Empire, later Alexander the Great, and subsequently the Greco-Bactrian Kingdom had control of this area until the collapse of the Asian Huns led to the flooding of Turkish tribes into Turkestan, including the Fergana Valley.

Anatolia, also known as Asia Minor, is an ancient land known as the cradle of civilization. Anatolia is derived from Greek and means "land of the sun." In addition to the ancient Greeks, other ancient peoples, such as the Hittites, Lydians, Phrygians, and Urartians, were in this peninsula, a meeting point between Europe, Asia, and Africa. Today, Anatolia is the mainland of the Republic of Turkey.

Pannonia was once a province of the Roman Empire. Geographically it is the largest basin of Europe. The Danube River divides this basin roughly in the middle. The Pannonian Plain constitutes the lowland parts of this basin. The area was the most suitable territory for nomadic lifestyle of the ancient Eurasian Steppe tribesmen of the past. The European Huns and the Avars chose this plain to house their tribesmen, but their command center was at Alföld, known as the Great Hungarian Plain, from where they carried out their military operations in Europe. Alföld is the largest part of the Pannonian Plain. Today the Pannonian Basin is located in Hungary in addition to eastern portions of Austria and Slovenia, northern Serbia, northern Croatia, and western Transylvania in Romania. The area was once home to the Turkish polities of the European Huns, Avars, On-Oghurs, Pečenegs, and Cumans.

The Balkan Peninsula, also known as the Balkans, is the southeastern corner of Europe, where modern-day Albania, Bulgaria, Bosnia, Croatia, Greece, Macedonia, Montenegro, Romania, Serbia, Slovenia, and Turkey's European component, Thrace, are located. Historically, it served as home to the Bulgar Turks and later to the Cuman Turks.

Another important geographic area in Turkish history is the Pontic Steppe in eastern Europe, also known as the Pontic-Caspian Steppe, the Qïpčak

Steppe, or the Qïpčak-Cuman Steppe, named after the old Turkish Qïpčak tribes from this area. This region was also referred to as Scythia and Sarmatia in antiquity. Today this area includes Moldova, Ukraine, and southern (European) Russia, extending to northwestern Kazakhstan up to the Ural Mountains.

Levant is a geographic term that came into use more and more starting in the sixteenth century. Often it was synonymous with the eastern Mediterranean territories, which were already under the control of the Ottoman Empire. Essentially it covers the same territories that the term Near East covers, but the latter often does not include Egypt in its coverage, whereas Levant does. In French, the people of European descent in the Levant are referred to as Levantin.

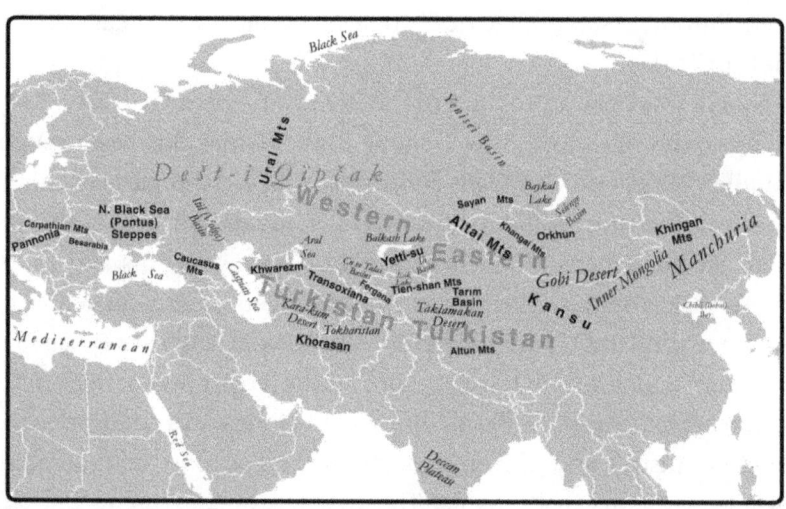

Map 3. Many of the important geographic locations across the vast Eurasian steppes are illustrated here. These locations are known to be related to the Turkish history.

THE TURKS AS DEMOGRAPHY CHANGERS

In the second century BCE, the powerful Xiong-nu (Asian Hun) presence in modern-day Mongolia either directly or indirectly began to push some of the tribes westward. Among these, the Yueh-chih were one of the largest groups of tribes in eastern Central Asia. The Yueh-chih's arrival in Transoxus and Khorasan caused the complete fall of the Greco-Bactrian Kingdom (250–125 BCE) in modern-day western Turkestan. Later, with the decline of Xiong-nu power in northern China in the first century CE, Turkish tribes began migrating westward to the Tarim basin, and most went farther west to present-day western Turkestan and also toward the western Kazakh Steppe. Therefore, because of the fall of the Huns in Asia, the process of turkization of all Central Asia began. The former heavily Persian character of the western part of Central Asia gradually changed in favor of the Turkish presence.

The Turks who had moved to the western Kazakh Steppe appeared to move to the Pontic Steppe early in the third century. Prior to the arrival of the European Huns in the fourth century, the makeup of Europe's demographics was very different from what it is today. On the eve of the Hun invasion of Europe in the fourth century, the Celts living under the Latin-speaking Roman Empire were the primary tribal people living in a large area extending from Iberia in the west to the Pannonian Basin in the east, including modern-day Ireland, Britain, and Scotland. The Roman Empire occupying these territories formed a barrier against the Germanic and Slavic tribes located to the east of the European border of the Roman realm, outside the Celtic territories.

In the fifth century, the Germanic tribes of the Angles and Saxons began to migrate north to the island of Britannia, away from mainland Europe. The time of their migration corresponds to the time the Huns pushed into the crowd of Germanic tribes, causing them to flee, as we will see later (chapter 4.2). The arrival of Germanic tribes into Celtic Britannia initiated the medieval period in Britain. Prior to the arrival of the Huns, the Goths were dominant in eastern Europe from the Danube River to the Volga River. When the Huns fell upon the Goths in 375–76, they conquered them and their territories. Many Goths fled in fear into the Roman domain, crossing the Danube River. From this point on, the Goths in the Roman Empire came to be known as the Visigoths (Western Goths), whereas the Goths under the Huns were called the Ostrogoths (Eastern Goths).

In 418 the Romans had to settle these Gothic tribes in Aquitaine, the southwestern region of modern-day France. In 590 the Visigoths gave their people living in Iberia the name Spania (early name of Spain) and in Gaul the name Gallia (early name of France).[517] However, the Romans had used the name Hispania for the Iberian Peninsula much earlier. The Huns' constant push deeper into the Western Roman Empire forced the Germanic tribes to continue relocating farther west, deeper into the Roman realm.[518] By the fifth century, the Germanic tribes were scattered across the territories of the Roman Empire in Europe, mixed with the native Celts, particularly in modern-day Spain, France, and the Celtic islands. As the Goths fled from the relentless push of the Huns, some of them reached the northeastern Italian coastline, where they forced the natives to look for more secure habitats. Consequently, these people, out of necessity for their security, began the foundation of Venice on the water.[519]

The Huns' continued push of the Germanic tribes into the Roman Empire and the subsequent influx of Goths through the weakened Roman defenses brought more Germanic tribes into Roman domains. The Franks, for example, who had lived along the Rhine River in the western portion of modern-day Germany, were now in Gaul (modern-day France). The Goths never established a large settlement in modern-day France as the Germanic Franks did. Therefore, Gaul later became the center of power of the future (German) Frankish Kingdom. Eventually, their territory became known as Francia, the earliest name of France, for the land of the Franks.

As the Goths and other Germanic tribes moved deep into Europe, pushed by the Huns, the Western Roman Empire was destined to collapse, and the demographics of western Europe and, to some extent, central Europe were permanently changed to create modern Europe. Meanwhile, the Goths living under the Huns learned their knowledge of cavalry.[520] In time this knowledge became very useful in the Gothic conquest of the ailing Western Roman Empire.

Following the death of Attila, the Ostrogoths set themselves free from the control of the Huns. Consequently, their leader, Theoderic the Great, under the command of the Eastern Roman emperor, arrived in the Italian Peninsula to take over the former seat of the Western Roman Empire from its non-Roman king, Odoacer. After he established the Ostrogothic Kingdom, Theoderic used the name Italia for the peninsula. Meanwhile, with the loss of Roman authority, the former territories of the Western Empire were now completely overtaken by the German tribes of the Visigoths, Ostrogoths, Franks, Burgundians, and Vandals. Of these, the last settled in the western portion of the northern African shores. The Burgundians established themselves in modern-day France, where their name lives on in the region of France known as Burgundy. In short, the Germanic tribes played a role in the evolution of western Europe. Indeed, power interactions between the Germanic Visigoths, Ostrogoths, and Franks in the fifth and the sixth centuries contributed to the formation of future Spain, Italy, and France.

The Frankish Kingdom, which overcame the remaining Germanic tribes, at its zenith included the territories of modern-day France, Germany, and northern Italy. In the year 800, the Frankish king Charlemagne was crowned as the emperor of the state now known as the Carolingian Empire, which in 843 at the Treaty of Verdun was divided into Eastern Francia, Central Francia, and Western Francia. The last eventually became known as France. Central Francia later became part of Eastern Francia, which became largely the medieval Kingdom of Germany. In 962 the territories of the Kingdom of Germany together with the territories of the Kingdom of Bohemia and the Kingdom of Burgundy were known as the Holy Roman Empire (962–1806).

Just as the early Germanic tribes of the Franks gave their name and their founding dynasty to the establishment of modern-day France, the Viking Rus' did the same for Russia (chapter 4.6) in the ninth century, while the Cuman Turks established the founding dynasties of Bulgaria and Romania (chapter 4.3) in the twelfth century. The evolution of new national groups of western Europe and the modern-day languages of Europe were indirect effects of the Hun penetration into Europe.

The Turks also played a significant role in the evolution of eastern European demographics. The On-Oghur Turkish tribes, having a symbiotic relationship with the Magyars, laid the foundation for present-day Hungary. The Bulgar Turks established the foundation of modern-day Bulgaria and contributed to the formation of Hungary as well. The Avar Turks (chapter 4.4) set the tone for the development of central and eastern European Slavic demographic changes that lasted into modern times. Furthermore, the Qïpčak-Cuman (chapter 4.8) tribes of the Turks caused additional changes in modern-day Hungary, Romania, Russia, and Ukraine.[521]

In Asia, modern-day Mongolia was the land of the Turks. But with the decline of the Xiong-nu (Asian Huns) after the first century CE, the Turkish tribes started their westward movement out of this land. By the time the Kyrgyz Qaghanate lost its battle against the Khitans in the tenth century, the Turkish population in Mongolia had dwindled to a minority. As a result, empires in this Eastern Eurasian Steppe, the center of the former Turkish steppe, began to change hands to the Mongols beginning in the eleventh century. Around this time, at the westernmost point of Asia, there was another demographic change. In 1071 the defeat of the Eastern Roman Empire by the Seljuk Turks at the Battle of Manzikert opened Anatolia to the Oghuz Turks, who flooded the peninsula in a matter of a few years, thus completely changing the Greek character of the land in favor of a Turkish one.

HISTORIC TURKISH TITLES AND GOVERNMENT

On the basis of Chinese archives, the very first supreme title for the ruler of the Turks was *shan-yu*, used by the Xiong-nu, or the Asian Huns. However, this title seems to have been used solely by the Huns, as it never appears again in the annals of history. Much later, the Buddhist Uighur Turks of the Qara-Khoja Kingdom in the ninth century used the Turkish title of *idi-qut* (sacred majesty). But this title was never used by any other Turkish political entity either. However, the title of "khan" was commonly used as an equivalent of the Western term *king*. The Turkish title of *gür-khan* (universal khan) was only known to be used by the Qara-Khitan monarch Küčlüg. It should be noted that among ancient Turks, just as in many other monarchies of the past, rulers were known by their regnal names, including their titles.

The pre-Islamic period Turkish title of *qaghan* (*qağan*) was used to denote "emperor." The title of *yabghu* (*yabğu*) was a lesser title, likely meaning "prince," usually a vassal of the qaghan or the ruler of a confederacy of tribes ultimately responsible to the qaghan.[522] In the Orkhon inscriptions from the eighth century, it is apparent that the Gök-Türks attributed a "lesser version" of the title *qaghan* to the Turkish Chinese rulers (Tabgač qaghan) and to the subordinate Turkish chieftains of the Türgeš and Kyrgyz tribes. Furthermore, the leader of the Toquz-Oghuz tribes in the Gök-Türk Empire was similarly given the title of *qaghan*. The ruling clan of the Toquz-Oghuz, which has been associated with the Uighurs by some historians, has been thought to be an "in-law" clan of the A-shih-na clan, the founder of the Gök-Türks.[523] Thus, this clan's leader carried the title of *baz qaghan*, meaning "vassal qaghan." But the supreme qaghan resided only in the house of the A-shih-na.

Tengri qaghan is a unique Turkish title, meaning "heavenly qaghan" or "heavenly emperor," in similar fashion to the Chinese monarch's title. The Turkish rulers of the Mongolian steppes demanded such a title from the Chinese emperors to attain at least an equal status with the rulers of China. The title was accorded to the rulers of the Gök-Türks, the Uighurs, and the Kyrgyz.[524] This title was similar to the title of *ch'eng-li ku-t'u shan-yu* (great son of heaven) of the Xiong-nu (Asian Huns).

The name Bumïn for the founder of the Gök-Türk Empire may have been of Persian origin. Just as present-day Turks use many Arabic names, owing to long-term Islamic influence, in the sixth century, there was heavy Sogdian (an Iranian race) influence on the Gök-Türks. In Persian *bum* indicated "earth," and *in* or *ina* was a common suffix. Accordingly, the Chinese referred to Bumïn as Tu-men, where Chinese *tu* meant "earth" and *men* meant "door, gateway" or "family."[525] Hence, Bumïn Qaghan probably meant "emperor of the world." In fact, this regnal title would have been fitting for the ideal of world domination, which was once a goal of the ancient Turkish people, who previously had a strong military character.[526] The actual recorded regnal title of Bumïn, the founder of Gök-Türk Empire, was *yili-kehan* (per the Chinese transliteration), which was identical with the Xiong-nu (Asian Hun) title *shan-yu*, according to the Chinese record of Zhou-shu, but according to the T'ang annals, the title *qaghan* itself was equivalent to *shan-yu*.[527] The word *yili* is thought to be a Chinese transliteration of the Turkish *el* or *il* for "having land," similar to the later title of *il-khan*,[528] hence the Chinese *yili-kehan* for the possible Turkish title *il-qaghan*. The regnal title of Il-teriš Qaghan, the founder of the Second Gök-Türk Empire, was Qutlugh Qaghan, which meant "blessed emperor." His actual name, Il-teriš, meant "he who collected (the people) of the realm." His younger brother and the second ruler of the Second Gök-Türk Empire was Qapghan Qaghan, with a regnal title Bügü Qaghan,[529] meaning "wise emperor."

For the Tengriist Turks, their qaghan was considered holy. For this reason, if there was need for the death penalty involving a royal family member, the person was put to death by strangulation with a silk cord because no one had the right to shed the blood of a royal person.[530] This ancient tradition was also followed by the Ottoman Turks. According to the ancient beliefs, the qaghan was created in heaven and placed on earth to carry out Gök-Tengri's missions through the throne. The qaghan had the power to bring "good (or blessed) fortune," known as *qut*, and he had the privilege of establishing traditional law, known as *törü* (or *töre*).

We learn from the Qara-Khanid Turks of the eleventh century about the hierarchical system of power of the ancient Turks. The supreme leader was the great qaghan, and the coqaghans governed their territories, usually only one of them being the great qaghan. This was somewhat similar to the tetrarchy created in 293 by the Roman emperor Diocletian, who shared one-fourth of the power with his coemperors.

The acquisition of ranks was an important trait among the ancient Turkish mounted archers. The ranking order of the ancient Turkish titles in sequence was qaghan (emperor), yabghu (prince), and šad, tigin, and tarkhan (commander).[531] The title *šad* was used as a high military ranking. *Tigin* or *tegin* was an old title; initially it was used for "prince" for the sons of the qaghans, but later it likely meant "commander" or "general," as noted by the Ghaznavids. *Kül čor* or simply *čor* was another high-ranking title possibly acquired by non-Gök-Türk princes among the Turks.[532]

Turkish history also shows the title of *khaqan* being used in a similar fashion as the term *qaghan*. The Qara-Khanids of the eleventh century used the title prominently. A khan was beneath a qaghan, in hierarchy, with an added totemistic title taken from an animal, such as *arslan* (lion), *buğra* (camel), *toğrïl* (also *tuğrul*, for "falcon, hawk"), and so on.[533] Interestingly, shamanic totemic names were used among Turks who were already following the Muslim faith.

In pre-Islamic Turkish armies, generals were known with the title of *tarkhan*, but in the Ottoman Empire, the term *paša* was used instead. Although modern-day Turkey has adopted the Western term *general*, the Ottoman Turkish word *paša* is still used in a loose manner for the generals of

Turkey. The title of *sü-bashï* was used either as a military gubernatorial title or for a high-ranking officer. The Turkish term *beg* or *bey* was used for Turkish warlords and leaders of principalities or tribes; it was common particularly among the Oghuz Turks, but it was used by other Turks as well. The title *atabeg* was used among the Seljuks for warlords who were mentors of princes destined to become future monarchs. The Turkish title *bagatur*, which we see being used by the Mongols much later in the twelfth century, was also used by the Bulgar Turks in the seventh century.[534] It meant "brave leader." Genghis Khan's father, Yesügei, in the twelfth century was known to have the Turkish title *bagatur*.[535]

When the Turks formed the Turkish Islamic empires, they began to use the Arabic title of "sultan," and consequently their states were known as sultanates. The latter was the equivalent of a kingdom of the Islamic state. The title of "sultan" had to be certified by the Abbasid caliph to the Turkish monarchs who defended orthodox (Sunni) Islam and offered protection to the caliph. Thus, for someone to have such title meant that the recipient needed to have Sunni piety while carrying out sharia (religious law). The Turkish rulers were the first to acquire this title. Mahmud of Ghazna was the first to have the title of "sultan," and the Seljuks had the first dynasty of sultans.[536] It has also been claimed that the first Turkish monarch to officially acquire the title of "sultan" was Tuğrul Bey of the Seljuk Turks.[537] This is because Mahmud of Ghazna proclaimed the title of "sultan" by himself, whereas Tuğrul Bey was given the title by the Abbasid caliph. Since the Seljuk power base was in Iran, they were not immune to the Persian influence; consequently, it was common for them to also use the Persian title of "shah" to indicate "king of Persia," even though they were not Persians.

The history of the Ottoman Empire shows an interesting evolution of acquired titles. The founder Osman had the title of *bey* as he was the leader of his Turkmen Qayï tribe. When he declared statehood, with the city of Bursa as his capital, he had the title of "khan." All his descendants subsequently had the title of "khan," indicating that they were the rulers of the Ottoman Turks. The military successes of Bayezït Khan in Christian Europe earned him the title of "sultan," given by the Abbasid caliph. The Ottoman monarchs acquired the titles of the localities that they acquired as well. For example, over time they were known as the king of Serbia, the king of Bulgaria, and so on. Upon the conquest of Constantinople, which was the capital of the (Eastern) Roman Empire (330–1453), Sultan Mehmet II acquired the title of Kayser-i Rum (Caesar of the Romans), which was the most prestigious title of the conquered lands. From this point on, the Ottoman Sultanate was known as the Ottoman Empire. In the West the Ottoman state was known as an Islamic empire. When the Shi'ite Turkmen group the Safavids established themselves as a power in Iran, they acquired the Persian title of "shah." To declare supremacy over the Safavids of Iran, the Ottoman monarch acquired the Persian title of *padishah*, meaning "father of the shah." The Persian title of *hünkar* was also used in the Ottoman court. But formally the Ottoman rulers used dual titles, such as Sultan Mehmet Khan; the former legitimized their Islamic character, while the latter showed their Central Asian heritage. The title of "sultan" was also used by the children of the Ottoman monarch. When attributed to males, the title was applied before the name, but when used for female children, it was used after the name. Among the female members of the royal family during the later years of the empire, the title of "sultan" was given only to the mother of the monarch. During the nineteenth century, the remaining female members were given the title of *kadın efendi*; *kadın* was derived from the Old Turkish word *khatun* (lady).

The capture and control of the Islamic holy lands in Mecca and Medina gave the Ottoman rulers significant prestige. The Ottoman government then began to use the term Sublime Porte for the Arabic term Bab-ï Ali (or simply the Porte in the West). This term was used because the sultans viewed themselves as God's representatives in the world, and the Porte was the gateway to heaven. In a way, this view of the "heavenly monarchy" was reminiscent of the "God-appointed heavenly qaghan" of the ancient Turkish rulers of the steppes.

In pre-Islamic Turkish tribal administration, there used to be a royal counseling group known as the *qurultai*, but the Ottomans used the Persian word *divan* to serve the same purpose. This government entity served not only as the chamber of counsels for the monarch but also later as the office of grand vizier, deciding on important state affairs, particularly after the sixteenth century.

STATE SYMBOLISMS: FLAG, TUGH, AND DRUMS

Based on ancient steppe traditions, 'state' and 'monarch' for the ancient Turks were heavenly symbols on earth given to them by Sky-God. For this reason among these Turks the monarch was considered to be God's representative on the planet. This tradition was continued most recently among the Ottoman Turks as their sultan was known to be 'God's shadow on earth.' Based on this tradition, the presence of a monarch allowed the existence of a state, which was God's grace to the nation.

During the process of ascension to the throne, the monarch was given both the flag of the nation and a drum, together symbolizing the power and independence. The material representation of earthly power was the flag, and the possession of such item was providing the legitimacy to the ruler of the nation. For the Turkish nation a flag has always been a symbol of honor and existence of the people but in reality the flag itself was not a mere piece of cloth but rather a sacred entity with an infinite influence stretching from the underground world to the heavenly place where the creator Sky-God resided. This concept was in fact embedded in the Tengriism that the early Turks followed.

The phrase from the legend of Oghuz "May the sun become our flag and tugh, and the blue sky be our domed tent" embodied this concept for the ages. There are multiple symbolisms that can be found in this simple phrase that has been present in many ancient legends. For example, association of the nomadic traditional domed tent with the blue sky represents living free across the land. Furthermore, it represented world domination since it suggested that the domed tent equated with the sky would be everywhere where the blue sky was.

In the legend of Manas of the Kyrgyz Turks, the phrase "Strike the flagpole to the ground and let the flag wave freely in the sky" was a pre-war cry intended to motivate the warriors. The symbolism here indicated that the location where the flagpole was to be hammered was going to be conquered, and then the free flowing flag was going to represent their independence under the sky.

The horsetail banner, known to the Turks as tugh (tuğ), was a special representation for respected power. Literally it was made out of horsetail hair hanging down from a pole. The number of separate horsetail clumps also indicated the rank of the power. For example, among the Qara-khanids of the eleventh century, the monarch could only have 'nine-tugh,' meaning nine separate horsetail clusters attached to a single flagpole. However, tugh could only be given to the lords and commanders by the monarch. It is clear that this horsetail banner carried significant importance for the ancient Turks. Yet, the tugh of the former Tengriist Turks of the steppes in time was replaced with the crescent as the insignia of the Ottoman Turks.

At times tugh was a horsetail clump attached to a flagpole and sometimes it was a combination of a flag attached to a horsetail flagpole and at other times tugh was a combination of horsetail pole with drums; indeed, both the drum and the tugh were considered to be part of the military equipment.[538] They were used to give momentum and direction for the movements of the army. But at the same time they could have both been used for ceremonial purposes as well. The tall horsetail tugh would indicate the locations of the fighting units on the battlefield. As a result, the commander-in-chief was able to make strategic moves during a battle whereas this tactical advantage was not available to the sedentary armies of the past. In the mean time, the playing of the drums in the mean time intended to give motivation to the warriors fighting the enemy.[539]

The state insignia that was designed for Sultan Selim III had flags as well as tugh and drum representations. Sultan Mahmud II Khan, making an effort to reform the decaying Ottoman Empire, issued a new state insignia, which illustrated multiple flags and a drum as centerpiece in addition to a tugh. Then at the time of Reformation (Tanzimat) Period during the reign of Sultan Abdulmecit the insignia included the flag as well as sultan's tughra (seal) embedded within sun rays, perhaps was influenced by ancient Oghuz legend where tugh was represented by the sun. Later, the fact that the reverse of the Osmaniye order issued for the first time 1862 by Sultan Abdulaziz carried a relief of a pair of drums was not a coincidence. Finally the Ottoman state insignia underwent further evolution and by 1882 under the rule of Sultan Abdulhamit II it gained numerous symbolisms among which the flag remained prominently whereas the tugh and the drum have disappeared. Nonetheless, if we consider that the tugh was once symbolized by the sun, the latest insignia's sun symbol could also be representing the tugh of the past.

THE PASTORALIST NOMADIC WARRIORS

In the steppes of Eurasia, nomadism started as a way of life in about the fourth and third millennia BCE among agricultural people who had been involved with stock breeding. For one reason or another, they were likely pushed into the steppe life from their former sedentary ways. But the horse was not immediately an important part of their lives until it was domesticated, possibly in the Pontic Steppe or Central Asia no later than the third millennium BCE. Early on in the history of the world, the horse was hunted for its flesh. In fact, it went extinct in the Americas, owing to those who crossed over from Asia to North America via the Bering Strait at the end of the Ice Age, whereas in Europe the return of the forests forced the horse to establish its habitat in the vast grasslands of the Eurasian Steppe, whose dwellers began to domesticate the animal initially for its flesh.[540] Once horseback riding was discovered, the horse became a war tool. The first evidence for the technology for sustaining mounted horsemen is from the middle of the second millennium BCE.[541] But this was not enough to cause a demographic change from a sedentary lifestyle to equestrian nomadic pastoralism. Horseback riding as a means of transportation and military use became important even later.

Riding a horse was known in the civilized world as early as the second millennium BCE. In fact the horseman was depicted in Egyptian art by 1350 BCE. It has been even suggested that perhaps it was the Assyrians who started to develop the beginning of the cavalry force, but it was the fearsome Scythians from Central Asia who contributed to the downfall of the Assyrian Empire by assisting the Babylonians in 605 BCE with their fearsome mounted archery. This event showed that horsemanship in the civilized world was not as advanced as it was among Central Asians. In fact, horse riding started in the steppes well before it did in the civilized world.[542]

The early Turks took pride in mastering horseback riding and their ability to shoot arrows with deadly accuracy while at full gallop. Many historians have accepted that the Scythians were the earliest known tribal nation to have adopted equestrian nomadism. Assuming these tribes were among the early Iranian-origin tribes, it has been suggested that the early Turks borrowed horsemanship from the Iranian nomads of the west.[543] According to Chinese records, the Turkish people of the Di tribes confronted the Chinese army on foot rather than on horseback as early as the sixth century BCE. But later, by 300 BCE, these early Turkish fighters were expert cavalrymen.[544] It is not clear whether all Turkish tribes adopted horsemanship into their lifestyles early on, but we know that the Huns (Xiong-nu) did (chapter 3.2).

Central Asian nomadic life was far more ordered than their sedentary neighbors gave them credit for.[545] Among the tribal nomadic societies of the Far East, including the Tibetans, Mongols, and Turks, the latter had the most advanced and complex organizational skills.[546] For example, the early Mongols did not have leader tribes to control other tribes to form tribal federations; therefore, generally speaking, their tribes were independent from one another. Furthermore, the Mongols were known primarily as cattle breeders and did not travel far.[547] By contrast, the Turks, who specialized primarily as horse breeders, had a hierarchical tribal system with leader tribes, where royal families could form tribal federations, leading to nomadic-state formation.[548]

Turkish-type tribal organization required seasonal displacement of the nomads. The Turkish nomads were not vagabonds but had predetermined seasonal settlement areas. They were forced to establish lower-altitude, warmer winter camps known as *kišla* (from the Turkish word *kiš* for "winter") and higher-altitude, cooler summer camps known as *yayla* (from the Old Turkish word *yay* for "summer"), thus creating the need for migration. Sometimes these tribal movements necessitated crossing distances of hundreds of miles, in which case tribal leaders needed to have experience in diplomacy and military skills for when they encountered other groups of people.[549] The horse-breeding Turkish tribes had a wider migration range than the Mongols and the Tibetans since the use of the horses allowed the tribesmen to travel farther distances. The ease of mobility of the horse breeders separated them from the other nomads. Eventually, the nomads on horseback, by developing military and diplomatic leadership, had enough knowledge to establish a state.[550] Early on in antiquity, their capability for distant migration was well demonstrated by the wide geographic distribution of the Turks across the large Central and Eastern Eurasian Steppes and the subsequent great Turkish migrations (chapter 4) that allowed the Turkish tribes to further spread out from the outskirts of the Eastern Eurasian Steppe in the Far East to the Western Eurasian Steppe in the heart of central Europe.

The Mongols, as part of the Tung-hu tribes, remained in Manchuria until the Asian Huns began to collapse in the second century CE. By acquiring the Turkish knowledge of horse breeding, they soon began to expand their pastoral territories, but they did not have known polities early on in their history. This was because early Mongolian society was based on loose federations of tribes, and no tribe took a leadership role over the others.[551] This Mongolian attitude changed when, in the thirteenth century, the Mongol leader Genghis Khan emerged as a true strong leader for the first time in Mongol history to subjugate all the Mongol tribes under his rule, thereby changing the Mongol way of life into a Turkish-style hierarchical organization system, with the help of the Uighur Turks (volume 2, chapter 3.3).

As stated earlier, prior to Islamization starting in the ninth and tenth centuries, the Turks were mostly nomadic people. They did not leave written records, yet their oral epic stories live on. Most of their history, way of life, faith, and language were discovered through the people they encountered. Even though they led a nomadic lifestyle in the early part of their history, their organizational skills, both military and administrative, were not as simple as most people imagined. Indeed, many sedentary civilizations underestimated the abilities of the Turks on their initial contact with them. The nomads formed a sophisticated society where individuals had specific roles in their tribal organizations. They were not mere horsemen or herders of animals; they were also carpenters, weavers, and smiths and metallurgists who had the knowledge to smelt iron from rocks.[552] Their adaptability to complex conditions also allowed them to take on a sedentary lifestyle while forming great empires, as noted later. However, the laws (*yasa*) of the nomadic Turks were simple; adultery, treason, and murder were punishable by death, and theft required a tenfold repayment.[553] Cowardice was considered a crime, and no chastisement was considered sufficient.

The Xiong-nu (Asian Huns), the Gök-Türks, and the Kyrgyz were mostly pastoralist Turkish nomads with limited agricultural activities. The Khazars and the Uighurs were, by contrast, seminomadic; they engaged in agricultural activities as well. But they all had the ability to build cities. The central activity of pastoral nomadism was maintenance of livestock, which was often exposed to the dangers of severe weather changes that adversely affected the animals.

For example, observations of the Gök-Türks by a Chinese ambassador in 627 CE described heavy snowfall wiping out a large portion of their sheep and horses and consequently leaving the population exposed to severe famine.[554] The best combination of animals was horses (for mobility), sheep (for food, clothing, and fuel), and cattle (for transport).[555] The nomads survived primarily on the products from their livestock, such as meat, dairy, wool, and hides. The early steppe nomads were warriors, but their economy required contact with sedentary societies and therefore access to their offerings, such as sustenance and other material goods. While peaceful trade often occurred in a symbiotic relationship, at other times the nomads used force to get access to the goods of the sedentary civilization if they were ignored.

The horse was their most important animal, not just for riding but also for its meat, skin, and milk, from which the Huns made a fermented drink known as *kïmïz* (koumiss), still consumed in many parts of Asia. Their experience in horseback riding was unmatched, which gave them an advantage over Chinese armies with chariots. Because of their effective use of horses as war machines, the Asian Huns were instrumental in introducing the concept of the cavalry in China.[556] Hun males were all trained to be warriors starting early in their childhood. Young children were taught to ride on the back of sheep and to shoot small animals with miniature bows. As soon as they could ride horses while shooting full-sized bows, they were recruited into the cavalry of the Huns.[557] This type of training was also practiced by subsequent Turkish nomadic tribes and states as well.

These Central Asian nomads were superb horsemen and extremely skillful archers on horseback, thus deserving of the term *mounted archers*.[558] However, the bow and the arrow were not the only weapons that they had. The Central Asian fighters were also expert in close combat skills. For example, they were known to use the mace (*topuz, gürz*), a weapon unknown to the Europeans until the early medieval period.[559] In addition, they used swords (*kïlïč*) daggers (*kama*) for close combat. Apparently, the Huns of Attila carried two swords each. Pečeneg graves from the ninth and tenth centuries reveal massive, slightly bent sabers, no longer than one meter. Spears and lances were also used by nomadic armies.[560] Making goblets out of the skulls of conquered peoples was an ancient warrior custom noted among the Scythians as well as the Xiong-nu (Asian Huns), the Bulgars, and later the Pečenegs.[561]

Each steppe warrior needed well over ten horses to change mounts on long-distance campaigns; Marco Polo observed in the thirteenth century that each rider had as many as eighteen changes of mount.[562] Before engaging in a battle, the Turks attempted to intimidate their enemies from a distance by showering them with arrows shot from their superior composite bows.[563] While their sedentary enemies formed lines of battle, the steppe Turkish warriors approached their targets in a loose crescent formation, outflanking them, but when they met resistance, they did not hesitate to retreat—with the intention of forcing their adversaries to break their line—only to return to finish them off.[564] The Turkish mounted archers terrorized the Western Roman Empire and forced payment of tributes from the emperors of China and the Eastern Roman Empire. Then they conquered the Middle East and India to lay the foundation for long-lasting empires. Hence, these warriors made significant historical impressions in both Europe and Asia for nearly two millennia.

The nomadic Turks were known as pastoralists, but some of their tribes pursued agriculture. Although the Huns themselves are not thought to have been involved in agricultural activities, other Turkish tribes in their confederacy, such as the Kyrgyz and the Tung-hu, appear to have been engaged in some agricultural pursuits. It is therefore not surprising to see that the Turkish language from this time already included vocabulary naming agricultural plants and instruments.[565] The historical data indicate that the Khazar and the Uighur Turks later on were also involved in agriculture.

The nomadic horseman wore a conical hat protecting the ears and the neck, a jacket resembling a caftan reaching down to the knees, loose trousers similar to *shalvar* suitable for horse riding, and finally boots made of felt or leather.[566] They did not have written records, primarily because they were not permanently sedentary, but there is evidence that they could write and read. However, the contracts among themselves, it is believed, were based purely on verbal agreement, owing to trust and honor.[567] For the Xiong-nu and later the Turks, the left side was considered to represent honor since the heart was on the left side of the body.[568] The arrow symbolized the chieftains and tribes, and ultimately power. Furthermore, the drum and the wolf head implied royal authority.[569] Centuries later we see that the drum was a symbol of authority for the Ottoman Turks.

The ancient Central Asian nomads did not have the social-class differences that the sedentary civilizations developed. In fact, nomadic life allowed everyone to have equal status within the old Turkish society. The tribal chief and his royal family always had the respect of the tribal people. But his family and he would have participated in the day-to-day activities of the tribe. Chinese archives clearly indicate that the Asian Huns (Xiong-nu) had an egalitarian society, where the ruling class and the common people had no significant social-status differences.[570] Nearly a millennium later, the Qïpčak tribal people were also an egalitarian society, but as their relations with neighboring sedentary societies increased, the tribal leadership began to distance themselves from their people, as the Xiong-nu leaders did when they increased relations with Chinese royalty. Marriages between tribal dynastic families and the aristocracy of their neighbors (such as Rus', Khwarezm, and Georgia) contributed to the evolution of class differences.[571] When this occurred, the tribal leaders also began to lose the respect of their followers.

Though the Ottoman Turks were heavily influenced by Arab and Persian cultures, they retained their Central Asian customs early on. Indeed, some similarities between the social practices of the Huns and the later-appearing Ottomans from the Oghuz Turks showed the preservation of old Central Asian traditions. The Hunnic dignitary in charge of the queen's household was a eunuch, just as the *qïzlar ağasi* was for the Ottoman Turks.[572] The black-coated horse (*qara tonlï at*) was apparently important in the Hunnic tradition and among their progeny, the Old Chuvashians and the Ottomans, as observed by Evliya Çelebi during the funeral procession of Sultan Murad IV.[573]

The ancient Turkish tribal states pursued commerce with their sedentary neighbors. The Turks received food items and clothing material such as silk from the Chinese and in turn gave them horses. As we will see later, no matter how much military superiority the Turkish nomadic states had over the sedentary Chinese, they did not intend to conquer them because of fear of being assimilated by the conquered. Instead, their wish was to have constant access to the goods of the sedentary world.[574] The type of interaction constantly shifted between trading and raiding. In the classical age, or the medieval period, cities such as Constantinople built fortified walls to protect themselves from their enemies and the nomads, and the Chinese began to build the Great Wall of China, starting with the first dynasty of China, the Qin (or Ch'in) dynasty (256–206 BCE), to protect themselves from the raids of the Xiong-nu (Asian Huns).

China's agrarian economy was sufficient to produce whatever the Chinese people needed, but they were always in need of horses. Ironically, they needed to acquire these animals from the very people who threatened them from the north, the nomads.[575] Through their contact with China, the nomadic Turks in turn began to use Chinese silk in exchange for horses. The Chinese realized that the lack of strong cavalry force as the Turks had was always giving them a disadvantage on the battlefield.

In his fight with the Xiong-nu (Asian Huns), Han emperor Wudi desired to acquire mythical horses from the far west with the hope to improve his odds against the nomadic mounted archers. The Fergana Valley (now in modern-day Uzbekistan and Kyrgyzstan) was previously known to the Chinese as Da-yüan, and this area was famous for its horses. As far as the Chinese were concerned, they were the best horses in the world. The Chinese referred to them as the "blood-sweating celestial steeds."[576] After 104 BCE, Wudi sent an envoy to acquire some of these horses, but his envoy was assassinated. Furious, Wudi sent an army with several tens of thousands of soldiers to the west to inflict punishment upon the locals of Fergana and to capture these special horses. During their march, the majority of the soldiers died, owing to starvation, and a few thousand remaining soldiers were killed by the locals. But his next campaign for these celestial horses, with an even larger army and an endless supply of provisions, was successful. Finally, after Da-yüan was punished, Wudi received the "celestial blood-sweating horses" he had coveted for so long.[577] Yet, these efforts soon proved to be in vain. Not only did the efforts of Wudi helped to drain the treasury, but the Xiong-nu also showed that they were unstoppable.

Neither the Scythians nor the Xiong-nu (Asian Huns) had heavily fortified walled cities, which were built originally to protect sedentary residents from outsiders, particularly the nomads. The steppe nomads instead wandered in search of water and vegetation for their animals. Nomadic life was not just a way of life but also the means for security against enemies. When facing larger forces, such as the Chinese, the nomadic movements gave the Turks a strategic advantage because it was more difficult for the enemy armies to locate them. In the eighth century, Kül Tigin, the co-ruler of the Gök-Türks, left a warning for all Turkish tribes on the Orkhon inscriptions (south side of the inscriptions). He cautioned that the Chinese were the enemy and that if the tribes decided to settle down, the Chinese would entice them and scheme to cause them tragedy, including death.[578]

Until the gunpowder era, the nomads of the steppes were more efficient and successful warriors than sedentary peoples were. This was true in the case of the European Huns against the Romans, and the Asian Huns and the Gök-Türks against the Chinese. They owed their military superiority to the maneuverability of their deadly cavalry and the difficulty the sedentary empires had in establishing adequate defenses against them.[579] But there were multiple reasons for the tactical and strategic superiority that the Turkish nomads had over sedentary peoples. These arose from multiple factors, including the harsh conditions in which they lived, their habits of hunting (their only means of sustenance, to which they were accustomed to since their early childhood), their unmatched skill in the use of the bow, making them unmatched hunters and formidable fighters, their dizzying mobility, and their organizational skills.[580]

The fall of the former great nomadic Turkish empires (Xiong-nu, Gök-Türks, and Uighurs) happened not because of direct outsider interference but often because of internal strife among the Turks themselves. In the case of both the Xiong-nu and the Gök-Türks, the Chinese applied their divide-and-conquer politics by getting different Turkish political entities to fight among themselves for power, which in turn caused the fall of the empires. In the case of the Uighur Empire, however, they did not fall because of self-destruction. Instead, their kinsmen the Kyrgyz Turks in the ninth century came down from the north unexpectedly to destroy Uighur rule in the Mongolian steppes.

In the sixteenth century, the military superiority of the nomadic warriors ended with the emergence of the gunpowder empires. The once-feared mounted archers of the Turks and the Mongols were no longer a match for muskets and cannon fire. Their era came to an abrupt end, and consequently, the domains they once ruled came under attack by outsiders. However, the pages of history demonstrate that the Turkish mounted archers were able to form gunpowder empires as well as the Europeans did. These were the empires of the Ottomans, Safavids, Uzbeks, and Mughals.

POLITICAL ESTABLISHMENT OF THE TURKISH STEPPE EMPIRES

Although the Xiong-nu Empire (Asian Huns; chapter 3) of the Mongolian steppes have been popularly known as pastoralist nomadic super-complex tribal confederacy, they were truly agro-pastoralist society by having mixture of true nomadic population with sedentary people dealing with agricultural activities.[581] Similar political setup can be seen in subsequent Gök-Türk as well as Uighur steppe empires. For example, an Arab merchant from the ninth century gave impressive descriptions of the Uighur cities, thriving with booming markets and agricultural activities.[582]

Each of these empires were led by a supreme leader. The Chinese recorded the title of the Hunnish supreme leader as "Shan-yu" but later Turkish empires used the title of "Qaghan" in their original language. In both instances the title was defined as 'emperor.' Typically the steppe empires were led by a government overlooking eastern (left) and western (right) halves of the empire. Each half were led by a lesser-king or sub-qaghans under the supreme leader. Then, each division had further subdivisions led by kings. Even though each administrator were acting like a monarch of their own territories, they were ultimately responsible to their supreme leader.

Furthermore, each of the tribal leaders had their autonomy within their tribes. The Xiong-nu government also allowed the conquered chieftains and kings to remain as rulers of their conquered people. Much later, the Ottomans acted similarly when they conquered Hungary in 1526, subsequently allowing the appointed Hungarian king to remain as vassal of the Turkish empire. The European Huns however treated the conquered German tribes as fiefs, and appointed Hunnish nobles to lead each of these tribes to ensure their loyalty to the state (more in chapter 4.2).

At this point it is not only important to describe how the pastoralist Central Asian peoples governed themselves but it is also equally critical to explain how Europe benefited from the administrative system of the Inner Asian conquerors. Much has been said about the evolution of the feudalist government system in medieval Europe following the cessation of the Roman Empire's authority in western and central Europe after the fifth century. Scholars have often suggested that feudalism was a byproduct of the administrative systems of the defunct Western Roman Empire and Germanic clan society. Furthermore, it has been suggested that feudalism was re-invented by William the Conqueror who upon becoming King of England in 1066 introduced a new form of feudal system of the land.

First we need to understand that the Roman Empire's administrative system had nothing to do with feudalism but rather it was based on absolute autocracy. In other words, the state was ruled by an emperor. Meanwhile, the Senate, which was once the dominant political institution of the Roman Republic, continued its existence under the emperor but without real political power. Within the imperial administration, the emperor overlooked a hierarchy of magistrates and provincial governors who were appointed by the emperor himself.

In reality neither the Roman Empire nor the Germanic clan society had feudalism at the heart of their administrative systems. Each of the Germanic tribes were governed by a tribal king (*könig*) who owned everything in his realm. In fact, feudalism in Europe did not become a native reality until the second half of the fifth century when the Huns already had lost their grip of power over the Germanic tribes (chapter 4.2). In order to understand the birth feudalism in medieval Europe, we need to understand how tribal Central Asians governed themselves.

The Inner Asian tribes were often not given proper credit by the sedentary peoples of the past. However, it was clear that they were not primitive barbaric hordes of warriors. A Roman chronicler's documented information gives us clear picture that the military sophistication of these Asian warriors was not only superior to that of the Romans but also this military superiority could not have been achieved without having a strong political unity.[583]

The military strength elevated the psyche of the nomadic society, thus giving them a sense of superiority over their sedentary rivals. During the times when they were at the zenith of their power, the Central Asian warriors exhibited some rightful grandiosity. For example, Attila viewed the Roman emperors as equals to his generals, not to himself.[584] Showing a similar attitude during nearly four century period of the rise of the Ottoman Empire, the sultans viewed themselves higher than any other monarch in Europe, in fact European monarchs were viewed only as equals to their viziers.

Within the political system of the steppe empires, the supreme leader always resided in the eastern half of the state. The only exception came with Attila when he murdered his brother and his supreme ruler Bleda from the eastern wing to move his command center to the western wing. Upon the death of Attila, the next supreme leader, Attila's eldest son Ellac stationed himself in the traditional eastern wing. Similarly, when the Gök-Türks split into two halves in the sixth century, the supreme qaghan was ruling from the eastern territories whereas the lesser qaghan resided in the western territories of the massive empire.

The steppe empire political system that was carried by the Huns who invaded Europe in the fourth century was actually 'feudal' or 'proto-feudal' system of governance that Europe adapted so eagerly following the fall of the Hunnish hegemony in Europe.[585] This governmental system was implemented for subsequent Turkish steppe polities as well, including those of the Gök-Türks (chapter 5.3) and the Volga Bulgars (volume 2, chapter 2.3).[586] Similar political system was also present among the Muslim Qara-Khanids of the eleventh century, who also had a subordinate king under each lesser-king (volume 2, chapter 2.4).[587]

Not only the Germans (more in chapter 4.2) but also the Slavs copied from the Turkish political system as well. The first Russian state that established by the Viking Rjurik dynasty imitated its neighbor the Khazar Qaghanate (chapter 4.6) in every way[588], and it became a vassal of the Turks with its monarch carrying the title of vassal qaghan.[589] As a result, within the steppe empire political system the Viking monarch had allegiance to the Khazar ruler. Hence, the first Russian state came to be known as the Qaghanate of Rus', a vassal of the Khazar Qaghanate.

Feudalism, which historically has been a governing system of medieval Europe, was essentially born from the culmination of Hunnish legal as well as military customs. Within this system the monarch assigned his closest vassals heritable fiefs, which were property of land and people, serving for the greater good of the nation under the monarch. In fiefdoms, the vassal nobility cultivated the land and raised taxes, ultimately paid to the central government. In time of war, the vassal nobility in ownership of the fiefs provided military personnel to the monarch. In essence a feudal society was based on a military hierarchy in which a monarch assigned his loyal mounted fighters a fief, in other words a territory to manage in exchange for military service in time of need. The loyal fief who accepted this assignment became a vassal. Essentially, this system also led to the formation of the knighthood of Europe.

In more recent history of the Turks, the Ottomans seemed to follow a similar governing pattern based on steppe traditions. While the sultan was the supreme leader of the state, he also had two high-ranking officials, each governing the European and Asian territories respectively. The title for this position was *'beylerbeyi'* meaning 'lord of the lords' in Turkish. One deviation from the steppe culture was the adoption of the position of vizier (equivalent to modern-day prime minister) into the Ottoman governmental system.

Furthermore, information from the Chinese archives demonstrate that the shan-yu also had a supreme aristocratic council, which included six top ranking nobles. Among these were the 'left' and 'right' kings who were the sons and brothers of the supreme leader, and below the council there were 24 imperial governor-commanders for the provinces of the Xiong-nu empire; each of these high-ranking commanders had their respective tribal leaders as their subordinates.[590] However, only the upper class of the imperial clan had access to key administrative and military positions within the empire.

Just as the governing body had complex hierarchy, the military was also a well-organized and disciplined institution. During wartime the Hunnish military was divided in decimal ranking system (tens, hundreds, thousands, etc) especially when large armies were needed; this allowed to form a more disciplined tighter system in preparation for the war. A routine census was also taken in order to determine the state's manpower and livestock status.

Scholars have concluded that the Xiong-nu (Asian Hun) state was not a mere tribal federation but rather with its imperial rituals and governmental system, its complex well-disciplined military organization, as well as its centralized political functions of trade and diplomacy, it was in fact a well-organized state just like sedentary established states were.[591] After all how could the Huns (known with their initial name as the Xiong-nu) exist for a long time after they formed their state initially in 209 BCE? Even though they experienced civil wars and splitting of their tribal confederations, their state building abilities kept them going into the eighth century CE.

HETEROGENEITY OF THE STEPPE EMPIRES

The Inner Asians, also referred to as the Central Asians, were once known for their superb skill in horsemanship as for their pastoralist nomadic lifestyle. These people once formed formidable steppe empires across the endless lands of Eurasia. Even though the ruling clan of the steppe empires were likely from a specific race, their polities were often composed from multiple ethnicities with a rich variety cultural backgrounds. The conquerors did not only possess vast grazing lands of Eurasia for their animals but they also acquired oasis merchant cities of the Silk Road, thus exposing themselves to other cultures commonly found on the historic Silk Road.

The main players of Inner Asia were the Altaic people. Among these Central Asians the most dominant ones were the Turks, but others were the Mongols and the Tungus. Until the advent of the gunpowder age by the fifteenth century, these mounted archers showed their military superiority over the sedentary people across a large geographic area over transcontinental Eurasia. The utilization of the Silk Road on the steppes, and therefore, the ongoing trade over the ages created constant interaction between multiple ethnic groups, both nomadic as well as sedentary.

The Turks, known as pastoralist nomads were once the masters in Inner Asia. As a result of their constant movements due to their migrations they were continuously exposed to a variety of cultures. To their southeast they had contact with Sino-Tibetan culture, to their southwest they were exposed to Iranian and Semitic cultures of the Middle East, and finally to the south of Inner Asia they showed interactions with Indo-Iranian peoples.

The Sogdians who spoke an eastern dialect of the Persian language were the ancestors of modern-day Tajiks, and they were once well-known as merchants of the Silk Road. They became prominent as skillful traders between the East and the West. The Sogdians however were not only carriers of goods between established sedentary civilizations but also they acted as conduit for transmission of technology as well as philosophy and faith. The Sogdians were particularly well-established as traders during the steppe empire periods of the Turks, including those of the Huns, Gök-Türks, and Uighurs.

The Inner Asian Turks through their direct interaction with the Chinese became acquainted with the teachings of Taoism and Confucianism. The Tengriism of the Turks and Mongols met with Zoroastrianism of the Sogdians and Iranians as well. In reality, the Silk Road was a place where different faiths constantly interacted with each other. With the help of the trading routes Buddhism also reached Inner Asia coming from its native India. In addition, the Sogdian merchants played a role in carrying Nestorian Christianity as well as Manichaeism from the Middle East into Central Asia. Later, it was Arab and Persian traders who transmitted the faith of Islam deep into the nomadic villages of the Inner Asian Turks. It is believed the once well-known giant Buddhas of the valley of Bamiyan, in central Afghanistan, were erected under the patronage of the White Huns (chapter 3.6), showing the religious tolerance of these Central Asian warlike people.[592] Unfortunately, these giant Buddha statues which were entered into UNESCO's World Heritage List, were destroyed by the Taliban in March of 2001.

Through these constant trading and interfaith relations the ethnic make-up of the steppe empires quickly became an amalgamation of multiple cultures. Even though the ruling force of the steppe empires may have been often from a single ethnic entity, they were indeed exposed to multiple cultural elements from their diverse environments. The exposure to different languages was one of the cultural elements showing the diversity of these horsemen. For example, Priscus, a Roman historian and diplomat, described that Attila's court had multicultural elements. In fact, the Hunnish empire was culturally heterogenous with Germanic Goths as well as Iranian language speaking Alans who were both part of the formidable empire of their Central Asian invaders. The Hunnish court was exposed to three main languages; the

Oghuric Turkish of the ruling elite, the Gothic German of the Huns' subjects, and Latin of the neighboring Romans.[593] The Hunnish Kidarite Empire of Central Asia (chapter 3.6), which was formed from the same stock of people who formed the European Hunnish Empire, was also exposed to multilingual environment, which included Sogdian, Bactrian, Persian as well as Brahmi.[594]

Nevertheless, stereotyping both in the West and in the East has led us to believe that the Central Asians have always been known as savages. For example, the Xiong-nu, known as the ancestors of the European Huns, have always been referred to as barbaric primitive people. Even though well established sedentary civilizations, such as those in China, Iran, as well as the Westerners, have viewed the Inner Asians as primitive and simple peoples, modern archeology has demonstrated that these Central Asian Turks were actually more sophisticated than originally thought.[595]

Throughout the history of Eurasia, while most Inner Asians remained as nomadic people, there were many of them who also chose to become sedentary. For example, modern archeological discoveries at Xiong-nu cemeteries illustrated the fact that the Xiong-nu were not merely wandering nomads. In fact, the Xiong-nu economy was not only based on pastoralism, and in fact, the diversity of the land that they commanded demonstrated agriculture being one of the important elements of their daily lives. Furthermore, new discoveries demonstrated multiple fixed buildings, suggesting that sedentary lifestyle was also present among these Asian Huns. Moreover, the Xiong-nu tombs revealed the presence of personal items originating not only from China but also from territories as far as from Bactria; these finds suggested these people were also actively engaged in trade as well.[596]

THE SILK ROAD

Controlling lucrative trade routes was vital for the empires of the past. Trade routes were important to allow both commercial and cultural exchanges between civilizations. The ports of the Mediterranean Sea were the initial important trading points among the early civilizations of the West and the Middle East. But the commerce between the civilizations of the Mediterranean basin and the ancient civilization of China led to the formation of new trading routes that would become the most important of premodern times. This was the well-known Silk Road.

The Silk Road was an important historic trade connecting China and the Mediterranean world through an east-west network of multiple trails. These commerce routes also included destinations on the Indian subcontinent. The historic Silk Road was actually never called by this name during more than two millennia; the term was invented by nineteenth-century German traveler and geographer Ferdinand von Richthofen, who in his native tongue called the network of Central Asian trade routes between East and West Seidenstraße.[597] Probably this name was used because of the West's insatiable appetite to acquire Chinese silk. China used the same routes to import horses (from the Fergana Valley, now in Uzbekistan and Kyrgyzstan), camels (from Bactria, now in Afghanistan and Tajikistan), luxury metalwork and textiles (from Persia), and jade (from Khotan). Although commerce was achieved primarily through land-based routes, the Silk Road also acquired maritime routes in the first century CE.[598] Just as silk became an important commodity for the Turks, jade became an important trade item for the Chinese. For the last two millennia, Turkestan—in other words, parts of Central Asia—has provided China the greater supply of its jade.[599]

The Silk Road was once an important communication and trade route for the exchange of merchandise, technology, and ideas between the agrarian communities of the East and the West. However, the Silk Road served a similar purpose between the agrarian and pastoralist peoples of the steppes. Merchandise ranged from the main commodity, silk, to agricultural goods and livestock, to goods such as ceramics, glass, and precious metals. The transfer of technological knowledge occurred in the form of military weapons, architecture, and construction. For example, the knowledge of paper making was carried by the Arabs from Asia to the West. The Turks brought tea from the Far East to the Middle East. Ideas were transported from one place to another in the form of epic stories, languages, and religious thoughts and beliefs, in addition to the exchange of medical knowledge. These trade routes helped to disseminate religious beliefs across the Eurasian steppes. These included Iranian Zoroastrianism and Manichaeism, Far Eastern and South Asian Buddhism, and Middle Eastern Christian Nestorianism and Islam.

The Silk Road was also a conduit for disease transmission, as in the case of the Black Death, resulting from the transmission of bubonic plague from the Mongol Empire to Europe in the fourteenth century. It is estimated that this pandemic resulted in more than one hundred million deaths across Europe.

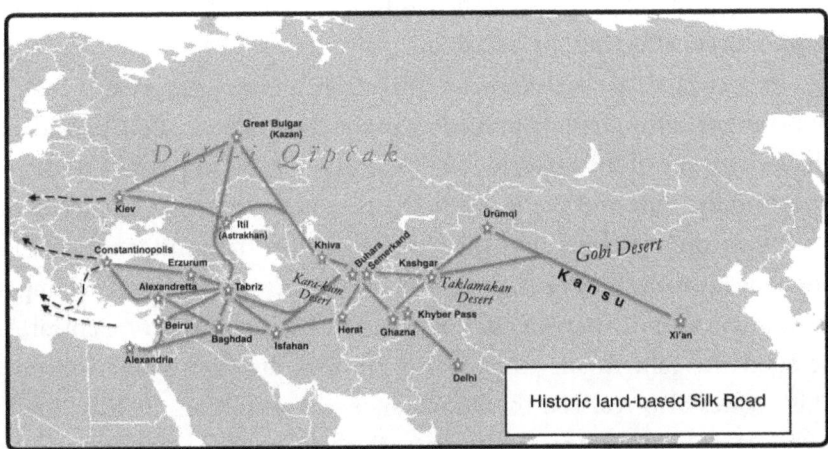

Map 4. Major trade cities are demonstrated along the historically well-known land-based Silk Road. These trade routes played a vital role in the evolution of many civilizations both in Europe and Asia.

Ultimately, the historic Silk Road took its name from the high demand for the famous Chinese silk in the West. The raising of silkworms and extracting silk yarn was already known in China in the third millennium BCE.[600] Chinese farmers paid taxes in grain and silk textiles. In turn, the Chinese government used silk textiles as a trading commodity with outsiders. The evolution of the trade between the East and the West helped the development of the civilizations of China and India in the East and the Western civilizations of Europe, as well as those of the Near East, such as Persia and Arabia. The Silk Road witnessed the first trade with the West, beginning late in the third century BCE with the Han dynasty of China.

The emergence of nomads on horseback in the Central Asian Steppe also brought the West and the East together.[601] Horseback riding, an important means of transportation, began about 600 BCE on the Eurasian Steppe.

Later, by 400 BCE, nomads to the north of the agricultural zone of Central and East Asia started to master horsemanship with archery, thus becoming military machines.[602] This capability of the nomads allowed them to often control the Silk Road, and thus, it also benefited them economically. The area where the nomads survived was in the southern Siberian territories, in other words areas difficult to reach by the Chinese military trying to overcome the nomadic forces affecting the Silk Road.

Z. V. Togan, a well-known Turkologist, has suggested that the establishment of the Great Hun Empire in the third century BCE played a role in the emergence of the historic Silk Road as the most important trade route connecting the East and the West.[603] The pastoralist nomads, spending most of their time on horseback, like the Huns, extended their influence over large areas; consequently, they became crucial in the network of these exchanges.[604] The Hunnish empire, having conquered the vital territories of Central Asia, controlled the Silk Road, which went through its dominion. Subsequent Turkish states also realized the importance of controlling the Silk Road for their benefit. Over the centuries some Turkish-controlled Central Asian cities became economically thriving centers, including Bukhara, Fergana, Kashgar, and Samarkand.

Early on, Chinese emperors traded silk textiles with the Huns to please them and to receive horses in exchange.[605] Besides silk diplomacy, the emperors also offered princesses of the Han court to appease the Hun aristocracy.[606] This was done with the hope that a future Hun prince or the future shan-yu from a Chinese princess might be friendlier toward China.[607]

Over time the fame of Chinese silk was known not only to the Huns but also beyond the steppes of Asia into the Mediterranean basin. During the period of the Gök-Türks, the Eastern Gök-Türks acquired silk from the Chinese; then their Western Gök-Türk cousins traded it to the West. The Chinese emperors began to understand the value of silk clothing in the West. Thus, silk became the main good China traded with the West. It was transported to the Middle East and Eurasia through commercial routes on land and later by sea. The land route for the most part was controlled by the Turks for nearly two millennia. Though Han China was briefly able to extend its territories into Central Asia in the first half of the first century BCE, the

Chinese emperor was not able to hold on to the oasis trading centers of the eastern Silk Road. In the mean time, these centers also allowed non-Chinese goods and ideas, particularly the teachings of Buddhism, to enter China.[608]

Over the centuries, vying for control of the Silk Road became a reason for war between empires. As a result, alternative routes were created. Between 655 and 692, corresponding to the absence of Gök-Türk authority in the steppes, control of the Tarim basin passed to the Tibetan Empire, which thus acquired access to the eastern portion of the Silk Road. Then, between 794 and 851, Tibet took Buddhist Khotan, the southern portion of the Tarim basin.[609] During the period of T'ang China (618–907), the Tibetans remained rivals of the Chinese for the claim of eastern Silk Road.

As stated earlier, the Silk Road's primary component was the land route, and its secondary route was the maritime one. Goods went from China to the initial stop in modern-day Xinjiang, or eastern Turkestan, and then to Khorasan and Khwarezm in western Turkestan. From any one of these places, the route continued in one of three directions: south toward India, west toward the Middle East, or north to end up in Europe by going around the Caspian Sea and then reaching the Pontic Steppe. The Silk Road's maritime route existed well before the European imperial colonizers were aware of the route's existence. It was limited to exchanges between China, India, Iran, and Arabia along the shores of the Indian Ocean.

The discovery of the Americas and the route around the southern tip of Africa in the late fifteenth and the early sixteenth centuries seriously diminished the importance of the land-based Silk Road. This transition period also corresponded to the emergence of the gunpowder empires. All these factors cut down the former glorious powers of the nomadic polities of the steppes, as the absolute advantage went to the sedentary peoples who then became industrial powers.

During the most powerful period of the Ottoman Empire, the Turks controlled nearly all trade routes across the Mediterranean Sea and the Black Sea. They essentially turned these water bodies, and the Red Sea, into virtual Turkish lakes. In addition, they controlled the entire Middle East. Essentially they had full control of the western end of the Silk Road. This forced Europeans to look for new trading routes; subsequently, maritime expeditions began in the fifteenth century. This also led to the little-known naval battles between the Ottomans and the naval forces of the Portuguese and the Spanish in the Indian Ocean.

WOMEN IN OLD TURKISH SOCIETY

On the basis of archaeological and literary evidence, in ancient times in Siberia, a widow would have been killed immediately after her husband's death, but this practice was not continued by the Xiong-nu (Asian Huns), according to Chinese records.[610] In Xiong-nu society, the sons of a dead father would marry their stepmothers but not their natural mothers. This custom provided shelter to the widows. Although the ancient nomadic Turks were known to be patriarchal, they had great respect for women. It is known that the Utrighur Turks had at least one woman tribal leader.[611] This was apparently also true for the Sabir Turks, who are believed to have been related to the European Huns. Chinese historical data show that the Chinese were impressed by the rough equality between men and women within Xiong-nu society.[612] Although the Turkish nomads were considered barbarians by the Chinese elite, the latter also reported that their nomadic laws, or *yasa*, did not allow for killing or robbing a woman.[613] Since ancient Turkish tribal societies are known to have had an egalitarian system, it is believed that women took part in the military force. In fact, the powerful Uighur military of the eighth century included women warriors.[614]

After Bilge Qaghan died, probably poisoned by one of his ministers, the Gök-Türk Qaghanate was to be ruled by his son and successor, Tengri Qaghan, who was a minor. For almost seven years, the empire was controlled by the child's mother until the dynastic rule was ended by the Basmïl Turks in 741.[615] Owing to the influence of the free lifestyle of the Central Asian nomads, including the Turks of antiquity, Chinese women in the northern dynasties (such as the Turkish T'o-pa Northern Wei dynasty) and the T'ang period enjoyed freedom and independence more than in the latter periods of China.[616] This is significant because particularly in ancient and medieval China, women did not have a say in the men's world. An exception is the reign of Empress Wu Zetian (690–705) of T'ang China. She is believed to have been of Central Asian origin. It is apparent that during the era of the Sui and T'ang dynasties of China, in the Turkish custom, the wife of the qaghan could participate in decision making for the state.[617] Turkish women were also seen as monarchs later. Sulafa Khatun, a female member of the Seljuk Atabey Ahmadilis, became the ruler of the principality in the last years of this small state in Azerbaijan, until the Mongols came to conquer it in 1221.[618] When Sultan Il-Tutmuš, the Turkish monarch of the Sultanate of Delhi, felt that he was ready to give up his kingship, he gave his throne to his daughter Raziyya (1236–40).[619] Her rule was short because she was murdered by a Hindu.

In the tenth century, Ibn Fadlan, the secretary of the Abbasid Caliphate's mission to the Volga Bulgar Khanate, just north of the Caspian Sea, observed that Oghuz Turkish women had remarkable freedom.[620] Similarly, the women of the Seljuk Dynasty appeared to have political and financial independence as well as prominent roles in public life.[621] The most well-known influential dynastic Seljuk woman was Terken Khatun, wife of Sultan Malik-Shah and daughter of the Qara-Khanid ruler Tamghach Khan. She unsuccessfully tried to oust the most powerful Seljuk vizier, Nizam al-Mulk. During the Seljuk period, many hospitals in Asia Minor were established by Turkish women of nobility.[622] Turkish Qara-Khanid women had physical freedom in their nomadic society, but they apparently lived in seclusion in their homes within the Irano-Islamic urban areas.[623]

It is believed that among the early Turks, at least women of relatively high position received as good an education as men did.[624] It appears that especially pre-Islamic Turkish women enjoyed equality with men in Central Asian societies. If this is the case, why is it that the women of the Middle East, where the Turks ruled for nearly a millennium, now seem to have unequal social status with their male counterparts? On the basis of the observation of Muslim social life, even though it seems women do not have equal rights with men in the Islamic realm, this social status is not a product of the religion itself but rather due to the cultural influences of the Middle East long before Islam took root across these territories. These were also not part of the old Turkish cultural portfolio. In other words, women's inferior social status in the Middle East is a result of local non-Turkish cultural influences. In regard to the Islamic view regarding women's status, the Qur'an clearly points out

God's declaration in 3:195 as follows: "You (men and women) are equal to one another."

In the fourteenth century, during the period of Orhan Bey, the second monarch of the Ottoman Turks, an observer recorded that "among the Turks and the Tatars their wives enjoy a very high position."[625] This was a result of Turco-Mongol tradition regarding women's influence in the life of the nomads of Central Asia.

Despite royal women's strong role in Ottoman politics, at the end of the seventeenth century, the status of women in the Middle East began to diminish because of the growing influence of the religious bigotry that began to shape the Ottoman realm. When Sultan Murad IV came to the Ottoman throne in 1623, he was only eleven years of age and thus a minor. His mother, Kösem Sultan, also known as Mahpeyker, ruled the mighty Ottoman Empire until her son took control in 1632. Murad IV became a strong leader but died at the age of twenty-seven in 1640. He was succeeded by his brother, Ibrahim I, also known as Deli Ibrahim (Crazy Ibrahim). He was not mentally stable enough to lead the empire. His mother, Kösem Sultan, continued to rule the empire in her son's name. When Ibrahim I was deposed in 1648, his son Mehmed IV was placed on the throne at the age of six. Once again, Kösem Sultan ruled the empire in the name of her grandson until he took power in 1651. Hence, a turbulent period of the Ottoman Empire, with two sultans (Osman II and Ibrahim I) being killed and Kösem Sultan directly and indirectly ruling an empire for nearly three decades, came to an end.

MAJOR TURNING POINTS

Turkish history officially began when the unprovoked attack of the first Chinese emperor from the Ch'in (Qin) dynasty forced the Xiong-nu (Asian Huns) to form a steppe empire to stand up against a unified China. The Huns' subsequent attacks on China forced the Chinese to build the Great Wall of China. Finally, the fall of the Huns in Asia led to the migration of the Turkish tribes, causing the turkization of Central Asia and most of the Eurasian steppes.

Following the fall of the Huns, the Tabgač Turks and other Turkish tribes who controlled northern China introduced Buddhism into China. The European Huns helped to change the demographics of Europe forever and facilitated the fall of the Western Roman Empire. The Gök-Türks came into power with the assistance of a branch of the Tabgač and formed the largest Turkish empire, stretching from the Manchu land in the east deep into eastern Europe in the west. Later in the eight century, the Uighurs adopted Manichaeism as their state religion, and the Khazar Turks adopted Judaism. But the fall of the Gök-Türks led to the eventual Islamization of the Turks of western Turkestan over a period of nearly two centuries, after the Qara-Khanid Khanate became the first Turkish state to accept Islam.

Following the fall of the Mongol Empire, the Turks formed three major gunpowder Islamic empires. These were the Ottoman Empire, the Safavid Empire, and the Mughal Empire. The Ottomans became the first superpower of the modern age and ended the Roman legacy by conquering the capital of the Eastern Roman Empire. They extended their control over Europe, Asia, and Africa. The Safavids became a power in Iran and introduced the Shi'ite faith into the mostly Persian-speaking country. The Mughals tried to revive the legacy of their ancestor Tamerlane. In India they left a lasting legacy by building one of the wonders of the world, the Taj Mahal.

The Republic of Turkey officially chose sixteen of the more prominent historical Turkish states for their influential role in world history. Because of this recognition, these historical states earned individual spots on the presidential seal of the Republic of Turkey. The seal is formed by a large sixteen-pointed star in the center representing the Republic of Turkey, with sixteen smaller stars surrounding it that symbolize these sixteen states. But as we will see, there were many more states formed by the Turks in the form of kingdoms (khanates) and empires (qaghanates) throughout the ages. The book will touch upon the tribes that formed these states and will elaborate more on their historical evolution and contribution to the development of the modern-day world.

Chapter 3:

THE RISE OF THE MOUNTED ARCHERS

3.1. ANCIENT CHINA AND THE NOMADS

How far Turkish history can be traced back is unclear not only because the origins of Turks remain unclear but also because it is difficult to trace back their history. The original homeland of Turks is thought to have encompassed a significant portion of the Central and Eastern Eurasian Steppes, including the vicinity of the Altai and the Tien Shan mountain ranges, an area shared by the modern-day territories of Mongolia, Kazakhstan, Kyrgyzstan, Russian Siberia, and the Chinese province of Xinjiang. A narrower homeland of the proto-Turks has also been described as encompassing a still-vast area, starting in the north with Lake Baikal in southern Siberia, then stretching to the south into Inner Mongolia, and then westward to the Altai Mountains and eastward to the Khingan Mountains in Manchuria.[626] Research has suggested that the early proto-Turkish geography included a large domain covering much of Siberia and Central Asia. The evidence consists primarily of matching rock-carving symbols across this large territory, which gives information about the lifestyle, culture, and religious beliefs of the people who made those rock carvings.[627] In fact, stone carvings and figures across the Asian steppes from ancient times have been attributed to the earliest Turkish tribes.[628]

Today most of the information about early Turkish history comes from Chinese historical archives. In these ancient records, numerous Turkish tribes are mentioned as being present to the north of China. However, since Chinese chroniclers sinicized their names, we do not know their original Turkish appellations. Some examples are the tribes of the Jung, Di (Ti), Ting-ling, and Hien-yün (or Hün-yu). The earliest appearance of the Xiong-nu (also referred to as the Hsiung-nu) may have been with the tribal people known as the Hien-yün. According to a Chinese legend, emperor Huang-di of the Celestial Empire waged a successful battle against the Hün-yu in about 2600 BCE.[629] This suggests that the proto-Turks were already organized and formidable, worth being mentioned in an ancient Chinese legend. We also find the presence of additional Turkish tribes in these Chinese annals, including the Gienkun (Kyrgyz) and the Hugie (Uighurs). The names of these latter groups, present in these records as early as the third century BCE, are still used by Turks in Central Asia today. However, scholars believe that the ancient Uighurs have disappeared, and instead the Turkish people of today's Xinjiang Uighur Province in China are a mixture of Turkish groups who remained in the territory of their former kinsmen for centuries.

The Scythians, known as the first formidable nomadic force of Asia, initially resided in the modern-day northern Turkestan steppes. But by the seventh century BCE, they had pushed the Cimmerians westward to occupy the Pontic Steppe for themselves. Later the Sarmatians moving westward—perhaps because of pressures exerted by the Xiong-nu to their east—pushed the Scythians farther west as well. TSubsequently, the Sarmatians completely disappeared by the fourth century CE with the dominant presence of the European Huns coming from Asia into the steppes of eastern Europe. Most written Western information regarding the Scythians, also known as the Saka, comes from Greek recorders.

While many historians accept them as part of the early Iranian tribes,[630] others consider them the earliest known Turkish conquerors.[631] The only historical evidence that supports the claim that the Scythians were of Persian origin is a few presumed Iranian-origin Scythian words recorded by Greek and Roman writers. However, one can argue that even if this is so, borrowing from the language of a conquered people had been a normal practice, as

Turks did later when the Seljuks, Mughals, and Ottomans, who once spoke Turkish proper, were heavily influenced by the Arabic and Persian languages of the peoples they conquered. Nevertheless, these conquerors were neither Arabs nor Persians. Similarly, the Scythians were in frequent contact with the established Persian civilization in Iran, and thus, it would not have been surprising for them to have borrowed Iranian words.

It is also conceivable that the Scythians were an Iranian people but dissimilar to the Persians. Nevertheless, there are many documented cultural similarities between the Scythians and the early Turkish peoples of the Xiong-nu of Asia and the European Huns[632] rather than the Persians of Iran. In fact, they seem to have been so similar that one could argue the Xiong-nu were a continuation of the Scythians.[633] As Greek historian Herodotus pointed out, the Saka (Scythians) had customs of horse sacrifice, water taboo, and the making of drinking vessels or goblets from the skulls of slain enemies; all these traditional practices were later found among the early Turkish tribal peoples as well.[634] In fact, unlike that the Indo-Europeans in general, the life of the Scythians was centered around their horses, just like that of the early Turks. The Scythians were experienced mounted archers, just as the Turks and the Mongols were until the gunpowder age began. Furthermore, when the Scythians and the Xiong-nu were riding horses, the rest of the world was only driving them. The history of the early civilized world of China, India, Mesopotamia, and Egypt shows that the horse was used primarily to pull heavy war chariots.[635]

During the first half of the first millennium BCE, the people in the territories to the north of China joined in the rise of the culture of pastoral nomadism in the Central Eurasian Steppe.[636] In other words, the nomads extended their territories all the way to the northern borders of China. The growth of the pastoral economy in the steppes also came to be associated with the rise of militant warlike aristocracy. Furthermore, advanced metallurgy and the use of specialized technology by these nomads became vital in managing their horses.[637] The Scythians emerged as the first pastoral nomadic people moving to the West from Central Asia.

Although there is no language information left by the Scythians, and even though it has been determined that the nomadic Scythians were enemies of the sedentary Iranian people, they are still thought by many Western scholars to have been of Iranian origin. Though the Scythians may have been the proto-Turks, the first official recorded history of the Turks begins in the third century BCE with the establishment of the first-known nomadic empire in the Eastern Eurasian Steppe. This was also the first-known confederation of the nomadic tribes. This empire was formed by the Xiong-nu or the (Asian) Huns, as we will see later.

TURKISH TRIBES DURING THE HUNNISH EPOCH

The powerful tribes of the Hien-yün and the Jung, whom the Western Zhou (also referred to as Chou, 1045–770 BCE) fought, were considered in later Chinese historiography to be the progenitors of the Xiong-nu.[638] It has also been said that the Xiong-nu arose as a subtribal group from the Jung.[639] Hence, both the Hien-yün and the Jung are considered to have been among the proto-Turks. Described as being "white-skinned and red-haired (likely blond)," the Ting-ling were a large group of tribal people who lived north of the Xiong-nu, in the southern Siberian plains; they occupied a territory stretching from Lake Baikal to the Yenisei River from the third century BCE to the third century CE.[640] They were subdued by Mo-tun Shan-yu, the founder of the Great Hun (Xiong-nu) Empire, between the years 203 and 200 BCE.[641] The legendary shan-yu then went on to conquer the Ko-k'un (also known as the Chien-k'un, or Gienkun, for the Kyrgyz), the Hün-yu, and the Xianbei of the Tung-hu.

The Wu-sun was another ancient Turkish tribal confederacy that existed during the period of the Asian Huns (Xiong-nu); it seems to have appeared in the third century BCE, lasting to about the fourth century CE. Anthropological studies show that these people had both Europoid and Mongoloid features. Chinese described them as having "red beards (probably blond)" and "blue eyes," but they spoke the Turkish language.[642] At the height of their power, they had control of the area from the banks of Issyk Kül to the basin of the Ili River, a large region shared by the modern-day states of Kyrgyzstan, eastern Kazakhstan, and western Mongolia. The Wu-sun occupied the Western Territories long coveted by China for the security of the Silk Road. They were conquered by their kinsmen, the Asian Huns, with whom they apparently shared the same traditions.[643] The Wu-sun remained for generations in the Western Territories, an area more recently referred to as Zungaria (northern half of Xinjiang).[644]

At times in Xiong-nu history, the Wu-sun were seen as revolting against their suzerain, the Huns, with the help of other tribes, such as the Wu-huan and Xianbei. The ethnic origin of the Wu-huan tribes is not clear, but it appears that they had a close cultural affinity with the Huns but were not as powerful.[645] There have been academic suggestions that they were another group of Turks.[646] It has been suggested that the Wu-huan, who initially invaded Liao-tung in China and were later pushed back in 207 to Manchuria, were likely the later-appearing Oghuz Turks.[647] By the first century CE, they had changed their alliance frequently. Although they preferred to be under the Hun influence, they did not hesitate to switch their allegiance to Han Chinese when the Huns were weak or involved in one of their civil wars.

Similarly, the ethnic background of the Xianbei tribes (chapter 5.1) is not well known. Some scholars believe that they were of Mongol origin from the Tung-hu ("eastern barbarians") group of tribes from Manchuria. Others yet have considered other ethnicities, such as Turkish or Tungus origin. However, they were more likely to be tribes of mixed ethnicity when they appeared in the fourth century CE in the northern borders of China. During the presence of the Southern Huns, many of the Xianbei, just as the Wu-huan did, preferred to be aligned with the Huns (Xiong-nu) rather than Han Chinese.[648] On many occasions the Southern Huns suppressed Xianbei revolts on behalf of the Chinese emperor. The southern shan-yu had a strong influence on the Xianbei as he did over other non-Chinese people of the north.[649] The Xianbei did not appear to have been politically unified; though some of them aligned themselves under the leadership of the Southern Huns, others preferred to remain independent but not as sovereigns of the steppes.

The Ting-ling were one of the oldest Turkish tribal unions, lasting from the third century BCE well into the sixth century CE under the Gök-Türks. The Ko-k'un (also known as Chien-k'un or Gienkun) were defined as the Kyrgyz,[650] a name that has been present since the early Xiong-nu era. The lifestyle of the Ting-ling was quite similar to that of the Huns, as was their way of attacking with lightning speed on horseback.⁶⁵¹ Chinese annals identify the Ting-ling with the Kao-ch'e, who in turn were thought to be the same as the Turkish Töles tribes; consequently, it has been concluded that the Ting-ling were also Turks.⁶⁵² Their tribal name was also associated with other forms of the name, such as T'ieh-le and Kao-ch'e, meaning "high carts."⁶⁵³ In Turkish, this name would have corresponded to the ancient Turkish tribal union of Qanglï. Their spoken language was Turkish and similar to that of the Huns.⁶⁵⁴ As will be seen later, the remnants of the Ting-ling or the Qanglï became part of the Kimek Qaghanate of the ninth and tenth centuries in the Kazakh steppes (chapter 4.8).

It appears that early in the first century CE, the Ting-ling served in the imperial armies of Emperor Wang Mang; in the fourth century, they resided around Baoding, in eastern China, but toward the end of the fifth century CE, they were allies of the T'o-pa of Northern Wei against the Jou-jan, or Juan-juan.⁶⁵⁵ The latter formed the second known Asian nomadic empire in the steppes, sometimes referred to as the empire of the Asian Avars. Perhaps such an alliance happened because the ruling T'o-pa dynastic family (chapter 5.2) were Turks, just the Ting-ling were.⁶⁵⁶ By the fifth and sixth centuries, the Ting-ling were spread out across western Mongolia, Altai, and Zungaria.⁶⁵⁷ Some of their tribes were also stretched out into modern-day Kazakh steppes. The Ting-ling (Qanglï) never established political unity but rather always had a loose tribal confederacy somewhat like the Turkish Qïpčaks of the eleventh and twelfth centuries. On the basis of their location in the north, in the ninth century, they might have contributed to the formation of the Kimek tribal confederation, which included the Qïpčak, Cuman, and Qanglï tribal groups. This large confederation is sometimes referred to as the Kimek Qaghanate. Meanwhile, the Kao-ch'e (for "high carts," or Qanglï), the descendants of the Ting-ling, came to be known as the T'ieh-le tribal confederation, which began to expand during the period of the Northern Wei dynasty (386–534). It has been suggested that the Gök-Türks (T'ü-chüeh) and the Uighurs were descendants of the Kao-ch'e (Qanglï) or, in other words, of the Ting-ling.⁶⁵⁸ More data from Chinese records suggest that the Uighurs probably originated from the Kao-ch'e tribes.⁶⁵⁹ As presented later, the Uighur, Qïpčak, and Cuman Turks, among others, played significant roles in world history.

T'ieh-le as an ancient tribal union of the Turks was in fact a continuation of former Ting-ling tribal federation entity. Chinese records (Sui-shu) describe the large T'ieh-le territory as stretching from Mongolia in the east to Caucasus and the Black Sea in the west, but it was also noted that the Uighurs (Wei-ho) were among the T'ieh-le tribes north of the Tola River.[660] At the end of the sixth century, Chinese mentioned the Uighurs (as part of the Toquz-Oghuz) being among the larger T'ieh-le confederation of tribes.[661] In the seventh and eighth centuries, the leading tribe of the Uighurs, who themselves were present since the times of the Asian Huns (Xiong-nu), were from the Toquz-Oghuz confederacy.

The Khalaj Turks were another prominent but little-known group of nomadic people. They were noted to be part of the tribal federation of the Ephtalites, or the White Huns.[662] They probably detached from the T'ieh-le federation of tribes before moving westward. According to Muslim chroniclers, they were probably one of the earliest Turkish tribes that crossed the Oxus. They apparently settled in the area between northern India and Ghur of Afghanistan.[663] This explains their presence there when, centuries later, the Persian Saffarids encountered the Khalaj Turks while penetrating into Afghanistan in the ninth century. By the eleventh century, the Turkish dynasty of the Ghaznavids had begun to employ them in their armies (volume 2, chapter 1.3).

While discussing about ancient Turkish tribes it is also worthwhile to mention here about Turkish nomadic presence reaching the Korean peninsula. Puyē was once an ancient Korean state centered in Manchuria and extending into northern Korea. Eventually it gave rise to the old Korean kingdoms of Paekje (18 BCE–660 CE) and Koguryo (Kokuryē) (53–668 CE). The latter was an ancient Korean state that reigned over the northern part of the Korean Peninsula. On the basis of the name of the state and the title *kočurka* used for its princes, it has been suggested that the royal family borrowed the title from Turks, or they were once from an ancient Turkish tribe, or they once lived in a tribal confederation of Korean, Turkish, and other tribes. Koguryo apparently was formed from five tribal groups, and the leading tribe, even though it was a minority among the others, is suggested to have been of Turkish origin.[664]

Before moving on to the beginning of Turkish history, we need to understand early Chinese history, which was affected by the presence of early Turkish elements.

GETTING TO KNOW ANCIENT CHINA

China, with a history of more than five thousand years, is one of the oldest civilizations of the world. However, the land has not always been home to a homogeneous nation; early in its history, it was overrun by various foreign invaders who were eventually assimilated into the Chinese culture.[665] Some of these invaders became successors to the Chinese civilization, and others became its promoters.

The indigenous Chinese people are initially thought to have lived around the Yellow and Yangtze Rivers, an area known as *Zhongguo* (中國), the center of the Chinese world. This is what the Chinese call their country, rather than China, which is a foreign denotation for the land. But in the past, just as Turkish tribes or states were known by the names of their founders or totems, China was more commonly known by its dynasty names. During the epoch of the Xiong-nu in the Eastern Eurasian Steppe, China was known by the name Han (206 BCE–220 CE) and later by the names of T'ang (618–907), Yuan (1271–1368), Ming (1368–1644), and Qing (1644–1912). During the period of the Liao dynasty (907–1125), established by the Khitans, also known as the Khitai, China came to be known to the Persians, Russians, and Greeks as Cathay.

Before the Khitans took northern China in the tenth century, Turks called the land Tabgač.[666] That is because the Tabgač Turks (chapter 5.2) established the Northern Wei dynasty in China between the fifth and sixth centuries, and therefore, most of the Turks of eastern Eurasia from the seventh century and onward referred to China as Tabgač up until the era of the Qara-Khanid Turks, who also used the word Tabgač (or Tamgač) as a name or a title since they ruled from western China, thus making a claim to the rule of China as well. The eighth-century Orkhon inscriptions of the Gök-Türks used the word Tabgač for China. The present-day name China, by contrast, is derived from the Ch'in (also known as Ts'in or Qin) dynasty (221–206 BCE).[667] This short-lived dynasty was known to have unified China for the first time in recorded history. The Turks, who had long relationship with China in the past, now refer to China as Čin (pronounced "chin").

Earlier Chinese history may have begun with the legendary Xia period, followed by the Shang period (1600–1045 BCE), and then the Zhou period (1045–256 BCE). The latter two periods were marked by scattered city-states ruled by royal families from the Shang and Zhou dynasties. In fact, China did not become a unified nation until the Chinese imperial period (221 BCE–1912 CE), beginning with the Ch'in dynasty (Qin) in 221 BCE. The Zhou dynasty (also referred to as the Chou dynasty), known as the longest-lasting dynasty, was formed by the union of the non-Chinese Ji and Jiang clans.[668] According to Mencius, a well-known Chinese philosopher and historian of ancient times (372–289 BCE), King Wen of his time was a "western barbarian."[669]

The Chinese Zhou city-states competed with one another, but they also faced warlike peoples of the Ti (Di) and Jung (also referred to as the Rung), who existed as independent non-Zhou (foreign) polities until the end of the fifth century BCE, when they were largely absorbed into the northern states of the Eastern Zhou period. The fierce Ti (Di) and Jung were considered to be proto-Turks.[670] The Ti people in the north were known to the Chinese as a political and military force to be reckoned with. At the time of the Eastern Zhou, the Ti had a large tribal union divided into at least two major groupings, the Ch'ih (Red) Ti and the Pai (White) Ti.[671] The presence of the Jung and Ti has been described by Chinese historians as the "first barbarian invasions" of China. In reality, however, these so-called barbarian invasions by the Jung and Ti in the Zhou (Chou) period were the result of the expansion of Chinese territory into nomadic lands.[672]

In the year 770 BCE, which also marked the beginning of the Spring and Autumn period of China, the Western Zhou collapsed under the attacks of the Jung.[673] The Spring and Autumn period (770–476 BCE) roughly corresponds to the first half of the Eastern Zhou dynasty (770–256 BCE), which immediately followed the Western Zhou period. During this new period, there was a major political shift between Zhou and non-Zhou northern (non-Chinese) peoples. Previously, during the Shang period (1600–1045 BCE) and the Western Zhou period (1045–770 BCE), there were frequent wars between the Chinese south and the non-Chinese north. In 562 BCE the Chinese signed a major treaty with the Ti and Jung; as a result, the only remaining adversary along China's northern borders was the Hien-yün (also from the Ti people and known as the progenitors of the future Xiong-nu), the founders of the state of Chung-shan.[674] This was possibly the first Turkish state in history. In 406 BCE Chung-shan was conquered by the Chinese Wei state, yet it regained its independence in 377 BCE only to fall later to the Chao state in 295 BCE. Nevertheless, the history of the Ti did not end there (chapter 5.1).

Essentially, during the Eastern Zhou period (770–256 BCE), most of the northern adversaries, the Ti and the Jung, were incorporated into the Zhou states. This was achieved particularly by the expansionist Zhou states of Ch'i, Ch'in, and Chin. Under (Eastern) Zhou policies, initially the Jung were brought under the control of the states, a necessary condition for the state's further expansion, yet these people remained difficult to control and were even hostile.[675] But the Jung eventually became an integral part of Zhou politics and also formed the military and farming forces of the states.[676] Later, most of the Ti were absorbed into Zhou polities as well. Subsequently, the foreign northern fighters, just like their descendants, the mamluk (Arabic for "slave") fighters of the Near East of the ninth to thirteenth centuries CE, were enlisted in the armies of the Zhou states to guard borders and to conquer new lands to support the states' competition for supremacy.[677] While during the Spring and Autumn period the stronger Zhou states swallowed non-Zhou communities and weaker Zhou states, during the subsequent Warring States period (480–221 BCE), the competition became tougher as the remaining powerful states were under pressure to improve their defensive and offensive capabilities against one another.[678] The monarchs of this period were constantly forced to remain a step ahead of their neighbors by maximizing their resources while trying to neutralize their adversaries' advantages.

THE RISE OF IMPERIAL CHINA AND THE HU

At the beginning of the Warring States period (480–221 BCE), the Zhou states included the Ch'in, Jin, Ch'u, Yen, and Ch'i. But the fall of the Jin in about 453 BCE gave rise to the states of Chao (also known as Zhao), Wei, and

Han. Beyond the captured northern territories of the Ti and Jung, the Zhou states were about to meet a new foe. While the central states could no longer expand, the northern states had a chance to expand into the steppes, where there were martial societies of aristocratic mounted nomads who excelled in archery on horseback. The Chinese referred to these people as the *Hu*, and the Chao state established the first contact with them, in 457 BCE. After the Eastern Zhou period and during the subsequent Han dynasty, the Hu became synonymous with the Xiong-nu.[679] As we will see in the next section, the Xiong-nu were Turks who formed the first-known nomadic empire.

It has been argued that the northern Hu people (later known as the Xiong-nu) were the descendants of the Hien-yün and the previously conquered Jung and Ti peoples, who were forced from a sedentary lifestyle to a nomadic one in the face of Zhou expansionism.[680] As these people turned to a pastoralist nomadic life, they also carried their knowledge of sedentary culture with them, hence making them more sophisticated and powerful than the other nomadic people, the Mongols and Tungus of Manchuria, later collectively known as the *Tung-hu*.

The reader should understand that the terms Mongolia and *the Mongolian steppes* are used only as geographic descriptives. They are actually misnomers; the Mongolians were part of the eastern tribes, thus known by the Chinese name "eastern barbarians" (Tung-hu). In fact, the territories mentioned were part of the Turkish homeland. It was not until Mongolia lost most of its Turkish population in early second millennium CE because of the westward 'great Turkish migrations' (chapter 4); hence, the land eventually became Mongolian in the thirteenth century CE, under the leadership of Genghis Khan.

In contrast to the Ti and the Jung of the seventh and sixth centuries BCE, the northern Hu (Xiong-nu) nomads were peaceful, at least between 450 and 330 BCE. The first mention of the Xiong-nu in Chinese records appears from the late fourth century BCE. According to Ssu-ma Ch'ien, in 318 BCE Xiong-nu mounted archers became part of the joint force of the states of Han, Chao, Wei, Yen, and Ch'i against the Ch'in.[681] This was also the first time that the Chinese began to pay attention to the cavalry, though Chinese contingencies were small. Being in contact with the northern mounted archers, in 307 BCE the state of Chao was, presumably, the first Chinese polity to adopt the concept of the cavalry, along with Hu clothing suitable for riding horses.[682] But the state was soon conquered by the Ch'in state, which continued its policy of taking on the Warring States one by one. Finally, the powerful Ch'in state became the champion and established the first unification of China under the short-lived Ch'in dynasty (221–206 BCE). By unifying the separate nation-states, Ch'in monarch Shih-huang-ti also became the first emperor of China.[683]

By this time, the Hu nomads in the north were known as the Xiong-nu. It was the Ch'in military expedition into the Ordos region in the geographic area of Inner Mongolia, located in modern-day northern China, that forced the Xiong-nu to transform into a formidable power. Though the Ch'in action presumably was intended to keep the nomadic mounted archers out of raiding range, the Chinese incursion into Xiong-nu territory led to the formation of a powerful nomadic steppe empire bordering northern China. While the former Northern Zhou states had found it easier to repulse these scattered nomads from their borders, the Xiong-nu as a unified state forced unified China into successive humiliating peace treaties up until the Common Era.[684]

With the beginning of the Chinese imperial period by the Ch'in dynasty in 221 BCE, China pursued a foreign policy to diminish and thwart the threat of the warlike peoples of Central and northern Asia.[685] To achieve this goal, the Chinese often used diplomacy, but when the nomadic warriors were weak, war also became a means to achieve these aims. Fed up with the humiliating posturing against the Xiong-nu (Asian Huns), Han emperor Wudi (141–87 BCE) took an aggressive approach against these fearsome mounted archers. T'ang emperor T'ai-tsung (also known as Taizong, 626–49 CE), taking advantage of the weakness of the T'u-Chüeh (Gök-Türks), marched into the territories of these previously powerful warriors to turn them into vassals of China. In the case of the Uighurs, the T'ang Chinese benefited from the power of these Turkish horsemen to crush the An Lushan Rebellion, which threatened the very existence of the T'ang dynasty.

Throughout the ages, even though China saw numerous invasions by northern tribes, and even though the land at times was ruled by a number of foreign monarchies, Chinese protected their national and cultural identity. Historical records indicate that the well-known Chinese dynasties of the Sui (581–618) and the T'ang (618–907) had non-Chinese origins in their makeup (chapter 5.2). During more than two millennia of imperial China, five major non-Chinese dynasties ruled part of or all the land for a total of more than seven centuries. These were all Altaic dynasties. In order of occurrence, they were the T'o-pa Wei (Tabgač Turks, 386–534), the Liao (Turco-Mongol Khitans, 907–1125), the Chin (Jürchen Tungus, 1115–1234), the Yuan (Mongols, 1271–1368), and the Qing (Manchu Tungus, 1644–1912) dynasties.[686] Furthermore, the Sha-t'o Turks formed three ephemeral imperial dynasties known as the Later T'ang (923–36), the Later Chin (936–46), and the Later Han (947–50).[687] The Xiong-nu tribes, descendants of the Southern Huns in China, formed the Zhou dynasty (557–81) in northern China in the fourth century. In addition there were smaller and short-lived non-Chinese kingdoms of China before and after the T'o-pa Wei dynasty. The emergence of this Turkish (T'o-pa) imperial dynasty marked the end of the Sixteen Kingdom period (304–439) of China. During this time the multiple non-Chinese kingdoms scattered in northern China were gradually absorbed by the T'o-pa Wei, who succeeded in unifying northern China. With this accomplishment, these Turks opened a new chapter in Chinese history known as the period of the Northern and Southern dynasties (420–589).

THE GREAT WALL

As it did during the Xiong-nu, Gök-Türk, and Uighur periods, beginning with the Northern Zhou states, China acquired horses and fur by trading with the northern pastoralist nomads.[688] Toward the end of the Warring States period (480–221 BCE), the increased commercialization of the northern frontier, Chinese interest in the northern plains, and the Chinese need for horses led to increased tensions in the area. With these changes, the Chinese states introduced extensive fortifications as a new type of defensive system.[689] The city-states built walls around themselves against one another and against the northern "barbarians." Long walls were built to mark state boundaries; an example is the walls of the Ch'i state. The earliest known walls were not the northern walls but rather those built by the states of Wei and Ch'u.[690] When it was built, the Ch'in wall (the early Great Wall) was nearly 1,775 kilometers

(1,103 miles) in length, consisting of several separate walls. The Great Wall of China was eventually born out of the earlier system of walled frontiers of the city-states from the Warring States period.[691] During the leadership of the Ch'in dynasty of unified China, there was no longer a need for walls between the nonexistent city-states; instead, the emperor, by connecting the northern walls, took the first step in creating the Great Wall to defend against the Xiong-nu (Hun) tribes in the north.

Today, this wall, which was built to halt Xiong-nu incursions into China, is nearly nonexistent. The ancient construction with a combination of stone, mud, and clay could not withstand the power of time and the elements of Mother Nature. Remnants of the original wall can be seen today in Zhangbei County in Hebei Province and in Guyuan County in Inner Mongolia. The present-day Great Wall of China was rebuilt starting with the native Ming dynasty after the Chinese pushed the Mongol Yuan dynasty out of China in the fifteenth century.

HAN CHINA AND THE BARBARIANS

Even though the Ch'in (Qin) dynasty had a short life, it left multiple legacies behind. These include the establishment of the first-known imperial class, the first unification of China, and the formation of the defensive northern walls (known today as the Great Wall of China) against the incursions of Xiong-nu (Huns) from the north. But it was the subsequent Han dynasty, which defended China against the powerful Xiong-nu Turks, that instilled a sense of lasting unity among the Chinese. Even though in modern times this Far Eastern country came to be known to foreigners as China after the name of its first imperial dynasty, the Ch'in, it was the subsequent Han dynasty that left its cultural footprint on modern Chinese identity. In fact, in modern times the ethnic Chinese people of China are referred to as the Han Chinese.

With more than four centuries of rule, the Han indeed left a lasting legacy in Chinese history. For the ruling class of this dynasty, non-Chinese or non-Han people were often judged by their social behavior. Those who had accepted the Han lifestyle were referred to as "cooked" (*shu*), in contrast to rejecters of the culture, who were "raw" (*sheng*).[692] In the case of the Huns, the Han Chinese were not able to force them to accept their sedentary lifestyle. Instead, the Han continuously faced the danger of Hun incursions into northern Chinese towns, and in most instances, they were not able to stop them.

When the Han Chinese faced military danger from outsiders and were not able to defeat them, they used various tactics to fend off their attackers; these included offering honors and materials or using one "barbarian" group against another. If all else failed, the tactic of sinicization was used to capture the invaders' attention with the rich culture and lifestyle of China.[693] This principle was based on a Confucian teaching: "If remote people are not submissive, all of the influences of civil culture and virtue are to be cultivated to attract them to be so."[694] Hence, the tactic of cultural assimilation was often successful against outside invaders, allowing China to keep its cultural identity alive despite multiple invasions.

The Han Chinese were a quite heterogeneous people as they included elements from the Xiong-nu, the Xianbei, and later from others, and they proved to be a dominant people by demonstrating a remarkable ability to constantly absorb other cultures into their own.[695] Their dominance came from their proud and strong heritage; Chinese perceived their culture to be superior to those of other nations, primarily because their land was thought to be the center of the world, since it was also supposed to be closest to the heaven; consequently, the Chinese empire was known as the Celestial Empire (Tianguo), and their emperor was referred to as the "son of heaven" (*tianzi*).[696] By contrast, the nonsinicized states outside China, whether in the Inner Asian zone (such as the nomadic states) or the outer zone (such as Europe and the Middle East), were often referred to as *yi*, *fan*, and *man*, all indicating "barbarians."[697] In other words, Chinese considered every other race besides themselves as barbarians, including Europeans who engaged in trade in Southeast Asia during the eighteenth and nineteenth centuries.[698] The Huns (Xiong-nu) too were considered barbarians, as recorded by Chinese chronicler Sima Qian (also referred as Ssu-ma Ch'ien) of the second century BCE.[699] But nearly a century later, another Chinese scholar documented that the Huns were more civilized than his predecessors thought, as they showed the capability of understanding the works of Confucius and were also able to defend Chinese values and way of life.[700]

Han China was not able to expand its territories to the north due to the powerful nomadic polity of the Xiong-nu; instead, it managed to extend its land into the south and southeast. In fact, most Chinese dynasties were not able to push their borders into the north beyond Inner Mongolia, with the exception of the Yuan (1271–1368) and the Qing (1644–1912) dynasties, which were both non-Chinese dynasties with northern roots. In dealing with the Huns, the Han court often preferred the bribery method to the military one. The Han chose to give the Hun leader a "fixed amount of annual imperial gifts" along with a "Han princess" in exchange for the Hun pledge of nonaggression.[701] From the Chinese point of view, this was bribery, but from the Hun point of view, it was a tribute. Between the Han period and the T'ang period of China, from the Chinese point of view, the Chinese princesses were given to the Turkish rulers or dynasties for various reasons, including as rewards for assistance, as bribery to foreign monarchs, or to create animosity within the foreign dynasty or regime, but ultimately to keep the peace.[702] While in the foreign dynastic house, the Chinese brides tried to protect the interests of their native country while maintaining pro-China relations. These princesses became Chinese diplomats, arbitrators, and even informants.[703] After the T'ang dynasty, the Chinese Song (960–1279) abandoned the marriage-alliance policy established by prior dynasties.[704] But neither the Song nor subsequent dynasties had to deal with the mounted archers of Turks, since most of the Turkish tribes had already left the Eastern Eurasian Steppe by the end of the tenth century.

THE WESTERN WORLD FROM THE THIRD BCE TO THE FIFTH CENTURY CE

In the third century BCE, when Turkish history was about to officially begin in the Far East, in the West a Macedonian king and commander threatened the East by marching from ancient Greece into western Central Asia. Alexander the Great of Macedonia (336–323 BCE) formed a great empire that was destined to break apart just as quickly as Genghis Khan's Great Mongol Empire disintegrated shortly after its formation more than a millennium later. As the Xiong-nu (Asian Huns) were confronting the Han dynasty of China in the East, Alexander's heirs in western Central Asia formed the Greco-Bactrian Kingdom (256–125 BCE) and the Seleucid Empire (312–63 BCE), both of which extended the Hellenistic influence in this region until the Persian Parthian Empire (247 BCE–224 CE) took control of this area. The Yueh-chih, who were chased away by the Asian Huns from modern-day western Mongolia, moved into western Central Asia, where they formed the Kushan Empire in place of the former Greco-Bactrian state, but by the third century CE, they were conquered by the Persian Sassanid Empire. Meanwhile, the western territories of Alexander's empire were eventually absorbed into the Roman Empire (27 BCE–476 CE), which emerged from its predecessor, the Roman Republic (509–27 BCE). These Western empires and states were the contemporaries of the Xiong-nu Turks of the East.

Until the sixth century, the political landscape of the West continued to change. With the splitting of the once-mighty Roman Empire and the eventual fall of the Western Roman Empire, Germanic kingdoms began to dominate much of western and central Europe, while in Asia, after the fall of the Hun (Xiong-nu) Empire, the Tabgač Turks ruled over northern China, and the Avars managed Central Asia until the Gök-Türks came to power in the mid-sixth century.

3.2. THE XIONG-NU

Turkish history officially begins with the establishment of the Great Hun Empire in 209 BCE. In the archives of China, the founders of the empire were known as the Xiong-nu (also referred to as the Hsiung-nu).[705] On the basis of mostly older information, some scholars believe that the Xiong-nu were not Turkish. For example, some suggested that they were related to the Chinese, others claimed that these nomads were from the Yenisei group of the southern Siberian tribes, and yet others supported the idea that the Xiong-nu were of Iranian stock. In addition, some Chinese scholars supported the idea that the Xiong-nu were proto-Mongols. Naturally, there are also Mongol historians who believe that the Xiong-nu were proto-Mongols. However, with the unearthing of more information, there has been more scholarly support for the idea that the Xiong-nu were among the early Turkish tribes. The eighteenth-century French historian Deguignes and later prominent modern scholars such as Hirth, de Groot, Shiratori, and Pritsak maintained that the Xiong-nu were Turks.[706] Many Chinese scholars accepted that the Xiong-nu were the ancestors of the later Turks and Mongols.[707] Yet, the Xiong-nu spoke a dialect of the Turkish (Turkic) language.[708] Since the Xiong-nu (also known as the Asian Huns) did not leave written records, today we find most of our information about them from Chinese, with whom they came into contact. We learn from the Chinese archives that the modern-day Turks are descendants of the Xiong-nu.[709]

The Xiong-nu Empire was a confederation of tribes, which may have incorporated some Mongol elements into their union in addition to mostly Turkish tribes. According to Chinese Han dynasty records, the word Xiong-nu was used to denote a specific tribal group of a specific ethnic origin, language, and culture, but it referred to a political entity formed under the dominance of that particular tribe as well.[710] The political confederation of the Xiong-nu had a significant Turkish component.[711] Indeed, the governing political tribe was the Turkish Huns, after whom the empire was thus named.[712] According to Chinese chronicles, the language of the Gök-Türks was similar to that of the Xiong-nu (Asian Huns), but these archives also suggest that their (contemporary) speech was a little different from that of the Huns.[713] After much research and debate, it has been concluded that the Asian Huns were ethnic Turks and spoke the Turkish language.[714] Chinese also recorded that these Huns were related to the later-appearing Uighur Turks.[715] In fact, according to Chinese annals, the Kao-ch'e tribes noted in northeastern Turkestan territories were descendants of the Huns and were thought to be the ancestors of the Uighurs.[716] However, in all likelihood, the early Uighurs were under the rule of Oghur Turkish–speaking Huns. Overall, the Chinese archives conclude that the nomadic Hun tribes were of ethnically Turkish origin.[717]

Were the Asiatic Xiong-nu – who had a political presence in the Far East from the third century BCE to the third century CE – the ancestral tribal people of those who threatened Europe in the fifth century as the Huns of Europe? The answer to this question lies in a fourth-century Sogdian letter (known to be written after the year 311), which refers to the Xiong-nu as the Hun, or *Xwn* in Sogdian, thus showing the connection between the name Hun and the Xiong-nu.[718] The Xiong-nu origins of the European Huns will be discussed later (chapter 3.5). Furthermore, the history of the Xiong-nu demonstrates how their descendants migrated into Europe. Hence, from this point on, we will refer to the Xiong-nu as the Huns, or more specifically, the Asian Huns.

WHO WERE THE XIONG-NU?

Today we know that the Asian Huns (Xiong-nu) were identical to the later-appearing European Huns and spoke Turkish.[719] It is thought that at least during the Eastern Zhou period (770–256 BCE) of China, the Asian Huns were scattered in the steppes and forests between the Khingan Mountains in the east (Manchuria, China) to the Sayan Mountains in the west (northwestern Mongolia), including central and northern modern-day Mongolia in addition to the large area around Lake Baikal (southern Siberia, Russia).[720] The Hun territories also included the grazing grounds of the steppes of Inner Mongolia, just north of the future (first) Great Wall of China, which was intended to halt the incursions of these nomadic warriors. Eventually these Huns formed the first known historical tribal union of Turks over this large geographic area just north of ancient China. With their expanding power, they displaced the Scyto-Siberian cultures, and they managed to establish the presence of the Hunnish art, millet agriculture, and iron technology in the vast eastern Eurasian steppes.[721]

Within the Asian Hun Empire Huns had twenty-four tribal entities,[722] which were known as *boy*. Each boy included multiple tent villages, known as *oba*. When the Huns formed their nomadic statehood in modern-day Mongolia, not even the Mongols lived in the same territory. In fact, they were known to be part of the "eastern barbarians" (referred to as Tung-hu in Chinese) along with the Manchu Tungus people, living in the eastern Siberian forests and Manchuria.[723] Among these so-called barbarians, the Manchu lived to the east of the Huns, and the Mongols lived to the far northwest of them. Chinese records also indicate that there were significant intermarriages, or interbreeding, between the Huns and the northern Chinese peoples.[724] Besides the tribes within Hun dominions, the tribes to the north of the Huns were Turkish as well.[725] In addition to the Ting-ling, the Yenisei Kyrgyz and the Yakut Turks were likely among these tribes in the north.

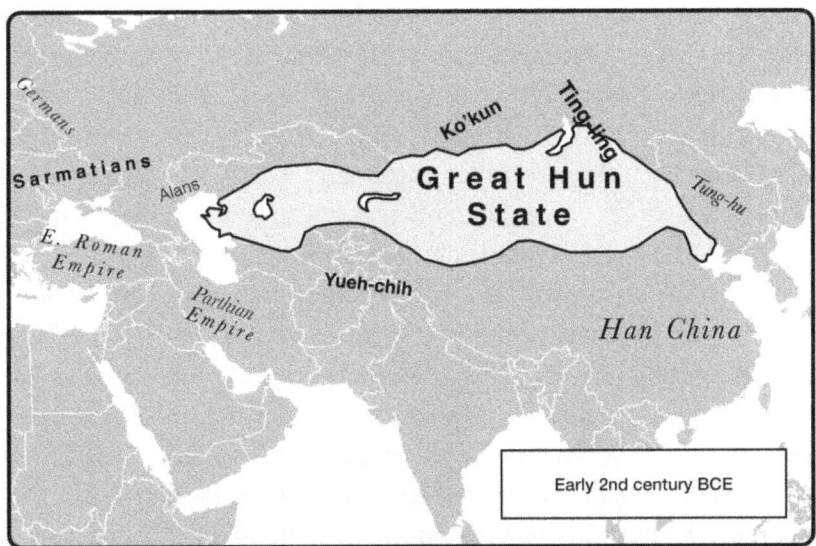

Map 5. The Great Xiong-nu, also known as the Asian Huns, were able to form the first known Turkish tribal confederation. Based on a letter sent by Mo-tun, the founder of the steppe empire, it has ben suggested that the western boundaries of the state reached the Caspian Sea.

The earliest presence of the Hun tribes, even prior to the establishment of their empire, appears to date back to the third century BCE, according to the annals of the Ch'in dynasty.[726] Prior to the appearance of the Asian Huns, their ancestors were known in the eighth and ninth centuries BCE as the Hien-yün (or Hsien-yün) in the Chinese records.[727] Furthermore, the same records show that the Rung (Jung) and the Di (or Ti) tribes were early Turkish tribal entities that were engaged in war with China in 714 BCE and 541 BCE respectively.[728] By contrast, the earliest mention of the Huns, according to some of the Chinese annals, dates back to the second millennium BCE.[729]

Today we have come to the conclusion that the earliest recorded confederation of tribes in Inner Asia was that of the (Asian) Huns, which formed the earliest powerful Turkish empire, known as the Great Hun Empire (209 BCE–216 CE). This pastoral state was a true confederation made up mostly of Turkish tribes but also including, to a lesser extent, tribes of the

Mongols and the Tungus. When the Huns showed up at the northern doorstep of China, they were called barbarians by the Chinese. Often, Chinese referred to these people of non-Chinese origin in the north as the Hu. Practically, these (northern) Hu were the Huns. Early Chinese civilization learned to build cavalries from these so-called barbarians.[730] After the disappearance of the Huns, the term Hu was used for other non-Chinese to the north of China.

The Asian Huns were the ancestors of the later-appearing European Huns.[731] We know that the "barbarian" label was attributed to the European Huns by the Romans as well. In addition, the Romans called Attila the Hun the "scourge of God." According to Roman historian Eunapius, the Huns came to Europe because "God sent them forth as a punishment for the sins of the world."[732] It was clear that those who recorded the history of the European Huns were biased against them. They described these conquerors in the most despicable ways. They were often described as "sub-human monsters."[733] Attila had such a reputation that it lingered for centuries; the later-appearing Turkish nomadic mounted archers, along with the non-Turkish Magyar tribes, took ownership of this reputation and regarded themselves as the heirs of Attila and his Huns.[734]

For the Central Asian nomads, just as collective action was crucial for the survival and prosperity of their tribe, war was considered a precondition for survival. Therefore, for their males, military service was a way of life. As a result, military training for the nomads began early in life.[735] Ssu-ma Ch'ien, a Chinese chronicler from around 200 BCE, wrote that military training among the Xiong-nu began in early childhood. He noted that young boys rode sheep, learning to shoot birds and rats with their bows and arrows, and as they got older, they shot foxes and hares for food. By the time they were young men, they were all able to become active members of the cavalry during wartime.[736] Highly skilled mounted archers were the hallmark of the Hun army. In the Chinese annals, the Huns were said to cloud the skies with their arrows more than rain or hail, and nearly a millennium later, the crusaders described the Seljuk Turks as being able to do the same by shooting arrows at a high rate.[737] But just as they could keep their enemies at a distance with their far-reaching arrows, they were also masterful with their close-combat talents. In describing the Huns, Ssu-ma Ch'ien mentioned that their military skills were part of their inborn nature.[738]

THE TRIBAL ECONOMY

On the basis of witness accounts by Chinese, the main occupation of the Huns was warfare.[739] Indeed, it seems the economic relations between the Huns and the Chinese were based on the military actions between the two; in many instances, trade talks were initiated after the end of successful Hunnish incursions into Chinese territories. The Chinese records claim that each time the Huns launched an attack, it was to secure a new treaty with the Han to increase the amounts and types of subsidies and to force the Han to open border markets. Negotiations with the Han included the means to reward the Hun noblemen, benefiting the shan-yu and creating peaceful trading opportunities for Hun tribesmen at the border markets.[740] However, the Asian Hun economy was not dependent solely on their *ho-ch'in* treaties with China. It also benefited from the sedentary communities that the Huns controlled. Large nomadic steppe empires such as that of the Asian Huns had numerous sedentary communities under their political control in a large geographic area stretching from the Tarim basin to northern China and to Manchuria. The Asian Huns maintained diplomatic as well as political and economic relations with the sedentary communities in addition to the nomadic entities situated in modern-day Xinjiang territory.

By the first half of the second century BCE, the Asian Huns had become a major military power in the Far East, with large territories stretching from Manchuria in the east to the Western Territories (modern-day Xinjiang) in the west and to Lake Baikal in the north.[741] However, according to Chinese, most of the Huns, after all, were nomads, living on horseback and in tents. Their needs were different from those of sedentary peoples. Chinese did not think highly of them or of the subsequent nomadic powers, including the Mongols. Early Chinese historians from the Han dynasty described them as savage plunderers. The name Xiong-nu, a sinicized version of the tribal name, has been defined in multiple ways. The word *xiong* in Chinese possibly meant "wild" or "mad," whereas *nu* indicated "slaves"; hence, Xiong-nu meant "mad slaves," since Chinese viewed them as their subjects even though in reality they were a free-spirited people who could not be enslaved. Another explanation of the term is "howling slaves."[742] One other interpretation is "fierce slaves."[743]

According to Chinese, the nomads needed goods such as grain and textiles from the sedentary Chinese, but when they were not able to acquire them through peaceful trade, they were forced to raid and loot northern Chinese towns.[744] The Huns understood the importance of including sedentary peoples within their political borders to ensure their supply of necessities. As a result, in addition to having the nomadic territories of southern Siberia and northern Mongolia, they conquered sedentary communities and states from the oases of the Tarim basin to northern China (Inner Mongolia) to Manchuria.[745] Excavations at an Inner Mongolia site revealed a Jung/proto-Hun graveyard dating back to the late Spring and Autumn period (770–480 BCE) and the early Warring States period (480–222 BCE) of China; the finds included not only typical Jung/proto-Hunnish artifacts such as arrowheads but also farming tools. These findings suggest the Jung/proto-Huns had knowledge of agriculture and a sedentary lifestyle.[746] The Hunnish tombs found in Noin-Ula, Mongolia, contained many Chinese products, such as silk, lacquer, and mirrors. Archaeological discoveries south of Ulan Ude, in southern Siberia, showed that some of the Huns (Xiong-nu) had sedentary lifestyle with agricultural and engineering achievements.[747] Hence, the sedentary experience was not limited to the territories near China but was also seen in areas far from Chinese influence.

Ancient Turks were known mostly to be nomads, but there is evidence that they had knowledge of commerce and agriculture, just like the sedentary peoples they encountered.[748] Rome and China became large commerce centers, which led to the development of caravan trafficking between the East and the West through a series of pathways collectively known as the Silk Road. These roads of commerce and cultural exchange passed through the domains of nomadic people. Hence, the Huns were the first Turks benefiting from the lucrative Silk Road trading routes.

China used silver coins for currency, and Rome used both silver and gold coins. Turks became involved in trade by means of either barter (Turkish horses for Chinese silk and tea) or coins. The oldest known Turkish coins were found in western Turkestan, belonging to the periods of both the Western Gök-Türks and the Türgeš.[749] This region used to be a major hub for the main arteries of the Silk Road, stretching between China in the Far East,

India in the south, the Middle East in the west, and eastern Europe in the north. The trading experience of the ancient Turks in Asia dates back to the time of their ancestors, the Huns, who initiated the commercial link between the Turks and the Chinese. The Huns traded their surplus in livestock for Chinese merchandise, particularly silk luxury items, and their descendants, the Gök-Türks, later did the same. More specifically, Turkish cattle and jade were generally traded for Chinese silk fabrics, tea, and grain, but for military purposes, Chinese state also purchased Turkish horses.[750]

XIONG-NU SOCIETY

Since the Huns (Xiong-nu) did not leave written records behind, most of the information about them has been passed down to us through the records of Chinese historians and chroniclers. Certainly, bias is prevalent throughout these archives. The Huns are painted as barbarians having no knowledge of a sedentary lifestyle. But as mentioned above, new archaeological data indicate that the Huns had knowledge of a sedentary lifestyle and had a highly organized society. According to the records, even though Chinese were astonished by the Huns' lack of permanent dwellings, they were also impressed by the Huns' military prowess and by the rough equality of the sexes in their society.[751] On the other hand, Chinese had a male-dominated society. Furthermore, in contrast to the status-conscious Chinese, the Huns had an egalitarian society where there was little differentiation between commoners and aristocracy[752] owing to mutual respect from both sides. Nevertheless, the common tribesmen still demonstrated high regard for their leaders, who benefited their tribes. Despite their warlike character, another Hunnish virtue was that they did not force conquered peoples to abandon their own cultures.[753] This indicated that the Asian Huns, despite being known as warlike people, showed tolerance for the traditions of their vassal subjects of various backgrounds. This was also true for their descendants, as can be seen during the reigns of the Seljuks, Mughals, Ottomans, and so on.

For the Huns, their most important animal was the horse. After all, not only was the horse used by the nomads for its mobility, facilitating animal herding during peacetime, but during wartime, it was also used as a war machine. Therefore, it was unthinkable for a Hun to be without a horse. In fact, the Huns were known to have an immense source of horses. While large herds of horses roamed free miles away from nomadic encampments under the supervision of few herders, the necessary number of horses for immediate need was kept by the tents with hobbles, allowing them sufficient freedom for grazing and water. The use of hobbles was a common technique among the nomads of Central Asia. Their general purpose was to prevent the horses from wandering off; in other words, hobbles were essentially devices for controlling domestic animals.[754]

The supreme leader of the Asian Huns was the shan-yu (referred to as *tanhu* in Turkish), the equivalent of an emperor. The power of shan-yu was limited internally by tribal leaders of the confederacy. His court included leaders from the Hunnish core tribes (*boy*) loyal to him. Shan-yu acted as the intermediary between the Han emperor of China and the tribes of the nomadic empire. He was a war leader for the nation and a negotiator to obtain goods and trade benefits from China.[755] Chinese thought they could corrupt shan-yu and weaken his authority by giving gifts and tribute, misreading shan-yu's frequent demands for Chinese goods as greed, when in fact he was asking them to keep his subordinate noblemen rewarded.[756]

According to Chinese records, Hun nobles met three times a year to "discuss national affairs, take a census of the Hun population, decide legal cases, and perform sacrifices to Heaven, earth, and the ancestors"; these ancient Hunnish rites were ultimately concluded with traditional games and displays of horsemanship.[757] The Hun Empire was autocratic and state-like in its foreign affairs but consultative and federally structured in its domestic affairs.[758]

Within the Hun Empire and most of the later Turkish states of the steppes, leadership did not necessarily pass from father to son; many times power instead was transferred to a more able leader within the royal family.[759] When a man died, his widows were then married to his surviving son, except for the mother of the son, but if there was no heir, then the deceased's brother would marry the widows. The practice was followed to protect husbandless women.[760]

XIONG-NU HORDES

According to Chinese records, the Huns (Xiong-nu) were also referred to as the Ten Horns (or Ten Hordes), and the Western Gök-Türks were known in both the Chinese records and the Orkhon inscriptions as the Ten Arrows.[761] The Hunnish word for "horn" is believed to indicate a unit of organization, division, or horde. The Turkish tribes that had the word *ughur* (*oghur*) in their names, such as the On-Oghur (ten horns or ten hordes), continued to carry on the tradition of using the "ten hordes" name even after the Huns ceased to exist.[762] The Bulgar Turks, for example, are thought to have had five hordes, and therefore, it has been postulated that they were once part of a larger tribal federation of ten hordes. In fact, this is true, since they were once part of the On-Oghur tribal union.

Since the Asian Huns were referred to as the Ten Hordes, it is possible that the Northern Huns who began to move westward toward the Kazakh Steppe in the northwest were the On-Oghurs who arrived in Europe, even though they had split earlier from their southern cousins. Nevertheless, if the Huns were composed of ten hordes, it is conceivable that the Northern Huns who migrated westward had five hordes with them, since the Southern Huns who remained in northern China also had five hordes.

The first group that broke off from the migrating Northern Huns may have been the first Turkish raiders of Europe, known as the European Huns, whereas the Bulgars, the remaining On-Oghurs, followed these Huns into Europe later. Linguistically, as mentioned in chapter 1.1, both the Huns (Xiong-nu) and the Bulgars spoke the Oghur dialect of the Turkish language, an ancient form of this Altaic language. The modern-day Chuvash language is said to be a direct descendant of ancient Bulgar Turkish, which was a version of European Hunnish, deriving from the Xiong-nu language in Asia.[763] Other ancient tribes whose names ended with *ughur* were the Kutrighur, Utrighur, Uighur, and even possibly Bašgur (possibly the Baškurt of today, also known as the Baškïr). Perhaps the word Avar was distorted from its original stem word *ugur*. It has been suggested that the name Oghuz (*oyuz*) of one of the largest known Turkish tribal confederations may have been derived from *ughur* (*oghur*), meaning "horde." Hence, the tribal confederation of Toquz-Oghuz would have meant Nine Hordes, in which the Uighur tribes were the primary power holders.[764]

XIONG-NU CULTURE

Throughout history, nomadic cultures have been considered lowly by sedentary societies. The Huns were not immune to such stereotyping by the Chinese. Modern research on Han Chinese archives suggests that the Huns were viewed as inferior to the Han and as "rebellious subjects" of the emperor despite their independent political and military power.[765] Indeed, Chinese elite's initial view of the Huns was negative; they thought that Huns were barbarians. But over time this view began to change with the later acceptance of Huns. For example, Yang Xiong, a Chinese scholar (53 BCE–18 CE), wrote that Huns were capable of studying the works of Confucius and that they could become more Chinese than the Chinese could.[766] However, others did not accept this view, because to be accepted into the civilized world, one had to be sinicized.

The Hun culture appears to have been similar to the culture of Scythian nomads of western Asia, who also rode horses.[767] The lifestyle of the Huns has been described in Chinese archives. Hunnish nomads kept moving to look for pastures for their animals, but each component group was granted certain land for its exclusive use as well. They lived in felt-walled dome-shaped tents known as *yurt*. They wore trousers and leather boots, and their upper costumes reached to the level of the knee and resembled caftans; Huns also had fur caps or hats.[768] In ancient China on the other hand, people wore loose robes as garments. But beginning in the third century, Chinese came to learn about the trousers of the Huns, and by the seventh century, the use of trousers had become common throughout China.[769] The Turkish nomadic outfit finally became fashionable among Chinese men particularly after the rule of the Turkish Northern Wei dynasty in China ended earlier in the sixth century. With the exception of Continental Celts, who apparently used trousers, most early Europeans, including ancient Germans, ancient Slavs, and Celts of the British Isles, wore skirts; furthermore, early Egyptians, ancient Greeks, and Romans never wore trousers.[770]

Archaeological digs in burial sites in eastern Central Asia have unearthed Hunnish pottery with geometrical designs. In addition to the having knowledge of pottery making, Huns were also known for their metalworking. The same archaeological discoveries show that the making of metal objects, particularly out of iron and bronze, was already known to Huns; their dead were also found to have gold and silver items.[771]

3.3. THE FIRST NOMADIC EMPIRE

Huns were present well before the formal establishment of the Great Hun Empire. It has been suggested that (Asian) Huns existed as early as 2000 BCE, according to Chinese chronicles.[772] Ancient Chinese records indicate that proto-Turks were raiding northern China as early as the eleventh century BCE.[773] But the actual year the Hunnish state was formed is not clear. Most sources consider 209 BCE as the year of establishment of the Hun Empire. It is clear that the founding tribe of the Hun Empire was in existence for some time before the actual establishment of the empire. Even though the Huns' first state is known as the Great Hun Empire by Turks, their statehood is thought to have been based on nomadic standards. Therefore, their governing body was often actively moving on horseback.

Until the third century BCE, Huns lived in relative peace in the northern territories in a scattered fashion without a known statehood. However, the peace would not last for long. The authors of the ancient Chinese chronicles might have described the Huns as barbarians, but history must be looked at in a more objective manner. Indeed, once historical facts are carefully analyzed, it appears that Huns or Turks were forced to enter history's spotlight because of actions taken by Shih-huang-ti, the first Chinese emperor of the Ch'in dynasty. China's unprovoked attack on the Asian Huns (Xiong-nu) brought major consequences not imaginable to the Ch'in (Qin) emperor. While the Chinese emperor intended to scare away the nomads with his assault upon them, the Huns instead became unified under one strong leader, who in turn launched devastating attacks upon China. Ultimately these clashes initiated the first international relations not only for the Chinese but also for the Turks.

The first treaty signed between these two nations in 198 BCE was followed by more than four centuries of relations involving war, diplomacy, and trade. The interactions were often described as the shepherd versus the farmer, the nomad versus the peasant, the cavalry versus the infantry, the horse versus the chariot, and the Hun versus the Han. We will now look into these relationships in a bit more detail.

When China was united as one empire under the Ch'in dynasty, the first emperor began the ambitious construction of the Great Wall of China against the nomadic Huns and sent General Meng T'ien to conquer the steppes to the north, where the nomads thrived. This Chinese action was seen by the nomads as an unprovoked attack. The assault forced the Huns to unite under the banner of their leader, Mo-tun Shan-yu (known as Mete in modern Turkish).[774]

Briefly we need to touch upon how the title shan-yu was utilized. According to the Chinese archives, the full title of the supreme Hun ruler was *ch'eng-li ku-t'u shan-yu*, which can be translated from ancient Turkish into English as "majesty son of heaven."[775] Another translation may be "emperor blessed by god." It has been determined that Chinese transliteration of *ch'eng-li* meant *tengri*, the Old Turkish word for God. Modern Turks of Central Asia and Mongols still use the word *tengri*, but Turks of Turkey have modified it to *tanrï*. In addition to identifying a deity, in ancient times the word *tengri* was used to denote heaven as well.

During the period of 209–141 BCE, Huns became a formidable power, and Chinese felt helpless to stop their incursions into China despite the Great Wall. Huns not only controlled their nomadic realm but also had control over Chinese peasants in the conquered territories of northern China.[776]

THE STORY OF MO-TUN (METE), THE FOUNDER

According to Chinese records, the story of Mo-tun and his rise to Hun leadership coincides with the rise of Huns into an Asian power. His remarkable story is as follows:

> In 214 when first emperor of China Shih-huang-ti sent his army into the territories of the nomads in the north, the *Xiong-nu* were caught

unprepared. The destruction that the Chinese brought upon them turned them weaker than other nomadic people in the vicinity. In order to seek peace Tumen (Teoman), the leader of the *Xiong-nu*, gave his eldest son, Mo-tun (Mete in contemporary Turkish) as a hostage to *Yueh-chih*, a rival nomadic group on the western side of the Asian Huns.

Meanwhile, in order to have protection in afterlife the emperor of the Ch'in (Qin) House had his people prepare an army of terra-cotta soldiers for his future tomb. In 210 when emperor of the Ch'in House died, the dynasty eventually collapsed and the Han Dynasty came to power.

The collapse of the Ch'in Dynasty allowed the Huns to move back to their former pastures. Tumen now saw an opportunity to get rid of Mo-tun and prepare his younger son from his favorite Chinese consort to be his future heir. Hence, when he later attacked the *Yueh-chih* he expected them to kill Mo-tun in retaliation. Instead, Mo-tun managed to escape in a heroic manner, which did not only impress his father Tumen but also earned the respect of the Huns. As a reward Tumen granted Mo-tun with 10,000 warriors.

At the same time Mo-tun was aware of his father's plans. He was now determined to take the control of the *Xiong-nu* for himself not only to secure his survival but also he wanted to exalt his people. After all he was unpleased with his father's passive stance against the Chinese aggression. Therefore, his first goal was to achieve absolute obedience and a discipline of steel from his troops. He provided his warriors with whistling arrows and drilled to shoot their targets from horseback. He in fact ordered soldiers to shoot wherever he aimed at. The cost of the disobedience was immediate death. The targets he chose included hunting animals and then his best horses. Those who did not follow his orders were immediately executed. But the successive trials became more difficult. The final test was his father's finest horses. When the warriors did not fail to shoot these horses Mo-tun knew that they were ready. On a hunting expedition when Mo-tun shot his father with his whistling arrow his guards did the same. Now Mo-tun was the ultimate leader of the Huns, their Shan-yu.[777]

Mo-tun Shan-yu in a short period formed a powerful, well-disciplined army, the strength of which was its cavalry. The following is a legendary story to show how Mo-tun went on to declare his supremacy over the Eastern Eurasian Steppe before turning his attention to China:

> After Mo-tun (Mete) took the leadership role of the *Xiong-nu* (Asian Huns) he was first confronted by the mixed *Tung-hu* tribes of the East. The leader of their confederation demanded Tumen's best horse to be handed over. Against the advice of his lieutenants he obliged. Then the *Tung-hu* assumed that Mo-tun was afraid. Consequently, the *Tung-hu* asked for one of Mo-tun's favorite wives. Again against the advice of his counselors he surrendered her. When the *Tung-hu* made a claim on a *Xiong-nu* territory, Mo-tun consulted with his advisers who suggested that the land in question could be yielded to the *Tung-hu*. Then Mo-tun angrily replied, *"The land is the root of a nation! How can we cede it?!"* Subsequently, he killed his advisers who gave the recommendation to yield the land. Afterwards he launched a campaign and crushed the *Tung-hu*. He then turned his attention to the West and drove away the *Yueh-chih*. Now Mo-tun was unchallenged in the steppes as he became absolute power over the nomads.[778]

By forming the first formidable confederation of tribes across the Eastern Eurasian Steppe, Mo-tun also formed the first union of Turkish tribes. According to the Chinese archives, Ting-ling Turkish tribal confederations were among those who joined the greater Hun confederation.[779] The Ko-k'un tribes joining Mo-tun's banner, as recorded by Chinese, were likely the Kyrgyz Turks, who have existed since the time of the Huns. It has been suggested that the tribes of Wu-huan, who were also incorporated into the Hun Empire, were claimed to be the Oghuz Turks.[780]

When Mo-tun had gathered Hunnish and non-Hunnish Turkish tribes under his banner, he defeated the Yueh-chih tribes twice. After the last and crushing defeat of the Yueh-chih in 174 BCE, Lao-shang Shan-yu of the Huns made a drinking vessel out the skull of the Yueh-chih king. Subsequently, the defeated people moved far away from the Huns, toward the Ili River basin.[781] The movement of the Yueh-chih was further forced by the Turkish Wu-sun tribes acting in concert with the Huns. Eventually the migration of the Yueh-chih to the Transoxus area caused the destruction of the Greco-Bactrian Kingdom. These events were the first in world history to be recorded by both Far Eastern (Chinese) and Western (Greek) sources.[782]

During the thirty-five years of his reign, Mo-tun's Xiong-nu Empire stretched from the Yellow Sea (marginal sea of the Pacific Ocean) in the east to the Aral Sea in the west, and from Lake Baikal in the north to the Yellow River in the south. His capital was in the Orkhon valley in modern-day Mongolia, near the future Mongolian capital Qarakorum.[783] Liu Pang (regnal name Kao-tsu or Gaozu, 202–195 BCE), the founder of the Han dynasty, died in 195 BCE, and Mo-tun, the founder of the Great Xiong-nu (Hun) Empire, died in 174 BCE.[784]

The army of Mo-tun Shan-yu was formed in groups of multiples of tens, hundreds, thousands, and tens of thousands; this was also an old Turkish military organizational system. When the hostilities began, the Chinese counted on their foot soldiers but mostly on their chariots. But the emperor soon realized that his chariots were no match for the superbly skilled mounted archers, who had high maneuverability on their horses. The nomads used their ability of speed and the element of surprise to their advantage in stunning the northern towns of China.[785] When Mo-tun Shan-yu solidified his control over the vast eastern Eurasian steppes, including Inner Mongolia, he sent a letter to the Chinese Han emperor indicating that "all the people who live by drawing the bow are now united into one family."[786] This declaration was similar to the statement of Mongol Genghis Khan, who proclaimed more than a millennium later that all the people in Mongolia living in felt tents, whether Turks or Mongols, were under his leadership. However, at the time of Mo-tun, the mounted archers were the Turks, and the Mongols were not skilled archers yet.

Today, the armed forces of the Republic of Turkey claim that the Turkish military is the oldest army of the world; it believes that throughout the centuries, since 209 BCE, the Turkish army has continued the military traditions of the armies of the Huns of Mo-tun (Mete) Shan-yu, the founder of the Great Hun Empire. Hence, its insignia today includes the year "209 BCE." Although the original Turkish name of Mo-tun is not known due to sinicization of Turkish names in the archives of China, it is believed that the proper name or title of Mo-tun was an old Central Asian title "Bagatur" meaning hero in Turkish.[787]

THE YUEH-CHIH NOMADS

While discussing the history of the Xiong-nu (the Huns) it would be appropriate to briefly touch upon the history of the Yueh-chih, who actually inadvertently gave impetus to Mo-tun's rise to power. While they were known to reside to the west of the Xiong-nu, they were once located near the border of China's western part of modern Chinese province of Kansu. However, they were ultimately forced to migrate westward to the territories of Bactria, and all the way to northern Indian peninsula to eventually establish the vast Kushan Empire. From being a nomadic people of the Eurasian steppes they turned into a dominant force over parts of Central Asia and south Asia as they ruled over an empire that thrived on pastoralism of the nomads as well as agriculturalism of the sedentary peoples.[788]

Who were these people? Did they belong to an Indo-European race, speaking a form of Persian language as many Western scholars claim? Or, as Turkish historians suggest, were they Turkish dialect speaking nomadic people originating from near Han China?

We know that the Yueh-chih were once involved in trading jade to China from Hotan region. They were also taking advantage of pastoralism as part of their economy. They were mostly described to be Europoid in appearance and based on this fact many Western scientists have claimed that the Yueh-chih were Indo-European origin but in chapter 2.2 we have already indicated that physical-anthropologic findings are not adequate to determine ethnicity of lost peoples of the past. In addition, to this date we have no formal record of their spoken language, and yet their unknown language has been considered to be part of Indo-European group of languages. On the other hand, ancient Han-shu records of China suggested that the Yueh-chih based on their pastoralism and traditions were very similar to the Xiong-nu (Asian Huns).[789]

The Yueh-chih have been thought to be the same people as Tokharians. Consequently, Tokharian language has also been considered to be Indo-European origin but there are no surviving records to prove this point of view as well. Indeed, it has been claimed that the Yueh-chih spoke a language that the Uighur Turks later referred to as 'Togar tili' or in another words in English as Tokhar language.[790] Today, the historical names Tokharians, Kushana, and Yueh-chih are considered to be different appellations for the same people.[791] On the other hand, in June of 2013 the presentation of Chinese scientists at a symposium in Vienna, Austria, claimed that based on archeologic and genetic studies the Yueh-chih and the Tokharians were not the same people.[792] Although Chinese did not leave much descriptive information in regards to their ethnicity, we find even more reference on the Yueh-chih from Greco-Roman historians after they established themselves in Bactria.

The Yueh-chih were engaged in war against the Xiong-nu (Asian huns) three times, and all of them ended with the victory of the Huns. First, after Mo-tun turned the Huns into a formidable military power, he convincingly defeated the Yueh-chih around 206/205 BCE. Secondly, around the year 177/176 BCE Mo-tun crushed the Yueh-chih one more time. Finally, around 172-161 BCE his son Chi-yü (Shan-yu Lao-shang) scored third Hunnish victory, which was disastrous for the Yueh-chih. The triumphant Hun leader severely humiliated the losers by turning their leader's skull into a golden goblet.[793] As a result, leaving their traditional Kansu area territory the Yueh-chih split into two groups. First, the smaller group known as the Little Yueh-chih remained at the foothills of the Tian-Shan Mountains (Qinghai plateau).[794] Then, the larger group known as the Great Yueh-chih, being chased by the Huns reached the Ili River basin, where they pushed the Saka (Scythian) tribes away from this territory.[795]

The displaced Saka tribes moved in two separate directions. Those who moved south reached India whereas those who migrated westward reached the eastern borders of Parthian Iran. In the mean time around 145-140 BCE their appearance caused the Bactrian kingdom to be severely weakened. Meanwhile, the fate of the Yueh-chih was going to be changed again, but this time by the Turkish Wu-sun.

According to the story of Chinese ambassador Zhang Qian (also referred to as Chang Ch'ien) in the Han-shu record, after the king of the Wu-sun was killed by the Yueh-chih, his people sought refuge with the Xiong-nu (Huns). By this time the murdered leader's infant son Kun-mo was being guarded by his assigned protector who was a yabgu (prince). According to a legend, after he hid the child in the bushes, he went away to look for food. When he came back he saw that a crow was feeding him meat while a wolf was giving the child her milk.[796] Yabgu immediately thought that Kun-mo was heavenly blessed child. He then took him to the shan-yu of the Huns who in turn gave shelter to Kun-mo as if he were his own son. The child eventually became a successful commander, and the emperor of the Huns gave Kun-mo the leadership of his Wu-sun people. Subsequently, when shan-yu granted Kun-mo the right to avenge his father, around 130 BCE the young Wu-sun fell upon the Yueh-chih to take his revenge for the death of his father.[797] Kun-mo, a legendary leader of the *Wu-sun,* became a powerful vassal of the Huns but upon the death of the shan-yu he made his people independent.[798] Interestingly, likely based on this legendary story the Chinese name of Wu-sun was defined as "the grandsons of the raven"[799] whereas the Yueh-chih meant the "moon people".[800] However, the original names of these nomadic peoples are not known.

Finally, continued Wu-sun attacks forced the Great Yueh-chih to flee westward towards Ta-hsia (Afghanistan). As a result, it is believed that by 130/129 BCE the new comers easily conquered the territories of former Greco-Bactrian Kingdom. When the Great Yueh-chih established themselves in this area, they appeared to be divided into five separate feudal polities. One of them, the Kushana, eventually became the dominant one taking over the remaining of their kinsmen as they formed the Kushan Empire named after their tribal name in the early first century CE. Despite their official name the Chinese still referred to the founders of the state as the Yueh-chih.[801]

Numismatic evidence shows that the Kushan Empire, built by the Yueh-chih over the ashes of the Greco-Bactrian Kingdom, utilized two official languages but neither of them was their own native language. Instead, the Yueh-Chih Kushans used spoken languages belonging to the majority of the native peoples. Hence, both Bactrian written in Greek alphabet and Sanskrit written in Kharosthi script were utilized by the Kushans.

THE TURKS

It appeared that the Kushan people spoke the Saka language whereas the Bactrians spoke Sogdian; furthermore, it has been demonstrated that the Kushan and the Saka wore the same type of costumes and used the same weapons.[802] What is known today is the fact that the Kushan people were practicing the flattening of the heads of their children as this was a common tradition among the tribes of the Eurasian steppes of the time.[803] Similar cranial deformation was also present among the European Huns who invaded Europe late in the fourth and the beginning fifth centuries.[804]

It is a fact that the Kushans had a multicultural society, and their ruling minority was exposed to multiple languages, including Greek and other native languages, thus forcing the Yueh-chih monarchs to adapt and make compromises for purposes of ruling and trading with other nationalities.[805] Just like any other empire where the ruling elite were minority, the character of the founders of these states eventually became assimilated within the culture of the native peoples. For example, although the Eastern Roman Empire was Roman, in other words Latin in character at the time of its foundation, it eventually turned into a Greek character by the time the Turks ended its existence in 1453 since the Roman elite over time were forced to accept the language and the culture of the Greek majority of their dominions.

Hence, using this example, were the Yueh-chih initially Altaic (in other words Turkish speakers) origin and yet later upon moving to the west did they become more persianized due to cultural assimilation by the vast majority of the population with Persian character? Or, were they part of early Indo-European tribes reaching the borders of the Far East? Some of the answers are given in chapter 2.2.

Now, we will turn our attention back to the Far East to the second half of the second century BCE. At the time, feeling desperate to break the military power of the Asian Huns, Han emperor Wudi looked for allies to stand up to the military might of the northern mounted archer warriors. He thus sent Zhang Qian (also referred to as Chang Ch'ien) as his envoy to Bactria to convince the Yueh-chih to join in a military alliance with China. When Chinese ambassador Zhang Qian arrived to Bactria in 129-8 BCE, he saw the Yueh-chih ruling over this territory.[806] After he failed to secure military support

243

of the Yueh-chih against the Xiong-nu, the ambassador later convinced his emperor to appeal to the Wu-sun to convince them to be their subjects and to take over the Kansu corridor territory to create an obstacle against the Xiong-nu. Nevertheless, it took decades before the Wu-sun participated in a joint attack with the Han Chinese against their Xiong-nu overlords only after they were weakened.

In the first half of the third century CE, the Kushan Empire was divided into two halves. The western half quickly came under the Persian Sassanid rule while the eastern part survived nearly for another century. By the middle of the fourth century the eastern Kushan Empire came under the influence of the Gupta Empire of India but by the year 360 the Kidarite Huns (chapter 3.6) prevailed over the Kushans but the newcomers also adopted the cultural heritage of the land as their own. Hence, by the end of the fourth century the Yueh-chih legacy came to an end.

THE ROLE OF CHINESE WOMEN IN PEACE TREATIES WITH THE HUNS

When the Ch'in dynasty unified China for the first time, Chinese first started engaging in foreign affairs—or in other words, they had their first international relations—with their northern neighbors, the Huns (Xiong-nu). After the Ch'in dynasty ended, the marriage alliances, known in Chinese as *ho-ch'in* (harmonious kinship), were used by the Han dynasty in an attempt to appease and pacify the powerful Huns. However, ho-ch'in for the Huns meant the achievement of equal status; in other words, the Xiong-nu shan-yu was considered the brother of the Chinese emperor of the Celestial Empire. In 198 BCE, when the first ho-ch'in marriage occurred between a Han princess and Mo-tun, the shan-yu and the founder of the Xiong-nu (Great Hun) Empire, the Huns considered themselves equal to China.[807] Even though in 134, Emperor Wudi sent a daughter of the royal house to marry the shan-yu of the Huns, he later decided to act against them by trying to make an alliance with a Hun ally, the Wu-sun, who were the kinsmen of the shan-yu's tribes. In 105 the Celestial Emperor established a ho-ch'in relationship with the Wu-sun by sending a Han princess. Finally, later in 71 BCE, Princess Chieh-yu in the Wu-sun court was instrumental in securing a joint military action between the Wu-sun and the Han Chinese against the Huns.[808]

The Hun-Han intermarriages were unidimensional, meaning while the Huns received Chinese brides, Turkish females never married Chinese males, or at least there are no established records of such marriages with the exception of Chinese ambassador Zhang Qian, whose story will be told below. While the shan-yu considered himself an equal to the Chinese emperor by marrying a princess from his house, the Han looked at the trading of their princesses from the point of view of gaining Chinese allies within the royal establishment of the Turkish Hun Empire.

There were multiple royal Han-Hun marriages where Chinese princesses were given to the shan-yu, particularly in the years 198, 192, 174, 156, 152, and 33 BCE. The multiplicity of royal marriages earlier on indicate the strength of the Huns, and the long gap between the years 152 and 33 BCE show the weakening period of the Huns. The Dyrestuj warrior tombs (in the Buryat Republic north of Mongolia, within Russian Siberia), attributed to the clan of the shan-yu, did not have Xiong-nu women but rather had Chinese women. Interestingly, the dead warriors were also found to have cowrie shells on or in their mouths;[809] the significance of this is unknown.

After the Huns split, the southern state's shan-yu in 33 BCE was given a Chinese bride, but in contrast to the prior ho-ch'in agreements, the Hunnish royalty was given son-in-law status rather than the brother status previously given; the Chinese took this action to diminish the prestige of the Northern Huns. As we will see later, when Wang Mang became emperor of China in the year 9 CE, the Huns were reunified against the Chinese threat. But after the Huns were defeated by the Wu-huan, they were once again split into northern and southern states around the year 48 CE. When the southerners were pressured by their northern kinsmen, they were given territories by the Han emperor within northern Chinese borders and military assistance, but again they were no longer given the equal status that their predecessors enjoyed.[810]

THE RISE OF HUN POWER

As we can see, the rise of the Huns came in three stages. The first was the invasion of the Xiong-nu territory in Ordos by Ch'in general Meng T'ien in 215 BCE. The second was the legendary rise of Mo-tun (Mete) to the throne of supreme ruler (shan-yu) in 209 BCE. The third and the final stage was the establishment of a centralized structure of government.[811] In a short period, Mo-tun succeeded in forming a highly disciplined powerful army based on a cavalry of mounted archers. According to Chinese annals, it is known that Mo-tun's highly skilled Huns crushed the Chinese in their encounters. In about the year 200 BCE, when the Chinese emperor was surrounded by Hun (Xiong-nu) armies, Mo-tun found himself having to choose between two options. One was to capture the emperor and invade China, followed by total military occupation, but Mo-tun realized that the option of full-scale invasion would have put his nation's way of life at risk of assimilation. Instead, by choosing to establish friendlier relations with the Chinese, he inadvertently started the history of Far Eastern diplomacy.[812]

Finally, with diplomacy a truce was achieved, resulting in the first ho-ch'in treaty (198 BCE), which forced the Chinese emperor to pay annual tribute.[813] In addition to the payment of tribute, the Chinese government committed itself to trading silk textiles and royal princesses to the Hun rulers in exchange for peace. However, when Chinese decided to break the peace contract by stopping the complex trading process, Huns began their attacks again.[814] With the ho-ch'in treaty, the emperor intended to gain some control of the Huns by giving his eldest daughter to acquire a grandson from among the "barbarians." But Huns had more to gain from their dealings with Chinese since in addition to receiving annual tributes, no other "barbarian" ruler was ever treated as the titular equal of the Chinese emperor.[815]

Essentially, the ho-ch'in treaty had four major provisions. The first was that Chinese would give Huns silk, wine, grain, and other foodstuff annually. Second, the Chinese emperor was to give a princess in marriage to the shan-yu. Third, both states would be recognized as coequal polities. Fourth, the Great Wall was to be known as the official boundary between the Xiong-nu and China.[816] While the goods were distributed to the political elite of the nomadic empire to ensure their support, the shan-yu also secured prestige for being recognized as an equal to the Han emperor and for having a Han princess as a consort. For nearly a century, even though the Chinese records do not clearly admit to it, Huns (Xiong-nu) received tribute from China as well as equal status, or the status of being brothers.[817]

As mentioned earlier, to prevent "barbarian" encroachments upon Chinese agricultural territories, the Ch'in (or Qin) emperor who had ordered the initial failed attempt to occupy Hun territories ordered the construction of the Great Wall of China. Building walls was an old military defense tool that was not unique to China. In ancient times, walls were built around well-established cities of the sedentary world to protect the people and their property against nomadic warriors more powerful than their armies. In fact, the city walls remained a useful defense mechanism until the advent of cannons in the fifteenth century. Indeed, in 1453, by bringing down the previously impregnable walls of Constantinople (the capital of the Eastern Roman Empire) with their gigantic cannons, the Turks changed the course of history by making the use of city walls in the art of warfare obsolete. However, with the Great Wall, the Chinese did what no other nation on earth has done: they built a wall with the intention of protecting an entire country rather than just cities. We will refresh our memory of the history of the Great Wall within the context of Hun (Xiong-nu) history.

Although there is evidence that there were small walls along the northern borders of the former Chinese kingdoms, the building of the actual Great Wall began after the unification of China under the Ch'in (or Qin) dynasty (221–207 BCE). The Chinese city-states during the Warring States period (480–221 BCE) had initially built walls around their cities to defend against one another as well as against the Huns, known as the northern "barbarians." Several walls were built beginning in the fifth century BCE, and they came to be collectively known as the Great Wall of China.[818] After the unification of China by the Ch'in dynasty, the walls of the northern cities were united to form the early Great Wall, which was rebuilt and maintained time after time from the third century BCE through the seventeenth century CE. However, only a small part of this historic original wall remains today. Most of the Great Wall that exists today was established during the Ming dynasty (1368–1644). Hence, the Great Wall of China was originally maintained to stop attacks by the Turks from the north for nearly a millennium, and later after the thirteenth century it was intended to thwart attacks by the Mongols.

The truth is, the Great Wall could not completely protect China from the nomadic invaders coming from the north. Despite the wall, the Turks and later the Mongols managed to menace China nearly until the modern age. During this time period Turks, Mongols, Manchu-Tungus tribal peoples did not only threaten China but also they were able to establish from time to time multiple dynasties within China. Ultimately, the Great Wall of China could not prevent the Huns from attacking and taking spoils from China. In addition to internal Chinese political turmoil after the unification of China, the rise of Hun power in modern-day Mongolia and northern China in the third century BCE likely precipitated the fall of the Ch'in (Qin) dynasty, which was succeeded by the Han dynasty. Even though the Han were just as helpless as their predecessors in preventing Hun attacks, the Xiong-nu had no intention of conquering China; instead, they chose to stay at a distance to exploit China without putting themselves in danger by exposing their weakness in numbers and without giving up their mobility and freedom.[819]

The intermittent periods of war and peace between the Huns and the Chinese Han went on for centuries. Despite the temporary achievements of peace, Hunnish offensives into the Chinese territories occurred for centuries. In the second century BCE, Emperor Wudi sent Zhang Qian as an envoy to Yueh-chih, also referred to as the Tokhar. The goal was to lure the Yueh-chih into an alliance against the Huns. Ultimately, the emperor wished to open a corridor to the West to secure the trading routes of the Silk Road. But during his round trip to modern-day western Turkestan, the location of the Yueh-chih, Zhang Qian was captured by the Huns on two occasions and forced to live among them. During his stay among the Huns, Zhang Qian recorded his observations, which are now valuable information about the Huns' lifestyle, political structure, and military organization. As a guest-prisoner, he was allowed to marry a Xiong-nu woman.

By the time Zhang Qian reached the Yueh-chih, he found that they had already been defeated and pushed from their homeland in eastern Turkistan by the Huns.[820] He was acutely aware of his emperor's frustrations since Hunnish raids on China could be stopped neither militarily nor by the Great

Wall. Hence, upon arrival to Bactria in 139 BCE Qian presented emperor Wudi's proposal of an alliance with the Yueh-chih of Bactria against the (Asian) Huns (Xiong-nu).[821] Yet, the offer was rejected. The Han emperor then looked for alternate routes to trade with the West in order to avoid the Huns. But the search was in vain. Finally, he was resigned to the fact that the trade route with the West had to remain under Hun control. Meanwhile, Chinese continued to extend the wall with hopes of protecting the route from Hun attacks.[822] This eventually proved to be a futile effort, and an expensive one for the Han treasury.

The tradition of Chinese princesses entering the shan-yu's tent continued for successive Hun rulers. However, over the next two centuries, Hun power began to wane. Eventually Chinese created divisions among the Huns. The decentralization of the Hun tribes further added to their weakness. The rise of the Hun Empire, known to the Turks as the Great Hun Empire, occurred during 209–126 BCE, followed by the weakening of the Hun power in 126–101 BCE, particularly during the reign of the Han emperor Wudi, who came to the Chinese throne in 141 BCE. In 126 BCE, upon the death of Günchen Shan-yu, the last of the great shan-yus of the Huns, the weakening period of the northern nomads began. Before the reign of Wudi, Chinese were always on the defensive, but the situation began to change in their favor after the year 126 BCE.

Wudi (141–87 BCE) became one of the most famous Han emperors of China. He established Confucianism as the official religion of China. He made efforts to change the existing ho-ch'in treaty stipulations, which were humiliating for China. These included a Chinese princess, silk goods, food, and other goods to be given by the Chinese emperor to the Hun shan-yu. Instead, Wudi intended to establish a tributary system as the framework of Chinese foreign relations. When China was finally able to defeat the Huns (Xiong-nu) in 119 BCE, Huns still requested a continuation of the old ho-ch'in policies, which was immediately rejected by Wudi. Instead, the Chinese requested a hostage be sent to the palace as payment of homage to the emperor and the offering of tribute to him. The shan-yu found these demands outrageous and immediately rejected them.[823] Similar peace-treaty demands by the Chinese were again declined by the Huns in 107 BCE. Finally, in the year 54 BCE, following the First Xiong-nu (Hun) Civil War (57–54 BCE), which ended in the splitting of the Great Hun Empire, the (southern) Huns caved in to the Chinese peace-treaty demands previously proposed by Wudi.[824]

After temporarily containing the Hunnish threat in the north, Emperor Wudi sought to expand China from the Korean Peninsula to Vietnam. In 111 BCE, Wudi also tried to make an alliance with the (Turkish) Wu-sun to break the Hun power in the Western Territories. The slow decline of the Hun Empire occurred particularly during 100–51 BCE. Chinese found a way to weaken the Huns by political means instead of using military confrontations. In the first century BCE, the Huns entered into a series of civil wars, and the Han Chinese played warring Hunnish factions against one another. Chinese women who married the shan-yu, the Hun leader, also played an important role in meddling in Sino-Hun political affairs.[825] In their relentless pursuit to weaken the Hun state, Chinese also sought economic factors to achieve their goals.

In the realm of the Huns, who had formed stronger and better organized polities than the former Scythians, steppeland trade was quite extensive.[826] When Han emperor Wudi's ambassador Zhang Qian visited the Huns, he was astonished to find that Chinese goods were already known to them. Chinese merchandise moved westward through Hun-controlled Xinjiang. Even after the Han Chinese established their trade route through Xinjiang, the Huns continued to control much of the Silk Road's eastern trade routes.[827] In effect, Huns were trading as well as collecting tributes in Xinjiang, which was a major hub for the Silk Road.[828] Hun tombs in northern Mongolia from the first century BCE contain materials brought from Bactria, Sogdiana, and Syria.

Starting with the reign of Emperor Wudi, China tried to instigate rebellions among the tribes against the Huns to diminish their strength and influence in these useful territories.[829] The ultimate goal was to establish pro-Chinese tribal allegiances in the area to achieve free trade through the Silk Road. Wu-sun was the primary tribal union that the Han Chinese tried to bring under their sphere of influence. But despite Chinese expectations of the decline of Hun power in the strategically important Western Territories, the strength of the Huns seemed to remain undiminished.

At the end of his reign, Emperor Wudi, who had always pursued expansionism, issued the Edict of Lantai of 89 BCE, where he declared that he would not pursue the conquest of Lantai. His expansionist policies had cost the Chinese treasury dearly. In his edict, Wudi gave the tale of the Huns and the hobbled horse:

> On a summer day of the year 90 BCE a group of Xiong-nu arrived to the walls of a Chinese outpost. The warriors tied a horse's foreleg(s) and after yelling, "Chinese! We give you a horse!" they left. The Xiong-nu intention was not clear. Was it an act of jest or raillery? Was it an act of boasting for showing off possession of excess amounts of their military mounts? Was it a threat? Was it an insult (equating horse's situation to the Chinese being confined to one area)? Was it a curse to the Chinese presented in the form of evil omen? The emperor and his counselors did not know how to interpret this act but he sent out a war campaign under his general Li Guangli. The result was a humiliating defeat with surrender to the Xiong-nu.[830]

After all the years of his expansionist efforts using the muscle of China, the undiminished strength of the Huns finally seemed to discourage Wudi. During the reign of Emperor Wudi, the Han changed their pacifist policy by going on the offensive and pursuing back-to-back military campaigns against Huns. Chinese became encouraged when they gained unfamiliar tactical victories and pushed Huns farther away from the Han border, but ultimately, Wudi realized that despite his best efforts, the power of the shan-yu and his Huns was not broken. As Wudi's relentless attacks drained China's economy, Huns resumed their attacks against the emperor's borders.[831]

Since the steppes were not logistically suitable for housing an army not heavily relying on the cavalry, Huns knew that the Chinese military could not occupy their grasslands. By contrast, the steppes were perfect for the mounted archers of the nomads. Yet, the Huns also knew that other tribes with their characteristics could attempt to dislodge them, if they dared to do so. Nevertheless, the Huns often overlooked their subject tribes.

The year 78 BCE marks the first nomadic attack on the Huns by the Wu-huan, resulting in the pillaging of the tombs of former shan-yus. The outraged

Huns retaliated and crushed the Wu-huan in return. A few years later, when the Wu-sun felt threatened by the Huns, they received military aid from the Chinese Han and subsequently launched a partially successful attack on the Huns. The Huns experienced successive disasters. While trying to avoid Chinese assaults, they moved their people and animals at unseasonable times of the year, ending in the catastrophic losses of both. Furthermore, following a successful counterattack on the Wu-sun, the Hun army was almost wiped out by a blizzard. In addition, in the year 68 BCE, famine struck the Huns, and their shan-yu died as well. Finally, when others became aware of these Hunnish misfortunes, the Huns came under attack by the Ting-ling from the north, the Wu-sun from the west, and the Wu-huan from the east.[832] It was Turk against Turk, brother against brother, and all Chinese needed to do was to watch these tribal forces weaken one another.

Despite all these catastrophic events, Hun power was still strong enough to continue their hegemony over the steppes.[833] The Chinese annals provide staggering statistics for the casualties of the Huns. These documents claim that following the disasters of the year 78 BCE and afterward, the Huns lost nearly 90 percent of their men and animals to the harsh winter; subsequently, nearly 30 percent of the remaining men and half of the animals died because of famine. The Chinese records suggest that in 68 BCE, when the Huns were hit by famine again, they lost about 60–70 percent of their men and animals.[834] Perhaps these numbers are exaggerated. The multitribal assaults against the Huns were repeated in 64 and 61 BCE. But when the Huns regained their strength, the liberated Ting-ling and Wu-sun tribal confederations of the Turks were once again subdued under their power. But the Huns faced another disaster between the years 60 and 57 BCE, when internal tensions began to rise, leading to a civil war.

3.4. THE SPLIT AND THE FALL OF THE EMPIRE

The distribution of Chinese goods among royal Hunnish clan members eventually created a situation where the Hun nobles became dependent on these materials from China. Furthermore, under Chinese influence, the Hunnish court, trying to imitate the Han Chinese court, with its ceremonial rituals and its aristocratic system, transformed into a more central bureaucratic government. Shifting away from its natural decentralized feudal system, Hunnish society began to experience tensions.[835]

In addition to receiving foodstuff as part of the tribute from China, Hun incursions into northern Chinese farming territories in the autumn allowed the Huns to secure supplementary food before the winter. It is believed that the reliance of Huns (Xiong-nu) on Chinese agricultural foodstuff may have caused them to stop practicing agriculture in their territories. This situation may have changed Huns from a balanced pastoral society into a warrior-nomad society. In the first century BCE, when Chinese could stop the influx of foodstuff into the nomadic territory, Huns were put under more stress.[836] By the middle of the first century BCE, the increasing internal tensions, the clear economic dependence on China, and the fractured control of non-Hunnish tribes had started to take a toll on Hun leadership, which began to fracture.

THE CIVIL WAR AND THE FIRST SPLIT

By 57 BCE, the Asian Huns (Xiong-nu) had fallen into civil war, with the internal political crisis exacerbated by a natural disaster destroying most Hunnish livestock.[837] The First Xiong-nu Civil War led to a final contest for the throne between two brothers. When Chih-chih, later known as the northern shan-yu, defeated his brother Huhanye and pushed him out of the Hunnish capital, Huhanye sought refuge with his followers within the borders of China.[838] Finally, the civil war ended in 54 BCE, when the split of the Hun Empire was formalized. However, many of the Southern Huns, to avoid submission to China, would not stay with Huhanye I Shan-yu and defected to the Northern Huns. Now facing the military superiority of Northern Huns, Huhanye I Shan-yu felt that he had no choice but to submit to Han China.[839]

In 54 BCE, Huhanye I Shan-yu of the Southern Huns accepted the Chinese peace terms as proposed by Former Han emperor Wudi, and he sent the required hostage.[840] Furthermore, he declared his surrender to the Han to ensure Chinese military aid in return for the protection of the northern Chinese borders against his kinsmen, the Northern Huns.[841] But the two sides viewed the treaty differently. While the Chinese now considered the (Southern) Huns under their suzerainty, the Southern Huns thought that they were free by acting independently within the borders of northern China. The peace accord happened not because of Hun weakness but rather because of the shan-yu's political aspirations. In fact, the Huns remained a sovereign power in northern China. Consequently, a new Hun-Han relationship began.

In 49 BCE, Huhanye I became the first shan-yu to visit the emperor's court. Even though the (southern) shan-yu had surrendered to the Chinese, the treaty recognized Hun sovereignty to the north of the Great Wall and Han rule of the territories south of the wall.[842] Huhanye I Shan-yu was treated with special respect and was given a rank above all Han nobility.[843] The Han did not attempt to absorb the Southern Huns into China.

When Chih-chih Shan-yu of the Northern Huns found out about this setup and realized that the Han tributary system was only ceremonial, he also showed his symbolic submission by sending a hostage to the Han palace, and in return he expected to receive lavish payments and gifts, just as his brother Huhanye I, the southern shan-yu, had obtained.[844] Because of these events and similar ones at a later time, symbolic or not, the tributary system allowed the use of the terms *submission, homage,* and *tribute*; this treaty was different than the earlier ho-ch'in treaties, which recognized the shan-yu as an equal to the emperor of China. But Huns did not view themselves as submitting to Chinese, who in fact considered Huns their subjects. Rather, the (Northern) Huns, aware of their military capability of disrupting China, figured that they could manipulate this tributary system to their own advantage, and Chinese, facing the threat, consequently complained about the greed of the nomads.[845]

In 1 BCE, another treaty was offered by the Chinese emperor to the (Southern) Huns, recognizing the Huns as the vassals of China, but Huns did not accept this view. Chinese tried to claim that China was the sole dominant world power by declaring the non-Hunnish tribes, such as the Turkish Wu-sun, their subjects and the Western Territories the emperor's natural lands.[846] Meanwhile, Huns refused to accept this interpretation of the former treaty policy, and the new proposed treaty was never ratified. Yet, Chinese still perceived the Southern Huns as vassals of Han China during the period of 50 BCE–8 CE. Even though within the Hunnish (Xiong-nu) world, the southern shan-yu was militarily weaker than his northern counterpart, he found a way to establish advantages such as receiving Chinese titles and a place within the Han administrative framework, all without outright submission to China.[847]

In 9 CE, Wang Mang, a powerful Han official, wrested the throne of China through a coup d'état to establish his short-lived Xin (Hsin) dynasty (9–23 CE) until the Han reestablished themselves in 24 CE. Hence, the period of Han China is divided into the Former (Western) Han (206 BCE–8 CE) and the Later (Eastern) Han (24–220 CE) periods.

It should be noted that before the reign of Wang Mang began in 9 CE, Chinese did not directly interfere in the Huns' internal affairs.[848] This policy changed under the new emperor, who also tried to change the advantages given to Huns, as he did not want them to benefit from the tributary system without having them accept the sovereignty of China. To divide and weaken the Huns, Emperor Wang Mang appointed fifteen different shan-yu names in 10 CE. Wuzhuliu Shan-yu of Huns responded by attacking northern towns of

China in Inner Mongolia. Then, in 15 CE, Wang Mang attempted to change the title of *shan-yu* and the name of the Huns by imperial order to diminish Hun influence over non-Chinese peoples. But despite all the muscle Chinese tried to muster against the nomadic fighters, Huns (Xiong-nu) proved to Wang Mang that a frontier war on the steppes was more expensive than Xiong-nu peace.[849] Ultimately, Wang Mang's policies failed because of the Huns' strong independence.[850] Hence, after Wang Mang, the Han court remained uninvolved in the Huns' domestic matters. Consequently, the succession of the shan-yu continued in a well-ordered manner under the control of the Hun government, with the exception of four shan-yus assigned by the Han during severely weakened times of the Southern Huns; these were Tingdu (95 CE), Hulan (143 CE), Qianqu (179 CE), and Qubei (216 CE).[851]

THE SECOND AND FINAL SPLIT OF THE EMPIRE

While Wang Mang worked hard, but in vain, to bring Huns under complete Chinese sovereignty, the shan-yu resisted these efforts and instead pushed for the reestablishment of the benefits of the ceremonial tributary system established by the Former Han dynasty. The death of Emperor Wang Mang at the hands of Chinese rebels brought on a civil war within China. The chaotic situation was an opportune moment for Huns to invade China, but instead the steppe warriors chose to stay neutral. Since the Hunnish economy was in large part supported by goods received from China, the Hunnish leaders preferred to deal with a stable Chinese government to get what they needed.[852] Finally, when the Chinese civil war ended, the Han dynasty was back in power, with China now entering the Later (Eastern) Han (24–220 CE) period.

As a result of Emperor Wang Mang's aggressive anti-Hun policies, Huns were once again unified. Nearly a century after the First Xiong-nu Civil War, Huns were again at the height of their power, ready to push Chinese to the old ho-ch'in treaty policy giving the shan-yu equal status with the Chinese emperor.[853] However, the death of Wu-tu-ti-hou Shan-yu in 46 CE within months of taking the throne led to the Second Xiong-nu Civil War as the result of a dispute over the position of the next shan-yu.[854] Soon after

P'u-nu became shan-yu, his adversary Bi began to work with the Chinese against him, beginning in 47 CE. Bi offered to defend the Chinese borders against his own kinsmen, and in addition, he later assumed the regnal name Huhanye II to legitimize his alliance with the Han. The result was the second and permanent division of the Great Hun Empire into its northern and southern parts.[855]

In 49 CE a new treaty was signed between the Han and the Southern Xiong-nu. The peace treaties made between the Han emperors and the Southern Xiong-nu shan-yus Huhanye I and Huhanye II in 54 BCE and 49 CE were viewed by the Chinese as complete submission of the Southern Xiong-nu to China. But the treaties in fact were bilateral agreements recognizing Southern Hun sovereignty over the Southern Hunnish peoples while assuring Han Chinese military support against the Northern Huns in exchange for a Xiong-nu oath of allegiance.[856] Hence, the treaties were essentially made for cooperation between the Southern Huns and the Han Chinese against incursions by the Northern Huns. Nevertheless, the ultimate Han policy regarding Xiong-nu culture was its eradication and, therefore, the elimination of the foreign power by means of cultural subversion when military means proved to be inefficient.[857] But the Han did not succeed.

Once again the Northern and Southern Huns diverged from each other. The court of Huhanye II was established in Yunzhong, in northern China (within Han borders) in 50 CE, but later a move to Meiji was made, owing to short-lived revolts against the (southern) shan-yu.[858] After capitalizing on his power over the southerners, he also wanted to take control of his northern kinsmen to reunite the Huns. But the Northern Huns refused to be allied with Chinese, and many of the southern noblemen also resisted this new arrangement. A rebellion followed, but the southern shan-yu overcame the difficulties and consolidated his power. When Huhanye II Shan-yu died in 56 CE, Chinese officials arranged for a burial in the presence of an honor guard, offering sacrifices and mourning gifts. From this time on, the practice became customary for Chinese.[859] This was the first time an honor was bestowed by the Chinese court to a non-Chinese.

The southern shan-yu followed successful strategies to weaken his northern counterpart. For nearly two and a half centuries, Huns had absolute control over the modern-day Mongolian steppes, but the southern shan-yu's move to block Chinese trade goods from reaching the north and his exclusive benefits from the lucrative tributary system began to attract Hunnish nomads to flock southward to join their southern kinsmen. These strategic moves not only had the eventual effect of pulling the Northern Hunnish economy down but also impaired the northern shan-yu's control over the Hunnish nobles, who expected to receive Chinese goods from their leader.[860] Despite all the disadvantages created by the southern shan-yu, P'u-nu Shan-yu of the Northern Huns remained a strong and capable ruler, preserving the strength of the north by keeping the economy alive by means of successive raids on China.[861] P'u-nu had a long reign, and when he died, probably around 83 CE, the Northern Huns (Northern Xiong-nu) remained stable.[862]

Meanwhile, the Southern Huns felt secure, having entered the Chinese sphere of influence, thereby guaranteeing Chinese military aid against their northern kinsmen. As the years went by, Chinese continued to supervise the activities of the Southern Huns within the borders of the "son of heaven." They also invited the Northern Huns to relocate within China. The ultimate goal was to remove the Hun leaders from the source of their power. However, the weakness of the central government of the Han dynasty became more apparent over time as the Southern Huns in return maintained their independence within the northern territories of China. Indeed, the shan-yu was never put under the Hans' direct control.[863] In the end, the Southern Hun–Chinese alliance depended on each other's goodwill. There was a mutually beneficial relationship between the southern shan-yu and the emperor. The Southern Huns took advantage of the availability of Chinese goods, and they received Han military assistance against their northern kinsmen when needed. The ultimate benefit of this alliance for China was the protection the Southern Huns provided to China at its northern borders.

The Han still viewed the southern shan-yu as China's subject, and therefore, any antigovernment action among the Huns was considered rebellion. However, Han would forgive the shan-yu for such actions in return for the execution of the instigators of the revolts. The Southern Huns revolted against the alliance in the years 109, 158, 166, and 187 BCE. In the first three of these rebellions, they were accompanied by the Wu-huan and Xianbei troops from the steppes.[864] The last Hun revolt, however, corresponded to the great Chinese peasant Yellow Turban Rebellion (184–205). This Hun revolt was against the emperor indirectly because this time the noblemen rebelled against the shan-yu. Even though the Han were finally able to crush the costly domestic rebellion of the Chinese peasants, the central government was severely weakened as governing control shifted to regional governors and commanders. This event eventually became a catalyst for the cessation of the Han dynasty in the year 220.

In the first century CE, while the Southern Huns controlled the territory known as Inner Mongolia bordering China proper and parts of (eastern) Turkestan (known as the Western Territories), the Northern Huns reigned over Outer Mongolia (modern-day Mongolia) as well as southern Siberia. In the days when Huns (Xiong-nu) had indisputable power over the steppes, those who challenged their rule had to flee from the Hunnish territories. But late in the first century CE, after the death of P'u-nu Shan-yu, the power of the Northern Huns declined fast. Suddenly the Wu-huan and the Xianbei tribes began to challenge the Huns. As long as they showed their intent to assault Huns, Chinese offered the benefits of the tributary system even to the leaders of small tribes. The Xianbei were given rewards for the heads of the Northern Xiong-nu.[865] These catastrophic events began to shift groups of Northern Huns westward, creating a new center of power over one thousand miles to the west. As a result of this major geographic shift, the loose polity formed by Northern Huns farther west is sometimes referred to as the Western Hun Empire. Eventually, the invaders of Europe in the fourth century emerged from this group of the Huns.

Even though the last mention of a northern shan-yu is from 91 CE,[866] the last documented Northern Hun raid into China was in 120 CE, and the last mention of their location, according to some records, was in 126 CE. But in Han diplomatic records, there is further mention of the presence of the Northern Hun court as late as 155 CE.[867] The continued use of the name Northern Xiong-nu suggests their ongoing presence and the lack of reunification with their southern kinsmen, who remained militarily allied with Han China against the north. Even though the north and the south remained separate, any Northern Huns who later surrendered to Han China were under Southern Hun control, thus benefiting Southern Hun strength and sovereignty overall.

The status of Northern Huns triggered assaults upon them by neighboring nomadic groups. In 85 CE the Ting-ling were once again freed from Hun control since Northern Xiong-nu had been severely weakened after the death of northern shan-yu P'u-nu around 83 CE. A series of attacks was launched by Ting-ling from the north and the Southern Huns from the south. The year 87 was disastrous for Northern Huns. After their shan-yu (Youliu) was captured, decapitated, and skinned by Xianbei, two hundred thousand Northern Huns surrendered to China.[868] The subsequent incursions of Ting-ling from the north and the attacks of Xianbei (Hsien-pi) from the east eventually turned Hun country into Xianbei country. Such attacks against Northern Huns by their neighbors were noted in the Chinese records as follows: "At this time the Northern bandits were weakening, and different groups rose against them. The Southern Xiong-nu attacked from the front (south); the (Turkish) Ding-Ling or Ting-ling invaded from behind (north); the Xianbei (mixed ethnicities) struck from the left (east), the Western regions (Turkish Wusun) from the right (west); they no longer knew how to retain their sovereignty and fled far into the desert."[869]

According to a Chinese record, some remnants of Northern Huns existed under the leadership of their "king" (probably a khan, not a shan-yu) from the year 119 until the end of the Han dynasty around the lakes of Barkol and Bosten (Pulei and Qin in Chinese respectively) in the northeastern Xinjiang area of China, but the last mention of Northern Hun existence north of China might have been from the year 120.[870]

Even though Huns continued with their nomadic life, their lifestyle by no means proved that they were illiterate. They did not leave an archive behind, but Chinese chronicles indicate that there was written communication between Hun leadership and the Chinese court. In 88 CE, a letter by Xiulan Shan-yu to the emperor mentioned his previous order to Wu-huan and Xianbei tribes to attack Northern Huns, and he indicated it was an opportune time to attack the northerners to unite the Hun nation under one banner.[871] In the year 89, a coalition of Southern Hun, Xianbei, and Han troops caused the northern shan-yu to flee farther north while nearly one hundred thousand tents of the

Northern Huns were forced to join the Xianbei confederation.[872] Southern Huns retained power over the northern non-Chinese peoples because of the Hun reputation, but they could not unify the entire north under a single polity, because the southern shan-yu continued to rule as a sovereign from within the Chinese borders.[873] Owing to their treaty with China, Southern Hun troops could not remain north of Han borders to exercise control of the land, even when they were capable of doing so.

Eventually, in the late second century CE, the northern non-Chinese peoples began to ally themselves with the Xianbei since they were viewed as antagonists of China, whereas the southern shan-yu appeared to be associated with the house of the Han.[874] But the Southern Huns never lost their ethnic identity during their stay within Chinese borders, even after the Han dynasty ended in the early third century.[875] The Huns who later invaded China and formed various dynasties in China were from the Southern Huns, whereas the Huns who later ravaged Europe were from the Northern Huns.[876]

Starting in 50 CE, the Chinese administration managed to include the commemoration of the Han family in Hunnish sacrificial rites. This process, even though Huns were still not sinicized, had a profound effect as Huns began to identify with the Han as well. Eventually, after the fall of the Han dynasty, China went into its Three Kingdoms/Six Dynasties period (220–589), and the remaining Hun nobles viewed themselves as carriers of the Han tradition. As a result, new Hunnish dynasties emerged in China, with the view of carrying on Han authority while also continuing the tradition of mythic descent from legendary Hun leader Mo-tun.[877]

THE FALL OF THE SOUTHERN HUNS

The Yellow Turban Rebellion (184–205), which eventually spelled the doom of the house of the Han, also brought down the Southern Hun government. In the year 187, the Southern Hun noblemen rebelled against their leader, Qiangqu Shan-yu, for fear their shan-yu would attack his own people as part of the Hans' efforts to quell the rebellion. Consequently, shan-yu was murdered, and his son Chizhi was placed to the throne of Southern Huns. But his reign was short. In the year 189, Huns were briefly ruled by their noblemen without a shan-yu. It appears they were governed in a more fragmented way, as the former Chinese emperors had hoped to achieve.

Southern Huns continued the administration of their territories until 216–220, or until the Han dynasty ended in the year 220. In 216 the southern shan-yu Huchuquan was retained at the Han court and replaced with the last shan-yu, Qubei by Chinese general Cao Cao, who then divided the Southern Huns into five groups, thus ending the single Southern Hun polity.[878] Beyond this time, there are no known Sino-Hunnish relations, since there was no single Chinese state and no single Hun polity. With the collapse of the Han dynasty in 220, Southern Huns witnessed the end of their state, but they did not disappear completely; they survived and resurfaced again in Chinese politics in the upcoming centuries.

3.5. THE OUTCOME OF THE HUNS

Following the formal cessation of the Southern Hun state in 216, the (Southern) Huns remained together in the northern territories of the Han Empire until the Han dynasty ended in 220. Suddenly China went from a unified state into the Three Kingdom period (220–280), which was followed by a brief unification of China under the Jin (also referred to as Tsin) dynasty (266–420). Meanwhile, in Mongolia, the former home of Asian Huns (Xiongnu), the control of the steppes was now with the multiethnic Xianbei tribal federation, which never formed a state as Huns did.

Most of Northern Huns were long gone westward, but Southern Huns remained in the northern territories of Former Han China. Initially, they were dispersed within the three short-lived Chinese kingdoms that followed the fall of the Han dynasty. Subsequently, when China was reunified under the Jin (Tsin) dynasty, the remnants of scattered Southern Huns came under the rule of the Chinese emperor until the empire suffered from revolts in the early fourth century, forcing the Jin dynasty to retreat to southern China as the north witnessed the evolution of the Sixteen Kingdoms period (304–439), also known as the Wu Hu period. Before the Chinese Sui dynasty rose to power in 589, Chinese history also saw the Six Dynasties period (266–589), which coincided with the above-mentioned historical periods mostly over the same geographic area. Only one dynasty was of Chinese origin; four were established by Southern Huns while the Tabgač Turks formed another one. In fact, Tabgač Turks ended the Sixteen Kingdoms (304–439) and forced Chinese history into the Northern and Southern dynasties (420–589).

THE SURVIVAL OF THE SOUTHERN HUNS

Huns continued to exist even after the Southern Hun polity ended in 216 CE. While Northern Huns' westward departure from the Mongolian steppes led to the eventual appearance of the Black (European) Huns and the White Huns (Ephtalites) in eastern Europe and western Turkestan respectively, it is clear that, as we will see later, the remnants of Southern Huns contributed to the establishment of multiple Turkish polities within China proper. The Hun entity in China also contributed to intermarriages with Tabgač Turks (T'o-pa), who established a royal dynasty in control of all northern China between the fourth and sixth centuries. Furthermore, in the fourth and fifth centuries, we find the Buddhist Chü-Ch'ü Huns, under whose dominions in Kansu the Gök-Türk royal clan lived until it later went on to establish the Gök-Türk Qaghanate in the mid-sixth century.[879]

During the rebellions against the Jin, Southern Huns also acted against the empire to form short-lived dynasties within China.[880] Southern Huns were familiar with Chinese internal politics from their earlier close interactions with the Han dynasty. Consequently, small fragmented Hunnish polities ruled parts of northern China from the early fourth century CE until the sixth century. The four Hun dynasties formed within China were the Han or Former Zhao (304–29), the Northern Liang (401–60), the Xia (406–31), and the Northern Zhou (557–81).[881] Even though these states were formed by nonsinicized Huns, their leaders did not use the title of *shan-yu* although they claimed to be descendants of Mo-tun. The remaining Hun groups, which were outside of China, joined the Juan-juan, the next nomadic power taking control of the northern steppes.[882] But this event did not take place until the fourth century.

The founder of the Xia (Hsia) dynasty came from the seemingly indestructible line of the descendants of Mo-tun, the founder of the former formidable Xiong-nu (Hun) Empire of the steppes.[883] The administration of the Xia refused to accept the Chinese ways of governing, and it turned into a powerful state, but it lost sovereignty to another Turkish-origin dynasty, the Northern Wei of the T'o-pa (Tabgač). Even after the fall of their short-lived small northern kingdoms, the Southern Huns continued to be present in the territories of northern China. Their existence is documented in Chinese archives from the fifth and sixth centuries.

The Northern Zhou (557–81) was the last known imperial dynasty of China established by Southern Hunnish clan. This dynasty became instrumental in introducing Chinese Buddhism to the Gök-Türks late in the sixth century.[884] One other interesting information is that Li-Yuan, the founder of the T'ang dynasty (618-907), was grandson of Dugu Xin, who was an aristocrat from the previous Northern Zhou dynasty.[885] Hence, through the Northern Zhou dynastic lineage the T'ang dynasty of China seemed to have Xiong-nu (Hun) ancestry as well.

THE FATE OF THE NORTHERN HUNS

When the Northern Huns began to leave their ancestral territories in modern-day Mongolia in the late first century CE, nearly one hundred thousand of them were assimilated by the Xianbei, but the bulk of them moved in westerly direction towards western Turkestan.[886] In the mean time, the apparent addition of the Huns into the Xianbei tribal group at least added more Turkish character to the ethnically mixed tribal federation. With their migration those who moved further west did not go into oblivion nor did they get absorbed by another political entity. In fact, nearly a century after their departure from the Far East, a Chinese source indicated that these Xiong-nu were in existence in the Altai mountain range region.[887] Meanwhile, the other contemporary Turkish tribal entity of Wu-sun was located at Yettisu (modern-day southeastern Kazakhstan) region. Later, Northern Wei records of China reiterated that many of the Xiong-nu were still present in the vicinity of the Altai under the same political name.

While the Wu-sun territory was absorbed by a group of the Xiong-nu, known as the Yüeh-pan Xiong-nu, the main core of the Northern Xiong-nu had moved further west and by the third century it began to mingle with another Turkish tribal federation of the Ting-ling. When the (Northern) Huns began to leave their ancestral territories, the Chinese became acquainted with the remaining Turkish tribes. The Yüeh-pan, an obscure group in the Chinese chronicles, were noted to be the same as the Northern Xiong-nu, and their language was similar to that of the Kao-ch'e (Qanglï Turks), and while the Töles were considered to be descendants of the Xiong-nu, the Chinese suggested that the Uighurs also were of Xiong-nu origin.[888]

We know that the Northern Huns' migratory movement came in response to the lack of security in the Mongolian steppes. From their south, the Southern Huns, in alliance with Chinese Han military support, were hostile, and from the east, the multiethnic Xianbei tribal forces were encouraged by China to keep pushing against the Northern Huns. Finally, as the Northern Huns began their westward migration to reach the Altai region. After more of them left the steppes north of China in the second century, the Northern Huns first settled in the territories of the Altai region and the Kazakh steppes before they eventually moved in two separate directions. By the third century it is clear that the bulk of the Northern Xiong-nu who in the end of the first century CE were leaving their homeland in the Mongolian steppes was now spread across the vast territories of modern-day north and northeastern Kazakhstan and western Siberia (the Irtysh and Middle Ob river regions). Some sources suggest that the Xiong-nu who had migrated westward away from the Mongolian steppes were now known to be as the Western Huns. However, it is from the Altai region that these so-called Western Huns (migrating core of the Northern Xiong-nu) further split into the European Huns and the White Huns who moved to Europe and Sogdia (modern-day Uzbekistan and Tajikistan) respectively.[889]

Those Huns, who moved in northwest direction after splitting from the main body of their tribal confederation, reached the northern shores of the Caspian Sea, and eventually gave rise to the European Huns of Attila, who in turn eventually caused the destruction of the Western Roman Empire.[890] Their vanguard group first appeared on the outskirts of eastern Europe by the late second century. Meanwhile, the remainder of the Huns who did not move towards Europe left the Altai region to reach modern-day southern Uzbekistan territory. Ultimately, by the fourth century, the westward-moving (Northern) Huns clearly came into military-political action as the 'Black' Huns (invading Europe; chapter 4.2) and the White Huns (making incursions into Persia and India; chapter 3.6).[891] In the ancient Turkish nomenclature of directions, colors were often used; in this instance, black indicated north, and white meant west. Even though there is evidence that this color-coded direction system existed since the time of legendary Hun leader Mo-tun (Mete), there is no known Chinese description of the Northern Huns as the Black Huns and the Southern Huns as the Red Huns.

FURTHER SPLIT OF THE NORTHERN HUNS

In the fourth century for whatever reason the Western Huns (formerly Northern Huns) split again. Due to scarcity of records, they did not seem to have international relations with established civilizations in their vicinity. The closest largest civilization was that of the Chinese. But, probably the activities in the steppes east to them may have prompted them to move again. Even though the Xianbei (chapter 5.1) did not formally form a state in the former seat of the Huns in Mongolia, the evolving tribal political action in the eastern Eurasian steppe led to the formation of the Juan-juan empire, also known as Ruanruan Qaghanate (chapter 5.1). Hence, the development of this new steppe power in the fourth century may have triggered the Huns to move on again. Yet, it is not clear why they did not move as a single tribal confederacy, when in fact, they split their forces to move in different directions. In all likelihood there was internal squabble for power that forced them to make their internal division. In the fourth century, while a group of Huns moved to the north of the Caspian Sea, some of the Huns began to move southward from the Kazakh steppes, but a third group of the Huns remained at the foothills of the Altai Mountains.

Regardless of where they were headed to, these Hunnish groups managed to maintain their political identity of the Huns. After the year 350, the Sassanid Persians met with the first group of Central Asian tribes, which they called Chionites, whereas the tribes referred to as the Ephtalites appeared in the following century from the Altai; meanwhile, the European (Black) Huns had begun to show up in large numbers between the Volga and the Don by 370.[892] Indeed, the Huns of Europe were from the same group of Huns (Xiong-nu) who left the steppes of Mongolia beginning late in the first century.[893] The European Huns who arrived in the Volga basin from the Altai were political and cultural descendants of the Xiong-nu.[894]

It is clear that after they abandoned the Mongolian steppes, the Huns first moved into western Central Asia. Because of the westward displacement of the Northern Xiong-nu, their relocated polity is sometimes referred to as the Western Xiong-nu (Hun) Empire by some modern historians, particularly Turkish historians. In other words, when the second split of the Xiong-nu

Empire occurred in the year 48 CE or 49 CE, leading to the formation of the northern and southern states, some scholars considered the beginning of the Western Xiong-nu Empire to have arisen from the northern state after its center of power shifted westward into the Kazakh Steppe. It is believed that the fragments of the Western (formerly Northern) Xiong-nu merging with the Uralic tribes in Siberia eventually formed the European Huns, whereas the Chionites, likely the remaining larger group from these so-called Western Huns, were known as Hunnas in India, Khun in eastern Turkestan, and White Huns in the Eastern Roman Empire.[895] In the old Turkish nomenclature of the directions, the color white would have indicated west, hence the name White Huns (Ak Hunlar) for the Western Huns. The Chinese used to call a country by the name of the capital of that country; hence, they called the Ephtalite Empire (White Huns) Hua, after its capital.[896]

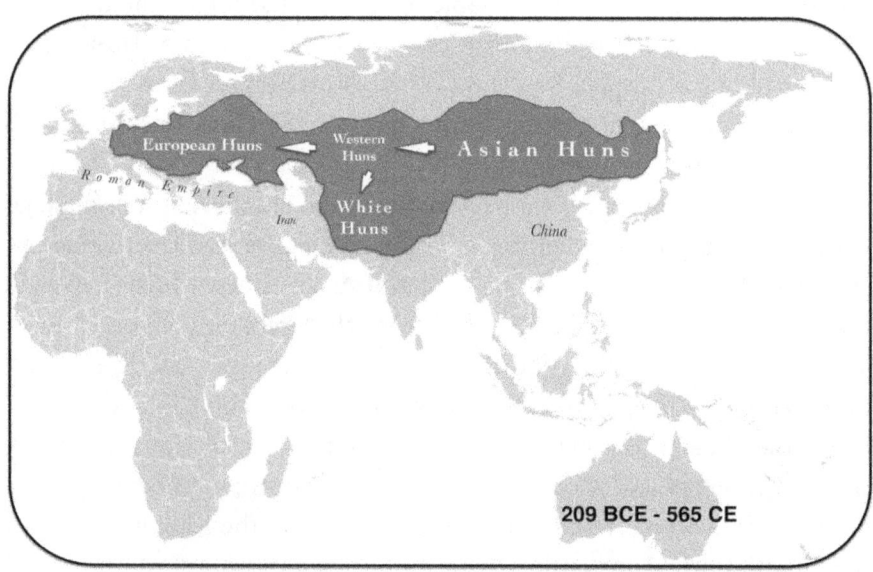

Map 6. *The Huns and the beginning of the great Turkish migrations. As shown in chapter 4, after the fall of the Huns, the Turkish tribes moving westward from their ancestral steppes in Mongolia began to emerge in world history one by one.*

THE EUROPEAN HUNS VERSUS THE ASIAN HUNS (XIONG-NU)

Where did the name 'Hun' originate from? As many of the early Turkish tribes carried totemic tribal names due to their shamanic traditions, the name 'Hun' may have derived from the ancient Turkish word 'khun' for sheep. But, was the name 'Hun' synonymous with the Chinese appellation 'Xiong-nu'? Previously there was a lack of information to link the European Huns to the Xiong-nu. In other words, were the Huns of Attila the descendants of the Xiong-nu? Were the White Huns who controlled northern India and turned the Sassanian Persian Empire into a vassal state the descendants of the Huns of Mo-tun?

Even before the European Huns showed up in the annals of the Roman Empire late in the fourth century, a Sogdian merchant's letter dated 313 CE clearly indicates without any doubt that the Xiong-nu of China's northern peoples were described as the Xwn in Sogdian, in other words the same proper name of the Central Asian tribes that showed up in eastern Europe. The term Xiong-nu was the Chinese description of the people rather than their proper political name. The Sogdian merchant's use of the term Xwn (or Hun) was the accurate name of the people who had threatened the security of China for nearly four centuries.[897]

Skeptical of the early fourth-century Sogdian letter, a historian suggested that the term Hun (in the Sogdian document) could have been used as generic term for "barbarian" in the West, since Eastern Roman sources often referred to the Hungarians and the Ottomans as the Huns, to label them as barbarians. But French historian de la Vaissière countered this suggestion by saying that there was no proof for the generic use of the term for a barbarian before the fourth century, before the Huns appeared in Europe.[898]

Could it be that the Sogdian term Xwn for Hun was a distorted version of the Chinese description Xiong-nu? This Sogdian was a merchant, and like all other merchants of Central Asia, he traded with all peoples, whether the Xiong-nu or the Chinese. Hence, he was in all likelihood in direct contact with the Xiong-nu as known to the Chinese, but these people must have called themselves Hun since this merchant referred to them as Xwn. In fact, it is clear that the Chinese referred to the Hun with the term Xiong-nu, which meant "howling slaves" among other possible meanings already mentioned earlier; hence, it was actually a derogatory term coined by the Chinese to describe the Hun.[899] It is known that the ancient Chinese never referred to the tribal people by their proper name, instead they often used another name they made up for them.

The name Hun appeared in different formats in different geographic areas; the Sogdian term Xwn, the Sassanid term Hyōn, the Indian word Hūna, and the term Xoŭvoi used by Ptolemy all described the people by the Don River in the second century CE. These descriptions show the extent of the migrations of the Huns over a large geographic area, from the Far East to central Europe in the west, from the Kazakh Steppe in the north to the Iranian world and northern India in the south.[900]

There are other references linking the European Huns to the well-known Xiong-nu of the past. Two Buddhist Indian texts, translated into Chinese around the end of the third century and the beginning of the fourth century, show that the Hūna were actually the Xiong-nu and describe them as neighbors of the Chinese. The translation was done by Chinese Zhu Fahu; the first document was completed in 280 CE, and the second in 308 CE. In the text, which includes a list of multiple peoples and locations, Zhu translated the term Hūna, without a doubt, as the Xiong-nu.[901] In conclusion, the Buddhist Indians and Zhu Fahu both must have known that the Xiong-nu were actually the Huns. Similarly, Sogdian merchant Nanaivandé must have had knowledge of the Chinese term Xiong-nu being properly known as Xwn, or the Hun.[902]

Archaeological studies in Mongolia and southern Siberia have revealed that the weapons, utensils, and ornamental objects used by both the (European) Huns and the Xiong-nu were very similar. Because these "two" tribal peoples lived on the same vast Eurasian steppes, one group on the western extreme point and the other on the eastern extreme point, scholars also consider that it was only natural for these "two" groups to use similar objects as a result of nomadic movements and interactions.[903] However, archaeological findings also demonstrate the cauldrons of the European Huns originated from those of the Xiong-nu, and in addition, their use in rituals was similar in the two distant places. Hence, these discoveries ultimately led to the conclusion that the likeness between the European Huns and the Xiong-nu of Eastern Eurasian Steppe were based not only on material similarities but also on cultural and ritual continuities. It should be noted that the prototype cauldrons of the Huns of Pannonia were found among the cauldrons of the Asian Huns in the Altai Mountains.[904]

Today, we know that the Xiong-nu of the Mongolian steppes and the Huns of Europe and Central Asia were the same people.[905] While we know that the European Huns were primarily Turks (chapter 4.2), the Central Asian (or Western) and the White Huns were likely Turks as well. While the latter group controlled Afghanistan starting in the fifth century, one of their remnants, the Khalaj Turks settled in northern India and Ghur of Afghanistan.[906] They were discovered by the Persian Saffarids who invaded Afghanistan in the 9th century,[907] and later joined their kinsmen the Ghaznavid Turks in the tenth century.[908] Interestingly, the Khalaj Turks (the remnants of the White Huns) also succeeded in establishing their own dynasties in India (volume 2, chapter 1:4) in addition to forming strong influence over Iran as the Sunni Ghilzai Afghans[909] who invaded Iran in the eighteenth century (volume 2, chapter 5:5).[910]

THE EASTERN STEPPES AFTER THE HUNS

Meanwhile, the Xianbei (also known as the Hsien-pi) established the next confederation of tribes in the Mongolian steppes, but this time with mixed ethnicity, as the union had clear Turco-Mongol character. Before the westward Hunnish migration, the Xianbei moving southward had caused the Huns to remain vulnerable between the Xianbei in the north and the Chinese in the south. After the ruling class of the Huns lost control, many Turkish tribes, including some of the Huns, joined the Xianbei confederation, and others moved westward. The Turco-Mongol federation eventually became part of a new nomadic state (407–552), which came to be known as the Juan-juan in the Chinese archives, meaning "unpleasantly wriggling insects."[911] In the West they were referred to as the (Asian) Avars.

THE WESTWARD MIGRATION OF THE TURKS

To summarize the fate of the Northern Huns, these nomads, also known as the Western Huns during their westward migration, seem to have split; one group remained in western Central Asia, where they formed the White Hun Empire (420–552), also known as the Ephtalites, and the other group continued to move northwest to become the European Huns (375–469) of Attila the Hun (chapter 4.2). Today we know that the European Huns were an extension of the Asian Huns (Xiong-nu).[912] In other words, the ancestors of the European Huns (chapter 4.2) and the later appearing (European) Avars (chapter 4.4) were the Northern Huns.[913] With the arrival of the European Huns in the fourth century, the turkization of the central Eurasian steppes also began.[914] It is worth mentioning again that research on the history of the Asian Huns shows that the White Huns were proto-Turks, just as the Europeans Huns were.[915]

Hun history encompassed three phases of existence in very different geographic locations: the Far Eastern, European, and Afghan-Indian phases.[916] The latter two phases were a consequence of the end of the first phase, thus initiated by the westward migration of the Turkish tribes. As we will see later, in the ninth century, the Turkish Khalaj tribes which were discovered during the invasion of Afghanistan by the Muslim Saffarids were the remnants of the White Huns (volume 2, chapter 1.3).

Ultimately, the fallout from the loss of Asian Hun power led to the westward migration of the Turkish tribes, which marked the beginning of the turkization process of the central Eurasian and eventually the western Eurasian steppes. By 500 CE, the Turkish language dominated the central and the western steppes, and by 1000 CE, the language dominated most of southern Central Asia as well.[917] Furthermore, the remarkable spread of the Turkish tribes in such a short time illustrates their vitality and military superiority over the sedentary peoples of their time. Within the fifth century, the Turks were in Europe (Attila near ancient Paris in 451), in China (the Tabgač as founders of the Northern Wei dynasty in 458), and in northwest India (the White Huns in 484).[918]

The arrival of the early Turkish tribes and the presence of Turkish loanwords in Europe were a direct result of the protracted Turkish migrations from the Far East due to the breakup of Asian Hun power in the Mongolian steppes north of China.[919] The disappearance of the Hunnish state in Asia led to significant consequences both in the Far East and in Europe, as well as in Turkestan. Chapter 4 deals with the great Turkish migrations and their consequences, resulting in the wide expansion of the Turkish tribes from the Eastern Eurasian Steppe into Turkestan and to the Western Eurasian Steppe in central and eastern Europe. Then, within the context of Turkish history, chapter 5 elaborates on the events in Asia in the aftermath of the fall of Hun power in northern China and Mongolia. By the fourth century, Turkish history was now evolving on two different continents. With the westward movement of the nomads known as the great Turkish migrations, many Turkish tribes migrated in the direction of eastern Europe, and others remained behind, scattered in Asia, particularly in the Kazakh and the Mongolian steppes and within northern Chinese territories. In short, we will see the evolution of Turkish history both in Europe (chapter 4) and in Asia (chapter 5, and volume 2 chapters 1 and 2) up until the Mongol invasion (volume 2 chapter 3). The subsequent chapters in volume 2 then illustrate the continued development of Turkish history into the modern age.

3.6. THE WHITE HUNS

The White Huns were a group people who arrived from Central Asia to form an empire that included modern-day territories of Uzbekistan as well as much of Afghanistan and Pakistan in addition to northern half of the Indian subcontinent. In the zenith of their power on the west they bordered the Sassanian Empire and on the east they reached the outskirts of modern-day Xinjiang of China. Starting their reign in the second half of the fourth century they immediately engaged themselves against the Persian Sassanians, who found themselves in a difficult position to defend their eastern borders against these Central Asian Turks while they were also dealing with unfriendly Eastern Roman Empire to their west. By the fifth century they began to expand into the Indian subcontinent at the expense of a major Indian empire. Although they had pastoralist nomadic lifestyle of Central Asia, they were quick to adapt to the culture and ways of life of the land, and yet, they were still able to retain their warlike character. The White Huns later came to be known as the Ephtalites but the founder of the empire was actually a different group of Hunnish tribal people.

THE ORIGIN OF THE WHITE HUNS

As stated in the previous chapter, the Northern Huns who left their ancestral territories in modern-day Mongolia likely settled initially in eastern present-day Kazakhstan and the Altai Mountain area. The Chinese records indicate that in the third century CE there was a group of people in the vicinity of the

Altai Mountain range, just outside the control area of the later appearing fifth century *Juan-Juan* (also known as *Ruanruan*; see chapter 5.1) of Mongolia; these were known to be descendants of the Northern Xiong-nu (Asian Huns) who then migrated towards western Turkestan by mid-fourth century CE.[920] By the middle of the fourth century, their tribal mass experienced another split. While a group of them moved southwest toward Persia, the other group migrated in a northwest direction toward eastern Europe, attracting other Turkish tribes behind themselves. As mentioned earlier, those who migrated to Europe came to be known as the European (Black) Huns, and those who eventually encroached upon the Sassanid territories were the White Huns. The latter group likely came from the Hun tribes leaving the Altai Mountains by mid-fourth century.[921] While the European Huns went on to leave their mark in the history of Europe, their cousins the White Huns who were left behind in Central Asia equally rose to prominence by affecting the course of history of Sassanid Persia and India.

The founding dynasty of the White Huns came to be known as the Kidarites (Chionites), who were later followed by another group of Hunnish people referred to as the Ephtalites by the Persians and Greeks. According to Wei-shu (Northern Wei) records, the Ephtalites also originated from the Altai.[922] The same sources later indicate that the Ephtalites initiated a relationship with China by sending an ambassador to the Northern Wei emperor in 456.[923] The Northern Wei had significant knowledge of the western countries since they sent envoys to them.

However, before the Ephtalites established themselves in the eastern Iranian world, an earlier group of Huns showed up at the doorstep of the Persians. In the mid-fourth century, the Chionites, a branch of the Western Huns (formerly the Northern Huns) in Kazakhstan, caused significant grief for the Persians.[924] In fact, these Central Asian Huns who eventually founded the White Hun Empire emerged from the Xiong-nu of the Mongolian steppes; it is said this group of people, who also gave rise to the European Huns, were from the Oghuric group of Turks.[925] Eventually, these Huns were joined by additional Hunnish tribes arriving from the Altai Mountain area to take the control of western Turkestan to settle there; these people finally came to be known as the White Huns. They were referred to as the Huns by Roman historians, and they were called *Huna* by the Indians.[926]

THE KIDARITE DYNASTY

As stated earlier, the founding dynasty of the White Hun Empire came to be known as the Kidarites, who formed their state neighboring the Persian Sassanid Empire. The Kidarite Huns did not only began to disturb the Persians but also they subsequently began to invade northern India. The Indian sources correctly refer to these Hunnish invaders of India as *"Sveta Huna"*, meaning White Huns. However, the word "white" was not used to describe a certain racial characteristic but rather it was used as an indicator of a "geographic location" or a "direction." In the old steppe culture white indicated "west", and hence, White Huns actually meant "Western Huns." These Inner Asians who first arrived to this region were labeled as Kermichiones from old Persian source meaning 'red,' and therefore, they were likely known as Al-Hun in proper Turkish for Red Hun. This made sense since they were actually the southern wing of the White Huns as the color "red" was used to indicate south.[927] However, it was also the Persians who originally referred to these invading Huns as "Chionites" (Kidarites).[928] But, it has been suggested that the word "Kidarite," possibly meaning Western Hun, was derived from old Turkish runic term *"kidirti"* meaning west.[929]

The arrival of these Inner Asian warriors forced Shapur II the Sassanian king (r. 309-79), to turn his attention away from the Eastern Romans to his eastern borders. After eight years of war (350-58 CE) the Persians made an uneasy truce with these Huns but gained their support for military expeditions against Constantinople. Later, however, Sassanian Bahram IV (r. 388-99) lost much of his eastern territories to the Huns, and in addition, the Persians were forced to pay tribute to the Huns.[930]

According to the Chinese sources, the Kidarite Huns conquered the territory of modern-day Afghanistan prior to 410 CE, and later, they brought the region of Gandhara (modern-day northeastern Afghanistan and northern Pakistan) under their rule. Consequently, they became a threat to the Gupta Empire of northern India. The desperate Indians were not able to stop the repeated Kidarite invasions; the Indians finally took a breather when the Kidarites fell to the new invaders, the Ephtalites, in the Gandhara region between the years 477 and 520 CE.[931]

Meanwhile, the Sassanian armies were repeatedly defeated by the Huns until Yazdgird II (r. 438-57) was able to push back the Central Asian warriors for nearly a decade (440s-450s). However, during this period of time the Kidarite White Huns were in retreat from the Ephtalite forces arriving from Central Asia. Hence, feeling the pressure both from the Ephtalites and the Persian Sassanians the Kidarite Huns pushed themselves against the Gupta Empire of India. Yet, when Yazdgird II felt unrealistic confidence to make a demand of the reversal of the tributes from the Kidarites by 454 or 456, the Huns came back to deal a decisive blow to the Persians. This defeat eventually led to a royal tragedy followed by a civil war in Persia.

THE FALL OF THE KIDARITES

Sassanian ruler Yazdgird II was not successful in his final battle against the Kidarites. Meanwhile, when the king died, his eldest son Hormizd III (r. 457-59) became the next ruler. His brother Peroz (also known as Firuz) instead sought the crown for himself, thus resorting to civil war. In order to secure the throne he sought help from the Ephtalites, the new warlike people from Inner Asia. After capturing the crown of Persia, Peroz I (r. 459-84) ceded some territory to these Central Asians to compensate them for their help.

When Kidarites renewed their offensive in 464 against the Persians, Peroz offered his sister in marriage to Kidarite king Khunkas, also known by the name Khushnavaz, a Sogdian rather than Turkish name. However, when the ruler of the Huns realized that the woman who was sent to him was not from the royal family, the hostilities were renewed. Peroz reached victory when he allied himself with the Ephtalites who finally captured the Kidarite capital in 467 and later killed the last ruler of the Kidarite dynasty. With the fall of the Kidarites the Ephtalites took over as the new dynasty of the White Hun Empire. Initially, the name Ephtalite was applied to the ruling dynasty, but later the name was used interchangeably for the empire that they ruled.[932]

THE RISE OF THE EPHTALITE DYNASTY

Who were these Ephtalites who came from Inner Asia as a new power? The Ephtalites were known to use a typical ancient Turkish title, *tigin*, leaving no doubt that they were Turkish people.[933] According to Chinese records (Wei-shu), the ethnic identity of the dynasty that controlled Sogdia (a land covering parts of modern-day Uzbekistan, Kyrgyzstan, and Tajikistan) for three generations starting in the fifth century was consistent with that of the Xiong-nu, and it was suggested that the Ephtalites were from the same stock as the Huns.[934] Since the Ephtalites were thought to be the same people with the earlier appearing Chionites, they were also referred to as the Chionites, who were first mentioned at about mid-fourth century CE.[935] But in reality, the Kidarite (Chionite) Huns were an earlier group of Huns who threatened the Eastern Roman Empire and Persia.[936]

According to Menander, an Eastern Roman historian, the Kermichiones (Chionites) were Turks previously known as the Massagetae, but for the Persians in the fourth and fifth centuries the Huns (Kušan Huns or White Huns) living east of Iran were known as the Turks.[937] The Ephtalites were a mixture of Turkish tribes like their predecessors, the Xiong-nu. For example, it has been suggested that the tribes joining them from the Pamir were related to the Qarluq Turks.[938] One other group of tribes within the Ephtalite federation was that of the Khalaj Turks,[939] who preserved their ethnic identity and culture until they came under the rule of their kinsmen, the Ghaznavid Turks, in Afghanistan late in the tenth century.

The Ephtalites were also referred to as the "Hua" people who were initially under the rule of the Juan-juan (also known as the Asian Avars; see chapter 5.1); it was suggested that this word in the Early Middle Chinese could have meant "Var," which possibly was derived from the word "Avar." In other words, this hypothesis would claim that the Ephtalites were the same people as the European Avars (see chapter 4:4) who rose to power in Europe in the sixth century.[940] This may make sense since after destroying the Ephtalite White Hun Empire, the Gök-Türks demanded the capture of these Avars from the Eastern Roman Emperor. The origin of the "Hua" perhaps indicated the region of Ghur from where the next dynasty of the White Huns rose to power, but according to another scholar's view the Ephtalite dynasty came from within the original Oghuric Turkish Huns who showed up from Central Asia.[941] Regardless, the Ephtalite Hunnish state was formed by a core of Turkish speaking military elite, and yet, they were rather quickly influenced by the neighboring Persian and Indian cultural and linguistic elements.[942]

In the history of the Asian Huns (Xiong-nu), it is also important to mention the Gaoju (or Kao-ch'e). These nomads corresponded to the ancient Turkish tribal union of Qanglï, their name meaning "high carts," and they apparently spoke a language similar to that of the Xiong-nu.[943] They were from the west of Mongolia, between Turfan and Jinshan, or in other words from Altai. They were once under the suzerainty of the Juan-juan (Asian Avars), but in 481 they came under the umbrella of another Turkish tribal confederation referred by the Chinese as the T'ieh-le; they established an independent state north of Urumchi (capital of modern-day Xinjiang Uighur Autonomous Region in China).[944] On the basis of information from the Northern Wei, the Ephtalites were from the same ethnic group as the Kao-ch'e, and therefore, they were of Turkish descent, more specifically from Oghuric tribes.[945] Hence, the Ephtalites, being Oghuric, possibly originated from the T'ieh-le tribes.[946] In other words, it is possible that the Ephtalites were not a political extension of the former Northern Xiong-nu but that, since they initially migrated with the Asian Huns, they were once under their leadership and hence the name White Huns. Besides the Ephtalites, the earlier-arriving Chionites and Kidarites were also likely Oghuric Turks who, like the Ephtalites, used the old imperial name of (Asian) Hun.[947]

In the fifth century, the Kidarite territories formerly known as the Kushan lands were overwhelmed by the Ephtalites, who dealt a huge blow to the western Central Asian Buddhist financial organization by destroying and plundering monasteries, but the natives continued to practice their Buddhist faith.[948] The Ephtalite invasion of Sogdia and Bactria (a land covering parts of modern-day Iran, Turkmenistan, Uzbekistan, and Afghanistan) occurred in the second half of the fifth century.[949] A document from the Northern Wei dynasty of China, from about 457 CE, suggests that the Xiong-nu ruler attacked and conquered Su-t'ê.[950] It was initially thought that Su-t'ê was in Crimea, and since the (European) Huns took the Alans in this land, an association between the (European) Huns and the Xiong-nu is also claimed on the basis of this document. However, a prominent Japanese historian suggested that Su-tě was actually Sogdia in Central Asia, not in Crimea, and the Ephtalites who ruled this area were the Xiong-nu.[951] The fact that Su-tě sent lions as gifts to the (Northern) Wei court in the fifth century indicates that the country described was actually Sogdia in Central Asia and not Crimea; during the Ming dynasty (1368–1644), Samarkand (modern-day Uzbekistan) and Herat (modern-day Afghanistan) still had lions in the wilderness. Meanwhile, Crimea had a location known as Sughdak (Sudak or Soldaïa), which was a Genoese entrepôt in the Middle Ages, but whether this place served as a significant trade center with direct connections with China before the fifth century is not known.[952] In short, according to the Tʼo-pa Wei records, Su-tě (Sogdia) was conquered by the Xiong-nu likely in the middle of the fourth century, and it is where they formed their kingdom. These Xiong-nu were also known as the Chionites or Chionitae, per Ammianus Marcellinus. According to the records of this Western chronicler, they formerly established their state in 356 CE. In the mean time, the name Ephtalites did not appear in the Chinese records until 456 CE.[953] Even though the Ephtalites conquered their kinsmen the Kidarites, according Western chroniclers Agathias and Procopius the Ephtalites were Hunnish people just as the Kidarites were.[954]

At the beginning of the sixth century, the Ephtalites held back the westward advancement of the Kao-chʼe (Qanglï) and the Juan-juan.[955] At the zenith of their power, they reigned over large territories, including Sogdia, much of modern-day Chinese Turkestan, and northern India.[956] These Huns interfered with the internal affairs of the Persian Sassanids by acting as kingmakers for the Iranian rulers.[957] For a brief period, they also conquered parts of Persia. Moreover, they controlled northern India.[958]

The Ephtalites were a confederation of tribes just like their predecessor the Xiong-nu were. Like other Turkish empires that occupied civilized areas, they came under the cultural influence of the occupied territories. Just as their kinsmen the Seljuks did late in the eleventh century, the Ephtalite Huns also adopted Iranian personal names. As a result, the Ephtalites seem to have become persianized over time. These nomads settled in an area where Persian-speaking people were the majority. As a result, the Ephtalites became exposed to the customs of the native peoples different than theirs. It has been suggested that polyandry was one of the customs of the Ephtalites (White Huns). This practice was however present in Bactria at least a century before the Ephtalites appeared in the area, and it was in fact a Bactrian tradition rather than an Ephtalite one.[959] Yet, the Chinese records erroneously attribute the culture of polyandry to the newcomers.

According to later records, the Ephtalite language was different from that of the Juan-juan and the Qanglï. Just as the Danubian Bulgar Turks lost their cultural and linguistic identity upon being absorbed into the numerically superior Slavic population, it is possible that the Ephtalites, who were Turks, over time became assimilated by the native Bactrian people.[960] According to texts from the 530s or 540s from Procopius, a Greco-Roman chronicler, the Ephtalites were from the same origin as the Huns, but their way of life was different from that of their kinsmen, owing to the fact that they had experienced cultural assimilation.[961] In other words, unlike the European Huns, they were no longer a nomadic people. Their kinsmen, the Tabgač Turks (Northern Wei, chapter 5.2), had been similarly assimilated by the Chinese population by the sixth century. Even though Western records from the sixth century indicate the Ephtalites were a sedentary people, Eastern records suggest that they followed a nomadic lifestyle.[962] However, it is conceivable that even though there were urban people in the Ephtalite Kingdom, there were also people living as nomads in felt tents, as noted in the records from the year 519.

RELATIONS WITH PERSIA AND INDIA

When the Ephtalites assumed the control of the White Hun Empire by taking over the Kidarite territory that the Persians opportunistically captured, Sassanian monarch Peroz challenged the White Huns. He subsequently lost back to back battles, in the years 467 and 471. He was captured twice and had to pay huge ransom-tributes. As the Ephtalite Huns exerted their power over the Persians they managed to intervene in the internal affairs of the Sassanian court, and as a result, Sassanian Persia became a vassal state of the White

Huns.⁹⁶³ In order to overcome his humiliation in 484 Peroz sought his final battle, which did not only cost him his life but also most of his army was slain by the victors.

We need to look into the historical Persian mind set in regards to dealing with the fact of the Sassanian Empire coming under the overlordship of the White Hun Empire. After the Parthian Empire (247 BCE–224 CE) of the Arsacids had been helpless to defend the Iranian capital Ctesiphon against their archrival the Romans, the Sassanian Empire (224–651) took the leadership of Persia by claiming its legitimacy based on their military success against their aggressors from Rome. Nevertheless, the appearance of the White Huns damaged this legitimacy due to their repeated humiliation against these Central Asian warriors. In addition, their position as a regional power was threatened when the Sassanian Empire fell into vassal status under the power of the White Huns. Even then, the Sassanian kings managed to stay in control of Persia by claiming lineage to the legendary Kayanian kings who went through similar ordeal but ultimately managed to defeat their enemies the Turanians. Nevertheless, the legitimacy of the Sassanians in kingship was seriously put in danger by the White Huns when they came under their vassalage.⁹⁶⁴ However, with the White Hun Empire being finally crushed by the Gök-Türks in mid-sixth century, the Sassanians took opportunity as being participants in this destruction, and hence, they seemed to gain some vindication for their fictitious Kayanian legitimacy. Yet, the Sassanian existence did not last long since Persia fell to Umayyad Arabs by mid-seventh century.

While the White Huns continued to collect tribute from the Persians until mid-sixth century, they reached the zenith of their power by the end of the fifth century. By this time they controlled nearly entire western and eastern Turkestan territories.⁹⁶⁵ By the beginning of the sixth century the Ephtalites also overcame the powerful Gupta Empire, and as a result, they conquered virtually entire northern India. By the second quarter of the sixth century the White Hun Empire may have been the largest empire of the world.⁹⁶⁶ In the east the Ephtalite White Hun Empire reached Urumchi (in modern-day Xinjiang), in the south central India, in the north the Kazakh steppes, and in the west the borders of Eastern Roman Empire through its vassal Sassanid Persia.

THE FALL OF THE EPHTALITE WHITE HUNS

Early in the first half of the sixth century, while the Ephtalites controlled the central portion of the Silk Road in western Turkestan, they also subjugated the Sassanid Persians to their west but by middle of the century on their eastern front they faced a new power, that of the Gök-Türks (chapter 5.3), who aimed to take control of the Silk Road.[967] Hence, the rise of the Gök-Türks added new political and military complicating factors for the Ephtalites, who in addition needed to deal with the Sassanians eager to eliminate the White Huns. Under the leadership of Khusrow Anušarwan I (r. 531-79) the Sassanians found an opportunity to regain respect with the help of the Gök-Türks, who had just crushed the Juan-juan (Asian Avars) to take control of the steps. Meanwhile, in the Far East, the Northern Wei dynasty in China had split into two smaller states. This was the status of politics of the time in Asia.

The Sassanian Persians did not waste time to take advantage of the opportunity as they sought an alliance with these Central Asian Turks in order to rid themselves from their White Hunnish overlords. In 557 the Gök-Türks immediately captured Tashkent and then faced the Ephtalites in a eight-day battle, which ended with a decisive victory for the Turkish qaghan from Mongolia. Finally, the last White Hun king surrendered himself to Sassanian monarch Khusrow around 560-563.

According to Menander Protector, an Eastern Roman chronicler, an Ephtalite played a critical role in the destruction of the Ephtalite Empire. This key player was Katulph, an important political figure and an Ephtalite nobleman who first served under Istemi Yabghu of the Western Gök-Türk Qaghanate and later became an important official of the Persian court.

According to Menander's record, because his wife was sexually assaulted by the king of the Ephtalites, Katulph went on to join the Gök-Türks. A former adviser to his king, he likely had valuable inside information. In time, the Gök-Türks, in alliance with the Persians, attacked the Ephtalites, and therefore, it seems that Katulph contributed to the fall of his former state.[968] The alliance of the Sassanid Persians and Gök-Türks did not last long, however. After the Ephtalite Empire was absorbed by the victors, who were now neighbors, the relationship eventually became hostile. Katulph again changed his allegiance, for an unknown reason; he became adviser to Persian monarch Khusraw I, and with his inside information about the Gök-Türks, he became a prominent politician within the Sassanid establishment. Consequently, he apparently recommended they stop trading with the Gök-Türks.[969]

When Istemi Yabghu's efforts to restore friendly relations failed, the Persian king, listening to his advisers, including Katulph, refused peaceful offers from Istemi, and instead he sent insults to the Turks, accusing them of being untrustworthy.[970] But poor political judgment and the underestimation of the Gök-Türks' resolve by the Sassanid administration eventually resulted in the isolation of the Persians as the Gök-Türks became allies with the Eastern Romans against the Sassanid Empire. After 570, when the Gök-Türks launched an invasion on the former Ephtalite territories occupied by the Sassanians, there is no more mention of the name of Katulph.[971] But the Ephtalite White Huns remained under the rule of the Yabghus of Tokharistan (630–758) (volume 2, chapter 2.2).

POLITICAL AFTERMATH AFTER THE WHITE HUNS

Neither the people of the crushed empire nor their military elite disappeared. In fact, despite the opportunistic Sassanians who wanted to claim the lands of the former White Huns, small polities of White Hun origin began to emerge in the area corresponding to modern-day Afghanistan, Pakistan, and Tajikistan. However, all this White Hunnish territory fell under the overlordship of the Gök-Türks in the second half of the sixth century, then later under that of the Western Gök-Türks early by seventh century when the Sassanians entered into an irreversible decline period.[972]

In the mid-sixth century Pravarasena, an Ephtalite White Hunnish king with hinduized name, took control over the territories of Gandhara and Kashmir; he also built a city named after him as Pravarasenapura (modern-day Srinagar) with a temple known as Pravaresha, and finally, Yudishthira became the last Ephtalite monarch from this dynasty in the sixth century to have ruled over northwestern India independently.[973]

In order to gain the support of the local White Hunnish elements the Gök-Türk leadership took ownership of the Hunnish heritage and titles. Particularly, after the Western Gök-Türk leadership disappeared beyond the year 630, the new Central Asian polity known as the Yabghu of Tokharistan (volume 2, chapter 2.2) was led by the rulers from the former Gök-Türk dynasty but also supported by many of the remaining White Hunnish military elite.[974]

At about 719 CE a local warlord named Tish the 'One-eyed', presumed to be an Ephtalite White Hun, took over much of northern Afghanistan as well as Tajikistan when the Yabghus of Tokharistan were weakened. Meanwhile, in 729 Chinese records indicate that the T'ang court received an embassy from a Turkish ruler known as Qutlugh Ton Tardu, thought to be from the Gök-Türk family or from the Ephtalite White Huns. In short, it appeared that the Ephtalite White Hunnish presence in the area of Afghanistan and Tajikistan may have continued until the mid-eighth century.[975] In fact, the resistance posed by Nizak Tirek (volume 2, chapter 2.2), known by his Turkish title name Tarkhan, showed that he was the last known defender of the White Hunnish territory against the Arab invaders early in the eight century; with his fall northern and western Afghanistan fell into the hands of the Muslims.[976]

Meanwhile, the Khalaj Turks, who were once part of the White Hun tribal confederation, survived in Afghanistan until they were discovered by Muslim Persians in the ninth century. It was these Turks who joined their kinsmen the Ghaznavids of Afghanistan in the tenth century, then formed some of the Muslim dynasties of the Sultanate of Delhi, before joining with the local Pashtuns of Afghanistan to form the dominant Ghilzai Pashtuns or Ghilzai Afghanis who ferociously fought against the invaders of Afghanistan, including the Safavids in the eighteenth century, the British in the nineteenth century, the Soviet Russians in the twentieth, and finally the Americans in the twenty-first century.[977]

The remnants of these White Hunnish dynasty however continued to remain in the political landscape of this part of the world. Later, in the seventh century another group of probable White Hunnish elite emerged in the areas of Kabul and Gandhara, where they formed a new dynasty, which came to be known as the 'Turk-shahis'; they reigned until about the mid-ninth century. Known with their Ephtalite Hunnish titles the Turk-shahis showed resistance against the Arab invaders and managed to keep them out of Kabul, Zabulistan (Ghazna), and Kandahar.[978] By the ninth century the Turk-shahis finally vanished with Kabul, Zabul, and Kandahar falling into the hands of Muslims, whereas in Gandhara a new dynasty known as the Hindu-shahis emerged.

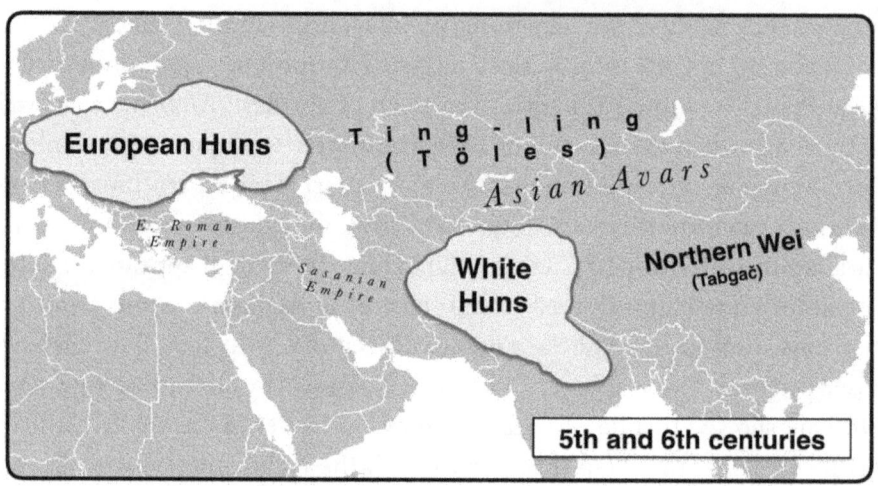

Map 7. By the middle of the fifth century both European Huns and White Huns in Afghanistan and northern India were powerful states. However, in the next century the lands of these formidable empires came under the influence of another emerging Turkish powerhouse, the Gök-Türks.

THE LEGACY OF THE HUNS IN ASIA

Due to biased reporting by previous chroniclers of the Chinese, Persians, Greeks, and Romans, the Huns have been given an unfair coverage in the annals of the history. They have been labeled as "barbarians," "savages," "goat herders," "scourge of God," and so on. However, they did not deserve any of the biased comments that they received in history. The Huns showed remarkable resilience, overcoming multiple hardships both from human and natural causes, and managed to demonstrate political presence over nearly the entire Eurasian vast lands for a long time. With their dominance over their adversaries they certainly had significant influence over them.

The Huns actually were unique group of Turks who did not only have long lasting political existence but also they had significant impact on well-established sedentary civilizations both in Asia and Europe. Their political presence in the arena of the world history in fact stretched from the late third century BCE until the middle of the seventh century CE. Hence, during their presence of nearly nine centuries they deeply affected old civilizations of China, Persia, India, and Europe, including the once invincible Roman Empire.

The Huns left multiple legacies behind. One of them was the formation of the first Turkish state in history with the unification of most Turkish tribes. Furthermore, their military dominance over China forced the Chinese to abandon their chariots in favor of the concept of the cavalry in order to keep up with the nomadic mounted archers.[979] Moreover, Mo-tun's establishment of the first organized army in Turkish history is immortalized today by the insignia of the army of the Republic of Turkey with the markings of "209 BCE." In addition, Hun control of the eastern end of the Silk Road, which the Chinese failed to overcome even with the extension of the Great Wall, allowed the Turks to play a significant role in commercial relations in the Far East for centuries to come. Finally, their presence in northern China allowed their Central Asian kinsmen to penetrate into these territories, which did not come under the full control of the Chinese until the Song dynasty took over late in the tenth century, when most Turks were already gone from the Far East.

Militarily the Huns succeeded in collecting tributes from Han China starting before common era then grabbing the political control of China in the fourth century, then they contributed in the fall of the Western Roman Empire in the fifth century after causing the split of once mighty Roman Empire a century earlier, and they also collected tributes from the Eastern Roman Empire; in addition, in the fifth century they turned the once proud Persian Sassanian Empire into a vassal state paying hefty tributes.[980]

One of the important historical outcomes of the White Hunnish presence in India was that these Central Asian warriors effectively prevented Arabs from invading India. It is thought that the White Hunnish military units together with native Indian fighters under the regime of Gurjara Pratihara in northern India did not allow Muslim expansion into India. It is believed that the Hunnish elements in India may have contributed to the evolution of the well known Rajputs for their warlike traditions.[981] Ultimately, Islam began to make inroads to the Indian peninsula later with the Ghaznavid Turks (volume 2, chapter 1.3) who penetrated into the Hindu territory after the tenth century.

The White Huns left deep marks in the history of Persia and India. Particularly in the case of the Persians the Hunnish overlordship created the galvanization of the Persian identity, which helped the Iranians later against the assimilation by their Arab invaders.[982] In the case of the Indians the Hunnish warriors protected Hinduism from becoming an early target by militant Islamic expansion of the Umayyad Arabs.

Besides Hinduism and Zoroastrianism, Buddhism was also a well-established religion of the land of the White Huns. When the Muslim Arabs reached the territories of Afghanistan in the seventh century, the Turks of the territory were already staunch Buddhists. Hence, in this rugged terrain while the people of the White Huns had accepted this Indian religion as their faith, their rulers the yabghus of Tokharistan from Gök-Türk dynastic family were also Buddhists. The well-known giant buddhas of the valley of Bamiyan in central Afghanistan, which were blown into pieces by the Taliban in March 2001 were originally built under the patronage of the White Huns.[983]

In the context of historical facts it is worth to mention here about the history of Nestorianism as it had part in the history of the Turks. After this view of Christianity was proclaimed to be a heretical faith by the the Council of Ephesus in 431 and the Council of Chalcedon in 451, its followers relocated themselves to the Sassanian Empire, where Nestorianism was declared to be the doctrine of the Persian Christian church in 484, the year Sassanian emperor Peroz died. Although we do not have any proof that White Huns accepted this faith as their religion, we know that the Turks of Mongolia at the time Genghis Khan were mostly Nestorian Christians (volume 2, chapter 3).

The Huns also provided cultural influence upon their neighbors as well. One significant Hunnish contribution, particular to China, was in the area of male dressing. The Chinese have always been very proud of their culture, and any cultural trait other than theirs has been looked down by them. In fact, the

Chinese despised Central Asian outfits as being the clothing of the low class people. In ancient China, people were accustomed to wearing loose robes as their garments. Meanwhile, the Central Asians being equestrians wore a caftan reaching down to the knees in addition to loose trousers suitable for horse riding and finally boots made of felt or leather.[984] Furthermore, the Huns were known for wearing fur caps or hats.[985] Despite the fact the Chinese men detested nomadic clothing, in 307 BCE the state of Chao presumably became the first Chinese polity to adopt the concept of the cavalry, and with it the nomadic male clothing suitable for riding horses.[986] However, the Hunnish influence over time became more and more visible upon the Chinese as by the beginning of the third century, the Chinese started to accept the trousers of the Huns, and by the seventh century, the use of trousers was more popular throughout China.[987] This conversion was facilitated by the Central Asian (Turkish) Northern Wei dynasty of China that lasted into the second-half of the sixth century. In fact, by the time the T'ang dynasty took the power in China in 618, Central Asian Chinese male clothing style was already adopted into the Chinese culture as their own.[988]

During the imperial period of Han China, the Chinese realized that their war chariots were completely ineffective against the deadly cavalry of the Huns. Hence, the Huns played a crucial role in introducing the concept of cavalry into China.[989] It is a fact that the Turks of the past were expert equestrian archers, thus receiving the historic nickname *mounted archers*.[990] Both the warriors from the Ting-ling tribal federation as well as the Huns were known for their way of attacking with lightning speed on horseback.[991] But they also used their equestrian skills for sports as well, and later, games such as polo have emerged from Asia (see chapter 1.2). Chinese have documented that the Huns also pursued diversions such as horse jumping and camel races.[992] Central Asian horsemen were also known for practicing falconry on horseback to hunt for foxes and pheasants. The Huns and other Turkish tribal customs allowed horse racing during funerals.[993]

Chapter 4:

THE GREAT TURKISH MIGRATIONS

4.1. THE TRIBAL MOVEMENTS

The beginning of mankind's urban life occurred before the Bronze Age, even possibly in the Paleolithic Age. But more advanced urbanization was particularly prevalent when agriculture began around 6000 BCE. As an alternative lifestyle, after the domestication of animals was realized, pastoralist nomadism came into existence between 4000 and 3000 BCE. Then with horseback riding starting around 1000-600 BCE in Central Asia, the nomads of the east gained ability to migrate to farther distances.

Among the major sedentary civilizations of all time we can give the examples of China in the Far East, Egypt and Persia in the Middle East as well as Greece and Rome in the West. On the other hand, among those who were known as nomads early on were the Scythians and Xiong-nu (Asian Huns) in the east, while the Germans and Slavs in the West, and finally the Arabs and Hebrews (Jews) in the Middle East were forced to migrate. But particularly the latter group experienced forced migrations due to persecutions. The Scythians were the first known migrating nomadic people on horseback, moving from Central Asia to eastern Europe. Another major group of migrating nomadic people of the Antiquities were the Turks who made an impact on the world history. Their westward movement on horseback from the heart of Central Asia began late in the first century CE or sometime in the second century CE. While the current section of this book touches upon the history of the Turkish tribes in the context of the great Turkish migrations, the movements of the large tribal federations of the Oghuz (volume 2, chapters 2.5 and 2.6) and Qarluq will be discussed in volume 2.

In the previous chapter, we saw that the Xiong-nu, who officially started Turkish history and established the first international relations in the Far East between the Turks and the Chinese, were the same people who later came to Europe as the European Huns to catalyze the destruction of the Roman Empire and showed up in Afghanistan and northern India as the White Huns. By causing the collapse of the Western Roman Empire, the European Huns contributed to the start of the medieval period, or the Middle Ages. The White Huns, their kinsmen, were called the Sveta Hûna by Sanskrit chronicles and were known as the Ephtalites by the Eastern Romans and the Greeks.[994] It was French historian de Guignes (in his *Histoire générale des Huns, des Turcs et des Mogols*, published in five volumes between 1756 and 1758) who first claimed that Attila's Huns were direct descendants of the Asian Xiong-nu tribes.[995] Recent discoveries of Buddhist Indian texts (third and early fourth centuries) shed more light on the (European) Hun–Xiong-nu connection; these texts and their translations by contemporary Chinese scholar Zhu Fahu refer to the Hun as the Xiong-nu, and vice versa. Similarly, the Sogdian merchant Nanaivandé in the early fourth century referred to the Xiong-nu as the Xwn,[996] or Hun.

With the beginning of the nomadic migrations, the westward movement of the Northern Xiong-nu (Asian Huns) must have pulled with them the non-Xiong-nu Turkish tribes within the prior tribal confederation. As mentioned in the previous chapter, it seems that when they finally settled in the area of the Kazakh Steppe, a group of the leading Xiong-nu moved farther west to Europe to form the European Huns, while another group migrated south to establish the White Hun Empire. Meanwhile, in the Kazakh Steppe, additional tribes remained behind, and/or more Turkish tribes came in from the Mongolian Steppe, possibly pushing the clans previously arrived there farther west. If we assume for a moment that the Scythians were not Turks (for more on the Scythians see chapter 2.3), the Huns were the first Turks who penetrated into eastern Europe. Then they were followed by successive other Turkish tribes coming to the European continent. The Bulgars first settled in modern-day Ukraine in the late fifth and early sixth centuries, followed by the Avars upon the rise of the Gök-Türks in Asia in the mid-sixth century.

With the movement of the Northern Huns away from the Far East starting in the first century CE, Turkish history continued not only in Asia but also in

Europe. The next chapter deals with Turkish history in Asia after the fall of the Xiong-nu, but the current chapter provides a glimpse into the past of the Turks in Europe, where the Turks had a long-lasting and significant influence on Western history. The Ottoman Empire (volume 2, chapter 5) is a well-known historical Turkish power that had a lasting impact on European and world history. But the Turkish entry into European history began about a millennium before the Ottoman Turks' appearance on the world stage.

As noted earlier (chapter 3.4), the decline in the strength of the Northern Huns in the first century CE in the Mongolian plains precipitated the migration of many Turkish tribes westward toward western Turkestan and in a northwest direction toward eastern Europe. The leading clans of this migration are believed to have been from the ruling Hunnish tribes (of the Northern Huns). Since the Huns spoke the Oghuric dialect of Turkish, it was natural that the first group of Turks arriving to Europe spoke this version of Turkish. These were successively the Huns, Bulgars, Avars, and Khazars.

The mass tribal movements started by the Huns are also known as the great Turkish migrations, and they continued for nearly a millennium. At the onset of the migrations, those who settled in western Turkestan formed the White Hun Empire, and those who reached the outskirts of eastern Europe by the fourth century were known as the European Huns.[997] In fact, the first-known Turkish intruders into Europe were the European Huns of Attila in the fourth century.[998] But there is evidence Turkish-speaking tribes arrived on the northern shores of the Black Sea before the European Huns. They are thought to have been a spearheading group of Turks before the actual invasion of Europe.[999]

Some scholars have hastily suggested that these European Huns might have been Mongols. This conclusion is based on their physical appearance (cemetery findings) and their Turkish names being confused for Mongolian names. Even their way of life has been confused with that of the Mongolians. But it is clear, on the basis of paleoanthropological research, that the European Huns were not of one single race but were rather a mixture of people. According to Chinese descriptions, at least some of the Xiong-nu (Asian Huns) had Europoid features, but for some Western scholars as these Turks mixed with the northern Chinese and the Mongols over a few centuries, many of them also had acquired Mongoloid features by the time their descendants reached eastern Europe as the Huns of Attila.[1000] Similar situation appears to be true for contemporary Central Asian Turks (Kazakhs, Kyrgyz, and Uzbeks) as well; many of them have Mongoloid features, whereas Turks in the Middle East have more Europoid features because of having been in this land for nearly a millennium. More on this subject was already discussed in chapter 2.

Both cultural practices and language (determined mostly from personal and tribal names and military ranks) have helped experts to determine that the European Huns were Turks.[1001] Turkologists have concluded that the archaeological findings leave no doubt that both the European Huns and the Asian Huns spoke Turkish.[1002] In fact, the Asian Huns have been shown to be the ancestors of the later-appearing European Huns.[1003] The Hunnish language, on the basis of etymological studies of words recorded by Roman and Greek chroniclers, was closest to Old Bulgarian and modern-day Chuvash, and it apparently had some significant lexical and morphological connections to Ottoman and Yakut Turkish.[1004] Furthermore, later-appearing Danube-Bulgarian is known to be a Hunnish language.[1005] It has been suggested that the language of the Huns (Xiong-nu) was not different from that of the Gök-Türks, who came to the world political arena in the sixth century in Asia.[1006]

After the Huns disappeared from Europe politically, the subsequent immediate Turkish threat came from the Avar Empire, which appeared in the northern Balkans in the sixth century. The European Avars are thought to have been led by the remnants of dispersed Hunnish tribal leaders. Meanwhile, in the early seventh century, the Gök-Türks successfully extended their influence from their base in modern-day Mongolia into the Eastern Roman Empire's territories in modern-day southern Ukraine. Later in the seventh century, the Bulgar Turks, also thought to be of Hunnish origin, established the Bulgarian Kingdom. Finally, the Bulgar Turks were forced to move to the Balkans when the Khazar Turks established an empire lasting nearly four hundred years in modern-day southern Ukrainian and Russian territories.

Starting in the late fourth century, the migration period of Europe followed the great Turkish migration, which brought the Hunnish Turks to the doorstep of eastern Europe. The westward push of these Turks forced European tribes to move deeper into Europe. This resulted in the weakening and permanent splitting of the Roman Empire in 395 CE. The forced relocation of the Germanic tribes of the Angles and Saxons (to modern-day Britain), Franks (to modern-day France), Vandals (to modern-day Spain), and Goths (Visigoths and Ostrogoths to modern-day Spain, Italy, and Greece) helped to shape modern European demographics. The outcome of the migratory patterns of these Germanic tribes finally pressured the Roman Empire to split into western and eastern empires in 395 CE. By the tenth century, the Magyars, from the Finno-Ugric race, had moved into central Europe following the appearance of the Bulgar Turks. The Magyars, associated with the On-Oghur Turks, formed the foundation of today's Hungary. It is an accepted fact that the name Hungary (or Hongrie, in French) etymologically evolved from the Turkish tribe name On-Oghur.[1007]

The great Turkish migrations that began in the first century CE with the weakening of the Northern Huns in the territories of modern-day Mongolia led to the formation of the White Hun Empire in western Turkestan and Afghanistan, but the migrations were followed by the movement of Oghur Turkish–speaking Hunnish tribes that formed successively the Hun, Avar, Bulgar, and Khazar polities in Europe. Later these migrations continued in the tenth and eleventh centuries with the decline of Turkish authority in Mongolia the non-Hunnish Turkish Pečenegs, Qïpčaks, and Cumans began to move in the direction of eastern Europe. By the eleventh century, the Oghuz Turks coming from eastern Europe had moved into the Middle East, where they found a permanent home. After the collapse of the short-lived Mongol Empire, many Turkish tribes in eastern Europe gradually returned to their ancestral steppes in Asia, but the Turkish presence in eastern Europe and Siberia continued until the eighteenth century. With the rise of Russian power then, the Turks were pushed farther back from eastern Europe, but they remained across Central and Northern Asia.

Ultimately, starting late in the first century CE, the westerly great Turkish migrations led to three major consequences. The first was their gradual exodus from the Mongolian steppes, and the second was the gradual turkization of western Central Asia. Finally, the third consequence of these migrations was the expansion of Turkish tribes into Europe. As will be seen later, these movements contributed to the eventual demographic evolutions in a vast geographic area, shaping up modern-day Europe, Central Asia, the Indian subcontinent, and the Middle East.

4.2. THE BLACK HUNS

The first Asiatic warriors who came from the east to change the history of Europe in the fourth and fifth centuries were none other than the Huns, who were undoubtedly Turks.[1008] The lack of written records by the European Huns has led to the question of whether they were the same as the Asian Huns. But it has been suggested that the Kenkol finds were helpful in establishing a missing link between these groups.[1009] These discoveries by the Kenkol River (Kyrgyzstan) showed that scores of Asian Hun tribes left their pastures for Europe via the Pontic Steppe north of the Caspian Sea and the Black Sea.[1010] Today we know the European Huns emerged from the former Xiong-nu warriors of the Far East.[1011] The European Huns were known to be a tribal confederacy, and like other large Central Asian tribal confederacies, which were subdivided into multiple clans with their chieftains, these Huns had a similar leadership system. It was Rua (Rogas), with his brothers Oktar and Mundzuk (Mundiuch), who began to lead the entire Hunnish confederacy into Europe. Upon his death in 434, leadership was passed to his two nephews, Bleda and Attila.[1012] The core language of the leading European Hunnish tribes was Oghuric Turkish, and we understand this better from the Turkish titles and names of the ruling elite of the Huns; for example, Attila's father was Mundzuk (Munčuk), his uncle was Oktar, another paternal uncle was Aibars (known to the Romans as Oebarsius), and before Rogas the uncle of Attila, the supreme leader of the European Huns was Qaraton (meaning black-coat in Turkish).[1013]

In the second half of the fourth century, the unexpected destruction of the large Ostrogothic Empire in the modern-day territories of Ukraine, as well as the surprise smashing of the Visigoths in present-day Romania by the Huns suddenly appearing from Asia, began to squeeze the Germanic tribes westward against the imperial borders of the Roman Empire. It was impossible for these fleeing tribes to resist the lightning-speed attacks of the Huns, who were described as destroying everything that got in their way. It was autumn of 376 when the first wave of Visigoths appeared on the Danubian imperial border, begging the dumbfounded Roman officials for safety in the Roman domain.[1014]

Today it is clear that (as we will see later) the European Huns played a significant role in the development of European history. The major power in the West at the time was the Roman Empire. However, when the Huns arrived in eastern Europe, the Roman Empire no longer had its former strength. Despite the efforts by Emperor Constantine I to reunify the politically divided state in the early fourth century, the Roman Empire could no longer muster enough power to revive its old glorious days. Theodosius the Great (379–95) was the last Roman monarch to rule over all Roman dominions. After his death in 395, the Roman Empire became permanently divided into western and eastern halves. It was under these conditions that the Huns entered Europe from Asia. Around 376 CE, the arrival of these Turkish tribes from the east caused the panic-stricken Germanic Goths to flee to the Danube basin away from the incoming Hunnish groups.[1015] Consequently, the Goths crossed the borders into the Roman Empire. The invasion by the Goths seriously weakened Roman authority in the European territories of the empire. Later, the attack of the Huns of Attila on both the Western and Eastern Roman Empires struck terror into the hearts of the Romans.

From the time the first wave of Germanic tribes hit the Roman border in 376 until the Western Roman Empire ceased to exist in 476 owing to the Hun warriors who conquered Italy, only one hundred years passed. The forced Gothic invasion through the lower Danube in 376 cost the Roman Empire the territories of Gaul; then the invasion by the second wave of Germanic invasion induced by the Huns in 406 forced the Romans to lose part of Spain and the northern African coastline. Finally, while the invasion of 455 took Italy out of the reach of the emperors in Constantinople, the coup d'état by a "barbarian" in 476 formally ended the once-mighty Western Roman Empire.

Before discussing the European Huns, it is important to understand the political health of the Roman Empire before the arrival of the Turkish invaders, and it is equally important to comprehend the eventual consequences of the Germanic tribal movements catalyzed by the Huns.

THE ROMAN EMPIRE BEFORE THE HUNS

The Roman Empire was once a formidable polity, setting the foundation for Western civilization. However, in the year 235, the assassination of Emperor Severus by his own soldiers led to widespread anarchy, known as the Crisis of the Third Century (235–84), which nearly brought the empire to its total collapse. As generals began civil wars to claim the throne, the state became vulnerable to external attacks by Germanic tribes and the Sassanid Persians. In the year 251, the Plague of Cyprian hampered defenses even further. In 258–60 the empire was divided into the Gallic Empire, the Roman Empire, and the Palmyrene Empire.

Finally, when Diocletian (284–305) became emperor, he thought the sheer size of the empire was too much for one man to rule. As the emperor, he was first able to stabilize the empire, thus ending the Crisis of the Third Century. He then created the controversial concept of tetrarchy (rule of four), which allowed the empire to be managed in four zones. He assigned his officer Maximian (286–305) as Augustus (coemperor) of the west, while he remained in charge of the east. In 293 he assigned Galerius and Constantius as junior coemperors to complete his tetrarchy. The latter was the father of Constantine the Great (324–37), who eventually became the sole emperor by ending the tetrarchy government system of Diocletian.

Initially a coemperor (306–24) with Licinius I (308–24), Constantine was instrumental in the proclamation of the Edict of Milan in 313, which declared religious tolerance throughout the Roman Empire, giving the Christians the freedom to practice their religion. In 325, as caesar of the empire, he called for the First Council of Nicaea, which issued the Nicaean Creed in 325, shaping up the doctrines of modern-day Christianity. In 324 he moved the capital from Rome to the Greek city of Byzantium on the Bosporus. In 330, to honor Emperor Constantine, the new capital was named Constantinopolis

(Constantinople) after him; it remained an impenetrable city and the capital of the empire for more than a millennium, until it was conquered by the Ottoman Turks in 1453.

Constantine's dynasty was followed by the reign of Jovian (363–64), who was succeeded by Emperor Valentinian I (364–75), who in turn appointed his brother Valens (364–78) as coemperor of the east. Theodosius I rose to the throne as coemperor of the east in 379, but after his coemperor Valentinian II died in 392, he became the last sole emperor to rule the Roman Empire as a single polity. As emperor, Theodosius I also made Christianity the official religion of the empire. Following his death in 395, the empire witnessed internecine politics for about a decade, and it became divided permanently into the Western and Eastern Roman Empires. While Constantinople remained the capital of the Eastern Roman Empire until the polity ceased to exist in the fifteenth century, in the west Milan served for a short while as the center of the western empire. Later, Ravenna became the seat of the Western Roman Empire from 402 to 440, while Rome reclaimed its capital status for the last time between 440 and 476, when the western empire ceased to exist. But under Odoacer, the first non-Roman (or non-Italian) ruler who deposed the last emperor Romulus Augustulus, Ravenna once again became the capital of the next regime.[1016]

THE MOVEMENTS OF THE GERMANIC TRIBES

During the years 341–48, the Goths became Christians with the help of Ulfilas the Greek, shortly before they were attacked by the Huns.[1017] Feeling the pressure from the Huns at their rear, the Germanic tribes, starting around 376, were on the move toward the frontier of the Roman Empire. The second German incursion into Roman territory did not occur until much later, about 405, when the Goths invaded northern Italy under their leader, Radagaisus. After this threat was defused and the German king was executed, the next wave of Germans crossed the Rhine River into Roman provinces in 406. The main tribal Germanic groups penetrating into the western imperial territories in Gaul were the Alamanni, Suevi, and Vandals.[1018] By 410 the Vandals and Suevi were roaming free within Iberia (modern-day Spain).

The western empire tried to deal with these invaders by subduing them and dispersing them into smaller units to minimize the security threat that they posed. But ultimately, the Roman armies had to deal with a series of German rebellions. The Goths revolted in the years 425, 430, and 436, the Franks followed suit in 428 and 432, and the Alamanni did the same in 430–31. In the face of these German activities within Western Roman imperial territories, Roman commander Aëtius called on the Huns for help against the Germans, who were then effectively subdued in Gaul (modern-day France) by these Asian warriors.[1019] Finally, with the Burgundians defeated in 436–37, the remaining German uprisings were pacified by 439.[1020]

While the Western Romans were managing the troubles caused by the Germanic tribes, they also had to deal with internal political rivalries. Any loss of territory also led to an immediate loss of tax revenue, which was essential to overcome internal political and fiscal difficulties. Hence, loss of revenues from Britain, Spain, and war-torn Gaul added to the financial burdens of the western empire. In 439 the Vandal takeover of the rich North African territories forced the Western and Eastern Roman forces to unite their strength against the Vandals (another Germanic tribal group). However, the serious threat posed by Attila and his Huns on the European frontier allowed the Vandals to keep their possessions. Eventually, the raids of Attila the Hun precipitated the demise of the Western Roman Empire, which was once a great power that ruled over the Western civilization. This event also ended the classic era (or antiquity) and marked the beginning of the Middle Ages (or the medieval period) in Europe.

THE HUN INVASION

The first presence of the European Huns northeast of the Sea of Azov appears to be about 200 CE. In fact, Ptolemy (90–168 CE), a Greco-Roman mathematician and geographer, illustrated in his maps the Hunnish tribes by the shores of the Black Sea in 160 CE,[1021] well before the demise of the Southern Hunnish polity in Asia in 216 CE. As stated in the previous chapter, the Northern Huns had begun to leave their command center in the territories of modern-day northern Mongolia by the end of the first century CE, moving westward and eventually giving rise to the White Huns and the European Huns. The latter group had a relatively short history, but their impact on European history was quite significant, as they contributed to the evolution of the modern-day demographics of Europe.

After crossing the Volga River, the Huns crushed the kingdom of the Alans in northern Caucasus in 374. Some scholars believe that the Alans were an offshoot of previous Scythian-Sarmatian tribal groups. Once their kingdom perished, some of them fled westward into Europe, while others joined their conquerors, the Huns. Another group of Alans fled southward and became the ancestors of the modern-day Ossetians in Caucasus. Then, after crossing the Don River, the Huns first destroyed the Eastern Gothic (Germanic) Kingdom in 375; subsequently, in 376, by crossing Dniester River, they eliminated the Western Gothic Kingdom, causing the Goths to flee.[1022] When the Goths showed up on the banks of the Danube River in 376 CE, the bulk of the Huns who pushed the Goths westward were still much farther east of the Danube by 395, probably around the Volga and the Don.[1023] By the end of the fourth century, the Alans and Goths, previously powerful nomads not conquered by the Romans, were subjects of the Huns.[1024]

In 395 a group of Huns moved south through Caucasus into eastern Anatolia and western Iran, where they attacked the Roman territories of Armenia, Cappadocia, and Syria, but as mentioned above, the bulk of the Huns remained around the Don and the Volga Rivers.[1025] After entering the Middle East from the north, a group of them moved eastward to attack Persia, while some moved into Anatolia and raided cities as far as Cilicia, Antioch, and Edessa.[1026] Hence, the first entry of the Turks into Anatolia did not occur in 1071, when the Seljuk Turkish sultan defeated the Eastern Roman emperor in Manzikert (Malazgirt), but in 395, when the Hunnish Turks penetrated this land coming down through Caucasus, though it was the later event that turned this land into a permanent Turkish home. While the majority of the Huns were establishing themselves in eastern Europe, neighboring the Roman Empire, a smaller group of them began their raids upon the rich eastern provinces of the empire, coming down through Caucasus to stretch into the eastern part of modern-day Turkey.[1027]

Ultimately, the Huns played a key role in the development of the modern-day demographics of Europe by forcing the relocation of European tribes. It is clear that they pushed the Germans permanently deep into Europe. But after the Huns lost control of the eastern European territories, owing to their own internal squabbles, the Slavs, who were previously trapped in the north by the more dominant Germans, began to move southward into the eastern European plains.

It is also clear that the Huns played a critical role in the dismemberment of the Western Roman Empire.[1028] The process was initiated when the Huns uprooted the Germanic Goths from their land in the Pontic Steppe and subsequently pushed the Goths deep into central Europe, into the Roman territories.[1029] In 406 the westward push of the Huns forced the Vandals, Sueves, and Alans beyond the Rhine frontier into Gaul, or modern-day France.[1030] While the Franks and the Burgundians were trapped in France, the Angles and the Saxons sought sanctuary in Britain. When the Goths, fleeing from the unstoppable Huns, reached the northeastern Italian coastline, the people there ran away, eventually to found Venice.[1031] It has also been suggested that when Attila and his Huns invaded northern Italy, the people retreated from the plains of Po to the islands along the northern shores of the Adriatic Sea, where Venice was later established.[1032] Most probably both the Goths and the Huns directly or indirectly precipitated the foundation of Venice, which most likely came out of necessity of establishing security against invaders in light of experiencing helplessness facing both the Goths and the Huns.

The westward pressure of the Huns on the Germanic tribes at the end of the fourth century and the declining strength of the Western Roman Empire facilitated the chaotic invasion of Roman territories by the Germanic tribes. The Roman state was not prepared to handle the sudden influx of barbaric people into their territories. Consequently, these population movements led to anarchy within the weakened empire, accelerating the definite disintegration of the Western Roman Empire.[1033] Mass migrations led to loss of revenue from areas caught up in warfare, which had a significant negative economic impact on the empire, ultimately leading to the loss of power. Thus, in essence, the Huns, by facilitating the end of European antiquity, caused the beginning of the Middle Ages (the medieval period), which was ended nearly a millennium later by other kinsmen of the Huns, the Ottoman Turks, when the Eastern

Roman Empire ceased to exist with the conquest of Constantinople in 1453, marking the beginning of the modern age.

The invasion of the Western Roman Empire by Germanic tribes was followed by the first-known Hunnish incursion into Roman domain in 408. Under their leader, Uldin, the Huns crossed the Danube with their Sciri allies to seize the Roman province of Dacia Ripensis (parts of modern-day Bulgaria and Serbia).[1034] As more Huns moved westward in the 420s, they exerted more pressure on the Roman territories of the middle Danubian regions west of the Carpathians, and the main body of the Huns appears to have been west of this mountain range by 425.[1035] However, it appears that in 409 about ten thousand Hunnish auxiliary forces arrived at the request of Western emperor Honorius, son of the late Theodosius I. Roman general Aëtius also used Hunnish forces to achieve his military goals and his domestic agenda. Hence, the Hun forces employed by the Romans served not only to temporarily stabilize the empire politically but also to put down German revolts, which the Huns caused in the first place by pushing these tribes into the Roman Empire.[1036]

Up to the year 440, the Huns occasionally raided both the western and the eastern empires, but they caused more problems by pushing the Germanic tribes across the imperial border.[1037] In the year 440, both halves of the empire lost their shared territory of Pannonia, a rich Roman province, to Attila. In Europe, the Alföld Plain, today known as the Great Hungarian Plain and the largest part of the Pannonian Plain, was the only suitable plain where the Huns could sustain their livestock and horses. Consequently, modern-day Hungary became their natural base, from where they launched their attacks upon the Roman Empire. Later this steppe would become logistic base for the European Avars as well. The ancestors of the modern-day Hungarians were not in this territory yet.

THE HUNS IN WESTERN AND CENTRAL EUROPE

Once situated in the steppes of central and eastern Europe, the next move of the Huns was to go deeper into Europe. Subsequently, the first quest of these Hunnish Turks appears to have been their penetration into modern-day central France. At the Battle of the Catalaunian Fields, also called the Battle of Châlons, in 451, the Huns of Attila were stopped by a coalition led by Roman general Flavius Aëtius and Visigothic king Theodoric I. The lack of grazing pastures for horses in western Europe did not allow the Huns to rely on their powerful cavalry, which was always the core of their army. Hence, when Attila faced Aëtius on June 20, 451, at the Battle of the Catalaunian Fields in modern-day France, he had to rely mostly on his infantry with limited cavalry.[1038] The cooperation of the Germanic Visigoths and the Romans led to the victory of Aëtius against Attila, and the new political picture with the Germans in Europe eventually contributed to the formation of the nucleus of the future (Germanic) Holy Roman Empire.[1039]

But the defeat did not stop the Huns, who remained strong. On the contrary, the Hunnish hegemony in Europe continued. In 452 they penetrated Italy, sacking cities in the Po valley. Many northern Italian cities, such as Milan, Pavia, and Aquileia, were devastated.[1040] Suddenly the Italian Peninsula, once the seat of the powerful Roman Empire, was at his mercy, ready for him to claim his great prize. To stop the Huns from reaching the capital of the Western Roman Empire, Pope Leo I and his delegation met with Attila to persuade him not to attack the capital.[1041] Subsequently, Attila appeared to turn back. Was this a miracle? Did this heathen Hun leader receive a divine intervention, as the Christians at the time believed? After all, Attila had long wanted to take the seat of the Roman Empire for himself. The meeting of Attila the Hun with Pope Leo I was immortalized in the fresco of Raphael (1483–1520), an Italian painter and architect of the Renaissance.

According to a Roman account, though Attila came to Italy with the intent of a full-scale invasion, he retreated not because of the words of the pope but rather to some extent because of the famine and the plague that had struck the northern Italians; the conqueror realized that the same danger also threatened his invaders. There was yet another factor, the fact that Eastern Roman emperor Marcian (450–57) had sent an army into the heartland of the Huns. Attila might have considered this a more serious concern. The Roman action could have triggered a rebellion of the Germans under Hunnish control, weakening Attila's power.[1042] In the end, whatever his true reason was, Attila retreated, but not because his army was in danger of being cut down by the Roman army; instead it seems he made a strategic move to return to his base in Pannonia.

From his base in modern-day Hungary, Attila stretched his empire from the Baltic in the north to the Balkans in the south and from the Rhine in the west to the coastline of the Black Sea in the east; he achieved all this and contributed to the collapse of the Roman Empire with the help of his mounted archers, who could shoot arrows with deadly accuracy and power while at full gallop.[1043] It was clear that the foot soldiers and the chariots of Europe were no match for the mighty cavalry and archers from Asia.

Finally, Eastern Roman emperor Theodosius II made a pact with Attila the Hun to stop the Hun attacks by paying the Huns a yearly tribute of seven hundred pounds of Roman gold. Theodosius II later changed his mind and did not pay the tribute, but he found it to be an expensive mistake. He painfully observed Attila crushing his armies at the gates of Constantinople. The Roman defeat resulted in the tripling of the tribute to the Huns.[1044] As the head of the Hun Empire in Europe, Attila received tribute from both the Western and Eastern Roman Empires. According to the sixth-century Roman historian Jordanes, Attila the Hun was referred to as the ruler of the world; he made the world cower and tremble by conquering the Scythian and German Kingdoms and capturing the cities of the two empires of the Roman world.[1045] Just as the Turks of the Asian steppes believed that their monarchs were heavenly appointed khans (*tengri khan*), Jordanes pointed out that the Huns thought their ruler Attila was appointed by Sky God (Gök-Tengri). But his contemporary Western chroniclers believed that God had sent Attila to punish the Christian world for its sins.[1046]

After the sudden death of Attila in 453, his successors could not maintain the power the Huns once had in Europe yet they did not politically disappear. Nevertheless, the demise of the great monarch led to a civil war within the once formidable empire. Once the Huns recovered they continued their political existence for nearly another century. But their descendants today are still surviving. Linguists believe that the closest language to the Huns of Attila is that of the modern-day Chuvash Turks, who live in the Chuvash Autonomous Republic in the European part of the Russian Federation. But their language appears to be near extinction, owing to the heavy influence of Russian in the Chuvash territory. It is conceivable that the contemporary Chuvash people are the descendants of the former Hun conquerors.[1047]

THE HUNNISH CIVIL WAR AND ITS OUTCOME

The Hunnish political system that helped its stability which in turn helped its control over most of the continental Europe worked against the empire after Attila's death. Until the great emperor's demise each new ruler assigned new fief rulers or local monarchs after eliminating previous supreme ruler's appointed fiefs. Within this system the Germanic tribes which were under the rule of the Huns received appointed Hunnish nobility as their leaders. As a result of the death of Attila the fief who had most to lose was Ardaric the king of the Gepids who was known as the most loyal supporter of Attila. Therefore, he had to make a move before the new supreme ruler made his.

Indeed, following the death of Attila the Huns became engulfed in a civil war in which his sons and other powerful Hunnish nobles fought with each other. The war however was not a war of liberation for Germanic tribes as it is often presented in recreated popular historiography, but rather it was about a dispute over royal inheritance and control of fiefs.[1048] In fact, the war was between Hun nobility of the western half of the empire in charge of fiefs and represented by Ardaric against the disenfranchised eastern half of the state led by Ellac son of Attila. In this war the Germanic fief tribes were also involved as belligerents for the western group. At the Battle of Nedao in 454 Ardaric managed to kill Ellac the new supreme ruler of the Huns; the victor however was not a German but rather a Hunnish prince placed in charge of a German tribe by Attila.[1049]

Besides initiating the disintegration of the extensive Hunnish empire, the civil war also exposed the extent of the Hunnish control of the Germanic tribes. After the war Valamer the ruler of the Ostrogoths parted from the surviving sons of Attila in the year 459 when he made an alliance with Eastern Roman emperor; around this time he also sent his son/nephew Theodoric (the Great) as a hostage to Contanstinople.[1050] Valamer was the founding king of the Ostrogoths, and yet, like Ardaric of the Gepids he was also a Hunnish prince, being a product of the eighty years of Hunnish rule over the Germans.[1051] In fact, during this period of time the royal Ostrogothic genealogy was more Hunnish than Gothic, and the dynasty was thought to be related to certain Hunuil, which etymologically suggested to be an eponymous name derived from the imperial indication 'Hun' and the Turkish word 'il' for people or state, thus with combined word meaning the 'Hun state'.[1052] According to Priscus, Valamer (also known as Balamer) was a Scythian, in other words a Hun.[1053]

After the death of Ellac, Dengizich and Ernakh, the remaining surviving sons of Attila, took the leadership of western and eastern halves of the empire respectively. Then the Huns of Dengizich moved to punish Valamer and his Goths. Meanwhile, Edeco, the Hunnish prince in charge of the Germanic Sciri tribe joined forces with the Huns to defeat and kill Valamer around 465-66.[1054] As a result, while some of the Goths came under the Hunnish rule, the Gepids also bowed to the hegemony of the Central Asian warriors. While Dengizich made attempts to reestablish his father's legacy, his subsequent ill-prepared war against the Eastern Romans in 467-69 ended with a disaster for the Huns.

Ernakh the supreme ruler in the east and elder brother of Dengizich warned his sibling not to engage the Eastern Romans since he himself was dealing with a rebellion of Oghuric Turkish tribes. However, Dengizich not taking the heed of his brother relied solely upon the Ostrogoths for his efforts against Constantinople and finally lost his battle and his life. Subsequently, the Germanic tribes under the Huns permanently abandoned the rule of the Huns who immediately began to lose their strength in central Europe. With the Ostrogoths freed, the Eastern Romans released Theodoric who went to lead the Ostrogoths as Theodoric the Great.

The process of disintegration of the western half of the Hunnish empire was facilitated by the fact that the eastern command could not spare its forces to provide military assistance to Dengizich as Ernakh was involved in a survival battle against the new arrival of Turkish tribes from the east starting at the time of the Hunnish Civil War that ended with the victory of Ardaric and Ellac's death.[1055] While the forces of the east were involved in a protracted civil war, the forces of the west depending on Germanic tribes dissolved with the departure of the Germans from the union. Finally, when decades long internal struggle ended by the end of the fifth century, Ernakh, Attila's youngest son, managed to reorganize the Huns with the new Central

Asian warriors. After all the Huns were Oghuric Turkish speakers and the newcomers were Oghuric speaking Turks as well. In the new realignment of the Hunnish polity the new state eventually came to be known Bulgar Hunnish state.

By this time, the once seemingly invincible Hunnish empire was reduced to a rejuvenated state occupying the plains of eastern Europe. In its former western territories in central Europe Germanic tribes led by their Hunnish princes were struggling with each other for supremacy. Meanwhile, Torcilingian Huns and the Sciri Germans under the command of Odoacer moved to Italy around 471-72.[1056] This young warrior was about to change the fate of the ailing Western Roman Empire.

The European Hun Empire's loss of power on the western front after the death of Attila actually became the doom of the Western Roman Empire. Upon the breakup of the Hunnish polity, many of the previously subdued barbarian tribes became free to attack Roman territories at will. Furthermore, the Hun forces previously used to quell German uprisings and establish peace in the imperial realm were no longer available.[1057] Moreover, the western state was now financially crippled after the devastations caused by Attila and his troops. All these conditions became vital factors in the collapse of the Western Roman Empire and the development of a new political order under the Germans in western Europe.

THE FIRST "BARBARIAN" KING OF ITALY

Late in the fifth century, the control of the Italian Peninsula, which had been the power base of the former (Western) Roman Empire, was suddenly in the hands of a non-Roman warrior. Who was this soldier of fortune? He and his mercenary fighters from the Torcilingi Huns, as well as from the Sciri Germans, have a prominent place in the pages of history for establishing a kingdom in Italy on the ashes of the defunct Western Roman Empire. This warrior became the first king of Italy, ruling the land from 476 until 493. Even though the popular Western view considers this non-Roman king to be a German warrior, there is a suggestion that he was in fact not German. Indeed, scholarly evaluations based on etymology and a review of the ethnic backgrounds of the tribes involved may indicate that Odoacer, who left his mark on Western history, was not from the Western world.

In the year 449, when a Roman ambassador crossed the border to meet Attila, he also became acquainted with the Hun leader's two most trusted officers. One was a Roman named Orestes, who acted as Attila's secretary. The other person was Edeco, who, according to information from the Romans, was a native-born Hun with an influential position, a famous warrior and a commander of the Hun army of Attila. These two officials of Attila traveled together as companions on a diplomatic mission to Constantinople, the capital of the Eastern Roman Empire. An unexpected twist of fate later on brought the sons of these two allies as adversaries against each other. Apparently, Orestes's son Romulus, also known as Romulus Augustulus, eventually became the last Western Roman emperor, whereas Odoacer, son of Edeco, became the first "barbarian" ruler of Italy by dethroning the son of Orestes in August of 476.[1058] Hence, Odoacer was a Hun, and at least some of his loyal soldiers were Huns as well.[1059]

One historical clue supporting this suggestion is Odoacer's tribal affiliation. He was the leader of the Sciri tribe and the Torcilingi tribe.[1060] The latter tribe, which was thought to be Turkish (Hunnish) and to be closely associated with the Sciri, played a key role in Odoacer's quest to depose Romulus Augustulus, the last emperor of the Western Roman Empire.[1061] When Odoacer became the first king of Italy (476–93), this change in monarchy ended the once-mighty (Western) Roman Empire. The usurper was thought to be from the tribe Sciri, which is not included in the list of the German tribes of this era, nor was it known to the Romans, but the members of this tribe were known to be bitter foes of the Ostrogoths.[1062] According to Jordanes, a Greco-Roman historian, Odoacer was also a royal of the Torcilingi, from the Rogas family, whose name was presumably derived from Rogas (Rua), one of Attila's uncles.[1063] The name of Odoacer is thought to be a Roman distortion of the Turkish compound *ot-toghar* (fire-born).[1064] This name was also used for another uncle of Attila.

The view that Odoacer the first 'barbarian' king of Italy was a Turk from the Turkish (Hunnish) tribe Torcilingi was supported by Roman historian Jordanes and Lombard historian Paul the Deacon.[1065] His son's name was Oklan, likely from Turkish Oghlan. In all likelihood Odoacer may have had a mixed lineage as he was Hunnish from his father side and possibly Germanic from his mother's side being from the Sciri tribe.[1066] His affiliation with the Sciri tribe was also through his father Edeco, likely from Turkish name Edgü (meaning 'good') who was the king of the Sciri tribe but a Hun as Priscus documented.[1067] In other words, Edeco was a fief king of a German tribe appointed by Attila as a reward.

There is another historical clue suggesting that Odoacer might have been a Hun but not a German. The records by Jordanes indicate that the father of Odoacer (sometimes referred to as Odovacer) was Edeco (written by some scholars as Edicon) and his brother was Hunoulphus. The latter's name was likely Germanized version of Turkish name possibly meaning 'Hun-wolf.' The Gothic practice of germanicization of original Hunnish names was common[1068] as the Chinese did with the original names of the Asian Huns known as the Xiong-nu.

According to the chronicles of Priscus, a well-known contemporary Greek historian, Edeco not only was the bodyguard of Attila but also was sent to Emperor Theodosius II as an ambassador of the Huns; Priscus went on to state explicitly that Edeco was a Hun.[1069] However, it is not clear whether Edeco, the bodyguard and ambassador (described by Priscus), was the same person as Edeco, father of Odoacer (described by Jordanes).[1070] If the Edeco described by these two contemporary historians was the same person, then Odoacer, who became the first king of Italy by deposing the last Roman emperor, was not a German but a Hunnish Turk. It is also known that with the Sciri tribe, Edeco led a retaliatory attack against the Ostrogoths who had betrayed the heirs of Attila.[1071]

After Attila died in 453, Hun power in central Europe quickly declined. The Great Hun's Roman lieutenant Orestes found opportunities to rise in the ranks of the Western Roman Empire. By 475 he was given by the emperor Julius Nepos the position of patrician with the supreme command of the imperial army. Taking advantage of his rank, Orestes managed to usurp the throne for his son Romulus Augustulus as the next emperor of the Western Roman Empire in place of Julius Nepos.[1072] In the meantime, it is postulated that Edeco, former friend and companion of Orestes, probably died in a battle in 469 while attacking the Ostrogoths. His son Odoacer, on the other hand, was rising in the ranks of the Roman army under Orestes.[1073] When Odoacer rebelled with his followers, Orestes was killed, and his son, the puppet emperor Romulus Augustulus, was dethroned. As a result, Odoacer the Hun achieved what his late chief Attila could not do. He ended the once-mighty Western Roman Empire; about a millennium later, another Turk, from the Ottomans, would end the Eastern Roman Empire. It should be noted that despite the chaotic times across the continent, during Odoacer's seventeen-year rule of Italy, the land saw domestic and foreign peace.[1074]

Many sources clearly show that he was not a Catholic, though the Germans had converted to Christianity a century before. The Romans, preferring to be in the hands of the Germans rather than under the rule of heretic Odoacer, were happy to see his fall at the hands of the Christian Goths. After all, they considered Odoacer to belong to the barbaric Hunnish people; described in an exaggerated way, his people were viewed as eating their older men, drinking blood, and sleeping on horseback.[1075]

When Theoderic the Great descended upon Italy with his Ostrogoths under the orders of the Eastern Roman emperor, Odoacer and his followers lost to the newcomers, yet peace was achieved between Theoderic and Odoacer. But on March 15, 493, Odoacer was treacherously murdered despite the treaty made with Theoderic. Why was he murdered? Rome and the Italian Peninsula were still sacred for Christians, and therefore, it was unthinkable for a non-Christian heathen to rule over the heartland of the former Roman Empire. Consequently, since it was believed that Odoacer was not a Christian, the Eastern Roman emperor ordered Theoderic the Great to end Odoacer's rule over Italy as king. Odoacer was first said to be a Christian so the people would accept his rule over Italy and to distance him from the pagan Huns. But when Theoderic the Great murdered him, he buried him in a Jewish synagogue to prevent "the pollution of the Christian church by an unworthy body," as Theoderic stated.[1076] These historical events suggest that Odoacer was neither a Christian nor a European but rather a Tengriist Hun warrior who conquered Italy, a dream his kinsman Attila wanted to accomplish earlier in the same century.

Meanwhile while Odoacer the Hun was eliminated Italy came under the kingdom of the Ostrogoths led by Theodoric the Great who likely accepted

Christianity while he remained as a hostage among the Eastern Romans. Once his father or uncle Valamer (Balamer) was killed by the Huns around 465-66, and the Goths split form the Hunnish union after the Eastern Romans prevailed in the battle of 467-69, the Roman emperor released Theodoric to lead the Ostrogoths as an ally of Constantinople. Nevertheless, this young warrior who came to be known as Theodoric the Great in history, was not a German but rather a Hun as his family was formerly appointed by Attila to the Ostrogoths as their fief ruler.[1077] Hence, even though the Roman emperor succeeded in seeing the elimination of the first Hunnish king of Italy, the birth place of the Roman Empire came under a German kingdom led by a warrior of Hunnish nobility.

ABOUT THE HUNS AND ATTILA AND THE HUNS

Attila was the best-recognized ruler of the European Huns. However, his name in its present-day form is a germanized version; the name Attila is possibly distorted from the Old Turkish composite word *es-til* meaning "universal ruler."[1078] Over time, the *st* consonant cluster became *tt* by assimilation, giving rise to Attila.

Known to the Roman realm as Flagellum Dei (Scourge of God), Attila was the most feared and admired nomadic monarch in Europe. The European peoples who were most affected by the Huns were the Germanic tribes (who became the subjects of the Huns) and the Slavs (who became aware of their national individuality after facing an outside threat).[1079] The Germanic tribes subdued by the Huns were so impressed by them that many of their sagas and legends were inspired by the Huns.[1080] But the Huns did not leave any written records behind. Most of the information about them comes from the Christian Romans and the Greeks whom they attacked. Even though Attila has been portrayed for ages as a monster, the prejudice against him and his Huns comes from Christian writers and chroniclers, owing to his attacks on the Christian world; this prejudice has continued until the present time.[1081] Similar prejudices surfaced nearly a millennium later, when Attila's kinsmen, the Ottoman Turks, were penetrating into Europe.

The Huns were not as primitive as the Western chroniclers led us to believe. Indeed, according to the same Latin and Greek recorders, these so-called barbarians of the Eurasian Steppe, both in Inner Asia and later in Europe, apparently had a rich and stratified society.[1082] However, the Greek and Roman historians were not kind to them when they recorded their historical events with their biased views. Just as their ancestors, the Xiong-nu (Asian Huns), created an organized state under their supreme leader Mo-tun in 209 BCE, the European Huns organized themselves to reach their zenith under the reign of their legendary leader Attila (444–53). About two years after his death, the Hunnish subjects of the Ostrogoths split from the Turkish Empire. Because of the internal struggle within the royal family and a lack of subordination within the military ranks, Hunnish power began to diminish. Even after they withdrew to the Dnieper basin, the continued existence of the Huns in the territories of modern-day Ukraine (375–560) allowed them to mix with the Slavs and with the influx of tribes coming from Asia, leading to the eventual Ukrainian ethnogenesis.[1083]

Despite the fact that the Huns of Attila were followers of a Tengriist faith, they also showed signs of influence from Chinese beliefs they carried from the Far East. For example, the use of yin and yang, well-known symbols of Taoism, as the emblems of the Roman auxiliary units the Armigeri and the Mauri Osismiaci can be explained only by the fact that these symbols were introduced to the Romans by the Huns.[1084] This suggests that there were Hun warriors in these units voluntarily serving Rome, but the situation was the focus of sore diplomatic relations between the Huns and Romans, as Attila frequently demanded the immediate return of the fugitives.[1085] In addition, this fact demonstrates to skeptical scholars that the European Huns had Far Eastern connections, thus having a link to the Xiong-nu (Asian Huns).

Another consequence of the arrival of the Huns in Europe was that, perhaps by their superior cohesion, political skill, and sense of survival, they eliminated the Indo-European nomads on the steppe.[1086] Many of these victimized tribes were pushed deeper into Europe. The ultimate actions of the Huns led to lasting changes, both political and ethnic, across Europe and Asia, leading to the migration and destruction of peoples and to the rise of new kingdoms and empires.[1087] In other words, the seeds of modern-day western European nations were sown by the Huns.

THE LEGACY OF THE HUNS IN EUROPE

Just as their ancestors in Asia have been given unfair coverage in the annals of the history, the European Huns were also given derogatory descriptions in Western historical chronicles written by Greek and Roman historians. Even well after the Huns were gone, their name continued to be loosely used by Westerners to describe many other people in a demeaning way. These included Turks, such as the Avars, Bulgars, Cumans, Kutrighurs, Utrighurs, Oghuz, Seljuks, and Ottomans, and non-Turks, such as the Goths, Hungarians, and Lombards.[1088] But the legacy of Attila lived on among the Germans who had been once part of his empire. His influence must have been profound for his name to have lingered in German folklore for such a long time. The funeral mounds in northern Germany were referred as Hunnenbette (Hun beds) until the twentieth century, and Norwegian and Danish stories of the Huns carry common themes of honor, justice, and vengeance.[1089] In the tenth century, the Germanic Vikings carried his name with them to Iceland and then to Greenland, where the Greenlandic Lay of Atli (Attila) came about.[1090] Nevertheless, when the events of the past are carefully analyzed by filtering out previous biased observations, one can clearly see that the Huns actually made significant impact on the evolution of modern-day Europe.

Upon their entry into Europe in the fourth century their biggest influence was upon the Germans who eventually formed the backbone of the development of modern-day western and central Europe. Prior to the arrival of the mounted archers from Central Asia, the predominant population of western Europe was the continental Celts. Hence, the abrupt arrival of the Huns into European arena precipitated a significant change of the demographics of Europe, thus initiating the evolution of modern-day European political landscape. In fact, the Huns contributed to the radical alteration of the political map of Europe as they forced the destruction of the Western Roman Empire, which once was a superpower in modern sense dominating the Mediterranean basin for nearly half a millennium. This was an important Hunnish factor in the history of the Western world since as a result of the Huns, Western Europe finally managed to break away from the political and cultural yoke of the Mediterranean world. By ending the hegemony of the Western Roman imperial presence and by creating a favorable medium to create a new "Western" culture from the amalgamation of Germanic, Central Asian (Hunnish), Mediterranean Greco-Roman, and Judeo-Christian cultural traditions, a new form of Western identity was born.[1091]

As discussed earlier, the Hunnish invasion of Europe beginning in the second half of the fourth century resulted in uprooting of the Germanic tribes, which moved into central and western Europe, thus creating havoc across the realm of the western territories of the Roman Empire. Out of multiple Germanic tribes, the Franks moved into Gaul (future France), the Visigoths settled in Iberia (future Spain), while the Vandals ended up in north Africa and the Anglo-Saxons in Britain. While the Huns and later the Avars (chapter 4.4) helped to shape the evolution of modern European demographics, Germans did not manage to remain dominant over western Europe. In fact, the German language in these areas was replaced with the Latin languages of French, Spanish, and Italian, except in Britain, where the Celtic language was pushed more to the periphery of the Celtic world in Wales, Scotland, and Ireland. However, among all the German tribes, the Franks became the most dominant of all. Yet, by entering Europe in an unopposed fashion, the Huns did not only conquer the Germanic people and forcing them to relocate to their present-day locations, but they also introduced their way of governing to the Germans, which was then renamed by Europeans as "feudalism" by creating Hunnish style supreme ruler with subservient fiefs and militarized aristocratic class.[1092]

The first monarch of the Merovingian Kingdom of the Franks was Childeric, who was once a vassal of Attila the Hun.[1093] It is also suggested that Childeric fought at Chalons (Gaul) as a commander of Attila against the Roman army of general Aëtius.[1094] Hence, one of the Hunnish contributions to the European history was the birth of the Frankish polity by a German noble who was strongly influenced by the Huns.[1095] After Childeric, his son Clovis took the throne and thrusted the Frankish kingdom into a powerful polity in post-Attila Gaul. With the Western Roman Empire vanished, the Frankish kingdom, as the dominant force of western Europe, quickly capitalized to gain control of central Europe. This polity then evolved into the Carolingian Empire, which then contributed to the formation of future Germany, France, Austria, Netherlands, and Switzerland.

Until the fall of the Roman Empire in the West, western Europe was only familiar with the rule of the emperor in Rome through his regional governors. However, after the Huns allowed the change of the political landscape of the continent, Europe entered a new period known as the Medieval Times, during which Europeans came to know about feudalism. In adopting this new system of governance, the Germans were heavily influenced by their former Central Asian overlords in addition to using Roman and German traditions; there is no question that the Germans adopted feudalism from the Huns.[1096]

In this feudal system, just as seen in the political structure of the steppe empires, the state control was divided between the supreme king and his highest level vassal aristocrats, including the dukes and barons, who were able to enjoy local autonomy, but ultimately, they were responsible with their political positions to their supreme king. One could make the argument that the Franks may have adopted their system from the Roman Tetrarchy, which was put in place by Diocletian in the third century, but the Roman experience was a failure and did not last more than two decades. Nevertheless, the governmental system utilized by the Franks was clearly copied from their former Inner Asian overlords; similarly, the Rurik Viking dynasty, the Rus', which established the early Russian state with its Slavic population imitated their governmental system after their Turkish overlords, the Khazars (chapter 4.6) as more detailed information can be found elsewhere in the reference.[1097] The eastern Slavs were in fact affected by the Turkish polity of the Khazars in eastern Europe. Indeed, there is clear evidence that the embryonic Russian state got a jumpstart in the ninth century by imitating the Khazars in every single aspect, including in its use of Turkish titles.[1098] It is a fact that the influx of Turkish tribes, first beginning with the Huns then followed by the Avars and the Bulgars, left deep political imprints across Europe. However, among all the early Turkish invaders the most influential ones were the Huns, whose political influence left behind in Europe was not only exclusive for the Germanic tribes, in fact, the Danes as well as the Slavs adopted, just as the Germans did, Central Asian style political structure for governing.[1099]

The Huns also made impact on the evolution of the European armed forces. Prior to the arrival of these Central Asian warriors the Germans were unruly fighters, who were not fit to take on well organized military force like that of the Roman Empire. However, both the Germans and the Romans were quick to recognize the military superiority of the Huns, and therefore, they both made efforts to reorganize their forces to imitate those of their adversaries from the east.[1100] While the Romans employed the fighters of the tribal Alans who coming from north of the Caspian Sea sought sanctuary from the Huns among the Romans. The Germans on the other hand, since many of them lived among the Huns as their subjects, began to form their forces after the Hunnish model, thus giving their rulers an opportunity to have disciplined fighting units.[1101]

The usefulness of mobile armies on horseback was also introduced into Europe by Huns, but later in the sixth century with the introduction of stirrups by another Turkish tribal group, the European Avars (chapter 4.4), the class of the knights arose from the nobility of Europe. With the adoption of this Turkish innovation the Eastern Romans were able to form the first early medieval cavalry, which then was introduced into western Europe.[1102]

The Hunnish impact over the Europeans was not limited to socio-political and military influences; archeological evidence has clearly shown the fact that the Huns also had cultural impact on the lives of the Europeans. Prior to the arrival of the Huns to Europe, the males of the Romans as well as the Germans were wearing a form skirt.[1103] All classes of Roman males in fact wore short-sleeved or sleeveless, knee-length tunic. But the national dress of the Romans included 'toga;' borrowed from their predecessors the Etruscans it was a form of lengthy cloth which was worn across the shoulders and around the body coming over a tunic. At the time, however, it appeared that Hunnish national dress for males included a caftan reaching the knees in addition to trousers and leather boots.[1104] It appeared that the influence of the Huns upon the Roman people was so strong that the citizens of Eastern Roman capital Constantinople began to dress imitation of Hunnish outfits as a show of fashion.[1105] But, as a result of the introduction of the cavalry concept into Europe by the migrating Turks, the Central Asian trousers and boots became the norm for the males of medieval Europe.

Before the fourth century the dominant people of western and central Europe were the Celts, who were at the time ruled by the Romans. However, before the arrival of Huns later in the fourth century the Celts had been already acquainted with a flavor of Inner Asian culture brought by the Scythians around mid-millennium BCE. This was then followed by the Sarmatians, who had similar culture to that of the Huns.[1106] Cranial deformation, for example, was a practice found among the Hunnish aristocracy but also among the leadership of the Germanic tribes. Even though cranial deformation was presented to Europe earlier by the Sarmatians and Alans, it was the Huns, who by dominating over the Germanic tribes, either by direct rule over them or through their strong influence, formally introduced to them the practice of cranial deformation. There is archeologic evidence that this practice was carried out among the Germanic tribes, including the Lombards, Thuringians, Rugians, Burgundians, as well as the Goths.[1107]

But, by bringing significant portion of Europe under their rule, it was the Huns who made a significant impact on the cultural evolution of early Europe; they in fact facilitated the birth of a new culture arising from an amalgamation of Hunnish, Alanic, German, and Greco-Roman influences of art. Eventually, it was this hybrid art from different ethnic backgrounds that became the impetus for the cultural development of the future Germanic Europe.[1108] However, early medieval Germanic art forms (particularly from the Danube basin), whether they are labeled as Gothic, Lombardian, or Frankish-Burgundian, actually show strong Hunnish influence.[1109] Neither the historical sources nor the archeological findings support the age long biased view that claim the Huns were 'primitive' and 'unrefined' people; unlike the popular belief that claimed that the Inner Asian invaders were affected by their Germanic subjects, it was in fact the Germans who were strongly influenced by the steppe art and material culture brought by the Huns from Eastern Eurasia.[1110]

The early medieval Germanic practice of making polychrome cloisonné style of jewelry and weapons adorned with precious stones cannot be claimed to be an original Germanic art since this art form was already present late in the first millennium BCE in the Altai region, home of the Huns.[1111] The archeological finds also demonstrate the fact that the early Germanic people imitated the Hunnish burial practices; for example, the tomb of Childeric clearly shows the aspiration of the Germanic aristocracy to associate itself with the Hunnish imperial elements.[1112] In addition, the archeological discoveries illustrate that the Hunnish cultural influence reached as far north as Scandinavia and as far west as Gaul and Spain.[1113] For this reason, it is not surprising to find that the motifs and patterns of epic stories of early Germanic peoples were likely borrowed from the Central Asian nomads migrating into Europe[1114]; an example is the story of Beowulf.

The Hunnish influence on Europe was so powerful that it lasted into our modern times. In fact, the Hun continued to appear in the culture of the land as well as in description of the Germans. The great Hun became the main character of Giuseppe Verdi's 1846 opera *Attila*, based on the 1809 play *Attila, König der Hunnen* (*Attila, King of the Huns*) by Friedrich Ludwig Zacharias Werner, a German writer. During World War I (1914–18) the Germans were equated with the Huns. For example, the publication *War Illustrated* on December 1, 1917, contained an article with the title of "The Footprints of the Hun," and at the end of the World War I, on November 10, 1918, publication of *News of the World* signaled the end of the war with the title "Hun Surrender Certain."

THE AFTERMATH OF THE HUNS IN EUROPE

After the decline of the Huns in central Europe later in the fifth century and particularly in the sixth century, many of their warriors joined the Eastern Roman armies as mercenaries. However as stated earlier, the Huns were able to come together to reform their empire in eastern Europe by the end of the fifth century after overcoming their civil war. Nevertheless, a small group of Huns split from the union to establish themselves in northwestern Caspian territory, in modern-day Dagestan. These people came to be known as Caucasian Huns since they rose to prominence with their military prowess in northern Caucasus. Their neighbors were the Sabir Turks to their north in Volga region, the Bulgar Huns to their west, and Sassanid Persia to their south. In the year 503 when these Huns invaded northern Persia, Sassanian king Kavadh was forced to abandon his successful military campaign against the Eastern Romans.[1115] These Huns of Dagestan were later absorbed by their kinsmen the Khazars, another Oghuric Turkish dialect speakers.

Many of the Huns served as mercenaries or allies for the Romans, as they formed special units of mounted archers with their skillful use of the bow and the arrow. In fact, Emperor Justinian the Great found their assistance quite crucial in his quest to recapture previously lost Roman territories. At the Battle of Dara in 530, the Romans defeated the larger Persian army with the help of 600 Hunnish cavalrymen; in Morocco, a Hunnish force with only 70 horsemen was able to defeat the Moors on behalf of Constantinople, and furthermore, the Hunnish forces assisted the Eastern Romans in reconquering Italy from the Ostrogoths in the year 530.[1116]

The next year Eastern Roman emperor Justinian received an intelligence that informed him that Persians were going to attack with the assistance of the Huns. However, he tricked the Persians into believing that the Huns were bought by his bribes. Terrified by the prospect of facing the Hunnish warriors Persians retreated.[1117] This event alone illustrated how much both the Romans and Persians feared facing the fierce warriors from Central Asia. The tactical advantage of the Hunnish cavalry over their enemies showed that the opposing forces could not cope with the rapid-firing and constantly moving mounted archers.[1118] But the disappearance of the Hun units eventually severely weakened the mounted-archer unit of the Roman army. By the next century, it was practically nonexistent. This weakness became clear in the ninth century, when the Eastern Roman armies were defeated by those of the Arab Abbasid caliph Mu'tasim, who used ten thousand skillful Turkish mamluk mounted archers against them.[1119]

The fall of the Black Huns did not end the Turkish presence in Europe. In fact, the continuous influx of (non-Hunnish) Turkish tribes eventually flooded not only Central Asia and modern-day Kazakhstan but also southern Siberia and the territories of southern modern-day European Russia in succeeding centuries.[1120] Significant Turkish presence in or domination over eastern Europe lasted more than a millennium after the Huns. The flow of Turkish tribes from Central Asia into eastern Europe continued intermittently at least until the advent of the Turco-Mongol invasion in the thirteenth century. The early arrivers were the Oghur Turkish–speaking tribes, likely related to the Huns of Asia. Following the fall of the European Huns, the remnants of these Huns survived in the eastern Pontic Steppe and northern Caucasus for many more years.[1121] After the cessation of the European Hun polity, Europe witnessed the formation of subsequent Turkish tribal states linguistically related to the Huns; these were formed by the Bulgars, Avars, and Khazars.

4.3. THE BULGARS

The Bulgar tribes of the Turks were first mentioned to be present north of Caucasus in the sixth century, and subsequently, for nearly seven centuries they played an important role mostly in the political history of eastern Europe.[1122] The Bulgars were part of an ancient branch of the Turkish race, likely related to the Huns,[1123] and today they are represented by the Chuvash Turks in the Volga region.[1124] It appears that they were from the Oghuric group of Turks.[1125] The name Bulgar was derived from the ancient Turkish word *bulgha* (to mix).

While the Huns faced a civil war after Attila's death they also needed to deal with an influx of Oghuric Turkish speaking Turkish tribes from Central Asia. Even though the civil war of the Huns led to the loss of territorial control in central Europe, Ernakh, Attila's youngest surviving son, by the end of the fifth century managed to reorganize his domain by forging a powerful state with incorporation of new Oghuric Turkish tribes under his command. The reestablished Hunnish state emerged with two wings, the Kutrighurs in the west and the Utrighurs in the east.[1126] Meanwhile, another group of Oghurs by the name On-Oghurs (chapter 4.5) came into the mix; these remained among the powerful Utrighurs. The new political stability only lasted until about mid-sixth century when Eastern Roman emperor Justinian managed to incite a new civil war by trickery between the western and eastern Hunnish wings. At the end of the conflict the eastern group emerged under a new political name known as Bulgars.[1127]

At the time when the Bulgar Huns were engaged in a civil strife among themselves, another newcomers from Asia showed up to change the course of history. These new immigrants in mid-sixth century came to be known as the European Avars. In about 557 the Avars first brought the Sabirs, On-oghurs, and Barsils from the Volga region under their control, and subsequently, most of the Bulgar Huns, with both their Kutrighur and Utrighur wings, joined into their tribal confederation as well. As a result, a new Oghuric speaking empire was formed. In a manner of speaking the Turkish Hun empire was recreated with an Avar leadership controlling the Hunnish military elite. It has been suggested that the ruling Avar clan may not have been Turkish but because they ruled among the majority Turkish tribes, they were quickly turkicized by adopting the Oghuric (Turkish) Hunnish language as their own.[1128]

Just as the Huns of Attila had established their hegemony over the Germans, the Avar-Huns also moved in quickly against the Germanic tribes. In 565-66 they defeated and captured Frankish king Sigibert, and in 567 they destroyed the Gepids and then forced the Lombards to leave modern-day Austria in 568. In a short period of time the Avars also conquered most of Roman Balkans and placed the Slavs of eastern Europe under their absolute control.[1129] Meanwhile, the Turkish hegemony over central and eastern Europe was divided between two separate powers. While the Kutrighurs joined forces with the European Avars, the Utrighur Turks allied themselves with the Eastern Romans but also they came under the expansion of the Gök-Türks into Europe in the late sixth century.

In 626 the Avars laid siege to Constantinople, the capital of the Eastern Roman Empire. However, when the siege failed a civil war threatened the Avar leadership as the Hunnish elite rose against the rulers of the qaghanate. Ultimately, the powerful empire broke into two halves; the western half remained under the Avars in Hungary and other parts of central Europe whereas the eastern half came under the leadership of the Bulgars led by Qubrat Khan.[1130]

Even before the Gök-Türk Empire was established in Central Asia in the sixth century, the Bulgar Turks were present in eastern Europe, in the territories of modern-day southern Ukraine. In the early years of his reign, Eastern Roman emperor Justinian the Great (527–65) had to face the incursions of the Bulgar Turks into the northern borders of the Balkans. Procopius, an Eastern Roman chronicler, wrote that in the years 539–40, the Bulgar Turks (described as Huns) fell as a scourge upon all Europe as they caused havoc from the Ionian Gulf to the suburbs of Constantinople.[1131] It appears that in 544, the Bulgar raiders reached the Roman province of Illyricum (Pannonia and Dalmatia), and then in 551, the Bulgars joined with the Germanic Gepids threatening Constantinople and Thessalonica.

Taking advantage of the lack of Gök-Türk authority early in the seventh century, the Bulgars, under the leadership of Qubrat Khan, formed their own khanate, known as Old Greater Bulgaria (also known as Magna Bulgaria, 632–81) in modern-day southern Ukraine along the northern shores of the Black Sea. Just like their kinsmen from Asia, they worshipped Gök-Tengri (Sky God) of their Tengriist faith. They refused to accept the overlordship of their kinsmen, the (European) Avars.

THE SPLITTING OF THE BULGAR UNION

After the death of Qubrat Khan in 642, the Bulgar tribal union began to fracture. According to Greek records, the tribal federation eventually split into five groups along the lines of their tribal affiliations. The great khan's eldest son, Bayan, stayed in the Kuban area with a group of On-Oghurs who later contributed to the formation of Hungary (chapter 4.5). Bayan remained in this region as the leader of Old Greater Bulgaria until the Khazars turned this state into a tributary in the latter part of the seventh century. The fate of the Kutrighurs is not clear, but they probably became subjects of the Avars in Pannonia. While one group of the Bulgars eventually formed the Baškïrs (volume 2, chapter 7.8), another group established a great khanate (Volga Bulgar Khanate) with a rather long existence from the late seventh century until the early thirteenth-century Mongol invasion. Finally, a smaller group of On-Oghur Turks moved toward the Balkans under the leadership of Qubrat's other son, Asparukh, to form the Danube Bulgars and lay the foundation of modern-day Bulgaria in the territory, which at the time was controlled by the Eastern Roman Empire.[1132] Indeed, when Asparukh showed up by the Danube River in 679 with less than half of the Bulgar On-Oghurs, the history of modern-day Bulgaria also began.

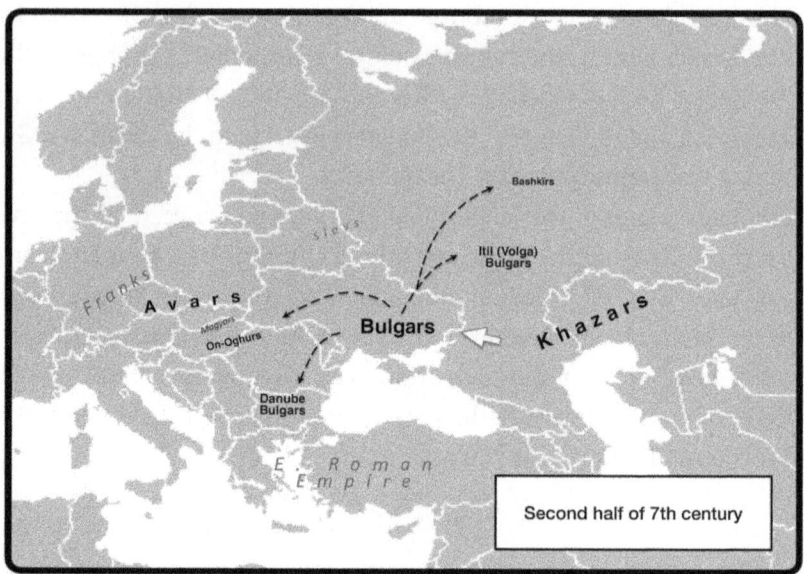

Map 8. In the sixth century upon arrival to the steppes in modern-day Ukraine Bulgars took over the control of the land from the Huns. But when their kinsmen Khazars exerted pressure upon them, Bulgars split into smaller groups, each migrating in different directions.

Because these Bulgar Turks initially settled by the Danube River, they were subsequently referred to as the Danube Bulgars; similarly, their kinsmen who moved north by the Volga River came to be known as the Volga Bulgars (volume 2, chapter 2.3). According to Greek observers, when the Danube Bulgars showed up in Thrace after 679, they pursued agriculture and construct buildings just as sedentary people did.[1133] It appears that the knowledge of sedentary life known to their kinsmen of the past, the Xiong-nu, was also known to the Bulgars. Once these Turks settled in the Balkans, they formed the Bulgar Khanate, which was later known in the West as the First Bulgarian Empire (681–1018). Now, in the Balkans, the Bulgar Turks came into constant contact with the Eastern Romans. Their interactions were sometimes hostile and at other times friendly. For example, during the Second Siege of Constantinople by the Muslim Arabs (717–18), the Bulgar Turks assisted the Eastern Romans in pushing back the Arabs. However, there is also evidence that in the seventh century, the Eastern Roman city of Corinth of the Morean Peninsula was captured by the Bulgars of the On-Oghur Turks.[1134]

It has been suggested that the On-Oghurs who remained in Kuban after the bulk of the Bulgar Turkish tribes left the area were actually the Finno-Ugric group of Magyars, who came to be known as the On-Oghurs because they lived so closely with the On-Oghur Bulgar Turks for a long time. Indeed, while this non-Turkish group of people living side by side with the On-Oghurs called themselves by their true Finno-Ugric name of the Magyars, they were known by others as the On-Oghurs, or Ungroi (for On-Oghurs), and hence they came to be known by non-Magyar people by the name Hungarians. An exception to this is the fact that the Turks have always called Hungarians by their true ethnic name, Majar, for Magyar. However, even though the Magyar people demonstrated definite Finno-Ugric characteristics, their chiefs were still On-Oghurs of Turkish Altaic origin when they were living together.[1135]

THE LOSS OF ETHNIC IDENTITY

The eventual spread of the Christian faith and the constant influx of Slavs into Danube Bulgar territory began to take a toll on the culture of these Turks. Indeed, by the late ninth century, Christianity and the slavicization of the population were gaining traction in the Bulgar Khanate. Under Krum Khan (802–14), the fusion of the Bulgar Turks and the Slavs was encouraged, leading to the slavicization of the Turkish state. This process was catalyzed by the Christianization of the population under Eastern Roman influence. Even the Bulgar nobles adopted Slavic names. When Vladimir, son and successor of Boris Khan (852–89), tried to reverse the process of Christianization by reinstalling the ancestral Tengriist faith with the help of some Bulgar nobles, Boris returned to power to remove his son from control. In the year 864, with the influence of Constantinople, he finally adopted Christianity as the state's official religion. Hence, the First Bulgarian Empire was the second Turkish state to adopt Christianity,[1136] after the (European) Avar Qaghanate. He also declared Slavic the official language.[1137]

Boris Khan then placed his second son, Symeon (893–927), in power after ensuring that Christianity was the official religion of the state. Boris was the last Bulgar noble to use the Turkish title of "khan" (king), and his son Symeon became the first czar (emperor) in history. Thus, this Slavic title was first ever used by a Christianized Turk under heavy Slavic influence, before the Russians began using it in the sixteenth century. The justification for the change in title was simple: the title of "khan" was associated with the pagan Central Asian culture, and therefore, it was thought that the use of a Slavic title could facilitate mass conversion from the Tengriist faith to Christianity. A change was needed, and it was made. The few remaining traditionalist Bulgar Turks had no option but to be assimilated within the grand process of slavicization and Christianization. With their ancient traditions and political past taken from them, they were doomed to lose their ethnic identity forever.

The Avar Qaghanate controlled the Slavs from the Great Hungarian Plain (known as Alföld). First when the Avars promoted the migration of Slavs into the Balkans, and later when they lost power over them late in the eighth century, the further influx of Slavs into the southern Balkans had a further negative impact on the Danube Bulgars. The Slavs, now freed, formed the Eastern Slavs (future Russians) in addition to beefing up the Balkan Slavs. Hence, over the next century, as the Slavs began to stretch into the Balkans, they put the Bulgar Turks through a heavy slavicization process by means of cultural assimilation.[1138] By the early tenth century, the ancient Turkish traditions and culture had faded away, and as a result, the Bulgars were now slavicized and Christianized.[1139] Even though they eventually lost their national identity, the Danube Bulgar Turks and their state building might have preserved the ethnic survival of the Slavs by preventing their assimilation by the Greeks of the Balkans.[1140]

Following the total collapse of the Avars, the Slavs also began to organize politically and establish new principalities in the early ninth century. As stated earlier, with the influence of the numerically superior Slavs, the Turkish identity and culture of the Bulgars inevitably disappeared. The Eastern Romans played a significant role in this process. Meanwhile, the Cyrillic alphabet was developed under the rule of the Bulgar ruler Boris with the help of Saint Cyril,

Saint Constantine, and Saint Methodius.[1141] The Cyrillic alphabet accepted by the Bulgarians eventually was introduced to the future Russians. Ultimately, the Turkish character of the Bulgars was lost forever, but the original name of the Bulgar Turks today lives in the name of modern-day Bulgaria, a Slavic nation in the Balkans.

In 925 Symeon declared himself as the emperor—hence the title of "czar"—of the Bulgarians and the Romans and elevated the Bulgarian Church to the level of patriarchate.[1142] After his death, the power of the Bulgar state began to decline. Finally, following their annihilation in 1018, the Bulgars came under the rule of the Eastern Roman Empire until about 1185, when the Turkish Cuman contribution to Bulgarian history proved to be significant for the revival of the Bulgarian polity (chapter 4.8); not only did the Cumans help the Bulgarians to regain their independence but they also established their first dynasty. But the independence of the Second Bulgarian Empire (1185–1396) lasted until the Bulgar lands were conquered by the Ottoman Turks.

THE BULGAR LEGACY IN THE VOLGA

In the north, the Volga Bulgars, the brothers of the Danube Bulgars, managed to keep their cultural and national identity. They remained with their traditional Tengriist faith until the tenth century, when the khan of the Volga Bulgars sent a request to the Abbasid caliph in 920 for teachers to educate his subjects in the Islamic religion.[1143] Subsequently, after 922, the Volga Bulgars eventually adopted Islam as their official state religion, and the Arabic script replaced the Old Turkic script (also known as the Orkhon alphabet).[1144] The Volga Bulgar Khanate by the end of the tenth century had become a prosperous Muslim state, controlling the trade routes between the Baltic Sea states in the north to the Middle East in the south and Central Asia in the east.[1145] Although the Qara-Khanid Khanate in eastern Turkestan was the first Muslim Turkish state in history (owing to mass conversions), the Volga Bulgar khan became the first Turkish monarch accepting Islam as his religion.

In the thirteenth century, Volga Bulgar independence ended with the conquest of the eastern European steppes by the Turco-Mongol hordes of the

Mongol Empire. Subsequently, the Bulgar Turks were absorbed by another Turkish group, known as the Tatars (volume 2, chapter 4.2). But the land of Volga Bulgaria later regained its independence as a Tatar khanate (Kazan) in the early fifteenth century.[1146] A few Bulgar legacies managed to survive to our modern times. Today, though the political tribal name of Bulgar remains in the official name of the Slavic-speaking Balkan state of Bulgaria, the Volga Bulgar dialect of the Turkish language has survived only with the Chuvash Turks of the Chuvash Autonomous Republic of the Russian Federation. Hence, only the Chuvash Turkish dialect of the old Hun-Bulgar language has survived to our modern times. While the Danube Bulgars disappeared in the pages of the history, the Volga Bulgars, another group from the former Hun-Bulgar confederation, will be discussed in more detail in volume 2, chapter 2.3.

4.4. THE AVARS

The name Avar was associated for the first time with a tribal federation in the fifth century in Asia. It has been thought that these (Asian) Avars were associated with the Tungus or Mongol ruling clan of Rouran, known as Juan-juan in Chinese Pinyin (Chapter 5.1). The Juan-juan (fourth to sixth century CE) formed an old tribal confederate state, like the Huns before them. The area was predominantly Turkish after the collapse of Asian Hun power, but the influence of these Avars in Asia was not as significant as that of the previous Hun rule. It has been suggested that the European Avars appeared in the area of northern Caucasus about a century before they invaded Europe in the sixth century.[1147] Linguists agree that their language was similar to that of the Huns, more specifically the Oghuric Turkish dialect.[1148] It has also been suggested that the European Avars linguistically belonged to the same branch of the Turkish language family as the Gök-Türks and the Huns.[1149] Indeed, the European Avars were Turks, most likely originating from a branch of the Bulgar Turks; in other words, they were the descendants of the Xiong-nu (Asian Huns).[1150]

A number of Oghuric tribes in eastern Europe called themselves Avars since the name still commanded some respect in the Eurasian Steppe.[1151] But it has been suggested that the Avars were actually the remnants of the Vigur nomadic group, a Turkish pastoralist people from western Siberia moving westward into Europe to avoid the leadership of the Gök-Türks, who became the dominant power in Asia in 552.[1152] The Avars in Europe, just like their Asian predecessors, had a mixture of tribes, mostly Turkish; though they may have included a minority group of the Mongols, the ruling class was Turkish.[1153]

It has been suggested that the leaders of the European Avars left Central Asia to avoid the rule of the emerging Gök-Türks, who conquered the Juan-juan (Asian Avars) in Asia. After they left Central Asia and crossed over the Pontic Steppe, they finally reached the lower Danube in the second half of the sixth century. They probably had Hunnish guides as they were led to the Alföld Plain, or the Great Hungarian Plain, as the Huns were. Hence, the Avars made their first political appearance in Europe in 558 at a time when the Eastern Roman emperor was being harassed by the Bulgar Turks. They first settled in Pannonia, which included the eastern provinces of modern-day Austria, previously occupied by the Germanic Lombards.[1154] This territory was the most suitable land for these nomads in Europe. Eastern Roman historian Theophylact Simocatta reported that the Avars had a core of Huns within their society.[1155] Soon after taking hold of central Europe, the Avar Qaghanate established diplomatic contact with the Eastern Roman Empire (also known as the Byzantine Empire in modern times).

Initially these Avars consolidated their power by bringing other Turkish groups under their power. These included the Kutrighurs, Utrighurs, and Sabirs. In 558, at the request of Eastern Roman emperor Justinian the Great, the Avars moved against the Turkish tribes menacing Constantinople; consequently, they put the Kutrighurs and the Sabirs under their rule and defeated the On-Oghurs. In 567 the Avars used the Germanic Lombards to destroy the kingdom of another Germanic group, the Gepids. But subsequently they acquired Lombard land in Pannonia for themselves, and the Lombards were forced to move to Italy, where they ruled for nearly two centuries.

In 568 Bayan Qaghan of the Avars laid siege to a key Roman city, Sirmium, in Pannonia and sent ten thousand Huns (Kutrighurs) to create havoc in Dalmatia. The Avars then crushed the Eastern Roman armies sent to stop them. In the end, the emperor in Constantinople had to pay tribute to the qaghan.[1156] But the Eastern Romans found themselves in a more difficult situation against the Avars when the Gök-Türk qaghan demanded the return of the Avar leaders from the Roman emperor. The Turkish qaghan in the Mongolian steppes justified his demands by declaring that these Avars were his escaped slaves. But when the Romans could not stop Avar attacks upon their territories, they continued to pay them annual tribute.

THE MAKERS OF CENTRAL EUROPEAN DEMOGRAPHY

After the European Huns uprooted the German and Slavic tribes permanently, nearly two centuries later, sixth-century Avar activities in Europe began to shape modern-day central Europe. As the German tribes moved west and south into Europe, their former territories in eastern Europe were eventually populated by Slavic tribes; those moving into Bohemia, vacated by the Lombards, were the future Czechs and Slovaks. The early Slavs came under the rules of the Germans (Goths) and the Turks (Huns, Bulgars, and Avars). Particularly under the Bulgars and the Avars, some Slavs found their way into Balkan territories.[1157] In 566 the Avar qaghan managed to take control of Silesia (a territory between modern-day Poland, the Czech Republic, and Germany) and Bohemia (modern-day Czech Republic and Slovakia), where the Slavs thrived under their Asiatic overlords. As mentioned, the Slavs in this area were the future Czechs and Slovaks. In 567, after the Avars forced first the German Gepids and then the German Lombards further west, they occupied the Hungarian Plain. Subsequently, when these Asian warriors invaded the Roman province of Noricum (modern-day Austria and Slovenia), the Slavs who encountered them became the forefathers of the Slovenes and Serbo-Croats.[1158]

Leaving their base in Hungary, the Avars eventually extended their territories into modern-day Slovakia, Romania, Serbia, Bosnia, and eastern Austria.[1159] Often allying themselves with the Eastern Roman Empire, the Avars struck fear into the hearts of their enemies, including the Germanic Franks. As mentioned earlier, when Germanic Lombard king Albuin (567–73) asked for help from the Avars against the Gepids, another Germanic tribe, the Avars first used them to get rid of the Gepids and then forced the Lombards to leave their territories in the western Hungarian plains out of fear of these Asian warriors.[1160]

The Slavs were also present near the settlement areas of the Avars, but they remained as subjects of these Asian warriors. It appears that the Slavs served an important function in extracting salt from the mines located in Transylvania in modern-day western Romania.[1161] In the Middle Ages, salt was as important a resource as gold and iron. After the fall of the Avar Qaghanate, the Bulgar Turks began to extend their control into this territory.

While the Avars were settling in modern-day Hungary, or more specifically in the Pannonian Plain, in the second half of the sixth century, the German Frankish Kingdom (Francia, 481–843) was gaining power. The demographics of modern-day Germany can be viewed as a composition of the tribes of the Saxons and Slavs in the north and the Teutonic peoples of Bavarian and Swabian tribes in the south, with considerable Slavic elements entering the southeastern area later on.[1162] The fall of the Ostrogothic Kingdom in the sixth century allowed the Bavarians to spread along the Danube River. Here they willingly entered under the protection of their kinsmen the Franks against the formidable pressure of the Avars, who stopped the southeasterly German expansion.[1163]

Beginning in the sixth century, the Avars promoted the migration of the Slavs into the Balkans, which eventually changed the demographics of this peninsula permanently.[1164] But these Slavs were used by their Avar overlords in the fights of the Avar Qaghanate against the Eastern Roman Empire. The Slavs, under the rule of the Avars, began to devastate the Roman Thrace late in the sixth century, beginning the permanent slavicization process north of the Greek lands. However, the arrival of a new wave of Turks began to change the political landscape of the region again. The victory of Bulgar Qubrat Khan over the Avars in 640–41 allowed the Bulgar Turks to eventually settle in the southern Balkan Peninsula, whereas the Avar Turks remained in Pannonia, in modern-day Hungary.

The Avar incursions on Roman Thrace continued during the reigns of emperors Justinian II and Maurice, and tribute payments to the Avars continued. But when Emperor Maurice struck a peace deal with Sassanid Persia in 592, the Eastern Roman army could then concentrate on the Avars and Slavs in Thrace. Consequently, there were bitter wars between the Avars and the Romans. In 597 Bayan failed to capture the port city of Thessalonica on the Aegean Sea coastline. In 600 a truce was established, and the Danube River became the border between the two dominions. Moreover, the Eastern Romans had to pay tribute to the Avars.[1165]

THE STRENGTH OF THE MOUNTED ARCHERS

According to a Roman military manual, the *Strategikon*, the Avars were the first people to use stirrups in Europe.[1166] The earliest use of stirrups appears to have been in Korea and Japan in about the fourth century CE. Stirrups, which were transmitted to the West by the Gök-Türk pastoralists, had a huge impact on the evolution of cavalry warfare, as it gave the rider a firmer seat on horseback. There is no proof that the Huns used them, but there is evidence that the Avars were using stirrups almost a century later, and they taught the Eastern Romans to use this device.[1167] In addition to bringing the iron stirrup to Europe, the Avars introduced the long lance.[1168] The Europeans also became reacquainted with the reflex bow, which the European Huns had brought previously. These Avar tools provided them a clear military tactical advantage over their enemies.

In the year 601, under the command of Priscus, the Romans pushed the Avars farther back into Pannonia. But after Emperor Maurice died in 602, the emperors Phocas and then Heraclius could not stop the loss of Roman territories. Soon the hostilities between the Eastern Romans and the Sassanid Persians were renewed. Suddenly Syria, Palestine, and Egypt fell into the hands of the Persians, and the border along the Danube River could no longer be controlled. On June 5, 617, the Avars laid siege to Constantinople. But Emperor Heraclius persevered and reorganized his army to crush the Persians (622–29). During the Persian wars, the Avars came down for their second siege of Constantinople in June 626. The Avar forces could be repulsed only in August of the same year. However, after this event, the strength of the Avars began to decline.

As mentioned in the earlier chapter, the Avar retreat became a trigger for the Hunnish elite within the political structure to revolt against the ruling clan. As a result of the civil war the Avar Qaghanate was split into two halves. While the Avar government continued to reign in Hungarian plains and parts of central Europe, the Bulgar Huns, particularly from the Utrighur tribal union, emerged as a new power in the eastern European plains. Taking advantage of the decline of the Gök-Türk power in the area, they formed the first Bulgar state under the leadership of Qubrat Khan. However, following the death of their revered leader and facing the rise of the Khazar Turks, the Bulgars split again; a group of them migrated towards the Balkans and came to be known as the Danubian Bulgars while another moved further north into the Volga basin to establish the Volga Bulgars (volume 2, chapter 2.3).

Meanwhile, even though the Eastern Roman Empire gained a respite after the Avars retreated, the Romans would face a new Turkish power on their Balkan borders, that of the Danubian Bulgar Turks, while on their eastern borders, they would face the Muslim Arabs who had conquered Sassanid Persia in 651.[1169] But by this time, Heraclius had secured an alliance with Bulgar Khan Qubrat of Old Greater Bulgaria, in 635–36[1170] in order to defend against the Avars together.

During their zenith, the Avars conquered nearly the entire Balkan Peninsula from the Eastern Romans. The Avar power in Europe owed much of its reputation to the celebrated efficiency of their cavalry units, their survival skills, and their strict discipline.[1171] But in the middle of the seventh century, they began to adopt a sedentary lifestyle around the Carpathians with Pannonia as their power center. As a result, they lost the traditional discipline imposed on them by their nomadic lifestyle. Though the Avars resisted the Christian influence brought by German monks, they were ultimately trapped between the Catholic Carolingian and the Orthodox Eastern Roman powers.

THE END AND THE LEGACY OF THE AVARS

One of the legacies of the (European) Avars is the formation of the specific Slavic groups that eventually led to the development of their modern national entities, and their influence on the Hungarians later catalyzed the development of modern-day central and eastern Europe; all these factors became vital turning points in Slavic history.[1172] Another major Avar legacy is the introduction of the stirrup, which essentially diminished the cavalry advantage that the Avars had since with the help of this vital equipment, the Europeans were now able to master equestrian arts. Consequently, with the emergence of the new armored cavalry force of the knights, a new feudal class in Europe came into existence.

By the end of the eighth century, the Avars were no longer as strong as they had been when they initially arrived in Europe. In comparison, the German Frankish Kingdom, also known as the Carolingian Empire, was now probably the most powerful polity of Europe. Under the rule of Charles the Great (Charlemagne), the Franks gave the Avars back-to-back defeats in the campaigns of 791, 793, and 796. Finally, the conquest of the Avar state was completed with the campaigns of 803 and 811. In the end, the Avars were forced to accept Christianity and abandon their Tengriist faith.[1173]

The elimination of the Avar state allowed the Germans and the southern Slavs to expand and colonize along the Danube, only to be stopped by the Bulgars, who moved into the Avars' former eastern territories.[1174] Nevertheless, the German sphere of influence extended beyond the Enns, the southern tributary of the Danube River. To the north of this main waterway, the German expansion stopped at the Theiss (Tisza in Hungarian) River basin, the northern tributary of the Danube, where the Magyars (ancestors of modern-day Hungarians) had settled by 896. But ultimately, the fall of the Avar state helped the southeastern German settlements in the area referred to as Ostmark initiate the building of future Austria by the tenth century.[1175]

The remaining Avars were assimilated by Turkish-Slavic state in Europe, the First Bulgarian Empire, but their fall had additional significant consequences in Europe. First, the Pannonian Plain in modern-day Hungary, once home to the Avars, became the permanent home of the newly arriving tribes, the Magyars, who were displaced from the Pontic Steppe by the Pečeneg Turks. Ultimately, this demographic change led to the evolution of modern Hungary. Furthermore, the Slavs, who had remained subdued until this time, found an opportunity to expand into eastern Europe and down to the Balkans. Some of them became the Eastern Slavs, who later became Russians.

A few artifacts from the Avars have been recovered. Superb-quality gold and silver artifacts have been found and are displayed in Vienna's Kunsthistorisches Museum. These finds in Avar graves not only reveal the social status of the deceased but also show that they were trading with the Eastern Roman Empire during times of peace, but at other times they were acquired by the Avars as tribute payments from Constantinople during times of war.[1176]

4.5. THE ON-OGHUR LEGACY

Although today's Hungarians consider themselves descendants of the Magyars, a distinct group of tribes not related to the Turks, there are historical facts that point a strong Turkish influence. Contemporary Hungary was formed from a mixture of tribes that were pushed into the Pannonian Basin in central Europe when they were forced out of the Pontic Steppe by the Pečeneg Turks (chapter 4.7) in the late ninth century.[1177] In central Europe in 843, the Germanic Carolingian Empire was divided into the Frankish kingdoms from which the future kingdoms of France and Germany were born. The disintegration of the Carolingian Empire allowed the Magyars, displaced by the Pečenegs, to settle in the Pannonian Plain, where they met with the remnants of the Avars. On this western end of the Eurasian steppes, once home to the Huns of Attila and the Avars, the Magyars formed a new state, which became the Kingdom of Hungary.

The Magyars, a Finno-Ugric group of peoples, were one of the founding tribes of modern-day Hungary. These ancient Hungarians initially moved from the western Siberian steppes toward the area of the Baškïr and Bulgar Turks around the year 500 CE.[1178] Their tribes finally settled in the lower Don and lower Dnieper regions, where they became part of the Turkish tribal federation of the On-Oghur. As a result, early Magyar culture had significant exposure to early Turkish culture.[1179] In fact, they came under both cultural and ethnic influences from the Turkish tribes, particularly the elements of agricultural and nomadic civilization.[1180]

Although the Magyars are Finno-Ugric, they initially joined with the Bulgar On-Oghur Turks in the fifth century while in western Siberia to the east of the Urals. The two nations lived almost as a single nation in symbiosis as they moved westward to the northern shores of the Black Sea. After the On-Oghur federation dissolved in the seventh century with the splitting of the Bulgar tribes, the ancient Hungarians encountered another group of Turks. By the end of the eighth century but no later than the ninth century, the Magyars came under the rule of the Khazar Qaghanate.[1181] In the second half of the ninth century, when they were pushed westward by another Turkish tribal union, the Pečenegs, their seven tribes left together with a Khazar tribe (Kabars or Kavars).[1182]

Once in eastern Europe, the Slavs called the Magyars On-Oghurs since they were part of the On-Oghur tribal federation of the Turks.[1183] Even though there is no clear historical record showing that the Magyars lived with the Huns of Attila, the contemporary Hungarians believe that their founder Arpad, from the ninth century, was a descendant of Attila the Hun of the fifth century; hence, to the Hungarians, Attila is a hero.[1184] But in reality, the Magyars moved to their final homeland in modern-day Hungary much later, after the Huns disappeared. According to Eastern Roman records, the Magyars moved into the Pannonian Steppe with the Ungroi tribes. The name Ungroi (in Greek), from which the name of Hungary is derived, was originally derived from the name On-Oghur of the Turkish tribes that formed the other major tribal union that contributed to the formation of modern-day Hungary.[1185] Hence, it is a fact that present-day Hungary was formed by a mixture of Magyar tribes and Turkish Oghuric tribes.[1186] It is no surprise that the contemporary Hungarian language has many common words with Turkish. The Turkish name Onogundur, likely from On-Oghur, survived among the Hungarians as Nándor, and interestingly, the Hungarian name for the Danube Bulgars was Nándor.[1187]

During the symbiotic relationship between the Magyars and the On-Oghur Turks, the Hungarian language borrowed multiple words from Turkish.[1188] The modern-day Hungarian language evolved from the Finno-Ugric group of languages, but there is evidence that it contains a considerable amount of Old Bulgar Turkish (Oghuric) loanwords related to social and moral codes, religious life, agriculture, and animal husbandry. The quality and quantity of these words proves that there was once an intense symbiosis between the On-Oghur Turkish tribes and the Magyars. Furthermore, in contemporary Eastern Roman and Arab sources, the Hungarians were described as Turks.[1189] By the ninth and the tenth centuries, the Magyar and On-Oghur confederation of tribes were more Turkish than Finno-Ugric. These tribes also absorbed the Slavs in their immediate vicinity.

It is plausible to assume that with long co-existence of early Hungarians with Oghuric Turkish dialect speaking Bulgar tribes and later with multiple Turkish tribes penetrating into the Hungarian society, there must be significant Turkish elements being present within Hungarian genetic make-up. Indeed, during the Middle Ages one can trace the Pečenegs, Cumans, Qïpčaks, as well as Turkmens being assimilated within the Hungarian population.

By the eleventh century, Hungary was a strong Christian state, a barrier protecting western Europe from incoming Turkish nomads from Asia. Meanwhile, the Pontic Steppe was undergoing a change as the Pečeneg and the Qïpčak-Cuman Turks became its new masters between the tenth and thirteenth centuries. However, by the eighteenth century, as the influence of Turkish lessened, the Hungarian language was more of Finno-Ugric origin. Interestingly, modern-day Hungary served as home to the former Turkish entities of the European Huns, Avars, On-Oghurs, Pečenegs, and Cumans. Later, the Ottoman Turks occupied Hungary in the sixteenth and seventeenth centuries. Today, the Hungarians still keep their cultural ties with the Turks alive through traditional festivities involving equestrian competitions, which include competitors from the modern-day Turkish states and territories.

4.6. THE NON-HEBREW JEWS

The Hun (Xiong-nu) legacy continued even after the fall of the Hunnish Oghuric Turkish–speaking Danubian Bulgars and European Avars. The Volga Bulgars (volume 2, chapter 2.3) and the Khazars were the last tribal entities that arose from the westerly migrating Xiong-nu coming from the Mongolian steppes. The Khazars were Turks[1190] who established international power for four centuries between the seventh and eleventh centuries in the Pontic Steppe in the area of modern-day Ukraine and southern Russia. The name Khazar emerged in the sixth century with the appearance of powerful tribes from the Sabirs, originating in the modern-day Dagestan region.[1191] These Turks showed a strong capability for political organization. The dominant language of the Khazar Turks was the Oghur dialect, similar to that of the European Huns and the European Avars before them.[1192]

The Khazars and their contemporary Bulgars were related to each other.[1193] It has been suggested that the ruling class may have come from the A-shih-na family, which had ruled the Gök-Türk Empire as well.[1194] Early on they used a lesser ruling title of *yabghu* since they were under the control of the Gök-Türks (chapter 5.3). They also made an alliance with the Eastern Roman Empire against the Persian Sassanid Empire in the south, as their former overlords, the Gök-Türks, did before them. Following the fall of the Gök-Türks, the Khazar rulers assumed the title of *qaghan*.

With the declining influence of the Western Gök-Türks in Asia and eastern Europe (corresponding to the end of the First Period of Türk, 552–630), two new Turkish states appeared in the Pontic Steppe, just north of the Black Sea, in about 630–50. As mentioned earlier, the Bulgar Turks, also speaking Oghuric Turkish like the Khazars, formed Old Greater Bulgaria (also known as Magna Bulgaria) to the west of the Khazars. But the defeat of the Bulgar Turks in 670 by the Khazar armies forced some of them to leave their territories in modern-day Ukraine. This victory allowed the Khazars to remain the primary Turkish power in the Pontic Steppe. But the great Turkish migrations that were initiated by the earlier movements of the Huns had brought other Turkish tribes to this area as well. Indeed, the Khazars had the Turkish groups of the Khotzirs, On-Oghurs, Volga Bulgars, and Huns (remnants of the European Huns) in their realm. The last group resided the basin of the Sulak River, north of Derbent in modern-day Dagestan.[1195] In the demographic makeup of the Khazar Empire, the majority of the population consisted of Bulgar Turks.[1196] The Khazars also ruled over Slavs (Ventič, Sever, and Slovene), Finnic groups (Ar, Ves, and Čeremis), and Germanic Goths (particularly between 786 and 810).[1197]

KHAZARIA AS AN INTERNATIONAL POWER

The center of power for the Khazars was just north of the Caspian Sea, near the Volga delta, where their capital was located. Until 722–23 Semender in northern Caucasus was the capital of Khazaria, but later the Khazar emperors ruled from the twin city of Amol/Atil (also known as Saričin/Khamlï) in the lower Volga region. While the western city of Amol (Saričin) was the center of government and rituals, the eastern city of Atil (Khamlï) was the commercial center. Their strength eventually reached Kiev in the west and the trans-Volgan-Khwarezmian steppes in the east, where the Oghuz Turks were situated. The Khazars ruled over the Pontic Steppe, northern Caucasus, Crimea, and the basins of Don, the lower two-thirds of the Volga, and the Oka.[1198] Between 642 and 737, the Khazars remained allies with the Eastern Roman Empire. Together they acted against the Persian Sassanids, who were later supplanted by the Muslim Arab Umayyads in the year 651.[1199]

The Khazars benefited from the northern trade routes of the Silk Road, connecting Central Asia in the east to the Baltic and the woodlands of Russia. Starting from their base in modern-day Dagestan in northern Caucasus, the Khazar Qaghanate turned into one of the greatest international powers of the ninth and tenth centuries in an area that had never possessed such wealth and power.[1200] During the zenith of its strength, both the Khanate of the Volga Bulgars and the Qaghanate of Rus' were under the suzerainty of the Khazar Empire.[1201] After the Persian Empire perished, the Khazars chose to become allies with the Eastern Romans against the Arabs to secure trade routes to Iran and secure Azerbaijan territories. Indeed, trade relations between the Eastern Romans and the Khazars remained friendly.[1202] The relationship with Constantinople also included dynastic intermarriages. Eastern Roman emperor Leo IV the Khazar (775–80), for example, was the offspring from the marriage of Emperor Constantine V and Khazar princess Tzitzak (Çiçek), baptized as Irene.[1203] Furthermore, the Khazars contributed to the Eastern Roman Empire by providing religious leaders and prolific writers; Photius from Khazaria, for example, was patriarch of Constantinople during 858–67 and then again in 877–86.[1204]

In the seventh century, the Khazars faced a series of wars with Muslim Arabs, who were not initially successful in penetrating Khazar territory. In 730 the Khazars destroyed the entire Muslim army just south of modern-day Azerbaijan. Later, in 737, Umayyad general Marwan (later known as Marwan II, the last Umayyad caliph) successfully invaded Khazar territories. The Arab general's violence in Khazar land forced the Khazar qaghan to accept Marwan's demand to convert to Islam.[1205] But the lack of communication lines between the Arab armies and the caliphate and the fall of the Umayyad dynasty in 750 meant the Arabs could not sustain their control over the Khazar realm. Soon after the departure of Marwan, the Khazar qaghan denounced Islam.

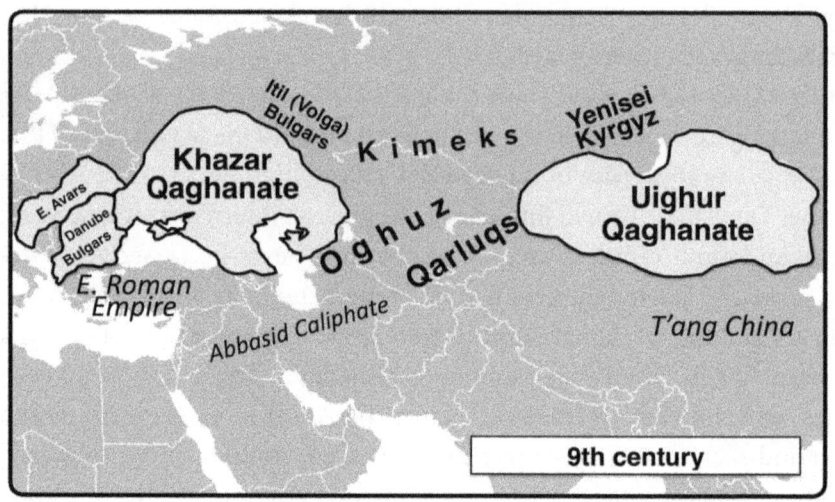

Map 9. In the ninth century Khazars were known to be a major economic and military power in eastern Europe, at the crossroads between the West and the Far East. With the fall of the Uighur Qaghanate near the middle of this century, this was also the last century of ages-long full Turkish control of the Mongolian steppes.

THE SOLE NON-HEBREW JUDAIC STATE

By the second half of the eighth century, the Khazar Turks began to convert to Judaism.[1206] In the first half of the ninth century, under the reign of Bulan Qaghan, Khazaria adopted rabbinic Judaism as its official religion.[1207] According to historical sources, the Khazar rulers began to use the title of "king" instead of *qaghan*. Many modern rabbinic scholars view the Khazar conversion to Judaism as a crucial event in Jewish history.[1208] In the year 864, Druthmar of Aquitaine, a Frankish Benedictine monk at the Corvey Monastery in Westphalia, referred to the Khazars as a Hunnish race living in the lands of Gog and Magog professing the Jewish faith, whereas their kinsmen (Danubian) Bulgars were Christians.[1209]

The religious tolerance demonstrated by the Khazar Turks was common to all nomadic empires of Asia.[1210] Just as, for example, the Gök-Türks showed tolerance to other religions in their realm, the Khazars allowed all three Semitic faiths to thrive within their borders. In fact, the Arsiyahwas, a

Khazar military unit, was formed from Muslims from the Khwarezm region. Meanwhile, the Eastern Roman Jews sought refuge in Khazar-dominated territories from the oppression imposed by Constantinople.[1211] As a direct consequence of increased trading opportunities in the Khazar Qaghanate—but also owing to the unbearable persecutions that the Jews experienced in Eastern Roman and Sassanid Persian territories—masses of Jews, particularly in the eighth century, began to seek sanctuary in the tolerant Tengriist Khazar Qaghanate.[1212] In their new Turkish homeland, the Jews, who became the forefathers of the contemporary Ashkenazi Jewry of Europe, prospered and began to exert religious influence upon the Khazar aristocracy. Much later, the descendants of the Khazars in Crimea eventually contributed to the formation of the Crimean Tatars and Crimean Jews.[1213] Khazaria collapsed in the late tenth century, but it is claimed that there is still a small Turkish Khazar element in the makeup of modern-day Ashkenazi Jews.[1214]

THE TURKISH JEWRY

Following the fall of Khazaria, the Jewish population in the lands, where the Turkish language remained prevalent for centuries to come, continued to survive. A peculiar group was the Karaim, who were Turkish-speaking followers of Judaism; the Crimean Turkish Jews were related to the Khazars, whereas the Polish ones spoke Qïpčak Turkish.[1215] Meanwhile, another group of Turkish-speaking Jews, known as the Krïmchaks, emerged after the arrival of the Tatars in the Crimean Peninsula.

Following the fall of the Khazar Empire, many Khazars survived in the Crimean Peninsula. During the late stages of the Golden Horde and later, a significant group of them became mixed with the Tatars, forming the future Crimean Tatar Khanate while adopting the religion of Islam, whereas others remained Jewish in faith. Together with incoming Jewish immigrants, the latter group formed the Krïmchak Jews, who were mostly artisans, farmers, gardeners, and traders.[1216] The Krïmchak Jews were a separate sect from the Karaim Jews, who were nontalmudic. These two Jewish groups were a minority of the total Jewry in the future Russian Empire. By 1939 there were nearly three million Jews living in Soviet Russia.[1217] However, during

World War II nearly 60 percent of Jews in the countries under the Axis domination, about six million of them, were murdered.[1218] According to records from the Nuremberg International Military Tribunal, the orders for the massacres of the Krïmchaks by the Nazi Germans came directly from Berlin. Their murders were carried out between November 16 and December 15, 1941, and as a result, the Krïmchaks were completely annihilated; only a small group of them remain in the United States.[1219]

THE KHAZAR ECONOMY

The Khazar economy was multifaceted, including animal husbandry, hunting, fishing, crafting, and agriculture along with both domestic and international trade. The Khazars' most important trade routes crossed over the basins of the Don and Volga. Eventually, with the fall of the Avars, the Khazars established a trading relationship with the Carolingian Empire through a transcontinental route, along which Vienna and Kiev turned into transit centers.[1220] The Khazar realm was also on the direct trading route of the northern branch of the historic Silk Road, connecting Europe to Asia as well as to the Middle East through Caucasus.

Archaeological discoveries illustrate that the Khazars used coins. The issue of dirhams by the Khazars started in 825.[1221] The first issue was a copy of the Islamic coins of the Abbasid Caliphate, even though the Khazars did not accept Islam as their official religion. But in 837 the Khazars issued three distinct coins, known as the Ard al-Khazar, Moses, and Tamgha dirhams.[1222] The first coin had an Arabic inscription meaning "land of the Khazars." The second coin had an Arabic inscription stating "Moses is the prophet of Allah." The third Tamgha coin carried an Old Turkish Orkhon alphabet letter as the seal. The significance of the use of the Old Turkish letter is unknown. Perhaps it was used as the symbol of the rulers. Or it could have been a reminder of their past and therefore their heritage. The apparent conclusion from these coins is also that the Khazars were expressing the legitimacy of their Judaic faith to the expansionist Abbasids in the south.

Khazaria remained an international power from the mid-eighth century to the mid-tenth century. But its fall came quickly. Perhaps the new Judaic faith of the Khazar elites and their abandonment of a pastoralist lifestyle did not allow the Khazar rulers to dominate the newly emerging Turkish entities near the Khazar Qaghanate. In fact, it was these new tribal entities that contributed to the downfall of the once-mighty Khazaria.

THE DECLINE

Beginning in the tenth century, the Pečeneg Turks (next chapter), driven westward by the Oghuz Turks in the territories of the modern-day Kazakh steppes, became the dominant force in the Pontic Steppe, as noted in Eastern Roman annals. The Pečeneg presence began to weaken the strength of the Khazars. Furthermore, multiple incursions upon the Eastern Roman Empire by the Pečenegs put the Roman legacy in danger as well.[1223] These occurred specifically in 934, 944, 1064, 1076, 1087, and 1090.

With the eventual collapse of Khazar power, the non-Khazar Turks in this area began to exert their own influence. The Muslim Volga Bulgar Turks in present-day Kazan became a strong military power in the tenth century. Hence, with the loss of trading routes in the Pontic Steppe and the Volga trading posts to the Bulgars, the Khazar economy began to decline in the tenth century. As it has always been in history, the loss of power of one group was to benefit the rise of another group.

When the Khazars were strong, the Slavic tribes remained under the control of the Khazar monarch.[1224] In fact, until the tenth century, the Slavs remained subjects of the successive Turkish polities (Avars, Bulgars, and Khazars) in eastern Europe. But taking advantage of the decline of the Khazar power, the Slavs of eastern Europe began to emerge in the second half of the tenth century. Interestingly, as will be pointed out later, the early Russian state was formed by a Viking prince, and the first Russian dynasty was therefore a Viking dynasty. The early rulers of Russia governing the Slavs fashioned their state after the Khazar Qaghanate. Thus, this state came to be known with its Turkish title name as the Qaghanate of Rus' (later known as Russia).

In the early Middle Ages, eastern Europe was home to three major states, the Khazar Qaghanate, the Volga Bulgar Khanate, and the Qaghanate of Rus' (also known as Kievan Rus'). All three were initially formed by pagan rulers. But by the tenth century, the leaders of all three states followed separate Abrahamic religions: the Khazars were Jewish, the Volga Bulgars were Muslims, and the Rus' were Orthodox Christians. However, when the Khazars were in power, both the Bulgars and the Rus' were under the rule of the Jewish Turks.

The Viking ruling class had their eyes on the Khazar territories' riches and trade organizations, and taking advantage of the decline of Khazar power, they began raids upon the Turkish state. When the Khazars sensed the threat of Varangian Viking presence in the modern-day territories of Ukraine, in 833 they asked for assistance from Eastern Roman emperor Theophilus to build a fortified position, which came to be known as Sarkel, at the mouth of the Don. In response, the government of Constantinople also built fortifications in the southern part of the Crimean Peninsula.[1225]

The Khazars repelled the Russian attacks only until 965, when (Russian Viking) Svyatoslav I of Kiev, with the assistance of the Oghuz Turks, caused the collapse of Khazar power. This event gave prominence to the Russian state, which benefited from Khazar commercial and political traditions, but despite the historical facts, the Russians in general have refused to accept that they owe the Khazars for playing a key role in the creation of the medieval Russian state.[1226] Svyatoslav later was killed at the hands of the Turkish Pečenegs.

The Khazar Qaghanate, also known as the Khazar Empire, lasted about four centuries. It appears in the annals of history as the only non-Hebrew Judaic state. The territories of the Khazars were known as Khazaria, but in the archives of the medieval Eastern Roman Empire, Khazaria was often referred to as Tourkia—in other words, Turkey—in Greek. The Khazar Turks, like the Huns and the Avars, were originally a nomadic people, though they eventually established a powerful settled civilization. So it has been hypothesized that the name Khazar might have been derived from the Turkish word *gezer* for "wandering" (old pronunciation, "khazar"). There is a theory that the word *khazar* was derived from the Latin word *caesar*,[1227] but this is not true. After all, the Khazars were strongly bound to their traditions and had no intention to imitate the Eastern Roman Empire.

At its zenith, the Khazar Qaghanate stretched from the Danube in the west to the Volga-Ural Steppe in the east. The empire was situated along the Silk Road's northern branch, between Asia and eastern Europe. This Turkish state was a strategically important empire that established good relations with the Eastern Roman Empire in the south. When the Romans came under attack from the Abbasid Caliphate's army, the Khazars came to the help of the Eastern Roman Empire to repulse the Arabs in the eighth century. The Khazars were highly productive people and able to manufacture goods for internal use and for export. They also appeared to be expert farmers and herders. Most Khazarians lived in felt tents known as yurts.[1228]

The Caspian Sea at the time was known as the Khazar Sea.[1229] Today, the Caspian Sea in the Turkish language is still known as the Hazar Denizi, named after the Khazars.

THE RISE OF THE RUS'

In the context of discussing the history of the Turks in the Pontic Steppe, it is worth mentioning the rise of the Russians in this geographic area. Russian history owes its emergence to the Viking leadership that took over the Eastern Slavic people in the area of western Khazaria, leading them to form the future Russian state.

In the first half of the ninth century, eastern Europe was divided into two spheres of interest: the southern zone, which was Turkish (Avars, Bulgars, and Khazars), and the northern zone, which was Danish/Swedish. It was from the northern zone that the Rus' emerged with their Viking leadership. The Frisians (a Germanic people) were known to be involved in maritime ventures in the northern seas, and they were involved in the Anglo-Saxon colonization of Britain about 440 CE. These were Scandinavians who began to learn from their maritime activities as they also became expert ship builders. The Frisian Danes formed a society known as the "nomads of the sea" and began their activities as Vikings in the eighth century. Their primary interest was trading. They finally formed the company of Rus' primarily for this purpose before settling along the Volga in the north. The economic cooperation between the nomads of the sea (Vikings) and the nomads of the land (Khazars) led to the eventual formation of a new state, known as the Rus' Qaghanate.

The Rus' Qaghanate went through three stages of development: Volga Rus' (839–930), Dnieper Rus' (930–1036), and Kievan Rus' (1036–1169). While the Rus' were establishing themselves along the Volga in eastern Europe, Charlemagne was making efforts to end Avar existence and secure a trade route from Regensburg to Khazar Itil; the cities of Vienna and Kiev were built along this route. In 930 the Viking Rus' shifted their trading operations center from the Volga to the Dnieper, where they later captured Kiev, the former Khazar garrison town. Thus, over a period of two centuries, what started as a social and economic entity of a low culture transformed into a Christian and linguistically Slavic high-culture entity known as Kievan Rus'.[1230]

After the invasion of the Pontic Steppe by the Pečeneg Turks, Khazar strength weakened, and consequently the Russo-Varangian Vikings took over the key commercial city of Kiev in 890. Subsequently, the Vikings put the Slavs under their rule. It is clear that the name of modern-day Russia was derived from the Viking name of Rus'.[1231] It appears that the early Rus' (Russian) state tried to emulate the Khazar Qaghanate.[1232] It was evident that the first Russian state "imitated many Khazar customs and terms in their legal, military, and administrative organizations, besides adopting a series of Khazar names of clothing, utensils, transport, and trade."[1233]

Interestingly, the Viking rulers took the Turkish title of *qaghan*, and therefore, the state in Kiev was known as the Qaghanate of Rus'. These Vikings either used this Turkish title to copy the Khazar Qaghanate's grandeur or were given the title by the Khazar qaghan to be known as vassal qaghans. According to the ancient Turkish code, the title of *qaghan* had to be accorded by a ruling qaghan. We see such an example in the Orkhon inscriptions, where Bilge Qaghan awarded the title of *baz qaghan* (vassal qaghan) to the ruling clan of the Toquz-Oghuz Turkish tribal union. Recent research suggests that the Qaghanate of Rus' in its early formation was a vassal of the Khazar Qaghanate and thereby received the title of *qaghan* from a ruling qaghan.[1234] In addition, there were possibly intermarriages between the two ruling families.

Russian history thus began in 839 with the formation of the Qaghanate of Rus', where its Viking monarch used the Turkish title of *qaghan*.[1235] As mentioned, the first dynasty of Russia was not Slavic but rather came from the descendants of Danish king Hrærikr (Rjurik) from the Ylfingar tribe. Consequently, this founding dynasty of the Russian history came to be known as the Rurikid (or Rurik) dynasty of the Vikings, and it lasted from 839 until 1598.

The Rus' made efforts to expand their territories by seeking land and booty from the Khazars and later from the Eastern Romans. According to Roman records, Kievan Rus' was led by a royal Viking group controlling its army of Slavs, Vikings, and Finns.[1236] By the mid-tenth century, the capital of the Qaghanate of Rus' was modern-day Kiev. By this time the Rus' were engaging the Eastern Romans as well as the Khazar Turks and the Pečeneg Turks.

For the Russians, the first true monarch of the Rurik dynasty was Svyatoslav I of Kiev, who emerged as a powerful prince of Kiev. He dealt a fatal blow to the Khazars in 965 with the help of Oghuz Turks. At the request of the Roman emperor, he also crushed Bulgaria in the Balkans. But subsequently, the Roman emperor employed the Pečeneg Turks to destroy Svyatoslav's army, and the prince was killed. However, the Viking-led dynasty of Svyatoslav pulled the scattered Slavic tribes under its rule to form the foundation of future Russia. By the eleventh century, the Russians were facing a new Turkish power on their eastern border, the Qïpčak-Cumans. The Russians often referred to them as the Polovtsy. In order to avoid confrontation with the newcomers, the Russian aristocracy eventually established intermarriages with the Qïpčak-Cuman aristocracy of the steppes.[1237] The Qïpčak-Cuman Turks will be discussed in chapter 4.8.

With the arrival of the Tatars under Mongol rule, the Russians were subdued into suzerainty. The state building in Kiev (in modern-day Ukraine) was destroyed, and the center of Russian politics was permanently moved to Moscow, farther away from the steppes. The new Russian polity also came to be known as Muscovy. From the thirteenth to the sixteenth century, Muscovy remained under Tatar control (volume 2, chapter 4.2). This period in Russian history is also referred to as the Tatar Yoke. With the crowning of Ivan IV from the Rurik dynasty as the first czar of Russia in 1547, the Russians began to take the weakened and disunited Tatar khanates one by one. The Crimean Tatar Khanate was the last Tatar polity to survive until it was annexed by the Russian Empire in 1783. With this event came the end of nearly fifteen hundred years of independent Turkish presence in eastern Europe, noted since late in the fourth century CE. However, Turkish entities continued to survive in this part of the continent. The Turks currently living in eastern European region include the Kazan Tatars, Lithuanian Tatars, Baškïrs, Chuvash, Gagauz, and Lithuanian Karaim.[1238]

4.7. THE WILD WARRIORS

In the tenth to thirteenth centuries, following the collapse of the Khazar Qaghanate, control of the Pontic Steppe and eastern Europe for the most part remained under the Turkish nomads. In the area north of the Caspian Sea, the Pečeneg, Oghuz, and Qïpčak-Cuman Turks dominated eastern Europe in the late tenth and early eleventh centuries.[1239] First the Pečenegs in the tenth century and then, beginning in the eleventh century, the Qïpčak-Cumans controlled the Pontic Steppe, keeping the Russian and Polish principalities in check. During the same time, south of the Caspian Sea, the Ghaznavid Turks occupied Iran.

Even though they had an obscure past and seemingly short existence, the Pečeneg Turks left a lasting legacy in European history. They displaced the Magyar tribes from the territories of modern-day Ukraine, forcing them to move into their new permanent home in modern-day Hungary, and they split the Slavs into northern and southern branches. Furthermore, they did not allow the Rus' (future Russians) to get strong enough to threaten the weakened Eastern Roman Empire.[1240]

The Pečenegs were first recognized in the steppes between the Volga and Ural Rivers in the ninth century. Their tribal union was formed by eight hordes, three of which acted as leaders of the union. They were situated along the northern branch of the Silk Road between Khwarezm and the domains of Khazaria and Volga Bulgaria. Under pressure from the Kimeks (next chapter) to their northeast and the Oghuz (volume 2, chapters 2.5, 2.6) to their east, around the mid-ninth century, they were forced to move westward against the Khazars. Some of the Pečenegs were under the control of the Oghuz, and another group came under the rule of the Khazars. Yet another group acted independently. Toward the end of the same century, this latter group became powerful.

Around 840–41, predicting danger from these newcomers, the Khazars, with the assistance of the Eastern Romans, built the fort of Sarkel/Sharkil on the left bank of the lower Don.[1241] But eventually the unruly presence of the Pečenegs weakened Khazar authority in the region. Crossing the Volga and Don Rivers, they pushed the Magyars farther west to take their grazing grounds.[1242] Late in the tenth century, control of the western part of the Pontic Steppe shifted from the Khazar Turks to the Pečeneg Turks, who shortly thereafter began to lose their grip against the powerful Qïpčak-Cuman tribes, who were moving in from the east following the disintegration of the Kimek Qaghanate in the Kazakh Steppe. The Pečenegs were a large tribal union and were thought to be associated with the Töles (previously known as the T'ieh-le), a huge Turkish tribal confederation, as mentioned in Chinese sources.[1243] The T'ieh-le were also present in the tribal confederation of the Xiong-nu (chapter 3.2).

Under pressure from the Oghuz Turkish tribal union and the Khazar Qaghanate, the Pečenegs moved to present-day western Ukraine in the late ninth century. By the 1030s, the Qïpčaks were in the modern-day Kazakh Steppe, the Oghuz were between the Ural (Yayïk) and Volga (Itil) Rivers, and the Pečenegs were situated between the Volga and the lower Danube. In addition, the Volga Bulgars (volume 2, chapter 2.3) were in the Volga basin.

In the twelfth century, the Cuman Turks were on the western end of the Qïpčak country, and the two Turkish confederacies loosely merged into one. It has been suggested the Cuman Turks were related to the Qanglï, an ancient Turkish tribal group[1244] known to the Chinese as the Kao-ch'e. Perhaps the Töles once incorporated the Pečenegs and the Qanglï, which later formed the Cumans. Or both might have originated from the Ting-ling, since the T'ieh-le (later known as Töles) were believed to have once been part of this larger tribal federation as well.

In any case, the Turkish tribal union of the Pečenegs established itself between Sarkel, the Khazar fortress on the Don, and Silistria, on the Danube. They had peaceful relations with the Slavs around Kiev and their eastern neighbors, the Khazar Turks and Persian-speaking Alans. Once again they enjoyed the benefits of the trade route crossing their lands. Like other nomadic peoples, they also thrived on their livestock.

Although the Pečenegs did not assist Russian leader Svyatoslav's campaigns against the Khazars, they joined in his campaign against Constantinople and Bulgaria. The Eastern Romans managed to convince the nomadic fighters to plunder Bulgaria instead. Then, while returning to Kiev after his defeat by the Eastern Romans, Svyatoslav was killed by the Pečenegs. Their leader, Kur Khan, turned Svyatoslav's skull into a drinking cup with the inscription "He who covets the property of others often loses his own."[1245] From this point on, the Pečenegs' relations with the Russians soured.

The Pečenegs, like their ancestors from Central Asia, followed the Tengriist faith. In the year 1008, German missionary Bruno arrived in the land of this Turkish pastoral people to convert them to Christianity. His efforts were successful to some extent, but the new converts did not follow their new religion for long.[1246] Bruno, having survived in the land of these pagan Turks, ironically was later murdered by his own kinsmen, the Prussians.

Meanwhile, the Russians took advantage of the void created by the collapse of the Khazar Empire. At the same time, a new group of Turks, the Cumans and the Qïpčaks, began to pressure the Pečenegs to move farther west as they forced the Oghuz southward to Khwarezm. The latter action eventually led to the formation of the Great Seljuk Empire (volume 2, chapter 2.5) by the Oghuz in the eleventh century. When the Pečenegs were defeated by the Varangian-led Russians in 1036, they began to move toward the basin of the Danube River in the Balkans.[1247] As a result, the Pečenegs pursued secure lands within Eastern Roman territories, particularly in the Balkans.

The armies of the emperor could not stop the incursions of these nomadic warriors looking for grazing lands for their animals. By 1036 Constantinople was forced to make a treaty with the Pečeneg khan, recognizing this group of Turks as allies. A group of Pečenegs, however, entered Hungary in 1051 and remained there as mercenary troops. Another group of Pečenegs was defeated by Yaroslav, the leader of the Russians. Consequently, he was viewed as the savior of Russia, but in reality, the true pacifier of the Pečenegs was another group of Turks, the Oghuz remnants. As a result, some Pečeneg chieftains sought refuge in the territories of Kievan Rus', where they served as frontier guards.[1248]

Kegen, a nonnoble Pečeneg rebel not satisfied by his supreme khan's failure to defend his tribes, valiantly stood up against the incursions by the Oghuz.

As a result, he gained respect from his people. However, trying to save himself and his followers from the wrath of the khan, he sought asylum in the Eastern Roman Empire. The emperor welcomed the refugees and baptized them. Ultimately, the Pečeneg tribal nation, owing to the peace treaty signed in 1053, was allowed to settle in central Macedonia and northeastern Bulgaria. The Pečeneg Turks were then incorporated into the Eastern Roman armies, soon to be used against the Seljuk Turks in Anatolia in the same century.[1249]

Indeed, the Eastern Romans tried to use the Pečenegs against the Seljuk Turks on at least two occasions (volume 2, chapter 2.5, 2.6). The first attempt was at the Battle of Manzikert in 1071, where the Pečeneg warriors changed sides to fight alongside their kinsmen against the emperor.[1250] The second event was during a civil war within the Eastern Roman Empire. At the Battle of Kalovryia (Calobyra) in Thrace, the skilled archery of the mercenary Seljuk mounted archers proved to be vital[1251] to the victory of the emperor Nicephorus Botaniates (1078–81) over his rebellious general Bryennius, who was abandoned by the Pečeneg Turks during the battle.[1252]

In the north, the remnants of the Oghuz in the Pontic Steppe disappeared as a political power when the Qïpčak-Cumans began to arise as the new power of the region. These Turks were pushed all the way to the Carpathians, and as a result, the Pečenegs felt the need to settle in the western regions of Hungary. Once here, they helped King Geysa defend his throne against his cousin Salamon. Meanwhile, the remnants of free Pečenegs in the northern Balkans fled from the Cuman Turks in 1085–86 by crossing the Danube into Eastern Roman territories. The imperial armies felt helpless to stop them. Consequently, with no alternative solution, they were allowed to settle. The Pečenegs in fact did not intend to eliminate the central power in Constantinople but rather wished to find a secure place to settle. When they offered their services to the Romans, emperor Alexius Comnenus refused and marched over them. But he found himself defeated by these pastoralist warriors, and ultimately, he allowed them to remain within his borders. When the Cumans arrived to slaughter the Pečenegs, the emperor sent them away with gifts instead.[1253]

The army of the Eastern Roman Empire employed Turkish warriors of the Pečeneg and Oghuz tribes, which sought sanctuary in the Balkans from the Qïpčak-Cumans in the eleventh century.[1254] These warriors were also recruited by the Russians against the Qïpčaks.[1255] In fact, in the Russian territories, the Pečenegs and the remnant Oghuz formed a new tribal federation, which came to be known as the Qaraqalpaqs (Black Hats).[1256] This new union gave the Russians a barrier against the Qïpčaks. The evolving friendly relations led to the practice of interracial marriages between the Russians and the Qaraqalpaq Turks, and later the Qïpčak Turks provided significant mixing of the Turkish genetic pool into the Russian Slavic stock.[1257]

The Pečeneg Turks who freely roamed in the Roman Balkan territories in the late eleventh and early twelfth centuries were erroneously referred to by former historians as the Scyths (a.k.a. the Scythians).[1258] In 1090, when the Pečenegs once again caused chaos across Thrace all the way to the impenetrable walls of Constantinople, Emperor Alexius used the services of Cuman mercenaries to crush the Pečenegs, whose survivors were placed in Macedonia and employed in the imperial army. There are records mentioning that they formed an important part of the armies of the Eastern Roman Empire until at least the mid-twelfth century.[1259] The remaining Pečenegs were trapped under the rule of the Cumans until they were freed, together with the remnants of the Oghuz, after the Russian victory over the Cumans in the early twelfth century. After the Cumans pulled back to the Don River, there were nearly fifty years of peace in the territories of modern-day Romania and southwestern Ukraine, where the remnants of the Pečenegs and Oghuz tried to regroup.

Finally, in 1122, the Pečenegs started their final clash with the Eastern Roman Empire with incursions into its northern borders. The emperor John Comnenus eliminated the Pečeneg threat by means of treachery; he first invited their leaders into various cities of the empire as guests and subsequently had them arrested, and then he had the leaderless people slaughtered with the battle-axes of English mercenaries. This day of slaughter was declared a special festival day, Pečeneg Day.[1260] Some survivors were sold into slavery; others were placed along the borders of Albania, forming a special legion. Those who managed to escape sought refuge in Hungary. After the tragic slaughter, the Pečenegs disappeared from the pages of history as an independent tribal entity. The surviving Pečenegs merged with the peoples of the Balkans and Hungary. They were integrated into Hungarian society, where they reached various ranks, from free peasants to noblemen.[1261] Eventually they were completely assimilated.

4.8. THE POLOVTSY

From the early Asian Hun (Xiong-nu) era, we know that the Ting-ling Turks resided in large territories of northern Mongolia and southern Siberia (chapter 3). However, after the Hun political establishment disappeared in the Far East, it seems the Ting-ling descended to the northern borders of China, and in the fifth century, they became allies with the Northern Wei dynasty of the Tabgač Turks (chapter 5.2) against the Juan-juan (Asian Avars). It appears that later the Ting-ling were likely part of the greater Turkish union of the Gök-Türks. We know from Chinese records that the Kao-ch'e (Qanglï Turks) were either descendants or at least part of the greater Ting-ling tribal confederation. Eventually the Qanglï moved in a northwesterly direction to the territories of modern-day Kazakhstan and western Siberia, where they were part of the Kimek union, which was part of the greater Gök-Türk Empire (chapter 5.3). Perhaps Ting-ling was the Chinese name for the Turkish Kimek tribal union, and it has been suggested that this tribal confederation included the Turkish tribes of the Qïpčaks in addition to the Cumans and the Qanglï as separate tribal union entities.

THE KIMEK TURKS OF SIBERIA

By the ninth and tenth centuries, it is thought, this large confederation was known as the Kimek Qaghanate. By this time, these Turks dominated the northern borders of the Eurasian Steppe in western Siberia.[1262] The ruling tribe of the Kimek state was known as Tatar, and the Qïpčak grouping was in the western section of this obscure state. The Selenga inscription of the Uighur Eletmish Qaghan (747–59) mentions the Turk Qïpčak. The Kimek Turks were engaged in the trade of fur and forest products, particularly with the Muslim market down south in the eastern Mediterranean region.[1263] The Kimeks largely followed the traditional shamanist Tengriist cult of Central Asia. In the early eleventh century, because of migration, the Kimek union fractured. But this political union may have fragmented because of political intertribal turmoil as well.[1264]

When the Kimek union collapsed, many tribes from this confederation migrated to join the Qarluq and Oghuz tribal unions. The Qïpčaks spread across vast territories extending from the Danube River in the Balkans to western Siberia and modern-day Kazakhstan—in other words, the lands north of the Qara-Khanid Qaghanate.[1265] Eventually the Kimek confederation was replaced by a loose confederation of tribes led by the Qïpčaks moving to the Pontic Steppe. Within this new restructured confederation, the western branch included the Cumans, and the eastern branch had the Qanglï. When they succeeded in driving off the Pečeneg and the Western Oghuz tribes into the Balkans—in other words, to the borders of the Eastern Roman Empire— the Qïpčak Turks became the undisputed owners of the large Pontic Steppe portion of the Western Eurasian Steppe stretching from the Danube in the west to Khwarezm in the east. By the eleventh century, the steppes of modern-day western Kazakhstan, between the Caspian Sea and the Aral Sea, were also occupied by the Oghuz Turks, the future powerhouse of the Turkish world. It was probably Qïpčak pressure that destabilized and pushed the warriors of the Oghuz Yabghu state closer to the Muslim lands in Khwarezm, leading to the rise of Seljuk power (volume 2, chapter 2.5), initially in the sphere of influence of the Abbasid Caliphate.[1266] During this time in Turkestan, southeast of the Pontic Steppe, the Turkish Islamic states of the Qara-Khanids (volume 2, chapter 2.4) and Ghaznavids (volume 2, chapter 1.3) were already established. While the Qïpčaks were settling themselves in estern European steppes, the Volga Bulgar Khanate (volume 2, chapter 2.3) continued their existence in modern-day Kazan region until the Mongol invasion of the thirteenth century.

THE RULERS OF THE PONTIC STEPPE

The Qïpčaks first appeared in eastern Europe in the steppe between the Volga and the Don Rivers. The Khazar Qaghanate had already been destroyed by the Oghuz Turks. But the Qïpčaks coming from western Siberia and in need of wider pastures pushed westward to displace most of the Oghuz to the south and to penetrate freely into the Pečeneg territories in modern-day Ukraine. In 1054 they appeared on the outskirts of the territories of the Rus', in 1070 they crossed the Carpathians, and in 1090 they reached the Danube River.[1267] In the mid-thirteenth century, Muslim chroniclers called the large territory between the Altai Mountains and the Carpathians the Qïpčak State, or Desht-i Qïpčak in Arabic. Despite the fact that the little-known loosely formed Qïpčak Khanate had declined by 1130, their domination of these territories lasted until the invasion of the hordes of Genghis Khan in the thirteenth century. These Turks of Desht-i Qïpčak were also known to be part of the Qïpčak-Cuman tribes. The name Qïpčak is believed to have originated from the old name of the great northwestern steppe of Asia, which is now known as the Kyrgyz Steppe (also as the Kazakh Steppe). The dialect of the Qïpčak Turks is believed to have been similar to that of the Qanglï Turks and close to Old Uighur.[1268]

With the fall of Khazaria, it seemed that the Western Eurasian Steppe was being flooded with a constant influx of nomads because of ongoing migrations of Turkish tribes from the east. The late arrival of the Qïpčak-Cuman Turks from the east and the Vikings from the north to eastern Europe, primarily as traders, began to change the demographic landscape of this geographic area once again. During this time, the Eastern Slavs were organizing into principalities. After being released from Khazar suzerainty, the early Russian development under the Viking dynasty known as the Rus' then had to face the Qïpčak-Cuman Turks. The Arabs and Georgians referred to these Turks by their proper name, the Qïpčaks, the Greeks called them the Cumans, the Hungarians acknowledged them as the Kun, the Transylvanian Saxons labelled them Valvi or Falben, and the Russians knew them as the Polovtsy.[1269]

The Qïpčaks menaced the border towns of the Eastern Roman Empire and the Hungarian Kingdom, but the Russian towns suffered the most under their incursions.[1270] Despite their military dominance of the region until the Mongol invasion of the thirteenth century, the Qïpčaks did not intend to conquer the

Russian lands but rather their goal was to protect their steppeland in eastern Europe and thus their way of life. Their legendary khans included Bonyak, Tugorkan, Sharukan, and Altunopa, whom these Central Asian nomads revered as great leaders seeking the best interest of their people. At the end of the eleventh century, during their internal struggles, the Russian princes began to seek alliances with the Qïpčak chieftain, Bonyak (Bönäk). In 1097 Bonyak assisted David of Volyn from the Rus' state to crush the Hungarians by using the traditional Central Asian nomadic tactic of feigned retreat.[1271]

The Qïpčaks, who overran the entire Pontic Steppe (also referred to as the Russian Steppe at times) at least from 1080 to 1100, occupied territories from north of the Caspian Sea in the eastern end of the steppe to the Carpathians in the west, invading both Eastern Roman and Hungarian territories. However, the Russians regrouped, and in 1117 they managed to break Qïpčak power by killing many of their chieftains. The Qïpčaks were pushed back to the Don River. For next half century, the Russian towns achieved some sense of security from the absence of the nomads in the area. In the second half of the century, internal political strife weakened Russian unity, and the Qïpčaks were hired as mercenaries in the Russian territories.[1272] During the fifty years of peace, the area at the western end of the steppe remained masterless; this area was bordered by the Dnieper on one end and the Balkans and the Carpathians on the other.

THE QÏPČAK MERCENARIES

Despite their excellent skills in the military arts, neither the Qïpčaks nor the Cumans showed the cohesiveness needed to form a true unified state that could have threatened the growing Slavic principalities of eastern Europe. Instead of being under the absolute control of their khans, their tribes often acted independently of one another. This appeared to be their biggest weakness. In fact, because of their fighting skills, they often served as mercenaries for the Russians and other polities in the area.

When the Georgians in Caucasus faced the threat of Seljuk invasion in the late eleventh and early twelfth centuries, the Georgian monarchs used these mercenaries. By this time, a group of Qïpčaks had left the northern steppe to move into Caucasus, where they eventually joined with the Georgians to fight the Seljuks on at least one occasion as an auxiliary cavalry unit in the Georgian army.[1273] The archives demonstrate that when in need, Georgian king Davit Agmanšenebeli (1089–1125) asked for help from Šaruqan, his Cuman father-in-law, and in return he received about forty thousand warriors, many of whom were Christians. Many Qïpčaks served Queen Tamar (1184–1213) as well. By this time, however, many other Qïpčaks had been assimilated into the Georgian population; these Christian Turks were referred to as the Naqivč'aqara, or Former Qïpčaks, in this mountainous country.[1274]

Qïpčak fighters were also hired soldiers in the Muslim territories of western Turkestan. At the end of the twelfth century, Qïpčak mercenaries joined the powerful armies of the Turkish Khwarezm-shah Empire (volume 2, chapter 1.5). In the same century, they also became slave (mamluk) soldiers in Saladin's military battles against the crusaders. Eventually these mamluk (Qïpčak) Turks grabbed power for themselves to rule Egypt following the fall of the Ayyubid dynasty, thus forming the Mamluk Sultanate of Egypt (1254–1517) (volume 2, chapter 1.6). Meanwhile, in Desht-i Qïpčak, beginning in 1170 and for nearly two decades under Konchak Khan, the Qïpčaks once again began their incursions into the southern Russian principalities.

While putting the Qïpčaks aside for now, we will discuss regarding Cumans who migrated further west from their kinsmen Qïpčaks after their Kimek union disintegrated in western Siberia. Cumans appeared being more active in the northern Balkan Peninsula, where they assisted their subjects, the Vlakhs, in forming Wallachia, the founding principality of modern-day Romania. They also helped the Bulgarians gain their independence from the Eastern Roman Empire. In fact, according to the Russian chronicles, the Cumans formed the new Bulgarian dynasties Asen and Tertery.[1275]

CUMANIA IN THE BALKANS

In the twelfth century, the Latin-speaking Vlakhs (also known as the Vlachs or Wlachs or Wallachs) lived in the Balkans side by side with the Bulgars under the rule of Byzantium (also known as Constantinople, the capital of the Eastern Roman Empire). Neither group was strong enough to wage rebellion against their rulers. Even their joint efforts could not overcome the

Greek-speaking Eastern Romans. With the help of the Cuman Turks, the Vlakhian nomads began to set up the upcoming Rebellion of 1185–86, which eventually led to the establishment of the Second Bulgarian Empire. The Vlakhians remained part of the subsequently formed empire, but it took 150 years until they began to form their own Romanian principalities, known as Wallachia and Moldavia. It is clear that without the help of the Cuman Turks, the Second Bulgarian Empire would not have come into its existence.[1276]

Even though the Second Bulgarian Empire (1185–1396) was a Bulgarian polity, the primary supporters of the Rebellion of 1185–86 were the Vlakhs, with the help of the Cuman Turks. Thus, the established state was properly known as the Bulgarian-Vlakhian Empire. However, as stated earlier, the Vlakhians eventually began to migrate farther north in the Balkans to the territories of modern-day Romania. Subsequently, with the separation of the two ethnic entities, the new states came to be known as the Second Bulgarian Empire and the Romanian principalities of Wallachia and Moldavia.

In Transylvania the Vlakhs encountered the remnants of the Pečeneg Turks. Just as the Finno-Ugric Magyars had lived together with Turkish On-Oghurs, in the thirteenth century in Transylvania, the Vlakhs had a symbiotic relationship with the Pečeneg Turks coming from Hungary to use the same pastures.[1277]

According to Western recorders, Cumania (land of the Cuman Turks) in the twelfth century was a large territory having the Danube River as its southern border and stretching to the Volga River in the east. But the Cumans were devastated in 1223 by the Tatars under Mongol leadership. Then, in 1241, the Qïpčak-Cuman tribal confederacy ended. Thus, the Tatar-Mongol conquest of eastern Europe was complete.[1278] Hungarian king Bela IV allowed the shattered Cumans to settle in his kingdom. In contrast to the Pečenegs, who settled there before them in a dispersed fashion, some of the Cumans remained in close groups, preserving their language and customs well into the sixteenth century.[1279] The name Cumania lived on as a geographical term until the fourteenth century, when the Romanian principalities of Wallachia and Moldavia emerged as new states in the Balkans.[1280] During their presence in the Balkans, the Cumans came under the influence of the Roman Catholic Church.

Interestingly, the Second Bulgarian Empire became a shared historical entity for modern-day Bulgaria and Romania. The brothers Asen and Peter who led the Bulgars in 1185 to revolt against the Eastern Roman yoke are claimed by some scholars to have been Vlakhs, but Bulgarian scholars claim they were actually Bulgars, not true Vlakhs.[1281] Nevertheless, the one fact most scholars agree on is that the Vlakhs and the Cuman Turks, who were erroneously referred to as the Scyths, were ultimately allies in instigating the Rebellion of 1185–86.[1282] In fact, the influx of Pečenegs and Cumans turned the land of the Bulgarians into a battleground between the Eastern Romans and the Turks, who also supported local revolts against the rulers in Constantinople.[1283] Since the Cuman Turks participated in the rebellion, it also became part of Turkish history. In fact, the leaders of the Rebellion of 1185–86, Asen (from the Turkish Cuman name Esen, meaning "sound, safe, healthy") and his brother Peter (likely a Christianized Cuman), were not only the founders of the Second Bulgarian Empire but also of Cuman aristocratic descent; hence, the founding dynasty of the empire was a Cuman dynasty, known as the Asenid dynasty.[1284]

During the Fourth Crusade, the Europeans took advantage of the hospitality of Constantinople to take control of the Eastern Roman Empire and establish the short-lived Latin Empire (1204–61). Meanwhile, in 1237, the Cumans fleeing the Tatar devastation of their homeland began to move into the Balkans in large numbers. As mentioned above, some moved into Hungary. Many of these Cumans were hired as mercenaries by the Latin emperors. In 1241 another wave of Cumans arrived into Bulgaria, but this time from Hungary. After being baptized by Hungarian king Bela IV, Cuman prince Köten (known as Prince Kotjan Sutoevic in the Russian annals) was killed after the Tatars attacked and devastated Hungary. Angered by the death of their leader, the Cumans began to plunder Hungary and then moved into Bulgaria.

In Bulgaria, the Cuman Turks formed the future Terterid and the Shishmanid dynasties.[1285] The slain prince Köten was from the Cuman Terter oba (or Terter clan). George Terter I, a member of the royal Cuman family, became the Bulgarian czar in 1280 and established the Terter dynasty. Later on, another Cuman-origin dynasty, Shishmanid, led Bulgaria from 1323 until the state was conquered by the Ottoman Turks in 1396, thus beginning the Ottoman Bulgaria period.

As mentioned earlier, in the thirteenth and fourteenth centuries, the territories where the Romanian principalities of Wallachia and Moldavia eventually formed were known as Cumania since the area was heavily occupied by Cuman Turks. This fact also influenced the formation of these Romanian principalities. Basarab, the first Wallachian ruler, and many other Romanian noblemen were Cuman descendants.[1286] He acquired the title of *voivode*, a Slavic borrowing for "warlord, prince." To honor him, the Vlakhs called the Romanian Plain Bessarabia, a word derived after his name, Basarab, which likely was formed from the Turkish words Bashar (Bašar) and *oba*; the former was a personal name, meaning "success" whereas the latter was used to indicate nomadic tent-village. In 1330, with the help of his brother-in-law, Bulgarian czar Ivan Alexander, he defeated the Hungarians at the Battle of Velbuzd, removing the Vlakhs from their vassal dependence on the Hungarian king. The Cumans here were eventually absorbed by the Vlakhs, who were a latinized population of central and eastern Europe. The name Wallachia was derived from these people. Romanian history includes the Cuman dynasty as its founder dynasty, just as Bulgarian history saw the Cumans form successive three dynasties of the Second Bulgarian Empire. In 1417 the Romanian principalities came under the suzerainty of the Ottoman Turks, who called Wallachia 'Eflak' and Moldavia 'Boğdan.'

THE FALL OF DESHT-I QÏPČAK

While the Western Qïpčaks, or the Cumans, were dispersed in the Balkans and Hungarian plains after the Mongol invasion, the Eastern Qïpčaks (true Qïpčaks) had a different fate. The Eastern Qïpčaks were influenced by the Great Seljuks in the south, but they saw only limited conversions to Islam until the late twelfth century, when widespread conversions started. Regardless of their faith, these Qïpčaks were quite involved with the political and military matters of the Turkish Muslim Khwarezm-shah state, a vassal of the Great Seljuks until 1194. At times, Muslim Turks were engaged in battles against their pagan kinsmen, but at other times, some Qïpčaks were found to be serving the ruling Khwarezmian dynasty and even establishing marital ties with them. For example, the well-known Khwarezmian figure Tergen Khatun was the Qïpčak wife of Takach or Tekiš (1172–1200) and mother of Ala al-Din Muhammad (1200–1220), the last monarch of the Khwarezm-shah state. Tergen Khatun became Muslim after she joined the court. At the end of the twelfth century, it was clear that the Qïpčaks at the lower Syr Darya were still not Muslims.

Upon the arrival of the Mongols in the Pontic Steppe in the thirteenth century, many Qïpčaks joined the Russians to defend against the invaders. When the Mongols demanded the Qïpčaks be handed back to them as their slaves, the Russians refused but lost at the Battle of Kalka River. After the Mongol victory, thousands of Qïpčaks were ruthlessly murdered by the victors. Others moved into Bulgaria, where they were gradually assimilated by the Slavs. Those who settled in Hungary, the Cumans, were more fortunate. Under the Hungarian king, they were treated well, and they served in the Hungarian army. In this kingdom they gave their name to the counties of Great and Little Kun-sag, where the Qïpčak-Cuman language appears to have survived until the eighteenth century.[1287] But the main body of the Qïpčak tribes came under the rule of the Golden Horde, where they joined the military and participated in the Tatar assaults upon eastern and central Europe.[1288]

The Qïpčaks who moved to Crimea were taken as slaves by Venetian and Genoese merchants. The slaves were then sold to Islamic leaders, under whom they became mamluks, or slave soldiers (volume 2, chapter 1.2). In the twelfth century, the Qïpčak mamluks formed the bulk of the armies of Saladin and helped him to regain Jerusalem from the crusaders. In Egypt, the Qïpčak mamluks had already become powerful by the early thirteenth century. After they toppled the descendant of Saladin, they established their Mamluk dynasty (volume 2, chapter 1.6). Sultan Baibars became their most prominent leader, who also defeated the seemingly invincible Mongols. By trying to acquire as many Qïpčak slaves as possible, the Mamluk leaders continued to show their interest in their kinsmen. Hence, the Mamluks had good relations with the Golden Horde in the north, where the bulk of the Qïpčaks remained.

Meanwhile, in Desht-i Qïpčak, or the Qïpčak Steppe, during the reign of Berke Khan (1257–67) of the Golden Horde, the Qïpčaks began to convert to Islam. Most Tengriist Qïpčaks were forced to convert to Islam under the rule of Özbek Khan (1312–41), and some those who resisted were captured and sent to the Qïpčak Mamluk sultan of Egypt. Still, even though many initially remained Tengriists, over time the Qïpčaks became Muslims by forming newer societies, in places like Egypt, Anatolia, eastern Europe, as well as in the old dominions of the Khwarezm-shahs (volume 2, chapter 1.5). The Cuman Qaračay-Balqar group emerged in northern Caucasus in the late seventeenth and early eighteenth centuries, and the Eastern Qïpčaks became the Kazakhs (volume 2, chapter 4.5), among whom the process of Islamization continued into the late eighteenth and early nineteenth centuries.[1289]

Qïpčak (Cuman) contributions to the histories of other nations are also notable. Through intermarriages, many rulers of Qïpčak origin sat on the thrones of Russia, Hungary, Bulgaria, Serbia, and Georgia.[1290] They are also present in Chinese chronicles; for example, Tu-tu-ha, a Qïpčak general, served in Qubilai's army, and his son Yentimur became a minister in China.[1291] The Qïpčaks also made significant contributions to the Hungarian army. But they prevented the Magyars from colonizing Bessarabia, and this allowed the Romanian principalities of Wallachia and Moldavia to flourish. Their continued presence along the northern Black Sea coastline also prevented the Russians from reaching this strategic area.[1292]

The arrival of the Mongols in eastern Europe only paused Turkish independence in the Western Eurasian Steppe. As will be discussed later (volume 2, chapter 4.2), the Turks continued living in this area well after the Mongol leadership here ended. Today the Qïpčak legacy survives in the spoken Qïpčak dialect of Turkish among the Turks who emerged from the Golden Horde Khanate (volume 2, chapters 4.2, 4.5). Even though the Qïpčaks lost their independence to the Mongols in the thirteenth century, their existence did not end. Since they remained an absolute majority in the land of the Golden Horde, governed by the Turco-Mongol administration, their Turkish dialect in time became the primary spoken dialect of this great empire. As a result, when the Golden Horde ended in 1502, the emerging people spoke a Qïpčak-based Turkish dialect. Hence, the Tatars as well as the Uzbeks and the Kazakhs spoke this dialect. The Uzbek language evolved further with exposure to the Čaghatai (Qarluq) Turkish spoken by the Timurid Turks of western Turkestan.

Chapter 5:

THE MASTERS OF THE EURASIAN STEPPES

5.1. TURKISH MONGOLIA AND CHINA

After completing the discussion of the great Turkish migrations that pulled many Turkish tribes from the Mongolian steppes toward western Turkestan and eastern Europe, we will now turn our attention back to the Mongolian steppes and China in the third century CE, following the fall of the Southern Xiong-nu (Asian Huns) state and the Han dynasty. Even though many Turkish tribes migrated westward, many other Turkish nomads roamed the Eastern Eurasian Steppe in Outer and Inner Mongolia.

Even though Mongolia, once the center of power of the Huns, received its name from the Mongols, the land did not actually become the property of the Mongols until they gained power in the Far East in the thirteenth century. Mongolia in its present form is not only the name of a country but also a geographic term meaning "land of the Mongols." Although today the word is used as the name of the state bordering the north of China, it is used by modern historians primarily as a geographic descriptor.

From history we know that Mongolia was initially home to the Turkish tribes but not to the Mongols. We also know that Turkish history officially began with the Huns (Xiong-nu), who were later followed in Asia by the Gök-Türks, Uighurs, and Yenisei Kyrgyz, all of whom once controlled Mongolia. The Mongols, who today live in Mongolia, used to live in the territories northeast of Mongolia, in the eastern Siberian forests and Manchuria. Together with the Manchu people, they were known to the Chinese as Tung-hu in Chinese Pinyin, meaning "eastern barbarians."

The Mongols were less civilized than their neighbors, the Turkish Huns. It appears that they were heavily influenced by their Hun (Xiong-nu) masters both politically and culturally.[1293] Under the leadership of their first ruler, Mo-tun Shan-yu, the Huns brought the Tung-hu, including the Mongols, under their rule and kept them out of Mongolia. The Hun leadership was believed to have resided in the Orkhon valley in central Mongolia, which was also the command center later for the Gök-Türks, the Uighurs, and the Mongol leader Genghis Khan.

The Gök-Türks had a capital known as Ötüken near the Khangai Mountains in the Orkhon valley. The area along the Orkhon valley in central Mongolia, where the former Turkish empires of the Huns (Xiong-nu) and the Gök-Türks established their headquarters, was considered sacred in the nomadic world.[1294] As stated on the Orkhon inscriptions from the eighth century, the Turks believed that a heavenly power known as *qut* emanated from these mountains, giving the qaghan a divine right to rule over his people from this place. The Turkish Tengriist tradition was later followed by the Mongols, who began to move into Mongolia after the tenth century. As a result, the Mongol city Qara-Qorum was founded in this area nearly four hundred years after the last Turkish empire of the Uighurs, who had founded their capital in Ordu-Balïq, known as the "city of the army," in place of Ötüken, the former Gök-Türk capital. The city's location today is in Arkhangai Province of Mongolia. The place is just north of Qara-Qorum, the capital of the Mongol Empire of Genghis Khan.

Today, the Orkhon valley in Mongolia is a site of ancient Turkish artifacts and monuments. These include the Orkhon inscriptions of the Gök-Türks and the ruins of Khar-Balgas of the Uighurs from Ordu-Balïq. The ruins of Qara-Qorum are near the capitals of the former Turkish nomadic states. The area is known as the Orkhon Valley Cultural Landscape, as noted in the list of UNESCO World Heritage Sites.

The breakup of the Hun (Xiong-nu) Empire ultimately resulted in the breakup of the first-known confederation of Turkish tribes, which were concentrated mostly in Mongolia and southern and eastern Siberia. Therefore, in the first century CE, with the splitting of the Hun Empire in the Eastern Eurasian Steppe, or Mongolia, the westward movement of the Turkish tribes began. After reaching the Central Eurasian Steppe, they eventually moved into the Western Eurasian Steppe in eastern and central Europe. This event is also known as the migration period in Turkish history, or the great Turkish migrations. As discussed in the previous chapter, the vanguard group of Turks, who had reached the outskirts of eastern Europe by 200 CE, were the Huns, known to the Chinese as the Xiong-nu. Subsequently, for the next millennium or so, the Turkish tribes had supremacy over nearly all the Eurasian steppes from the west to the east.

The other consequence of the loss of Hun power was the release of the Hun grip on the Tung-hu. Consequently, the Xianbei and Wu-huan tribes emerged (chapter 3.1). Among them were Mongol-speaking tribes. Despite the westward movement of multiple Turkish tribes, Mongolia was still dominated by the Turks. Ultimately, the fall of the Xiong-nu authority in the steppes and Han authority in China early in the third century led to a huge power vacuum across the Eastern Eurasian Steppe and the Far East. Taking advantage of the political chaos across this large area, many small states mushroomed, particularly in northern China, while in the northern steppes, the Xianbei freely roamed the pasturelands. Between the third and sixth centuries in Asia, three politically significant states emerged from the Central Asian nomadic world. These were the Northern Wei in northern China, the Asian Avars in Mongolia, and the Ephtalites in the Kushan lands.[1295] While the founders of the Northern Wei and the Ephtalites were Turks, the ethnicity of the Asian Avars is in dispute. During the same period in Europe, the rise of the European Huns and the European Avars followed each other.

THE XIANBEI

The Xianbei tribal confederation, which took over the former Xiong-nu (Hun) territories in the northern steppe, was in effect a loose tribal union with a lack of confederate leadership, unlike the Huns, who had strong leadership establishing a nomadic empire.[1296] The inability of the Xianbei to form a true nomadic confederacy and a nomadic state probably arose from the fact that they were made up from tribes of mixed ethnicities, whereas the Huns (Xiong-nu) were more cohesive, owing to a more homogenous ethnic background. Furthermore, the Hunnish tribal union was modeled after the Turkish tribal system, with strong leadership, whereas the Xianbei was based more on the Mongol tribal system, with a lack of leadership.[1297] In fact, the Huns had a strong leader in the shan-yu (emperor), whereas Xianbei leadership was confined to the chieftain level.[1298] An exception occurred briefly during the period of T'an-shih-huai, who became the only known unifying leader of the Xianbei (156–80 CE). During his rule, T'an-shih-huai organized successive raids, and unlike the Huns before his time, he turned down every offer of a peace treaty from China. This resulted from a Chinese lack of understanding of the fact that the Xianbei tribal leaders relied on being in constant war to remain in power.[1299]

As discussed in chapter 3, the declining power of the Northern Xiong-nu was precipitated by their inability to withstand combined attacks from the Wu-sun, Wu-huan, and Xianbei along with the Southern Xiong-nu allied with imperial China. Ultimately, the Northern Huns (Xiong-nu) did not fall because of the Xianbei; instead the collapse of Hun control of the northern steppes allowed the Xianbei to rise to power.[1300] After the year 89 CE, following the defeat of the northern shan-yu, a large mass of Northern Huns merged with the Xianbei, leading to a significant infusion of Turkish blood into the multiethnic makeup of the Xianbei confederacy. In fact, nearly one hundred thousand Northern Huns became absorbed into the Xianbei federation.[1301] As a result, they added more Turkish character to the tribal makeup. This nomadic union indeed had multiethnic tribal groups, including Turkish, Mongol, and Tungus. The Xianbei confederation had nomads previously coined by the Chinese as the Tung-hu, which was previously suppressed by Mo-tun of the Xiong-nu. Just like the Turks and the Mongols, the Tungus are linguistically from the Altaic language family; the name Tungus is not part of the Tungus language but rather is from Turkish, meaning "swine."[1302] One of the prominent tribes within the Xianbei federation was the Tabgač Turks, known to the Chinese as the T'o-pa (or Tuoba). As we will see in the next chapter, these Turks came to play an important role in the history of China.

As most Northern Xiong-nu started to migrate westward, the Xianbei eventually began to have influence over the Mongolian steppes, which were once the power base of the Asian Hun (Xiong-nu) Empire. By the end of the second century CE, the Xianbei had extended their control over the Eastern Eurasian Steppe, but they could not penetrate into China. One of their clans, the Mu-jung, managed to settle in northern China under the name Yen, but they were annihilated by the Tabgač (T'o-pa) Turks in 436.[1303]

In their military, the Xianbei (also known as Hsien-pi) preferred to have a pure cavalry force but often forced their armies to remain small and comparatively weak, whereas the Turkish tribal forces, while still relying on a strong cavalry, included infantry and nontribal forces as well.[1304] This flexibility gave the Turks a better chance of sustaining statehood in the lands they conquered. The Xianbei, unlike the Xiong-nu, were purely tribal people without a permanent leader; they had an elected military leader only during wartime.[1305] Unlike the name Xianbei, which does not have political identification, the name Xiong-nu has both ethnic and political significance.[1306] For this reason, the Xianbei never existed as a state but only as a loose tribal confederation, whereas the Xiong-nu (Asian Huns) did not only have a tribal confederation but also have a powerful supreme leader governing a well-organized state. It is apparent that the Xianbei evolved through cultural interaction with the Xiong-nu.[1307] Indeed, Xianbei art was partially influenced by the Xiong-nu.[1308]

The Southern Xiong-nu collapsed in 216, and by the year 280, as the (Southern) Xiong-nu remnants were regrouping in the south in Shanxi, within the territories of northern China, the leadership role in the Eastern Eurasian Steppe was with the Xianbei north of China.[1309] But even though they became dominant in the steppes, the Xianbei did not establish a nomadic state as the Xiong-nu did previously.

THE POLITICAL CLIMATE IN NORTHERN CHINA AFTER THE HAN

Beginning in the third century CE, the Far East faced political chaos. The collapse of the Southern Xiong-nu in northern China in 216 and the fall of the Chinese Han dynasty in 220, following the Yellow Turban Rebellion (184–205) of Chinese peasants, created an unstable political environment. Many

Turkish tribes started their westward movement in an event known as the great Turkish migrations when Northern Xiong-nu power faded in modern-day Mongolia in the second half of the first century CE. Consequently, many of the leading Xiong-nu tribes also moved west, where they eventually formed the historical states of the European Huns and the White Huns. While most of the remaining Northern Xiong-nu joined their southern kinsmen, others were absorbed into the multiethnic Xianbei tribal federation, which was formed by the Tung-hu tribes long suppressed by the Xiong-nu. The remaining non-Xiong-nu Turkish tribes were scattered in the northern outskirts of the Chinese territories, and some were in the Xianbei confederation. Hence, in the Eastern Eurasian Steppe, the Xianbei readily took advantage of the power vacuum created by the decline of Xiong-nu strength.

In China more than four centuries of unity had been disrupted. Following the collapse of the unified empire of the Han dynasty, China fractured, and the land entered the Three Kingdoms period (220–80), which witnessed the formation of the Chinese kingdoms of the Cao Wei (220–65) in the north, the Shu Han (221–63) in the west, and the Wu (229–80) in the south. But these kingdoms had short life-spans. The Cao Wei, with its capital in Luoyang, appeared to be the most prominent. But by 265 China's Three Kingdoms period began to fall apart, and successive weak non-Chinese monarchs started to rule northern China; most of these were Xiong-nu (Huns).[1310] During this period, the remnants of the former Southern Huns were composed of five tribes, and they had settled in T'ai-yüan (Shanxi).[1311] In the meantime, the Chinese Sima family under the Cao Wei became influential and powerful enough to eventually form the new Jin dynasty (also known as Tsin or Chin, 266–420) at the expense of these Chinese kingdoms.

At the end of the Three Kingdoms period, the Chinese Jin dynasty managed to reunite China for a short period. The new empire was formed when the last monarch of Cao Wei abdicated his throne to Sima Yan, the founder of the Jin dynasty, on February 4, 266. The reunification of China was completed when the third and last kingdom of Wu in the south was taken by the Jin in 280. An interesting point is that the Jin showed respect to the Southern Huns (Southern Xiong-nu), who had been in northern China since the days of the Later Han period. The invitation of the Xiong-nu shan-yu to the coronation of the Jin (Chin) emperor was an honor; even though he was viewed as a barbarian, he was the only foreign participant at the event.[1312]

Despite Jin efforts to keep China united, the years between 301 and 439 witnessed a lack of strong Chinese authority in northern China, since the area was populated by "disobedient" Central Asian nomadic tribes, known to the Chinese as the "barbarian" tribes. As was pointed out earlier, the Southern Asian Huns (Southern Xiong-nu) had been residing in northern China territories since the first century CE with the prior approval of the Han emperor on the basis of the old treaty policy. Since then, other Central Asian tribes had settled in the same area as well. These tribes were referred to by the Chinese as the Wu Hu, meaning "five barbarian tribes." These were the Xiong-nu, Xianbei, Ti, Qiang, and Jie.[1313] The Xiong-nu (Asian Huns), Ti, and Jie were of Turkish origin, whereas the Xianbei were a Turco-Mongol mixture. Now, the political pressures from these tribes and the revolt led by the Xiong-nu tribes in particular began to threaten the authority of the Jin dynasty.

Finally, in the early fourth century, the Jin had to abandon northern China to the tribal entities, which began to form short-lived kingdoms in this part of China. As a result, the Western Jin period (266–317) of the Jin dynasty ended, and subsequently, with the royal family moving to southern China, the Eastern Jin period (318–420) began.[1314] The new chaotic times in northern China, also referred to as the Sixteen Kingdoms period or the Warring Kingdoms period, eventually led one of the tribal entities to form the Northern Wei dynasty, controlling all northern China, where peace and prosperity were restored.

With the start of the Warring Kingdoms period (or the Sixteen Kingdoms period) by the end of the third century CE, northern China witnessed the mushrooming of multiple non-Chinese states. In the early medieval era, the Ti resided in the northern and northwestern areas of Chang'an, the Lushui and other Xiong-nu groups were present in northeast Chang'an territories, within the Fengyi and Xinping commanderies.[1315] Selecting Chang'an as their capital, the Xiong-nu formed the Former Zhao (304–329), and the Ti established the Later Zhao (328–350), while the Ting-ling lived to the northeast of the future Northern Wei capital Pingcheng.[1316] The latter may have formed late in the fourth century the ephemeral Zhai Wei Kingdom, which was in eastern part of Henan. The state of Cheng Han (or Great Cheng)

(304–347) was established by Ti tribesmen, who were from an earlier group of Turks. The kingdom of Chouchi (297–371) was considered the first of multiple states established after the Three Kingdoms period.[1317] This state was also established by the Turkish tribes of Ti. In 322, however, they were defeated by and came under the vassalage of the Former Zhao (or also known as Chao) Kingdom (304–329) of the Xiong-nu Turks. But the vassalage of the Chouchi came to an end when they were conquered by the Former Qin, founded by the Ti Turks as well.

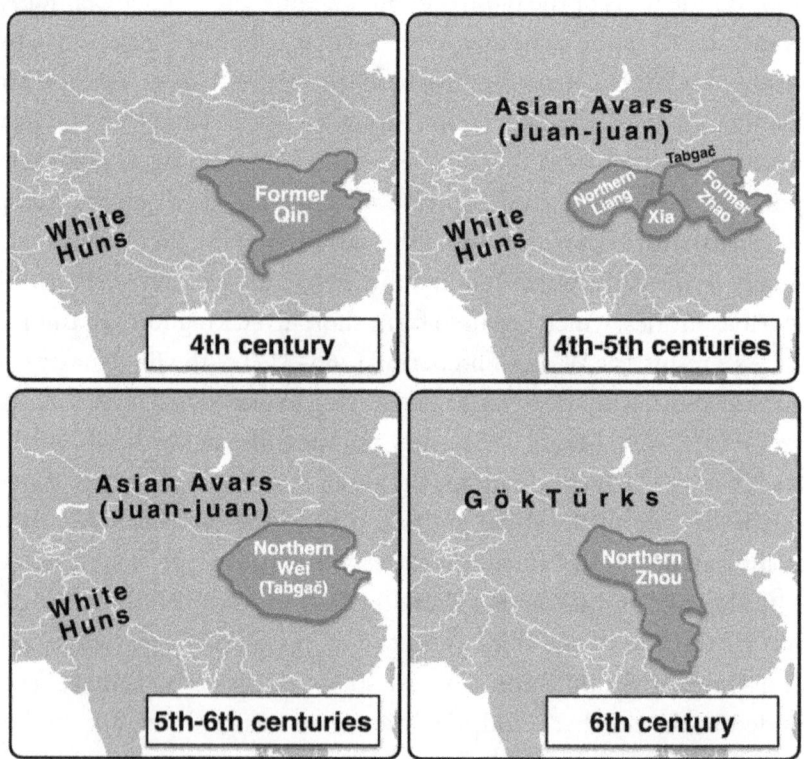

Map 10. After the fall of the Han dysnaty in China, the land went into political chaos. As a result, multiple small states erupted across China. The map illustrates some of these states formed by Ti (Former Qin), Huns (Former Zhao, Northern Liang, Xia, and Northern Zhou) and Tabgač Turks (Northern Wei).

Meanwhile, the Northern Han (also known as Former Zhao) Kingdom (304–329) of the Xiong-nu was established by their leader, Liu Yüan. The royal clan was represented by the Liu family, who were the descendants of the shan-yu line of the former Southern Xiong-nu.[1318] In fact, with the Han royal name Liu, Liu Yüan claimed that he was a descendant of a Han princess given to Mo-tun, the legendary leader of the Huns (Xiong-nu).[1319] Therefore, he claimed descendance from royal houses of both the Han and the Xiong-nu. In the year 289, before he established his kingdom and while he was under the service of the Jin, he was given by the Jin emperor the title of "commander of all Southern Xiong-nu tribes." But taking advantage of the civil war within the Jin dynasty, he declared himself the shan-yu by the year 304.[1320]

In 311 Liu Cong, the Xiong-nu leader of the Northern Han state, took the Jin capital Luoyang, and subsequently, the reigning Jin emperor Sima Zhi died as a prisoner in the Xiong-nu capital, Pingyang. These events had a significant outcome, as a capital city (Luoyang) and a Chinese emperor had both fallen into foreign hands for the first time in Chinese history.[1321] Only a few years later, history repeated itself when Sima Ye, nephew of the late Sima Zhi, confronted Liu Cong of the Xiong-nu and became a prisoner in 316 with the fall of Chang'an to the Huns.[1322]

In 319 the state's name was changed, and the kingdom of Northern Han, founded by Liu Yüan in 304, came to be known as the Former Zhao.[1323] The inability to overcome the forces of the Hunnish power in the north forced the Jin to abandon northern China. With the exception of the Liang state in the northwest and the Xianbei states in the northeast, all northern China came under the rule of the Huns (Xiong-nu).[1324] Consequently, the Western Jin period came to an end, and with the movement of the royal capital to southern China, the Eastern Jin period began. With this political change in the north, small kingdoms emerged, and thus the Sixteen Kingdoms period (or the Warring Kingdoms period, 304–439) of northern China officially began.

In 319 a great warrior, Shi-le from the Jie tribe of the Xiong-nu, while serving the emperor of the Former Zhao, went on to establish his own kingdom, known as the Later Zhao (319–51). A Buddhist, Shi-le became instrumental in the foundation of the early Buddhist monasteries in China.[1325] But according to other sources, the Later Zhao was formed by the Ti during a different period of 328–50.[1326] The Mu-jung tribe established the first Xianbei dynasty in China following the fall of the Xiong-nu Zhao (Chao) state.[1327]

In 329 when the Former Zhao, under the rule of the Xiong-nu Chieh, fell in northern Honan, the conquering Chinese commander ordered the extermination of the captured people, and the majority of these two hundred thousand Xiong-nu people were reportedly Europoid in appearance.[1328] The Xiong-nu established the Former Zhao in the fourth century, but later they also formed the kingdoms of the Northern Liang (401–60), the Xia (406–31), and the Northern Zhou (557–81).[1329] The latter replaced the Western Wei of the T'o-pa Turks in northern China.

The kingdom of Dai, one of the prominent sixteen kingdoms of northern China, was formed by the Tabgač Turks (known as T'o-pa or Tuoba to the Chinese) of the Xianbei federation. T'o-pa Li-wei was the first-known monarch, starting in 220/221 CE, shortly after the fall of the Han dynasty.[1330] T'o-pa Kuei (or Gui) came to the throne at the age of six in 377, but as a minor, he was unable to stop the invasion of the formidable forces of the Former Qin of Fu Chien, and as a result, he was taken hostage in Chang'an.[1331] Later Kuei found sanctuary among the Xiong-nu tribes, the natural T'o-pa allies. More on the T'o-pa will be presented in the next chapter.

During the Sixteen Kingdoms period of China, the Former Qin (also known as Ch'in) of the House of Fu (352–94) from the Ti tribes of the Turks became probably the most dominant kingdom. The Ti were one of the oldest Turkish tribes, present in northern China territories even before the foundation of the great Xiong-nu Empire.[1332] The founder, Fu Hong, a Ti chieftain, was once in the service of Later Zhao before proclaiming himself the great shan-yu and king of Sanqin in 350. His son Fu Jian took the title of "heavenly king" (*tian wang*), and after defeating the imperial Jin army, he declared himself the emperor of the Former Qin in 352.[1333] The fourth monarch, Fu Chien (Jian) (357–85), became Former Qin's greatest and most devastating ruler. He declared Buddhism the official religion of the state.[1334] He also went on to expand his territories ambitiously. In addition to all northern China, vast territories from Korea to Turkestan came under his rule. Finally, after securing the entire north, he intended to conquer the Eastern Jin in the south to claim all China for himself. One of the turning points in Chinese history was the Battle of Fei River in the year 383. When Fu Chien attacked the Jin with a large force, he first met his adversary at Huai only to find decisive defeat at Fei. If he had been successful in conquering the Jin, the last bastion of Chinese culture, the future of Chinese civilization could have been quite different.[1335]

After the annihilation of the Former Qin, the T'o-pa (Tabgač Turks) began to regroup under their leader, Kuei, who declared himself in 386 the king of Dai (*dai wang*), also known as the king of Wei (*wei wang*).[1336] This event was the start of the Northern Wei dynasty of China (see the next chapter).

Meanwhile, the fall of the Former Qin again led to the formation of multiple kingdoms in northern China. Among these, in addition to the Kingdom of Wei of the T'o-pa Turks, there were those of the Xiong-nu and the Xianbei as well. The Kingdom of Xia (406–31) was formed by Liu Bobo, coming from the Xiong-nu Liu family, which led the earlier prominent Former Zhao Kingdom. He assumed the title of "heavenly king of the great Xia" (*da xia tian wang*).[1337] But by the mid-fifth century, most of the kingdoms of northern China had been conquered by the Northern Wei of the T'o-pa Turks, who were once a tribal group split from the Xianbei nomadic federation.[1338] One of the legacies of the Turkish tribes being part of the Sixteen Kingdoms period (or the Warring Kingdoms period) is that they permanently introduced Buddhism into China, where the prevalent faith was based on Taoism and Confucianist teachings.

THE JUAN-JUAN AS THE NEW NOMADIC POWER

Upon the breakup of the Xiong-nu federation in the third century, many new tribal entities emerged in the northern steppes, and the Juan-juan (also known as Ruanruan) emerged as one these tribal entities as well.[1339] Who were these people?

Beginning in the early fourth century CE, just about a century after the Southern Xiong-nu (Southern Asian Hun) state ceased to exist in 216 CE, a new nomadic empire was established north of China, in the vast territories of the Mongolian steppes. The Chinese referred to these nomads, who filled the void left by the Asian Huns, as the Juan-juan. It is not clear whether these tribes were actually from the Xiong-nu tribes or their nomadic federation. However, it is suggested that the Juan-juan may have been a separate branch of the Xiong-nu.[1340]

In the history of Central Asia warlords often yearned to become like their successful predecessors in order to leave their legacy behind. For example, in the thirteenth century it is a fact that Genghis Khan and his Mongols established a favorable reputation among all the nomads living in felt tents, and similarly, the Xiong-nu (209 BCE–216 CE) also had a strong and long reputation among the mounted archers of Central Asia. Hence, just as the Central Asian Turkish monarchs beyond the thirteenth century viewed themselves as descendants of Genghis Khan, many Central Asian peoples from the fourth century to the eighth century considered themselves to be affiliated with the Xiong-nu.[1341] The Juan-juan followed suit by trying to recreate the glory the Asian Huns had previously over the steppes of Mongolia.

Interestingly, these new Central Asian warriors were not mentioned on the eighth-century Orkhon inscriptions of the Gök-Türks as the Juan-juan (also known as the Rouran or Ruanruan); rather they were called the Avars. Indeed, while the Chinese called them Ruanruan (or Juan-juan), the people of Rouran referred to themselves as Avars.[1342] The Juan-juan, also known as the Asian Avars, had a powerful tribal confederation ruling over the Eastern Eurasian Steppe in the fifth century and the first half of the sixth century until they were crushed by the Gök-Türks. Many scholars have accepted that the Juan-juan were the predecessors of the European Avars noted in the Eastern Roman archives starting in the second half of the sixth century.[1343] Northern Wei records indicate that the Juan-juan extended their control as far west as north of the Kushans; hence, their dominion stretched to the west of Lake Balkhash.[1344] At their zenith, these Asian Avars occupied territories from the Turfan area in the west to Manchuria and the borders of modern-day Korea in the east, from the Gobi Desert in the south to Lake Baikal in the north.[1345]

It appears that the Kao-ch'e (T'ieh-le) tribes of the Turks moved southward from the Lake Baikal area to find new pastures, but in 402 they were defeated by the Juan-juan (Avars). But the Juan-juan never brought the Kao-ch'e under their complete control, and in fact these tribes from time to time rebelled against their overlords.[1346] According to Greek records, between 461 and 465 CE, the Avars chased the Savir people (likely Greek for the Sabir Turks), who in turn pushed other Turkish tribes, the Saraguri (likely Greek for Saragur or Sarï-Oghur) and Onoguri (On-Oghur).[1347] The latter group of Turks, the

On-Oghurs (chapter 4.5), as mentioned earlier, established themselves in the sixth century north of the Black Sea. It was this Turkish tribal federation that gave rise to Old Greater Bulgaria (chapter 4.3) in the territories of modern-day Ukraine; in the seventh century, this first Bulgarian state, under pressure from the Khazar Turks, split into the Volga Bulgar Khanate (seventh to thirteenth century) and the Danubian Bulgar Khanate (also known as the First Bulgarian Kingdom, 681–1018).

It has been suggested that the Chinese name Juan-juan (also referred to as Jou-jan) may have been derived from the Turkish word for crimson or for the insect from which crimson dye was obtained.[1348] According to Chinese historians, their leading clan name was Yu-chiu-lü, which has been linked to Mu-ku-lü, the ancestor and leader of the clan. Initially a servant in the T'o-pa court, Mu-ku-lü later served in the T'o-pa military until he escaped into modern-day Mongolia, where he gathered fugitives like himself to form the nucleus of the Juan-juan leading clan.[1349] On the basis of Wei records, the name Mu-ku-lü is implied to be the same as Yu-chiu-lü, a different pronunciation of the same name. Although the Juan-juan may have been an Altaic-speaking people, there is no surviving language evidence to confirm their ethnicity. Only if the Juan-juan were the true predecessors of the later-appearing European Avars, who were known to be Turkish speakers, could one say that the Juan-juan were also Turks.

Another hypothesis has been put forth about the ethnicity of the founder of this nomadic empire. After Mu-ku-lü died, his son Che-lu-hui extended his power over the neighboring tribes and called his own tribe Rouran, which was called by the emperor of China Ru(an)ru(an), or "wriggling ones" for being "mindless and wormlike."[1350] There are many theories about the origin of the name Ruanruan among historians. It has been suggested that since the word Ruanruan seem to give a Chinese description for "pint-sized worms," perhaps the word's non-Chinese meaning may have derived from the Turkish word *cüce* (pronounced "jüjé") for "dwarf" or "tiny"; in other words, the name Ruanruan was given to a tribe of dwarves since these people, who had migrated south from the north, were short people.[1351] Ancient Turks called the Tungus peoples and their land *cürcet* (probably for Jürchen of the Jin dynasty), likely derived from the Turkish word *cüce* for "dwarf," and therefore, the name Ruanruan may have been used for the *cürcet* (Tungus) people.[1352]

During much of the fifth century, the T'o-pa Turks (known as Tabgač to the Turks) of the Northern Wei (next chapter) militarily had the upper hand over the Juan-juan of the steppes. In 429, after the nomadic army was defeated, marriages were set up between the royal houses to pacify the nomads. During the 449 conflict, the Northern Wei again scored a victory against the Asian Avars. But when the Revolt of the Six Garrisons broke out in 523, the balance of power tilted in favor of the Juan-juan, who assisted the northern emperor in quelling the rebellion.[1353] By 534 the state of the Northern Wei was divided into the Western and Eastern Wei. When the Juan-juan were at the zenith of their power, in 545, another nomadic power emerged. This was the Gök-Türks (chapter 5.3), who set up an alliance with the Western Wei through a marriage in 551. This event allowed the Gök-Türks to gain political recognition. A year later the Gök-Türks crushed the Juan-juan and established their own nomadic empire in the Eurasian steppes.

THE RELATIONS BETWEEN THE NOMADS AND CHINA

The Central Asian nomadic confederacies could turn themselves into effective steppe empires when they were also able to establish a viable link between their economy and that of China.[1354] Hence, to ensure the stability of the economies of their steppe empires through the steady acquisition of Chinese goods, the Turkish nomadic empires of the Xiong-nu, the Gök-Türks, and the Uighurs preferred to have a strong China on their border rather than a weak China. Therefore, the Turks had no intention of invading and destroying the principal resource of their economies. However, the Mongolian and Manchurian nomads acted differently, waiting for the opportune moment to take advantage of a weakened China by invading or conquering Chinese territories.[1355] The exception were the T'o-pa Turks of the fifth and sixth centuries and also the Sha-t'o Turks of the tenth century, who briefly managed to rule Chinese territories as emperors of China. But being at the helm of a much larger foreign population led to the eventual assimilation of these Central Asian conquerors by the natives.

The T'o-pa Turks in fact formed the first formal non-Chinese dynasty within China proper. The subsequent major foreign-origin dynasties in

China were all Altaic, including the Khitan Liao dynasty (907–1125) of the Turco-Mongols, the Jürchen Jin dynasty (1115–1234) of the Tungus, the Yuan dynasty (1206–1368) of the Mongols, and the Qing dynasty (1616–1912) of the Manchu (Tungus). By contrast, the native Chinese dynasties were the Ch'in (221–206 BCE), Han (206 BCE–220 CE), Jin (266–317, 317–420), Song (960–1279), and Ming (1368–1644) dynasties. However, there is evidence that the founders of the Sui (581–618) and the T'ang (618–907) had strong non-Chinese elements in their families (chapter 5.2).

In the latter half of the sixth century, the Gök-Türks formed a powerful empire over a vast territory. Their strength caused the Chinese to fear them, and as a result, the leaders of China paid large subsidies, or tributes, in silk in exchange for peace.[1356] However, neither their awareness of their own strength nor the fall of the Sui dynasty persuaded the Gök-Türks to pursue the conquest of China. The Uighurs did not hesitate to send their troops to assist the T'ang emperor to crush a rebellion that threatened the viability of the Chinese government's existence. While one reason to provide military assistance to China was to ensure the continuity of economic ties with the Chinese, another reason for their support for China was actually to eliminate the Gök-Türk elements within the same rebellion (chapter 5.4). In fact, the Uighur qaghan saw these elements as a threat to his throne.

DEMOGRAPHIC CHANGES IN MONGOLIA

Mongolia did not become the home of the Mongols until the last of the Turks began to leave the Eastern Eurasian Steppe after the Turkish Kyrgyz Qaghanate lost its battle with the Manchurian-origin (or Tungus or Turco-Mongol) Khitan (also known as the Khitai) in the tenth century. After that, as the Mongol tribes began moving into this territory, the Turkish tribes, which had been on the move since the fall of the Huns, mostly pulled out from this ancient Turkish homeland by the end of the first millennium. A few powerful Turkish tribes were still present in Mongolia, as we will see later (volume 2, chapter 3), when Genghis Khan became the ruler of the Mongols. After conquering the remaining Turkish tribes and uniting the Mongol tribes under his banner in 1206, Genghis Khan turned Mongolia into a true Mongolian homeland.

In the second millennium, after most of the Turks had left Mongolia, they occupied mostly central and western Eurasia. The former included the western and eastern Turkestan territories, and the latter had the Pontic Steppe (eastern Europe), which came to be known as the Qïpčak Steppe later on. But between the tenth and thirteenth centuries, neither the Turks nor the Mongols could make a claim on Mongolia. The Khitans, a powerful tribal federation of Turco-Mongols, did not remain in Mongolia; instead they occupied northern China to form the Liao dynasty. After the fall of the Yuan dynasty in China in 1368, the Mongols of Mongolia did not remain united. In the eighteenth century, Mongolia was conquered by the Qing dynasty of China.

THE SIXTH AND SEVENTH CENTURIES

While the Gök-Türks reigned supreme across the Eurasian steppes in the sixth century, it has been suggested that a little-known Turkish-Mongolian federation was present in Korea in the seventh century;[1357] Koguryo (53–668 CE), an ancient Korean state in northern peninsula, was led by an obscure Turkish tribe. During this time, western and central Europe came under the rule of the Germanic states of the Visigoth Kingdom (Iberian Peninsula), the Frankish Kingdom (Gaul), the Burgundian Kingdom (Gaul), and the Ostrogoth Kingdom (Italian Peninsula). When the European Huns had withdrawn deep into the outskirts of eastern Europe, the (European) Avar Turks were on the rise in eastern Europe. The Eastern Roman Empire, controlling the Balkans, Anatolia, and most of the Middle East, including Egypt, was in a rivalry with the Persian Sassanid Empire. In Asia, the Sui dynasty in the late sixth century reunited China for the first time since the Han dynasty's fall in 220 CE.

The Eastern Roman and Sassanid rivalry continued in the early seventh century; however, by the second half of the seventh century, the Persian Sassanids had lost their freedom to the Muslim Arab Rashidun Caliphate. Meanwhile, most of western Europe remained under the rule of multiple Germanic states, of which the Frankish Kingdom was predominant. The Turkish Avar Qaghanate was now the dominant power in eastern Europe, and the Khazar Turks were on the rise just north of the Caspian Sea.

5.2. THE CHINESE TURKS

After the fall of the Han dynasty of China, many Central Asian nomadic tribes began to settle in northern China, owing to the political power vacuum in the area. Most of these were Turkish tribes, many of them remnants of the Southern Xiong-nu. There were also the Xianbei tribes, from which the T'o-pa tribes of the Turks split to eventually form the Northern Wei dynasty. It appears from the fifth-century art and literature of the Northern Wei that males of the time, like the Xiong-nu of the past, wore caftan-like tops, trousers, and boots. In fact, this form of male clothing used to be an ethnic trademark of the nomadic Turks. In the sixth and seventh centuries, Chinese art illustrated Chinese men wearing trousers and boots as well. In other words, by the time the T'ang dynasty was in power in China in 618, Chinese men had already adopted the male clothing style formerly known only to the Central Asians.[1358]

As stated earlier, the fall of Xiong-nu (Asian Hun) power in the modern-day territories of Mongolia and northern China did not lead to the complete disappearance of the Turkish presence in this area. On the contrary, the political instability in this region created new opportunities for the Turkish-speaking tribes. To understand the new political developments, it is important to understand how events evolved during the third century. It was within this Chinese and nomadic tribal political turmoil in Inner Mongolia (northern Chinese territory) that a unique Turkish tribe began to surface as a new power. This tribal entity was known to the Chinese as the T'o-pa and to the Turks as the Tabgač. The T'o-pa are considered proto-Turks by some scholars, simply Turks for others.[1359]

Benefiting from the power vacuum created by the fall of the Xiong-nu in the northern steppes, the Xianbei, considered to be a confederation of tribes of mixed ethnicities from western Manchuria, moved down to the northern border of China.[1360] It is believed that the Xianbei probably had a major Tungusic component.[1361] Its other ethnic components included Turks and Mongols. The Tungus and the Mongols of the Xianbei were part of the Tung-hu ("eastern barbarians") tribes initially subdued by Mo-tun of the Huns.[1362] As mentioned earlier, in 155 the Xianbei absorbed some of the remaining Northern Huns into their confederacy. After the collapse of the Southern Hunnish state in the year 216, the remaining Turkish tribes were dispersed, without a central authority. Taking advantage of the absence of the iron-fisted authority of the Huns, the Xianbei now executed all scattered Northern Hun remnants along the way as they moved closer to China.

Although some scholars believe that the Xianbei were mostly Mongols, others believe that there were also many Turkish-speaking tribes, on the basis of an examination of linguistic elements.[1363] In fact, during the reign and after the fall of the Asian Huns, the Turkish language became the prominent language in a large geographic area covering the Central and Eastern Eurasian Steppes. While the majority of the Xianbei might not have been Turkish, their leadership appeared to be Turkish speakers.

Indeed, during the early third century, the Tabgač (T'o-pa) tribes of the Turks were in control of the Xianbei just north of the Great Wall, and these tribes eventually founded the Northern Wei dynasty of China.[1364] Before the Tabgač Turks began their southward movement under the leadership of Khan Lin in the year 160, they apparently had ten hordes, seven of which were led by his brothers.[1365] It is believed that sometime in the third century, owing to discord within the Xianbei confederation, the Tabgač split from the union and moved farther into China. After they formed the powerful Northern Wei dynasty (386–535), the royal family's T'o-pa name was replaced with its sinicized form, Yuan.[1366] Interestingly, nearly eight centuries later, the Mongols used the same dynastic name during their occupation of China. Meanwhile, as these events were taking place in China and in the steppes immediately north of China, in the greater Eastern Eurasian Steppe, a new nomadic empire was shaping up; its rulers were known to the Chinese as Juan-juan. This nomadic state was discussed in the previous chapter. The founding tribe could have been from the Xianbei as well.

THE STEPPES IN THE FOURTH CENTURY

According to some sources, the Tabgač leaders previously served as generals in the Xiong-nu (Asian Hun) armies. The Tabgač, who were mentioned in the eighth-century Orkhon inscriptions of the Gök-Türks, eventually established a strong footing in northern China when the Hun influence waned in Asia.[1367] During the civil war of the Xianbei tribal confederation sometime in the third century, the T'o-pa, who had controlled this federation, split from this union. It has been suggested that the Tabgač were a branch of the Xianbei, but around 160–70 CE, they began to migrate southward to the northern China, where the Southern Xiong-nu used to reside.[1368] As mentioned earlier, by the fourth century the control of the steppes now passed to the Juan-juan Empire, also known as the Asian Avar Empire. Another theory for the formation of the Juan-juan is that a renegade officer of the T'o-pa state went to gather warriors to form a new nomadic steppe empire.[1369] However, other scholars suggest that the new leadership in the Xianbei formed the Juan-juan. But unlike the nomads of the Huns or other Turkish tribal confederations, the tribes within the Xianbei union showed loyalty not to their federation but only to their individual tribes. The Tabgač were the first-known Xianbei tribal entity splitting from the greater union, and later the Mu-jung were probably another such entity that split before moving into China. Meanwhile, as discussed in the previous chapter, due to the collapse of the Xiong-nu, the Turkish tribes across the Eastern Eurasian Steppe remained dispersed, with many of them moving west. Finally, in the power struggle, the defeat of the Chile (Turkish) tribe in 399 allowed the Juan-juan to come to power in the steppes to the north of China.[1370]

The territories of modern-day Mongolia, where the Huns traditionally ruled, were now under a new confederation of Turco-Mongol and probably mostly Tungusic tribes. The new empire came to be known as the Juan-juan or the (Asian) Avar Qaghanate. Although it has frequently been suggested that this Avar Empire, which replaced the Xiong-nu (Asian Huns) on the steppes of Central Asia, was formed under the leadership of the Mongol tribes, there are also claims that ethnolinguistically, the Avars were not Mongolic but rather from the Turkish Utrighur group of nomads.[1371] These Avars are thought to have been connected with the mid-sixth-century European Avars, who are known to be Turks, most likely originating from the Bulgar Turks—in other words, descendants of the (European and Asian) Huns.[1372] Eventually, in the year 552, the (Asian) Avars lost power to another rising Turkish power, the Gök-Türks, from modern-day Mongolia (see the next chapter).

THE RISE OF TURKISH POWER IN CHINA

The T'o-pa began to surface in the pages of recorded history by the third century CE in Shanxi (Shansi) Province of northern China. As they began to make their conquests, they finally reached the Yellow River until the Houai-ho basin by the end of the fourth century, when they began to make an impact on Chinese politics.[1373] The T'o-pa (Tabgač) were a unique Turkish group.[1374] They were actually a Turkish-led federation of the Tabgač tribes with mostly Turkish elements, including Xiong-nu remnants along with some Xianbei clans.[1375]

Scholars have erred in interpreting the ethnicities of certain prominent dynasties in Turkish history. For example, the Gök-Türks referred to the Tabgač as Chinese, and the Ottomans referred to the Mughals as Indians, but this does not mean that these dynasties were not Turkish. The Tabgač, for example, were situated in China, and they were accurately described as being from China by the Gök-Türks; the Mughals ruled from India, and consequently, the Ottomans did not refer to them by their ethnic identity but rather called them Indians (Hintli). But it should also be noted that because the Tabgač remained a prominent political entity in China, even after they declined and disappeared following the year 550, China came to be known as Tabgač by the Turks and later as Tamgaj by the Arabs.[1376] Indeed, in the eighth-century Orkhon inscriptions, the Gök-Türks called China Tabgač. Even in the eleventh century, the Qara-Khanids of the Qarluq Turks used the ancient tribal name Tabgač or Tamgaj as a title for having control over part of the Chinese territories.

The T'o-pa spoke an ancient form of Turkish,[1377] as seen in the titles and proper names used by these Central Asian nomadic warriors. The useful linguistic data were obtained from Chinese records. Turkish titles such as *tigin*, *khatun*, and *qaghan* (or *khaqan*) were used by the T'o-pa elite.[1378] In addition to these titles, names and adjectives were also found to be related mostly to Old Turkish and partly to the Xiong-nu (Hun) language.[1379] Overall, a review of T'o-pa vocabulary demonstrated that the primary language was Turkish with some Mongol elements.[1380] A study of the T'o-pa language also revealed that the Turkish title *qaghan* was used by the T'o-pa before the Juan-juan (Asian Avars). Not only their language but also their social structure showed their Turkishness. The organizational pattern of the T'o-pa subjects into inner (ruling class) and outer (common class) tribes is considered a Turkish-type organization style. Even more recent linguistic evidence suggests the core of the T'o-pa spoke the Turkish language.[1381]

The recorded history of the T'o-pa began in the third century with Li-wei (also known as Shen-yüan-ti), the ancestor of the founder of the dynasty, and his wife, Lady Tou, whose clan eventually contributed to the royal line of the future Chinese T'ang dynasty with the mother of well-known T'ang emperor T'ai-tsung (also known as Taizong).[1382] In 261 CE the T'o-pa leader Li-wei sent his eldest son, Sha-mo-han, as a hostage to the Chinese court of Jin. This was done as a goodwill gesture to establish peace between the two peoples. About sixteen years later, the heir returned home. Yet, owing to fears that Sha-mo-han might attempt to impose Chinese influence on his people, the T'o-pa elite managed to convince Li-wei to kill his son in 277. Shortly thereafter Li-wei died, but the Chinese Jin succeeded in temporarily weakening T'o-pa strength in northern China by creating dissension among the T'o-pa with the help of Wu-huan prince K'u-hsien by spreading rumors that Li-wei had intended to punish those who had conspired against his late son.[1383]

Li-wei was succeeded by his sons Hsi-lu (277–86) and Cho (286–93). But instead of his third son, Lu-kuan, it was slain Sha-mo-han's youngest son, Fu (293–94), who became leader in place of his third uncle. When in need of a new monarch, there was an old tradition of choosing a more capable ruler from within the royal family; it had happened among the Xiong-nu previously, and the T'o-pa elite believed that Fu was a more capable military leader than Lu-kuan. This was typical in the nomadic administration system; even though the hereditary aristocracy was maintained, the ablest male of the dynastic family would take leadership. Furthermore, Fu was probably chosen over his half brothers because their mother was Chinese.

After Fu and during the reign of his half brother Yi-lu (295–316), Sino-T'o-pa relations began to improve. In 313 Yi-lu moved the center of the T'o-pa into Datong (Ta-t'ung) in Shanxi Province. As his grandfather had, Yi-lu remained in alliance with the Jin court. Interestingly, later Chinese T'ang historians depicted Yi-lu's Chinese mother, Lady Feng, as an empress, whereas Fu's mother, Lady Lan, was considered to be a concubine, but in fact it was Lady Lan's lineage that later became the royal line of the T'o-pa Northern Wei dynasty. Indeed, Lady Lan was the great-great-grandmother of T'o-pa Kuei, the founder of the dynasty. But Lady Feng was preferred by later Chinese historians not only because of her Chinese ethnicity but also because she was married to a T'o-pa with presumed pro-Chinese attitudes and was the mother of a T'o-pa ally against the Xiong-nu.[1384]

After Yi-lu's death in 316, his nephew P'u-ken from Yi-yi and his Chinese mother, Lady Wei, took control. At the helm, P'u-ken dismissed his Chinese advisers, and instead he tried to engage in relations with the Xiong-nu (Asian Huns) remnants in the area. After his death one month into his reign, his cousin and Fu's son, Yü-lü (316–21), took leadership. Yü-lü did not favor maintaining a relationship with the Xiong-nu, owing to the squabbles within their leadership. Lady Wei, however, had Yü-lü killed only to have her second son Ho-ju to take over. For unknown reasons, Ho-ju actually took control in 324, and therefore, Lady Wei managed to govern the T'o-pa from 321 to 324 by herself.[1385]

THE TURKISH RULE OF CHINA

On the eve of the establishment of the Northern Wei dynasty, T'o-pa intermarriages with the Liu Xiong-nu and the Ho-lan Xianbei politically strengthened the position of the T'o-pa house. Moreover, by having interdynastic marriages with the house of Mu-jung (Asian Avars), the T'o-pa eventually expanded their sphere of influence into the steppelands of Asia. T'o-pa Shih-yi-chien's marriage to the Mu-jung princess produced Shih, who became father of T'o-pa Kuei, the founder of the dynasty.[1386]

In 377, when they were attacked from the south by the armies of the Former Qin, the T'o-pa found themselves leaderless, their chieftain being ill. Therefore, they were temporarily forced to move to the north. But once in the northern territories, the T'o-pa were assaulted by their kinsmen the Kao-ch'e (Qanglï Turks). These events demonstrated that the T'o-pa were still not sedentary; in fact their core group was still nomadic and thus quite mobile.[1387] Upon their return to the south, Shih-yi-chien and his sons were murdered by the Jin, but his grandson Kuei, still a minor, sought refuge along with his mother with T'o-pa ally Xiong-nu Liu K'u-Jen, who himself was the son of the late Shih-yi-chien's sister. When an internal struggle began among the Xiong-nu in 385, Kuei, at the age fourteen, returned to his people and married a princess from the Xiong-nu clan. After the establishment of the dynasty, his son Ssu was later to become the second emperor in the T'o-pa house. Once in power, Kuei firmly established the administrative strength of the T'o-pa by diminishing the influence of the other clans in the tribal confederacy. In 391 Kuei punished the Mu-jung for holding his half brother hostage, and in 397 he took more than four hundred thousand Mu-jung captive.

Finally, in 398, T'o-pa Kuei, the founder of the T'o-pa state and the Wei king (*wei wang*), assumed the title of "emperor" (*huangdi*) and changed the name of his state to Northern Wei (398–534), which was otherwise a continuation of the kingdom of Wei (or Dai, 386–98).[1388] The T'o-pa first engaged against the Juan-juan (Avars) in 391 and then against the Kao-ch'e in 399 even before consolidating their power over China.[1389] The presence of this Turkish dynasty is also associated with the Sixteen Kingdom period (304–439), but the Northern Wei dynasty is not included in the Sixteen Kingdoms. Also, the Northern Wei dynasty should not be confused with the Cao Wei Kingdom (220–65) during the Three Kingdoms period. In fact, the Northern Wei dynasty of the Tabgač Turks is part of the Southern and Northern dynasties period (420–589).

It was T'o-pa Kuei's son T'o-pa Dao who initiated and completed the reunification of northern China before the mid-fifth century. He also faced and chased out the Juan-juan from the northern borders of China in 424–25.[1390] In fact, facing the Juan-juan invasion, the T'o-pa quickly regrouped to stage a counterattack in which they caught the steppe nomads by total surprise. Then, in 429, the T'o-pa staged another campaign on the steppe to crush the Juan-juan and subdue them. In 492 the T'o-pa managed to deal another blow to the Juan-juan by causing them to split.[1391] Ultimately, the Tabgač Turks succeeded through perseverance in showing their strong presence in the Chinese territories with the establishment of a prominent polity known in the Chinese annals as the Northern Wei state, and by the year 450 CE, these Turks had claimed supremacy over all northern China.[1392] Indeed, the Tabgač Turks managed to establish the Northern Wei dynasty, which lasted about 150 years (386–534). However, the Turkish Wei, known as the (Northern) Wei dynasty to the Chinese, was not able to conquer southern China, where the Chinese Jin dynasty remained in firm control. Hence, the period of the Northern and Southern dynasties officially began when the Tabgač Turks ended the Sixteen Kingdom period by conquering all the small kingdoms in the north. The reunification of northern China by the non-Chinese Northern Wei dynasty brought a sense of unity to China, which had been fragmented since the fall of the Han dynasty in 220 CE.

The T'o-pa, or the Tabgač, had a diverse population: 60 percent Turkish, 35 percent Mongol, and 5 percent Tibetan or Tungus.[1393] However, over time, under the heavy influence of Chinese culture, they eventually became assimilated by this powerful Asian culture. When the T'o-pa, through their Northern Wei dynasty, reached the climax of their power in 439, they controlled all China north of the Yellow River in addition to the steppes in the Ordos in the north and the Western Territories in Turfan area. The capital was Pingcheng (near modern-day Datong). But late in the fifth century, the emperor Xiao Wen-ti (Hung) not only outlawed the Tabgač language but also moved his capital to Luoyang, farther south into the Chinese territories,[1394] even though the T'o-pa nomadic class was still in the Ordos Steppe. The situation was further testament to the sinicization of the ruling class. The evolving conditions eventually created a political rift between the sinicized ruling class and its supporting warrior class maintaining its Turkish character.

THE ESTABLISHMENT OF BUDDHISM IN CHINA

In the early part of their reign over northern China, the T'o-pa Turks followed the old Turkish faith of Tengriism. Like the old Turks following this creed, they buried their dead on top of the mountains.[1395] Eventually the T'o-pa, particularly their ruling class, adopted Buddhism as their religion. Although Buddhism began to firmly establish itself in China during the Sixteen Kingdoms period with the help of kingdoms led by Central Asian chieftains, this Indian-origin faith would actually start taking root with the strong rule of the T'o-pa Turks. Hence, the most significant contribution of the Tabgač Turks to Chinese history was providing strong footing for Buddhism in China, declaring it the official religion of the state.[1396] During the Turkish Northern Wei rule of northern China, Buddhism as the faith from India replaced the native Confucianism and Taoism. The founder of the Northern Wei dynasty, T'o-pa Kuei (Gui), who was a follower of the Chinese Taoist faith, issued an edict favoring Buddhism. The T'o-pa in fact realized that not only would their support of a religion popular in Central Asia help them to govern most of the non-Chinese in their territory, since they were followers of Buddhism, but by converting the Chinese into this religion, their administration over the natives would also be eased.

In fact, the conquest of northern China, where Central Asians carried the Buddhist creed with them, allowed the rapid spread of the faith across the large Chinese domain of the Northern Wei.[1397] In the early fifth century, the T'o-pa, the conquerors from Central Asia, not only united the northern Chinese territories but also provided unprecedented patronage to Buddhism in the land of Confucianism and Taoism. Consequently, Buddhist temples flourished across China, where more than 30,000 temples were established; the capital Luoyang alone had 1,367 monasteries.[1398] As mentioned above, by the year 439, the T'o-pa moved the Northern Wei capital from Pingcheng (Datong) in Shanxi Province to Luoyang (a.k.a. Lo-yang) in Henan Province. Hence, Luoyang turned into the political, religious, and artistic center of the Turkish T'o-pa Empire.[1399] In essence, it also became the center of Buddhism in China.

However, the records indicate that for a short period, the royal attitude toward Buddhism suddenly changed, perhaps because of the influence of Chinese officials who followed the native faiths of Taoism and Confucianism. In the year 438, during the reign of T'o-pa Dao, the persecution of Buddhism began. In 444 an edict was issued to kill Buddhist monks, owing to their alleged practice of sorcery. Because of the significant influence on the emperor by his Taoist minister, Cui Hao, and Taoist patriarch Kou Qianzhi, an order was issued to suppress Buddhism, with the subsequent declaration of Taoism as the official religion of the state.[1400] Consequently, owing to the state's intolerant attitude toward Buddhism, the Gaiwu Rebellion broke out in 445, led by Gaiwu's Lushui-hu branch of the Xiong-nu (Huns) against the Northern Wei dynasty. The revolt turned into a large movement with the assistance by the Han Chinese and the Ti and Qiang peoples. Ultimately it threatened the Turkish dynasty.

The emperor Taiwudi acted personally by leading his army to suppress the rebellion easily. During his campaign in 446, because of his discovery of weapons in a Buddhist monastery, he assumed the monks were assisting the rebels, and he issued an edict for the complete eradication of Buddhism.[1401] In addition to this discovery, tensions between the T'o-pa ruling class and the ethnic groups who opposed them also motivated the Northern Wei emperor to suppress Buddhism. After all, at the time, the Lushui-hu branch of the Xiong-nu was a group of devout Buddhists who fought side by side with other Buddhist people against the T'o-pa.[1402] But after the pro-Buddhist efforts of the crown prince T'o-pa Huang, persecution of Buddhists began to decline; after the state execution of Taoist minister Cui Hao took place in 450 for his strong anti-Buddhist stance, the harsh penalties were practically removed. In 453 Emperor Jun issued a decree allowing the practice of Buddhism in Northern Wei.[1403]

During the reign of Xiao Wen-ti (471–99), there was also a drastic change in the artistic rendering of Buddhist sculptures. Foreign Buddhist imagery, which was predominant until the early part of the fifth century, was now replaced with the Chinese style.[1404] Hence, by the early sixth century, previously Indian-appearing Buddha sculptures were completely transformed to Chinese-looking figures. Nevertheless, the male figurines of this evolving

Buddhist art had Central Asian–style clothes, with over-the-knee tunics, trousers, and boots.[1405] While in control of northern China, the T'o-pa Turks also built the well-known Buddhist caves of Yün-kang in Shanxi and Lungmen in Honan. The T'o-pa, just like the other ancient Turks, had a cave cult just as the Gök-Türks (chapter 5.3) did. Well before establishing themselves within northern China late in the fourth century, while they were wandering around Lake Baikal in 260 CE, they were noted to be venerating a cave where they lived for generations after their ancestral animal totem (a wolf) appeared there.[1406] Thus, these Buddhist caves may have been merely an adaptation of the old Turkish cult into the Buddhist faith in China.[1407] Today, they are UNESCO World Heritage Sites.

THE CULTURE OF FORCED SUICIDE

The ability of the Tabgač Turks to survive in the harsh political and warlike environment depended on their elected leadership's capability in the military arts, as was typical of Central Asian nomads. But with the establishment of the sedentary Northern Wei state, their culture and customs began to change under Chinese influence. For example, the father-to-son succession in ruling, children's accession to the throne, and the suicide of the mother of the heir apparent were all part of the Chinese dynastic system adopted into T'o-pa law in 398. According to Wei-shu records, likely modified by T'ang historians, the suicide system was an ancient T'o-pa tradition, but there are no such records of suicides of mothers of earlier heirs to the T'o-pa throne. Apparently the suicide system in Chinese dynastic history began in 88 BCE, when Han emperor Wudi ordered the suicide of the mother of his young heir apparent son to prevent her from taking power after his death.[1408] The elimination of female influence in imperial operations was encouraged by the Chinese; Chinese records are abundant with fears of empresses, concubines, and distaff interfering in state affairs, leading to disaster.[1409] The accession of a child was not part of the nomadic Tabgač tradition. Under the ancient Turkish tradition, a candidate for leadership had to prove his ability in military skills, as this was necessary for the survival of the tribal society. Nevertheless, beginning with the declaration of the new sinicized law by Emperor Kuei, T'o-pa society was destined to become more Chinese than Central Asian in character. Furthermore, at the end of the fifth century, T'o-pa Hung, a sinicized monarch, outlawed the T'o-pa (Turkish) language in favor of Chinese alone.[1410]

Even though the Chinese promoted the removal of a female regent in the dynastic house for fear of female interference in state affairs, the adoption of the Chinese filial accession system at the end of the fourth century opened the T'o-pa state to the political interference of empresses, empress-dowagers, concubines, and distaff groups; a similar system in the Ottoman Empire had a negative impact beginning late in the sixteenth century. Another deviation from the Central Asian nomadic tradition was that, even against his mother's objections, Emperor Kuei married his mother's sister, a situation allowed in the Chinese imperial system.[1411]

There is another ancient custom worth mentioning that the T'o-pa Turks kept alive when they ruled over northern China. While facial metal casting for the selection of their leader was done among the Xiong-nu, the same custom was used only for the selection of an empress among the T'o-pa (Tabgač Turks). However, it appears that the implementation of this custom occurred after T'o-pa Kuei declared his Northern Wei state in the late fourth century. The successful casting of the image of a candidate allowed that person to become the empress.[1412]

THE ENSUING EVENTS AND THE FALL

In 429 the Tabgač pushed the pastoralist Juan-juan (Asian Avars) to the west. Then, in 430, they destroyed the Xia (Hsia) dynasty, the last to be ruled by the descendants of Mo-tun of the Huns. By 440 the Northern Wei dynasty controlled all northern China and much of modern-day Mongolia.[1413] In 458 they once again pushed the Juan-juan farther west after capturing Turfan. During this time, the Turkish Ting-ling appeared as allies of the T'o-pa of the Northern Wei against the Juan-juan.[1414] In 526, the two enemies decided to make an alliance. The last Juan-juan leader, A-na-kuei, was recognized as an equal to the Northern Wei emperor.

In the spring of 534 CE, a great fire in Luoyang consumed a one-thousand-foot-high pagoda, a symbol of Buddhism in China in the sixth century. This was also a sign of political disturbance within the government of Northern Wei. A few months later, this great dynasty of the Turks came to an end when it divided into the Western Wei (Xi-Wei, 534–57) and the Eastern Wei (Tung-Wei, 534–50), governed by the split T'o-pa house.

It has been suggested that the fall of the Northern Wei dynasty in China came from a direct loss of communication between the ruling T'o-pa and their power base, the Turkish-speaking T'o-pa tribes following their Central Asian customs. When the T'o-pa initially arrived in northern China, their aristocratic class settled in their new capital, a Chinese city, while their tribesmen remained as stock breeders and warriors in the pasturelands. Over time this arrangement led to T'o-pa leaders and noblemen adopting the manners of the Chinese gentry as they became disconnected from their tribesmen in the Ordos steppes. Eventually the Northern Wei broke apart, owing to social tensions within T'o-pa society rather than Chinese resistance. Consequently, the lower-class T'o-pa, splitting from their leaders, became part of the western state, and the aristocratic class remained in the eastern polity.[1415] Later, the Xi-Wei played an important role in the destruction of the Juan-juan by assisting the rising Gök-Türks, who unified the Turks under one banner for the last time in history. However, the western kingdom was later replaced by the Xiong-nu-origin Northern Chou (or Northern Zhou, Bei Zhou, 557–81), and the eastern kingdom gave away to the Chinese Northern Ch'i (or Northern Qi, Bei Qi, 550–77). Finally, in 581, China was once again united under the Chinese dynasty of the Sui house (581–618).

By the middle of the sixth century, despite the fact Buddhism was the primary religion of China including among its nonnative population with Central Asian background in northern China, the new power in the north in the steppes of Mongolia, the Gök-Türks, were staunch adherents to the faith of Tengriism. Indeed, the Turkish Northern Wei was the first formal Buddhist state in Chinese history, and yet for this reason the Gök-Türk qaghan described their faith as idolatry to the Eastern Roman emperor Maurice.[1416]

In later years China would again experience foreign dynasties in its territory. These were the Altaic (Turco-Mongol) Liao dynasty (907–1125), the

Mongol Great Yuan dynasty (1279–1368), and the Manchu Tungus–led Qing dynasty (1644–1912). As will be seen later, there would be one more, albeit very short-lived, Turkish dynasty in northern China (chapter 5.5).

THE LEGACIES OF THE T'O-PA TURKS

Chinese culture has always had a powerful assimilating influence on non-Chinese peoples within and around of China. However, the traditions of the same non-Chinese peoples had strong effects on the Chinese lifestyle as well. For example, equestrianism was introduced to China with the help of the Xiong-nu. Though the Chinese were already familiar with the dress style of the Xiong-nu warriors, the use of the Central Asian trousers and boots became adopted by Chinese men with the strong influence of the T'o-pa.[1417] These Turks were also instrumental in the permanent establishment of Buddhism within China. As mentioned above, in creating Buddhist sculptures, the T'o-pa created their own style, which became adopted into the Chinese style.[1418] It should also be noted that the T'o-pa not only established the Northern Wei dynasty (386–534) but also produced the imperial heirs in the subsequent Sui (581–618) and T'ang (618–907) dynasties.[1419]

Another legacy of the T'o-pa appears to be the legend on which Disney's famous 1998 animated film *Mulan* was based. It has been suggested that the name Mulan was derived from the T'o-pa tribal name Pulan.[1420] The story of Mulan, in fact, was derived from the folk tradition "The Mulan Poem," from the period when the Northern Wei dynasty of the T'o-pa fought the Juan-juan. The implication here is that, in the legendary story, Mulan was not Chinese. Was she a Turk living in northern China, or was she a Chinese girl living in a land ruled by a Turkish dynasty? The hero of the story illustrates how steppe women had a strong social role that was absent in earlier Chinese history.[1421] In the poem, the heroine is born in the large old province of Henan, south of the Yellow River, where the Turkish T'o-pa clans settled after the Northern Wei capital was moved from Pingcheng to the old Chinese capital city of Luoyang. Interestingly, in the official form of the ballad, the ruler of China is not referred to as *huangdi*, the Chinese term for "emperor," but instead as *kehan*—in other words *qaghan*, the Turkish term.[1422] In literary Chinese, *mulan* means "fragrant and delicate flower." In the story, however, when Mulan reveals her identity, her fellow soldiers are amazed that she is a girl. This suggests that when the story emerged, the word *mulan* likely did not mean "flower," and that it was not likely to be a Chinese-origin word. It has been suggested that the heroine's name was derived from Old Turkish word *bulān* for "elk" or "unicorn." It appears that among the T'o-pa Turks, there was a cultural obsession with the unicorn.[1423] Furthermore, it should be kept in mind that it was a common practice among the Central Asian Turks of the past to use animal names under the influence of their traditional Tengriist faith.

Was the story of Mulan a shared legend of two different peoples? Even though the people in northern China historically were a product of mixed populations at least since the Chou (1046–256 BCE, later known as the Zhou), preceded by the Shang dynasty, there is no present-day evidence for Mulan being a shared legend, likely because there is no trace of the Turkish T'o-pa population today. The name of its hero was perhaps derived from Turkish, but today it is known as a Chinese legend. The Northern Wei dynasty of the T'o-pa Turks ruled over northern China; to outsiders, the land that they controlled was known as China, and the vast majority of the population was Chinese. Furthermore, the legend tells us that its hero fought the Huns, whose polity ceased to exist in the early third century CE, long before the T'o-pa Turks rose to power in the late fourth century, when the legend presumably surfaced and when there was no Hunnish state in existence. The exception is the short-lived Hunnish Xia Kingdom in northern China arising in the early fifth century, as mentioned above, but the T'o-pa eliminated this polity with relative ease.

Furthermore, at the time when the T'o-pa controlled China, the steppes came under the new nomadic empire of the Juan-juan. Since the prior Xiong-nu (Asian Huns) had established a strong favorable reputation among the nomadic tribes of Central Asia, it was a tradition and a privilege for a tribal political entity to assume an association with the existing or former powerful tribe or confederation of tribes. Possibly, the Juan-juan at the time viewed themselves or were viewed as the Xiong-nu, even though they were not. Certainly, the story of Mulan is open for debate.

According to Chinese records, after a civil war was quelled, General Kao Huan decided to install young prince T'o-pa Hsiu as the next emperor. The T'o-pa ceremonies described are reminiscent of ancient Turkish coronation rituals, which we also find among the later Gök-Türks. Seven high officials held up a black felt rug on which the new emperor paid his respects to heaven; black was traditionally the official and most honored color for the T'o-pa Turks.[1424] For the ancient Turks, the color black indicated royalty. This was in contrast to the use of gold color by the imperial Chinese dynasties. Later, in Western sources in the thirteenth century, a similar ritual is reported during the coronation of Mongol Genghis Khan, but Eastern sources do not mention this event.[1425] Much later (the fourteenth century and later), the Ottoman Turks honored black as the royal color as well.

Another T'o-pa legacy is the Northern Wei governmental system, which was adopted by the next government of the T'ang dynasty.[1426] There is one other important legacy of the Tabgač that should be mentioned. This legacy lies in the answer of the next question. After the Northern Wei dynasty collapsed in the sixth century, did the Tabgač disappear?

As mentioned earlier, when the Gök-Türks came to power in 552, northern China was already divided between the Western and Eastern Wei of the T'o-pa (Tabgač). Hence, when the Gök-Türks erected the stone Orkhon inscriptions in the eighth century, why did they refer to China as Tabgač? Was it because they associated the country with the founders of the Northern Wei dynasty or because the contemporary eighth-century T'ang dynasty had T'o-pa ancestry? The Gök-Türks were well aware that neither the Sui nor the T'ang were politically the same as the Northern Wei dynasty formed by the Tabgač Turks. But in the eighth century, they were still referring to China as Tabgač.

Interestingly, the founder of the T'ang dynasty, Li Yuan, was the nephew of Yang Jian, who was the founder of the preceding Sui dynasty. However, Li Yuan was also grandson of Dugu Xin, who was a nobleman from the Northern Zhou dynasty, which was from a Xiong-nu clan.[1427] The Li family that established the T'ang dynasty was possibly descended from the T'o-pa, and furthermore, there are records showing that the Li family used the T'o-pa language as their family language.[1428] Even later, many of the powerful aristocrats of the T'ang court were either able to speak Turkish or they were themselves Turks in command of the Turkish troops in the service of the Chinese army; even some of the emperors were known to speak the Turkish language.[1429] Indeed, the historical records indicate that the T'o-pa language was the primary or family language of both the Yang and Li clans, which formed the Sui and T'ang dynasties respectively.[1430] If this is indeed true, then both the Sui and the T'ang dynasties may have originated from the ancient Turkish Tabgač tribe, or T'o-pa in Chinese Pinyin. Nevertheless, by this time, the remnants of the T'o-pa, as well as most other northern peoples of "barbarian" background, had been culturally sinicized.

The "Li" imperial family that eventually formed the T'ang dynasty was known to have been heavily influenced by the Inner Asians.[1431] Hence, even before taking the imperial throne, the family had close connections with the Turks of the Mongolian plains. The ascension of the Li family to the Chinese imperial status was facilitated by the assistance from these Turks. As it will be mentioned in the next chapter the Li family benefited from the formidable Turkish cavalry of the Gök-Türks, which helped to achieve reunification of China under the T'ang dynasty.[1432]

5.3. THE CELESTIAL TURKS

Earlier we saw that following the fall of the Huns (Xiong-nu) in eastern Central Asia in the third century CE, the large territories encompassing the Central and Eastern Eurasian Steppes were populated by Turkish-speaking tribes, but they lacked the authoritative leadership and protection that the Xiong-nu had provided against a large state like China. The control of the eastern steppes, the original home of the Huns, eventually passed from the Xianbei to the Juan-juan. As mentioned previously, during the short Xianbei period in the second and third centuries, the scattered (Northern) Hun tribes were chased out. Many sought sanctuary in the central Eurasian steppes, while others gathered around the Altai Mountains, where the Turks believed they originated. According to an ancient Central Asian myth, the Turks were descendants of a wolf.[1433] According to this legend, this mountain range was the birthplace of the Turks, and with the emergence of the Gök-Türks, it became a place of rebirth, as explained in the following synopsis of the anonymous epic story of Ergenekon:

> The Epic of Ergenekon is the story of the Turkish people who were pushed to extinction but with sheer determination and patience they were able to make a comeback to power by defeating the enemy who had inflicted their earlier tragedy upon them. The prior tragic events showed that the Turkish tribe was annihilated by the enemy but only one young boy remained alive. In a supernatural event (likely influenced by shaman beliefs) the boy found protection with a grey-wolf which gave birth to his children. Eventually he fathered a reborn nation closed in a "locked" valley. The people became

expert blacksmiths making exquisite swords (kïlïnch), arrows (ok), and spears (mïzrak). Centuries passed by. When the nation was ready for their next task, a grey-wolf appeared and showed them an exit from the locked valley thru a closed iron wall. The blacksmiths opened a gateway to the outside world through this wall. Then the gray-wolf led them to their new homeland where they became a world power.

CONNECTION TO THE HUNS

It has been suggested that well before the Gök-Türks established their empire in the mid-sixth century, during the fourth and fifth centuries, the royal clan of the Gök-Türks resided in Kansu (Gansu province in modern-day China) and later in Qočo, under the dominion of the Buddhist Chü-Ch'ü Huns, while many of the aristocratic Turkish families lived in China, where they served the Northern Wei dynasty of the T'o-pa (Tabgač Turks).[1434] It is believed that the A-shih-na clan, the founders of the future Gök-Türk Empire, after settling in the Kansu area, may have later relocated to the Altai Mountains in the fifth century.[1435] It has been suggested that the Gök-Türks (T'ü-chüeh in Pinyin Chinese) were the descendants of the Kao-ch'e (Qanglï)—in other words, they originated from the ancient tribal union of the Ting-ling.[1436] If true, this origin would separate the Gök-Türks from the Huns. Regardless of their origin, later it appears that the A-shih-na clan worked as blacksmiths for the Asian Avars.[1437]

According to a Chinese story, the A-shih-na, a royal Turkish family or clan within the Türk tribe, were initially noted to be Hunnish refugees who had fled from the Xianbei in the second century and lived by the majestic Altai Mountains.[1438] Chinese historians of the T'ang dynasty believed that the Gök-Türks were descendants of the Asian Huns (Xiong-nu).[1439] As described in chapter 3, a group of Huns remained by the Altai Mountains after they left their ancestral Mongolian steppes. Hence, this Chinese input may be shedding light on the origins of the Gök-Türks. After remaining by these majestic mountains for a few centuries, they became stronger in strength. By the mid-sixth century, the A-shih-na and the Türk tribes were adversaries of the Juan-juan, or the Asian Avars. In 552 the Gök-Türks, gathered under the leadership of the A-shih-na clan, conquered the Juan-juan, and by the end of the same century, they had become a world power stretching from Manchuria in the east to the western outskirts of the Pontic Steppe in eastern Europe in the west. They fulfilled the epic of Ergenekon by taking control of the Turkish world. It has been suggested that the rulers of the Xiong-nu, Gök-Türks, and Khazars all belonged to the house of the A-shih-na.[1440] According to Chinese recordings from the seventh century, the leading Turkish tribes within the Gök-Türk Qaghanate, also known as the Türk Empire, were—based on linguistic findings—descendants of the Xiong-nu.[1441] Hence, it has been suggested that the language of the Gök-Türks was not different from that of the Huns (Xiong-nu).[1442]

The Gök-Türks built on the traditions that came down from the Xiong-nu. Later the Uighurs improved on these Central Asian Turkish customs, and finally the Khitans and later the Mongols borrowed from the imperial and cult traditions of the Gök-Türks and the Uighurs.[1443] Being descendants of the Huns, the Gök-Türks chose their leader from within the royal clan. According to Chinese records, the Gök-Türks, being from a branch of the Xiong-nu (Asian Huns) followed the same imperial traditions as the Huns did, and their great khan or qaghan of the empire was selected from within the royal A-shih-na family.[1444] The royal dynasty of legendary Mo-tun existed as the rulers of the Xiong-nu until 216 CE, when the Southern Xiong-nu ceased to exist. However, it has been said that the royal house continued ruling the Xiong-nu tribes that moved westward and eventually established the states of the White Huns in western Turkestan and the Black (European) Huns in eastern Europe. The A-shih-na family, which ruled over the Gök-Türk Empire, is also thought to have been a continuation of the royal Xiong-nu clan.[1445] Moreover, the Khazar Empire's ruling dynasty came from the A-shih-na family as well.[1446] If this is all true, then the royal house of Mo-tun had quite a long existence, ruling over a large geographic area from the Eastern Eurasian Steppe to the Western Eurasian Steppe until the Khazar Empire ceased to exist in the tenth century CE. Furthermore, the demise of the state of the Southern Huns in 216 did not, in fact, end their existence. As illustrated earlier, the Huns continued to exist in northern China. They succeeded in establishing four short-lived dynasties within northern China between the early fourth century and the late sixth century.[1447] The Xiong-nu also contributed to the Northern Wei dynasty of the T'o-pa Turks of northern China by intermarrying with their royal house. Later, in the tenth century, the Sha-t'o Turks (chapter 5.5), whose origins are obscure but who were perhaps descendants of the Xiong-nu, also established two short-lived dynasties in China (923–36 and 936–46).[1448]

THE COLOR BLUE AND ITS SIGNIFICANCE

Historical records show that when the Türk tribes under the control of the A-shih-na were ready, they began diplomatic interactions with the Western Wei (Xi-Wei) in the year 545. Upon freeing themselves from the authority of the Juan-juan, the Gök-Türks secured an alliance with the Western Wei in 551 with a marriage.[1449] Only a year later, in 552, the Gök-Türks utterly crushed the Juan-juan to take control of the entire Eastern Eurasian Steppe and more. When Bumïn Qaghan reclaimed the contemporary territories of Mongolia from Juan-juan rule, he also was quick to expand the dominions of his empire to the former Hunnish borders and beyond. This was likely facilitated by the scattered Turkish tribes readily accepting the leadership role of their powerful kinsmen. As a result, the Gök-Türk Empire, which we know from the Chinese archives as the empire of the T'u-Chüeh, was formed. On the basis of recordings by Chinese historians, the wolf was the principal totem of the Gök-Türks.[1450] It has been suggested that the head of the gray wolf was also used on their flag. According to a Chinese historian in 581, the Gök-Türks had a golden wolf head on top of the staff of their flag.[1451] This was in homage of the wolf that saved the Türk nation, a commemoration of the epic of Ergenekon.

The ethnonym Türk appears for the first time in history with the Gök-Türks. The corresponding Chinese name, T'u-Chüeh, is believed to be derived from its Mongolian plural form, Türküt, from the singular Türk. It literally meant "strong."[1452] According to Eastern Roman records, the Gök-Türks were numerous and free people, but they did nothing other than train to fight the enemy with courage.[1453] According to Roman *Strategikon* notes, the Gök-Türks trained in shooting arrows from horseback.[1454] Their state name, Gök-Türk, can be translated as the Blue Turks, or as the Eastern Turks, since according to the ancient color-coded cardinal-direction system, *gök* (blue) also meant "east." The color blue was sacred to the ancient Turks, and *gök* also meant "sky" or "heaven." Perhaps the founding clan used this term purposefully to distinguish itself as the royal banner carrier among the Turks. Consequently, the name Gök-Türks could also be translated as Heavenly Turks or Celestial Turks. The founding tribe could have claimed to have been appointed by Gök-Tengri (Sky God) of the Tengriist Turks.

The historical adjective *gök* (blue) of these Turks was transmitted to us through the recordings by the merchants of the Silk Road. The ruling clan A-shih-na was in contact with Persian-speaking Sogdian traders in the vicinity, and the name A-shih-na appears to have been derived from the Sogdian term for "blue." Therefore, even though the founding clan was known to be Turkish, they seem to have been known among merchants by a Sogdian-based word. Ultimately, they gave their name of "blue" to the empire that they led.

As stated above, possibly by adding their clan name "blue" (i.e., heavenly) to their ethnic name, the founders of the Gök-Türks intended to unite all the Turkish tribes under their banner by claiming divine appointment for leadership. Following an ambitious quest, similar to what Mongol leader Genghis Khan would achieve less than a millennium later, the Gök-Türks united most of the Turkish-speaking tribes over a large geographic area stretching from Korea in the east to the western outskirts of modern-day Ukraine in the west. The major Turkish tribes under Gök-Türk rule were the Toquz-Oghuz, Qarluq, Kimek, Khalaj, Oghuz, Pečeneg, On-Ok (Türgiš), Adkiš, Khišek, and Kyrgyz.[1455] But there may have been other unknown tribal entities as well, including groups of Ogurs.

The GökTürks chose to use their ethnic name as well as the founding clan's name (blue) as the name of their state. They were the only Turks to politically declare their ethnic identity prior to modern times. But even though during premodern times, the Central Asian Turks honored the names of their leaders, their shamanic totems, and their tribes by using them for their state names, they never forgot their ethnic origins. Mahmud of Kashgar from the eleventh century, likely from the Qarluq tribes in the Qara-Khanid state, glorified the

Turkish race in his literary work and pointed out the Turkish character of every tribal grouping across Asia. In the twelfth century, when Anatolia was no longer a Greek-majority land under the rule of the Seljuks, this westernmost territory of Asia came to be referred to as Turchia by the Greeks (in other words, Turkey, for "land of the Turks"). The Gök-Türks by the end of the sixth century formed the first trans-Eurasian state in history, linking Europe with East Asia. Indeed, it was the first largest nomadic empire in history, stretching from the Pontic Steppe of the Black Sea in eastern Europe in the west to the forests of Manchuria in the east.[1456]

The economy of the Gök-Türks primarily relied upon their pastoralist nomadism. Just like the Asian Huns did before them, they traded with the Chinese, getting silk and other agricultural products in exchange for horses and animal based merchandise. The Turks of the Gök-Türk Qaghanate—also referred to as the Türk Empire by historians—were also known as ironsmiths, and their legends suggested that they descended from a wolf.[1457]

Map 11. The Gök-Türk Qaghanate (Empire) at its greatest extent at the end of the sixth century. Even though the empire was loosely divided within the ruling family after the death of its founder, the eastern ruler was still considered the supreme ruler (qaghan). The nomadic empire was the last to encompass the majority of the Turkish tribes within its domain. After the fall of GökTürks, Turks were never united again.

THE RISE AND THE DIVISION OF THE STATE

Upon the death of Bumïn Qaghan, his empire was divided into two halves between his son Mughan and his brother Istemi, who brought the Turkish tribes under their control and solidified their control from Manchuria in the east to the Black Sea in the west; nevertheless, as mentioned above, the Gök-Türk Empire under its founder had become the first trans-Eurasian state in history, linking Europe to the Far East.[1458] As a result, the size of the state was able to support an extensive trade network allowing for the exchange of goods and ideas between the East and the West with ease.[1459] While Bumïn's son Mughan took the title of "(supreme) qaghan" to govern the eastern half under the Eastern Gök-Türk Empire, Bumïn's brother Istemi (known as Shih-tie-mi in the Chinese annals), with the title of *yabghu*, governed the Western Gök-Türk Empire. According to some records, the division of the state occurred later, in 581–83.[1460] After Istemi when his successor Tardu (582-603) came to power in Western GökTürk state led by a yabgu was under the power of Eastern GökTürk stater governed by supreme qaghan. However, in contrast to this traditional Turkish steppe rule Tardu attempted to bring the eastern half of the state under his authority. Taking advantage of this turmoil Chinese drove a wedge between Tardu of the West and Isbara Qaghan of the East, and as a result, they weakened Turkish unity by forcing the two states to remain apart from each other. The fact is that the administration of the qaghanate remained divided into eastern and western halves, each managed by a qaghan from the A-shih-na clan, but the eastern qaghan was politically considered the supreme ruler. From time to time, successors of the western qaghanate sought to capture the seat of the eastern qaghan; this situation led to internal struggles, which eventually drained the strength of the state.[1461]

The Western Gök-Türks later faced massive revolts of the Töles (T'ieh-le; see chapter 6) and other Turkish tribal federations.[1462] But eventually, authority was reestablished each time. While the Eastern Gök-Türks pushed the Khitan horde out of their territories, the Western Gök-Türks extended their sphere of influence into modern-day southern Ukraine to establish a border with the Eastern Roman Empire, a.k.a. the Byzantine Empire. Hence, during this period, the Gök-Türks had international relations with the empires of the Eastern Romans, the Sassanid Persians, and the Chinese. When the Gök-Türks reached the zenith of their power at the end of the sixth century, in China the land was once again reunited under the Sui dynasty (581–618) for the first time since the Han dynasty (206 BCE–220 CE). Gök-Türk power was still quite formidable, and the Chinese realized that they could not defeat the Turks militarily. Until the Gök-Türks emerged, no state other than the Asian Huns had managed to collect tribute from China.[1463] But once again the Chinese found themselves in the uncomfortable position of paying tribute to the Turks.

The principal (northern) branch of the A-shih-na ruled over the Eastern Gök-Türks from 552 to 742 over a large geographic area from the Gulf of Chihli (former name of Bohai, the innermost gulf of the Yellow Sea) to the Aral Sea, whereas the second (western) branch, the Western Gök-Türks, reigned between 580 and 658 over Turkestan and extended their control from Khorasan to the Don River area. Possibly between the years 557 and 563, the Gök-Türks, with their Persian Sassanid allies, annihilated the Ephtalites.[1464] After the Western Gök-Türk rule ended, control of their territories passed to another powerful union of Turkish tribes, known as the Türgiš (or Türgeš) tribes, from 658 to roughly 766. Subsequently, control passed to the Qarluq Turks. Meanwhile, the Yabghus of Tokharistan, a dynasty derived from T'ung Yabghu of the Western Gök-Türks, administered the western Turkish tribes in the area south of the Sogdian Iron Gate, extending their influence down to Herat (Afghanistan) between the years of about 600 and 758.[1465] Meanwhile, the Khalaj Turks, who had been in Afghanistan since the days of the White Huns (Ephtalites), were also governed by the Gök-Türks through the local leadership of the Yabghus of Tokharistan, and later they came under the rule of their kinsmen the Ghaznavids in the eleventh century.[1466] Much later, these Khalaj warriors would form the Turkish dynasties of pre-Mughal India as well (volume 2, chapter 1.4).[1467]

RELATIONS WITH ROME

In the sixth century, in the west, after the Gök-Türks ended the state of the Ephtalites (White Huns), they found themselves neighbors of Persia. At the time the Persians were enemies of the Eastern Roman Greeks. The Gök-Türks chose to establish an alliance with the Eastern Roman Empire against their formidable western neighbor, the Persian Sassanid Empire. In the year 562 or later, the qaghan sent the Roman emperor his (first) embassy, asking for intelligence on the Avars, who had escaped the wrath of the Gök-Türks. Later in the same year, the Roman embassy paid a visit to the Turks. Greek records indicate the Turks were formerly called the Sakai.[1468] This Greek term possibly referred to the ancient Saka people, also known as the Scythians, who are often referred to by some scholars as an Iranian people even though many of their cultural traits and their lifestyle fit that of the ancient Turks. According to Roman archives, the Roman envoy likely met with the western khan of the Turks at a place referred to as Ektag, or Ak Tag in Turkish (White Mountain). But the Romans described this place as the Golden Mountains (also referred to as such by the Chinese)—in other words, likely the Tien-shan Mountains, which was possibly the center of the Western Gök-Türks.

Meanwhile, the eastern khan was the supreme khan of the entire Gök-Türk dominion, ruling from the Orkhon valley. It appears that the eastern khan used the title of *zieghu*[1469] or possibly *shan-yu* of the former Xiong-nu. It is clear that during the reign of Roman emperor Justinian II, the Gök-Türk Empire was already being managed as two separate states known as the eastern and western empires, but in the face of a common enemy, they apparently united as one force.

In 568, when the Gök-Türk embassy reached Constantinople, the Turks asked the Avars to be handed back to them. By this time, as the European Avars settled in Pannonia, the former base of Attila the Hun, they were causing much distress in the Balkan territories of the Eastern Roman Empire, but the emperor in Constantinople chose to buy off or pay tribute to the Avars instead. In 576, when the second Eastern Roman embassy paid a visit to the Gök-Türks, Tardu Qaghan accused the Eastern Romans of "speaking with ten tongues and lying with all of them."[1470] During the same visit, the ambassador of Eastern Roman emperor Tiberius observed that the supreme Turkish qaghan was residing by a place called Ektel, where the ambassador and his staff met with him; this was likely Ötüken, as mentioned in the Orkhon inscriptions of the Gök-Türks. In 598 the Turks sent an embassy of diplomatic politeness to the Roman emperor Maurice. The Romans described the Turkish monarch by self-proclamation as the "Great Lord of Seven Peoples and Controller of

Seven Climes of the World."[1471] A similar description was also used by their kinsmen the Ottoman sultans almost nine centuries later.

In addition to the Roman records, Chinese writings also attest to the fact that Ötüken was important for the Gök-Türks. According to Chinese annals, the great Turkish qaghan (*k'o-han* in Chinese Pinyin) of the Gök-Türks lived on the mountain Yu-tou-kin (Ötüken in the Orkhon inscriptions), where the nobles of the state met annually at an ancestral burial site in a cave to make sacrifices. Its exact location is elusive. It seems that the Gök-Türks followed a similar cave cult as their kinsmen Tabgač Turks. According to these records, about four hundred to five hundred li (Chinese measurement; about 200-250 km) to the west of this mount, there was a high mountain, which at its zenith had no plants and no trees. It was called the "spirit of the sky" (spirit of heaven) in Chinese, but according to another description, it was known as the "god of earth" in Chinese. It has been thought that sacrifices were made on this mountain as well. Near the site of the mount, the people gathered by the T'a-jen River on the fifth month to make sacrifices to Gök-Tengri.[1472] The name Ötüken is a likely a contraction of two words; while the significance of *ötü* is not certain, the word *ken* (*kan*, *kän*) indicated "sovereign." Instead of being a single mountain, Ötüken may have been a chain of mountains that also included the "god of earth."[1473]

During the second year of the reign of Emperor Tiberius, the second Roman ambassador, Valentinus, was given a complaint by Turxanthus (Turhan?) Qaghan for the Gök-Türk perception of Greeks allying themselves with the Avars, who were viewed as the subjects of the qaghan. Theophylactus, the Eastern Roman historian, reported that in the Turkish qaghan's letter to Emperor Mauricius, dated 598, he boasted about his past victories over multiple peoples, including the Avars and the Oghurs. It is believed that the tribes Var and Hunni, splitting from the Oghur Turks, fled from the Gök-Türks and arrived in Europe during the reign of Justinian (527–65) under the name of Avars; the Hunni were actually the Bulgar Turks, referred to as the Huns by the Greeks.[1474] In fact, the Bulgars and the Huns were likely very similar, both speaking the same Oghur dialect of Turkish. Again, according to the Greek recordings, the Gök-Türk qaghan in his letter to the Eastern Roman emperor referred to the European Avars as the Varchonites (distorted Greek word for Avars).[1475]

RELATIONS WITH CHINA

While the Northern Ch'i (Qi) (550–77) replaced the Eastern Wei, the Northern Zhou (557–81) established itself in place of the Western Wei. The latter was formed by the remnants of the resilient Xiong-nu. Both of these new short-lived dynasties in northern China competed for the favors of the Gök-Türk qaghan, who favored the Northern Zhou (also known as the Northern Chou) by giving them his daughter, who became a respected empress of Northern Zhou in 568; in return, in 580 a princess was sent to marry Gök-Türk Taspar Qaghan.[1476] The alliance allowed the Zhou to defeat the Ch'i. Declaring that his "two loyal sons to the south were feuding," Taspar Qaghan of the east empire took advantage of the rivalries of China's Northern Ch'i and Northern Zhou to economically benefit his empire.[1477]

Later, in 581, Yang Chien, a powerful minister, usurped the throne of the Northern Zhou to establish his own Sui dynasty, which succeeded in unifying all China in 589. Ch'ien-chin, a Northern Zhou princess and the wife of Išbara Qaghan, forced the Gök-Türks to attack the Sui to revenge her father's death by the Sui. The Chinese dynasty in turn tried to drive a wedge between the Gök-Türk hierarchy by giving princess brides to lesser officials rather than to the qaghan. Aware of the intent of the Sui, Shih-pi Qaghan attacked the Sui, and the Chinese emperor barely escaped with the intervention of the qaghan's Chinese wife, I-ch'eng, a Sui princess who became the bride of Ch'u-lo Qaghan of the Western Gök-Türks in 614.[1478] In the meantime, while the little-known Kao-ch'ang Kingdom of the Töles (T'ieh-le) Turks were in charge at Turfan, the Sui Chinese emperor sent a princess to wed their Turkish king, Po-ya, who traveled with the emperor on his campaign to Korea in 612. The Sui dynasty pursued conquests in Vietnam and Koguryo (Korea), but the military campaigns became quite expensive. Consequently, China erupted with rebellions against the Sui, which were supported by the Eastern Gök-Türks.[1479]

In 617 a duke of T'ang, Li Yuan, a Sui general in T'ai-yüan (Shanxi), together with the rebel leaders in northern China, staged a coup against the Sui emperor, but he was only able to establish his own T'ang dynasty a year later in 618. Li Yuan wrote a letter to Shih-pi Qaghan seeking his protection of T'ai-yüan while hiding his true intention of building an empire. His proposal offered Chinese treasures in return for Turkish military assistance and a promise of noninvolvement in any future operations by Li Yuan, but in return the Turkish qaghan demanded the Chinese accept his suzerainty.[1480] Li Yuan reluctantly accepted the Turkish offer. In compliance with the Turks' demands, Li Yuan began to use the white banners that the Turks were using, but he did not completely abandon the crimson banners of the Sui dynasty; he did not want to appear too obvious in his allegiance. Shih-pi Qaghan sent his officials to T'ai-yüan and bestowed a Turkish title upon Li Yuan.

By August 10, 617, Li Yuan had managed to gather thirty thousand Chinese fighters for his army, but he also received a contingent of Turkish warriors from the Western Gök-Türks, led by A-shih-na Ta-nai Tigin.[1481] In addition, Gök-Türk Shih-pi Qaghan sent his commander with a Turkish cavalry of about twenty thousand upon request to help Li Yuan (Kao-tsu) in his uprising against the Sui dynasty.[1482] The records do not detail the breakdown of the Sui forces. But it appears that when Li Yuan reached the battlefield, his core army was down to about twenty-five thousand fighters, after some his detachments that headed back to T'ai-yüan. Accounts of the battle suggest that there were only a few hundred cavalry, most of which were Turkish mounted archers.[1483] The Battle of Huo-i on September 8, 617, ended with the capture of the Sui capital, Ta-hsing Ch'eng, by Li Yuan, who a year later formerly established the T'ang dynasty of China.

Even though he had defeated the Sui elite force, when his son lost to another rebel warlord, Li Yuan again sought help from Tong Yabghu, future Xieli or Illig Qaghan.[1484] In response the Turks sent military assistance to his son Li Shimin, who eliminated the opposing rebel forces of Xu Ju. Hence, in their relations with their eastern neighbor, the Gök-Türks also acted as dynasty makers in China. By supplying cavalry horses and Turkish warriors, the Eastern Gök-Türks provided assistance to Li Yuan, who defeated the Sui dynasty and formed the T'ang dynasty in 618 as the first emperor with the regnal name Kao-tsu (also known as Gaozu).[1485] However, after the T'ang dynasty took over, Princess I-Ch'eng persuaded her husband to attack the T'ang Chinese and provided sanctuary to the surviving Sui royal family within Gök-Türk territories.[1486]

Starting with the Huns, the Turkish ruling clans in modern-day Mongolia had close ties with prominent Chinese families, including the royal families. The Ch'ü family, which controlled Kao-ch'ang and cultivated the monarchs of the Sui and T'ang dynasties, established ties with the Turks through intermarriage with Tong Yabghu of the Western Gök-Türks.[1487] The founder of the T'ang dynasty, Koa-tsu, was from the Li family, which was related to the royal families from the Northern Zhou (Xiong-nu) and the Sui and to the Northern Wei of the Tabgač Turks.[1488] Hence, the T'ang family of the T'ang dynasty (618–907) was of mixed ethnic background.[1489] This mixture included significant Turkish ethnicity. As mentioned earlier, the Li family that founded the T'ang dynasty spoke the T'o-pa (Turkish) tongue as their primary language.[1490] According to Chinese historians, Crown Prince Chengqian, heir apparent of powerful T'ang emperor T'ai-tsung, who brought down the Eastern Gök-Türk Qaghanate in 630, acted inappropriately within the T'ang court, openly rejecting his Chinese heritage by using the Turkish language and dressing in Turkish costumes; the records indicate that other Li family members continued to speak the Turkish language as well.[1491] But it seems most others did not act in a way to alienate their Chinese subordinates. Later on, Emperor Xuanzong (712–56) was apparently the last monarch to prefer Turkish companions during his outings; during his reign, the influence of the Turkish language in the T'ang court was already diminishing.[1492]

The T'ang rulers were cognizant of the difficulties that the Han dynasty of the Chinese classical period had with the Turkish nomadic power of the Asian Huns (Xiong-nu). Therefore, they did not feel comfortable having a powerful foreign entity on their border. To influence their own people against the Turks, the T'ang filled the environment with misinformation, in other words with anti-Turkish propaganda in order to justify the actions of the state against their northern neighbors. But claims that the Gök-Türks repeatedly invaded Chinese territories at will were not true; in fact, such information was continuously disseminated to justify later aggression by the T'ang forces against the Turks.[1493] Most military interactions across the border were carried out in response to the perceived need for self-protection and for economic reasons. Now with China reunified under a single dynasty, the Turks began to think that rather seeing a strong China at their border, having an unstable

China better suited their needs. Hence, with only five hundred Turkish cavalrymen, they began to support the rebel activities of Liu Wuzhou, who began to seriously threaten the new T'ang. After the T'ang began to regroup, the Turks executed the rebel leaders. Nevertheless, it soon became clear that the T'ang would no longer act as vassals of the Gök-Türks.[1494]

Ch'u-lo Qaghan planned a massive attack upon T'ang China from four different directions, but when he died late in 620, the invasion plans were abandoned. The T'ang continued to consolidate power within Chinese territories, but disturbed by the changes in China, in 622, 150,000 cavalrymen at the command of Xieli (Tong) Qaghan crushed the T'ang defenses at Yanmen. With the city of Chang'an in danger, the Chinese sought peace with diplomacy and "gifts." Xieli decided to turn back, but in return the Chinese were forced to pay annual tribute for the price of peace; after all, the T'ang military was inferior to that of the Gök-Türks.[1495] In 626 Emperor Kao-tsu (Li Yuan) abdicated for his son Li Shimin, who took the regnal name of T'ai-tsung (also known as Taizong). Shortly thereafter, Xieli Qaghan invaded China with a force of two hundred thousand cavalrymen, putting the T'ang capital in danger. But once again Xieli returned after negotiations with T'ai-tsung.[1496]

THE END OF THE FIRST PERIOD

Tong Yabghu (618–30), with the regnal name Xieli (Chinese name) Qaghan, was the last great Turkish monarch to restrengthen the Western Gök-Türk Qaghanate by stretching his rule to southern Afghanistan; furthermore, in 628 he became an integral contributor to the Eastern Roman victory over Sassanid Persia.[1497] But when he was assassinated because of civil war in 630, the Western Gök-Türk state ceased to exist, and it was temporarily replaced by the On-Oq (Ten Arrows) tribal union of the Turks (see chapter 6).

There were multiple factors in the fall of the Eastern Gök-Türk Empire. When natural disasters led to starvation and the wasting of large numbers of their herds, Xieli Qaghan faced discontentment among his tribal leaders. Certainly the great famine of 628 hit the (eastern) Turks quite hard as well when they lost most of their animals in the harsh winter and were severely weakened. Furthermore, the confrontation between the qaghan and his popular commander and his nephew Tölis, also a "sworn brother" of T'ang emperor T'ai-tsung, created a huge rift within the steppe society. The T'ang masterfully played the warring factions against one another to keep the Turks preoccupied. After 628, tribes began to split from the vast empire, starting a chain reaction leading to the disintegration of the great steppe empire. Emperor T'ai-tsung, taking advantage of the discord among the Turks, went on the offensive in 630, thus ending the rule of the Eastern Gök-Türks in the Eastern Eurasian Steppe. In 630 T'ai-tsung also accepted the Turkish title of "heavenly qaghan" (in Chinese, *tian kehan*) when the Turks in the territories of the Western Gök-Türks accepted his suzerainty.[1498]

The T'ang emperor was successful in dividing the aristocracy of the Turkish empire through political tactics. Since the Eastern Gök-Türk Qaghanate had natural borders with China, he eventually managed to place it under the overlordship of the T'ang. When the Eastern Gök-Türk Qaghanate lost its authority in 630, as many as one million nomads may have been allowed to relocate within China's northern territories. Many Gök-Türk chieftains and nobles received Chinese titles and offices, and some had successful military careers in the T'ang armies.[1499] Finally, in 630 the First Gök-Türk Qaghanate Period ended. T'ai-sung declared himself the emperor of China and the qaghan of the Turks. Following the fall of the Western Qaghanate, two powerful Turkish states emerged from within the Gök-Türk realm in eastern Europe. As discussed in the previous chapter, these were the Bulgar confederation of tribes and the Khazar Qaghanate. The latter was formed by a branch of the Gök-Türk ruling family, A-shih-na.[1500]

THE GÖK-TÜRK INTERREGNUM

According to Chinese records, Li Yuan's son Li Shimin (known by his regnal name, T'ai-tsung) was fluent in Turkish and established "sworn brotherhoods" with several Turkish personalities.[1501] These prominent Turks included noblemen from both the Eastern and Western Gök-Türk states. Hence, it would make sense why the Turks of the fallen Eastern Gök-Türk Qaghanate and those of the dissolved Western Gök-Türk Qaghanate submitted to Emperor T'ai-tsung willingly after 630, if they knew that the Chinese emperor had Turkish ancestry.

After T'ai-tsung ended the government of the Eastern Gök-Türks, he followed the policy of bringing Turkish tribes into Chinese territories to be relocated among Chinese peasants. Ultimately he wanted to culturally assimilate them, hoping to eliminate the threat to China north of the Great Wall.[1502] In the meantime, the tribal leaders were to be kept as "hostages" in the Chinese capital so that without leadership, the tribal people ultimately would not be able to pose any threat to China.[1503]

According to an oral legend, Kür Šad was a Gök-Türk prince who was saddened and upset by the misfortunes of his people. So he gathered thirty-nine loyal noblemen around himself, and together they swore on a mission to assassinate Emperor T'ai-tsung or force him to assure the freedom of their people. But they also knew that their task could become a suicide mission. This mission became known in Turkish history as the quest of forty daredevils. The events presumably took place around the year 639. Against all odds, they were to going to storm the palace and capture the monarch. But their plans failed. Ultimately, all forty of them were killed. The news was inspiration for the patriotic Gök-Türks, but the assassination attempt appalled the T'ang court. Consequently, the emperor decided to relocate the Turkish tribes out of Chinese territories, to the north of the Ordos region, to create a buffer region between China and the Xueyantuo, who were thought to be part of ancient Töles (T'ieh-le) Turkish tribes in the north. These Turks formed short-lasting Sir-Tardush (Hsiyento) Khanate. Kür Šad and his daredevils did not achieve total freedom, but at least by sacrificing their lives, they prevented the assimilation of their people within Chinese territories. Perhaps their story was an inspiration to Il-teriš Qaghan and his followers when the Gök-Türks rose to power again in the year 682.

In 658 the Turkish tribal union of the Türgiš began to rule over the former Western Gök-Türk realm. By the early seventh century, the Eastern Gök-Türk rule was also weakening. The T'ang were quick to take advantage of this opportunity and actively pursued their "divide, dominate, assimilate" policy toward the Gök-Türks as the Han did against the Huns.[1504] The T'ang aimed to revive the Chinese expansionism of the Former Han at the expense of the Turks of Central Asia. Consequently, the T'ang created political unrest and internal divisions within the Gök-Türk aristocracy.

In the year 659, the fragmented Western Gök-Türks came under the suzerainty of the T'ang Chinese, who for a short time extended their influence to Afghanistan and the borders of Iran. But this situation put considerable economic pressure on the T'ang. The Turkish rebellions taking place in the Eastern and Western Gök-Türk territories weakened T'ang authority.[1505] But the Chinese still had significant influence over the area. With the fall of Gök-Türk authority in the western half of the empire in the early seventh century, the Turkish Töles (T'ieh-le) tribes gained independence in western Turkestan, and into the next century they often allied themselves with China against the Eastern Gök-Türks.[1506] In 646 T'ang emperor T'ai-tsung peacefully accepted Töles tribes into Chinese territory in the northern parts of modern-day Xinjiang Province.[1507]

With the Gök-Türk domain now under the influence of the T'ang, the Turkish qaghans were appointed by the Chinese emperor. Once again, as they did with the Huns (Xiong-nu), the Chinese politics temporarily succeeded against the Gök-Türks to control the lucrative Silk Road, the vital economic route connecting the East and the West. In all battles with the Chinese throughout old Asian history, the Turks found themselves in a struggle for this vital trade route. The Turks were not silk producers, but through the Silk Road they engaged in trade, selling horses to the Chinese and Chinese silk to the Eastern Romans. They employed Persian-speaking Sogdians as their merchants. The Turks also continued their alliance with the Eastern Romans against the Persian Empire to ensure the safe passage of westbound silk merchandise.[1508]

After the Eastern Turks lost control of their dominions to T'ang China in 630, a Turkish tribal group called Hsüeh-yen-t'o by the Chinese gained power in the steppes, but in 646 they too were brought under the suzerainty of T'ang China. While the Eastern Gök-Türks were under T'ang Chinese suzerainty, the emperor sent a princess bride to No-ho-po Qaghan to reward him for his adoption of pro-Chinese policies.[1509] In 652 the T'ang, acting against the Tibetans, agreed with T'u-yü-hun Qaghan to set up an alliance, which was consolidated with royal marriages between the Turkish monarchy and Chinese princesses. But in 682 the Eastern Gök-Türks regained power; now able to launch attacks against China, they again demanded interdynastic marriages.[1510] This was the beginning of the Second Gök-Türk Empire.

THE SECOND RISE OF THE STATE

The Tonyuquq inscriptions in Orkhon, erected in 726, describe how a small band of seven hundred warriors managed to rise to power in 682 to create the Second Eastern Gök-Türk Qaghanate under the leadership of Il-teriš Qaghan of the A-shih-na clan.[1511] In 682 the Second Gök-Türk Qaghanate period began as the Turks reorganized under the banner of Il-teriš Qaghan (also known as Qutlugh Qaghan, 682–91) from the royal family. With the help of Tonyuquq, an educated man from China, Il-teriš Qaghan reestablished Türk sovereignty by defeating the T'ang forces.

After Qutlugh Qaghan died, his brother Qapghan became the second emperor. According to an inscription on the tomb of his daughter, Qapghan ruled over thirty tribes.[1512] His empire included Oghuz tribes. Initially nine tribes joined this rejuvenated state. However, according to contemporary Tibetan and Chinese records, the Eastern Gök-Türks actually had twelve tribes.[1513] The Toquz-Oghuz were among the remaining eighteen tribes. According to the Chinese, the large T'ieh-le tribal union was also part of the new Gök-Türk state, and again according to Chinese records, in 620 the leading ten clans of this federation came to be known with the name Uighur.[1514] In this area the Khitans were also under the rule of the Eastern Gök-Türks starting in 697.[1515]

At the time the T'ang dynasty had lost power temporarily; late emperor Gaozong's consort Wu Tse-t'ien (690–705) rose to power until the T'ang reclaimed the throne. Qapghan Qaghan (691–716) of the Gök-Türks offered to give his daughter to a Chinese prince with the hope of having an insider in the Chinese court, perhaps with the intent to receive information and to interfere with state affairs. But when Chinese empress Wu Tse-t'ien made a counterproposal offering one of her relatives to marry the Turkish princess instead, Qapghan threatened to declare war to replace her with someone from the Li family to restore the T'ang.[1516] This event showed the strength of the Gök-Türks, which the T'ang dreaded.

Until it ended in 716, Qapghan's reign involved ambitious campaigns. Between the years 706 and 714, the Gök-Türks launched western military campaigns carried out by Qapghan's son Inal Tigin, Tarduš Šad (son of late Il-teriš Qaghan and future Bilge Qaghan), and Tonyuquq.[1517] Initially, the campaign was fought by Turk against Turk. In 706–7 they first defeated the Turkish tribe of Bayïrqu, in 709 they were victorious over the Kyrgyz, and in 710–11, marching through the Altai, they defeated the Türgiš. Perhaps their successes made them believe they were unstoppable, or they dreamed about recreating what their ancestors Bumïn Qaghan and Istemi Yabghu had achieved when, in the sixth century, these two brothers succeeded in forming one of the two true Eurasian Steppe empires in world history. But their hasty push would end up costing them. According to Muslim records, in 712–13 these mounted archers, after having initial difficulty crossing the Syr Darya, finally reached the Iron Gate in Tokharistan, somewhere between Samarkand and Balkh. But the Muslim Arabs managed to stop the Turks and force them to turn around.[1518] The Orkhon inscriptions do not mention any defeat.

After Qapghan passed away, his son Inal became qaghan. However, internal quarrels led to the death of Inal. Then Il-teriš Qaghan's son Tarduš Šad came to the throne with the acquired regnal name Bilge Qaghan (716–34). He ruled together with his brother Kül Tigin. The name or title *kül* among the Gök-Türks was used to indicate "glorious."[1519] According to the Orkhon inscriptions, together they turned the Gök-Türk Empire into an Asian giant. It is believed that under the rule of Kül Tigin and his brother Bilge Qaghan (Mo-ki-lien in Chinese), the empire reached its new zenith.

The Chinese unsuccessfully tried to break up the empire by pushing other Turkish tribes and hordes against the Gök-Türks. As a result, Kül Tigin and Bilge Qaghan (716–34) created their biggest legacy, the stone inscriptions known as the Orkhon inscriptions, sometime in the early eighth century. These inscriptions were intended to remind the Turkish nation of past lessons and urge them to remain unified against outsiders. They also warned the nation about Chinese inducements and intentions to destroy the Turkish unity. Hence, in a manner of speaking, these inscriptions, located in the Orkhon valley of modern-day Mongolia, carry nationalistic sentiments. One can compare these eighth-century inscriptions to the early twentieth-century warnings of Mustafa Kemal Atatürk in his famous "Address to the Youth," which made the Turkish nation aware of similar dangers that threatened its existence. Hence, the Orkhon inscriptions and Atatürk's address are similar in warning the Turkish nation to remain unified against external dangers.

Despite their superior numbers, the imperial Chinese military efforts to suppress the reemergence of Gök-Türk power were unsuccessful. The Chinese preferred to have a weak Turkish rule in Central Asia to protect their economic interests with the outside world. In 721 the Chinese T'ang were finally forced to make peace with the Turks. Once again, the famous Silk Road was in the hands of the Turks. For the most part, the Gök-Türks used a barter system for trading, but it appears that they also used some form of a monetary system. Coins with Turkish *tamghas* (seals) from as early as the mid-sixth century from the Gök-Türks and their vassals the Toquz-Oghuz, Türgiš, and Qarluq Turks have been found.[1520] These coins are among the earliest known Turkish coinage in history.

The second rise of the Gök-Türks did not last long, and they succumbed to internal political struggles once again. Soon after Bilge Qaghan was poisoned in 734, the Gök-Türks declined, their fall aided by subsequent revolts by primarily the Qarluqs and the Uighurs. After the fall of the Gök-Türks, the Sha-t'o Turks, a little-known people, left the territories of the former Western Gök-Türks and joined the Uighurs before moving on to China (chapter 5.5), where they ruled over northern China during most of the Five Dynasties (907–60) period.[1521]

THE FALL AND BETRAYAL

The Uighur Turks eventually became the masters of the Eastern Eurasian Steppe by betraying first their former masters, the Gök-Türks, and later their accomplices, the Basmïl and Qarluq Turks.[1522] The end of the Gök-Türk Qaghanate came during the rebellion events between 742 and 744.

The process started when the supreme qaghan of the Eastern Gök-Türks was overthrown by a coalition of the Basmïl, Qarluq, and Uighur tribes. The chief of the Basmïl Turks was made qaghan, but about two years later, he was brought down by the joint efforts of the Qarluqs and Uighurs. The Basmïls were annihilated. Ultimately, the Qarluqs were also betrayed, and the Uighurs finally took control of the territories of the former Eastern Gök-Türk Qaghanate and established their own state,[1523] which became the last Turkish nomadic empire centered in the territories of modern-day Mongolia.

The Basmïl tribes initially resided in the snowy regions to the north of the Gök-Türks, but later they moved south, to the Turfan area, before the Uighurs settled there.[1524] According to an eighth-century document written in Tibetan, the Basmïl territories were divided among other Turkish tribes of the Käštim, Bayïrqu (previously mentioned in the Orkhon inscriptions), and Hi-dog-kas (an unknown tribe).[1525] Meanwhile, in the west the Türgiš tribes, who used to be within the former Gök-Türk Empire, gave the Umayyad Arabs a difficult time in the eighth century, but they were also in conflict with their kinsmen the Qarluqs. In the year 739, after they lost their leader they were crushed between Arab and Chinese forces, and their territories were gradually taken by the Qarluqs.[1526]

THE AFGHANI GÖK-TÜRKS

According to the Chinese records, in 726 the territory of Gandhara (former name of Peshawar, Pakistan) was governed by a king from Gök-Türk stock, and his nephew governed Zabulistan (southern Afghanistan province by Ghazna); according to historians Biruni (973–1048) and Hsüan-tsang, Böri Tigin, born in a cave like the ancestor of the A-shih-na family, came to establish the Turk Shahi dynasty in this area in 630 or earlier.[1527] The Turk Shahis ruled a large area of eastern Afghanistan and northwestern Pakistan territories between the seventh and ninth centuries CE. The city of Puškulavati on the Indus was the Turkish king's winter residence, and Kapisa was the city of summer residence. In 664 the Muslim Umayyad Arabs met with fierce resistance by Turkish soldiers in this area. Interestingly, the Central Asian *böri* (wolf) head appeared on coins minted from the eighth century in the areas of Khorasan and Zabulistan, most likely attributed to the dynasty of Böri Tigin.[1528] This dynasty, which followed Buddhism, was also known as the Kabul Shahi, and late in the ninth century, it was replaced by non-Turkish Hindu Shahi dynasty of the Hindu faith. In summary, while A-shih-na clan was claimed to be related to the royal Xiong-nu (Asian Huns), it also formed the ruling body of the Gök-Türk Empire as well as the dynasties of the Khazars and the Kabul Shahi (also known as Turk Shahi). More will be presented in volume 2, chapter 2.2.

AFTER THE GÖK-TÜRKS

At its zenith the Gök-Türk Empire became so extensive that at different points it bordered the four great sedentary civilizations of its time: China, India, Persia, and the Eastern Roman Empire.[1529] It also united most Turkish tribes under one banner for the last time in history. In other words, with the collapse of the Gök-Türk Qaghanate, Turkish political unity in history ended. Suddenly the Turkish tribes found themselves dispersed over a wide geographic area from China to eastern Europe. But what they lost in unity they gained in land ownership. Over time, their scattering also played a role in their individual cultural differentiation as they became influenced by the locations they were in. In modern times those closer to China came under Chinese influence, those in western Turkestan underwent Russian influence, and those in the Middle East were affected more by Arab and Persian cultures.

5.4. THE POWER BROKERS OF CHINA

As presented in the previous chapter, the T'ang dynasty followed an expansionist policy against the Gök-Türks, as the Former Han dynasty had (unsuccessfully) during the era of the Huns. Both Chinese dynasties, when they realized that they could not bring down these Turkish powers militarily, resorted to their individual "divide, conquer, assimilate" policies. Thus, by stirring political intrigue within the nomadic confederation structure of the Gök-Türks, the T'ang were indirectly successful in weakening the Türk Empire in the seventh century. Finally, the mid-eighth-century rebellion of the Uighurs, Qarluqs, and Basmïls led to the fall of the Turkish giant to the north of China. Now, in an attempt to secure the Silk Road, the Chinese hoped to take full control of Central Asia. But to the dismay of the T'ang, the Chinese encountered a new threat in Turkestan with the advance of the Muslim Arabs. Furthermore, Mongolia, the former territory of the Eastern Gök-Türks in the north, was now claimed by the powerful Uighur Turks. Shortly after the Uighurs established their rule, they faced another Turkish threat from the north, the Kyrgyz, who wanted to move into Eastern Gök-Türk territories. But the Uighurs pushed back their kinsmen to the north in 758. Where did the Uighurs come from?

The Ting-ling were an ancient group of Turks present at least since the Asian Hun (Xiong-nu) Empire (chapter 3.1). It is believed that the Ting-ling gave rise to the Kao-ch'e (Qanglï) and T'ieh-le (later known as Töles) tribal federations.[1530] It has been suggested Uighurs came from the Töles (T'ieh-le) tribes.[1531] A similar suggestion is that Uighur Turks belonged to the Töles Turkish tribal confederation, which previously resided along the Selenga River in northern

Mongolia.[1532] According to Chinese archives, Uighurs are also believed to have originated from the Kao-ch'e (Qanglï), who were in turn descendants of the ancient Ting-ling tribes.[1533]

In short, it seems that the Uighurs may have originated from Kao-ch'e/Töles (see chapter 6) tribal groupings. However, it appears that the Uighurs later joined a tribal federation known as the Toquz-Oghuz, which, by the end of the sixth century, according to the Chinese, had previously been among the larger Töles (T'ieh-le) confederation of tribes.[1534] While the Turkish Töles (T'ieh-le) tribes in command of the former Western Gök-Türk territories in western Turkestan remained allies of China beginning in the seventh century, the Uighurs emerging from this large tribal federation in the eighth century had a tradition of alliance with China as well.[1535] As soon as the Uighurs came out of the domination of the Gök-Türks, they cooperated with T'ang China to deal with the remnants of the Gök-Türks. The leader of the Toquz-Oghuz tribal union was the Uighur qaghan from the single Uighur tribe, which was in a tribal federation with eight Oghuz tribes, hence the name Toquz-Oghuz (Nine Oghuz) for this union, which was to the west of the Gök-Türk qaghan's location. Yaghlaqar, the royal clan of the Uighurs, carried nine ornaments, as described in the Tibetan document,[1536] likely indicating nine *tugh* (horsetail insignia on flagpole), each representing a Toquz-Oghuz tribe. Uighur qaghan Ku-li P'ei-lo (744–47) was the founder of the Uighur Empire, and his son and his heir Mo-yen-ch'o (747–59) consolidated Uighur power over the Basmïl, Oghuz and Qarluq Turks and built the Uighur capital city and his imperial palace.[1537]

After taking over the territories of the Eastern Gök-Türks, the new Uighur qaghan intended to collect intelligence about his neighbors. Such information, which is found in Tibetan documents from the eighth century, was gathered when the Uighur qaghan sent envoys across the Eurasian steppes and beyond to understand his surroundings. The tribes or kingdoms surrounding his empire were mostly Turkish speaking, like his. There were the Kherged (likely meaning the Karait, who became prominent in the age of Genghis Khan—see volume 2, chapter 3) in the northeast, the Bükli tribes (mentioned in the Orkhon inscriptions) to the east, or in the direction of Koguryo (the area including northern Korea and southern Manchuria), the Naimans (volume 2, chapter 3) in the northwest, along with other unidentifiable Turkish tribes in the north, the Kyrgyz (volume 2, chapter 4.5) beyond these tribes in the north, the Pečeneg Turks (assisting the Uighur in their battles) in the northwest, and the Qarluq to the west.[1538] It is interesting to note that the Turkish Bükli tribe is described as being located in the direction of the former Korean state Koguryo, but in the eighth century, the tribe was identified with the Po-hai (also Bohai or Balhae, seventh to tenth century) state between modern-day northern Korea and southern Manchuria.[1539]

Just as the Huns and the Gök-Türks had, the Uighurs tried to establish control over other Turkish tribes. However, Chinese records suggest that in doing so they treated them harshly. Perhaps the excessive demands of the Uighurs or the decline of their authority toward the end of the eighth century allowed the rival Tibetan Empire to gather the Turkish tribes of the Qarluq, Gök-Türk (T'ü-chüeh), and Sha-t'o against the Uighurs to capture Pei-t'ing around the year 790.[1540] After the Uighurs lost this strategic territory, their efforts to recapture it were unsuccessful. Meanwhile, the Qarluq captured the Shen-t'u Valley from the Uighurs. Political turmoil among the nobility began to increase, and in the same year, the qaghan was poisoned by one of the *khatun*s (ladies) of the court.[1541] The domestic difficulties continued until 795, when Ku-tu-lu (Qutluğ) Qaghan turned the Uighur Empire into a formidable empire again.

THE ROLE OF RELIGION

Just like the other Turks of their time, the Uighurs followed the Tengriist faith. But in the eighth century, after they came to power, the Uighurs became acquainted with a new religion. Manichaeism was not actually a new religion, but since it could not find a place in Persia, where it originated in the third century CE, it found its way to China with the help of Persian-speaking Sogdian traders. In 762 Bügü Qaghan (Mou-yü), under whom the Uighurs reached the zenith of their power, met with the followers of Manichaeism while he was in Luoyang assisting the T'ang Chinese against the An Lushan Rebellion (755–63). Bügü Qaghan not only became a convert but also imposed his new

Manichaeist faith upon his own people. According to an ancient Turkish document, the Uighur people joyfully accepted their emperor's decision to embrace Manichaeism over their traditional Tengriism.[1542] Whether this is true is debatable.

In any case, under the influence of these traders, who wanted to have more influence than the Buddhist traders along the route of the traditional Silk Road, the Uighur Turks in 762 under Bügü Qaghan adopted Manichaeism as a state religion.[1543] Manichaeism was a gnostic religion synthesized from Christianity, Zoroastrianism, and Buddhism. In the ninth century, while the Uighurs in Mongolia followed the Manichaeist faith, the Xinjiang Province of modern-day China was inhabited by people of Buddhist and Nestorian Christian faiths, whereas China was mostly Buddhist. Since Manichaeism was the religion of the Persian-speaking Sogdians, the adoption of this faith as the official religion of the Uighurs allowed the Sogdians to increase their influence in the Turkish emperor's court.[1544] However, the influence of the Sogdians and the Manichaeist faith on Bügü Qaghan was not welcomed among conservative groups of Turkish nobility, who wanted to see the traditional cult of Central Asia return to their empire.

THE RELATIONS WITH CHINA

The Uighurs established peaceful relations with the T'ang dynasty of China. The T'ang, who pursued expansionism against the Gök-Türks, could no longer pursue the same policies, since they were considerably weakened. The annihilation of the Chinese at the Battle of Talas in 751 by the Muslim Arabs of the Abbasids was a devastating defeat for T'ang China, resulting in the loss of both morale and authority for the T'ang. Moreover, the Uighurs posed potential military threat to the Chinese. Another interesting point is that during the era of the Gök-Türk/Uighur Turks, many Turkish monarchs had Chinese princesses as wives. By contrast, the marriage of a Uighur princess to a Chinese prince in 756 was important and unique historically. A non-Chinese woman had not previously been admitted to the Chinese dynastic house; such an action was viewed as beneath Chinese royal standards. Another first is that, during the Uighur era, three daughters (Ning-kuo, Hsien-an, and T'ai-ho) of Chinese emperors married Turkish qaghans; previously the Chinese had always sent daughters of imperial kinsmen or kinswomen.[1545] By attempting to create their own terms, the Chinese tried to avoid giving the Uighurs the status of brothers; instead they preferred to view the Uighur monarchy as sons-in-law. The Chinese wanted to view the Chinese-Uighur relationship in their own way, as a superior/inferior family relationship.[1546] Nearly a millennium before, the Asian Hun (Xiong-nu) shan-yus politically were more successful than the Uighurs by obtaining equal status with the Chinese emperors of the Han dynasty during the pre-Wudi period by getting the coveted status of brothers.

THE AN LUSHAN REBELLION

An Lushan was a powerful Turkish official adopted by the Chinese T'ang emperor in his youth and serving in the Chinese army.[1547] Being from mixed Sogdian-Turkish stock, he was a governor general of the Ying prefecture.[1548] But a few years after the defeat of T'ang China by the Abbasid Arabs in 751, he rebelled against his emperor. The Chinese were not able to quell the rebellion. Hence, T'ang emperor Suzong (756–62) asked for help from the Uighurs, who responded by sending a cavalry force, which quelled the An Lushan Rebellion (755–63) and saved the T'ang dynasty from extinction.[1549] By starting a general rebellion, An Lushan initiated a series of civil wars that brought T'ang China to the brink of complete destruction; if it were not for the might of Uighur military power, China would have collapsed. Instead, the Uighurs launched successive military campaigns into China in 756, 757, 759, and 762; the last finally crushed the rebellion.[1550]

During the years when the Uighurs were helping the T'ang crush the An Lushan Rebellion, they were said to be involved in looting Chinese cities as well. These tragic stories were told only from the point of view of T'ang historians, but the Chinese were eager to demonize the Uighurs, even though the violence and pillage were at times started by the Chinese themselves.[1551] These events occurred during the reigns of Bügü Qaghan (759–79) and T'ang emperor T'ai-tsung (762–79). Clearly the Chinese feared that the Uighurs might invade China.[1552] In fact, the Uighurs, with their strong military, could have possibly overtaken China. In 779 Bügü Qaghan's Sogdian advisers encouraged him to invade China, but his chief minister and first cousin Tun Mo-ho opposed this idea, had him assassinated, and took over as the next qaghan.[1553] This drastic action was taken to prevent another drastic action, the invasion of China, which could have threatened the Uighur identity by assimilation into the Chinese culture.

The 755–63 insurgency not only exposed the weakness of T'ang China but also revealed the presence of powerful Turkish commanders and administrators within the Chinese governmental ranks. A-shih-na Ts'ung-li, from the Gök-Türk ruling clan, was among many Turkish aristocrats serving in the T'ang army to avoid Uighur rule. Many other non-Chinese commanders had joined in this rebellion against the rule of T'ang China as well.[1554] When the Uighurs responded to the appeal for help from the Chinese emperor, El-Etmiš Bilge Qaghan himself entered the military campaign in 756 as the general of his army. The direct involvement of the Turkish monarch in this military campaign indicated that the event was quite important for the Uighurs.

Indeed, it became clear that the 756 campaign was also intended to crush the troops of A-shih-na Ts'ung-li, who was in the process of gathering scattered Gök-Türk clans in the Ordos (Inner Mongolia) region in addition to the Toquz-Oghuz tribes, who opposed the rule of the Uighur clan of Yaghlaqar. It is apparent that A-shih-na Ts'ung-li split from the insurgents of the An Lushan Rebellion to organize the rebellious Turks for civil war and overthrow the Uighurs. In the eyes of the nomads, A-shih-na Ts'ung-li, from the royal Gök-Türk clan, was viewed as the rightful leader of the Turks.

The Uighur monarch, perceiving the danger, came with a large Uighur force joined by the Chinese forces of the T'ang, who also did not want to see the revival of the Gök-Türks. Even though the forces of A-shih-na Ts'ung-li were crushed, the leader escaped and joined the rebel forces under his relative General A-shih-na Ch'eng-ch'ing. Together they served under An Ch'ing-hsu, son of An Lushan. The An Lushan Rebellion brought the alliance of the Uighurs Turks and the T'ang Chinese against the Gök-Türk A-shih-na clan siding with the insurgents against the Chinese political establishment. Ultimately, the Uighur military assistance to T'ang China not only helped the T'ang regain their limited power but also, more importantly, weakened the hopes of the exiled Gök-Türks within China of restoring their former Gök-Türk Empire.[1555] When the Uighurs successfully ended the rebellions, they were allowed to sack the Chinese royal capitals as a reward. Taking advantage of T'ang weakness, the Uighurs went on to exploit China by acquiring large quantities of silk and other goods; in return they supplied many moribund horses in the name of trade.[1556]

POST-REBELLION SINO-TURKISH RELATIONS

Certainly the loss of the Battle of Talas in 751 against the Muslim Arabs was a serious blow to the T'ang Chinese. But the subsequent An Lushan Rebellion, suppressed in 762 with the help of the Uighur Turks, was even more damaging to T'ang control over China and its sphere of influence. Consequently, the Tibetans in 789, with the help of the Qarluq Turks and the remnants of the Western Gök-Türks, tried to seize the Turfan region from T'ang China. Once again, the Uighurs from Mongolia came down to defend the T'ang and eventually, in 803, occupied the area (Qočo) for themselves.[1557] The authority of the T'ang in the region was permanently weakened.

The continued reliance of the T'ang court on Uighur military strength allowed the Uighurs more freedom to dictate their terms to the Chinese.[1558] The T'ang managed to stay in power by defeating their enemies only with the help of the Uighur cavalry.[1559] An interesting note is that these Uighur chargers were known to wear masks during war.[1560] The once-expansionist T'ang dynasty, which came to power with the help of the Gök-Türks and then intended to conquer the Turkish territories in the seventh and eighth centuries, now found itself in an unfamiliar situation, depending on the Turks for their survival. Following the devastating An Lushan Rebellion, T'ang China was forced to make an alliance with the Uighurs against powerful Tibet, and this peace relationship was sealed with seven dynastic marriages.[1561] The power of the Uighurs over the Chinese is apparent from the fact that after Bügü

Qaghan's conversion to Manichaeism, the T'ang emperors had to tolerate this faith until the Uighur Empire fell in 840, after which Emperor Wu-tsung (840–46), known for his religious intolerance, persecuted Manichaeists and other foreign religions within China.[1562] However, while the Turks remained strong T'ang China benefited from the formidable Uighur cavalry, which included women warriors as well.[1563]

Even though Uighur embassies to China were considered to be tributary, according to Chinese records, in fact the Uighurs, who had military might on their side, did not accept being vassals or servants of China.[1564] Instead, the Uighur Turks, who had no intention of conquering China, considered themselves the protectors of the T'ang dynasty.[1565] The situation was a golden opportunity for the Uighurs. The price for peace was a tribute in Chinese goods that the Chinese had to pay the Turkish qaghan, just as the former Chinese emperors had paid the Huns (Xiong-nu) and the Gök-Türks in the previous centuries. Furthermore, the practice of giving Chinese princesses to Uighur rulers, as was also done for the Huns and the Gök-Türks, was resumed.[1566]

There was, however, a brief low point in the relations between China and the Uighur Empire. This became apparent by the end of the reigns of Bügü Qaghan, the Turkish emperor, and T'ai-tsung, the Chinese emperor. After the An Lushan Rebellion, upon coming to the Uighur throne, Tun Mo-ho Qaghan tried to improve relations with China. However, Emperor Te-tsung had a deep hatred of the Uighurs. When the Chinese emperor decided to deport Uighur and Sogdian merchants from China, the Sogdians tried to persuade the Chinese to kill the Uighur merchants, but instead the Chinese massacred both the Sogdians and the Uighurs and later sent their coffins to the Uighur qaghan with Chinese envoys. Tun Mo-ho initially intended to take revenge on the Chinese envoys, but he showed restraint and demanded a hefty price for their atonement and payment for the previously traded horses that were not paid for in exchange for the lives of the T'ang envoys.[1567]

The Chinese were able to deal with the disastrous An Lushan Rebellion (755–63) only with the vital assistance of the Uighur cavalry. However, the troubles of the Chinese dynasty were not over yet. New domestic problems arose with the rise of the revolts (782–84) of Chu T'ao and Chu Tz'u. The

T'ang again asked for help from the Uighurs, but this time the Turks decided to give tacit assistance to the rebels.[1568] In 787, when Tun Mo-ho Qaghan sent his envoys to demand a Chinese princess bride for peace, Emperor Te-tsung had to overcome his bitter feelings to give his daughter in marriage.[1569] From this point on, however, the relations began to improve again.

The weakened T'ang dynasty chose to be at peace with the Uighurs, thus pursuing a friendly relationship. Sogdian traders once again became agents for the Turks to engage in horse/silk trading, as they were for the Gök-Türks previously. According to T'ang records, the Uighurs sold one hundred thousand horses annually for one million bolts of silk.[1570] The excess silk was then sold to the West with the help of Sogdian merchants. Consequently, trade between these two nations began to grow, allowing the Uighurs to prosper.[1571] The primary exchange between them was Chinese silk and tea for Uighur horses, as was the case for prior nomadic Turkish empires. Turkish land was also used for agriculture. Uighur prosperity led to the formation of two well-known historic Uighur cities, Ordu-Balïq, in the Orkhon River valley, and Beš-Balïq, close to the Selenga River.

THE CHANGE IN DYNASTY AND DECLINE

In 779, after Bügü Qaghan was murdered in a coup d'état, Sogdian influence over the court declined. However, after the death of Tun Mo-ho Qaghan in 789, political turmoil followed and consequently led to the temporary decline of Uighur power and prestige. Finally, in 795, the authority of the royal clan Yaghlaqar (Yao-lo-ko) passed to the Hsieh-tieh tribe.[1572] Ku-tu-lu (known to the Chinese as Huai-hsin) Qaghan, the founder of the new Uighur dynasty, restored the power of the empire, and after taking Pei-t'ing from the Tibetan Empire, he extended his dominion as far west as Fergana.[1573] During his reign, the influence of the Sogdians and the Manichaeist faith in the Uighur Empire once again increased. However, after the death of Pao-i Qaghan in 821, the irreversible decline of the empire began.

There were multiple factors in the decline of the Uighurs, including the nobility's addiction to a luxurious lifestyle, skirmishes with the powerful

Kyrgyz Turks in the north, and domestic problems complicated by a rebellion. In 839 the attack upon the Uighur palace by powerful minister Chüeh-lo-wu with the assistance of the Sha-t'o Turks resulted in the qaghan committing suicide, and Prince Ho-sa was placed on the throne.[1574] Finally, the severe winter of 839 led to the wasting of a significant portion of livestock, which crippled the Uighur economy. In 840, an Uighur rebel invited the nemesis of the state, the Kyrgyz, who fell upon the Uighur Empire bringing widespread destruction. Chü-lu-mo-ho, a Uighur general at odds with Minister Chüeh-lo-wu, returned leading one hundred thousand Kyrgyz cavalry, with the intent to kill the qaghan and Minister Chüeh-lo-wu and destroy the Uighur fortress and palace.[1575] Suddenly the once-powerful Uighurs became stateless. But as the pages of history illustrate, the Uighur Turks did not disappear after the fall of their empire at the hands of the Kyrgyz. Instead, they demonstrated their resilience with their political continuation, and they excelled culturally and socially.[1576]

THE CITY BUILDERS OF CENTRAL ASIA

According to the Chinese, before 744 the Uighurs were a nomadic people with excellent skills in horsemanship and archery.[1577] After they established their empire, they began the transition to a sedentary lifestyle. Archaeological finds have demonstrated that the Uighurs had metallurgists, potters, engravers, blacksmiths, sculptors, stonemasons, weavers, and jewelers, and they also had the ability to mine iron ore, copper, gold, and silver.[1578] Agriculture apparently gained significant acceptance among the Uighur populace as well. Nevertheless, even with the social transformation from a nomadic to a sedentary lifestyle, the nomads still contributed to the Uighur economy with their livestock.

The Uighur Turks were a highly educated people who used three different scripts to produce documents: the Sogdian script of Aramaic-Syriac origin, the Turkic-Runic script that the Gök-Türks used, and the Tibetan script. It seems that the Uighurs used the Tibetan language to produce either sacred Buddhist texts or administrative documents.[1579] The Uighurs were also known for building cities, and their capital, Ordu-Balïq, was founded by the Orkhon River in 757.[1580] A ninth-century Muslim traveler described the Uighur royal city of Ordu-Balïq as a populous city rich in markets and agricultural activities.[1581] He was given a reception in a golden tent able to house one hundred people on the flat roof of the monarch's castle.[1582] This building was a multistoried palace in brickwork, decorated with stucco and bronze doors ornamented in the Central Asian style of tamghas.[1583] The city is known as Khar-Balgas (also referred to as Karabalghasun) in modern-day Mongolia, and it is today part of the Orkhon Valley Cultural Landscape, a UNESCO World Heritage Site. Tarim Ibn Bahr, the Arab visitor to the Uighur capital in the early ninth century, described his amazement at the size, wealth, and power of the Uighur Empire.[1584]

THE UIGHUR TRAGEDY

As mentioned above, toward the middle of the ninth century, Uighur strength declined in the face of internal power struggles, famine, and disease. Finally, paying a heavy price for their luxurious sedentary lifestyle by compromising their security, they were overrun by the nomadic raiders of the Kyrgyz Turks.[1585] These newcomers from the north were once the vassals of the Uighurs, but by taking advantage of the Uighurs' chaotic rule, the Kyrgyz dealt a fatal blow to the Uighurs in 840.[1586] Unlike the Uighurs, who were educated and successful builders in Central Asia, the Kyrgyz were known simply as livestock breeders and providers of merchandise from the Siberian forests.[1587] As stated earlier, the fall of the Uighurs was also facilitated by internal struggle, rebellion, and natural disaster.

After the crushing fall of their state, a group of Uighurs moved southwest from the territories of contemporary Mongolia into the Turfan region in present-day Xinjiang in China, where they formed the nucleus of the modern-day Uighurs. The remaining Uighurs in the steppes migrated south into T'ang China in two groups to seek sanctuary there; they were unaware they were moving toward their doom.[1588]

The first group arrived under the leadership of a commander (*tigin*). These newcomers inadvertently created a refugee crisis in northern China. The

Chinese were initially unaware of what had happened to the Uighurs in the steppes and were caught unprepared. After they informed the T'ang emperor that the Uighur homeland in modern-day Mongolia had been overtaken by the Kyrgyz Turks, the Uighurs officially requested asylum.[1589] Later, in 842, the second group of Uighur people arrived with Öge Qaghan (the emperor). Negotiations continued in order to find a solution for these newcomers seeking asylum in the Chinese empire, but T'ang officials were secretly scheming to solve the refugee crisis. Ultimately, in 843, the T'ang massacred the Uighurs who were seeking asylum in China.[1590] Öge Qaghan barely escaped the carnage and remained in exile with his remaining followers. After the qaghan died in 846, his wife, T'ang princess T'ai-ho, returned to China, where she was awarded a high rank.[1591]

THE REVIVAL OF THE UIGHURS

Turfan, in central part of modern-day Xinjiang Uighur Autonomous Region of China, historically came under Chinese rule during the T'ang dynasty (618–907) and later during the Qing dynasty (1756–1912). In the mid-ninth century, when the Uighurs took over this region, the land came to be known as Qočo, probably deriving its name from the Chinese Kao-ch'ang.[1592] Turfan and its environs had been a territory of the former Uighur Empire since the year 803, but the Uighurs settled here in large numbers after their state was destroyed in 840 by the Kyrgyz. Under their leader, P'u-ku Chün, in 866 they managed to transform Turfan into a new Uighur Kingdom with the old city Kao-ch'ang as the capital. Over time as the name of the city became Qočo, the polity was named the Qočo Uighur Kingdom (866–1283).[1593]

Until the Uighur Qaghanate collapsed, the Uighur Turks followed the Manichaean faith, but when a group of them moved to Turfan to flee the Kyrgyz Turks, they converted to Buddhism. Consequently, their leader dropped the use of the traditional Turkish title *qaghan* in favor of another Turkish one, *idiqut*, meaning "sacred majesty," a typical Buddhist nomenclature. Therefore, these Buddhist Uighurs were also known as Idiqut Uighurs. The state that they formed in Turfan was eventually known as the Qara-Khoja Kingdom, also known as the Gaochang Kingdom.

The change of religion was likely a strategic one for these Uighurs. At the time, Turfan and its environment were dominated by multiple religious faiths, and the Uighurs were known for their tolerance.[1594] In the Uighur Qočo Kingdom, the Turks were exposed to three religions: Manichaeism, Buddhism, and Nestorian Christianity.[1595] After the destruction of the Uighur Empire at the hands of the Kyrgyz, who followed the Tengriist faith, the surviving Uighurs chose Buddhism in order to be accepted by the other Buddhist peoples in the region, the Chinese and the Tibetans.

The Uighurs were also a very educated people, with a literacy rate similar to that of the former Roman Empire, the seat of the Western civilization (5–30 percent). In fact, it has been suggested that the literacy rate within the Uighur Qočo Kingdom was about 30 percent.[1596] The level of education facilitated to the cultivation of the Manichaeist faith among the Uighurs. But in time as they converted to Buddhism, they became great patrons of this Indian religion as well.

The Qara-Khoja Khanate (Gaochang) lasted from the ninth century into the late thirteenth century, almost four centuries. During this time they abandoned their Orkhon Turkic script in favor of a new script, which later came to be known as the Uighurjin script. The Buddhist Uighurs remained in relative peace. In 907, they witnessed the fall of the T'ang dynasty, which in 843 had massacred their tribesmen who were seeking asylum in northern China. In Turfan, now their new home, the Idiqut Uighurs prospered, benefiting from being right in the middle of the Silk Road. They not only thrived in commerce and agriculture but also developed a great knowledge base.

By the middle of the twelfth century, the Qočo Uighurs were in command of the Taklamakan oases, but in 1130 they decided to become vassals of the rising power of the Western Liao, or the Qara-Khitans, governing northern China. Later, Barchuq Art Tigin, the king of the Qočo Uighurs with the title *idiqut*, decided to side with Genghis Khan rather than the Khitans. In 1209, having assassinated the Khitan official, the state declared allegiance to the Mongol Empire. When the Mongols of Genghis Khan came to power, they called upon the Uighur elite to guide them into their future.[1597] The vassal status of the Uighurs remained under the Mongol Yuan dynasty of China, but their polity continued to be known as the Qočo Uighur Kingdom.

Finally, the Uighur state fell victim to a Mongol internal feud for the throne in 1283. The surviving royal Uighur family and people fled into China and settled in Yung-ch'ang, a county in Kansu Province.[1598] Following the departure of some Uighurs from Turfan, the area was governed after 1368 by the Čaghatai Mongols, who were expelled from western Turkestan by rising Turkish warlord Timur (Tamerlane) (volume 2, chapter 4.4). This area, which already had Muslim inhabitants but also significant Budhist population, eventually became Muslim majority.[1599] In the 1670s the Turfan region and its remaining Uighur inhabitants came under Zunghar (also referred to as the Junghar) Mongol rule, but in 1720 the Chinese forces of the Qing (Ch'ing) dynasty pushed the Mongols out and took the land for China. In the early 1900s, the local people referred to Qočo as Idiqut Shahri (King's City),[1600] reflecting the proud past of the Uighur people.

Starting with the Asian Huns (Xiong-nu), for over a millennium, the Turks had a multilevel relationship with the Chinese. But the collapse of the Uighur Qaghanate in the ninth century and the continued migration of Turkish tribes toward the west essentially ended such interactions. The Sha-t'o Turks (see the next chapter), who succeeded in establishing short-lived dynasties within China,[1601] were the last of the Turks to have close contact with the Chinese in the tenth century. After this point, the Chinese would deal with the Mongols and the Tungus.

THE TUTORS OF THE MONGOLS

With the fall of the T'ang dynasty came a power vacuum in China. Southern China eventually came under the rule of the Song dynasty (960–1279), and the north came under the influence of the Khitan (known as the Liao dynasty, 907–1125). But after they were pushed out by the Tungusic Jin dynasty, the Khitans (likely with mixed ethnicities of Tungus and Turco-Mongol presence) moved to the southern portion of modern-day Kazakhstan to form the Qara-Khitan Khanate (1125–1218). Here they became a power in Central Asia, and the Buddhist Uighurs chose to become their vassals. It appears that under the Khitan, the Uighurs had favorable positions. But in 1209, believing in the promising future of young Mongol ruler Genghis Khan, the Uighur Turks voluntarily submitted to the Mongol Empire instead.

Genghis Khan paid back the Uighurs by hiring them into the ranks of the Mongol Empire's hierarchy, where the Idiqut Uighurs served as educators and advisers for the Mongol elite.[1602] In essence, the Idiqut Uighurs were able to influence the Mongols, who by the end of the thirteenth century had converted to Buddhism as well (volume 2, chapter 3.3). The Mongols borrowed many cultural traits from the Uighur Turks, including the Uighurjin alphabet.[1603] Overall, the Uighur Turks played a key role in the development of the political institutions of the Qara-Khitan Khanate and later of the Mongol Empire of Genghis Khan.[1604] Under the Mongol Ilkhanid rule of Iran, the Buddhist Uighurs were also prominent in the Iranian Mongol court. In fact, they appeared to be active throughout the Mongol Empire's territories, particularly in administrative and religious roles.[1605] Educated Uighurs entered the Mongol court to serve as bureaucrats as well.[1606]

THE CONVERSION TO ISLAM

The Islamization process of Turfan and the Tarim basin—where the Buddhist Uighurs lived—began when the Turkish (Qarluq) Qara-Khanids used this territory as their base in the eleventh century. Over time, as the people began to abandon their Buddhist faith in favor of Islam, Uighur identity also seemed to weaken. The process of conversion was slow. Between the eleventh and sixteenth centuries, the Uighurs remained a sophisticated society and eventually converted to the Sunni sect of Islam.[1607] Between the late fourteenth and seventeenth centuries, the Čaghatai Mongols, previously pushed out of western Turkestan, became instrumental in solidifying the presence of Islam in this area. Although the land remained heavily Turkish, the Uighur name was no longer used by the end of the eighteenth century. It was not until the 1921 Soviet Convention for Central Asia in Tashkent that the Soviets decided to call the Turks living in Xinjiang Uighurs in order to create "national" groups of people in Central Asia. The ultimate hope for the creation of national groups rather than ethnic groups was to prevent pan-Turkish revolt in Central Asia against the rule of Moscow.[1608]

5.5. THE DESERT PEOPLE

Living in the territories of the former Wu-sun Turks (chapter 3), the Sha-t'o Turks were once a small tribal confederacy originally part of the larger Western Gök-Türk federation.[1609] Its ruling clan's name came from its royal family name, Ch'u-yüeh,[1610] as recorded in Chinese records. In another description of historical events, it is said that the Sha-t'o tribal confederacy was a descendant of the Ch'u-yüeh tribe within the Western Gök-Türk tribal union.[1611] The Sha-t'o were probably a group of three tribes; the leading royal clan was the Ch'u-yüeh, and the second tribe, the So-ko, apparently previously belonged to the Türgiš, but the name of the third one is not clear.[1612] The Chinese name of the leading clan, Ch'u-yüeh, is thought to have been Čiğil in Turkish.[1613] It is believed that the Chinese name Sha-t'o was actually a translation of the Turkish word *čöl* for "desert."[1614] In other words, these people were known as the Desert Turks or Sand Turks.[1615] Under the Western Gök-Türks, they lived near Lake P'u-lei (Barköl) in eastern Turkestan, with their capital in Beš-Balïq.[1616]

MOVING TO CHINA

When the Western Gök-Türk polity completely ceased to exist in 643 owing to an internal power struggle, the Sha-t'o came under Chinese T'ang control until about 712, when they had to run away from the incursions of the Tibetans. Later, they joined their kinsmen the Uighurs. When the Uighurs assisted the T'ang Chinese in their attempt to quell the An Lushan Rebellion, the Sha-t'o joined the Uighurs in their military activities. Consequently, a group of the Sha-t'o remained in the Shanxi area in China until about 810.[1617] The remaining group came under the rule of the Uighurs in 789.[1618] In the beginning of the ninth century, the Sha-t'o were all forced to leave the Uighur city of Beš-Balïq.[1619] This group of Sha-t'o moved into territories under the control of the Tibetans. In the year 808, living in the present-day Kansu area, they rebelled against their Tibetan overlords, and eventually in 809, they settled in the northern stretch of the Chinese Ordos region.[1620]

However, their escape from Tibet was not an easy task; in fact it became an epic story. In 808 the Sha-t'o, following very rugged terrain, succeeded in accomplishing their most difficult retreat from the Tibetan troops.[1621] It has been suggested that after escaping Tibetan control, they first moved toward the Ötüken Mountains, a sacred place for the former Gök-Türks, where they wanted to build an independent state. After they failed in their quest, they moved to Yen-chou, in northern China, where they joined with the previously settled Sha-t'o in Shanxi.[1622] But they split again and finally settled in separate groups in T'ai-yüan (Shanxi), northern Kansu, and the eastern Ordos Steppe. The last group eventually succeeded in developing significant military strength; they overthrew the Later Liang dynasty and formed their own Later T'ang dynasty in northern China. Upon their arrival in China, the Sha-t'o Turks appear to have followed both Tengriist and Buddhist faiths, but upon becoming rulers of northern China, they adopted Chinese religious rites into their culture. The Sha-t'o emperors of China visited the well-known Buddhist caves in China at Yün-Kang and Lung-men (both are UNESCO World Heritage Sites), which were built previously by the T'o-pa Turks.[1623]

THE GUARDS OF THE T'ANG

Upon the Sha-t'o's initial arrival in China, the Chinese military governor of this area welcomed the Sha-t'o warriors and admitted them into the Chinese army.[1624] As guards of the Chinese army along the northern Chinese borders, the Sha-t'o Turks also provided security for the Chinese by crushing rebellions within the Celestial Empire. Consequently, with their military abilities, they were able to rise to power.[1625] According to Chinese records, in 880 the governor of the Chiang-chou was a Sha-t'o Turk, and in 882 there is mention of seventeen thousand tribal warriors of the Sha-t'o coming down from the north to assist the Chinese royals.[1626] During the Huang Ch'ao Rebellion, when T'ang emperor Hsi-tsung realized that he could not retake his imperial city, Ch'ang-an, from the rebels by using Chinese forces alone, he asked for assistance from Sha-t'o Turk leader Li K'o-yung, who pushed the rebels back with his warriors in 883.[1627] The Sha-t'o Turks were described by the Chinese as courageous warriors, having provided meritorious service in war, and from 830 they became the dominant non-Chinese element in the Chinese army.[1628] Through the remainder of the ninth century, the Sha-t'o defended China against incursions by Central Asian nomads, and it is believed that they also may have played a role in the fall of the Uighur Empire in the same century.[1629]

By 874 many Sogdians (Iranian people) in the Ordos region of China had joined the Sha-t'o tribes, known as the Three Tribes of the Sha-t'o.[1630] According to the records, although many Sogdians acquired Turkish titles and, similarly, many Turks took on Sogdian surnames, the influence of Turkish culture was quite powerful.[1631] Even though, the Sha-t'o culture remained strongly Turkish, many of its features were borrowed from the Chinese.[1632] It is interesting to note that the Sha-t'o, having great interest in the art of sculpture, became imitators of the T'o-pa style.[1633] Chinese cultural dominance over time was going to have its effect in assimilating the Sha-t'o later in the tenth century.

THE FALL OF THE T'ANG

The Huang Ch'ao Rebellion (874–84) in China late in the ninth century precipitated the rapid decline of the T'ang dynasty. The final years of the last T'ang emperor were riddled with political power struggles between warlords within the Chinese empire. Preparing to usurp the throne, Zhu Quanzhong, a powerful warlord, ordered the death of Emperor Zhaozong. The assassination took place in September 904, followed by the coronation of the deceased emperor's nine-year-old son, Li Zhu (Aidi).[1634] Then, early in 905, Zhu Quanzhong had the late emperor's brothers killed. The observation of two comets between May and June 905 was interpreted as a sign of what was to come. In the summer of 905, by his order, all high court officials were gathered at a place known as the White Horse postal station, just north of Bianzhou. That night they were all butchered, and their lifeless bodies were thrown in the Yellow River. This event on July 5, 905, came to be known as the White Horse massacre.[1635] Even though Zhu Quanzhong was now in an opportune position to achieve his imperialist ambitions, he still had strong opponents, such as Li K'o-yung (or Li Keyong), the Sha-t'o Turk leader.[1636] But Zhu Quanzhong finally succeeded in forcing young puppet emperor Li Zhu to abdicate the imperial throne to him in 907, and a year later, he had Li Zhu poisoned. Zhu Quanzhong then established his Later Liang dynasty (907–23). With this move, the emerging political chaos across China allowed the warlords to declare their own polities, and as a result, the Five Dynasties (907–60) and Ten Kingdoms (902–79) periods in China began.

During this time of political upheaval in China, the T'ang gave birth to multiple small states. Hence, China once again was disunited. Among the five dynasties during this period, three of them were founded by the Sha-t'o; these were the Later T'ang, the Later Chin (or Jin), and the Later Han.[1637] Though these three dynasties were formed by people of Turkish stock, these foreign state builders continued to respect the old Chinese bureaucratic system.[1638] Hence, they protected the T'ang governmental system, which was itself an adaptation of the prior Turkish Northern Wei governmental system.[1639] In addition, when the Five Dynasties and Ten Kingdoms period began, the Khitan tribal organization established itself in the northeast of China as the Liao dynasty (907–1125), but this polity did not become part of proper Chinese history.

THE KHITAN INFLUENCE ON CHINA

The Khitan became power brokers for China just as the Uighurs were in the prior century. Particularly in northern China, they had significant influence. Even though it was the Chinese Song dynasty (960–1279) that later reunited China, the land of the Celestial Empire came to be known in the West by the tribal name of the Liao dynasty—Khitan, also known as Khitai—and therefore China was known in medieval times as Cathay.[1640] However, for the majority of Turks, even as late as the eleventh century among the Qara-Khanids, China remained to be known as Tabgač or Tamgač, after the Tabgač (T'o-pa) Turks, who formed the Northern Wei dynasty of China late in the fourth century.

The Khitan, like the Xianbei before them, were heterogeneous tribes of different ethnicities. Initially their weakness came from their Mongol-style social organization, as their tribes remained independent from one another within their loose federation. But beginning in the period of T'ang China, they came under strong Turkish influence with possible Turkish domination over large groups of Khitan and intermarriages with the Turks.[1641] The Khitan tribes formed a confederacy, which included Turkish, Mongol, and Tungus elements.[1642] The imperial Xiao clan of the Khitans has been suggested to have been of Turkish origin.[1643]

As stated earlier the Later Liang (907-923) was the first of the Five Dynasties seen after the T'ang fell, but this dynasty had short lasting life when it was conquered by the Sh'a-to Turks in 923. Meanwhile, the strategic region of the Sixteen Prefectures was under the control of these Turks, and the Khitans coveted this territory. As a result, they instigated rebellion among the Turks, and this insurrection led to the formation another dynasty by the Sh'a-to Turks known as the Later Jin. However, eventually the Khitans did not only confiscate the Sixteen Prefectures by 938 but also they took over the Later Jin dynasty's realm by 946. Subsequently, they adopted their dynastic name Da Liao in 947. Yet, there are also records suggesting that the name Liao was already present as early as 938. The Khitans remained in northern China until they were pushed out to Central Asia by the Jin dynasty of the Jurchens in 1125 (volume 2, chapter 3.2).

THE RISE AND FALL OF THE SHA-T'O

It is believed that the entire Sha-t'o population may have been around one hundred thousand. Therefore, it is important to note that the Sha-t'o maintained their hegemony in northern China with a small group of fighters.

When Li K'o-yung, the Sha-t'o leader, formed his army, the core group of his force was his ten thousand Sha-t'o Turk warriors, but he also had Chinese and Tatar soldiers. The bulk of the Turkish army consisted of the cavalry.[1644] Finally, in 923 Li K'o-yung, the leader of the Sha-t'o Turks, with the assistance of the Khitans of the Liao dynasty, rebelled against the Later Liang to start the rule of the Sha-t'o over northern China. Consequently, the Sha-t'o Turks formed three successive dynasties demonstrating imperial control over most of northern China for a period of about twenty-seven years. These imperial states successively were the Later T'ang (923–36), the Later Chin (936–46), and the Later Han (947–50).[1645]

After declaring himself the emperor of China, Li K'o-yung moved his capital back to the former T'ang capital of Luoyang. To keep a large cavalry force, the Sha-t'o administration decided in 925 to confiscate all horses from Chinese citizens, and the southern Ordos provided the necessary pastures needed for these horses. But the maintenance of one cavalry warrior became quite costly, the equivalent of maintaining five ordinary soldiers, and the cavalry force required nearly 70 percent of the entire budget.[1646] Later, taking advantage of the political unrest in the state, another member of the Sha-t'o Shi Jingtang, with the help of the Khitan, proclaimed the rule of the Later Chin dynasty (936–46) in Kaifeng, thus ending the Later T'ang. As a result, with the backing of the powerful Khitan, the Sha-t'o remained in control of most of the northern territories of China, including Shanxi and Beijing. When this dynasty defied the Khitans, the Later Jin ceased to exist after it attracted the wrath of the Khitans. However, even though the invaders penetrated into northern China, they did not intend to stay, and therefore, upon their return, another Sha-t'o Turk, Liu Zhiyuan, declared his Later Han dynasty (947–50), which became the shortest dynastic rule ever in Chinese history. When a Han Chinese commander staged a rebellion, the dynasty fell, thus ending the imperial rule of the Sha-t'o Turks of northern China.

The fall of the Later Han gave away to the formation of the Northern Han Kingdom (951–79) of the Sha-t'o Turks and the Later Zhou dynasty (951–60) of the Han Chinese. The latter became the last imperial house of the Five Dynasties and Ten Kingdoms period. In 960 Chinese general Zhao Kuangyin staged a coup d'état and established the Chinese Song dynasty (960–1279), which began to take the scattered smaller kingdoms within China proper one by one. In 979 the Northern Han Kingdom of the Sha-t'o Turks was the last remaining kingdom within China when the Song came to take it. Because of this conquest, fifty-six years of Sha-t'o Turkish rule in China ended, and China was once again reunified.

Did the Sh'a-t-o Turks disappear after the tenth century? Archival Chinese records indicate that this group of nomadic warriors continued to exist in northern Chinese territory at least until the rise of the Mongols in the thirteenth century. In fact, based on the Song dynasty records there has been some remarks regarding the ethnic relationship between the Sh'a-to and the Tatars as well as Genghis Khan of the thirteenth century; more on this matter is provided in volume 2, chapter 3.2.

In 1976 a stele with inscriptions was discovered in the historic Hexi Corridor, also known as the Gansu Corridor which was once a well-known historical trading route connecting the East to the West in China's present-day Gansu province along the Silk Road. These writings were thought to be referring to a prominent Tangut family's history in this region during the rule of the Mongol Empire. However, in 1983 a Chinese scholar suggested that principal characters mentioned in these texts were likely the descendants of the tenth century Sh'a-to (Shatuo) Turks who were later subjects of the Tangut Empire and subsequently the Mongol Empire.[1647] The Sh'a-to were not the only Turks in Gansu province, in fact, their kinsmen the Uighurs were also living in this vicinity. Indeed, this region, also known by its historic name of Suzhou or Sügčü, was residential place for a large Uighur population especially during the Yuan dynasty period.[1648]

Guazhou, (formerly known as Anxi) in present-day Guozhou County in Gansu province in China, is known to be home to famous Buddhist Yulin Grottoes (also referred to as the Ten Thousand Buddhas' Gorge) on the cliffs of Qilian Mountains on the banks of the Yulin River, south of Anxi. These grottoes possess largest amount of Uighur inscriptions discovered, and this fact suggested that the Uighur language was once very popular in this territory. Indeed, Uighur influence in many aspects of life in Yuan China was quite apparent, and this was true from the presence of their artists, military and government officials as well as their Buddhist clergy in the Hexi Corridor;[1649] more on this subject matter is discussed in volume 2, chapter 3.3.

The Song remained in control of the Celestial Empire until it fell to the Mongols of Genghis Khan in the thirteenth century. By the end of the first millennium, the Turks no longer had serious political or economic interactions with the Chinese since only a minority of Turks was left in the Eastern Eurasian Steppe. Hence, the Far Eastern Turkish experience for the most part had ended by the end of the tenth century. In the second volume of 'The Turks' we will therefore turn our attention to Turkish history evolving in western Central Asia, eastern Europe, and the Middle East.

Chapter 6:

TRIBAL ENTITIES UNTIL THE EIGHTH CENTURY

Many nations evolved from their own tribal past experiences. The Turks also had proud rich tribal past history. In fact, many of their tribes did not only made an impact on the evolution of modern-day Turkish nation but also, they contributed to the gradual development of world civilizations as well. Today we know that Turkish history officially began with the emergence of warlike Turkish tribes under the leadership of the Xiong-nu, or the Asian Huns. These steppe nomadic people felt the necessity to form a state for security purposes when they faced an unprovoked attacked by the Ch'in (Qin) emperor of China in 214 BCE. Until this challenge by the Chinese, the primary relationship of the Xiong-nu with their giant southern neighbor essentially involved trade interactions. Chinese trade items such as silk as well as agricultural goods were important merchandise for the Huns. But disagreements and negative factors, such as the Chinese not wanting to trade with their northern neighbors, often led to skirmishes between the nomads and the peasants of northern China. Eventually, Ch'in (Qin) emperor began building long defense wall by uniting existing walls of separate northern towns initially constructed in the fifth century BCE. The intent of this project was to protect the northern borders of China from the incursions of the Huns.[1650] Essentially the unification of northern city walls led to the construction of the greatest military structure of the world known as the Great Wall of China. However, the contemporary Great Wall of China is the product of reconstruction accomplished by the native Ming dynasty (1368–1644) after the Mongol Yuan dynasty (1271–1368) was pushed out of China. Only very limited ruins of the original wall remain today.

ANCIENT TURKISH TRIBES

Although the Hunnish warriors may have formed the earliest known state in the Turkish history, there were older Turkish speaking tribes, well before the emergence of the Huns. For the most part we rely on Chinese records for ancient history of the Turks.

In ancient Chinese history we know that during the Shang dynasty period (1600–1045 BCE) the Chinese met a formidable foe in ancient powerful tribal people known as the *Kuei-fang*. Subsequently, the Shang dynasty was brought down by the new conquerors of China known as the *Zhou*, who were a warlike foreign tribal people.[1651] Both the Kuei-feng and the Zhou emerged from the northern peoples. With the latter coming to power, the Western Zhou dynasty period (1045–770 BCE) of China began. Although the ethnic identities of these two tribal peoples are not well known, it is plausible to think that they were likely proto-Turks since at the time they were the dominant entities north of China. In fact, it is believed that Kuei-fang and Hien-yün (or *Hün-yu*) were from the same ethnic group of people.[1652] Both the Hien-yün and contemporary Jung were new tribal federations emerging from the north, and they both continued to exist during the dynastic rule of Western Zhou.

The eighth century BCE led to a political change in China with the start of the Eastern Zhou dynasty period (770–256 BCE). At about this time a new group of tribal people known as the Ti came down from the north. While the Ti settled in northern frontier of China, the Jung were residing to the west of China. Both of these warlike tribal groups were considered to be proto-Turks.[1653] The Ti and Jung tribes continued their existence until the end of the fifth century BCE, when they mostly became assimilated by the northern states of the Eastern Zhou period. Although the names of dominant tribal federations were disappearing after a period of time, in all likelihood many of the nomads to the north of China maintained their existence in perpetuity. For example, while the name of Hien-yün faded away during the Eastern Zhou period, the tribes that made up this federation eventually contributed to the formation of the Xiong-nu. Moreover, the Xiong-nu have been said to be an offshoot from the Jung as well.[1654] Indeed, Chinese archives indicate that the powerful tribes of the Hien-yün and the Jung, contemporary to the Western Zhou (1045–770 BCE) period of China, were considered to be the progenitors of the Xiong-nu.[1655] Hence, an appellation of a tribal federation ceased to exist in time, yet it was often replaced by that of a new dominant tribal name.

The Scythians (more in chapter 2.3) were known as one of the oldest tribal peoples of Asia. The beginning of their history however appears to be linked to the Jung (Rong) nomadic tribes.[1656] When the Ch'in state of the Chinese began to push against the Jung tribes, their western branch began a westward migration during the second half of the seventh century B.C.E., and when they reached Ili-Chu basin they came to be known to the Persians as Saka people and to the Greeks and Romans as Scythians.[1657] The Jung tribesmen who remained behind were eventually addressed as the Yueh-chih people (more in chapter 3.3), who then later formed the Kushan Empire in the early first century CE after they migrated to Bactria.

During the rise of the Huns in Mongolian plains, the Ting-ling nomadic federation occupied a large territory from Lake Baikal to the Yenisei River Basin in southern Siberia.[1658] These Turks came under the banner of their kinsmen the Huns between the years 203 and 200 BCE.[1659] Later, with the addition other Turkish tribal unions such as those of the Ko-k'un (Kyrgyz), Hün-yu and Wu-sun, a first unification of Turkish nation was achieved.

Furthermore, Mo-tun, the legendary leader of the Xiong-nu, brought the Tung-hu under his power. These tribes included the Wu-huan as well as Xianbei. The latter were a group of loose tribal federation of mixed racial groups. Even though there is no clear evidence to pinpoint the ethnic origin of the Wu-huan tribes, it is known that they had close cultural ties with the Xiong-nu (Huns).[1660] There have been academic claims that Wu-huan were Turkish speakers as well.[1661] There has been also claim for the Wu-huan for being the ancestors of the Oghuz Turks.[1662]

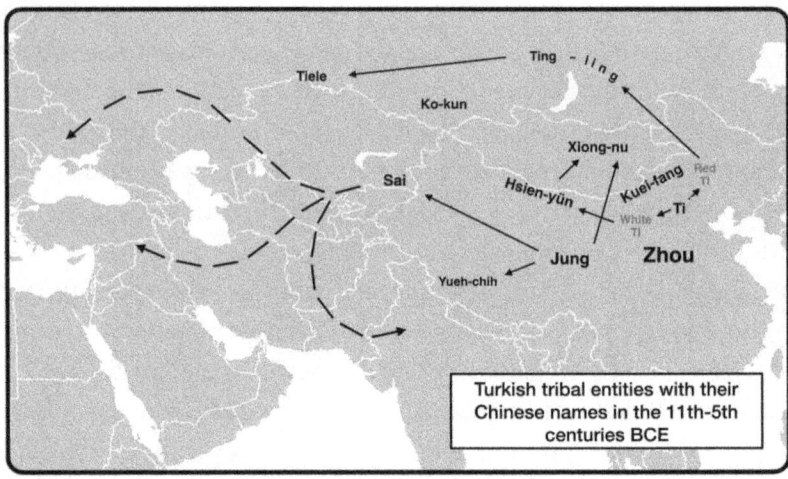

Map 12. Prominent northern tribal federations of proto-Turks have played a role in the evolution of the history of China. However, many of their names are only known by their Chinese given names based on ancient archives.

AFTER THE BREAK-UP OF THE FIRST UNION

Under the powerful rule of Mo-tun, known to the Turks as Mete, Turkish tribes were united under the banner of the Huns. This national union lasted more than two centuries until the Hunnish empire weakened by permanently splitting into two parts (Northern and Southern Huns) near the middle of the first century CE. Soon after each individual tribal federation formerly under Hun sovereignty began to act independently.

Southern Huns continued to have their political existence until 216 CE when China itself was about to enter into political chaos. After the Southern Huns lost their polity in northern China, their five tribes remained within Chinese territories. These Huns formed successive short-lived dynasties within China (volume 1, chapter 3.5): the Han or Former Zhao (304–29), the Northern Liang (401–60), the Xia (406–31), and the Northern Zhou (557–81).

Meanwhile, starting in the second century CE Northern Huns moved westward thus giving a start to the Great Migrations of Turkish tribes in the direction of the Western Eurasian Steppe (central and eastern Europe). The Northern Huns migrated westward, first settling in Altai Mountain and modern-day Kazakhstan plains and later splitting into two groups. One group continued to move towards Bactria while the other migrated to Europe to form the formidable Huns of Europe that menaced the Roman Empire (more in chapter 4.2). The Huns were speakers Oghuric-dialect of Turkish, and after the death of Attila in 453, the Huns began to absorb new Oghuric speaking tribes from the East. Early in the sixth century the Hunnish polity came to be known as the Bulgar-Hun state but later it emerged as Old Greater Bulgaria (also known as Magna Bulgaria, 632–81). Essentially with the Hunnish political power fading away in Europe early in the sixth century, we see the appearance of multiple new tribal unions with "oghur" or "ughur" name derivatives in Eastern Europe. Among these were the Utighurs, Kutrighurs as well as On-Oghurs. All of these tribal federation names were associated with the Bulgar Turks (chapter 4.3) who came to prominence after the disappearance of the Huns of Europe. Today while tribal Bulgar name survives with the modern Slavic nation of Bulgaria, the Oghuric-dialect of Bulgar Turkish is only spoken by Chuvash Turks living in the Chuvash Autonomous Republic of the Russian Federation.

The Ting-ling as the subjects of the Asian Huns were either a group of a larger Turkish federation known as the T'i-eh-le or they were the same as the T'i-eh-le. But eventually the latter name became more prominent in southern Siberian territories. Ko-k'un known as the Yenisei Kyrgyz remained in the Yenisei basin in southern Siberia and northern Kazakhstan plains. Wu-sun on the other hand remained in the Yetti-su region, in modern southeastern Kazakhstan territory. Yakut Turks were also contemporaries of the Huns, and they used to live in northern Siberia. It has been suggested that present-day Yakut Turks who are also known as Saha (Saka) Turks living in the Autonomous Saka (Yakutistan) Republic of Russian Federation are descendants of one of the branches of former Scythians.[1663]

After the Hun power completely disappeared in Mongolian steppes by the second century CE, the fate of the Wu-sun tribal federation remained obscure. However, it is believed that they eventually gave rise to the Karait Turks of Mongolia (volume 2, chapter 3).[1664] The Karaits were prominent in Mongolia before the rise of Genghis Khan, and they continued to play important roles within the Mongolian Empire even after the death of the Great Khan. However, after the thirteenth century they did not have political independence ever again. Instead, it is believed that their descendants survived by forming the Kireis branch of the contemporary Kyrgyz.[1665]

THE FORMER GREAT STATES

The Huns had powerful armies in ancient times. Perhaps they did not form the first Turkish state but they likely formed the first state uniting most of the Turkish tribes under one single banner. With their unstoppable mounted archers, Asian Huns were able to subdue China and collect tribute from the Han Chinese Empire. Later their descendants, the European Huns of Attila, did the same from both the Western and Eastern Roman empires. The legacies of the Huns include the splitting of the once-mighty Roman Empire and eventual cessation of the Western Roman Empire and consequently, the making of modern-day western Europe demographics. As Hun power declined in Europe, their core group retreated eastward and eventually became mixed with the populations of northern Caucasus. Although the Huns gradually disappeared after the death of Attila in 453.

The Volga Bulgar Khanate was built by Bulgar Turks who were mixed with the remnants of European Huns. They were the first to accept Islam as their religion in Europe, but they were later taken over by the hordes of Genghis Khan. Today they are represented by their descendants, the Chuvash Turks, living in the Russian Federation.

The GökTürk Qaghanate was not only the second state that unified Turkish tribes for the last time under a single banner but also it became the first true transcontinental Eurasian empire in the history of the world. Just like the Huns they were able to control the Chinese at will owing to their military superiority. GökTürks were survived by the Uighurs who formed a formidable empire in eastern Eurasian steppe and supported the existence of the T'ang dynasty of China.

The Khazar Turks established the first and only known non-Hebrew Judaic state in the history of the world. At the zenith of their power, they formed an alliance with the Eastern Roman Empire against the Umayyad Arabs and later against the Abbasid Arabs. In essence in the eighth and ninth centuries they were a formidable force in eastern Europe. Their economic power became the envy of the first Russian principality, formed in the ninth century under the rule of the Vikings. Their name today lives on among the Turks, who call the Caspian Sea 'Hazar Denizi' (Khazar Sea).

THE SECOND AND FINAL UNION OF TURKS

In the middle of the sixth century with the rise of the power of GökTürks (more in chapter 5.3) the nation was once again united as Turkish speaking tribes were brought together under a single banner. However, this was also the final reunification of the Turks in their history. Following the disappearance of GökTürks, multiple new empire building powerful tribes eventually emerged.

The T'i-eh-le tribes were also known as Chile tribes in Chinese. However, they also have been associated with the K'ao-che tribes of the Turks. Their tribal federation name meant "High Carts", and in Turkish these tribes were called Kanglı or Tegrek (tekerlek) because they were known for their chariots. By the time GökTürks took control of the Asian steppes in the middle of the sixth century this prominent Turkish tribal federation was known as the Töles. However, Turkish academicians continue to use the appellation 'Töles' synonymously for ancient large T'i-eh-le tribal federation as well.

In the year 627 GökTürks began to experience uprisings by the Turkish tribes. By this time the tribes of Töles were much stronger, and each sub-federation was able to act independently and not being concerned about safety issues. Subsequent to the end of the first GökTürk period in the early seventh century, the name of Töles tribal confederation became history. Those who remained in eastern Eurasian steppes to the east of Tola (Tuul) River were known as Tokuz-Oghuz tribal federation while those who resided in modern-day Kazakhstan steppes came to be known as On-Ok (Ten Arrows) tribal federation.[1666] The Chinese mentioned that at the end of the sixth century the Uighurs (Wei-ho) were among the T'ieh-le tribes as part of the Tokuz-Oghuz sub-federation north of the Tola River.[1667] While the Uighurs (chapter 5.4) emerged with control of the Tokuz-Oghuz and thus forming a powerful empire in eastern Eurasian steppes, the On-Ok in western Turkistan gave rise to the Türgiš Qaghanate (volume 2, chapter 2.2), which was able to delay Muslim Arab expansion into Central Asia until the middle of the eighth century. It appeared that the Türgiš eventually became the Oghuz Turks. These rose again to prominence starting in the eleventh century (see more in volume 2, chapters 2.2, 2.5, 2.6 and chapter 5).

Meanwhile, in northern modern-day Kazakhstan and in vast western Siberian territories of the former T'i-eh-le there was the tribal confederation of the Kimek Turks (chapter 4.8). This union later was also known as the Kimek Qaghanate, and it incorporated the Cuman, Qïpčak, and Qanglï (perhaps old dominating part of T'i-eh-le) tribal sub-federations. Following the fall of the Kimek union in the tenth century Cuman- Qïpčak tribal warriors moving westward eventually played important roles in the world history by exerting their influence in the history of large territory stretching from Hungary to Tataristan and from Egypt to India.[1668]

In summary, the most prominent byproducts of the Töles (formerly T'i-eh-le) confederation of tribes were the Tokuz-Oghuz, On-Ok, and Kimek tribal federations. However, with the fall of the GökTürks there were still other tribal entities that appeared in the annals of the history. These were the Sha-t'o, Pečenegs, and Qarluqs.

Following the end of the first GökTürk period the Sha-t'o Turks (chapter 5.5) left their territories in western Turkistan and eventually came to reside in northern China. In their new dominions, they provided support to the ailing T'ang dynasty of China. Following the fall of T'ang dynasty, Sha-t'o formed three dynasties during the period of Five Dynasties (907–60) and Ten Kingdoms (902–79) of China's history. These were successively the Later T'ang (923–36), the Later Chin (936–46), and the Later Han (947–50). Then, before the Five Dynasties and Ten Kingdoms period ended, these Turks formed the ephemeral Northern Han Kingdom (951–79). After they lost political control to the Chinese Song dynasty (960–1279). However, they appeared to continue their existence well after the tenth century as their descendants came to be known as the Önggüt Turks thriving in thirteenth century Mongolian plains (volume 2, chapter 3.2).[1669] It has been suggested that Sha-t'o Turks also formed some of the Tatar groups in Mongolia during the era of Genghis Khan.[1670] Indeed, Önggüt Turks were also referred to as White Tatars by the Chinese.[1671]

Another tribal group that emerged from the fall of the GökTürks was that of the Pečeneg Turks. As mentioned in Chinese sources Pečenegs' tribal union was thought to have emerged from the Töles, formerly known as the

T'ieh-le.[1672] These nomadic warriors displaced the Magyars (Hungarians), pushing them from the plains of Ukraine farther west into central Europe, where they formed Hungary. After Pečenegs disturbed the territories of the Eastern Roman Empire, many of them were massacred by Greeks. Some survivors became assimilated by Greeks, and others were absorbed into the Hungarian population in the north. Other Pečenegs who remained outside the Balkans in southern Russian territories possibly formed the new Qaraqalpaq tribal federation with Oghuz Turks who stayed in Europe rather than following Seljuks into western Turkestan in the eleventh century. Eventually, Qaraqalpaqs moved to Central Asia, and today they live in Uzbekistan.

Finally, one other notable tribal federation that rose to prominence after the GökTürks was that of Qarluqs. Their tribes were known to be living over a large area between Altai and Tien-shan Mountains. They contributed to the evolution of the histories of Turkistan. After the fourteenth century they came to be known mostly as the Čaghatai Turks.

THE LOST ANCIENT TRIBES

The T'o-pa (Tabgač) Turks (volume 1, chapter 5.2), after leaving the Xianbei tribal federation, settled in northern China after the fall of the Han dynasty. They emerged as the most powerful polity among the multiple kingdoms in Chinese territory and established the Northern Wei dynasty of China. The Tabgač replaced the Chinese religions of Confucianism and Taoism with the Indian-origin religion of Buddhism. Furthermore, they made Central Asian male costumes acceptable to the Chinese, who began to wear trousers and boots, which their ancestors despised. However, after their dynasty fell, these Turks became assimilated by the Chinese population.

The Kao-ch'e (Qanglï) were an ancient Turkish tribal union that replaced the name Ting-ling and possibly this name was synonymous with large Turkish tribal federation of T'i-eh-le, later known as Töles by the sixth century. It has been claimed that the leading clans of the once-mighty Gök-Türks and Uighurs were formed by this tribal union.[1673] The Qanglï Turks were still present as late as the ninth century as part of the great tribal union forming the Kimek Qaghanate in the territories of western Siberia (volume 1, chapter 4.8). After the Kimek broke apart in the tenth century, while the Cumans and Qïpčaks moved westward into the steppes of Europe, the Qanglï likely remained in western Siberia, where they probably came under the control of the Golden Horde Khanate. On the basis of their last location, they may have contributed to the formation of the Kazakhs together with the Tatars (Qïpčaks), but they may also live on among the present-day Siberian Turks, such as the Altai, Khakas, and Tuva.

CONTRIBUTIONS OF THE EARLY NOMADS TO SETTLED CIVILIZATIONS

Central Asian nomadic mounted archers of the past were warlike people once feared by great civilizations of the world, including China in the Far East and the Roman Empire in the West.

The economy of these Tengriist pastoralist nomads of the Eurasian steppes relied heavily on the animal husbandry. Hence, their animals were vital to them. The horse in particular had a very special place for these tribal peoples.

The horse was ridden initially by the nomadic warriors but not by sedentary peoples, like the Chinese. Nomadic fighters like the Scythians and the Xiong-nu rode horses for military use. From Chinese records we know that by 300 BCE the Xiong-nu were expert cavalrymen.[1674] While the Asian Huns were riding horses, the rest of the world was driving horses. In fact, in early civilizations in China, India, Mesopotamia, and Egypt, the horse was used primarily to pull heavy war chariots.[1675] The Chinese fought against the Turkish Xiong-nu with chariots but quickly realized that these war machines were no match for the superb mounted archers of the Xiong-nu. Consequently, the Xiong-nu were instrumental in introducing the concept of the cavalry in China in the third century CE,[1676] as well as the use of nomadic trousers, since these were more suitable for horseback riding.[1677] But the use of trousers and nomadic boots did not gain full acceptance until the reign of the Tabgač (T'o-pa) Turks in northern China, which ended in the sixth century.

Stirrup was an extremely important military invention. Its use first appeared in between the fourth and sixth centuries CE, and since it was the Turkish horsemen who first applied its use to the horseback riding, they also revolutionized the art of warfare.¹⁶⁷⁸ Europeans came to know about the strategic importance of stirrup from the European Avars.¹⁶⁷⁹ With the increase use of this equipment particularly after the eighth century nomadic Turks indirectly made a significant contribution to the medieval European military history since stirrup allowed the emergence of armored knights on horseback. Hence, with the rise of this new cavalry force in Europe, a new feudal class was born, and in times of need for the state European monarchs provided land in return for the pledges of armored knights on horseback.¹⁶⁸⁰ With exposure to Turkish military technology, the Europeans also began to acquire the strategic skills of the Central Asians. The (European) Avars, who initially subdued Europe in the sixth century from their base in the Hungarian Plain, introduced the scimitar,¹⁶⁸¹ and the long lance in Europe.¹⁶⁸² Eventually, armored knights became a formidable cavalry force, and with such new advantage Frankish Germans under Charlemagne overcame the Avars of Europe.

Ancient Turkish nomadic federative states were governed based on the principles of feudalism (more in chapter 2.4). We know that GökTürks as Volga Bulgars had clear evidence of applying such political system.¹⁶⁸³ Moreover, feudalism was also present in the state of Qara-Khanids of the eleventh century.¹⁶⁸⁴ Yet, tracing back to the earliest times of the Turkish history we see that the Huns applied 'feudal' or 'proto-feudal' system of governance, which Europeans eagerly adopted after their Hunnish overlords politically disappeared.¹⁶⁸⁵ Germans were not the only Europeans who embraced Turkish feudalism as their governance system but early Russians led by Viking Rjurik dynasty also adopted this Turkish political system.¹⁶⁸⁶ Moreover, the first Russian state became a vassal of Khazar Turks with its monarch carrying the Turkish title of vassal qaghan.¹⁶⁸⁷ Indeed, the very first the first Russian state was known as the Qaghanate of Rus', which was a vassal of the Khazar Qaghanate.

Another contribution of the Central Asian nomads was shadow theater, which was perhaps the most popular entertainment of the medieval period. Research has shown that it was likely introduced into China by the Turkish tribal people.¹⁶⁸⁸ One other contribution of ancient nomadic Turkish tribes to the global culture was hand woven carpets which have been one of the oldest cultural traditions of the world. Certainly many of Central Asian nomadic trademark dairy products particularly yogurt and its derivastives should not be forgotten as Turkish heritage being passed on to global civilizations.

One of the legacies of the Khazars is the present-day city of Kiev, which the Khazars built and originally named Sambat, a compound of two Turkish words, *sam* (high) and *bat* (power). In this context the Khazar name Sambat meant "high fortress," and the Eastern Romans added the Greek suffix *as* to make the name Sambatas.[1689] The city was on the border between the Slavic area northwest of the great plain and the Turkish area southeast.[1690] The newer name Kiev was a Turkish compound from *küi*, an ancient word for "lower place" or "bank of a river" or "cove, bay" (present-day Turkish *koy*), and *ev*, meaning "settlement" or "home." Therefore, the compound *küi-ev* meant "harbor settlement" or "lower town" on the Dnieper River.[1691] Finally, the Khazar Turks contributed to the formation of the Russian state. Indeed, by taking the Turkish title of *qaghan* and copying the administrative style of the Khazar Turks, the first Russian state, known as the Qaghanate of Rus', started by emulating the Khazar state.[1692]

Perhaps one of the most important legacies of the Khazar Turks is their contribution to the Jewish diaspora of modern times. By allowing the Jews from the Eastern Roman and Persian Sassanid Empires to settle in their territories and by proclaiming Judaism the state religion, they allowed eastern European (Ashkenazi) Jewry to take solid root in this part of the world. Furthermore, as stated earlier in this book (chapter 4.6), Khazars contributed to the formation of Crimean Jews as well. These were known as the Karaim Jews and Krïmchak Jews. During World War II, they were mostly exterminated by German Nazis.

SELECTED BOOK RECOMMENDATIONS

Agoston, Gabor. *Guns for the Sultan: Military Power and the Weapons Industry in the Ottoman Empire.* Cambridge University Press, 2005.

Balabanlilar, Lisa, *Imperial Identity in the Mughal Empire.* I. B. Tauris, 2012.

Beckwith, Christopher I. *Empires of the Silk Road: A History of Central Eurasia from the Bronze Age to the Present.* Princeton University Press, 2009.

Bosworth, Clifford Edmund. *The Ghaznavids: Their Empire in Afghanistan and Eastern Iran 994–1040.* Edinburgh University Press, 1963.

Bosworth, Clifford Edmund. *The Later Ghaznavids: Splendour and Decay—the Dynasty in Afghanistan and Northern India 1040–1186.* Columbia University Press, 1977.

———. *The New Islamic Dynasties: A Chronological and Genealogical Manual.* Edinburgh University Press, 1996.

———. "The Origins of the Seljuqs." In *The Seljuqs: Politics, Society and Culture*, edited by Christian Lange and Songül Mecit. Edinburgh: Edinburgh University Press, 2012.

Brook, Kevin Alan. *The Jews of Khazaria.* Rowman & Littlefield, 2006.

Brose, Michael C. *Subjects and Masters: Uyghurs in the Mongol Empire.* Center for East Asian Studies, Western Washington University, 2007.

Cahen, Claude. *Pre-Ottoman Turkey: A General Survey of the Material and Spiritual Culture and History 1071–1330.* Taplinger, 1968.

Christian, David. *A History of Russia, Central Asia, and Mongolia. Volume I: Inner Eurasia from Prehistory to the Mongol Empire.* Wiley-Blackwell, 1998.

Clauson, Gerard. *Studies in Turkic and Mongolic Linguistics.* Routledge, 1962.

Di Cosmo, Nicola. *Ancient China and Its Enemies: The Rise of Nomadic Power in East Asian History.* Cambridge University Press, 2005.

Drompp, Michael R. *Tang China and the Collapse of the Uighur Empire.* Brill Academic, 2005.

Eberhard, Wolfram. *Conquerors and Rulers: Social Forces in Medieval China.* 2nd ed. E. J. Brill, 1970.

Findley, Carter Vaughn. *The Turks in World History.* Oxford University Press, 2005.

Fisher, Alan. *The Crimean Tatars, Hoover Institution Press.* Stanford: Stanford University, 1978.

Golden, Peter B. *Central Asia in World History.* Oxford University Press, 2011.

Golden, Peter B. *Nomads and Their Neighbours in the Russian Steppe: Turks, Khazars and Qipchaks.* Variorum, 2003.

———. *Turks and Khazars.* Ashgate Variorum, 2010.

Grousset, René. *The Empire of the Steppes: A History of Central Asia.* New Brunswick: Rutgers University Press, 1999.

Johanson, Lars. "The History of Turkic." In *The Turkic Languages*, edited by Lars Johanson and Eva A. Csato. Routledge, 2006.

Klopsteg, Paul E. *Turkish Archery and the Composite Bow.* 2nd ed. Derrydale Press, 1947.

Lattimore, Owen. *Inner Asian Frontiers of China.* Oxford University Press, 1940.

Luther, Kenneth Allin, and C. Edmund Bosworth. *The History of The Seljuq Turks: From the Jami' al-Tawarikh: An Ilkhanid Adaptation of the Saljuq-nama of Zahir al-Din Nishapuri.* Routledge, 2001.

Mackerras, Colin. *The Uighur Empire: According to the T'ang Dynastic Histories, a Study in Sino-Uighur Relations 744–840.* University of South Carolina Press, 1972.

Maenchen-Helfen, Otto J. *The World of the Huns: Studies in Their History and Culture.* University of California Press, 1973.

McCarthy, Justin. *Death and Exile: The Ethnic Cleansing of Ottoman Muslims, 1821–1922.* Princeton: Darwin Press, 1995.

———. *The Ottoman Peoples and The End of Empire.* Oxford University Press, 2001.

McGovern, William Montgomery. *The Early Empires of Central Asia: A Study of the Scythians and the Huns and the Part They Played in World History.* University of North Carolina Press, 1939.

Rorlich, Azade-Ayşe. *The Volga Tatars: A Profile in National Resilience.* Stanford, CA: Hoover Institution Press, 1986.

Roux, Jean-Paul. *Histoire Des Turcs: Deux mille ans du Pacifique à la Méditerranée*. Fayard, 2000.

Shaw, Stanford J., and Ezel Kural Shaw. *History of the Ottoman Empire and Modern Turkey: Volume II: Reform, Revolution, and Republic: The Rise of Modern Turkey, 1808–1975*. Cambridge University Press, 1997.

Somuncuoglu, Servet. *The Turks on the Rocks*. Istanbul: At-Ok, 2011.

Soucek, Svat. *A History of Inner Asia*. Cambridge University Press, 2000.

Thompson, E. A. *The Huns*. Wiley-Blackwell, 1996.

SELECTED JOURNAL-ARTICLE RECOMMENDATIONS

Boswell, A. Bruce. "The Kipchak Turks." *Slavonic Review* 6, no. 16 (June 1927): pp. 68–85.

Bosworth, C. E. "The Development of Persian Culture under the Early Ghaznavids." *Iran* 6 (1968): pp. 33–44.

Brose, Michael C. "Uyghur Technologists of Writing and Literacy in Mongol China." *T'oung Pao,* 2nd ser., 91, no. 4/5 (2005): pp. 396–435.

Bury, J. B. "The Turks in the Sixth Century." *English Historical Review* 12, no. 47 (July 1897): pp. 417–26.

Bussagli, Mario. "Pages of Euro-Asian History: Attila and the Huns." *East and West* 4, no. 3 (October 1953): pp. 191–97.

Chen, Sanping. "Succession Struggle and the Ethnic Identity of the Tang Imperial House." *Journal of the Royal Asiatic Society*, 3rd ser., 6, no. 3 (November 1996): pp. 379–405.

———. "Turkic or Proto-Mongolian? A Note on the Tuoba Language." *Central Asiatic Journal* 49, no. 2 (2005): pp. 161–74.

Daim, Falko. "The Avars: Steppe People of Central Europe." *Archaeology* 37, no. 2 (March/April 1984): pp. 33–39.

de la Vaissière, Étienne. "Huns et Xiongnu." *Central Asiatic Journal* 49, no. 1 (2005): pp. 3–26.

Di Cosmo, Nicola. "Ancient Inner Asian Nomads: Their Economic Basis and Its Significance in Chinese History." *Journal of Asian Studies* 53, no. 4 (1994): pp. 1092–126.

Esin, Emel. "The Horse in Turkic Art." Proceedings of the 7th Meeting of the Permanent International Altaistic Conference, August 29 to September 3, 1964. *Central Asiatic Journal* 10, no. 3/4 (December 1965): pp. 167–227.

Golden, Peter B. "Religion among the Qïpčaqs of Medieval Eurasia." *Central Asiatic Journal* 42, no. 2 (1998): pp. 180–237.

Hambis, Louis. "The Ancient Civilizations of Manchuria." *East and West* 7, no. 3 (October 1956): pp. 218–228.

Hess, Andrew C. "The Evolution of the Ottoman Seaborne Empire in the Age of the Oceanic Discoveries, 1453–1525." *American Historical Review* 75, no. 7 (December 1970): pp. 1892–919.

Kamalov, Ablet. "Turks and Uighurs during the Rebellion of An Lu-shan Shih Ch'ao-yi (755–762)." *Central Asiatic Journal* 45, no. 2 (2001): pp. 243–53.

MacArtney, C. A. "On the Greek Sources for the History of the Turks in the Sixth Century." *Bulletin of the School of Oriental and African Studies* 11, no. 2 (1944): pp. 266–75.

———. "The Petchenegs." *Slavonic and East European Review* 8, no. 23 (December 1929): pp. 342–55.

Maenchen-Helfen, Otto. "The Ting-Ling." *Harvard Journal of Asiatic Studies* 4, no. 1 (May 1939): pp. 77–86.

Minorsky, Vladimir. "The Qara-qoyunlu and the Qutb-shāhs (Turkmenica, 10)." *Bulletin of the School of Oriental and African Studies* 17, no. 1 (1955): pp. 50–73.

———. "Tamīm ibn Baḥr's Journey to the Uyghurs." *Bulletin of the School of Oriental and African Studies* 12, no. 2 (1948): pp. 275–305.

———. "The Turkish Dialect of the Khalaj." *Bulletin of the School of Oriental Studies* 10, no. 2 (1940): pp. 417–37.

Pritsak, Omeljan. "The Hunnic Language of the Attila Clan." *Harvard Ukrainian Studies* 6, no. 4 (December 1982): pp. 428–76.

———. "The Khazar Kingdom's Conversion to Judaism." *Harvard Ukrainian Studies* 2, no. 3 (September 1978): pp. 261–81.

Psarras, Sophia-Karin. "Han and Xiongnu a Reexamination of Cultural and Political Relations (II)." *Monumenta Serica* 52 (2004): pp. 37–93.

Pulleyblank, Edwin G. "The 'High Carts': A Turkish-Speaking People before the Türks." *Asia Major*, 3rd ser., 3, no. 1 (1990): pp. 21–26.

Samolin, William. "Hsiung-Nu, Hun, Turk." *Central Asiatic Journal* 3, no. 2 (1957): pp. 143–50.

Sinor, Denis. "The Inner Asian Warriors." *Journal of the American Oriental Society* 101, no. 2 (April–June 1981): pp. 133–44.

Turan, Osman. "The Ideal of World Domination among the Medieval Turks." *Studia Islamica*, no. 4 (1955): pp. 77–90.

ABOUT THE AUTHOR

Erol I. Yorulmazoglu has previously served as secretary general and regional vice president for the Assembly of Turkish American Associations (ATAA). A board-certified physician and educator, he has voluntarily served as a history teacher at Chicago's Turkish American School.

Yorulmazoglu comes from a family of patriots. His grandmother Nuriye Idil as a young girl had a picture with the founder of Turkey, Mustafa Kemal Atatürk. Her father Sıtkı Gür was selected to founding Turkish assembly (Grand National Assembly of Turkey, or TBMM) on April 23, 1920. Her husband Resat Idil was sent by President of Turkey Atatürk to UCLA Berkeley to study agricultural engineering. Upon his return he established country's first vineyard in the postwar era.

An extensive traveler, Yorulmazoglu has visited many historical sites throughout central Asia. He enjoys giving lectures on Turkish history to adults and children alike. He is passionate about educating Turkish youth living outside of Turkey to help them better understand their culture and history. Yorulmazoglu is married and has three children.

APPENDICES

A.1. THE TURKISH UNESCO WORLD HERITAGE LIST

Petroglyphic Complexes of the Mongolian Altai

Location: Mongolia

From: likely proto-Turks

Time: 11,000–1000 BCE

The Turks believe that they originated in the Altai mountain range. The area of the Mongolian Altai mountain range has numerous rock carvings (petroglyphs) and funerary and ritual monuments. These findings reflect the development of human culture over a period of twelve thousand years. During 11,000–6000 BCE the area was forested and suitable for hunters of large game. But during the period of 6000–4000 BCE, steppe vegetation became dominant, and consequently, herding became a new way of life. These petroglyphs are a perfect visual record of human prehistory demonstrating the transition of lifestyles over the ages. The transition from hunting to herding as dominant way of life and then the transition to a horseback-riding lifestyle during the first millennium BCE are well illustrated. Among the earliest animals depicted are the rhinoceros and the mammoth. When the area became forested (Early Holocene, 11,000–6000 BCE), the aurochs, the elk, and the ibex became the predominant illustrated animals.

Petroglyphs within the Archaeological Landscape of Tamgaly

Location: Kazakhstan

From: likely proto-Turks

Time: 2000 BCE to twentieth century

The five thousand rock carvings found around the Tamgaly Gorge near the Chu-Ili mountains toward the western end of the Tien Shan mountains provide valuable information about the social, cultural, and religious lifestyle of the pastoral nomads in this area. Burial sites in this area include numerous tombs and kurgans.

THE BUDDHIST CAVES OF CHINA

Location: China

From: T'o-pa (Tabgač) Turks (Northern Wei)

Time: fifth to sixth century

Both the Yün-kang Buddhist Cave (also known as the Yungang Grottoes) and the Lung-men Caves (also referred to as the Longmen Grottoes) are UNESCO World Heritage Sites, true cultural legacies left behind by the T'o-pa Turks.

THE ORKHON VALLEY CULTURAL LANDSCAPE

Location: Mongolia

From: Huns, Gök-Türks, Uighurs, and Genghis Khan's followers

Time: sixth to thirteenth century

This site covers a large area of pastureland on the banks of the Orkhon River with numerous archaeological artifacts dating all the way back to the sixth century. This area, which was home to a strong culture of nomadic pastoralism over two millennia, was the command center for the old Turkish nomadic empires of the Huns, Gök-Türks, and Uighurs, until the latter had to leave in the ninth century. The Mongols first established themselves in this area in the thirteenth century, when they established their capital, Qara-Qorum, in 1220 under the leadership of Genghis Khan. The area was sacred for the ancient Turkish nomads, with the sacred mountain Ötüken in the vicinity. The land became a crossroads of civilizations, linking the East to the West. Particularly during the period of the Gök-Türks, strong trade relations between China and the Eastern Roman Empire were established by the Turks in this area. The pastureland is home to numerous Turkish memorial sites, including the Orkhon inscriptions of the eighth centuries, the Uighur capital of Khar Balgas, and the thirteenth and fourteenth centuries' ancient imperial Mongol capital of Qara-Qorum.

The Madara Rider
Location: Bulgaria
From: Bulgar Turks
Time: eighth century

The Madara Rider is a relief carved into a hundred-meter-high cliff near the village of Madar in northeast modern-day Bulgaria. The figure, which illustrates a knight triumphing over a lion, was made at the beginning of the eighth century. Madara used to be a sacred place for the First Bulgarian Empire before Bulgaria's conversion to Christianity in the ninth century from the Bulgars' traditional Tengriist faith. The relief is the only one of its kind in Europe. The inscriptions by the relief include a chronicle of important events in the reigns of famous Bulgar khans Tervel, Kormisos, and Omurtag.

A.2. CHINESE NAMES FOR TURKISH TRIBES AND STATES

Most of the original Turkish names of ancient tribal groups are unknown today. Their Chinese names do not necessarily reflect their true names but are rather descriptions given to them by the Chinese of the time. This section gives the Chinese names of some ancient Turkish tribal groups.

丁零 Ting-ling

鐵勒 T'ieh-le (Töles)

勅勒 Chile

匈奴 Xiong-nu (Hiung-nu: Hun)

維吾爾 Uighur

鬲昆 Ko-k'un (Kyrgyz)

鮮卑 Xianbei (nomads of mixed ethnicities)

東胡 Tung-hu (eastern barbarians)

胡 Hu (barbarian)

烏孫 Wu-sun

烏桓 Wu-huan

高車 Kao-ch'e (Qanglï)

拓拔 T'o-pa (Tabgač)

柔然 Jou-jan (Juan-juan 蠕蠕 – Asian Avars (non-Turkish group)

狄 or 氐 Ti (Di)

西戎 Jung (Rung)

突厥 T'u-chüeh (GökTürk)

欽察 Qïpčak

沙陀 Shatuo (Sh'a-to)

NOTES

INTRODUCTION

1. James Baker, *Turkey* (Henry Holt, 1877), 121.
2. William Ewart Gladstone, *The Bulgarian Horrors and the Question of the East* (London: John Murray, 1876), 12–13; Andrew Wheatcroft, *The Ottomans* (London: Penguin Books, 1993), 234.
3. Ernest Jackh, *The Rising Crescent: Turkey Yesterday, Today, and Tomorrow* (New York: Farrar and Rinehart, 1944), 37.
4. Giovanni Curatola, *Turkish Art and Architecture: From the Seljuks to the Ottomans* (New York: Abbeville Press, 2010), 11.

CHAPTER 1: LANGUAGE AND CULTURE

5. Theodore G. Schurr and Lenore Pipes, "The Prehistory of Mongolian Populations as Revealed by Studies of Osteological, Dental, and Genetic Variation," in *Mapping Mongolia: Situating Mongolia in the World from Geologic Time to the Present*, ed. Paula L. W. Sabloff (Philadelphia, PA: University of Pennsylvania Museum of Archaeology and Anthropology, 2011), 130.
6. Claus Schönig, "Turko-Mongolic Relations," in *The Mongolic Languages*, ed. Juha Janhunen (Abingdon, Great Britain: Routledge, 2003), 403.
7. Han-Woo Choi, "Notes on Some Ancient Korean Titles," *Central Asiatic Journal* 36, no. 1/2 (1992): 34.
8. Yoshizo Itabashi, "A Comparative Study of the Old Japanese and Korean Nominative Case Suffixes with the Altaic Third Person Singular Pronouns," *Central Asiatic Journal* 37, no. 1/2 (1993): 111–12.
9. Martine Robbeets, "If Japanese Is Altaic, How Can It Be So Simple?" in *Evidence and Counter-Evidence: Essays in Honour of Frederik Kortlandt. Volume 2: General*

Linguistics, Studies in Slavic and General Linguistics, vol. 33 (Boston, MA: Brill, 2008), 363.

10. Gerard Clauson, "The Case against the Altaic Theory," *Central Asiatic Journal* 2, no. 3 (1956): 182–83.

11. Ibid., 183.

12. Schönig, "Turko-Mongolic Relations," 404.

13. Gerard Clauson, *Studies in Turkic and Mongolic Linguistics* (Abingdon, Great Britain: Routledge, 1962), 217.

14. Schönig, "Turko-Mongolic Relations," 410–11.

15. Clauson, *Studies in Turkic and Mongolic Linguistics*, 216–17.

16. Clauson, "The Case against the Altaic Theory," 184.

17. Peter B. Golden, "The Turkic Peoples: A Historical Sketch," in *The Turkic Languages*, ed. Lars Johanson and Eva A. Csato (Abingdon, Great Britain: Routledge, 2006), 16; Carter Vaughn Findley, *The Turks in World History* (New York: Oxford University Press, 2005), 21.

18. Clauson, *Studies in Turkic and Mongolic Linguistics*, 2.

19. René Grousset, *The Empire of the Steppes: A History of Central Asia* (New Brunswick, NJ: Rutgers University Press, 1999), 20; Clauson, *Studies in Turkic and Mongolic Linguistics*, 9–10; David Christian, *A History of Russia, Central Asia, and Mongolia. Volume I: Inner Eurasia from Prehistory to the Mongol Empire* (Hoboken, NJ: Wiley-Blackwell, 1998), 195.

20. Clauson, *Studies in Turkic and Mongolic Linguistics*, 10.

21. Owen Lattimore, *Inner Asian Frontiers of China* (New York: Oxford University Press, 1940), 451.

22. Christian, *A History of Russia, Central Asia, and Mongolia*, 248.

23. Lars Johanson, "The History of Turkic," in *The Turkic Languages*, ed. Lars Johanson and Eva A. Csato (Abingdon, Great Britain: Routledge, 2006), 85.

24. C. E. Bosworth, "The Development of Persian Culture under the Early Ghaznavids," *Iran* 6 (1968): 39.

25. Johanson, "The History of Turkic," 85–86.

26. Lars Johanson, "Linguistic Convergence in the Volga Area," *Studies in Slavic and General Linguistics* 28 (2000): 165.

27. Helmut Nickel, "Tamgas and Runes, Magic Numbers and Magic Symbols," *Metropolitan Museum Journal* 8 (1973): 168.

28. Andras Rona-Tas, "Turkic Writing Systems," in *The Turkic Languages*, ed. Lars Johanson and Eva A. Csato (Abingdon, Great Britain: Routledge, 2006), 127.

29. Nickel, "Tamgas and Runes, Magic Numbers and Magic Symbols," 170–73.
30. Ibid., 171.
31. Peter B. Golden, "Religion among the Qïpčaqs of Medieval Eurasia," *Central Asiatic Journal* 42, no. 2 (1998): 184.
32. Rona-Tas, "Turkic Writing Systems," 129–35.
33. Ibid., 131.
34. Mario Bussagli, "Pages of Euro-Asian History: Attila and the Huns," *East and West* 4, no. 3 (October 1953): 194.
35. Clauson, *Studies in Turkic and Mongolic Linguistics*, 17.
36. Jean Paul Roux, "Historical Introduction," in *The Turkic Peoples of the World*, ed. Margaret Bainbridge (Abingdon, Great Britain: Routledge, 1993), 12.
37. Dieter Kuhn, "The Spindle-Wheel: A Chou Chinese Invention," *Early China* 5 (1979–1980): 14–18.
38. Karl Reuning, "Turkish Contributions to Western Vocabularies," *Monatshefte für deutschen Unterricht* 35, no. 3/4 (March–April 1943): 125.
39. Sabri Koz and Kemalettin Kuzucu, *Turkish Coffee* (Istanbul, Turkey: Yapi Kredi Yayinlari, 2013), 21.
40. Reuning, "Turkish Contributions to Western Vocabularies," 127.
41. Jane Hathaway, "The Ottomans and the Yemeni Coffee Trade," *Oriente Moderno*, n.s., 25 (86), no. 1 (2006): 163; Koz and Kuzucu, *Turkish Coffee*, 9, 21, 25.
42. Hathaway, "The Ottomans and the Yemeni Coffee Trade," 161.
43. James C. Davis, ed., *Pursuit of Power: Venetian Ambassador's Reports* (New York: Harper and Row, 1970), 140.
44. Reuning, "Turkish Contributions to Western Vocabularies," 127.
45. Koz and Kuzucu, *Turkish Coffee*, 9.
46. Ibid., 15, 24.
47. Emine Gürsoy Naskali, "When Coffee Is Cooked," *Skylife*, June 2014, 115–16.
48. Benedict S. Robinson, "Green Seraglios: Tulips, Turbans, and the Global Market," *Journal for Early Modern Cultural Studies* 9, no. 1 (Spring–Summer 2009): 96.
49. Hathaway, "The Ottomans and the Yemeni Coffee Trade," 164.
50. Ibid., 164.
51. Karl Reichl, *Singing the Past: Turkic and Medieval Heroic Poetry* (Cornell University Press, 2000), 12.
52. Denis Sinor, "The Scope and Importance of Altaic Studies," *Journal of the American Oriental Society* 83, no. 2 (April–June 1963): 194.
53. Reichl, *Singing the Past*, 8.
54. Ibid., 12–13.
55. Julian Baldick, *Animal and Shaman: Ancient Religions of Central Asia* (New

York University Press, 2012), 8, 59.
56. Reichl, *Singing the Past*, 22.
57. Fan Pen Chen, "Shadow Theaters of the World," *Asian Folklore Studies* 62, no. 1 (2003): 25–26.
58. Ibid., 29, 47.
59. Ibid., 29.
60. Ibid., 47–48.
61. Ibid., 30, 40.
62. Peter B. Golden, *Central Asia in World History* (New York: Oxford University Press, 2011), 89.
63. Bussagli, "Pages of Euro-Asian History," 194.
64. Ibid.
65. C. A. MacArtney, "The Petchenegs," *Slavonic and East European Review* 8, no. 23 (December 1929): 354.
66. Wolfram Eberhard, *Conquerors and Rulers: Social Forces in Medieval China*, 2nd ed. (Boston, MA: E. J. Brill, 1970), 155.
67. Marios Philippides, ed., "Tetaldi: A Treatise on the Fall of Constantinople," in *Mehmed II the Conqueror and the Fall of the Franco-Byzantine Levant to the Ottoman Turks: Some Western Views and Testimonies* (Tempe, AZ: Mrts, 2007), 179.
68. Mehmet Ali Sanlikol, *The Musician Mehters* (London: Isis, 2011), 26.
69. Rhoads Murphey, *Ottoman Warfare, 1500–1700* (New Brunswick, NJ: Rutgers University Press, 1999), 157.
70. Sanlikol, *The Musician Mehters*, 38–39.
71. Charles Perry, "Nomadic and Medieval Turkic Cuisines," in *The Turkic Speaking Peoples: 2,000 Years of Art and Culture from Inner Asia to the Balkans*, ed. Ergun Cagatay and Dogan Kuban (Munich, Germany: Prestel, 2006), 117.
72. Ibid.
73. E. Hart, "Kefir, A New Milk-Ferment," *British Medical Journal* 1, no. 1167 (May 12, 1883): 925.
74. C. W. Hesseltine, "A Millennium of Fungi, Food, and Fermentation," *Mycologia* 57, no. 2 (March–April 1965): 188–89.
75. Jon A. Vanderhoof and Rosemary Young, "Probiotics in the United States," *Clinical Infectious Diseases* 46 (February 1, 2008): S67–S69.
76. Maija Saxelin, "Probiotic Formulations and Applications, the Current Probiotics Market, and Changes in the Marketplace: A European Perspective," *Clinical Infectious Diseases* 46 (February 1, 2008): S76.
77. Tuğrul Şavkay, "Turkish Cuisine—from Nomadism to Republicanism," in *The Turkic Speaking Peoples: 2,000 Years of Art and Culture from Inner Asia to the Balkans*, ed. Ergun Cagatay and Dogan Kuban (Munich, Germany: Prestel, 2006), 267.

78. Perry, "Nomadic and Medieval Turkic Cuisines," 118.
79. Ibid., 121.
80. Ibid., 124.
81. Ibid.
82. Ibid., 127.
83. Ibid., 126.
84. Ibid., 130.
85. Albert E. Dien, "The Stirrup and Its Effect on Chinese Military History," *Ars Orientalis* 16 (1986): 33.
86. Denis Sinor, "The Inner Asian Warriors," *Journal of the American Oriental Society* 101, no. 2 (April–June 1981): 137.
87. András Róna-Tas, "The Periodization and Sources of Chuvash Linguistic History," in *Chuvash Studies*, ed. A. Róna-Tas (Budapest: Akadémiai Kiadó, 1982), 121.
88. Ibid., 120, 122.
89. Dien, "The Stirrup," 33.
90. Emel Esin, "The Horse in Turkic Art" (proceedings of the 7th Meeting of the Permanent International Altaistic Conference, August 29 to September 3, 1964), *Central Asiatic Journal* 10, no. 3/4 (December 1965): 167.
91. Ibid., 171.
92. Ibid., 171, 175.
93. Ibid., 199.
94. Ibid., 168.
95. Ibid., 173.
96. Ibid., 171, 177–79.
97. Ibid., 172–73, 179.
98. Ibid., 198.
99. Ibid., 194–95.
100. Ibid., 199.
101. Ibid., 195–96.
102. Dominique Collon, "Hunting and Shooting," *Anatolian Studies* 33 (1983): 51.
103. Edward H. Schafer, "Falconry in T'ang Times," *T'oung Pao*, 2nd ser., 46, no. 3/5 (1958): 293.
104. Hans J. Epstein, "The Origin and Earliest History of Falconry," *Isis* 34, no. 6 (Autumn 1943): 497–98.
105. Ibid., 500.
106. Ibid., 499.
107. Schafer, "Falconry in T'ang Times," 294–95.
108. Epstein, "The Origin and Earliest History of Falconry," 508–9.
109. Schafer, "Falconry in T'ang Times," 294.
110. Eberhard, *Conquerors and Rulers*, 153.
111. Tülay Artan, "A Book of Kings Produced and Presented as a Treatise on Hunting," *Muqarnas* 25 (2008): 300–1.
112. Ibid., 303.
113. Wallace McLeod, "The Range of the Ancient Bow," *Phoenix* 19, no. 1 (Spring 1965): 2.
114. Sinor, "The Inner Asian Warriors," 137.

115. Ibid., 139.
116. Ibid., 140.
117. Paul E. Klopsteg, *Turkish Archery and the Composite Bow*, 2nd ed. (New York: Derrydale, 1947), 36.
118. Ibid., 36–42.
119. Ibid., 54.
120. Ibid., 68.
121. People of Central Europe," *Archaeology* 37, no. 2 (March–April 1984), 33.
122. Eberhard, *Conquerors and Rulers*, 153.
123. Ibid., 154.
124. Klopsteg, *Turkish Archery*, 2.
125. McLeod, "The Range of the Ancient Bow," 9.
126. Klopsteg, *Turkish Archery*, 17–18, 24, 26–28.
127. Ibid., 3.
128. Ibid., 29.
129. Kenneth Allin Luther and C. Edmund Bosworth, *The History of the Seljuq Turks: From the Jami' al-Tawarikh: An Ilkhanid Adaptation of the Saljuq-nama of Zahir al-Din Nishapuri* (Abingdon, Great Britain: Routledge, 2001), 63.
130. Esin, "The Horse in Turkic Art," 172–74.
131. Eberhard, *Conquerors and Rulers*, 155.
132. Baldick, *Animal and Shaman*, 5.
133. Percy M. Young, *A History of the British Football* (Sportsmans Book Club, 1968), 2.
134. Ibid.; F. P. Magoun, *History of Football: From the Beginnings to 1871* (Johnson Reprint, 1938), 2.
135. Eberhard, *Conquerors and Rulers*, 154.
136. Katharina Otto-Dorn, "Figural Stone Reliefs on Seljuk Sacred Architecture in Anatolia," *Kunst des Orients* 12, no. 1/2 (1978, 1979): 104.
137. Ernst Diez, "The Zodiac Reliefs at the Portal of the Gök Medrese in Siwas," *Artibus Asiae* 12, no. 1/2 (1949): 101.
138. Charles Melville, "The Chinese-Uighur Animal Calendar in Persian Historiography of the Mongol Period," *Iran* 32 (1994): 84.
139. Ibid., 83.
140. Benedict S. Robinson, "Green Seraglios: Tulips, Turbans, and the Global Market," *Journal for Early Modern Cultural Studies* 9, no. 1 (Spring–Summer 2009), 107.
141. Reuning, "Turkish Contributions to Western Vocabularies," 131–32.
142. Ibid., 132.
143. Robinson, "Green Seraglios," 98.
144. Ibid., 95.
145. Ibid., 97.
146. Emel Esin, "Tös and Moncuķ Notes on Turkish Flag-Pole Finials," *Central Asiatic Journal* 16, no. 1 (1972): 16.
147. Esin, "The Horse in Turkic Art," 175.

148. Bahaeddin Ögel, *Türk Kültür Tarihine Giriş*, cilt 6, (Ankara: Kültür Bakanlığı Yayınları, 1991), 393, 457.

149. William Ridgeway, "The Origin of the Turkish Crescent," *Journal of the Royal Anthropological Institute of Great Britain and Ireland* 38 (July–December 1908): 247.

150. Ögel, *Türk Kültür Tarihine Giriş*, cilt 6, (Ankara: Kültür Bakanlığı Yayınları, 1991), 459.

151. Ibid., 385, 407, 419.

152. Ibid., 403-05, 418.

153. Ibid., 400-01, 415.

154. Ibid., 479-82.

155. Ibid., 429, 457, 462.

156. Hyun Jin Kim, *The Huns* (New York, NY: Routledge, 2016), p. 49.

157. Talat Tekin, *Irk Bitig: The Book of Omens* (Wiesbaden, Germany: Harrassowitz, 1994), 1.

158. S. Schechter, "An Unknown Khazar Document," *Jewish Quarterly Review*, n.s., 3, no. 2 (October 1912): 182.

159. Henri Stierlin, *Islamic Art and Architecture: From Isfahan to the Taj Mahal* (London: Thames & Hudson, 2002), 34.

160. Ibid., 36.

161. Maria Ribeiro, *Iznik: Pottery and Tiles* (London: Scala, 2009), 15.

162. Ibid., 17.

163. Walter B. Denny, *Iznik: The Artistry of Ottoman Ceramics* (London: Thames & Hudson, 2004), 10.

164. Ribeiro, *Iznik: Pottery and Tiles*, 105.

165. "The Ottoman Empire," *Metropolitan Museum of Art Bulletin*, n.s., 26, no. 5 (January 1968): 204.

166. Ribeiro, *Iznik: Pottery and Tiles*, 15, 21–23.

167. Ibid., 33.

168. Ibid., 51.

169. Ibid., 105.

170. Denny, *Iznik: The Artistry of Ottoman Ceramics*, 229.

171. Richard J. Wolfe, *Marbled Paper: Its History, Techniques, and Patterns* (Philadelphia, PA: University of Pennsylvania Press, 1990), 1.

172. Ibid., 5–6.

173. B. Tevfik Akgun, "The Digital Art of Marbled Paper," *Leonardo* 37, no. 1 (2004): 49.

174. Wolfe, *Marbled Paper*, 8, 10–11.

175. Oktay Aslanapa, *One Thousand Years of Turkish Carpets* (Istanbul, Turkey: Eren, 1988), 7.

176. "The Ottoman Empire," 210.

177. Mehmet Ates, *Turkish Carpets: The Language of Motifs and Symbols* (Istanbul, Turkey: Yeni Alas Matbaasi, 1997), 9.

178. Aslanapa, *One Thousand Years of Turkish Carpets*, 10.

179. Harald Böhmer and Jon Thompson, "The Pazyryk Carpet:

A Technical Discussion," *Notes in the History of Art* 10, no. 4 (Summer 1991): 30, 34.
180. J. Iten-Maritz, *Turkish Carpets* (New York: Kodansha International, 1977), 9.
181. Ates, *Turkish Carpets*, 12.
182. Iten-Maritz, *Turkish Carpets*, 9.
183. Ates, *Turkish Carpets*, 7.
184. Iten-Maritz, *Turkish Carpets*, 24; Böhmer and Thompson, "The Pazyryk Carpet," 30.
185. Böhmer and Thompson, "The Pazyryk Carpet," 31.
186. Esin, "The Horse in Turkic Art," 196–97.
187. Ibid., 198–99.
188. Ates, *Turkish Carpets*, 12.
189. Ibid., 12–13.
190. Ibid., 17.
191. Aslanapa, *One Thousand Years of Turkish Carpets*, 12.
192. Ibid., 12.
193. Iten-Maritz, *Turkish Carpets*, 8.
194. "The Ottoman Empire," 210.
195. Ates, *Turkish Carpets*, 10; Aslanapa, *One Thousand Years of Turkish Carpets*, 37–46, 61.
196. Aslanapa, *One Thousand Years of Turkish Carpets*, 61.
197. "The Ottoman Empire," 211.
198. Ates, *Turkish Carpets*, 10.
199. Daniel Walker, "Turkish Rugs," *Bulletin (St. Louis Art Museum)*, n.s., 18, no. 4 (Summer 1988): 5.
200. Denis Sinor, "The Origin of Turkic Balïq 'Town'" (proceedings of the 23rd Meeting of the Permanent International Altaistic Conference, Vienna, July 27 to August 1, 1980), *Central Asiatic Journal* 25, no. 1/2 (1981): 95.
201. Koray Özcan, "Notes on Turkish Towns in Central Asia (Pre-Islamic Period)," *Central Asiatic Journal* 52, no. 2 (2008): 186.
202. Edwin G. Pulleyblank, "Ji and Jiang: The Role of Exogamic Clans in the Organization of the Zhou Polity," *Early China* 25 (2000): 3–4.
203. Nicola Di Cosmo, "Ancient Inner Asian Nomads: Their Economic Basis and Its Significance in Chinese History," *Journal of Asian Studies* 53, no. 4 (1994): 1098–99.
204. Emel Esin, "Baliq and Ordu (The Early Turkish Circumvallations, in Architectural Aspects)," *Central Asiatic Journal* 27, no. 3/4 (1983): 173, 176.
205. Sophia-Karin Psarras, "Xiongnu Culture: Identification and Dating," *Central Asiatic Journal* 39, no. 1 (1995): 104.
206. Nicola Di Cosmo, *Ancient China and Its Enemies: The Rise of Nomadic Power in East Asian History* (Cambridge, England: Cambridge University Press, 2005), 107, 116–24.
207. Ibid., 115.

208. Esin, "Baliq and Ordu," 182.
209. Ibid., 190.
210. Sinor, "The Origin of Turkic Balïq 'Town,'" 96.
211. Ibid., 97.
212. Esin, "Baliq and Ordu," 169.
213. Ibid., 170–71.
214. Golden, *Central Asia in World History*, 18.
215. Esin, "Baliq and Ordu," 187.
216. Ibid., 173–78, 183–84.
217. Ibid., 183–87.
218. Richard J. H. Gottheil, "The Origin and History of the Minaret," *Journal of the American Oriental Society* 32, no. 2 (March 1910): 133, 138.
219. Ibid., 147.
220. Esin, "Baliq and Ordu," 186.
221. V. Minorsky, "Tamīm Ibn Baḥr's Journey to the Uyghurs," *Bulletin of the School of Oriental and African Studies* 12, no. 2 (1948): 283, 303.
222. Esin, "Baliq and Ordu," 177.
223. Ibid., 177.
224. Ibid., 182.
225. Eberhard, *Conquerors and Rulers*, 148.
226. Esin, "Baliq and Ordu," 195–96.
227. Jung-Pang Lo, "The Controversy over Grain Conveyance during the Reign of Qubilai Qaqan, 1260–94," *Far Eastern Quarterly* 13, no. 3 (May 1954): 262.
228. Esin, "Baliq and Ordu," 195.
229. Francis Woodman Cleaves, "An Early Mongolian Loan Contract from Qara Qoto," *Harvard Journal of Asiatic Studies* 18, no. 1/2 (June 1955): 10.
230. J. Brutzkus, "The Khazar Origin of Ancient Kiev," *Slavonic and East European Review*, American series, 3, no. 1 (1994): 111.
231. Ibid., 112–13.
232. Ibid., 115; Donald Ostrowski, "City Names of the Western Steppe at the Time of the Mongol Invasion," *Bulletin of the School of Oriental and African Studies* 61, no. 3 (1998): 465.
233. Esin, "Baliq and Ordu," 193.
234. Ibid., 195.
235. Stierlin, *Islamic Art and Architecture*, 8–9.
236. Maurice Dimand, "Turkish Art of the Muhammadan Period," *Metropolitan Museum of Art Bulletin*, n.s., 2, no. 7 (March 1944): 211–12.
237. George Michell and Amit Pasricha, *Mughal Architecture and Gardens* (Antique Collectors Club Dist., 2011), 19.
238. Mary Lee Settle, *Turkish Reflections: A Biography of a Place* (New York: Touchstone, 1992), 77.
239. Stierlin, *Islamic Art and Architecture*, 30.
240. Ibid., 32–33.
241. Ibid., 34.

242. Giovanni Curatola, *Turkish Art and Architecture: From the Seljuks to the Ottomans* (New York: Abbeville Press, 2010), 34.
243. Ibid., 86.
244. Stierlin, *Islamic Art and Architecture*, 43.
245. Ibid., 46–47.
246. Ibid., 52.
247. Elizabeth Schotten Merklinger, "Possible Seljuq Influence on the Dome of the Gol Gumbad in Bījāpūr," *East and West* 28, no. 1/4 (December 1978): 261.
248. Lisa Golombek and Donald Wilber, *The Timurid Architecture of Iran and Turan* (Princeton University Press, 1988), 188.
249. Stierlin, *Islamic Art and Architecture*, 58–79.
250. Bernard O'Kane, *Timurid Architecture in Khurasan* (Edinburgh, Scotland: University of Edinburgh, 1987), 110.
251. Golombek and Wilber, *The Timurid Architecture of Iran and Turan*, 216.
252. Ebba Koch, *The Complete Taj Mahal and the Riverfront Gardens of Agra* (London: Thames & Hudson, 2006), 89.
253. Dimand, "Turkish Art of the Muhammadan Period," 214.
254. Curatola, *Turkish Art and Architecture*, 241.
255. Ibid., 158.
256. Dimand, "Turkish Art of the Muhammadan Period," 214.
257. John E. Kicza, "The Peoples and Civilizations of the Americas before Contact," in *Agricultural and Pastoral Societies in Ancient and Classical History*, ed. Michael Adas (Philadelphia, PA: Temple University Press, 2001), 183.
258. Hans-J. Klimkeit, "Christians, Buddhists and Manichaeans in Medieval Central Asia," *Buddhist-Christian Studies* 1 (1981): 46–47.
259.259. Jean Paul Roux, "Historical Introduction," 4; Grousset, *The Empire of the Steppes*, 60–66.
260. Peter B. Golden, "Religion among the Qïpčaqs of Medieval Eurasia," 230.
261. Ibid.
262. Ibid., 234–36.
263. Ibid., 236.
264. Kevin Alan Brook, *The Jews of Khazaria* (Rowman & Littlefield, 2006), 227–28.
265. Roberte Hamayon, "Shamanism and the Turkish Peoples of Siberia and Central Asia," in *The Turkic Speaking Peoples: 2,000 Years of Art and Culture from Inner Asia to the Balkans*, ed. Ergun Cagatay and Dogan Kuban (Munich, Germany: Prestel, 2006), 311.
266. Osman Turan, "The Ideal of World Domination among the Medieval

Turks," *Studia Islamica*, no. 4 (1955): 77.
267. Mario Bussagli, "Pages of Euro-Asian History: Attila and the Huns," *East and West* 4, no. 3 (October 1953): 194.
268. Turan, "The Ideal of World Domination among the Medieval Turks," 79.
269. Sinor, "The Inner Asian Warriors," 134.
270. Baldick, *Animal and Shaman*, 39.
271. Grousset, *The Empire of the Steppes*, 20.
272. Turan, "The Ideal of World Domination among the Medieval Turks," 80-81.
273. Ibid., 81-82.
274. Baldick, *Animal and Shaman*, 29, 42.
275. Turan, "The Ideal of World Domination among the Medieval Turks," 82.
276. Hansgerd Göckenjan, "The World of the Early Nomadic Horsemen," in *The Turkic Speaking Peoples: 2,000 Years of Art and Culture from Inner Asia to the Balkans*, ed. Ergun Cagatay and Dogan Kuban (Prestel, 2006), 74.
277. Ibid., 70.
278. Ibid., 75.
279. Nicola Di Cosmo, "The Northern Frontier in Pre-Imperial China," in *The Cambridge History of Ancient China: From the Origins of Civilization to 221 BC*, ed. Michael Loewe and Edward L. Shaughnessy (Cambridge, England: Cambridge University Press, 1999), 952.
280. Baldick, *Animal and Shaman*, 41.
281. Ibid., 3.
282. Turan, "The Ideal of World Domination," 83-84.
283. Ibid., 88.
284. Emel Esin, *Türk Kozmolojisine Giriş* (İstanbul: Kabalcı Yayınevi, 2001), 39-41.
285. Ibid., 42-4.
286. Dursun Yıldırım, "Köktürk Çağında Tanrı mı Tanrılar mı vardı?" - *Türk Mitolojisine Giriş*, editörler Fatma Ahsen Turan ve Meral Ozan, 4. Baskı (Ankara: Gazi Kitabevi, 2018), 23.
287. Ibid., 23-26.
288. Fatma Ahsen Turan, "Eski Türklerde Tek Tanrı İnancı" - *Türk Mitolojisine Giriş*, editörler Fatma Ahsen Turan ve Meral Ozan, 4. Baskı (Ankara: Gazi Kitabevi, 2018), 37.
289. Yıldırım, "Köktürk Çağında Tanrı mı Tanrılar mı vardı?", 28-29.
290. Ibid., 29-31.
291. Esin, *Türk Kozmolojisine Giriş*, 62.
292. Turan, "Eski Türklerde Tek Tanrı İnancı", 34.
293. Ibid., 41-42.
294. Golden, "Religion among the Qïpčaqs of Medieval Eurasia," 209-13.

295. Turan, "Eski Türklerde Tek Tanrı İnancı", 42-44.
296. John Andrew Boyle, "Turkish and Mongol Shamanism in the Middle Ages," *Folklore* 83, no. 3 (Autumn 1972): 178.
297. Golden, "Religion among the Qïpčaqs of Medieval Eurasia," 206.
298. Süheyla Sarıtaş, "Türk Mitolojisinde Ak İyeler" - *Türk Mitolojisine Giriş*, editörler Fatma Ahsen Turan ve Meral Ozan, 4. Baskı (Ankara: Gazi Kitabevi, 2018), 49-50.
299. Sarıtaş, "Türk Mitolojisinde Ak İyeler", 49-50; Meral Ozan, "Türk Mitolojisinde Kara İyeler" - *Türk Mitolojisine Giriş*, editörler Fatma Ahsen Turan ve Meral Ozan, 4. Baskı (Ankara: Gazi Kitabevi, 2018), 63.
300. Ozan, "Türk Mitolojisinde Kara İyeler", 63-68.
301. Pervin Ergun, "Türk Mitolojisinde Ağaç Kültü" - *Türk Mitolojisine Giriş*, editörler Fatma Ahsen Turan ve Meral Ozan, 4. Baskı (Ankara: Gazi Kitabevi, 2018), 109.
302. İskender Oymak, "Türk Mitolojisinde Su Kültü" - *Türk Mitolojisine Giriş*, editörler Fatma Ahsen Turan ve Meral Ozan, 4. Baskı (Ankara: Gazi Kitabevi, 2018), 92.
303. Bahaeddin Ögel, *Türk Mitolojisi*, Cilt II, (Ankara: Türk Tarih Kurumu, 2014), 611.
304. Ergun, "Türk Mitolojisinde Ağaç Kültü", 116-18.
305. Ögel, *Türk Mitolojisi*, Cilt II, 610-17.
306. Ergun, "Türk Mitolojisinde Ağaç Kültü", 130.
307. Meral Ozan, "Türk Mitolojisinde Dağ Kültü" - *Türk Mitolojisine Giriş*, editörler Fatma Ahsen Turan ve Meral Ozan, 4. Baskı (Ankara: Gazi Kitabevi, 2018), 139.
308. Ögel, *Türk Mitolojisi*, Cilt II, 621.
309. Ozan, "Türk Mitolojisinde Dağ Kültü", 134, 137-38.
310. Ibid., 143-44.
311. Ögel, *Türk Mitolojisi*, Cilt II, 583.
312. Baldick, *Animal and Shaman*, 172; Wolfram Eberhard, *Conquerors and Rulers: Social Forces in Medieval China*, 2nd ed. (Boston, MA: E. J. Brill, 1970), 146-47.
313. Rezan Karakaş, "Türk Mitolojisinde Taş Kültü" - *Türk Mitolojisine Giriş*, editörler Fatma Ahsen Turan ve Meral Ozan, 4. Baskı (Ankara: Gazi Kitabevi, 2018), 163.
314. Bahaeddin Ögel, *Türk Mitolojisi*, Cilt I, (Ankara: Türk Tarih Kurumu, 2014), 25.
315. Ülkü Kara Düzgün, "Türk Mitolojisinde Ateş Kültü" - *Türk Mitolojisine Giriş*, editörler Fatma Ahsen Turan ve Meral Ozan, 4. Baskı (Ankara: Gazi Kitabevi, 2018), 150.

316. Ögel, *Türk Mitolojisi*, Cilt II, 631.
317. Kara Düzgün, "Türk Mitolojisinde Ateş Kültü", 156-57.
318. Karakaş, "Türk Mitolojisinde Taş Kültü", 164-65.
319. Gülten Küçükbasmacı, "Türk Mitolojisinde Yılan" - *Türk Mitolojisine Giriş*, editörler Fatma Ahsen Turan ve Meral Ozan, 4. Baskı (Ankara: Gazi Kitabevi, 2018), 200-05.
320. Mehmet Aça, "Türk Mitolojisinde Kartal" - *Türk Mitolojisine Giriş*, editörler Fatma Ahsen Turan ve Meral Ozan, 4. Baskı (Ankara: Gazi Kitabevi, 2018), 231.
321. Ibid., 232.
322. Ibid., 234-35.
323. Ögel, Türk Mitolojisi, Cilt I, 637-8.
324. Ibid., 637-8.
325. Baldick, *Animal and Shaman*, 39.
326. Ibid, 173.
327. Boyle, "Turkish and Mongol Shamanism in the Middle Ages," 179, 184, 190.
328. Ibid., 190.
329. Minorsky, "Tamīm Ibn Baḥr's Journey to the Uyghurs," 285.
330. Golden, "Religion among the Qïpčaqs of Medieval Eurasia," 207–8.
331. Ibid., 213.
332. Ibid., 206.
333. Baldick, *Animal and Shaman*, 8.
334. Ibid., 39.
335. Paul Pelliot, "Neuf notes sur des questions d'Asie centrale," *T'oung Pao*, 2nd ser., 26, no. 4/5 (1929): 216.
336. Richard Foltz, *Religions of the Silk Road: Overland Trade and Cultural Exchange from Antiquity to the Fifteenth Century* (New York: St. Martin's Griffin, 1999), 26.
337. Golden, "Religion among the Qïpčaqs of Medieval Eurasia," 197–99.
338. Eberhard, *Conquerors and Rulers*, 145, 155–56.
339. Baldick, *Animal and Shaman*, 46.
340. Golden, "Religion among the Qïpčaqs of Medieval Eurasia," 192–93.
341. Ibid., 194.
342. Esin, "The Horse in Turkic Art," 170.
343. Baldick, *Animal and Shaman*, 23, 30.
344. Namu Jila, "Myths and Traditional Beliefs about the Wolf and the Crow in Central Asia: Examples from the Turkic Wu-Sun and the Mongols," *Asian Folklore Studies* 65, no. 2 (2006): 167.
345. E. G. Pulleyblank, "The Wu-sun and Sakas and the Yüeh-chih Migration," *Bulletin of the School of Oriental and African Studies* 33, no. 1 (1970): 155; Jila, "Myths and Traditional Beliefs about the Wolf and the Crow in Central Asia," 163.
346. Jila, "Myths and Traditional Beliefs about the Wolf and the Crow in

Central Asia," 164; Pulleyblank, "The Wu-sun and Sakas and the Yüeh-chih Migration," 156–57.
347. Baldick, *Animal and Shaman*, 41; Jean Paul Roux, *Faune et flore sacrées dans les sociétés altaïques* (Paris: A. Maisonneuve, 1966), 199, 211, 229, 246–49, 285, 298, 315–16.
348. Emel Esin, "Tös and Moncuḳ Notes on Turkish Flag-Pole Finials," *Central Asiatic Journal* 16, no. 1 (1972): 22.
349. Robert L. Reynolds and Robert S. Lopez, "Odoacer: German or Hun?," *American Historical Review* 52, no. 1 (October 1946): 49.
350. Baldick, *Animal and Shaman*, 49.
351. Esin, "Tös and Moncuḳ Notes on Turkish Flag-Pole Finials," 14.
352. Ibid.
353. Ibid., 15.
354. Ibid., 22.
355. Ibid., 17, 22.
356. Golden, "Religion among the Qïpčaqs of Medieval Eurasia," 187–89.
357. Étienne de la Vaissière, "Huns et Xiongnu," *Central Asiatic Journal* 49, no. 1 (2005): 7.
358. Esin, "Tös and Moncuḳ Notes on Turkish Flag-Pole Finials," 15.
359. Ibid., 15–16.
360. Ibid., 29.
361. Choi, "Notes on Some Ancient Korean Titles," 37–38.
362. Ibid., 39–40.
363. Baldick, *Animal and Shaman*, 46.
364. Esin, "Tös and Moncuḳ Notes on Turkish Flag-Pole Finials," 30.
365. Ibid., 32.
366. Ibid., 24.
367. Golden, "Religion among the Qïpčaqs of Medieval Eurasia," 189–91.
368. Esin, "The Horse in Turkic Art," 171.
369. Volker Rybatzki, "Titles of Türk and Uigur Rulers in the Old Turkic Inscriptions," *Central Asiatic Journal* 44, no. 2 (2000): 226.
370. Baldick, *Animal and Shaman*, 7, 42–43.
371. Rybatzki, "Titles of Türk and Uigur Rulers in the Old Turkic Inscriptions," 220.
372. Baldick, *Animal and Shaman*, 27.
373. Ibid., 29–30.
374. Ibid., 42.
375. Golden, "Religion among the Qïpčaqs of Medieval Eurasia," 203–5.
376. Ildiko Ecsedy, "Chinese Historical Connections with the Turkic Empires and Their Heirs," in *The Turkic Speaking Peoples: 2,000 Years of Art and Culture from Inner Asia to the Balkans*, ed. Ergun Cagatay and Dogan Kuban (Munich, Germany: Prestel, 2006), 142.
377. Esin, "The Horse in Turkic Art," 198.

378. Baldick, *Animal and Shaman*, 42.
379. Ibid., 44, 46, 53.
380. A. Bruce Boswell, "The Kipchak Turks," *Slavonic Review* 6, no. 16 (June 1927): 84.
381. Golden, "Religion among the Qïpčaqs of Medieval Eurasia," 194.
382. Ibid., 195–96.
383. Koch, *The Complete Taj Mahal*, 85.
384. Valerie Hansen, "The Path of Buddhism into China: The View from Turfan," *Asia Major*, 3rd ser., 11, no. 2 (1998): 37.
385. Ibid., 41.
386. Ibid., 46.
387. Ibid., 57.
388. Eberhard, *Conquerors and Rulers*, 126–27.
389. Ibid., 148.
390. Ibid., 146.
391. Ibid., 144.
392. Hans-J. Klimkeit, "Buddhism in Turkish Central Asia," *Numen* 37, no. 1 (June 1990): 54.
393. Esin, "Baliq and Ordu," 177.
394. Klimkeit, "Buddhism in Turkish Central Asia," 54.
395. Ibid., 54.
396. Ibid., 56.
397. Ibid., 56–60.
398. Ibid., 56.
399. Ibid., 61.
400. Michael R. Drompp, *Tang China and the Collapse of the Uighur Empire* (Boston, MA: Brill Academic, 2005), 23; Roux, "Historical Introduction," 13.
401. Z. V. Togan, *Umumi Türk Tarihine Giriş* (Istanbul: Ismail Akgün, 1946), 149.
402. Ibid.
403. Claude Cahen, *Pre-Ottoman Turkey: A General Survey of the Material and Spiritual Culture and History 1071–1330* (New York: Taplinger, 1968), 5.
404. Foltz, *Religions of the Silk Road*, 69–70.
405. Ibid., 70.
406. Golden, "Religion among the Qïpčaqs of Medieval Eurasia," 227–30.
407. Ibid., 218–19.
408. Brook, *The Jews of Khazaria*, 94.
409. Klimkeit, "Christians, Buddhists and Manichaeans in Medieval Central Asia," 46.
410. Ibid., 47.
411. Golden, "Religion among the Qïpčaqs of Medieval Eurasia," 232.
412. Golden, *Central Asia in World History*, 69.
413. Ibid., 69.
414. Golden, "Religion among the Qïpčaqs of Medieval Eurasia," 233.
415. Golden, *Central Asia in World History*, 99.
416. Otto-Dorn, "Figural Stone Reliefs on Seljuk Sacred Architecture in Anatolia," 104.

417. Ibid., 146.
418. Turan, "The Ideal of World Domination," 90.
419. Gy. Káldy-Nagy, "The Holy War (Jihād) in the First Centuries of the Ottoman Empire" (Part 1. Eucharisterion: Essays Presented to Omeljan Pritsak on His Sixtieth Birthday by His Colleagues and Students), *Harvard Ukrainian Studies* 3/4 (1979–1980): 467.
420. Ibid., 468.
421. Ibid., 469.
422. Ibid., 470.
423. Clifford Edmund Bosworth, "Notes on Some Turkish Names in Abu'l-Faḍl Bayhaqī's Tārīkh-i Mas'ūdī," *Oriens* 36 (2001): 299.

CHAPTER 2: OVERVIEW OF THE PAST OF THE TURKS

424. Peter B. Golden, *Central Asia in World History* (New York: Oxford University Press, 2011), 9.
425. Çiğdem Atakuman, "Architectural Discourse and Social Transformation During the Early Neolithic of Southeast Anatolia," *Journal of World Prehistory*, Vol. 27, No. 1 (March 2014): 1.
426. David W. Anthony, The Horse, the Wheel, and Language: How Bronze-Age Riders from the Eurasian Steppes Shaped the Modern World. (2010, Princeton University Press, Princeton, NJ), 416.
427. Ibid, 67.
428. Alan K. Outram, Natalie A. Stear, Robin Bendrey, Sandra Olsen, Alexei Kasparov, Victor Zaibert, Nick Thorpe, Richard P. Evershed, The Earliest Horse Harnessing and Milking, Science, 6 March 2009, vol 323, 1332-35.
429. Egemen Çağrı Mızrak, Savaş-Arabaları'nın İç Asya – Çin Cephesi (M.Ö. XII. – M.Ö. VIII. Yy.) (The Inner Asia – China Aspect of War-Chariots (c. XII. – VIII. BCE)), International Journal of History, Vol 12 (5), October 2020, 2399; Xiang Wan, The Horse in Pre-Imperial China, Phd. Thesis in Eastern Asian Languages and Civilizations, University of Pennsylvania, Advisor: Victor H. Mair, 2013, 19; David W. Antony, The Horse, the Wheel, and Language: How Bronze-Age Riders from the Eurasian Steppes Shaped the Modern World, Princeton University Press, 2007, s. 371- 75, 397-405.
430. Jianjun Mei, Yongbin Yu, Kunlong Chen, Lu Wang, "The Appropriation of Early Bronze Technology in China", Appropriating Innovations (Entangled Knowledge in Eurasia, 5000-1500 BCE.), ed. Philipp. W. Stockhammer-Joseph Maran,

Oxbow, Oxford&Philadelphia, 2017, s. 232; Mızrak, Savaş-Arabaları'nın İç Asya – Çin Cephesi (M.Ö. XII. – M.Ö. VIII. Yy.) (The Inner Asia – China Aspect of War-Chariots (c. XII. – VIII. BCE)), 2401-02.

431. Jianjun Mei, "Cultural Interaction between China and Central Asia during the Bronze Age", Proceedings of the British Academy, 121, The British Academy 2003, 31; Michael Puett, "China in Early Eurasian History: A Brief Review of Recent Scholarship on the Issue", The Bronze Age and Early Iron Age Peoples of Eastern Central Asia, ed. Victor H. Mair, vol. 2, 1998, 705; Stanley J. Olsen, "The Horse in Ancient China and Its Cultural Influence in Some Other Areas", Proceedings of the Academy of Natural Sciences of Philadelphia, vol. 140, No. 2, 1988, 163; Mızrak, Savaş-Arabaları'nın İç Asya – Çin Cephesi (M.Ö. XII. – M.Ö. VIII. Yy.) (The Inner Asia – China Aspect of War-Chariots (c. XII. – VIII. BCE)), 2403.

432. Esther Jacobson-Tepfer, "The Image of the Wheeled Vehicle in the Mongolian Altai: Instability and Ambiguity", The Silk Road, 10 (2012), 3-8.

433. V. V. Barthold, *Four Studies on the History of Central Asia* (Boston, MA: E. J. Brill, 1962), 1.

434. Paul J. Alexander, "The Strength of Empire and Capital as Seen through Byzantine Eyes," *Speculum* 37, no. 3 (July 1962): 340.

435. Ibid.

436. Peter B. Golden, "The Turkic Peoples: A Historical Sketch," in *The Turkic Languages*, ed. Lars Johanson and Eva A. Csato (Abingdon, Great Britain: Routledge, 2006), 16; Carter Vaughn Findley, *The Turks in World History* (New York: Oxford University Press, 2005), 21; William Montgomery McGovern, *The Early Empires of Central Asia: A Study of the Scythians and the Huns and the Part They Played in World History* (Chapel Hill, NC: University of North Carolina Press, 1939), 96.

437. John Man, *Attila: The Barbarian King Who Challenged Rome* (New York: St. Martin's Griffin, 2009), 32.

438. René Grousset, *The Empire of the Steppes: A History of Central Asia* (New Brunswick, NJ: Rutgers University Press, 1999), 19; Jean-Paul Roux, *Histoire Des Turcs: Deux mille ans du Pacifique à la Méditerranée* (Fayard, 2000), 43; Z. V. Togan, *Umumi Türk Tarihine Giriş* (Istanbul: Ismail Akgün, 1946), 39.

439. Alan Sanders, "The Turkic Peoples of Mongolia," in *The Peoples of the*

World, ed. Margaret Bainbridge (Routledge, 1993), 179.
440. William W. Fitzhugh and Jamsranjav Bayarsaikhan, "Mapping Ritual Landscapes in Bronze Age Mongolia and Beyond: Interpreting the Ideoscape of the Deer Stone-Khirigsuur Complex," in *Mapping Mongolia: Situating Mongolia in the World from Geologic Time to the Present*, ed. Paula L. W. Sabloff (University of Pennsylvania Museum of Archaeology and Anthropology, 2011), 170.
441. Denis Sinor, "The Scope and Importance of Altaic Studies," *Journal of the American Oriental Society* 83, no. 2 (April–June 1963): 194.
442. Togan, *Umumi Türk Tarihine Giriş*, 164; David Christian, *A History of Russia, Central Asia, and Mongolia. Volume I: Inner Eurasia from Prehistory to the Mongol Empire* (Hoboken, NJ: Wiley-Blackwell, 1998), 279.
443. Anatole V. Baikaloff, "Notes on the Origin of the Name 'Siberia,'" *Slavonic and East European Review* 29, no. 72 (December 1950), 288–89.
444. Ibid., 289.
445. Servet Somuncuoglu, *The Turks on the Rocks* (Istanbul: At-Ok, 2011), 19–20.
446. Ibid., 12, 18, 25.
447. Servet Somuncuoglu, *Saimaluu-Tash: Sky Horses* (Istanbul: At-Ok-Yay, 2011), 24, 42–43.
448. Ildiko Ecsedy, "Chinese Historical Connections with the Turkic Empires and their Heirs," in *The Turkic Speaking Peoples: 2,000 Years of Art and Culture from Inner Asia to the Balkans*, ed. Ergun Cagatay and Dogan Kuban (Munich, Germany: Prestel, 2006), 133.
449. Egemen Çağrı Mızrak, *Bozkır Kavimleri: M.Ö. VII. Yüzyıldan M.S. VI. Yüzyılın Ortalarına Kadar Batı Türkistan ve Kuzey Hindistan'daki Bozkırlar* (İstanbul: Ötüken, 2017), 231.
450. McGovern, *The Early Empires of Central Asia*, 94–96.
451. Ibid., 96.
452. Julian Baldick, *Animal and Shaman: Ancient Religions of Central Asia* (New York University Press, 2012), 44.
453. Egemen Çağrı Mızrak, *Bozkır Kavimleri: M.Ö. VII. Yüzyıldan M.S. VI. Yüzyılın Ortalarına Kadar Batı Türkistan ve Kuzey Hindistan'daki Bozkırlar* (İstanbul: Ötüken, 2017), 230-232.
454. Ibid., 30.
455. Ibid., 265.
456. Lalueza-Fox, C., Sampietro, M. L., et al (2004), "Unravelling migrations in the steppe:

mitochondrial DNA sequences from ancient Central Asians", *Proceedings of the Royal Society B: Biological Sciences (Proc. Biol. Sci.)*, 271, 941-947.

457. Mızrak, *Bozkır Kavimleri: M.Ö. VII. Yüzyıldan M.S. VI. Yüzyılın Ortalarına Kadar Batı Türkistan ve Kuzey Hindistan'daki Bozkırlar*, 263.

458. Ibid., 258-59.

459. Ibid., 255-56.

460. Victor Henry Mair, "The Mummies of East Central Asia," *Penn Museum Expedition*, 52 (3) (Winter 2010), 25.

461. Mızrak, *Bozkır Kavimleri: M.Ö. VII. Yüzyıldan M.S. VI. Yüzyılın Ortalarına Kadar Batı Türkistan ve Kuzey Hindistan'daki Bozkırlar*, 262-63, 280-81.

462. Mair (2010), "The Mummies of East Central Asia," 32.

463. Gonzalez-Ruiz, M., Santos, C., et al,, "Tracing the Origin of the East-West Population Admixture in the Altai Region (Central Asia), *PLoS ONE*, 7 (11) (November 2012), 9-10.

464. V.I. Molodin, "The Frozen Scythian Burial Complexes of the Altai Mountains: Conservation and Survey Issues", Preservation of the Frozen Tombs of the Altai Mountains, UNESCO, World Heritage Convention (2008), 25-26.

465. Mızrak, *Bozkır Kavimleri: M.Ö. VII. Yüzyıldan M.S. VI. Yüzyılın Ortalarına Kadar Batı Türkistan ve Kuzey Hindistan'daki Bozkırlar*, 89-90.

466. Paul Pelliot, "L'origine du nom de 'Chine,'" *T'oung Pao*, 2nd ser., 13, no. 5 (1912): 731–32.

467. Nicola Di Cosmo, *Ancient China and Its Enemies: The Rise of Nomadic Power in East Asian History*, Cambridge University Press, 2005, 165.

468. Ibid., 87, 107.

469. Owen Lattimore, *Inner Asian Frontiers of China*, Oxford University Press, 1940, p. 455.

470. Di Cosmo, *Ancient China and Its Enemies: The Rise of Nomadic Power in East Asian History*, 109.

471. William Montgomery McGovern, The Early Empires of Central Asia: A Study of the Scythians and the Huns and the Part They Played in World History, The University of North Carolina Press, 1939, 99-101.

472. Mızrak, *Bozkır Kavimleri: M.Ö. VII. Yüzyıldan M.S. VI. Yüzyılın Ortalarına Kadar Batı Türkistan ve Kuzey Hindistan'daki Bozkırlar*, 65-66.

473. Ibid., 198-201, 281-284.

474. Ibid., 199.

475. Ibid., 283.

476. Ibid., 199.

477. Ibid., 283-284.

478. Ibid., 284.
479. Ibid., 285.
480. Ibid., 286.
481. Alessandro Achilli et al., "Mitochondrial DNA Variation of Modern Tuscans Supports the Near Eastern Origin of Etruscans," *American Journal of Human Genetics* 80, no. 4 (April 2007): 759–68.
482. A. Piazza et al., "Origin of the Etruscans: Novel Clues from the Y Chromosome Lineages— Abstract of paper read at the 39th European Human Genetics Conference in Nice, France, in June, 2007," *European Journal of Human Genetics* 15, supplement 1 (conference abstracts; 2007); 19; T. A. Maugh II, "Genetic Tests: Italians Were from Turkey," *Los Angeles Times*, June 18, 2007.
483. Turkish Historical Society, "A Profile from History: The Etruscans" (proceedings from the TKK Symposium on the Etruscans, June 2–4, 2007).
484. Helmut Nickel, "Tamgas and Runes, Magic Numbers and Magic Symbols," *Metropolitan Museum Journal* 8 (1973): 173.
485. Andras Zakar, "Sumerian-Ural-Altaic Affinities," *Current Anthropology* 12, no. 2 (April 1971): 215; Jonathan R. Ziskind, "The Sumerian Problem," *History Teacher* 5, no. 2 (January 1972): 41; Jerrold Cooper, "Sumerian and Aryan: Racial Theory, Academic Politics and Parisian Assyriology," *Revue de l'histoire des religions* 210, no. 2 (April–June 1993): 187.
486. Istvan Fodor, "Are the Sumerians and the Hungarians or the Uralic Peoples Related?" *Current Anthropology* 17, no. 1 (March 1976): 118.
487. Togan, *Umumi Türk Tarihine Giriş*, 13.
488. Andrew Bell-Fialkoff, *The Role of Migration in the History of the Eurasian Steppe: Sedentary Civilization vs. "Barbarian" and Nomad* (London: Palgrave Macmillan, 2000), 275.
489. E. A. Thompson, *The Huns* (Hoboken, NJ: Wiley-Blackwell, 1996), 186.
490. Jean Paul Roux, "Historical Introduction," in *The Turkic Peoples of the World*, ed. Margaret Bainbridge (Abingdon, Great Britain: Routledge, 1993), 4.
491. Ibid., 5–6.
492. Grousset, *The Empire of the Steppes*, 220.
493. Egemen Çağrı Mızrak, *Bozkır Kavimleri: M.Ö. VII. Yüzyıldan M.S. VI. Yüzyılın Ortalarına Kadar Batı Türkistan ve Kuzey Hindistan'daki Bozkırlar* (İstanbul: Ötüken, 2017), 265.

494. William Montgomery McGovern, *The Early Empires of Central Asia: A Study of the Scythians and the Huns and the Part They Played in World History*, The University of North Carolina Press, 1939, 99-101.
495. Mızrak, *Bozkır Kavimleri: M.Ö. VII. Yüzyıldan M.S. VI. Yüzyılın Ortalarına Kadar Batı Türkistan ve Kuzey Hindistan'daki Bozkırlar*, 65-66.
496. Ibid., 50.
497. Ibid., 52.
498. Ibid., 57-8.
499. Ibid., 54.
500. Ibid., 230-32.
501. Ibid., 265.
502. Christopher I. Beckwith, *Empires of the Silk Road: A History of Central Eurasia from the Bronze Age to the Present* (Princeton University Press, 2009), 405; R. C. Blockley, *The History of Menander the Guardsman: Introductory Essay, Text, Translation and Historiographical Notes*, Arca Classical and Medieval Texts, Papers, and Monographs (Barnsley, Great Britain: Francis Cairns, 1985), 116-17.
503. Togan, *Umumi Türk Tarihine Giriş*, 23.
504. Ibid.
505. Baldick, *Animal and Shaman*, 5.
506. Nikolaos Sekoundinos, "An Epitome on the Family of the Ottomans for Aeneas," in *Mehmed II the Conqueror: and the Fall of the Franco-Byzantine Levant to the Ottoman Turks: Some Western Views and Testimonies*, ed. Marios Philippides (Tempe, AZ: Mrts, 2007), 57.
507. Tadeusz Milewski, "Similarities between the Asiatic and American Indian Languages," *International Journal of American Linguistics* 26, no. 4 (1960): 265.
508. Olga Rickards et al., "Genetic Relationships among the Native American Populations," *Anthropologischer Anzeiger* 52, no. 3 (September 1994): 193–96.
509. Gabriel E. Novick et al., "Polymorphic Alu Insertions and the Asian Origin of Native American Populations," *Human Biology* 70, no. 1 (February 1998): 24; Rickards et al., 196.
510. Novick et al., "Polymorphic Alu Insertions," 29, 37.
511. Samuel G. Franklin et al., "Albumin Naskapi Variant in North American Indians and Eti Turks," *Proceedings of the National Academy of Sciences of the United States of America* 77, no. 9 (September 1980): 5480–82.
512. Peter B. Golden, "The Turkic Nomads of the Pre-Islamic Eurasian Steppes," in *The Turkic Speaking Peoples: 2,000 Years of Art*

and *Culture from Inner Asia to the Balkans*, ed. Ergun Cagatay and Dogan Kuban (Prestel, 2006), 85.

513. David Christian, *A History of Russia, Central Asia, and Mongolia. Volume I: Inner Eurasia from Prehistory to the Mongol Empire* (Hoboken, NJ: Wiley-Blackwell, 1998), 248.

514. Golden, *Central Asia in World History*, 1–2.

515. Michal Biran, *Chinggis Khan* (London: Oneworld, 2007), 7; Thompson, *The Huns*, 22.

516. Ching-Lung Chen, "Trading Activities of the Turkic Peoples in China," *Central Asiatic Journal* 25, no. 1/2 (1981): 52.

517. Herwig Wolfram, *History of the Goths* (Oakland, CA: University of California Press, 1990), 10.

518. Thompson, *The Huns*, 33.

519. Ibid., 22.

520. Isaac Asimov, *Asimov's Chronology of the World: The History of the World from the Big Bang to Modern Times* (New York: Harper Collins, 1991), 102–5.

521. Istvan Vasary, *Turks, Tatars and Russians in the 13th–16th Centuries* (Ashgate, 2007), i–33.

522. Ecsedy, "Chinese Historical Connections," 134.

523. Peter B. Golden, *Nomads and Their Neighbours in the Russian Steppe: Turks, Khazars and Qipchaks* (Variorum, 2003), vi–84.

524. Michael R. Drompp, *Tang China and the Collapse of the Uighur Empire* (Boston, MA: Brill Academic, 2005), 126–27.

525. Volker Rybatzki, "Titles of Türk and Uigur Rulers in the Old Turkic Inscriptions," *Central Asiatic Journal* 44, no. 2 (2000): 218.

526. Osman Turan, "The Ideal of World Domination among the Medieval Turks," *Studia Islamica*, no. 4 (1955): 79, 83–84.

527. Rybatzki, "Titles of Türk," 207.

528. Ibid., 207.

529. Ibid., 222–23.

530. Golden, *Nomads and Their Neighbours in the Russian Steppe*, vi–85.

531. C. Edmund Bosworth, "The Origins of the Seljuqs," in *The Seljuqs: Politics, Society and Culture*, ed. Christian Lange and Songül Mecit (Edinburgh: Edinburgh University Press, 2012), 14, 16.

532. Emel Esin, "Tabarī's Report on the Warfare with the Türgiš and the Testimony of Eighth Century Central Asian Art" (proceedings of the 15th Meeting of the Permanent International Altaistic Conference August 7–12, 1972), *Central Asiatic Journal* 17, no. 2/4 (1973): 131.

533. Clifford Edmund Bosworth, *The New Islamic Dynasties: A Chronological and Genealogical*

Manual (Edinburgh: Edinburgh University Press, 1996), 184.
534. Hansgerd Göckenjan, "The World of the Early Nomadic Horsemen," in *The Turkic Speaking Peoples: 2,000 Years of Art and Culture from Inner Asia to the Balkans*, ed. Ergun Cagatay and Dogan Kuban (Munich: Prestel, 2006), 75.
535. Leo De Hartog, *Genghis Khan: Conqueror of the World* (London: Tauris Parke, 2008), 12.
536. Douglas E. Streusand, *Islamic Gunpowder Empires: Ottomans, Safavids, Mughals* (Boulder, CO: Westview Press, 2011), 18–19.
537. Claude Cahen, *Pre-Ottoman Turkey: A General Survey of the Material and Spiritual Culture and History, 1071–1330* (New York: Taplinger, 1968), 24.
538. Bahaeddin Ögel, *Türk Kültür Tarihine Giriş*, Kültür Bakanlığı Yayınları, cilt 8, Ankara 1991, 19-21.
539. Ibid., 19.
540. John Keegan, *A History of Warfare* (New York: Alfred A. Knopf, 1994), 156.
541. Ibid., 177–78.
542. Peter B. Golden, "Nomads and Sedentary Societies in Medieval Eurasia," in *East Central and Eastern Europe in the Early Middle Ages*, ed. Florin Curta (Ann Arbor, MI: University of Michigan Press, 2008), 75.
543. McGovern, *The Early Empires of Central Asia*, 100–1.
544. Ibid., 101.
545. Benjamin E. Wallacker and Ruth I. Meserve, "The Emperor of China and the Hobbled Horse of the Xiongnu," *Central Asiatic Journal* 49, no. 2 (2005): 287.
546. Wolfram Eberhard, *Conquerors and Rulers: Social Forces in Medieval China*, 2nd ed. (Boston, MA: E. J. Brill, 1970), 115–16.
547. Ibid., 116.
548. Nicola Di Cosmo, *Ancient China and Its Enemies: The Rise of Nomadic Power in East Asian History* (Cambridge University Press, 2005), 167; Eberhard, *Conquerors and Rulers*, 116–18.
549. Eberhard, *Conquerors and Rulers*, 118.
550. Di Cosmo, *Ancient China and Its Enemies*, 167.
551. Eberhard, *Conquerors and Rulers*, 115–16.
552. Man, *Attila*, 34–35.
553. James Baker, *Turkey* (New York: Henry Holt, 1877), 123.
554. Göckenjan, "The World of the Early Nomadic Horsemen," 69–70.
555. McGovern, *The Early Empires of Central Asia*, 104; Golden, "Nomads and Sedentary Societies in Medieval Eurasia," 75.
556. Nicola Di Cosmo, "The Northern Frontier in Pre-Imperial China,"

in *The Cambridge History of Ancient China: From the Origins of Civilization to 221 BC*, ed. Michael Loewe and Edward L. Shaughnessy (Cambridge, England: Cambridge University Press, 1999), 952.
557. McGovern, *The Early Empires of Central Asia*, 105.
558. Denis Sinor, "The Inner Asian Warriors," *Journal of the American Oriental Society* 101, no. 2 (April–June 1981): 139.
559. James Waterson, *The Knights of Islam: The Wars of the Mamluks* (Barnsley, England: Greenhill Books, 2007), 62.
560. Sinor, "The Inner Asian Warriors," 141.
561. Golden, "The Turkic Nomads of the Pre-Islamic Eurasian Steppes," 84.
562.562. Keegan, *A History of Warfare*, 187.
563. Ibid., 162.
564. Ibid., 161–62.
565. McGovern, *The Early Empires of Central Asia*, 104.
566. Göckenjan, "The World of the Early Nomadic Horsemen," 70.
567. Ibid., 72.
568. Baldick, *Animal and Shaman*, 25.
569. Ibid., 42–43.
570. Di Cosmo, *Ancient China and Its Enemies: The Rise of Nomadic Power in East Asian History*, 274–75.
571. Peter B. Golden, "Religion among the Qïpčaqs of Medieval Eurasia," *Central Asiatic Journal* 42, no. 2 (1998): 182.
572. Omeljan Pritsak, "The Hunnic Language of the Attila Clan," *Harvard Ukrainian Studies* 6, no. 4 (December 1982): 455.
573. Ibid., 437–38.
574. Peter B. Golden, "Nomads and Sedentary Societies in Eurasia," in *Agricultural and Pastoral Societies in Ancient and Classical History*, ed. Michael Adas (Philadelphia, PA: Temple University Press, 2001), 87.
575. Drompp, *Tang China*, 11.
576. McGovern, *The Early Empires of Central Asia*, 133, 149.
577. Ibid., 150–51.
578. Talat Tekin, *A Grammar of Orkhon Turkic* (Abingdon, Great Britain: Routledge Curzon, 1997), 262.
579. Drompp, *Tang China*, 24.
580. Mario Bussagli, "Pages of Euro-Asian History: Attila and the Huns," *East and West* 4, no. 3 (October 1953): 194.
581. Hyun Jin Kim, *The Huns* (New York, NY: Routledge, 2016), 12.
582. V. Minorsky, "Tamīm Ibn Baḥr's Journey to the Uyghurs," *Bulletin of the School of Oriental and African Studies* 12, no. 2 (1948): 283, 303; Colin Mackerras, *The Uighur Empire: According to the*

T'ang Dynastic Histories, A Study in Sino-Uighur Relations 744–840 (Columbia, SC: University of South Carolina Press, 1972), 13; Peter B. Golden, *Central Asia in World History* (New York: Oxford University Press, 2011), 45.

583. Kim, *The Huns*, 81-82.
584. Ibid., 82.
585. Ibid.,, 149-159.
586. Ibid., 14.
587. Peter B. Golden, *Central Asia in World History* (New York: Oxford University Press, 2011), 70; Peter B. Golden, *The Turkic World in Mahmûd al-Kâshgharî*, Complexity of Interaction along the Eurasian Steppe Zone in the First Millennium CE, ed. Jan Bemmann and Michael Schmauder (Rheinische Friedrich-Wilhelms-Universität Bonn, 2015), 509.
588. Omeljan Pritsak, "The Origin of Rus," *Russian Review* 36, no. 3 (July 1977): 268; Peter B. Golden, *Nomads and Their Neighbours in the Russian Steppe: Turks, Khazars and Qipchaqs* (Farnham: Variorum, 2003), vi-87-89; J. Brutzkus, "The Khazar Origin of Ancient Kiev," *Slavonic and East European Review*, American series, 3, no. 1 (1994): 111.
589. Golden, *Nomads and Their Neighbours in the Russian Steppe*, vi-96-97; Pritsak, "The Origin of Rus," 268.
590. Kim, *The Huns*, 14-15.
591. Ibid.
592. Ibid., 60.
593. Ibid., 8.
594. Ibid.
595. Wolfram Eberhard, *Conquerors and Rulers: Social Forces in Medieval China*, 2nd ed. (Boston, MA: E. J. Brill, 1970), 115–16; Kim, *The Huns*, 4; John Man, *Attila: The Barbarian King Who Challenged Rome* (New York: St. Martin's Griffin, 2009), 34–35; Nicola Di Cosmo, *Ancient China and Its Enemies: The Rise of Nomadic Power in East Asian History* (Cambridge University Press, 2005), 167; Eberhard, Conquerors and Rulers, 116–18.
596. Kim, *The Huns*, 4, 32-34.
597. Richard Foltz, *Religions of the Silk Road: Overland Trade and Cultural Exchange from Antiquity to the Fifteenth Century* (New York: St. Martin's Griffin, 1999), 1–2.
598. Milo C. Beach, "The Ear Commands the Story: Exploration and Imagination on the Silk Road," *Art Institute of Chicago Museum Studies* 33, no. 1 (2007): 10–12.
599. Berthold Laufer, *Jade: A Study in Chinese Archæology and Religion*, Anthropological Series, vol. 10 (Field Museum of Natural History, February 1912), 5.

600. Xinru Liu, *The Silk Road in World History* (New York: Oxford University Press, 2010), 1.
601. Ibid., 1.
602. Ibid.
603. Togan, *Umumi Türk Tarihine Giriş*, 115.
604. David Christian, "Silk Roads or Steppe Roads? The Silk Roads in World History," *Journal of World History* 11, no. 1 (Spring 2000): 10.
605. Liu, *The Silk Road in World History*, 3.
606. Ibid., 5.
607. Ibid.
608. Foltz, *Religions of the Silk Road*, 49.
609. Ibid., 58.
610. Baldick, *Animal and Shaman*, 24.
611. Thompson, *The Huns*, 186.
612. Golden, "The Turkic Nomads of the Pre-Islamic Eurasian Steppes," 85.
613. Ecsedy, "Chinese Historical Connections," 134.
614. Golden, *Central Asia in World History*, 45.
615. Golden, "Nomads and Sedentary Societies in Medieval Eurasia," 95.
616. Jennifer Holmgren, "Women and Political Power in the Traditional T'o-Pa Elite: A Preliminary Study of the Biographies of Empresses in the Wei-Shu," *Monumenta Serica* 35 (1981–1983): 33.
617. Pan Yihong, "Marriage Alliances and Chinese Princesses in International Politics from Han through T'ang," *Asia Major*, 3rd ser., 10, no. 1/2 (1997): 123.
618. Bosworth, *The New Islamic Dynasties*, 198.
619. Roux, *Histoire des Turcs: Deux mille ans du Pacifique à la Méditerranée*, 197.
620. Golden, "Nomads and Sedentary Societies in Medieval Eurasia," 73.
621. G. E. Tetley, *The Ghaznavid and Seljuk Turks: Poetry as a Source for Iranian History* (Abingdon, Great Britain: Routledge, 2009), 14.
622. Fanny Davis, *The Ottoman Lady: A Social History from 1718 to 1918* (Westport, CT: Greenwood, 1986), 265.
623. Golden, *Central Asia in World History*, 71.
624. Davis, *The Ottoman Lady*, 45.
625. Leslie P. Pierce, *The Imperial Harem: Women and Sovereignty in the Ottoman Empire* (New York: Oxford University Press, 1993), 275.

CHAPTER 3: THE RISE OF THE MOUNTED ARCHERS

626. Peter B. Golden, "The Turkic Nomads of the Pre-Islamic Eurasian Steppes," in *The Turkic*

Speaking Peoples: 2,000 Years of Art and Culture from Inner Asia to the Balkans, ed. Ergun Cagatay and Dogan Kuban (Munich: Prestel, 2006), 83.

627. Z. V. Togan, *Umumi Türk Tarihine Giriş* (Istanbul: Ismail Akgün, 1946), 164.

628. Ildiko Ecsedy, "Chinese Historical Connections with the Turkic Empires and their Heirs," in *The Turkic Speaking Peoples: 2,000 Years of Art and Culture from Inner Asia to the Balkans*, ed. Ergun Cagatay and Dogan Kuban (Munich: Prestel, 2006), 133.

629. William Montgomery McGovern, *The Early Empires of Central Asia: A Study of the Scythians and the Huns and the Part They Played in World History* (Chapel Hill, NC: University of North Carolina Press, 1939), 88.

630. Ibid., 43.

631. Rıza Zelyut, *Yabancı Kaynaklara Göre Türk Kimliği* (Ankara: Kripto, 2009), 380.

632. McGovern, *The Early Empires of Central Asia*, 43–45.

633. Julian Baldick, *Animal and Shaman: Ancient Religions of Central Asia* (New York: New York University Press, 2012), 5.

634. Richard Foltz, *Religions of the Silk Road: Overland Trade and Cultural Exchange from Antiquity to the Fifteenth Century* (New York: St. Martin's Griffin, 1999), 25.

635. McGovern, *The Early Empires of Central Asia*, 45.

636. Nicola Di Cosmo, *Ancient China and Its Enemies: The Rise of Nomadic Power in East Asian History* (Cambridge, England: Cambridge University Press, 2005), 87.

637. Ibid.

638. 638. Ibid., 107.

639. Owen Lattimore, *Inner Asian Frontiers of China* (New York: Oxford University Press, 1940), 455.

640. Otto Maenchen-Helfen, "The Ting-Ling," *Harvard Journal of Asiatic Studies* 4, no. 1 (May 1939): 77–78, 80.

641. Ibid., 77.

642. Namu Jila, "Myths and Traditional Beliefs about the Wolf and the Crow in Central Asia: Examples from the Turkic Wu-Sun and the Mongols," *Asian Folklore Studies* 65, no. 2 (2006): 162.

643. Ibid., 163.

644. E. D. Phillips, "New Light on the Ancient History of the Eurasian Steppe," *American Journal of Archaeology* 61, no. 3 (July 1957): 279.

645. Sophia-Karin Psarras, "Han and Xiongnu a Reexamination of Cultural and Political Relations (II)," *Monumenta Serica* 52 (2004): 62.

646. Gerard Clauson, *Studies in Turkic and Mongolic Linguistics* (Abingdon: Routledge, 1962), 20.
647. Louis Hambis, "The Ancient Civilizations of Manchuria," *East and West* 7, no. 3 (October 1956): 221.
648. Psarras, "Han and Xiongnu a Reexamination," 62.
649. Ibid., 62–63.
650. Edwin G. Pulleyblank, "The 'High Carts': A Turkish-Speaking People before the Türks," *Asia Major*, 3rd ser., 3, no. 1 (1990): 21.
651. Maenchen-Helfen, "The Ting-Ling," 79.
652. Ibid., 83, 86; Pulleyblank, "The 'High Carts,'" 21.
653. Pulleyblank, "The 'High Carts,'" 22.
654. Ibid., 23, 26.
655. Maenchen-Helfen, "The Ting-Ling," 83–84.
656. Ibid., 86.
657. Pulleyblank, "The 'High Carts,'" 22.
658. T. Senga, "The Toquz Oghuz Problem and the Origin of the Khazars," *Journal of Asian History* 24, no. 1 (1990): 64–65.
659. Peter B. Golden, "Religion among the Qïpčaqs of Medieval Eurasia," *Central Asiatic Journal* 42, no. 2 (1998): 185.
660. Senga, "The Toquz Oghuz Problem," 64.
661. Ibid., 62.
662. V. Minorsky, "The Turkish Dialect of the Khalaj," *Bulletin of the School of Oriental Studies* 10, no. 2 (1940): 426.
663. Ibid., 430.
664. Han-Woo Choi, "Notes on Some Ancient Korean Titles," *Central Asiatic Journal* 36, no. 1/2 (1992): 34, 40–41.
665. Q. Edward Wang, "History, Space, and Ethnicity: The Chinese Worldview," *Journal of World History* 10, no. 2 (Fall 1999): 286.
666. Edwin G. Pulleyblank, "Ji and Jiang: The Role of Exogamic Clans in the Organization of the Zhou Polity," *Early China* 25 (2000): 3–4.
667. Ibid., 22.
668. Paul Pelliot, "L'origine du nom de 'Chine,'" *T'oung Pao*, 2nd ser., 13, no. 5 (1912): 731–32.
669. Ibid., 736–40.
670. McGovern, *The Early Empires of Central Asia*, 99–101.
671. Di Cosmo, *Ancient China and Its Enemies: The Rise of Nomadic Power in East Asian History*, 109–10.
672. Lattimore, *Inner Asian Frontiers of China*, 349.
673. Di Cosmo, *Ancient China and Its Enemies: The Rise of Nomadic Power in East Asian History*, 109.
674. Ibid., 114–15.
675. Ibid., 110–11.
676. Ibid., 123.
677. Ibid., 124–25.
678. Ibid., 139.

679. Ibid., 127–29.
680. Ibid., 130, 165.
681. Ibid., 157.
682. Ibid., 131, 134.
683. Owen Lattimore, "Origins of the Great Wall of China: A Frontier Concept in Theory and Practice," *Geographical Review* 27, no. 4 (October 1937): 536.
684. Di Cosmo, *Ancient China and Its Enemies: The Rise of Nomadic Power in East Asian History*, 161–62.
685. Colin Mackerras, *The Uighur Empire: According to the T'ang Dynastic Histories, A Study in Sino-Uighur Relations 744–840* (Columbia, SC: University of South Carolina Press, 1972), 1.
686. Thomas J. Barfield, *The Perilous Frontier: Nomadic Empires and China* (Hoboken: Blackwell, 1992), 13.
687. Johannes L. Kurz, "A Survey of the Historical Sources for the Five Dynasties and Ten States in Song Times," *Journal of Song-Yuan Studies* 33 (2003): 188.
688. Di Cosmo, *Ancient China and Its Enemies: The Rise of Nomadic Power in East Asian History*, 131.
689. Ibid., 138–39.
690. Ibid., 144.
691. Lattimore, "Origins of the Great Wall of China: A Frontier Concept in Theory and Practice," 529.
692. Wang, "History, Space, and Ethnicity," 287.
693. Ibid., 288–89.
694. Ibid., 295.
695. Arif Dirlik, "Timespace, Social Space, and the Question of Chinese Culture," *Monumenta Serica* 54 (2006): 425.
696. Wang, "History, Space, and Ethnicity," 291.
697. Ibid., 290.
698. Julia Lovel, *The Opium War: Drugs, Dreams, and the Making of China* (Picador, 2011), 79.
699. Wang, "History, Space, and Ethnicity," 293.
700. Psarras, "Han and Xiongnu a Reexamination," 75.
701. Wang, "History, Space, and Ethnicity," 295.
702. Pan Yihong, "Marriage Alliances and Chinese Princesses in International Politics from Han through T'ang," *Asia Major*, 3rd ser., 10, no. 1/2 (1997): 125.
703. Ibid.
704. Ibid., 126.
705. Justin McCarthy and Carolyn McCarthy, *Who Are the Turks?* (New York: American Forum for Global Education, 2003), 9; Claude Cahen, *Pre-Ottoman Turkey: A General Survey of the Material and Spiritual Culture and History 1071–1330* (New York: Taplinger, 1968), 1.

706. Di Cosmo, *Ancient China and Its Enemies: The Rise of Nomadic Power in East Asian History*, 163–65.
707. Ibid., 165.
708. Lattimore, *Inner Asian Frontiers of China*, 451.
709. William Samolin, "Hsiung-Nu, Hun, Turk," *Central Asiatic Journal* 3, no. 2 (1957): 149.
710. Paul R. Golding, "Steppe Nomads in Classical China," in *Mapping Mongolia*, ed. Paula L. W. Sabloff (University of Pennsylvania Museum of Archaeology and Anthropology, 2011), 227.
711. Claus Schönig, "Turko-Mongolic Relations," in *The Mongolic Languages*, ed. Juha Janhunen (Routledge, 2003), 405.
712. René Grousset, *The Empire of the Steppes: A History of Central Asia* (New Brunswick: Rutgers University Press, 1999), 24; David Christian, *A History of Russia, Central Asia, and Mongolia. Volume I: Inner Eurasia from Prehistory to the Mongol Empire* (Hoboken: Wiley-Blackwell, 1998), 184.
713. Andrew Bell-Fialkoff, *The Role of Migration in the History of the Eurasian Steppe: Sedentary Civilization vs. "Barbarian" and Nomad* (Palgrave Macmillan, 2000), 216; Clauson, *Studies in Turkic and Mongolic Linguistics*, 8.
714. McGovern, *The Early Empires of Central Asia*, 99.
715. Bell-Fialkoff, *The Role of MigrationI*, 216; Clauson, *Studies in Turkic and Mongolic Linguistics*, 8.
716. McGovern, *The Early Empires of Central Asia*, 405.
717. Grousset, *The Empire of the Steppes*, xxiv
718. Clauson, *Studies in Turkic and Mongolic Linguistics*, 11; Bell-Fialkoff, *The Role of MigrationI*, 216.
719. Gerard Clauson, "The Case against the Altaic Theory," *Central Asiatic Journal* 2, no. 3 (1956): 182.
720. Galina S. Martynova, "The Beginning of the Hunnic Epoch in South Siberia," *Arctic Anthropology* 25, no. 2 (1988): 61–63.
721. Ibid., 61–63.
722. Hansgerd Göckenjan, "The World of the Early Nomadic Horsemen," in *The Turkic Speaking Peoples: 2,000 Years of Art and Culture from Inner Asia to the Balkans*, ed. Ergun Cagatay and Dogan Kuban (Munich: Prestel, 2006), 72.
723. Clauson, *Studies in Turkic and Mongolic Linguistics*, 10.
724. McGovern, *The Early Empires of Central Asia*, 96.
725. Clauson, *Studies in Turkic and Mongolic Linguistics*, 19.
726. Grousset, *The Empire of the Steppes*, 19.

727. Ibid., 19; McGovern, *The Early Empires of Central Asia*, 99–101.
728. McGovern, *The Early Empires of Central Asia*, 99–101.
729. Clauson, *Studies in Turkic and Mongolic Linguistics*, 19.
730. Nicola Di Cosmo, *The Northern Frontier in Pre-Imperial China*, *The Cambridge History of Ancient China: From the Origins of Civilization to 221 BC*, ed. Michael Loewe and Edward L. Shaughnessy (Cambridge, Great Britain: Cambridge University Press, 1999), 952; Grousset, *The Empire of the Steppes*, 19.
731. McGovern, *The Early Empires of Central Asia*, 102.
732. E. A. Thompson, *The Huns* (Hoboken: Wiley-Blackwell, 1996), 22.
733. Otto J. Maenchen-Helfen, *The World of the Huns: Studies in Their History and Culture* (Oakland, CA: University of California Press, 1973), 363.
734. Göckenjan, "The World of the Early Nomadic Horsemen," 74.
735. Denis Sinor, "The Inner Asian Warriors," *Journal of the American Oriental Society* 101, no. 2 (April–June 1981): 135; Di Cosmo, *Ancient China and Its Enemies: The Rise of Nomadic Power in East Asian History*, 276.
736. Sinor, "The Inner Asian Warriors," 135.
737. Ibid., 140.
738. Di Cosmo, *Ancient China and Its Enemies: The Rise of Nomadic Power in East Asian History*, 276.
739. Ibid., 269–70.
740. Thomas J. Barfield, "The Hsiung-nu Imperial Confederacy: Organization and Foreign Policy," *Journal of Asian Studies* 41, no. 1 (November 1981): 53.
741. Nicola Di Cosmo, "Ancient Inner Asian Nomads: Their Economic Basis and Its Significance in Chinese History," *Journal of Asian Studies* 53, no. 4 (November 1994): 1094–95.
742. Étienne de la Vaissière, "Huns et Xiongnu," *Central Asiatic Journal* 49, no. 1 (2005): 7.
743. Lattimore, *Inner Asian Frontiers of China*, 455.
744. Di Cosmo, "Ancient Inner Asian Nomads: Their Economic Basis and Its Significance in Chinese History," 1093.
745. Ibid., 1094, 1096.
746. Ibid., 1098–99.
747. Ibid., 1102.
748. Ching-Lung Chen, "Trading Activities of the Turkic Peoples in China," *Central Asiatic Journal* 25, no. 1/2 (1981): 38.
749. Ibid., 47.
750. Ibid., 39–40, 52.

751. Golden, "The Turkic Nomads of the Pre-Islamic Eurasian Steppes," 85.
752. Di Cosmo, *Ancient China and Its Enemies: The Rise of Nomadic Power in East Asian History*, 274–75.
753. Sophia-Karin Psarras, "Xiongnu Culture: Identification and Dating," *Central Asiatic Journal* 39, no. 1 (1995): 103.
754. Benjamin E. Wallacker and Ruth I. Meserve, "The Emperor of China and the Hobbled Horse of the Xiongnu," *Central Asiatic Journal* 49, no. 2 (2005): 287, 291, 293.
755. Barfield, "The Hsiung-nu Imperial Confederacy: Organization and Foreign Policy," 48–49.
756. Ibid., 56.
757. Psarras, "Han and Xiongnu a Reexamination of Cultural and Political Relations (II)," 56.
758. Barfield, "The Hsiung-nu Imperial Confederacy: Organization and Foreign Policy," 47.
759. McGovern, *The Early Empires of Central Asia*, 106.
760. Ibid.
761. Peter A. Boodberg, "Marginalia to the Histories of the Northern Dynasties," *Harvard Journal of Asiatic Studies* 4, no. 3/4 (December 1939): 235.
762. Ibid., 236.
763. Gerard Clauson, "The Earliest Turkish Loan Words in Mongolian," *Central Asiatic Journal* 4, no. 3 (1959): 179.
764. Boodberg, "Marginalia to the Histories of the Northern Dynasties," 238–39.
765. Psarras, "Xiongnu Culture: Identification and Dating," 103.
766. Psarras, "Han and Xiongnu a Reexamination of Cultural and Political Relations (II)," 75.
767. McGovern, *The Early Empires of Central Asia*, 102–3.
768. Ibid., 103.
769. Ibid., 48.
770. Ibid.
771. Ibid., 105, 108.
772. Charles Warren Hostler, *The Turks of Central Asia* (Praeger, 1993), 7.
773. Ecsedy, "Chinese Historical Connections," 133.
774. Di Cosmo, *The Northern Frontier in Pre-Imperial China, The Cambridge History of Ancient China: From the Origins of Civilization to 221 BC*, 964–65.
775. Grousset, *The Empire of the Steppes*, 20.
776. Göckenjan, "The World of the Early Nomadic Horsemen," 73.
777. Christian, *A History of Russia, Central Asia, and Mongolia*, 184–85; Christopher I. Beckwith, *Empires of the Silk Road: A History of Central Eurasia from the Bronze Age to the Present* (Princeton University Press, 2009), 5; Peter

B. Golden, *Central Asia in World History* (New York: Oxford University Press, 2011), 27; Sinor, "The Inner Asian Warriors," 135.
778. Lattimore, *Inner Asian Frontiers of China*, 464.
779. Clauson, *Studies in Turkic and Mongolic Linguistics*, 20–21.
780. Ibid., 20.
781. E. G. Pulleyblank, "The Wu-sun and Sakas and the Yüeh-chih Migration," *Bulletin of the School of Oriental and African Studies* 33, no. 1 (1970): 154, 156.
782. David Christian, "Silk Roads or Steppe Roads? The Silk Road in World History," *Journal of World History* 11, no. 1 (Spring 2000): 5.
783. John Man, *Attila: The Barbarian King Who Challenged Rome* (St. Martin's Griffin, 2009), 38.
784. Lattimore, *Inner Asian Frontiers of China*, 476.
785. Xinru Liu, *The Silk Road in World History* (New York: Oxford University Press, 2010), 2.
786. Golden, "The Turkic Nomads of the Pre-Islamic Eurasian Steppes," 85.
787. Hyun Jin Kim, *The Huns* (New York, NY: Routledge, 2016), p. 20.
788. Xinru Liu, "Migration and Settlement of the Yuezhi-Kushan: Interaction and Interdependence of Nomadic and Sedentary Societies," *Journal of World History*, 12, No. 2 (Fall, 2001): 261.).
789. Egemen Çağrı Mızrak, *Bozkır Kavimleri: M.Ö. VII. Yüzyıldan M.S. VI. Yüzyılın Ortalarına Kadar Batı Türkistan ve Kuzey Hindistan'daki Bozkırlar* (İstanbul: Ötüken, 2017), 27.
790. Otto Maenchen-Helfen, "The Yüeh-Chih Problem Re-Examined," *Journal of the American Oriental Society*, 65, No. 2 (Apr. - Jun., 1945): 71.
791. Liu, "Migration and Settlement of the Yuezhi-Kushan: Interaction and Interdependence of Nomadic and Sedentary Societies," 265.
792. Mızrak, *Bozkır Kavimleri: M.Ö. VII. Yüzyıldan M.S. VI. Yüzyılın Ortalarına Kadar Batı Türkistan ve Kuzey Hindistan'daki Bozkırlar*, 264.
793. Ibid., 38-39, 47.
794. Liu, "Migration and Settlement of the Yuezhi-Kushan: Interaction and Interdependence of Nomadic and Sedentary Societies," 270.
795. E. G. Pulleyblank, "The Wu-sun and Sakas and the Yüeh-chih Migration," *Bulletin of the School of Oriental and African Studies*, University of London, 33, No. 1, In Honour of Sir Harold Bailey (1970): 157.
796. Ibid., 155-156.
797. Ibid., 157, 159.
798. Namu Jila, "Myths and Traditional Beliefs about the Wolf and the Crow in Central Asia: Examples

from the Turkic Wu-Sun and the Mongols," *Asian Folklore Studies*, 65, No. 2 (2006): 164.
799. Pulleyblank, "The Wu-sun and Sakas and the Yüeh-chih Migration," 156; Maenchen-Helfen, "The Yüeh-Chih Problem Re-Examined," 74.
800. Maenchen-Helfen, "The Yüeh-Chih Problem Re-Examined," 80.
801. Ibid., 72.
802. Ibid., 73.
803. Ibid.
804. Hyun Jin Kim, *The Huns*, 20.
805. Liu, "Migration and Settlement of the Yuezhi-Kushan: Interaction and Interdependence of Nomadic and Sedentary Societies," 261, 272.
806. Maenchen-Helfen, "The Yüeh-Chih Problem Re-Examined," 71.
807. Yihong, "Marriage Alliances and Chinese Princesses," 95–96.
808. Ibid., 98–100.
809. Ibid., 108–9.
810. Yihong, "Marriage Alliances and Chinese Princesses," 101–2.
811. Di Cosmo, *Ancient China and Its Enemies: The Rise of Nomadic Power in East Asian History*, 174.
812. Wolfram Eberhard, *Conquerors and Rulers: Social Forces in Medieval China*, 2nd ed. (Boston, MA: E. J. Brill, 1970), 119.
813. Carter Vaughn Findley, *The Turks in World History* (New York: Oxford University Press, 2005), 33.
814. Stephen Turnbull, *The Great Wall of China 221 BC–AD 1644* (Oxford, Great Britian: Osprey, 2007), 5.
815. Findley, *The Turks in World History*, 33.
816. Barfield, "The Hsiung-nu Imperial Confederacy: Organization and Foreign Policy," 52.
817. Eberhard, *Conquerors and Rulers*, 119.
818. Grousset, *The Empire of the Steppes*, 47; Liu, *The Silk Road in World History*, 4.
819. Barfield, "The Hsiung-nu Imperial Confederacy: Organization and Foreign Policy," 55–56.
820. Liu, *The Silk Road in World History*, 6–8.
821. Foltz, *Religions of the Silk Road*, 2.
822. Ibid., 8–12.
823. Barfield, *The Perilous Frontier: Nomadic Empires and China*, 59–60.
824. Ibid., 60.
825. Psarras, "Han and Xiongnu a Reexamination of Cultural and Political Relations (II)," 40–42.
826. Christian, "Silk Roads or Steppe Roads?" 16.
827. Ibid., 18.
828. Ibid., 17.
829. Psarras, "Han and Xiongnu a Reexamination of Cultural and Political Relations (II)," 43.

830. Wallacker and Meserve, "The Emperor of China," 284–86, 289, 295.
831. Barfield, "The Hsiung-nu Imperial Confederacy: Organization and Foreign Policy," 57.
832. Maenchen-Helfen, "The Ting-Ling," 79.
833. Barfield, *The Perilous Frontier: Nomadic Empires and China*, 59.
834. Psarras, "Han and Xiongnu a Reexamination of Cultural and Political Relations (II)," 83–84.
835. Eberhard, *Conquerors and Rulers*, 120.
836. Ibid., 120–21.
837. Barfield, "The Hsiung-nu Imperial Confederacy: Organization and Foreign Policy," 47.
838. Barfield, *The Perilous Frontier: Nomadic Empires and China*, 61.
839. Ibid., 62.
840. Ibid., 60, 62.
841. Psarras, "Han and Xiongnu a Reexamination of Cultural and Political Relations (II)," 84.
842. Ibid., 40–41.
843. Barfield, *The Perilous Frontier: Nomadic Empires and China*, 62.
844. Ibid., 62.
845. Ibid., 62–63.
846. Psarras, "Han and Xiongnu a Reexamination of Cultural and Political Relations (II)," 45.
847. Barfield, *The Perilous Frontier: Nomadic Empires and China*, 63.
848. Psarras, "Han and Xiongnu a Reexamination of Cultural and Political Relations (II)," 42.
849. Barfield, *The Perilous Frontier: Nomadic Empires and China*, 69.
850. Psarras, "Han and Xiongnu a Reexamination of Cultural and Political Relations (II)," 47, 85.
851. Ibid., 55–56.
852. Barfield, *The Perilous Frontier: Nomadic Empires and China*, 70.
853. Ibid., 71.
854. Ibid., 76.
855. Ibid., 76–77.
856. Psarras, "Xiongnu Culture: Identification and Dating," 104–5.
857. Sophia-Karin Psarras, "Upper Xiajiadian," *Monumenta Serica* 47 (1999): 82.
858. Psarras, "Han and Xiongnu a Reexamination of Cultural and Political Relations (II)," 51–52, 86–87.
859. Ibid., 87.
860. Barfield, *The Perilous Frontier: Nomadic Empires and China*, 77.
861. Ibid., 78–79.
862. Ibid., 79.
863. Psarras, "Han and Xiongnu a Reexamination of Cultural and Political Relations (II)," 56.
864. Ibid., 62.
865. Barfield, *The Perilous Frontier: Nomadic Empires and China*, 77.

866. Psarras, "Han and Xiongnu a Reexamination of Cultural and Political Relations (II)," 68.
867. Barfield, *The Perilous Frontier: Nomadic Empires and China*, 80.
868. Psarras, "Han and Xiongnu a Reexamination of Cultural and Political Relations (II)," 88; Barfield, *The Perilous Frontier: Nomadic Empires and China*, 79.
869. Psarras, "Han and Xiongnu a Reexamination of Cultural and Political Relations (II)," 58.
870. Ibid., 73.
871. Ibid., 60.
872. Barfield, *The Perilous Frontier: Nomadic Empires and China*, 80.
873. Psarras, "Han and Xiongnu a Reexamination of Cultural and Political Relations (II)," 64.
874. Ibid.
875. Ibid., 75.
876. McGovern, *The Early Empires of Central Asia*, 364.
877. Psarras, "Han and Xiongnu a Reexamination of Cultural and Political Relations (II)," 56.
878. Ibid., 55–56, 93.
879. Emel Esin, "Baliq and Ordu (The Early Turkish Circumvallations, in Architectural Aspects)," *Central Asiatic Journal* 27, no. 3/4 (1983): 174–75.
880. Phillips, "New Light on the Ancient History," 279.
881. Psarras, "Han and Xiongnu a Reexamination of Cultural and Political Relations (II)," 72–73.
882. Ibid., 73.
883. Barfield, *The Perilous Frontier: Nomadic Empires and China*, 119.
884. Hans-J. Klimkeit, "Buddhism in Turkish Central Asia," *Numen* 37, no. 1 (June 1990): 54.
885. Sanping Chen, "A-Gan Revisited—the Tuoba's Cultural and Political Heritage," *Journal of Asian History* 30, no. 1 (1996): 54.
886. Psarras, "Han and Xiongnu a Reexamination of Cultural and Political Relations (II)," 62–63.
887. Hyun Jin Kim, *The Huns* (New York, NY: Routledge, 2016), 38.
888. Samolin, "Hsiung-Nu, Hun, Turk," 149–50.
889. Kim, *The Huns*, 38-39.
890. Lattimore, *Inner Asian Frontiers of China*, 509.
891. Phillips, "New Light on the Ancient History," 279.
892. De la Vaissière, "Huns et Xiongnu," 22–23.
893. Louis Hambis, "The Ancient Civilizations of Manchuria," *East and West* 7, no. 3 (October 1956): 219.
894. 8 Étienne de la Vaissière, "Is There a 'Nationality of the Hephtalites'?" *Bulletin of the Asia Institute*, n.s., 17 (2003): 122.
895. Samolin, "Hsiung-Nu, Hun, Turk," 148–49.

896. K. Enoki, "The Origin of the White Huns or Hephthalites," *East and West* 6, no. 3 (October 1955): 231.
897. De la Vaissière, "Huns et Xiongnu," 4.
898. Ibid., 6.
899. Ibid., 7.
900. Ibid., 8.
901. Ibid., 11–13.
902. Ibid., 15.
903. K. Enoki, "Sogdiana and the Hsiung-Nu," *Central Asiatic Journal* 1, no. 1 (1955): 43–44.
904. De la Vaissière, "Huns et Xiongnu," 17, 22.
905. Kim, *The Huns*, p. 6.
906. V. Minorsky, The Turkish Dialect of the Khalaj, Bulletin of the School of Oriental Studies, University of London, Vol. 10, No. 2 (1940): 426; Clifford Edmund Bosworth, The Ghaznavids: Their Empire in Afghanistan and Eastern Iran 994-1040, (Edinburgh, University Press, 1963) 35-36, 206.
907. Minorsky, p. 430.
908. Ibid., p. 431.
909. Ibid., p. 418.
910. Clifford Edmund Bosworth, The New Islamic Dynasties: A Chronological and Genealogical Manual (Edinburgh University Press, 1996) 280-281.
911. Grousset, *The Empire of the Steppes*, 61.
912. Findley, *The Turks in World History*, 29; Christian, *A History of Russia, Central Asia, and Mongolia*, 203.
913. James Baker, *Turkey* (Henry Holt, 1877), 122.
914. Findley, *The Turks in World History*, 37; Christian, *A History of Russia, Central Asia, and Mongolia*, 203.
915. Roux, "Historical Introduction," 5; Clifford Edmund Bosworth, *The Ghaznavids: Their Empire in Afghanistan and Eastern Iran 994–1040* (Edinburgh: Edinburgh University Press, 1963), 205–6.
916. Bosworth, *The Ghaznavids*, 206.
917. Christian, *A History of Russia, Central Asia, and Mongolia*, 203.
918. Roux, "Historical Introduction," 5.
919. Ecsedy, "Chinese Historical Connections," 133.
920. Kim, *The Huns*, 46.
921. Golden, *Central Asia in World History*, 36; De la Vaissière, "Is There a 'Nationality of the Hephtalites'?" 121.
922. De la Vaissière, "Is There a 'Nationality of the Hephtalites'?," 120.
923. Ibid., 121.
924. McGovern, *The Early Empires of Central Asia*, 404.
925. Kim, *The Huns*, 46–49.

926. McGovern, *The Early Empires of Central Asia*, 404–5.
927. Kim, *The Huns*, 49.
928. Ibid., 52.
929. Ibid., 48.
930. Ibid., 52-53.
931. Ibid., 50.
932. Szabolcs Felföldi, "A Prominent Hephthalite: Katulph and the Fall of the Hephthalite Empire," *Acta Orientalia Academiae Scientiarum Hungaricae* 54, no. 2/3 (2001): 191–92.
933. Jean Paul Roux, "Historical Introduction," in *The Turkic Peoples of the World*, ed. Margaret Bainbridge (Abingdon, Great Britain: Routledge, 1993), 5; Paul Pelliot, "L'origine de Tcou-kiue, nom chinois des Turcs," *T'oung Pao* 16, no. 5 (1915): 688.
934. De la Vaissière, "Huns et Xiongnu," 19, 21.
935. C. A. Macartney, "On the Greek Sources for the History of the Turks in the Sixth Century," *Bulletin of the School of Oriental and African Studies* 11, no. 2 (1944): 271.
936. Ibid.
937. Ibid., 272–73.
938. Emel Esin, "The Horse in Turkic Art" (proceedings of the 7th Meeting of the Permanent International Altaistic Conference, August 29 to September 3, 1964), *Central Asiatic Journal* 10, no. 3/4 (December 1965): 168.
939. Minorsky, "The Turkish Dialect of the Khalaj," 426.
940. Kim, *The Huns*, 47.
941. Ibid.
942. Ibid., 51.
943. Pulleyblank, "The 'High Carts': A Turkish-Speaking People before the Türks," 22–23, 26.
944. Enoki, "The Origin of the White Huns or Hephthalites," 232.
945. De la Vaissière, "Is There a 'Nationality of the Hephtalites'?" 119, 121.
946. Ibid., 121.
947. Ibid., 119, 124.
948. Foltz, *Religions of the Silk Road*, 47.
949. Samolin, "Hsiung-Nu, Hun, Turk," 148.
950. Enoki, "The Origin of the White Huns or Hephthalites," 233.
951. Enoki, "Sogdiana and the Hsiung-Nu," 44–45; De la Vaissière, "Huns et Xiongnu," 4.
952. Enoki, "Sogdiana and the Hsiung-Nu," 52–53.
953. Enoki, "The Origin of the White Huns or Hephthalites," 233.
954. Kim, *The Huns*, 54.
955. Enoki, "The Origin of the White Huns or Hephthalites," 236.
956. Golden, *Central Asia in World History*, 36.; Enoki, "The Origin of

957. Golden, *Central Asia in World History*, 36.
958. Mario Bussagli, "Pages of Euro-Asian History: Attila and the Huns," *East and West* 4, no. 3 (October 1953): 192.
959. De la Vaissière, "Is There a 'Nationality of the Hephtalites'?," 119.
960. De la Vaissière, "Is There a 'Nationality of the Hephtalites'?," 119, 121.
961. Ibid., 119, 123.
962. Ibid.
963. Kim, *The Huns*, 54.
964. Ibid., 61.
965. Ibid., 54.
966. Ibid., 55.
967. Felföldi, "A Prominent Hephthalite," 192.
968. Ibid., 193–94.
969. Ibid., 194.
970. Ibid., 195.
971. Ibid.
972. Kim, *The Huns*, 56.
973. Ibid., 58.
974. Ibid., 57.
975. Ibid.
976. Ibid.; Emel Esin, "Tabarī's Report on the Warfare with the Türgiš and the Testimony of Eighth Century Central Asian Art" (proceedings of the 15th Meeting of the Permanent International Altaistic Conference August 7–12, 1972), *Central Asiatic Journal* 17, no. 2/4 (1973): 132.
977. Kim, *The Huns*, 57.
978. Ibid., 58.
979. Nicola Di Cosmo, "The Northern Frontier in Pre-Imperial China," in *The Cambridge History of Ancient China: From the Origins of Civilization to 221 BC*, ed. Michael Loewe and Edward L. Shaughnessy (Cambridge, England: Cambridge University Press, 1999), 952.
980. Kim, *The Huns*, 174-175.
981. Ibid., 64.
982. Ibid., 62.
983. Ibid., 60.
984. Hansgerd Göckenjan, "The World of the Early Nomadic Horsemen," in *The Turkic Speaking Peoples: 2,000 Years of Art and Culture from Inner Asia to the Balkans*, ed. Ergun Cagatay and Dogan Kuban (Munich: Prestel, 2006), 70.
985. McGovern, *The Early Empires of Central Asia*, 103.
986. Di Cosmo, *Ancient China and Its Enemies: The Rise of Nomadic Power in East Asian History*, 131, 134.
987. McGovern, *The Early Empires of Central Asia*, 48.
988. Kate A. Lingley, "Naturalizing the Exotic: On the Changing Meanings of Ethnic Dress in Medieval China," *Ars Orientalis* 38 (2010): 56.

989. Nicola Di Cosmo, "The Northern Frontier in Pre-Imperial China," 952.
990. Denis Sinor, "The Inner Asian Warriors," *Journal of the American Oriental Society* 101, no. 2 (April–June 1981): 139.
991. Maenchen-Helfen, "The Ting-Ling," 79.
992. Julian Baldick, *Animal and Shaman: Ancient Religions of Central Asia* (New York University Press, 2012), 5.
993. Ibid., 27.

CHAPTER 4: THE GREAT TURKISH MIGRATIONS

994. Mario Bussagli, "Pages of Euro-Asian History: Attila and the Huns," *East and West* 4, no. 3 (October 1953): 191.
995. John Man, *Attila: The Barbarian King Who Challenged Rome* (St. Martin's Griffin, 2009), 31–32.
996. Étienne de la Vaissière, "Huns et Xiongnu," *Central Asiatic Journal* 49, no. 1 (2005): 3–15.
997. Carter Vaughn Findley, *The Turks in World History* (New York: Oxford University Press, 2005), 29.
998. Peter Heather, "The Huns and the End of the Roman Empire in Western Europe," *English Historical Review* 110, no. 435 (February 1995): 5; Claude Cahen, *Pre-Ottoman Turkey: A General Survey of the Material and Spiritual Culture and History 1071–1330* (New York: Taplinger, 1968), 1; Findley, *The Turks in World History*, 29; Z. V. Togan, *Umumi Türk Tarihine Giriş* (Istanbul: Ismail Akgün, 1946), 41.
999. Otto J. Maenchen-Helfen, *The World of the Huns: Studies in Their History and Culture* (Oakland: University of California Press, 1973), 23.
1001. E. D. Phillips, "New Light on the Ancient History of the Eurasian Steppe," *American Journal of Archaeology* 61, no. 3 (July 1957): 271.
1001. Cahen, *Pre-Ottoman Turkey*, 1; Findley, *The Turks in World History*, 29; Maenchen-Helfen, *The World of the Huns*, 358–443; Andrew Bell-Fialkoff, *The Role of Migration in the History of the Eurasian Steppe: Sedentary Civilization vs. "Barbarian" and Nomad* (London: Palgrave Macmillan, 2000), 217.
1002. Maenchen-Helfen, *The World of the Huns*, 403, 441.
1003. William Montgomery McGovern, *The Early Empires of Central Asia: A Study of the Scythians and the Huns and the Part They Played in World History* (Chapel Hill, NC: University of North Carolina Press, 1939), 102.

1004. Omeljan Pritsak, "The Hunnic Language of the Attila Clan," *Harvard Ukrainian Studies* 6, no. 4 (December 1982): 470.

1005. Ibid., 444.

1006. Phillips, "New Light on the Ancient History," 280.

1007. Togan, *Umumi Türk Tarihine Giriş*, 150.

1008. Bussagli, "Pages of Euro-Asian History," 192; John Keegan, *A History of Warfare* (Alfred A. Knopf, 1994), 180.

1009. Maenchen-Helfen, *The World of the Huns*, 368.

1010. David Christian, *A History of Russia, Central Asia, and Mongolia. Volume I: Inner Eurasia from Prehistory to the Mongol Empire* (Hoboken: Wiley-Blackwell, 1998), 203.

1011. Louis Hambis, "The Ancient Civilizations of Manchuria," *East and West* 7, no. 3 (October 1956): 219.

1012. K. Enoki, "Sogdiana and the Hsiung-Nu," *Central Asiatic Journal* 1, no. 1 (1955): 60.

1013. Hyun Jin Kim, *The Huns* (New York, NY: Routledge, 2016), p. 7.

1014. E. A. Thompson, *Romans and Barbarians: The Decline of the Western Empire* (Madison, WI: University of Wisconsin Press, 1982), 16.

1015. Heather, "The Huns," 5–6.

1016. Andrew Gillett, "Rome, Ravenna and the Last Western Emperors," *Papers of the British School at Rome* 69 (2001): 131–32.

1017. J. M. Wallace-Hadrill, *The Barbarian West: The Early Middle Ages A.D. 400–1000* (New York: Harper Torchbooks, 1962), 23.

1018. Heather, "The Huns," 12–14, 16.

1019. Wallace-Hadrill, *The Barbarian West*, 27.

1020. Heather, "The Huns," 25.

1021. Bussagli, "Pages of Euro-Asian History," 196; Christian, *A History of Russia*, 203.

1022. Christopher I. Beckwith, *Empires of the Silk Road: A History of Central Eurasia from the Bronze Age to the Present* (Princeton University Press, 2009), 94–95; Hansgerd Göckenjan, "The World of the Early Nomadic Horsemen," in *The Turkic Speaking Peoples: 2,000 Years of Art and Culture from Inner Asia to the Balkans*, ed. Ergun Cagatay and Dogan Kuban (Munich: Prestel, 2006), 73.

1023. Heather, "The Huns," 9, 16.

1024. E. A. Thompson, *The Huns* (Hoboken: Wiley-Blackwell, 1996), 26–27.

1025. Heather, "The Huns," 8, 10; Thompson, *The Huns*, 31–32.

1026. Heather, "The Huns," 8.

1027. Thompson, *The Huns*, 31–32.

1028. Heather, "The Huns," 11.

1029. Thompson, *The Huns*, 22.
1030. Ibid., 33.
1031. Ibid., 22.
1032. Keegan, *A History of Warfare*, 187.
1033. Bussagli, "Pages of Euro-Asian History," 197; Heather, "The Huns," 23.
1034. Heather, "The Huns," 14.
1035. Ibid., 16–17.
1036. Ibid., 26.
1037. Ibid., 28.
1038. Beckwith, *Empires of the Silk Road*, 98–99.
1039. Bussagli, "Pages of Euro-Asian History," 196.
1040. Gillett, "Rome, Ravenna," 147.
1041. Beckwith, *Empires of the Silk Road*, 99; Keegan, *A History of Warfare*, 187.
1042. Thompson, *Romans and Barbarians: The Decline of the Western Empire*, 151.
1043. Man, *Attila*, 1–3.
1044. Beckwith, *Empires of the Silk Road*, 97.
1045. Göckenjan, "The World of the Early Nomadic Horsemen," 73.
1046. Ibid., 74.
1047. McGovern, *The Early Empires of Central Asia*, 469–70.
1048. Hyun Jin Kim, *The Huns* (New York, NY: Routledge, 2016), 110, 113.
1049. Ibid., 111-112.
1050. Ibid., 123.
1051. Ibid., 116.
1052. Ibid.
1053. Ibid., 122.
1054. Ibid. 124.
1055. Ibid., 132-133.
1056. Ibid., 127.
1057. Heather, "The Huns," 29, 38.
1058. Thompson, *Romans and Barbarians: The Decline of the Western Empire*, 61.
1059. Wallace-Hadrill, *The Barbarian West*, 33.
1060. Robert L. Reynolds and Robert S. Lopez, "Odoacer: German or Hun?," *American Historical Review* 52, no. 1 (October 1946), 38.
1061. Ibid., 38–39.
1062. Ibid., 40–41.
1063. Ibid., 44–45.
1064. Ibid., 45.
1065. Kim, *The Huns*, 114-115.
1066. Ibid., 115-116.
1067. Ibid., 114-115.
1068. Ibid., 111.
1069. Bruce Macbain, "Odovacer the Hun?" *Classical Philology* 78, no. 4 (October 1983), 323; Reynolds and Lopez, "Odoacer: German or Hun?," 47–48.
1070. Macbain, "Odovacer the Hun?" 324.
1071. Reynolds and Lopez, "Odoacer: German or Hun?," 40.

1072. Thompson, *Romans and Barbarians: The Decline of the Western Empire*, 62.

1073. Ibid., 63–64.

1074. Ibid., 69.

1075. Wallace-Hadrill, *The Barbarian West*, 33.

1076. Macbain, "Odovacer the Hun?" 327.

1077. Kim, *The Huns*, 122-123.

1078. Pritsak, "The Hunnic Language of the Attila Clan," 444.

1079. Bussagli, "Pages of Euro-Asian History," 193.

1080. Ibid., 196.

1081. Man, *Attila*, 4, 289.

1082. Julian Baldick, *Animal and Shaman: Ancient Religions of Central Asia* (New York University Press, 2012), 171.

1083. Pritsak, "The Hunnic Language of the Attila Clan," 429.

1084. Bussagli, "Pages of Euro-Asian History," 195.

1085. Ibid.

1086. Phillips, "New Light on the Ancient History," 280.

1087. Bussagli, "Pages of Euro-Asian History," 192.

1088. Kenneth M. Setton, "The Bulgars in the Balkans and the Occupation of Corinth in the Seventh Century," *Speculum* 25, no. 4 (October 1950): 503.

1089. Man, *Attila*, 298.

1090. Ibid., 299.

1091. Kim, *The Huns*, 176.

1092. Ibid., 175-176.

1093. Ibid., 146.

1094. Istvan Bona, *Les Huns: Le grand Empire barbare d'Europe (IVe-Ve siècles)*, translated by Katalin Escher (Paris: Editions Errance, 2002), p. 69.

1095. Kim, *The Huns*, 146-148.

1096. Ibid., 149-150.

1097. Ibid., 149-159.

1098. Ibid., 157.

1099. Ibid., 149-159.

1100. Ibid., 160-161.

1101. Ibid.

1102. Ibid., 160, 162-163.

1103. William Montgomery McGovern, *The Early Empires of Central Asia: A Study of the Scythians and the Huns and the Part They Played in World History* (Chapel Hill, NC: University of North Carolina Press, 1939), 48.

1104. Hansgerd Göckenjan, "The World of the Early Nomadic Horsemen," in *The Turkic Speaking Peoples: 2,000 Years of Art and Culture from Inner Asia to the Balkans*, ed. Ergun Cagatay and Dogan Kuban (Munich: Prestel, 2006), 70.

1105. Kim, *The Huns*, 160.

1106. Ibid., 166.

1107. Ibid., 164-165.

1108. Ibid., 166-167.

1109. Ibid., 167-168.
1110. Ibid., 169.
1111. Ibid., 170.
1112. Ibid.
1113. Ibid.
1114. Karl Reichl, Singing the Past: Turkic and Medieval Heroic Poetry (Cornell University Press, 2000), 8.
1115. Kim, *The Huns*, 136.
1116. Ibid., 136-137.
1117. Ibid. 137.
1118. Walter Emil Kaegi Jr., "The Contribution of Archery to the Turkish Conquest of Anatolia," *Speculum* 39, no. 1 (January 1964): 98–99.
1119. Ibid., 99.
1120. Phillips, "New Light on the Ancient History," 280.
1121. Kevin Alan Brook, *The Jews of Khazaria* (New York: Rowman & Littlefield, 2006), 10–11.
1122. Istvan Vasary, *Turks, Tatars and Russians in the 13th–16th Centuries* (Farnham, UK: Ashgate, 2007), i–28.
1123. Robert Lee Wolff, "The 'Second Bulgarian Empire.' Its Origin and History to 1204," *Speculum* 24, no. 2 (April 1949): 168; Beckwith, *Empires of the Silk Road*, 99; Brook, *The Jews of Khazaria*, 13; Peter B. Golden, "Nomads and Sedentary Societies in Eurasia," in *Agricultural and Pastoral Societies in Ancient and Classical History*, ed. Michael Adas (Philadelphia, PA: Temple University Press, 2001), 101.
1124. Claus Schönig, "Turko-Mongolic Relations," in *The Mongolic Languages*, ed. Juha Janhunen (Routledge, 2003), 405; McGovern, *The Early Empires of Central Asia*, 469–70.
1125. Christian, *A History of Russia, Central Asia, and Mongolia*, 285; Brook, *The Jews of Khazaria*, 13.
1126. Kim, *The Huns*, 133.
1127. Ibid., 135.
1128. Ibid., 139.
1129. Ibid.
1130. Ibid., 139-140.
1131. Setton, "The Bulgars in the Balkans," 506-7.
1132. Golden, "Nomads and Sedentary Societies in Eurasia," 95; Setton, "The Bulgars in the Balkans," 505-6.
1133. Setton, "The Bulgars in the Balkans," 505.
1134. Ibid., 502.
1135. Ibid., 505-6.
1136. Togan, *Umumi Türk Tarihine Giriş*, 149.
1137. Wolff, "The 'Second Bulgarian Empire,'" 169.
1138. Przemyslaw Urbanczyk, "Early State Formation in East Central Europe," in *East Central and Eastern Europe in the Early Ages*, ed. Florin Curta (Ann Arbor:

University of Michigan Press, 2005), 144.
1139. Peter B. Golden, "Nomads and Sedentary Societies in Medieval Eurasia," in *East Central and Eastern Europe in the Early Middle Ages*, ed. Florin Curta (Ann Arbor: University of Michigan Press, 2008), 101.
1140. Vasary, *Turks, Tatars and Russians*, i–28.
1141. Göckenjan, "The World of the Early Nomadic Horsemen," 75.
1142. Wolff, "The 'Second Bulgarian Empire,'" 170.
1143. Cahen, *Pre-Ottoman Turkey*, 5.
1144. Allen J. Frank, *Islamic Historiography and "Bulghar" Identity among the Tatars and Bashkirs of Russia* (Brill, 1998), 63; Brook, *The Jews of Khazaria*, 140.
1145. Frank, *Islamic Historiography*, 7.
1146. Vasary, *Turks, Tatars and Russians*, i–29.
1147. William Samolin, "Some Notes on the Avar Problem," *Central Asiatic Journal* 3, no. 1 (1957): 62.
1148. David Christian, *A History of Russia, Central Asia, and Mongolia*, 280.
1149. C. A. Macartney, "On the Greek Sources for the History of the Turks in the Sixth Century," *Bulletin of the School of Oriental and African Studies* 11, no. 2 (1944): 273.
1150. Schönig, "Turko-Mongolic Relations," 406.
1151. Peter B. Golden, *Turks and Khazars* (Farnham, UK: Ashgate Variorum, 2010), i–14.
1152. Allen Leeper, "Germans, Avars and Slavs," *Slavonic and East European Review* 12, no. 34 (July 1933): 121.
1153. Gerard Clauson, *Studies in Turkic and Mongolic Linguistics* (Abingdon: Routledge, 1962), 26.
1154. Leeper, "Germans, Avars and Slavs," 119.
1155. Göckenjan, "The World of the Early Nomadic Horsemen," 74.
1156. Setton, "The Bulgars in the Balkans," 508–9.
1157. Leeper, "Germans, Avars and Slavs," 120.
1158. Ibid., 121–22.
1159. Falko Daim, "The Avars: Steppe People of Central Europe," *Archaeology* 37, no. 2 (March–April 1984): 33.
1160. Ibid., 33–34.
1161. Alexandru Madgearu, "Salt Trade and Warfare: The Rise of Romanian-Slavic Military Organization in Early Medieval Transylvania," in *East Central and Eastern Europe in the Early Middle Ages*, ed. Florin Curta (Ann Arbor: University of Michigan Press, 2008), 103–6.

1162. James Westfall Thompson, "German Medieval Expansion and the Making of Austria," *Slavonic Review* 2, no. 5 (December 1923), 263.

1163. Ibid., 264.

1164. Christian, *A History of Russia, Central Asia, and Mongolia*, 281.

1165. Setton, "The Bulgars in the Balkans," 510–12.

1166. Christian, *A History of Russia, Central Asia, and Mongolia*, 281.

1167. Denis Sinor, "The Inner Asian Warriors," *Journal of the American Oriental Society* 101, no. 2 (April–June 1981): 137.

1168. Daim, "The Avars," 33.

1169. Setton, "The Bulgars in the Balkans," 512–13.

1170. Ibid., 513.

1171. Göckenjan, "The World of the Early Nomadic Horsemen," 75.

1172. Denis Sinor, "The Scope and Importance of Altaic Studies," *Journal of the American Oriental Society* 83, no. 2 (April–June, 1963): 194.

1173. Togan, *Umumi Türk Tarihine Giriş*, 149.

1174. James Westfall Thompson, "German Medieval Expansion," 267.

1175. Ibid., 269.

1176. Daim, "The Avars," 36–38.

1177. Brook, *The Jews of Khazaria*, 142.

1178. Istvan Fodor, "On Magyar-Bulgar Turkish Contacts," in *Chuvash Studies*, ed. A. Róna-Tas (Budapest: Akadémiai Kiadó, 1982), 49.

1179. Brook, *The Jews of Khazaria*, 140.

1180. G. Roheim, "Hungarian Calendar Customs," *Journal of the Royal Anthropological Institute of Great Britain and Ireland* 56 (1926): 361.

1181. Margaret Pallo, "The Bulgar-Turkish Loanwords of the Hungarian Language as Sources of Chuvash Prehistory," in *Chuvash Studies*, ed. A. Róna-Tas (Budapest: Akadémiai Kiadó, 1982), 111.

1182. Istvan Fodor, "Are the Sumerians and the Hungarians or the Uralic Peoples Related?" *Current Anthropology* 17, no. 1 (March 1976): 115–16.

1183. Setton, "The Bulgars in the Balkans," 504.

1184. Man, *Attila*, 4–5, 309.

1185. Brook, *The Jews of Khazaria*, 140–43; Fodor, "Are the Sumerians and the Hungarians or the Uralic Peoples Related?," 116.

1186. Golden, *Turks and Khazars*, i–21.

1187. Fodor, "On Magyar-Bulgar Turkish Contacts," 55, 59.

1188. András Róna-Tas, "The Periodization and Sources of Chuvash Linguistic History," in *Chuvash Studies*, ed. A. Róna-Tas (Budapest: Akadémiai Kiadó, 1982), 147.

1189. Vasary, *Turks, Tatars and Russians*, i-30-31.
1190. Brook, *The Jews of Khazaria*, 2-6.
1191. Christian, *A History of Russia, Central Asia, and Mongolia*, 283.
1192. Ibid., 283.
1193. Brook, *The Jews of Khazaria*, 140.
1194. Christian, *A History of Russia, Central Asia, and Mongolia*, 281-83; Stephen G. Wheatcroft, *Challenging Traditional Views of Russian History* (London: Palgrave Macmillan, 2002), 9; Peter B. Golden, *Nomads and Their Neighbours in the Russian Steppe: Turks, Khazars and Qipchaqs* (Farnham: Variorum, 2003), vi-78, 85.
1195. Omeljan Pritsak, "The Khazar Kingdom's Conversion to Judaism," *Harvard Ukrainian Studies* 2, no. 3 (September 1978): 263.
1196. Pallo, "The Bulgar-Turkish Loanwords of the Hungarian Language," 111.
1197. Pritsak, "The Khazar Kingdom's Conversion to Judaism," 265.
1198. J. Brutzkus, "The Khazar Origin of Ancient Kiev," *Slavonic and East European Review*, American series, 3, no. 1 (1994): 111.
1199. Golden, *Nomads and Their Neighbours in the Russian Steppe*, vi-79.
1200. David Christian, "Silk Roads or Steppe Roads? The Silk Road in World History," *Journal of World History* 11, no. 1 (Spring 2000): 20.
1201. Ibid., 20.
1202. S. H. Cross, "The Scandinavian Infiltration into Early Russia," *Speculum* 21, no. 4 (October 1946), 511.
1203. Pritsak, "The Khazar Kingdom's Conversion to Judaism," 266-67.
1204. Ibid., 267.
1205. Beckwith, *Empires of the Silk Road*, 149; Christian, *A History of Russia, Central Asia, and Mongolia*, 286-87; Golden, *Nomads and Their Neighbours in the Russian Steppe*, vi-79; Pritsak, "The Khazar Kingdom's Conversion to Judaism," 266.
1206. Beckwith, *Empires of the Silk Road*, 149; Christian, *A History of Russia, Central Asia, and Mongolia*, 286-87; Golden, *Nomads and Their Neighbours in the Russian Steppe*, vii-74.
1207. Brook, *The Jews of Khazaria*, 94.
1208. Pritsak, "The Khazar Kingdom's Conversion to Judaism," 269.
1209. Ibid., 271.
1210. Ibid., 266.
1211. Rudolf Loewenthal, "The Extinction of the Krimchaks in World War II," *American Slavic and East European Review* 10, no. 2 (April 1951): 130.
1212. Brook, *The Jews of Khazaria*, 90-91.

1213. Brutzkus, "The Khazar Origin of Ancient Kiev," 116.
1214. Brook, *The Jews of Khazaria*, 226.
1215. V. Minorsky, "A New Book on the Khazars," *Oriens* 11, no. 1/2 (December 31, 1958): 143; Peter B. Golden, "Religion among the Qïpčaqs of Medieval Eurasia," *Central Asiatic Journal* 42, no. 2 (1998): 222.
1216. Loewenthal, "The Extinction of the Krimchaks in World War II," 131.
1217. Ibid., 132.
1218. Ibid., 133.
1219. Ibid., 135–36.
1220. Pritsak, "The Khazar Kingdom's Conversion to Judaism," 265.
1221. Roman K. Kovalev, "Creating Khazar Identity through Coins: The Special Issue Dirhams of 837/8," in *East Central and Eastern Europe in the Early Middle Ages*, ed. Florin Curta (Ann Arbor: University of Michigan Press, 2008), 225.
1222. Ibid., 226.
1223. Jean Paul Roux, "Historical Introduction," in *The Turkic Peoples of the World*, ed. Margaret Bainbridge (Abingdon: Routledge, 1993), 9.
1224. Brutzkus, "The Khazar Origin of Ancient Kiev," 111.
1225. Cross, "The Scandinavian Infiltration into Early Russia," 512.
1226. Christian, *A History of Russia, Central Asia, and Mongolia*, 298; Wheatcroft, *Challenging Traditional Views of Russian History*, 7.
1227. Kovalev, "Creating Khazar Identity through Coins," 222.
1228. Brook, *The Jews of Khazaria*, 59–68.
1229. Cross, "The Scandinavian Infiltration into Early Russia," 507.
1230. Omeljan Pritsak, "The Origin of Rus'," *Russian Review* 36, no. 3 (July 1977): 265–72.
1231. Christian, *A History of Russia, Central Asia, and Mongolia*, 335.
1232. Pritsak, "The Origin of Rus'," 268; Golden, *Nomads and Their Neighbours in the Russian Steppe*, vi–87–89.
1233. Brutzkus, "The Khazar Origin of Ancient Kiev," 111.
1234. Golden, *Nomads and Their Neighbours in the Russian Steppe*, vi–96–97.
1235. Pritsak, "The Origin of Rus'," 268.
1236. Christian, *A History of Russia, Central Asia, and Mongolia*, 344.
1237. Vasary, *Turks, Tatars and Russians in the 13th–16th Centuries*, xxi–28.
1238. Dmitri Bondarenko, Alexander Kazankov, Daria Khaltourina and Andrey Korotayev, "Ethnographic Atlas XXXI: Peoples of

Easternmost Europe," *Ethnology* 44, no. 3 (Summer 2005): 261–89.

1239. A. Bruce Boswell, "The Kipchak Turks," *Slavonic Review* 6, no. 16 (June 1927): 68.

1240. C. A. MacArtney, "The Petchenegs," *Slavonic and East European Review* 8, no. 23 (December 1929): 342.

1241. Peter B. Golden, *The Turkic World in Mahmûd al-Kâshgharî, Complexity of Interaction along the Eurasian Steppe Zone in the First Millennium CE*, ed. Jan Bemmann and Michael Schmauder (Rheinische Friedrich-Wilhelms-Universität Bonn, 2015), 515.

1242. MacArtney, "The Petchenegs," 343.

1243. Golden, *Nomads and Their Neighbours in the Russian Steppe*, vii–75.

1244. Istvan Vasary, *Cumans and Tatars: Oriental Military in the Pre-Ottoman Balkans, 1185–1365* (Cambridge, UK: Cambridge University Press, 2005), 8–9.

1245. MacArtney, "The Petchenegs," 345.

1246. Ibid., 346.

1247. Golden, *The Turkic World in Mahmûd al-Kâshgharî*, 521.

1248. MacArtney, "The Petchenegs," 346–47.

1249. Ibid., 347–48.

1250. Kaegi Jr., "The Contribution of Archery," 105.

1251. Ibid., 107.

1252. MacArtney, "The Petchenegs," 348.

1253. Ibid., 349.

1254. Boswell, "The Kipchak Turks," 71.

1255. Ibid., 74.

1256. Ibid., 75.

1257. Ibid., 76.

1258. Wolff, "The 'Second Bulgarian Empire,'" 175.

1259. MacArtney, "The Petchenegs," 350.

1260. Ibid., 351–52.

1261. Ibid., 353.

1262. Christian, *A History of Russia, Central Asia, and Mongolia*, 354–56.

1263. Golden, "Religion among the Qïpčaqs of Medieval Eurasia," 180–86.

1264. Golden, "Nomads and Sedentary Societies in Eurasia," 99.

1265. Golden, *The Turkic World in Mahmûd al-Kâshgharî*, 516, 518.

1266. Golden, "Religion among the Qïpčaqs of Medieval Eurasia," 180–86.

1267. Boswell, "The Kipchak Turks," 71.

1268. Ibid., 70–71.

1269. Ibid., 70.

1270. Ibid., 71.

1271. Golden, "Religion among the Qïpčaqs of Medieval Eurasia," 186–87.

1272. Boswell, "The Kipchak Turks," 78.
1273. Ibid., 77–78.
1274. Golden, "Religion among the Qïpčaqs of Medieval Eurasia," 217–18.
1275. Boswell, "The Kipchak Turks," 79.
1276. Vasary, *Cumans and Tatars: Oriental Military in the Pre-Ottoman Balkans*, 17.
1277. Ibid., 29.
1278. Ibid., 10.
1279. Vasary, *Turks, Tatars and Russians in the 13th–16th Centuries*, 2007, i–32.
1280. Vasary, *Cumans and Tatars: Oriental Military in the Pre-Ottoman Balkans*, 33.
1281. Wolff, "The 'Second Bulgarian Empire,'" 175, 180–81.
1282. Ibid., 183.
1283. Ibid., 179–80.
1284. Vasary, *Turks, Tatars and Russians in the 13th–16th Centuries*, i–31; Vasary, *Cumans and Tatars*, 33–42.
1285. Vasary, *Turks, Tatars and Russians in the 13th–16th Centuries*, i–32; Vasary, *Cumans and Tatars*, 65–66.
1286. Vasary, *Turks, Tatars and Russians in the 13th–16th Centuries*, i–32; Vasary, *Cumans and Tatars*, 112.
1287. Boswell, "The Kipchak Turks," 81.
1288. Ibid., 85.
1289. Golden, "Religion among the Qïpčaqs of Medieval Eurasia," 224–26.
1290. Boswell, "The Kipchak Turks," 82.
1291. Ibid.
1292. Ibid., 85.

CHAPTER 5: THE MASTERS OF THE EURASIAN STEPPES

1293. Claus Schönig, "Turko-Mongolic Relations," in *The Mongolic Languages*, ed. Juha Janhunen (Routledge, 2003), 404.
1294. Michal Biran, *Chinggis Khan* (London: Oneworld, 2007), 13.
1295. Peter B. Golden, *Central Asia in World History* (New York: Oxford University Press, 2011), 35.
1296. Thomas J. Barfield, *The Perilous Frontier: Nomadic Empires and China* (Hoboken: Blackwell, 1992), 85.
1297. Wolfram Eberhard, *Conquerors and Rulers: Social Forces in Medieval China*, 2nd ed. (Boston, MA: E. J. Brill, 1970), 115–16.
1298. Barfield, *The Perilous Frontier*, 85.
1299. Ibid., 89–91.
1300. Ibid., 87.
1301. Sophia-Karin Psarras, "Han and Xiongnu a Reexamination of Cultural and Political Relations

(II)," *Monumenta Serica* 52 (2004): 62–63.

1302. William Samolin, "Hsiung-Nu, Hun, Turk," *Central Asiatic Journal* 3, no. 2 (1957): 150.

1303. Louis Hambis, "The Ancient Civilizations of Manchuria," *East and West* 7, no. 3 (October 1956): 221.

1304. Eberhard, *Conquerors and Rulers*, 125.

1305. Pan Yihong, "Marriage Alliances and Chinese Princesses in International Politics from Han through T'ang," *Asia Major*, 3rd ser., 10, no. 1/2 (1997): 103.

1306. Sophia-Karin Psarras, "Xiongnu Culture: Identification and Dating," *Central Asiatic Journal* 39, no. 1 (1995): 102–3.

1307. Sophia-Karin Psarras, "Exploring the North: Non-Chinese Cultures of the Late Warring States and Han," *Monumenta Serica* 42 (1994): 5.

1308. Psarras, "Xiongnu Culture: Identification and Dating," 118.

1309. Étienne de la Vaissière, "Huns et Xiongnu," *Central Asiatic Journal* 49, no. 1 (2005): 14.

1310. Gerard Clauson, *Studies in Turkic and Mongolic Linguistics* (Routledge, 1962), 25–26.

1311. Owen Lattimore, *Inner Asian Frontiers of China* (New York: Oxford University Press, 1940), 526.

1312. Barfield, *The Perilous Frontier*, 98.

1313. Piero Corradini, "The Barbarian States in North China," *Central Asiatic Journal* 50, no. 2 (2006): 166.

1314. Michael C. Rogers, "The Myth of the Battle of the Fei River (A.D. 383)," *T'oung Pao*, 2nd ser., 54, no. 1/3 (1968): 50.

1315. Liu Shufen, "Ethnicity and the Suppression of Buddhism in Fifth-Century North China: The Background and Significance of the Gaiwu Rebellion," *Asia Major*, 3rd ser., 15, no. 1 (2002): 4.

1316. Ibid., 5.

1317. Corradini, "The Barbarian States in North China," 179.

1318. Ibid., 183–84.

1319. Lattimore, *Inner Asian Frontiers of China*, 526–27.

1320. David Christian, *A History of Russia, Central Asia, and Mongolia. Volume I: Inner Eurasia from Prehistory to the Mongol Empire* (Hoboken: Wiley-Blackwell, 1998), 234; Corradini, "The Barbarian States in North China," 184.

1321. Barfield, *The Perilous Frontier*, 101.

1322. Corradini, "The Barbarian States in North China," 174–75, 185.

1323. Lattimore, *Inner Asian Frontiers of China*, 527.

1324. Barfield, *The Perilous Frontier*, 101–2.

1325. Corradini, "The Barbarian States in North China," 187–88.

1326. Shufen, "Ethnicity and the Suppression of Buddhism," 5.

1327. Barfield, *The Perilous Frontier*, 105–6.

1328. Otto J. Maenchen-Helfen, *The World of the Huns: Studies in Their History and Culture* (Oakland: University of California Press, 1973), 372.

1329. Psarras, "Han and Xiongnu a Reexamination of Cultural and Political Relations (II)," 72–73.

1330. Corradini, "The Barbarian States in North China," 190–91.

1331. Ibid., 193.

1332. William Montgomery McGovern, *The Early Empires of Central Asia: A Study of the Scythians and the Huns and the Part They Played in World History* (Chapel Hill, NC: University of North Carolina Press, 1939), 99–101.

1333. Corradini, "The Barbarian States in North China," 198–99.

1334. Ibid., 200.

1335. Michael C. Rogers, "The Myth of the Battle of the Fei River (A.D. 383)," *T'oung Pao*, 2nd ser., 54, no. 1/3 (1968): 51.

1336. Corradini, "The Barbarian States in North China," 194.

1337. Ibid., 226; Sanping Chen, "Sino-Tokharico-Altaica—Two Linguistic Notes," *Central Asiatic Journal* 42, no. 1 (1998): 35.

1338. Katherine R. Tsiang, "Changing Patterns of Divinity and Reform in the Late Northern Wei," *Art Bulletin* 84, no. 2 (June 2002): 222.

1339. Kursat Yildirim, "An Opinion on the Meaning of the Name 'Ruanruan,'" *Central Asiatic Journal* 56 (2012–2013): 35.

1340. Samolin, "Hsiung-Nu, Hun, Turk," 150.

1341. K. Enoki, "The Origin of the White Huns or Hephthalites," *East and West* 6, no. 3 (October 1955): 233.

1342. Golden, *Central Asia in World History*, 36.

1343. C. A. Macartney, "On the Greek Sources for the History of the Turks in the Sixth Century," *Bulletin of the School of Oriental and African Studies* 11, no. 2 (1944): 266, 270.

1344. Ibid., 268–69.

1345. Golden, *Central Asia in World History*, 36.

1346. Barfield, *The Perilous Frontier*, 120, 132.

1347. Macartney, "On the Greek Sources," 266.

1348. Ruth W. Dunnell, "Who Are the Tanguts? Remarks on Tangut

Ethnogenesis and the Ethnonym Tangut," *Journal of Asian History* 18, no. 1 (1984): 86.

1349. Peter A. Boodberg, "Marginalia to the Histories of the Northern Dynasties," *Harvard Journal of Asiatic Studies* 4, no. 3/4 (December 1939): 230–31.

1350. Yildirim, "An Opinion on the Meaning of the Name 'Ruanruan,'" 36.

1351. Ibid., 37.

1352. Ibid., 38.

1353. Yihong, "Marriage Alliances," 95.

1354. Barfield, *The Perilous Frontier*, 9.

1355. Ibid.

1356. Ibid., 14.

1357. Han-Woo Choi, "Notes on Some Ancient Korean Titles," *Central Asiatic Journal* 36, no. 1/2 (1992): 37.

1358. Kate A. Lingley, "Naturalizing the Exotic: On the Changing Meanings of Ethnic Dress in Medieval China," *Ars Orientalis* 38 (2010): 56.

1359. Louis Bazin, "Recherches sur les parlers T'o-pa," *T'oung Pao*, 2nd ser., 39, no. 4/5 (1950): 228.

1360. Christian, *A History of Russia, Central Asia, and Mongolia*. 233–35.

1361. Rémi Mathieu, "Croyances des Toungouses de Chine," *Anthropos* 86, no. 1/3 (1991): 112.

1362. Sophia-Karin Psarras, "Upper Xiajiadian," *Monumenta Serica* 47 (1999): 5; Lattimore, *Inner Asian Frontiers of China*, 527.

1363. Clauson, *Studies in Turkic and Mongolic Linguistics*, 20, 27.

1364. Q. Edward Wang, "History, Space, and Ethnicity: The Chinese Worldview," *Journal of World History* 10, no. 2 (Fall 1999): 298; Patricia Eichenbaum Karetzky and Alexander C. Soper, "A Northern Wei Painted Coffin," *Artibus Asiae* 51, no. 1/2 (1991): 5; Andrew Eisenberg, "Retired Emperorship in Medieval China: The Northern Wei," *T'oung Pao*, 2nd ser., 77, no. 1/3 (1991): 57.

1365. Boodberg, "Marginalia to the Histories of the Northern Dynasties," 245.

1366. Eisenberg, "Retired Emperorship in Medieval China," 57.

1367. René Grousset, *The Empire of the Steppes: A History of Central Asia* (New Brunswick: Rutgers University Press, 1999), 17.

1368. Yildirim, "An Opinion on the Meaning of the Name 'Ruanruan,'" 35.

1369. Boodberg, "Marginalia to the Histories of the Northern Dynasties," 230–31.

1370. Mark Edward Lewis, *China between Empires: The Northern and Southern Dynasties* (Cambridge, MA: Belknap Press, 2009), 149.

1371. Christopher I. Beckwith, *Empires of the Silk Road: A History of Central Eurasia from the Bronze Age to the Present* (Princeton University Press, 2009), 103, 406–7; R. C. Blockley, *The History of Menander the Guardsman: Introductory Essay, Text, Translation and Historiographical Notes*, Arca Classical and Medieval Texts, Papers, and Monographs (Barnsley, Great Britain: Francis Cairns, 1985), 172–73, 178–79; Clauson, *Studies in Turkic and Mongolic Linguistics*, 27.

1372. Schönig, "Turko-Mongolic Relations," 406.

1373. Bazin, "Recherches sur les parlers T'o-pa," 228, 231.

1374. Otto J. Maenchen-Helfen, "The Ting-Ling," *Harvard Journal of Asiatic Studies* 4, no. 1 (May 1939): 86; Jean Paul Roux, "Historical Introduction," in *The Turkic Peoples of the World*, ed. Margaret Bainbridge (Abingdon: Routledge, 1993), 4; Christian, *A History of Russia, Central Asia, and Mongolia*, 209, 235–38; Jean-Paul Roux, *Histoire Des Turcs: Deux mille ans du Pacifique à la Méditerranée* (Paris: Fayard, 2000), 53–55.

1375. Bazin, "Recherches sur les parlers T'o-pa," 228–29.

1376. Ibid., 228.

1377. Clauson, *Studies in Turkic and Mongolic Linguistics*, 20, 39, 125, 217.

1378. Peter A. Boodberg, "The Language of the T'o–Pa Wei," *Harvard Journal of Asiatic Studies* 1, no. 2 (July 1936): 168–72.

1379. Ibid., 173–84.

1380. Ibid., 185.

1381. Sanping Chen, "Turkic or Proto-Mongolian? A Note on the Tuoba Language," *Central Asiatic Journal* 49, no. 2 (2005): 164, 171.

1382. Jennifer Holmgren, "Women and Political Power in the Traditional T'o-Pa Elite: A Preliminary Study of the Biographies of Empresses in the Wei-Shu," *Monumenta Serica* 35 (1981–1983): 36.

1383. Ibid., 37.

1384. Ibid., 38–40, 42.

1385. Ibid., 45.

1386. Holmgren, "Women and Political Power in the Traditional T'o-Pa Elite," 50–51.

1387. Ibid., 52.

1388. Corradini, "The Barbarian States in North China," 228.

1389. Barfield, *The Perilous Frontier*, 123.

1390. Corradini, "The Barbarian States in North China," 228.

1391. Barfield, *The Perilous Frontier*, 123–24.

1392. Boodberg, "The Language of the T'o–Pa Wei," 168.

1393. Hansgerd Göckenjan, "The World of the Early Nomadic Horsemen," in *The Turkic Speaking Peoples: 2,000 Years of Art and Culture from Inner Asia to the Balkans*, ed. Ergun Cagatay and Dogan Kuban (Munich: Prestel, 2006), 78.
1394. Golden, *Central Asia in World History*, 35.
1395. Eberhard, *Conquerors and Rulers*, 145.
1396. Roux, "Historical Introduction," 4; Grousset, *The Empire of the Steppes*, 60–66.
1397. Corradini, "The Barbarian States in North China," 228–29.
1398. Wai-Kam Ho, "Three Seated Stone Buddhas," *Bulletin of the Cleveland Museum of Art* 53, no. 4 (April 1996): 84.
1399. Ibid.
1400. Corradini, "The Barbarian States in North China," 230.
1401. Liu Shufen, "Ethnicity and the Suppression of Buddhism in Fifth-Century North China: The Background and Significance of the Gaiwu Rebellion," *Asia Major*, 3rd ser., 15, no. 1 (2002): 1–2.
1402. Ibid., 3.
1403. Corradini, "The Barbarian States in North China," 232.
1404. Katherine R. Tsiang, "Changing Patterns of Divinity and Reform in the Late Northern Wei," *Art Bulletin* 84, no. 2 (June 2002): 222.
1405. Ibid., 223.
1406. Julian Baldick, *Animal and Shaman: Ancient Religions of Central Asia* (New York: New York University Press, 2012), 172.
1407. Eberhard, *Conquerors and Rulers*, 146–47.
1408. Holmgren, "Women and Political Power in the Traditional T'o-Pa Elite," 57–60.
1409. Ibid., 60.
1410. Bazin, "Recherches sur les parlers T'o-pa," 231.
1411. Holmgren, "Women and Political Power in the Traditional T'o-Pa Elite," 60–61.
1412. Ibid., 56.
1413. Christian, *A History of Russia, Central Asia, and Mongolia*, 236.
1414. Maenchen-Helfen, "The Ting-Ling," 83–84.
1415. Eberhard, *Conquerors and Rulers*, 130–31.
1416. Ho, "Three Seated Stone Buddhas," 84.
1417. Lingley, "Naturalizing the Exotic," 56.
1418. Eberhard, *Conquerors and Rulers*, 147.
1419. Chen, "Turkic or Proto-Mongolian? A Note on the Tuoba Language," 161; Sanping Chen, "From Mulan to Unicorn," *Journal of Asian History* 39, no. 1 (2005): 23.

1420. Chen, "From Mulan to Unicorn," 27; Chen, "Turkic or Proto-Mongolian? A Note on the Tuoba Language," 161.
1421. Chen, "From Mulan to Unicorn," 23.
1422. Ibid., 24, 28.
1423. Ibid., 24–26, 31–32, 33.
1424. Boodberg, "Marginalia to the Histories of the Northern Dynasties," 242, 245, 246.
1425. Ibid., 242–43.
1426. Wolfram Eberhard, "Remarks on the Bureaucracy in North China during the Tenth Century," *Oriens* 4, no. 2 (December 31, 1951): 281.
1427. Sanping Chen, "A-Gan Revisited—the Tuoba's Cultural and Political Heritage," *Journal of Asian History* 30, no. 1 (1996): 54.
1428. Sanping Chen, "Succession Struggle and the Ethnic Identity of the Tang Imperial House," *Journal of the Royal Asiatic Society*, 3rd ser., 6, no. 3 (November 1996): 381.
1429. Hyun Jin Kim, *The Huns* (New York, NY: Routledge, 2016), p. 32.
1430. Chen, "A-Gan Revisited—the Tuoba's Cultural and Political Heritage," 53.
1431. Kim, *The Huns*, p. 32.
1432. Ibid.
1433. Lattimore, *Inner Asian Frontiers of China*, 528.
1434. Emel Esin, "Baliq and Ordu (The Early Turkish Circumvallations, in Architectural Aspects)," *Central Asiatic Journal* 27, no. 3/4 (1983): 174–75.
1435. Golden, *Central Asia in World History*, 37.
1436. T. Senga, "The Toquz Oghuz Problem and the Origin of the Khazars," *Journal of Asian History* 24, no. 1 (1990): 64–65.
1437. Golden, *Central Asia in World History*, 37.
1438. Clauson, *Studies in Turkic and Mongolic Linguistics*, 27.
1439. C. E. Bosworth and Gerard Clauson, "Al-Xwārazmī on the Peoples of Central Asia," *Journal of the Royal Asiatic Society of Great Britain and Ireland*, no. 1/2 (April 1965): 3.
1440. Kevin Alan Brook, *The Jews of Khazaria* (New York: Rowman & Littlefield, 2006), 47.
1441. Clauson, *Studies in Turkic and Mongolic Linguistics*, 8–9.
1442. E. D. Phillips, "New Light on the Ancient History of the Eurasian Steppe," *American Journal of Archaeology* 61, no. 3 (July 1957): 279.
1443. Peter B. Golden, "Religion among the Qïpčaqs of Medieval Eurasia," *Central Asiatic Journal* 42, no. 2 (1998): 215.
1444. J. B. Bury, "The Turks in the Sixth Century," *English Historical Review* 12, no. 47 (July 1897): 417.

1445. Brook, *The Jews of Khazaria*, 47.
1446. Christian, *A History of Russia, Central Asia, and Mongolia*. 281–83; Stephen G. Wheatcroft, *Challenging Traditional Views of Russian History* (Palgrave Macmillan, 2002), 9; Peter B. Golden, *Nomads and Their Neighbours in the Russian Steppe: Turks, Khazars and Qipchaqs* (Variorum, 2003), vi–78, 85; Emel Esin, "Tös and Moncuḳ Notes on Turkish Flag-Pole Finials," *Central Asiatic Journal* 16, no. 1 (1972): 21–22.
1447. Psarras, "Han and Xiongnu a Reexamination of Cultural and Political Relations (II)," 72–73.
1448. Roux, "Historical Introduction," 19.
1449. Yihong, "Marriage Alliances," 108.
1450. Brook, *The Jews of Khazaria*, 3.
1451. Robert L. Reynolds and Robert S. Lopez, "Odoacer: German or Hun?" *American Historical Review* 52, no. 1 (October 1946): 49.
1452. Grousset, *The Empire of the Steppes*, 81.
1453. Denis Sinor, "The Inner Asian Warriors," *Journal of the American Oriental Society* 101, no. 2 (April–June 1981): 137.
1454. Ibid., 139.
1455. V. Minorsky, "The Turkish Dialect of the Khalaj," *Bulletin of the School of Oriental Studies* 10, no. 2 (1940): 427–28.
1456. Golden, *Central Asia in World History*, 37.
1457. Baldick, *Animal and Shaman*, 7.
1458. Golden, *Central Asia in World History*, 37.
1459. Ibid., 49.
1460. Zhang Guangda and Rong Xinjiang, "A Concise History of the Turfan Oasis and Its Exploration," *Asia Major*, 3rd ser., 11, no. 2 (1998): 17.
1461. Golden, *Central Asia in World History*, 39.
1462. Guangda and Xinjiang, "A Concise History of the Turfan Oasis and Its Exploration," 17.
1463. Mark Edward Lewis, *China between Empires: The Northern and Southern Dynasties*, 149.
1464. Golden, *Central Asia in World History*, 38.
1465. Esin, "Tös and Moncuḳ Notes on Turkish Flag-Pole Finials," 26.
1466. Minorsky, "The Turkish Dialect of the Khalaj," 431.
1467. Clifford Edmund Bosworth, *The Ghaznavids: Their Empire in Afghanistan and Eastern Iran 994–1040* (Edinburgh: Edinburgh University Press, 1963), 36.
1468. Macartney, "On the Greek Sources," 267.
1469. Bury, "The Turks in the Sixth Century," 417–18, 421, 425–26.

1470. Golden, *Central Asia in World History*, 38–39.
1471. Bury, "The Turks in the Sixth Century," 420–22, 423, 426.
1472. Paul Pelliot, "Neuf notes sur des questions d'Asie centrale," *T'oung Pao*, 2nd ser., 26, no. 4/5 (1929): 212–16, 218.
1473. Ibid., 218.
1474. Macartney, "On the Greek Sources," 268, 273.
1475. Ibid., 273.
1476. Yihong, "Marriage Alliances," 108.
1477. Golden, *Central Asia in World History*, 39.
1478. Yihong, "Marriage Alliances," 109–10.
1479. Golden, *Central Asia in World History*, 41.
1480. Wang Zhenping, "Ideas concerning Diplomacy and Foreign Policy under the Tang Emperors Gaozu and Taizong," *Asia Major*, 3rd ser., 22, no. 1 (2009): 240–41.
1481. David A. Graff, "The Battle of Huo-i," *Asia Major*, 3rd ser., 5, no. 1 (1992): 33–37.
1482. Ching-Lung Chen, "Trading Activities of the Turkic Peoples in China," *Central Asiatic Journal* 25, no. 1/2 (1981): 41.
1483. Graff, 42.
1484. Zhenping, "Ideas concerning Diplomacy and Foreign Policy under the Tang Emperors Gaozu and Taizong," 242–44.
1485. Beckwith, *Empires of the Silk Road*, 124.
1486. Yihong, "Marriage Alliances," 111–12.
1487. Valerie Hansen, "The Path of Buddhism into China: The View from Turfan," *Asia Major*, 3rd ser., 11, no. 2 (1998): 57.
1488. Beckwith, *Empires of the Silk Road*, 124.
1489. Wang, "History, Space, and Ethnicity," 299.
1490. Chen, "Succession Struggle and the Ethnic Identity of the Tang Imperial House," 381.
1491. Ibid., 385–87.
1492. Ibid., 387.
1493. Beckwith, *Empires of the Silk Road*, 125.
1494. Zhenping, "Ideas concerning Diplomacy and Foreign Policy under the Tang Emperors Gaozu and Taizong," 246–47.
1495. Ibid., 248–49.
1496. Ibid., 251–53.
1497. Golden, *Central Asia in World History*, 40.
1498. Zhenping, "Ideas concerning Diplomacy and Foreign Policy under the Tang Emperors Gaozu and Taizong," 280.
1499. Golden, *Central Asia in World History*, 41.

1500. Peter B. Golden, "Nomads and Sedentary Societies in Eurasia," in *Agricultural and Pastoral Societies in Ancient and Classical History*, ed. Michael Adas (Philadelphia, PA: Temple University Press, 2001), 94.

1501. Chen, "A-Gan Revisited—the Tuoba's Cultural and Political Heritage," 55; Chen, "Succession Struggle and the Ethnic Identity of the Tang Imperial House," 386.

1502. Zhenping, "Ideas concerning Diplomacy and Foreign Policy under the Tang Emperors Gaozu and Taizong," 262.

1503. Ibid., 263.

1504. Beckwith, *Empires of the Silk Road*, 126.

1505. Golden, *Central Asia in World History*, 42.

1506. Colin Mackerras, *The Uighur Empire: According to the T'ang Dynastic Histories, A Study in Sino-Uighur Relations 744–840* (Columbia, SC: University of South Carolina Press, 1972), 8.

1507. Zhenping, "Ideas concerning Diplomacy and Foreign Policy under the Tang Emperors Gaozu and Taizong," 280.

1508. Xinru Liu, "The Silk Road: Overland Trade and Cultural Interactions in Eurasia," in *Agricultural and Pastoral Societies in Ancient and Classical History*, ed. Michael Adas (Philadelphia, PA: Temple University Press, 2001), 168.

1509. Yihong, "Marriage Alliances," 113.

1510. Ibid., 114–15.

1511. Golden, *Central Asia in World History*, 42.

1512. K. Czeglédy, "On the Numerical Composition of the Ancient Turkish Tribal Confederations," *Acta Orientalia Academiae Scientiarum Hungaricae*, Lvdovico ligeti septvagenario hoc volvmen damvs dicamvs dedicamvs, 25 (1972): 275.

1513. Ibid., 276.

1514. Ibid., 277.

1515. Mihály Dobrovits, "The Great Western Campaign of the Eastern Turks (711–714)" (proceedings of the 1st International Conference on the Mediaeval History of the Eurasian Steppe: Szeged, Hungary, May 11–16, 2004: Part II), *Acta Orientalia Academiae Scientiarum Hungaricae* 58, no. 2 (2005): 179.

1516. Michael R. Drompp, "Centrifugal Forces in the Inner Asian 'Heartland': History 'versus' Geography," *Journal of Asian History* 23, no. 2 (1989): 142.

1517. Dobrovits, "The Great Western Campaign of the Eastern Turks (711–714)," 181.

1518. Ibid., 182.
1519. Pelliot, "Neuf notes sur des questions d'Asie centrale," 210.
1520. Roman K. Kovalev, "Creating Khazar Identity through Coins: The Special Issue Dirhams of 837/8," in *East Central and Eastern Europe in the Early Middle Ages*, ed. Florin Curta (2008), 230.
1521. Drompp, "Centrifugal Forces in the Inner Asian 'Heartland': History 'versus' Geography," 145.
1522. Mackerras, *The Uighur Empire*, 8.
1523. Federica Venturi, "An Old Tibetan Document on the Uighurs: A New Translation and Interpretation," *Journal of Asian History* 42, no. 1 (2008): 4, 28.
1524. Emel Esin, "The Horse in Turkic Art" (proceedings of the 7th Meeting of the Permanent International Altaistic Conference, August 29 to September 3, 1964), *Central Asiatic Journal* 10, no. 3/4 (December 1965): 178.
1525. Venturi, "An Old Tibetan Document on the Uighurs," 28–29.
1526. Ibid., 30.
1527. Esin, "Tös and Moncuḳ Notes on Turkish Flag-Pole Finials," 19–20, 26.
1528. Ibid., 26.
1529. John Keegan, *A History of Warfare* (New York: Alfred A. Knopf, 1994), 191.
1530. Edwin G. Pulleyblank, "The 'High Carts': A Turkish-Speaking People before the Türks," *Asia Major*, 3rd ser., 3, no. 1 (1990): 22.
1531. E. G. Pulleyblank, "The Name of the Kirghiz," *Central Asiatic Journal* 34, no. 1/2 (1990): 106.
1532. V. Minorsky, "Tamīm Ibn Baḥr's Journey to the Uyghurs," *Bulletin of the School of Oriental and African Studies* 12, no. 2 (1948): 286.
1533. Senga, "The Toquz Oghuz Problem," 64–65; Golden, "Religion among the Qïpčaqs of Medieval Eurasia," 185.
1534. Golden, *Central Asia in World History*, 44; Senga, "The Toquz Oghuz Problem," 62.
1535. Mackerras, *The Uighur Empire*, 8.
1536. Venturi, "An Old Tibetan Document on the Uighurs," 24.
1537. Mackerras, *The Uighur Empire*, 8–9.
1538. Venturi, "An Old Tibetan Document on the Uighurs," 22–31.
1539. Ibid., 22.
1540. Mackerras, *The Uighur Empire*, 102–3.
1541. Ibid., 105.
1542. Ibid., 9.
1543. Johan Elverskog, *Buddhism and Islam on the Silk Road* (Philadelphia, PA: University of

Pennsylvania Press, 2010), 42; Golden, "Nomads and Sedentary Societies in Eurasia," 96.

1544. Mackerras, *The Uighur Empire*, 10.

1545. Yihong, "Marriage Alliances," 118.

1546. Ibid., 124.

1547. Ildiko Ecsedy, "Chinese Historical Connections with the Turkic Empires and their Heirs," in *The Turkic Speaking Peoples: 2,000 Years of Art and Culture from Inner Asia to the Balkans*, ed. Ergun Cagatay and Dogan Kuban (Prestel, 2006), 143.

1548. Ablet Kamalov, "Turks and Uighurs during the Rebellion of an Lu-shan Shih Ch'ao-yi (755–762)," *Central Asiatic Journal* 45, no. 2 (2001): 243.

1549. Michael R. Drompp, *Tang China and the Collapse of the Uighur Empire* (Brill, 2005), 24–25; Liu, "The Silk Road," 169.

1550. Kamalov, "Turks and Uighurs," 243.

1551. Mackerras, *The Uighur Empire*, 32–34.

1552. Ibid., 35.

1553. Ibid., 10.

1554. Kamalov, "Turks and Uighurs," 246.

1555. Ibid., 250–53.

1556. Golden, *Central Asia in World History*, 44.

1557. Guangda and Xinjiang, "A Concise History of the Turfan Oasis and Its Exploration," 20.

1558. Michael C. Brose, *Subjects and Masters: Uyghurs in the Mongol Empire* (Bellingham, WA: Center for East Asian Studies, Western Washington University, 2007), 61–62.

1559. Tsvetelin Stepsnov, "Ruler and Political Ideology in Pax Nomadica: Early Medieval Bulgaria and the Uighur Qaganate," in *East Central and Eastern Europe in the Early Ages*, ed. Florin Curta (Ann Arbor: University of Michigan Press, 2005), 154.

1560. Esin, "The Horse in Turkic Art," 198.

1561. Yihong, "Marriage Alliances," 124.

1562. Mackerras, *The Uighur Empire*, 43.

1563. Golden, *Central Asia in World History*, 45.

1564. Mackerras, *The Uighur Empire*, 42.

1565. Liu, "The Silk Road," 169.

1566. Drompp, *Tang China*, 22; Brose, *Subjects and Masters*, 65.

1567. Mackerras, *The Uighur Empire*, 36–39.

1568. Ibid., 39.
1569. Ibid., 41.
1570. Liu, "The Silk Road," 169.
1571. Brose, *Subjects and Masters*, 65.
1572. Mackerras, *The Uighur Empire*, 10.
1573. Ibid., 11.
1574. Ibid., 125.
1575. Ibid., 12, 124–25.
1576. Ibid., 13.
1577. Ibid.
1578. Ibid.
1579. Venturi, "An Old Tibetan Document on the Uighurs," 5.
1580. Golden, *Central Asia in World History*, 45.
1581. Minorsky, "Tamīm Ibn Baḥr's Journey to the Uyghurs," 283, 303; Mackerras, *The Uighur Empire*, 13.
1582. Minorsky, "Tamīm Ibn Baḥr's Journey to the Uyghurs," 283, 303.
1583. Esin, "Baliq and Ordu," 189.
1584. Golden, *Central Asia in World History*, 45.
1585. Ibid., 47.
1586. Golden, "Nomads and Sedentary Societies in Eurasia," 96.
1587. Golden, *Central Asia in World History*, 47, 49.
1588. Drompp, *Tang China*, 7–8.
1589. Ibid., 46.
1590. Ibid., 7–123.
1591. Yihong, "Marriage Alliances," 121.
1592. Guangda and Xinjiang, "A Concise History of the Turfan Oasis and Its Exploration," 13–14.
1593. Ibid., 20.
1594. Michael C. Brose, "Uyghur Technologists of Writing and Literacy in Mongol China," *T'oung Pao*, 2nd ser., 91, no. 4/5 (2005): 404.
1595. Hans-J. Klimkeit, "Christians, Buddhists and Manichaeans in Medieval Central Asia," *Buddhist-Christian Studies* 1 (1981): 47.
1596. Golden, *Central Asia in World History*, 47.
1597. Roux, "Historical Introduction," 13.
1598. Guangda and Xinjiang, "A Concise History of the Turfan Oasis and Its Exploration," 20–21.
1599. Ibid., 21.
1600. Ibid., 22–23.
1601. Roux, "Historical Introduction," 19.
1602. Ibid., 13; Drompp, *Tang China*, 22.
1603. Drompp, *Tang China*, 23; Roux, "Historical Introduction," 13.
1604. Aleksandr Kadirbaev, "Turks and Mongols," in *The Turkic Speaking Peoples: 2,000 Years of Art and Culture from Inner Asia to the Balkans*, ed. Ergun Cagatay and Dogan Kuban (Munich: Prestel, 2006), 105.

1605. Elverskog, *Buddhism and Islam on the Silk Road*, 150.

1606. Svat Soucek, *A History of Inner Asia* (Cambridge, England: Cambridge University Press, 2000), 105.

1607. Linda K. Benson, "The Turkic Peoples of China," in *The Peoples of the World*, ed. Margaret Bainbridge (Routledge, 1993), 55; Brose, *Subjects and Masters: Uyghurs in the Mongol Empire*, 78.

1608. Gardner Bovingdon, *The Uyghurs: Strangers in Their Own Land* (New York: Columbia University Press, 2010), 28.

1609. Eberhard, *Conquerors and Rulers: Social Forces in Medieval China*, 140–41.

1610. Paul Wittek et al., "Notes and Communications," *Bulletin of the School of Oriental and African Studies* 17, no. 2 (1955): 376.

1611. Minorsky, "Tamīm Ibn Baḥr's Journey to the Uyghurs," 288.

1612. Eberhard, *Conquerors and Rulers: Social Forces in Medieval China*, 141, 143.

1613. Wittek et al., "Notes and Communications," 376.

1614. Ibid.

1615. Minorsky, "Tamīm Ibn Baḥr's Journey to the Uyghurs," 289, 304.

1616. Karl A. Wittfogel and Fêng Chia-Shêng, "History of Chinese Society Liao (907–1125)," *Transactions of the American Philosophical Society*, n.s., 36 (1946): 107.

1617. Eberhard, *Conquerors and Rulers: Social Forces in Medieval China*, 141.

1618. Edwin G. Pulleyblank, "A Sogdian Colony in Inner Mongolia," *T'oung Pao*, 2nd ser., 41, no. 4/5 (1952): 342.

1619. Minorsky, "Tamīm Ibn Baḥr's Journey to the Uyghurs," 290.

1620. Edwin G. Pulleyblank, "Gentry Society: Some Remarks on Recent Work by W. Eberhard," *Bulletin of the School of Oriental and African Studies* 15, no. 3 (1953): 593; Minorsky, "Tamīm Ibn Baḥr's Journey to the Uyghurs," 289.

1621. Chen, "Sino-Tokharico-Altaica—Two Linguistic Notes," 34.

1622. Eberhard, *Conquerors and Rulers: Social Forces in Medieval China*, 141.

1623. Ibid., 146–47.

1624. Pulleyblank, "A Sogdian Colony in Inner Mongolia," 342.

1625. Pulleyblank, "Gentry Society: Some Remarks on Recent Work by W. Eberhard," 594.

1626. Edward H. Schafer, "The Auspices of T'ang," *Journal of the American Oriental Society* 83, no. 2 (April–June 1963): 221.

1627. Howard S. Levy, "The Righteous Uprising of Huang Ch'ao. By Chang Hui; The Righteous Uprising of Huang Ch'ao. By Hsi Chih-Pien," *Journal of Asian Studies* 16, no. 4 (August 1957), 613.

1628. Pulleyblank, "A Sogdian Colony in Inner Mongolia," 343.

1629. Pulleyblank, "Gentry Society: Some Remarks on Recent Work by W. Eberhard," 594.

1630. Karl Krippes, "Sociolinguistic Notes on the Turcification of the Sogdians," *Central Asiatic Journal* 35, no. 1/2 (1991): 70.

1631. Ibid.

1632. Pulleyblank, "Gentry Society: Some Remarks on Recent Work by W. Eberhard," 596.

1633. Eberhard, *Conquerors and Rulers: Social Forces in Medieval China*, 147.

1634. Kwok-Yiu Wong, "The White Horse Massacre and Changing Literati Culture in Late-Tang and Five Dynasties China," *Asia Major*, 3rd ser., 23, no. 2 (2010): 34, 36.

1635. Ibid., 37–39, 45.

1636. Ibid., 46.

1637. Pulleyblank, "A Sogdian Colony in Inner Mongolia," 346; Wittfogel and Chia-Shêng, 107.

1638. Eberhard, "Remarks on the Bureaucracy in North China during the Tenth Century," 281.

1639. Ibid.

1640. Paul Pelliot, "L'origine du nom de 'Chine,'" *T'oung Pao*, 2nd ser., 13, no. 5 (1912): 730.

1641. Eberhard, *Conquerors and Rulers: Social Forces in Medieval China*, 125–26.

1642. James Wasserman, *The Templars and the Assassins: The Militia of Heaven* (Merrimac, MA: Destiny Books, 2001), 129.

1643. Chen, "Turkic or Proto-Mongolian? A Note on the Tuoba Language," 171.

1644. Eberhard, *Conquerors and Rulers: Social Forces in Medieval China*, 141, 152.

1645. Johannes L. Kurz, "A Survey of the Historical Sources for the Five Dynasties and Ten States in Song Times," *Journal of Song-Yuan Studies* 33 (2003): 188.

1646. Eberhard, *Conquerors and Rulers: Social Forces in Medieval China*, 152–53.

1647. Otgon Borjigin, A Brief Introduction to the Historical Relics of the Hexi Corridor from the Time of the Mongol Empire, Mongolian Studies vol. 34 (2012), 81.

1648. Ibid.

1649. Ibid., 83.

CHAPTER 6: TRIBAL ENTITIES UNTIL THE EIGHTH CENTURY

1650. Rene Grousset, *The Empire of the Steppes: A History of Central Asia* (New Brunswick: Rutgers University Press, 1999), 47; Xinru Liu, *The Silk Road in World History* (New York: Oxford University Press, 2010), 4.

1651. Paul Pelliot, "L'origine du nom de 'Chine,'" *T'oung Pao*, 2nd ser., 13, no. 5 (1912): 731–32.

1652. Nicola Di Cosmo, *Ancient China and Its Enemies: The Rise of Nomadic Power in East Asian History*, Cambridge University Press, 2005, 165.

1653. William Montgomery McGovern, *The Early Empires of Central Asia: A Study of the Scythians and the Huns and the Part They Played in World History*, The University of North Carolina Press, 1939, 99–101.

1654. Owen Lattimore, *Inner Asian Frontiers of China* (New York: Oxford University Press, 1940), 455.

1655. Di Cosmo, *Ancient China and Its Enemies: The Rise of Nomadic Power in East Asian History*, 2005, 107.

1656. McGovern, *The Early Empires of Central Asia*, 99–101.

1657. Egemen Çağrı Mızrak, *Bozkır Kavimleri: M.Ö. VII. Yüzyıldan M.S. VI. Yüzyılın Ortalarına Kadar Batı Türkistan ve Kuzey Hindistan'daki Bozkırlar* (İstanbul: Ötüken, 2017), 65-66.

1658. Otto Maenchen-Helfen, "The Ting-Ling," *Harvard Journal of Asiatic Studies* 4, no. 1 (May 1939): 77–78, 80.

1659. Ibid., 77.

1660. Sophia-Karin Psarras, "Han and Xiongnu a Reexamination of Cultural and Political Relations (II)," *Monumenta Serica* 52 (2004): 62.

1661. Gerard Clauson, *Studies in Turkic and Mongolic Linguistics* (Abingdon: Routledge, 1962), 20.

1662. Louis Hambis, "The Ancient Civilizations of Manchuria," *East and West* 7, no. 3 (October 1956): 221.

1663. Z. V. Togan, *Umumi Türk Tarihine Giriş* (Istanbul: Ismail Akgün, 1946), 23.

1664. Namu Jila, "Myths and Traditional Beliefs about the Wolf and the Crow in Central Asia: Examples from the Turkic Wu-Sun and the Mongols," *Asian Folklore Studies* 65, no. 2 (2006): 167.

1665. D. M. Dunlop, "The Karaits of Eastern Asia," *Bulletin of the School of Oriental and African Studies* 11, no. 2 (1944): 289.

1666. Ahmet Taşağıl, Töles Boylarının Stratejik Önemi (6. Ve 7. Yüzyıllar), *İnsan ve Toplum Bilimleri Dergisi*, no. 3 (Spring 2014): 312.

1667. T. Senga, "The Toquz Oghuz Problem and the Origin of the Khazars," *Journal of Asian History* 24, no. 1 (1990): 62, 64.

1668. Taşağıl, Töles Boylarının Stratejik Önemi (6. Ve 7. Yüzyıllar), 313.

1669. Bahaeddin Ögel, Türk Mitolojisi, Cilt I, (Ankara: Türk Tarih Kurumu, 2014), 638.

1670. Chad D. Garcia, A New Kind of Northerner: Initial Song Perceptions of the Mongols, *Journal of Song-Yuan Studies*, Vol. 42 (2012), 319.

1671. Paul Pelliot, "Chrétiens d'Asie centrale et d'Extrême-Orient," *T'oung Pao*, 2nd ser., 15, no. 5 (1914): 630; De Hartog, *Genghis Khan*, 5.

1672. Peter B. Golden, *Nomads and Their Neighbours in the Russian Steppe: Turks, Khazars and Qipchaqs* (Variorum, 2003), vii–75.

1673. Senga, "The Toquz Oghuz Problem and the Origin of the Khazars," 64–65; Peter B. Golden, "Religion among the Qïpčaqs of Medieval Eurasia," *Central Asiatic Journal* 42, no. 2 (1998): 185.

1674. McGovern, *The Early Empires of Central Asia*, 101.

1675. Ibid., 45.

1676. Nicola Di Cosmo, *The Northern Frontier in Pre-Imperial China*, The Cambridge History of Ancient China: From the Origins of Civilization to 221 BC, ed. Michael Loewe and Edward L. Shaughnessy (Cambridge, UK: Cambridge University Press, 1999), 952.

1677. McGovern, *The Early Empires of Central Asia*, 48.

1678. András Róna-Tas, "The Periodization and Sources of Chuvash Linguistic History," in *Chuvash Studies*, ed. A. Róna-Tas (Budapest: Akadémiai Kiadó, 1982), 120-122.

1679. Denis Sinor, "The Inner Asian Warriors," *Journal of the American Oriental Society* 101, no. 2 (April–June 1981): 137.

1680. Albert E. Dien, "The Stirrup and Its Effect on Chinese Military History," *Ars Orientalis* 16 (1986): 33.

1681. Hansgerd Göckenjan, "The World of the Early Nomadic Horsemen," in *The Turkic Speaking Peoples: 2,000 Years of Art and Culture from Inner Asia to the Balkans*, ed. Dogan Kuban (Munich: Prestel, 2006), 75.

1682. Falko Daim, "The Avars: Steppe People of Central Europe," *Archaeology* 37, no. 2 (March–April, 1984): 33.

1683. Hyun Jin Kim, *The Huns* (New York, NY: Routledge, 2016), 14.

1684. Peter B. Golden, *Central Asia in World History* (New York: Oxford University Press, 2011), 70; Peter B. Golden, *The Turkic World in Mahmûd al-Kâshgharî*, Complexity of Interaction along the Eurasian Steppe Zone in the First Millennium CE, ed. Jan Bemmann and Michael Schmauder (Rheinische Friedrich-Wilhelms-Universität Bonn, 2015), 509.

1685. Kim, *The Huns*, 149-159.

1686. Omeljan Pritsak, "The Origin of Rus," *Russian Review* 36, no. 3 (July 1977): 268; Golden, *Nomads and Their Neighbours in the Russian Steppe*, vi-87–89; J. Brutzkus, "The Khazar Origin of Ancient Kiev," *Slavonic and East European Review*, American series, 3, no. 1 (1994): 111.

1687. Golden, *Nomads and Their Neighbours in the Russian Steppe*, vi-96–97; Pritsak, "The Origin of Rus," 268.

1688. Fan Pen Chen, "Shadow Theaters of the World," *Asian Folklore Studies* 62, no. 1 (2003): 25–26, 29, 47–48.

1689. Brutzkus, "The Khazar Origin of Ancient Kiev," 112–13.

1690. Ibid., 117–18.

1691. Ibid., 118.

1692. Omeljan Pritsak, "The Origin of Rus," 268; Golden, *Nomads and Their Neighbours in the Russian Steppe*, vi-87–89; Brutzkus, "The Khazar Origin of Ancient Kiev," 111.

INDEX

A

Abaqan 77
Abbasid Caliphate 74, 87, 203, 344, 347, 356
Adriatic Sea 302
adultery (death penalty) 185
Aëtius (Western Roman General) 300, 303, 304, 315
Afghanistan 19, 25, 26, 31, 39, 69, 81, 83, 86, 116, 162, 169, 170, 196, 198, 213, 242, 271, 272, 274, 276, 278, 279, 280, 284, 285, 286, 288, 292, 295, 405, 411, 414, 418, 455, 503, 523
Agra 90, 476
Ahmad Ibn Tulun 79, 87
Alamanni 299, 300
Alans 196, 279, 301, 302, 317, 318, 351
Albanians 40, 50
Alexander the Great 138, 139, 170, 171, 222
Alexius Comnenus (Eastern Roman Emperor) 353
Alföld 171, 303, 326, 330
Ali (cousin of the Prophet and the fourth Caliph) 91, 128, 180, 470
Alp Arslan 101
Altai Mountains 43, 72, 111, 142, 207, 267, 271, 275, 357, 398, 399, 485
Amol 340
Amu Darya (Ceyhun) River 162, 170

Anatolia (Asia Minor) 19, 20, 22, 23, 24, 52, 66, 75, 79, 82, 84, 85, 101, 130, 134, 137, 153, 154, 158, 162, 171, 176, 301, 353, 364, 380, 403, 472, 481, 482, 510
Anglo-Saxons 315
An Lushan Rebellion (755–63) 422, 424, 427
Antioch 301
Aq-Qoyunlu Khanate 20, 34, 118
Aquitaine 173, 342
Arab 20, 38, 39, 45, 52, 53, 70, 71, 74, 80, 83, 87, 90, 95, 98, 110, 125, 127, 129, 130, 131, 132, 188, 191, 196, 285, 286, 288, 320, 338, 341, 380, 418, 419, 430, 449
Aral Sea 145, 170, 239, 356, 405
archery 58, 60, 152, 183, 200, 217, 353, 429
Armenian 37, 50, 84, 126
arrow 58, 59, 60, 62, 98, 100, 146, 157, 183, 186, 187, 228, 237, 305, 319, 399, 402
Asen (Cuman Turkish) 359, 361
A-shih-na (the blue tribe) 177, 339, 399, 400, 401, 402, 404, 405, 409, 412, 415, 418, 419, 425
Ashkenazi Jews 343
Asparukh, son of Qubrat Khan 323
atabeg 179
Atil or Itil (Khamlï) 340

535

Attila 22, 26, 73, 93, 99, 120, 140, 157, 174, 186, 193, 196, 228, 266, 269, 272, 292, 293, 294, 296, 297, 300, 302, 303, 304, 305, 306, 307, 308, 309, 310, 311, 312, 313, 314, 315, 319, 321, 322, 336, 337, 406, 447, 448, 459, 460, 469, 477, 483, 489, 490, 491, 499, 505, 506, 507, 508, 509, 512

Aurangzeb (Mughal Sultan) 121

Avars (European) 22, 35, 54, 58, 93, 94, 98, 124, 143, 156, 167, 171, 212, 223, 271, 272, 278, 279, 283, 292, 293, 294, 303, 314, 315, 316, 317, 320, 322, 323, 326, 329, 330, 331, 332, 333, 334, 335, 336, 338, 339, 344, 345, 346, 347, 355, 367, 376, 377, 378, 384, 385, 386, 387, 392, 399, 406, 407, 453, 459, 511, 512, 533

Ay-Beg (founder of the Sultanate of Delhi) 61, 87

Ayyubid 88, 359

Azerbaijan 19, 21, 28, 31, 34, 37, 83, 203, 341

B

Bab-ï Ali (Porte) 180

Babur (founder of Mughal Dynasty) 22, 89

Babylonians 155, 183

Bactria, Greco-Bactrian Kingdom 147, 197, 198, 240, 241, 243, 249, 250, 279, 281, 445, 447

Bactrian 171, 173, 197, 223, 239, 241, 242, 281

bagatur 179, 240

Baibars (Mamluk Sultan) 363

Baikal Lake 147

Balasagun (Quz Ordu) 37, 69, 78, 118

balbal 100, 101, 108, 120, 121

Balkan Peninsula (Balkans) 24, 171, 332, 334, 359

Balkh 416

Barbarian 308, 483, 486, 491, 496, 499, 506, 507, 508, 509, 517, 518, 520, 521

Barkol (Pulei) lake 260

Baškïrs 323, 349

Basmïl 55, 98, 202, 417, 418, 421

Battle of Châlons (a.k.a.) 304

Bayezït II Khan, (Ottoman Sultan) 60

Beethoven, Ludwig Van 47

beg or bey 179

Beijing 81, 440

Bela IV (King of Hungary) 118, 360, 361

Bengal 87, 132

Beš-Balïq 77, 428, 435, 436

Bibi Khanïm Mosque 88

Bible in Hunnish (Turkish) 126

Bilge 99, 202, 348, 416, 417, 425

Bishop Kardost (Armenian missionary) 126

Black Death (bubonic plague) 199

Black Sea 24, 44, 57, 68, 96, 152, 157, 161, 162, 201, 213, 293, 296, 300, 305, 323, 337, 340, 364, 377, 403, 404

blood oath 113

Bodrum 154

Bohemia, Kingdom of 175, 331

Bosten (Qin) lake 260

Botai Culture 137, 138

bow 42, 58, 59, 60, 62, 100, 164, 186, 190, 239, 319, 333

Bögü Qaghan (Uighur qaghan) 95, 124

Brahms, Johannes 48

Britain 64, 135, 173, 295, 300, 302, 315, 347, 467, 468, 469, 472, 473, 483, 486, 487, 490, 492, 497, 504, 512, 520, 522

Britannia 173

Buddha 122, 196, 390

Buddhism 21, 79, 92, 93, 94, 95, 122, 123, 124, 127, 129, 196, 198, 201, 205, 265, 288, 374, 375, 389, 390, 393, 394, 419, 423, 431, 432, 434, 451, 481, 502, 517, 518, 521, 524, 526, 529
Bukhara 72, 80, 130, 200
Bulgaria 19, 83, 171, 175, 180, 303, 323, 327, 328, 334, 340, 349, 350, 352, 353, 361, 362, 363, 364, 377, 447, 465, 527
Bulgars 13, 35, 37, 58, 93, 94, 96, 97, 118, 121, 125, 126, 143, 156, 165, 167, 187, 193, 233, 292, 293, 314, 316, 320, 321, 322, 323, 324, 325, 326, 327, 328, 331, 334, 335, 337, 339, 340, 341, 342, 345, 346, 347, 351, 359, 361, 407, 453, 465, 509, 510, 511, 512
Bumïn Qaghan, founder of GökTürk 177, 401, 404, 416
Burgundians 22, 175, 300, 302, 318
Burgundy, Kingdom of 175
Bursa 39, 40, 179
Byzantine 23, 140, 330, 404, 470, 483, 487
Byzantium 140, 298, 359

C

Cairo 74
calendar 64, 65, 66, 85, 112
caliph of the al-Rashidun 128
camel (*buğra*) 62, 178, 289
Cao Cao (Chinese general) 262
caravanserai 86
Carolingian Empire 175, 315, 335, 336, 344
Carpathians , Mountains 303, 334, 353, 357, 358
carpenters 185
carpets 71, 72, 73, 74, 75, 163, 453

Caspian Sea 20, 81, 96, 143, 158, 162, 201, 203, 227, 266, 267, 296, 317, 340, 347, 350, 356, 358, 380, 449
Catalaunian Fields, Battle of the 304
Catholic 126, 311, 334, 360
Caucasus 49, 75, 126, 164, 213, 301, 319, 320, 321, 329, 340, 341, 344, 358, 364, 448
Celtic 64, 148, 173, 174, 315
Celts 63, 173, 174, 234, 314, 317
ceramics 70, 71, 82, 198
Chariots 136, 482, 483
charity as tradition 131
Charlemagne (king of the Franks) 94, 124, 175, 335, 348, 453
Chihli (Bohai), Gulf of 116, 405
Ch'in 57, 150, 161, 189, 204, 214, 215, 216, 217, 218, 219, 220, 227, 235, 236, 237, 244, 246, 247, 248, 374, 379, 443, 445
Ch'in (Qin) 216, 219, 370, 371, 438, 440, 450
Chin (Jürchen) 216, 219, 370, 371, 438, 440, 451
China 13, 20, 21, 23, 24, 26, 28, 31, 38, 39, 43, 44, 45, 52, 53, 54, 57, 58, 60, 61, 64, 69, 70, 71, 72, 75, 76, 91, 92, 94, 95, 96, 97, 98, 100, 101, 102, 107, 109, 115, 122, 123, 124, 127, 135, 137, 138, 139, 141, 142, 143, 147, 149, 150, 156, 157, 158, 159, 160, 168, 169, 170, 173, 177, 186, 187, 189, 197, 198, 199, 200, 201, 202, 203, 204, 205, 207, 208, 209, 210, 211, 212, 214, 215, 216, 218, 219, 220, 221, 222, 223, 224, 226, 227, 228, 229, 230, 232, 233, 234, 235, 236, 238, 239, 240, 243, 244, 245, 246, 247, 248, 249, 250, 251, 253, 254, 255, 256, 257, 258, 259, 260,

261, 263, 264, 265, 266, 269, 272,
273, 274, 275, 279, 280, 283, 287,
288, 289, 291, 355, 364, 365, 367,
368, 369, 370, 371, 372, 373, 374,
375, 377, 378, 379, 380, 381, 382,
383, 384, 385, 386, 387, 388, 389,
391, 392, 393, 394, 395, 396, 397,
398, 399, 400, 401, 405, 408, 409,
410, 411, 412, 413, 414, 415, 417,
419, 420, 421, 422, 423, 424, 425,
426, 427, 430, 431, 432, 433, 435,
436, 437, 438, 439, 440, 441, 443,
444, 445, 446, 448, 450, 451, 452,
453, 455, 456, 459, 464, 465, 468,
469, 470, 474, 477, 478, 481, 482,
483, 485, 488, 489, 490, 491, 493,
494, 495, 496, 497, 498, 499, 500,
501, 502, 505, 506, 516, 517, 518,
519, 520, 521, 522, 523, 524, 527,
528, 529, 530, 531, 532

Chionites (Kidarite) 267, 268, 275, 276,
278, 279, 280

Christianity 21, 22, 23, 37, 93, 94, 96, 116,
124, 125, 126, 127, 129, 131, 196,
288, 298, 299, 311, 312, 325, 326,
335, 352, 423, 432, 465

Chuvash 29, 33, 34, 36, 125, 233, 294, 305,
306, 321, 328, 349, 447, 448, 471,
512, 532

Chü-Ch'ü Huns 264, 399

Cilicia 301

Cimmerians 164, 165, 208

civil war 252, 254, 256, 277, 305, 306, 307,
319, 321, 322, 333, 353, 373, 383,
396, 411, 425

classic era (or antiquity) 300

Codex Cumanicus 35, 110

Coffee 40, 41, 469

Confucianism 122, 196, 249, 389, 390, 451

Confucius 221, 234

conquest of Constantinople 53, 180, 303

Constantine I (Roman Emperor) 297

Constantinople (Istanbul) 41, 46, 53, 66, 80,
102, 140, 180, 189, 247, 276, 297,
299, 303, 305, 307, 309, 312, 317,
320, 322, 323, 324, 325, 330, 333,
335, 341, 343, 346, 352, 353, 354,
359, 361, 406, 470

costumes 67, 234, 243, 410, 451

Cowardice (a crime) 185

Crimea 96, 279, 280, 340, 343, 363

Crisis of the Third Century (235–84) 298

Cuisine 48, 470

Cumania 359, 360, 362

Cumans 112, 118, 120, 121, 126, 143, 171,
295, 314, 327, 338, 349, 350, 351,
352, 353, 354, 355, 356, 357, 358,
359, 360, 361, 362, 363, 452, 515,
516

czar 25, 116, 158, 326, 327, 349, 361, 362

D

Dacia Ripensis 303

Dagestan 319, 339, 340, 341

Damascus 128

Danube Bulgars Khanate 165, 323, 324, 326,
327, 328, 337

Danube River 162, 171, 173, 301, 323, 324,
332, 333, 335, 352, 356, 357, 360

Dede Korkut (folk tale) 43, 67, 117

Delhi 35, 61, 73, 86, 87, 203, 285

Derbent 340

Desht-i Qïpčak 357, 359, 363

divan 180

Dniester River 301

Dolmabahče Palace 91

Don River 270, 301, 354, 358, 405

drum 45, 46, 181, 182, 188

Dyrestuj 245

E

eagle (*kartal*) 58, 109
Eastern Roman Empire 22, 23, 38, 69, 73, 84, 95, 111, 112, 139, 140, 143, 164, 176, 187, 205, 243, 247, 268, 274, 278, 282, 287, 294, 299, 302, 309, 311, 322, 323, 327, 330, 331, 332, 334, 335, 339, 340, 341, 345, 346, 347, 350, 353, 354, 356, 357, 359, 361, 380, 404, 405, 406, 419, 448, 451, 465
Edessa (Urfa) 301
Edict of Lantai 251
Edict of Milan 298
Edirne (Adrianopolis) 91
egalitarian society 188, 231
Egypt 24, 35, 40, 41, 43, 44, 74, 79, 83, 87, 88, 118, 128, 137, 138, 155, 162, 172, 209, 291, 333, 359, 363, 364, 380, 450, 452
England 63, 66, 192, 474, 477, 490, 493, 505, 529
Ephtalite 78, 126, 153, 157, 213, 264, 267, 268, 272, 274, 275, 276, 277, 278, 279, 280, 281, 282, 283, 284, 285, 292, 367, 405
equestrian (art, sports) 58, 62, 118, 164, 183, 289, 334, 338
equestrianism 58, 119, 394
equestrians 289
Erlik 92, 93, 104, 105, 106, 109
Etruscans 138, 153, 154, 155, 317, 486
(Roman historian) 228
Evliya Çelebi (Ottoman explorer) 188

F

Falconry 57, 58, 471
falcons (*sungur, doğan*) 57, 58, 62
Far East 19, 21, 26, 38, 57, 65, 71, 94, 102, 115, 143, 161, 166, 184, 198, 222, 225, 229, 230, 243, 265, 270, 273, 283, 287, 291, 292, 296, 313, 355, 365, 367, 369, 404, 452
Fei River, Battle of 374, 517, 518
Fergana Valley 170, 171, 189, 198
First Bulgarian Empire (681–1018) 324
First Council of Nicaea 298
flag 115, 117, 181, 182, 401
flagpole 116, 118, 181, 182, 421
football (soccer) 63, 64
Former Zhao (Xiong-nu) 264, 371, 372, 373, 374, 375, 446
France 26, 41, 173, 174, 175, 295, 300, 302, 304, 315, 336, 486
Francia 174, 175, 332
Frankish Kingdom 174, 175, 332, 335, 380
Franks 22, 101, 174, 175, 295, 300, 302, 315, 316, 331, 332, 335
French 19, 24, 52, 54, 141, 145, 172, 224, 269, 292, 295, 315

G

Gagauz 19, 34, 125, 349
Gaiwu Rebellion (445) 390, 517, 521
Gaul (*Gallia*) 63, 173, 174, 297, 299, 300, 302, 315, 318, 380
Genghis Khan 28, 32, 60, 78, 80, 93, 99, 101, 110, 127, 160, 165, 179, 185, 217, 222, 239, 288, 357, 366, 376, 379, 396, 402, 421, 432, 434, 441, 442, 447, 448, 450, 464, 465, 489, 532
Georgia 188, 364
Georgians 357, 358
Gepids 306, 307, 322, 323, 330, 331
German 47, 134, 136, 140, 151, 174, 175, 191, 197, 198, 299, 300, 303, 305, 306, 308, 309, 310, 312, 314, 315,

316, 318, 319, 331, 332, 334, 335, 352, 454, 480, 508, 512, 523
Germanic 42, 152, 173, 174, 175, 192, 196, 223, 294, 295, 297, 298, 299, 300, 301, 302, 303, 304, 306, 307, 308, 310, 312, 314, 315, 316, 318, 319, 322, 323, 330, 331, 336, 340, 347, 380
Germany 174, 175, 314, 315, 331, 332, 336, 470, 473, 476, 480, 484
Ghazna 164, 179, 286, 418
Ghaznavid 35, 39, 69, 86, 178, 213, 271, 278, 285, 288, 350, 356, 405, 455, 459, 468, 492, 503, 523
Gobi Desert 376
Golconda Sultanate 34
Golden Horde Khanate 35, 36, 68, 96, 364, 452
Golestan Palace 90
Gol Gumbad 87, 476
Goths 22, 152, 173, 174, 196, 295, 297, 299, 300, 301, 302, 307, 311, 312, 314, 318, 331, 340, 488
Gök-Medrese 65, 79, 85
Gök Tengri 103
GökTürk Qaghanate 13, 448
Great Seljuk (Sultanate) 20, 74, 84, 87, 352
great Turkish migrations 184, 217, 268, 273, 291, 293, 295, 340, 365, 367, 370
Great Wall of China 21, 189, 204, 220, 226, 236, 247, 248, 444, 495, 500
Greece 19, 58, 83, 171, 222, 291, 295
Greeks 20, 22, 25, 35, 40, 44, 50, 53, 58, 62, 63, 69, 98, 126, 161, 170, 171, 214, 234, 275, 286, 292, 312, 326, 357, 403, 405, 407, 445, 451
gunpowder 20, 24, 56, 190, 191, 195, 201, 205, 209
gür-khan 176

H

Han 57, 64, 73, 103, 114, 123, 139, 141, 170, 189, 199, 200, 211, 214, 217, 218, 219, 220, 221, 222, 223, 225, 229, 232, 234, 236, 237, 239, 240, 242, 243, 244, 245, 247, 248, 249, 250, 251, 252, 253, 254, 255, 256, 257, 258, 259, 260, 261, 262, 263, 264, 266, 287, 289, 365, 367, 369, 370, 371, 372, 373, 374, 379, 380, 381, 388, 390, 391, 405, 410, 413, 414, 420, 424, 438, 440, 441, 446, 448, 450, 451, 460, 467, 492, 493, 494, 495, 498, 500, 501, 502, 516, 517, 518, 519, 523, 531
hawk (*tuğrul, atmaca*) 58, 178
Haydn, Franz Joseph 47
Heraclius (Eastern Roman Emperor) 126, 333, 334
Herat 280, 405
Hien-yün (*Hün-yu*) 77, 144, 149, 208, 210, 216, 217, 227, 444, 445
Hindu 84, 89, 121, 203, 286, 288, 419
Hindu Shahi 419
Hittites (Empire) 134, 137, 138, 171
hobbles 232
ho-ch'in (between China and Asian Huns) 229, 244, 245, 246, 249, 255, 256
Holy Roman Empire 23, 139, 175, 304
Horse (*at, yund*) 438, 459, 471, 472, 474, 479, 480, 482, 483, 489, 498, 504, 526, 527, 530
Huang Ch'ao Rebellion 437
Huang Ch'ao Rebellion (874–84) 437
Huhanye I (Shan-yu of Southern Huns) 254, 255, 257
Huhanye II (Shan-yu of Southern Huns) 257

Hungary 83, 118, 141, 152, 157, 169, 171, 175, 191, 295, 303, 305, 322, 323, 331, 332, 335, 336, 337, 338, 350, 352, 353, 354, 360, 361, 363, 364, 450, 451, 525

Huns 13, 22, 26, 32, 33, 35, 37, 38, 42, 45, 48, 50, 51, 54, 57, 58, 59, 60, 62, 73, 77, 78, 92, 93, 94, 98, 100, 103, 107, 112, 114, 115, 116, 119, 120, 124, 125, 126, 139, 140, 142, 143, 144, 145, 149, 152, 153, 156, 157, 158, 159, 164, 165, 167, 170, 171, 173, 174, 176, 177, 184, 185, 186, 187, 188, 189, 190, 191, 192, 193, 195, 196, 197, 200, 202, 204, 205, 208, 210, 211, 212, 213, 218, 219, 220, 221, 222, 223, 224, 225, 226, 227, 228, 229, 230, 231, 232, 233, 234, 235, 236, 237, 238, 239, 240, 241, 242, 243, 244, 245, 246, 247, 248, 249, 250, 251, 252, 253, 254, 255, 256, 257, 258, 259, 260, 261, 262, 263, 264, 265, 266, 267, 268, 269, 270, 271, 272, 274, 275, 276, 277, 278, 279, 280, 281, 282, 283, 284, 285, 286, 287, 288, 289, 291, 292, 293, 294, 295, 296, 297, 298, 299, 300, 301, 302, 303, 304, 305, 306, 307, 308, 309, 310, 311, 312, 313, 314, 315, 316, 317, 318, 319, 320, 321, 322, 323, 324, 329, 330, 331, 333, 336, 337, 338, 339, 340, 346, 365, 366, 367, 368, 369, 370, 371, 372, 373, 375, 376, 379, 380, 382, 383, 384, 386, 390, 392, 395, 398, 399, 400, 403, 405, 407, 410, 413, 414, 419, 420, 422, 427, 433, 443, 444, 445, 446, 447, 448, 452, 453, 456, 457, 459, 464, 469, 473, 477, 480, 483, 485, 486, 487, 488, 490, 491, 492, 493, 497, 499, 500, 502, 503, 504, 505, 506, 507, 508, 509, 510, 517, 518, 522, 531, 533

Huo-i Battle of 409, 524

I

Iberian Peninsula (*Hispania, Spania*) 174, 380

Ibn Tulun Mosque 79, 87

Iconium - see *Konya* 130

Idiqut 93, 431, 432, 433, 434

Ili River 210, 238, 241

Ilkhanid 118, 434, 456, 472

Il-teriš Qaghan (Qutlugh Qaghan, Gök-Türk) 177, 413, 415, 416

Il-Tutmuš (Sultan of Delhi) 203

India 22, 25, 39, 43, 57, 61, 69, 70, 72, 73, 75, 81, 83, 86, 87, 88, 89, 101, 122, 127, 153, 161, 187, 196, 199, 201, 205, 209, 213, 231, 241, 244, 266, 268, 269, 270, 271, 272, 275, 276, 277, 280, 281, 282, 284, 286, 287, 288, 292, 384, 389, 405, 419, 450, 452, 455

Indian Ocean 24, 40, 201, 202

Inner Mongolia 76, 97, 169, 207, 218, 220, 222, 226, 230, 239, 256, 259, 365, 381, 425, 529, 530

Iran (as a geographic descriptor) 19, 22, 24, 25, 39, 44, 61, 65, 70, 71, 72, 75, 81, 83, 84, 85, 86, 89, 90, 94, 97, 101, 158, 162, 170, 179, 180, 197, 201, 205, 209, 241, 271, 278, 279, 301, 341, 350, 414, 434, 455, 459, 468, 472, 476, 503, 523

Isfahan 61, 85, 473

Islam 21, 22, 23, 25, 37, 49, 65, 69, 71, 79, 81, 83, 84, 87, 93, 94, 95, 96, 97, 99, 101, 105, 113, 118, 119, 125, 127, 128, 129, 130, 131, 132, 158, 160,

179, 196, 198, 203, 205, 288, 327, 341, 343, 344, 362, 363, 434, 448, 490, 526, 529
Issyk Kül 56, 170, 210
Italy 27, 75, 138, 153, 154, 175, 295, 297, 299, 302, 304, 308, 309, 310, 311, 312, 320, 330
Iznik (Nicaea) 70
idiqut 431, 432

J

jade 198, 231, 240
Japan 72, 333
Japanese 31, 32, 62, 64, 146, 150, 280, 467
javelins (jirid) 62
Jews 126, 291, 339, 343, 344, 454, 455, 476, 481, 510, 511, 512, 513, 514, 522, 523
Jin 216, 263, 264, 370, 371, 373, 374, 375, 377, 379, 385, 386, 387, 388, 433, 438, 439, 440, 473, 490, 499, 500, 502, 507, 508, 522, 533
Jordanes (Roman historian) 58, 152, 305, 309, 310
Juan-juan (Asian Avars) 54, 156, 165, 212, 264, 267, 271, 278, 279, 280, 281, 283, 329, 330, 355, 375, 376, 377, 378, 382, 383, 385, 387, 388, 392, 393, 394, 395, 398, 399, 400, 401
Juan-juan (Asian Avars) 54, 279, 283, 330, 355, 385, 392
Jung (Jiang) 77, 144, 149, 150, 161, 208, 210, 215, 216, 217, 227, 230, 444, 445, 475
Justinian, the Great (Eastern Roman Emperor) 319, 320, 321, 322, 330, 332, 406, 407
Justinian II (Eastern Roman Emperor) 332, 406

K

Kabul 285, 286, 419
Kalka River, Battle of 126, 363
Kalovryia (Calobyra) 353
Kansu 116, 124, 137, 240, 241, 244, 264, 399, 433, 436
Kao-ch'ang, see *Uighur Qočo* Kingdom Kingdom 408
Kao-tsu or Gaozu 239
karagöz 44
Karaim Jews 343, 454
Karait 96, 114, 125, 421, 447
Karbala 128
Kashgar 37, 51, 64, 69, 113, 141, 200, 402
Kazakh 34, 36, 61, 62, 95, 148, 162, 163, 173, 212, 233, 266, 267, 268, 270, 273, 282, 292, 345, 351, 357
Kazakhstan 19, 28, 31, 37, 51, 72, 83, 88, 130, 137, 138, 142, 143, 147, 161, 168, 169, 170, 172, 207, 210, 265, 266, 274, 275, 320, 355, 356, 433, 447, 449, 450, 464
Kazakh Steppe 95, 173, 233, 268, 270, 292, 351, 357
Kazan 328, 345, 349, 356
Kenkol River 296
Khakassia (or Khakas) 33, 36
Khalifatabad 87
khan 23, 26, 99, 100, 110, 121, 126, 165, 176, 177, 178, 179, 260, 305, 323, 326, 327, 352, 353, 400, 406
Khan-Balïq 81
Khangai Mountains 366
khaqan 178, 385
Khar-Balgas 366, 430
khatun 180, 203, 363, 385
Khazar Qaghanate 193, 337, 341, 343, 345, 346, 348, 350, 351, 357, 412, 453

Khazar Sea (Caspian) 347, 449
Khingan Mountains 207, 226
Khitans 32, 176, 214, 219, 380, 400, 415, 432, 433, 439, 440
Khiva 86
Khorasan 82, 85, 88, 97, 101, 130, 170, 173, 201, 405, 419
Khotan 122, 198, 201
Khwâja Bahâ ad-Din Naqshband (founder of Naqshbandiyya Order 130
Khwarezm 83, 84, 85, 88, 101, 118, 130, 170, 188, 201, 343, 350, 352, 356, 359, 362, 363, 364
Khwarezm-shah 84, 101, 359, 362, 363
Kidarite Huns 244, 276, 277
Kiev 81, 340, 344, 346, 348, 349, 351, 352, 454, 475, 491, 513, 514, 533
Kievan Rus' (Varangian) 345, 347, 348, 349, 352
Kimek 23, 95, 111, 212, 351, 355, 356, 359, 402, 450, 451
Kimek Qaghanate 95, 212, 351, 355, 450, 451
kingdoms of Paekje 213
Koca Mimar Sinan (Ottoman architect) 91
Koguryo (Kokuryē) 213
Ko-k'un 210, 211, 238, 445, 447
Konya (Iconium) 130
Korea 39, 213, 333, 374, 376, 380, 402, 408, 421, 422
Korean peninsula 213
koumiss 48, 49, 160, 186
Krïmchak Jews 343, 454
Krum Khan (Danubian Bulgar monarch) 325
Kuei-fang 138, 149, 444
kurgan 72, 92, 121
Kushan Empire 146, 223, 240, 242, 244, 445
Kutadgu Bilig (Wisdom of Royal Glory) 118
Kutrighurs 314, 321, 322, 323, 330, 447

Küčlüg (Naiman and Qara-Khitan monarch) 176
Kül Tigin (Gök-Türk prince) 99, 123, 190, 416
Kyrgyz 21, 25, 34, 36, 42, 50, 51, 55, 58, 61, 62, 93, 94, 97, 105, 121, 124, 145, 146, 168, 176, 177, 181, 185, 187, 190, 208, 210, 211, 226, 238, 294, 357, 365, 379, 402, 416, 420, 422, 429, 430, 431, 432, 445, 447, 448
Kyrgyz Qaghanate 176, 379
Kyrgyzstan 19, 28, 31, 37, 51, 142, 143, 144, 145, 157, 169, 170, 171, 189, 198, 207, 210, 278, 296
Kyrgyz Steppe 357

L

Lahore 89
lance 100, 117, 333, 453
Later Chin (Sha-t'o) 219, 438, 440, 450
Later Han (Sha-t'o) 219, 370, 438, 440, 450
Later T'ang (Sha-t'o) 219, 436, 438, 440, 450
Levant 71, 172, 470, 487
lion (*arslan*) 118, 119, 131, 178, 465
Li Shimin (regnal name T'ai-tsung, Taizong) 409, 411, 412
Li Yuan (Kao-tsu) (the Duke of T'ang) 409
Lombards 22, 314, 318, 322, 330, 331
Lydians 171

M

mace 186
Magyars 175, 295, 325, 335, 336, 337, 338, 351, 360, 364, 451
Mahmud of Kashgar 37, 51, 64, 69, 113, 141, 402
Mamluk 35, 40, 44, 87, 88, 91, 105, 118, 359, 363, 364
Mamluk Sultanate of Egypt 359

Manchuria 141, 142, 167, 169, 185, 207, 211, 213, 217, 226, 229, 230, 366, 376, 382, 400, 403, 404, 421, 422, 460, 494, 502, 507, 517, 531
Manichaeism 21, 93, 94, 95, 124, 127, 129, 196, 198, 205, 422, 423, 427, 432
Manzikert 73, 176, 301, 353
Manzikert (Malazgirt) 301
Marcian (Eastern Roman Emperor) 304
mask, *death mask* 120
Massagetae 161, 162, 278
mausoleum (türbe) 55, 87, 91, 120, 130, 131
Mazdaism 129
Mecca 128, 180
Medina 127, 128, 180
Mediterranean Sea 67, 197, 201
Mehmet II Khan (the Conqueror) (Ottoman Sultan) 46, 53, 80, 101, 180
Menander (Eastern Roman historian) 278, 283, 487, 520
Mendelssohn Bartholdy, Jakob Ludwig Felix 47
Meng T'ien (Chinese General leading first attack on the Xiong-nu) 236, 246
Menkermen (Kiev) 81
mercenary 308, 352, 353
Merv 80, 87, 125
Mesopotamia 82, 134, 136, 155, 162, 209, 452
metallurgists 185, 429
Mevlana, Jalal ad-Din Muhammad Rumi 130
Middle East 22, 24, 28, 31, 38, 39, 52, 53, 57, 67, 71, 81, 82, 83, 84, 85, 90, 94, 128, 132, 136, 137, 138, 158, 161, 162, 187, 195, 196, 197, 198, 200, 201, 203, 204, 221, 231, 291, 294, 295, 301, 327, 344, 380, 419, 442
Ming 71, 123, 214, 220, 247, 280, 379, 444
Moldova 125, 172

Mongolia (as a geographic descriptor) 19, 20, 21, 25, 29, 33, 36, 72, 76, 81, 96, 97, 99, 111, 114, 117, 125, 127, 138, 142, 145, 153, 157, 165, 168, 169, 172, 176, 207, 210, 212, 213, 217, 218, 220, 222, 223, 226, 230, 239, 245, 248, 250, 256, 259, 263, 265, 267, 268, 270, 273, 274, 275, 279, 283, 288, 294, 295, 301, 355, 365, 366, 367, 370, 376, 377, 379, 380, 381, 383, 384, 392, 393, 401, 410, 417, 418, 420, 421, 423, 425, 426, 430, 431, 447, 450, 455, 463, 464, 467, 468, 483, 484, 488, 496, 498, 503, 507, 510, 511, 512, 513, 514, 515, 517, 519, 520, 521, 523, 529, 530
Mongols 26, 28, 32, 33, 35, 44, 65, 68, 80, 81, 93, 96, 99, 101, 105, 112, 114, 124, 125, 126, 127, 137, 139, 142, 143, 145, 159, 160, 164, 165, 168, 169, 176, 179, 184, 185, 190, 195, 196, 203, 209, 217, 219, 224, 226, 228, 229, 236, 239, 248, 293, 329, 363, 364, 365, 366, 368, 376, 379, 380, 382, 400, 432, 433, 434, 441, 442, 464, 479, 493, 500, 528, 531, 532
Moscow 349, 434
Mo-tun (Mete) (founder of the Xiong-nu empire) 236, 238, 239, 246, 266
Mozart, Wolfgang Amadeus 47
Mughal (Timurid) 25
Mu-jung 369, 373, 383, 386, 387
Mulan (Chinese legend) 394, 395, 521, 522
Murder 113
music 44, 45, 46, 47
Mussorgsky, Modest 48

N

Naiman 96
Native Americans (Indians) 159, 166

Near East 22, 26, 27, 72, 81, 83, 93, 127, 133, 134, 145, 154, 155, 172, 199, 216
Nestorian 37, 94, 96, 109, 125, 126, 127, 129, 196, 288, 423, 432
Nicaea (see *Iznik*) 70, 298
Nicaean Creed 298
Northern Han Kingdom (Sha-t'o) 440, 441, 450
Northern Huns 233, 245, 254, 257, 258, 259, 260, 261, 263, 264, 265, 266, 267, 272, 274, 275, 292, 293, 295, 300, 368, 382, 446
Northern Liang (Xiong-nu) 117, 122, 264, 372, 374, 446
Northern Wei (Tabgač) 94, 107, 117, 122, 160, 202, 212, 214, 234, 264, 265, 272, 275, 279, 281, 283, 289, 355, 367, 371, 372, 375, 376, 378, 381, 382, 386, 387, 388, 389, 390, 391, 392, 393, 394, 395, 396, 399, 401, 410, 438, 439, 451, 464, 518, 519, 521
Northern Zhou (Xiong-nu) 410

O

Odoacer (First King of Italy) 174, 299, 308, 309, 310, 311, 480, 508, 523
Odyssey 42
Oghur 29, 33, 34, 35, 36, 157, 165, 167, 175, 225, 233, 295, 320, 323, 325, 336, 337, 338, 339, 376, 407
Oghuz 21, 23, 29, 34, 35, 36, 43, 54, 55, 56, 80, 81, 92, 93, 98, 103, 113, 118, 121, 132, 154, 157, 176, 177, 179, 181, 182, 188, 203, 211, 213, 233, 238, 291, 295, 314, 340, 345, 346, 348, 349, 350, 351, 352, 353, 354, 356, 357, 402, 415, 417, 421, 425, 445, 449, 450, 451, 494, 522, 526, 532
Oghuz Yabghu state 356
Ogurs 402

Old Greater Bulgaria 323, 334, 340, 377, 447
One Thousand and One Nights 74
On-Oghurs 157, 171, 233, 321, 323, 325, 330, 337, 338, 340, 360, 377, 447
On-Oq 411
Ordos (Inner Mongolia) 425
Ordu 77, 78, 80, 366, 428, 430, 474, 475, 481, 502, 522, 528
Ordu-Balïq 77, 80, 366, 428, 430
Orkhon River 111, 428, 430, 464
Orkhon valley 33, 36, 80, 112, 239, 366, 406, 417
Ortaköy Mosque 91
Orthodox 96, 125, 126, 128, 334, 346
Ostrogothic Kingdom 174, 332
Ostrogoths 57, 173, 174, 175, 295, 306, 307, 309, 310, 311, 312, 313, 320
Ottoman 20, 24, 25, 26, 34, 36, 39, 40, 41, 44, 45, 46, 47, 48, 50, 51, 53, 54, 56, 58, 59, 60, 62, 63, 66, 68, 70, 71, 72, 74, 75, 84, 85, 89, 90, 91, 97, 99, 101, 102, 121, 132, 139, 140, 158, 159, 164, 172, 178, 179, 180, 181, 182, 188, 193, 194, 201, 204, 205, 293, 294, 299, 302, 312, 327, 338, 362, 392, 396, 407, 455, 456, 457, 460, 470, 473, 474, 481, 482, 487, 489, 492, 495, 506, 511, 515, 516
Öd 56, 103
Ötüken 107, 111, 112, 366, 406, 407, 436, 465, 484, 486, 499, 531

P

padishah 180
Pakistan 25, 83, 116, 162, 274, 276, 284, 418
Pamir Mountains 146, 162, 170
Pannonia 171, 271, 303, 305, 323, 330, 332, 333, 334, 406
Paris 272, 480, 509, 520
Parthian Empire 223, 282

Paša (pasha) 40, 91
Pazïrïk 56, 72, 73, 74, 116, 148, 163
Pečeneg Day 354
Pečenegs 37, 45, 95, 121, 143, 156, 171, 187, 295, 336, 337, 338, 345, 346, 350, 351, 352, 353, 354, 360, 361, 450, 451
Pegasus 56
Persians 26, 39, 40, 53, 82, 126, 139, 150, 161, 168, 170, 179, 209, 214, 267, 275, 276, 277, 278, 281, 282, 283, 284, 285, 286, 288, 298, 320, 333, 404, 405, 445
petroglyphs 56, 74, 138, 144, 463
Phrygians 171
Plague of Cyprian 298
Poland 136, 331
Polish 96, 343, 350
polo 60, 61, 62, 289
Pontic Steppe (Northern Black Sea Steppe) 33, 96, 97, 157, 158, 167, 171, 173, 183, 201, 208, 296, 302, 320, 330, 335, 336, 338, 339, 340, 345, 347, 348, 350, 351, 353, 356, 357, 358, 363, 380, 400, 403
Pope Leo I (The Great) 304
Portugal 26, 40
Portuguese 19, 202
princesses (Chinese) 200, 222, 245, 246, 249, 415, 423, 427
Priscus (Greek historian) 73, 196, 307, 310, 333
Procopius (Eastern Roman chronicler) 280, 281, 322
Protestants 23
Ptolemy (Greco-Roman mathematician and geographer) 270, 300
P'u-nu (Northern Xiong-nu ruler) 257, 258, 259, 260

Q

qaghan 26, 43, 55, 56, 80, 94, 99, 100, 103, 110, 111, 112, 116, 117, 123, 176, 177, 178, 180, 193, 203, 283, 330, 331, 339, 341, 342, 348, 366, 379, 385, 393, 395, 400, 403, 404, 406, 407, 408, 409, 412, 416, 418, 421, 422, 425, 427, 429, 431, 453, 454
Qaghanate 13, 35, 95, 124, 169, 176, 193, 202, 212, 264, 267, 283, 325, 326, 330, 332, 333, 337, 341, 342, 343, 345, 346, 347, 348, 349, 350, 351, 355, 356, 357, 379, 380, 383, 400, 403, 410, 411, 412, 413, 415, 417, 418, 419, 431, 433, 448, 449, 450, 451, 453, 454
Qaghanate of Rus' (Varangian) 193, 341, 345, 348, 349, 453, 454
Qajar 65, 90
qam 105, 110
Qanglï 110, 212, 265, 279, 280, 281, 351, 355, 356, 357, 387, 399, 420, 421, 450, 451, 452
Qapghan Qaghan (GökTürk) 177, 415
Qara-Khanid Khanate 37, 69, 118, 205, 327
Qara-Khanids 35, 96, 178, 193, 356, 384, 434, 439, 453
Qara-Khitan 176, 433, 434
Qaraqalpaqs 354, 451
Qara-Qorum 366, 465
Qara-qoyunlu 34, 118, 460
Qara-Qum (desert) 169
Qarluqs 35, 417, 418, 420, 450, 451
Qayï 179
Qing (Manchu) 39, 214, 219, 222, 379, 380, 394, 431, 433
Qïpčaks 104, 105, 116, 121, 143, 156, 212, 295, 338, 351, 352, 354, 355, 356, 357, 358, 359, 362, 363, 364, 452

Qïpčak Steppe 171, 363, 380
Qubrat Khan (Bulgar monarch) 322, 323, 332, 333
Quebec, Canada 166
qurultai 180
Quwwat al-Islam Mosque 87

R

rainstone 110
Ravenna 299, 507, 508
Raziyya (1236–40) (Turkish woman monarch) 203
rebellion 126, 257, 258, 259, 261, 304, 307, 359, 361, 378, 379, 390, 417, 420, 424, 425, 429, 430, 439, 440
Rebellion (184–205) 259, 261, 369
Rebellion of 1185–86 360, 361
Red Sea 24, 201
Rhine River 174, 299
Ritter von Gluck, Willibald 47
Roman Empire 22, 23, 38, 69, 70, 73, 84, 95, 111, 112, 138, 139, 140, 143, 153, 154, 164, 171, 173, 174, 175, 176, 180, 187, 192, 205, 223, 243, 247, 266, 268, 269, 274, 278, 282, 287, 292, 294, 295, 297, 298, 299, 300, 301, 302, 303, 304, 305, 308, 309, 310, 311, 312, 314, 315, 316, 317, 322, 323, 327, 330, 331, 332, 334, 335, 339, 340, 341, 345, 346, 347, 350, 353, 354, 356, 357, 359, 361, 380, 404, 405, 406, 419, 432, 447, 448, 451, 452, 465, 506
Romania 83, 140, 171, 175, 297, 331, 354, 359, 360, 361
Roman Republic 154, 192, 223
Rome 58, 115, 140, 230, 282, 291, 298, 299, 311, 313, 316, 405, 483, 491, 499, 506, 507, 508
Romulus and Romus 154

Romulus Augustulus (the last Western Roman Emperor) 299, 309, 310, 311
Rossini (Gioacchino Antonio) 47
Russia 19, 28, 72, 73, 78, 117, 125, 142, 158, 163, 172, 175, 226, 320, 339, 341, 343, 345, 348, 349, 352, 364, 455, 468, 484, 488, 496, 498, 503, 507, 510, 511, 512, 513, 514, 515, 517, 519, 520, 521, 523

S

Sabirs 93, 143, 322, 330, 339
Safavid 23, 24, 25, 26, 34, 39, 46, 61, 70, 75, 84, 89, 90, 97, 180, 191, 205, 285, 489
Safranbolu 83
Saimaluu-Tash 144, 484
Samanid 130
Samarkand 88, 101, 200, 280, 416
Samarra 74, 79, 80
Sarmatians 164, 165, 208, 318
Sassanid Persia 38, 39, 275, 282, 319, 332, 334, 411
Sayan Mountains 226
Scythians (Saka) 13, 26, 57, 58, 60, 73, 145, 146, 147, 148, 149, 150, 152, 153, 156, 161, 162, 163, 164, 165, 183, 187, 189, 208, 209, 210, 250, 291, 292, 317, 354, 406, 445, 447, 452, 456, 483, 485, 487, 493, 506, 509, 518, 531
Sea of Azov 300
Second Bulgarian Empire 327, 360, 361, 362, 510, 511, 515, 516
Selenga River 117, 420, 428
Selenga valleys 77
Selimiye Camii 91
Seljuk 20, 23, 24, 45, 58, 59, 61, 72, 73, 75, 79, 81, 82, 83, 84, 85, 86, 87, 88, 90,

91, 101, 109, 125, 130, 131, 164, 176, 179, 203, 228, 301, 352, 353, 356, 358, 472, 481, 492
Seljuks of Rum 65, 75, 84, 130
Seljuk sultan 87, 101, 131, 164
Semender 340
Semirechye (see *Yettisu*) 170
Serbia 83, 171, 180, 303, 331, 364
Serbians 40
shadow theater 43, 44, 453
shaman 45, 93, 98, 104, 105, 110, 135, 398
shan-yu 33, 99, 114, 115, 176, 177, 194, 200, 210, 211, 229, 232, 236, 242, 244, 245, 246, 249, 250, 251, 252, 254, 255, 256, 257, 258, 259, 260, 261, 262, 264, 368, 370, 373, 374, 406
Sha-t'o 45, 58, 59, 64, 109, 112, 122, 219, 378, 401, 417, 422, 429, 433, 435, 436, 437, 438, 439, 440, 441, 450
Shi'ite 23, 97, 128, 180, 205
Shishmanid (Cuman Turkish) 361
Siberia 21, 25, 26, 31, 36, 63, 97, 105, 107, 117, 120, 132, 138, 142, 143, 144, 145, 147, 152, 153, 161, 162, 169, 202, 207, 226, 230, 245, 259, 266, 268, 270, 295, 320, 329, 337, 355, 356, 357, 359, 366, 445, 447, 451, 452, 476, 484, 496
siege of Constantinople 46, 333
Silistria 351
Silk Road (Seidenstraße) 13, 38, 39, 70, 77, 92, 94, 115, 127, 169, 171, 195, 196, 197, 198, 199, 200, 201, 210, 230, 248, 250, 283, 287, 341, 344, 346, 350, 402, 414, 417, 420, 423, 432, 441, 455, 479, 481, 483, 487, 491, 492, 493, 498, 499, 500, 504, 507, 508, 510, 513, 520, 524, 525, 526, 527, 528, 529, 531

Sima Qian (Chinese chronicler) 114, 221
Slavs 193, 234, 291, 302, 312, 313, 316, 322, 325, 326, 331, 332, 335, 337, 338, 340, 345, 348, 349, 350, 351, 357, 363, 511
Sogdia (Sogdiana) 266, 278, 279, 280
Sogdian (Persian) 81, 95, 104, 163, 177, 196, 197, 225, 243, 269, 270, 277, 292, 402, 405, 422, 424, 425, 427, 428, 429, 437, 529, 530
Song 43, 70, 222, 287, 379, 433, 438, 441, 442, 450, 495, 530, 532
Southern Huns 211, 219, 233, 254, 255, 256, 257, 258, 259, 260, 261, 262, 263, 264, 266, 370, 400, 446
Soviet Union 37, 158
Spain 26, 173, 174, 175, 295, 297, 299, 300, 315, 318
Ssu-ma Ch'ien (Chinese chronicler) 98, 217, 221, 228
stirrup 54, 55, 333, 334, 453
Suevi 299
Sufism 129
Sui 122, 203, 213, 218, 263, 379, 380, 393, 394, 396, 397, 405, 408, 409, 410
Sulak River 340
Sultan 46, 53, 55, 58, 59, 60, 61, 70, 80, 87, 90, 91, 101, 180, 182, 188, 203, 204, 363, 455
Sultanate of Delhi 203, 285
Sunni 23, 97, 128, 129, 130, 179, 271, 434
sü-bashï 179
Svyatoslav I (Russian Prince from Viking Dynasty) 346, 349
sword 45, 100, 113, 118, 129
Symeon (Czar of Bulgars) 116, 326, 327
Syr Darya (Seyhun) Rivers 170

T

Tabgač 32, 92, 94, 107, 117, 122, 123, 160, 176, 205, 214, 219, 223, 263, 264, 272, 281, 355, 368, 369, 372, 374, 375, 378, 381, 382, 383, 384, 385, 387, 388, 389, 391, 392, 396, 397, 399, 407, 410, 439, 451, 452, 464
Tabriz 75, 88
T'ai-tsung 218, 385, 410, 411, 412, 413, 414, 425, 427
T'ai-tsung (also known as Taizong, 626–49 CE) 218
T'a-jen River 407
Tajik 130
Tajikistan 157, 169, 170, 171, 198, 266, 278, 284, 285
Taj Mahal 89, 90, 205, 473, 476, 481
Taklamakan Desert 170
Talas (751), Battle of 423, 426
tamgha 36, 37, 57, 144
T'ang 44, 60, 70, 72, 80, 95, 96, 105, 117, 122, 123, 177, 201, 202, 203, 214, 218, 219, 222, 265, 285, 289, 379, 381, 385, 386, 391, 394, 396, 397, 399, 408, 409, 410, 411, 412, 413, 414, 415, 416, 417, 420, 421, 422, 423, 424, 425, 426, 427, 428, 430, 431, 432, 433, 435, 436, 437, 438, 439, 440, 448, 450, 456, 471, 490, 492, 495, 517, 525, 529
Taoism 196, 313, 375, 389, 390, 451
Tarim basin 122, 170, 173, 201, 229, 230, 434
tarkhan 178, 285
Tashkent 283, 434
Tatars 61, 81, 96, 109, 157, 204, 328, 343, 349, 360, 361, 364, 441, 450, 452, 456, 488, 510, 511, 513, 514, 515, 516

tengri 32, 33, 56, 67, 92, 93, 99, 100, 102, 103, 104, 106, 107, 108, 111, 112, 114, 119, 122, 142, 159, 177, 178, 202, 236, 305, 323, 402, 407
Tengriism 38, 92, 94, 95, 97, 98, 104, 108, 122, 123, 129, 159, 181, 196, 389, 393, 423
Tere-köl Lake 80
Tertery (Cuman Turkish) 359
Theiss (Tisza in Hungarian) River 335
Theoderic the Great (king of the Ostrogoths) 174, 311
Theodosius II (Eastern Roman Emperor) 305, 310
Theodosius the Great (the last Roman Emperor) 297
The Republic of Venice 139
Thessalonica 323, 332
Tibetan 37, 45, 195, 201, 388, 415, 418, 421, 422, 428, 429, 436, 526, 528
T'ieh-le 167, 212, 213, 279, 351, 376, 404, 408, 413, 414, 415, 420, 421, 449, 451
Tien Shan mountains 464
Tigin 80, 99, 123, 178, 190, 409, 416, 418, 419, 432
Timurid 22, 25, 72, 75, 84, 88, 89, 90, 91, 132, 364, 476
Timurid Renaissance 88
Timurid Renaissance (1405–1506) 88
Ting-ling 115, 146, 150, 167, 208, 210, 211, 212, 213, 226, 238, 252, 260, 265, 289, 351, 355, 371, 392, 399, 420, 421, 445, 447, 451
Tokharians 153, 156, 241
Tokharistan (*Yueh-chih*) 56, 124, 284, 285, 288, 405, 416
Tola River 213, 449
Tonyuquq (Gök-Türk minister) 123, 415, 416

Topkapï Palace 58, 80, 91
Toquz-Oghuz 176, 177, 213, 233, 348, 402, 415, 417, 421, 425
totem 104, 105, 116, 117, 118, 391, 401
totemism 104, 117
Töles 115, 116, 212, 265, 351, 404, 408, 413, 414, 420, 421, 449, 450, 451, 532
tös 105, 117, 118, 472, 480, 523, 526
trade 13, 39, 86, 94, 115, 169, 186, 195, 197, 198, 199, 200, 201, 221, 229, 230, 232, 236, 249, 250, 258, 280, 327, 341, 344, 346, 348, 351, 356, 404, 414, 426, 428, 443, 465
Transoxus (Transoxiana, *Mawarannahr*) 88, 147, 157, 170, 173, 239
treason (death penalty) 185
tribute 50, 222, 232, 246, 247, 249, 253, 255, 276, 282, 305, 330, 332, 335, 405, 406, 411, 427, 448
trousers 187, 234, 289, 317, 381, 391, 394, 451, 452
Tughluq 89
tuğ 55, 68, 118, 181
tulip 66
Tulunid 87
tumaq 111
Tung-hu 185, 187, 210, 211, 217, 226, 238, 366, 367, 368, 370, 382, 445
Tungus (Tungusic) 31, 32, 146, 148, 150, 195, 211, 217, 219, 226, 228, 248, 329, 368, 377, 379, 382, 388, 394, 433, 439
Turan 162, 170, 460, 476, 477, 478, 479, 482, 488
Turchia 20, 403
Turfan 116, 122, 124, 279, 376, 388, 392, 408, 418, 426, 430, 431, 432, 433, 434, 481, 523, 524, 527, 528
Turkestan 20, 24, 33, 36, 37, 50, 56, 63, 65, 72, 73, 74, 75, 77, 78, 80, 81, 88, 97, 124, 125, 127, 129, 143, 157, 158, 167, 168, 169, 170, 171, 173, 198, 201, 205, 208, 225, 230, 248, 259, 264, 265, 268, 273, 275, 280, 282, 283, 293, 295, 327, 356, 359, 364, 365, 374, 380, 400, 405, 414, 419, 420, 421, 433, 434, 435, 451
Turkey 19, 20, 21, 23, 27, 28, 31, 34, 37, 40, 43, 44, 50, 51, 54, 61, 62, 63, 65, 66, 67, 71, 72, 74, 75, 79, 83, 85, 86, 89, 113, 117, 131, 134, 135, 153, 154, 166, 171, 178, 179, 205, 236, 239, 287, 301, 346, 403, 455, 457, 461, 467, 469, 473, 481, 486, 489, 495, 503, 506, 511
Turkmenistan 19, 28, 31, 34, 36, 37, 75, 83, 87, 143, 169, 170, 279
Turkmens 25, 113, 338
Turk Shahi (Kabul Shahi) 418, 419
Tuscany 138, 153, 154
Tuva 19, 33, 36, 54, 148, 452
Türgeš Qaghanate 124
Türgiš (or Türgeš) 405

U

učmaq 111
Uighur Qaghanate 342, 431, 433
Uighur Qočo Kingdom 124, 432
Uighurs 32, 35, 37, 51, 65, 76, 77, 93, 94, 95, 97, 98, 102, 107, 116, 124, 127, 168, 177, 185, 190, 196, 205, 208, 212, 213, 218, 225, 265, 365, 366, 378, 379, 400, 417, 418, 420, 421, 422, 423, 424, 425, 426, 427, 428, 429, 430, 431, 432, 433, 434, 435, 436, 438, 441, 448, 449, 451, 460, 464, 526, 527, 528
Ukraine 33, 81, 161, 163, 172, 175, 292, 294, 296, 313, 322, 323, 324, 339, 340,

346, 349, 350, 351, 354, 357, 377,
402, 404, 451
Ulan Ude 77, 230
Ulugh Khan Jahan 87
Umay 103, 111
Umayyad 79, 128, 129, 282, 288, 341, 418,
448
Umayyad Caliphate 128
Ural Mountains 162, 172
Ural (Yayïk) Rivers 350
Urartians 171
Urumchi 279, 282
Utrighurs 314, 321, 330
Uzbekistan 19, 21, 28, 31, 37, 75, 83, 143,
157, 169, 170, 171, 189, 198, 266,
274, 278, 279, 280, 451
Uzbeks 25, 35, 36, 61, 62, 63, 191, 294, 364

V

Vandals 22, 175, 295, 299, 300, 302, 315
Varangian Viking 346
Venice 139, 174, 302
Venice (the Republic of) 139
Vienna 47, 241, 335, 344, 348, 474
Vikings (Varangian) Rus' (862-1598) 93,
314, 347, 348, 349, 357, 449
Visigoths 173, 175, 295, 297, 304, 315
Vlakhs 359, 360, 361, 362
Volga Bulgar Khanate 203, 323, 327, 345,
356, 377, 448
Volga (Itil) River 116, 173, 301, 324, 360

W

Wang Mang (Emperor of China) 212, 245,
255, 256
werewolf 116
Western Huns 266, 267, 268, 272, 275, 276
Western Roman Empire 21, 22, 140, 174,
187, 192, 205, 223, 266, 287, 292,
297, 299, 300, 302, 303, 304, 308,
309, 310, 311, 314, 315, 448
whirling dervishes 130
White Huns (Ephtalites) 264, 405
wishing tree 113
wolf (börü, kurt) 62, 67, 99, 109, 114, 115,
116, 117, 118, 152, 154, 188, 242,
310, 391, 398, 399, 401, 403, 418
World War II 96, 344, 454, 513, 514
wrestling 58, 61, 62, 63, 119
Wudi (Han Emperor of China) 189, 218,
243, 244, 248, 249, 250, 251, 254,
391, 424
Wu-huan 211, 238, 245, 251, 252, 258, 259,
260, 367, 368, 385, 445
Wu-sun 114, 115, 210, 211, 238, 241, 242,
244, 245, 250, 252, 255, 265, 368,
435, 445, 447, 479, 480, 499, 500

X

Xia (Xiong-nu) 215, 264, 372, 374, 375, 392,
395, 446
Xianbei 165, 210, 211, 221, 258, 259, 260,
261, 263, 265, 266, 267, 271, 367,
368, 369, 370, 371, 373, 374, 375,
381, 382, 383, 384, 386, 398, 399,
439, 445, 451
Xinjiang 19, 28, 94, 122, 124, 142, 143, 156,
169, 170, 201, 207, 208, 211, 229,
250, 260, 274, 279, 282, 414, 423,
430, 431, 434, 523, 527, 528
Xiong-nu 21, 32, 33, 38, 45, 50, 51, 54, 59,
62, 67, 73, 76, 77, 78, 93, 94, 98, 99,
100, 103, 112, 114, 115, 116, 119,
121, 122, 123, 141, 142, 144, 145,
146, 149, 156, 159, 167, 168, 169,
172, 173, 176, 177, 184, 185, 187,
188, 189, 190, 191, 194, 195, 197,
202, 204, 208, 209, 210, 211, 213,
214, 216, 217, 218, 219, 220, 221,
222, 223, 224, 225, 226, 227, 228,

229, 230, 231, 233, 234, 235, 236, 237, 238, 239, 240, 241, 242, 244, 245, 246, 247, 248, 249, 250, 251, 253, 254, 255, 256, 257, 258, 259, 260, 263, 264, 265, 266, 267, 268, 269, 270, 271, 272, 275, 278, 279, 280, 291, 292, 293, 294, 296, 310, 313, 324, 329, 339, 351, 355, 365, 366, 367, 368, 369, 370, 371, 372, 373, 374, 375, 376, 378, 381, 382, 383, 384, 385, 386, 387, 390, 392, 393, 394, 395, 396, 398, 399, 400, 401, 406, 408, 410, 414, 419, 420, 424, 427, 433, 443, 445, 452

Y

Yabghu 80, 81, 176, 178, 283, 284, 285, 339, 356, 404, 405, 409, 410, 411, 416
Yabghus of Tokharistan 124, 284, 285, 405
Yaghlaqar 421, 425, 428
Yaghma 23
Yakuts 36, 121, 163
Yangï-kent 80, 81
Yangtze Rivers 214
Yasawi Mausoleum 88
Yek 104
Yellow River 239, 384, 388, 394, 438
Yellow Sea 116, 239, 405
Yellow Turban Rebellion 259, 261, 369
Yemen 24, 40, 132
Yenisei River 143, 210, 445
yer 108, 111
Yesevi (Yasawi) 97, 130
Yettisu 170, 265
Yuan 160, 214, 219, 220, 222, 265, 379, 380, 382, 394, 396, 408, 409, 411, 412, 432, 441, 444, 495, 530, 532
Yunzhong 257
yurt 32, 74, 76, 77, 82, 85, 119, 160, 234

Z

Zhang Qian (Chinese ambassador) 242, 243, 245, 248, 250
Zhongguo (China) 214
Zoroastrianism 94, 108, 162, 196, 198, 288, 423
Zungaria 211, 212
Zunghar (Dzungar) 433

www.ingramcontent.com/pod-product-compliance
Lightning Source LLC
Chambersburg PA
CBHW031304150426
43191CB00005B/74